AND BOOK TRAINING PACKAGE AVAILABLE

ExamSim

Experience realistic, simulated exams on your own computer with Osborne's interactive ExamSim software. This computer-based test engine offers knowledge- and scenario-based questions like those found on the actual exams. ExamSim also features a review mode that helps build your testing confidence by allowing you to analyze the questions you missed.

Knowledge-based questions present challenging material in a multiple-choice format. Answer treatments not only explain why the correct options are right, they also tell you why the incorrect answers are wrong.

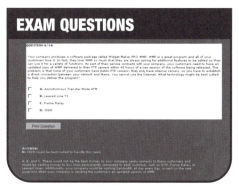

Realistic **scenario-based questions** challenge your ability to analyze and synthesize complex information in realistic scenarios similar to the actual exams.

Additional CD-ROM Features

- Complete hyperlinked **e-book** for easy information access and self-paced study

System Requirements:

A PC running Internet Explorer version 5 or higher

The **Score Report** provides an overall assessment of your exam performance as well as performance history.

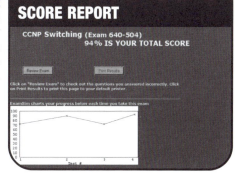

CCNP™ Switching Study Guide

(Exam 640-504)

CCNP™ Switching Study Guide

(Exam 640-504)

This study/training guide and/or material is not sponsored by, endorsed by or affiliated with Cisco Systems, Inc. Cisco®, Cisco Systems®, CCDA™, CCNA™, CCDP™, CCNP™, CCIE™, CCSI™, the Cisco Systems logo and the CCIE logo are trademarks or registered trademarks of Cisco Systems, Inc. in the United States and certain other countries. All other trademarks are trademarks of their respective owners.

This publication may be used in assisting students to prepare for an exam. Osborne/McGraw-Hill does not warrant that use of this publication will ensure passing any exam.

Syngress Media, Inc.

Osborne/McGraw-Hill
Berkeley New York St. Louis San Francisco Auckland Bogotá Hamburg London Madrid Mexico City
Milan Montreal New Delhi Panama City Paris São Paulo Singapore Sydney Tokyo Toronto

Osborne/**McGraw-Hill**
2600 Tenth Street
Berkeley, California 94710
U.S.A.

For information on translations or book distributors outside the U.S.A., or to arrange bulk purchase discounts for sales promotions, premiums, or fund-raisers, please contact Osborne/**McGraw-Hill** at the above address.

CCNP™ Switching Study Guide (Exam 640-504)

Copyright © 2001 by The McGraw-Hill Companies. All rights reserved. Printed in the United States of America. Except as permitted under the Copyright Act of 1976, no part of this publication may be reproduced or distributed in any form or by any means, or stored in a database or retrieval system, without the prior written permission of the publisher, with the exception that the program listings may be entered, stored, and executed in a computer system, but they may not be reproduced for publication.

1234567890 MMN MMN 019876543210

Book p/n: 0-07-212538-1 and CD p/n: 0-07-212539-X
>parts of ISBN: 0-07-212540-3

Publisher Brandon A. Nordin	**Editorial Management** Syngress Media, Inc.	**Copy Editor** Beth A. Roberts
Vice President and Associate Publisher Scott Rogers	**Project Editor** Maribeth A. Corona	**Production and Editorial** Black Hole Publishing Services
Editorial Director Gareth Hancock	**Acquisitions Coordinator** Jessica Wilson	**Series Design** Roberta Steele
Associate Acquisitions Editor Timothy Green	**Series Editor** Mark Buchmann	**Cover Design** Greg Scott
	Technical Editor Chris Olsen	

This book was published with Corel VENTURA™ Publisher.

Information has been obtained by Osborne/**McGraw-Hill** from sources believed to be reliable. However, because of the possibility of human or mechanical error by our sources, Osborne/**McGraw-Hill**, or others, Osborne/**McGraw-Hill** does not guarantee the accuracy, adequacy, or completeness of any information and is not responsible for any errors or omissions or the results obtained from use of such information.

ABOUT THE CONTRIBUTORS

About Syngress Media

Syngress Media creates books and software for Information Technology professionals seeking skill enhancement and career advancement. Its products are designed to comply with vendor and industry standard course curricula, and are optimized for certification exam preparation. You can contact Syngress via the Web at www.sygnress.com.

Contributors

David Bennett (CCNA, CCNP, CCDA, CNE, MCNE, MCSE, ASE) is a Senior Consultant for CoreTech Consulting Group, Inc. Based in King of Prussia, PA. He has an extensive and diverse background working with network operating system platforms (Novell and NT) and internetworking devices (routers, bridges and gateways). He has been involved in many large-scale, mission critical projects. Dave has been working in the information technology industry for over 7 years.

Dave holds an Associates Degree in computer engineering technology from CHI Institute in Southampton, PA. His many certifications include Cisco Certified Network Associate (CCNA), Cisco Certified Network Professional (CCNP), Cisco Certified Design Associate (CCDA), Novell Certified Network Engineer (CNE), Novell Master CNE, Microsoft Certified System Engineer (MCSE) and Compaq Accredited Systems Engineer (ASE). Dave, his wife, Barbara, and their son, Nicholas reside in Levittown, PA.

Herbert Borovansky (CCIE # 6037) is a Director in the Consulting business unit of Calence, Inc., a network integrator based in Phoenix, AZ. He gained his bachelor's degree in Management Information Systems from the University of Arizona. He is currently leading the analysis and design of a multi-service WAN and LAN infrastructure for a large financial services company. Herb has deep skills and experience in all aspects of internetworking including switching, routing, security and multi-service network convergence.

Russell Brown (CCNP, MCSE+I, A+) is an Independent Consultant in Minneapolis, MN. He focuses on networking and security, and specializes primarily in integrating Microsoft products with Cisco Routing. He has over 3 years of computer consulting experience but still finds time to play the guitar in several bands around the Twin Cities. Some of the projects Russ has worked on include LAN/WAN troubleshooting for small companies, Firewall and Proxy design and implementation, designing procedures for desktop rollouts, and various routing and switching implementations.

Russ lives in Minneapolis, MN and can be reached at brown@isd.net. His Web site is http://ruebarb.tripod.com.

Chuck Church (CCNP, MCNE, MCSE) is a Senior Network Engineer working for Magnacom Technologies (http://www.magnacom.com), a technology integration company based in Valley Cottage, NY, on the outskirts of New York City. He designs and supports Cisco switched and routed networks, in addition to Novell and Microsoft network operating systems. He has 7 years of computer consulting experience in both small business and large corporate networks. Chuck has worked on many diverse projects, including NOS migrations and upgrades, LAN/WAN redesigns revolving around switched core networks, and recently, many security projects involving VPN and firewall technology. Currently he is working on the Cisco CCIE certification, with an expected date of January, 2001.

Chuck lives with his dog Hogan and two cats in Nyack, NY and can be reached via email at cchurch@magnacom.com or cchurc2@banet.net.

Ricardo Daza (CISSP, CCNP (LAN-ATM, Voice Access), CCDA, SCNA (Solaris 7), IBM CSE (AIX 4.3 Sys Admin, AIX Firewall), MCSE+I, MCT, CNA) is a Channel Systems Engineer for Cisco Systems (http://www.cisco.com/), working out of Cisco's Seattle, WA office. He has over 10 years of computer consulting experience and has passed nine Cisco Certified Exams including the CCIE Written Qualification Exam (lab scheduled for later this year). During his career, Ricardo has worked on many extensive and diverse projects, including, network infrastructure and security analysis, network design and implementation, network management and documentation, project management and end-user training. He is proficient in a number of different vendor products ranging from Cisco, Microsoft, Sun, Novell, IBM, Bay, and 3Com to name a but a few.

Benoit Durand (CCNA, CCDA, CCNP, CCDP, CCIE #5754) is the Midwest Region Network Engineer for Tivoli Systems (www.tivoli.com), located in Indianapolis, IN. Ben designs and integrates high-end network solutions for Tivoli's worldwide operations while maintaining his own Cisco powered network in Indianapolis. He has over 10 years of networking engineering experience in a wide range of environments. Prior to working at Tivoli, Ben worked on many high-profile military projects for the Canadian Air Force, deploying wide-area network solutions to peacekeeping forces in Kuwait, Yugoslavia, and other exotic locations. His latest projects involve Voice-over-ATM, Virtual Private Network solutions, and Wide-Area Network switching.

Ben lives with his wife Dr. Christy Snider in Kingston, GA and can be reached at ccie5754@hotmail.com.

James Ewing (CCNP,CCSE,CNE,MCSE) is a Senior Network Engineer for USi, the leading Application Service Provider, headquartered in Annapolis, MD. He has a wide range of experience in the communications industry, including designing high-speed LAN switching solutions and diagnosing advanced LAN and WAN access problems. James will soon be a Cisco Certified Internetworking Expert.

John Friedrich (CCNA, CCI, CCA, MCSE+I, MCT, CNE) is a Senior Technical Training Consultant for Productivity Point, International. Based out of Fort Lauderdale, FL. He has an extensive and diverse background working with network operating system platforms (Novell and NT), and internetworking devices (routers, bridges and gateways). John started Dynacomp Systems, Inc., which provides LAN/WANs solutions. John has been working in the Information Technology industry for over 11 years.

John has taught thousands of students over the last few years how to configure Cisco routers and switches, design and troubleshoot complex networks, and to earn various Cisco/Microsoft/Citrix certifications. John is currently working on www.dynacomp.com, which will offer a virtual lab solution for the CCNA/CCNP certifications.

John, his wife Gail, and their son Christopher and daughter Julia reside in Fort Lauderdale, FL.

Barry Gursky (CCSI, CCNP) is currently employed as an Instructor for Global Knowledge. He has been in the networking industry for 12 years and has been responsible for managing networks in a variety of markets, including the legal, financial, and retail industries. In addition to classroom training, Barry has served as a mentor for other instructors. Barry keeps current technically by providing consulting services including network audits, design, and implementation.

Anthony Kwan (CCNP, CCDP, Master ASE, MCSE, CCA, Master CNE, and A+) has been working in the Internetworking arena over 8 years. Currently, he holds 14 Internetworking career certifications; such as CCNP, CCDP, Master ASE, MCSE, CCA, Master CNE, and A+. Anthony is a Senior Consultant for S3Networks, a Chicago-based consulting company, where he is specializes in LAN/WAN design and troubleshooting, as well as voice, video, and VPN integration. He can be reached at anthonykwan47@hotmail.com.

Andy McCullough (CCNA, CCDA) has been in the network consulting industry for over 5 years. He is currently working at Lucent NPS as a Chief Technical Architect. Andy has done design work for several global customers of Lucent Technologies including, Level 3 Communications, Sprint, MCI/WorldCom, London Stock Exchange, and Birch Telecom. Prior to working for Lucent, Andy ran his own consulting company, Cisco reseller, and ISP. Andy is a CCNA and CCDA and is also an assistant professor teaching Cisco courses at a community college in Overland Park, KS.

Technical Editor

Chris Olsen (CCSI, CCNA, MCT, MCSE, MCP, MCNI, MCNE, CNE) has been working in IT networking full time since 1993 in the areas of training, technical editing, outsourcing, and consulting. In 1996 he founded System Architects, Inc., a training and consulting firm in information technologies. Chris teaches over 30 different courses in Cisco, Microsoft, and Novell, has designed custom courses for corporations, performs a wide array of consulting assignments, does technical editing and outsources numerous IT consultants and trainers for a full range of clientele.

Chris is a Cisco Certified Systems Instructor (CCSI), Cisco Certified Network Administrator (CCNA), Microsoft Certified Trainer (MCT), Microsoft Certified System Engineer (MCSE), Microsoft Certified Professional (MCP), Master Certified Novell Instructor (MCNI), Master Certified Novell Engineer (MCNE), and a Certified Novell Engineer (CNE).

Chris also holds a Bachelor and Masters of Science degree in Mechanical Engineering from Bradley University and is actively pursuing Cisco's CCIE certification. Chris lives in Chicago, IL and can be reached at Chrisolsen@earthlink.net.

Series Editor

Mark Buchmann (CCIE, CCSI) is a Cisco Certified Internetworking Expert (CCIE) and has been a Certified Cisco Systems Instructor (CCSI) since 1995. He is the owner of MAB Enterprises, Inc., a company providing consulting, network support, training, and various other services. Mark is also a co-owner of www.CertaNet.com, a company providing on-line certification assistance for a variety of network career paths including all the various Cisco certifications.

In his free time he enjoys spending time with his family and boating. He currently lives in Raleigh, NC. Mark is Series Editor for Syngress Cisco books.

ACKNOWLEDGMENTS

We would like to thank the following people:

- All the incredibly hard-working folks at Osborne/McGraw-Hill, especially, Brandon Nordin, Scott Rogers, Timothy Green, Gareth Hancock, and Jessica Wilson.
- The Black Hole Publishing Services staff for their help in fine tuning the project.

CONTENTS AT A GLANCE

1	Introduction to Emerging Switching Technologies and the Campus Network	1
2	Switch Block Concepts	37
3	Virtual Local Area Networks (VLANs)	93
4	Redundant Links and the Spanning Tree Protocol	165
5	InterVLAN Routing Concepts	225
6	MultiLayer Switching	291
7	Hot Standby Routing Protocol (HSRP)	347
8	Switching and Routing IP Multicasting	393
9	Switch Diagnostics and Remote Management	477
10	Cisco Switching Product Line	525
A	About the CD	563
	Glossary	569
	Index	613

CONTENTS

About the Contributors .... *v*
Acknowledgments .... *xi*
Preface .... *xxv*
Introduction .... *xxxi*

1 Introduction to Emerging Switching Technologies and the Campus Network 1
  Origins and Directions of Switches/LAN Segmentation-Broadcast
    Issues 2
      Broadcast Issues 3
      Internetworking Equipment 6
      OSI Model 6
      Hubs 8
      Bridges 9
      Routers 10
      Switches 10
      Exercise 1-1: OSI Layer Matching 12
  Introduction to VLANs 13
      Layer 2 VLANs 13
      Layer 3 VLANs 13
      Exercise 1-2: Examples of VLANs 16
  Switching at Different Layers of the OSI Model 17
      Layer 2 17
      Layer 3 18
      Layer 4 19
      Multilayer Switching 21
      Exercise 1-3: Benefits of Switching at Different Layers 21
  Introduction to the Switch Block 22
      Design Layers 22

		Types of Blocks	23
		Exercise 1-4: Blocks and Their Components	25
	✓	Two-Minute Drill	26
	Q&A	Self Test	27
		Lab Question	31
		Self Test Answers	32
		Lab Answer	34

2 Switch Block Concepts 37

Switch Block 38
Fast Ethernet Implementations 41
    Exercise 2-1: Choosing the Correct Media Type 44
Duplex Settings 44
    Exercise 2-2: Selecting the Correct Duplex 46
Gigabit Ethernet 46
Connections 48
    Cabling 48
    Exercise 2-3: Console Connection to Your 1900/2800
        Or 2900XL Switches 51
    Exercise 2-4: Console Connection to Your 5000 Series
        Switches 53
    Ethernet Connection to Both Switch Types 54
    Exercise 2-5: Cabling Switch Block Devices 57
Fundamental Switching Commands 58
    IP Address 58
    sc0 60
    Description 60
    Defining Link Speed 62
    Full Duplex 63
    Ping 64
    Traceroute 67
    Hostnames/Prompts 68
    Passwords 68
    Exercise 2-6: 2900 Fundamental Switching Commands . . . 70
✓ Two-Minute Drill 72

	Q&A	Self Test	75
		Lab Question	80
		Self Test Answers	89
		Lab Answers	91

3 Virtual Local Area Networks (VLANs) 93

VLAN Overview 94
    Creating Virtual LANs 98
    Exercise 3-1: Unpacking and Installing a Core Catalyst
        Switch 99
    Static vs. Dynamic VLANs 103
    Trunking 108
    VTP 132
    Command Details 142
   ✓ Two-Minute Drill 150
  Q&A Self Test 152
    Lab Question 157
    Self Test Answers 159
    Lab Answer 163

4 Redundant Links and the Spanning Tree Protocol 165

Redundant Links 166
    Pros/Cons 169
    Exercise 4-1: Redundant Links 169
Bridging Loops, Spanning Tree, BPDUs 170
    Bridging Loops 170
    What Is the Spanning Tree Protocol? 172
    Understanding How STP Works 173
    STP Port States 179
    Spanning Tree per VLAN 182
    Spanning Tree Protocol in Action 183
    Enabling Spanning Tree 186
    Exercise 4-2: Enabling Spanning Tree 187
Fast EtherChannel 188
    PAgP Functionality 191

	Commands Related to Fast EtherChannel	191
	Exercise 4-3: Enabling Fast EtherChannel	193
PortFast, UplinkFast, BackboneFast		194
	PortFast	194
	UplinkFast	195
	BackboneFast	197
	Exercise 4-4: Enabling PortFast, BackboneFast, and UplinkFast	199
Commands		201
	set spantree (All of the Variables to the Command; Timers, Cost, etc.)	201
	show spantree	203
	show port	204
	show spantree uplinkfast	205
	Exercise 4-5: Using Set and Show Commands	205
✓	Two-Minute Drill	209
Q&A	Self Test	212
	Lab Exercise	216
	Self Test Answers	218
	Lab Answer	221

5 InterVLAN Routing Concepts ... 225

InterVLAN Environments	226
Basic Routing Operations	228
Exercise 5-1: Finding the Correct Address	233
Legacy Routing Environments	234
Router-on-a-Stick	236
VLAN Routing Environments	238
Internal Route Processors	244
Catalyst 5000 Series	244
Exercise 5-2: Hardware Configuration of the RSFC	249
Catalyst 6000 Series	252
Commands	258
enable	259
show running-config	259

configure terminal 260
ip routing 261
appletalk routing 261
ipx routing 261
interface 261
encapsulation 262
ip address 263
ipx network 263
appletalk 264
end 265
<ctrl>-z 266
show ip route 266
Exercise 5-3: Showing Specific Route Entries 267
show ipx route 268
show appletalk route 268
ping 269
traceroute 271
copy running-config startup-config 271
✓ Two-Minute Drill 274
Q&A Self Test 276
Lab Question 283
Self Test Answers 285
Lab Answer 289

6 MultiLayer Switching 291

Introduction to HSRP 291
Data Flow 292
    MLS Flow Mask 297
    Exercise 6-1: The Correct Flow Mask 300
How Different Hardware Platforms Handle Flows of Data through
    MLS 301
MLS-SE, MLS-RP, MLSP 302
    MLS-SE 302
Configuring the MLS-SE for IPX MLS 305
    MLS-RP 306

	MLSP	310
	MLS Topologies	311
	Exercise 6-2: MLS Topology Validation	314
	MLS Cache, Access-Lists, and Other MLS Restrictions	316
	Disabling Combinations	316
	Exercise 6-3: A World Full of Features	318
	MLS Cache Issues	319
	Commands	322
	Set-Based Commands to Configure the MLS-SE	323
	Exercise 6-4: Filtering the Output of the MLS Cache Table	325
	IOS-Based Commands to Configure the MLS-RP	326
✓	Two-Minute Drill	330
Q&A	Self Test	332
	Lab Question	340
	Self Test Answers	341
	Lab Answer	345

7 Hot Standby Routing Protocol (HSRP) 347

Introduction to HSRP 347
HSRP Groups, Virtual IP Address, HSRP Messaging Between Routers . . 350
    Basic Concepts 351
    Basic Configuration 353
    Exercise 7-1: Enabling HSRP 353
Learn States 354
    Exercise 7-2: Using the Debug Feature on a Lab Router . . . 354
Commands 359
    standby [group-number] ip [virtual ip-address [secondary]] . . . 359
    standby [group-number] preempt [**delay** [**delay in seconds**]] . . 361
    standby [group-number] priority [**number from 1 to 255**] 361
    standby [group-number] timers **hellotime holdtime** 362
    standby [group-number] authentication **string** 362
    standby [group-number] track type number [interface-priority] 362
    standby use-bia 364

	show standby	365
	Verifying HSRP in Switched Environments	366
	Configuration Exercises	368
	Exercise 7-3: Configuring HSRP	368
	Advanced HSRP Configuration Examples	371
	Access List Configuration	374
✓	Two-Minute Drill	377
Q&A	Self Test	379
	Lab Question	383
	Self Test Answers	385
	Lab Answer	390

8 Switching and Routing IP Multicasting 393

Understanding the Differences between Multicast, Broadcast, and
  Unicast Addresses 396
    Exercise 8-1: Converting an IP Address to Binary 397
    Exercise 8-2: Calculating the Broadcast Address of
      a Given Network 399
Translating Multicast to Ethernet Addresses 401
    Converting Multicast to Ethernet Addresses in Binary 402
    Exercise 8-3: Converting an IPMC Address to Its MAC
      Address Equivalent 403
Understanding Multicast Protocols 405
    Client-Router Protocols 405
    Multicast Switching Protocols 416
    Multicast Routing Basics 428
    Multicast Routing Protocols 433
    Exercise 8-4: Configure PIM Dense Mode with CGMP ... 437
Monitoring and Troubleshooting Commands 447
    show ip route 447
    show ip igmp groups 448
    show ip igmp interface 449
    show ip pim interface 449
    show ip pim neighbor 450
    show ip pim rp 450

show ip rpf 450
show ip mroute 451
show ip mroute summary 453
show ip mroute active 453
debug ip igmp 455
debug ip pim 455
debug ip mrouting 455
mtrace 457
mstat 457
Exercise 8-6: Monitoring and Troubleshooting IPMC 458
✓ Two-Minute Drill 462
Q&A Self Test 464
Lab Question 469
Self Test Answers 471
Lab Answer 474

9 Switch Diagnostics and Remote Management 477

SNMP Support 479
GET 479
Set 485
Traps 486
Exercise 9-1: Setting Up SNMP to Allow Access and
Trap Acceptance 493
MIBs 493
Web Interface 494
Remote Monitoring (RMON) 497
Exercise 9-2: Adding RMON Support to a Switch 503
Switch Port Analyzer (SPAN) 503
Exercise 9-3: Configuring SPAN for Port Analysis 506
✓ Two-Minute Drill 513
Q&A Self Test 514
Lab Question 518
Self Test Answers 520
Lab Answer 522

Contents   xxiii

10 Cisco Switching Product Line **525**

Cisco IOS-Based Switching Products 526

    Catalyst 1900 and 2820 527

        Exercise 10-1:   Observing and Diagnosing Catalyst Issues
        Using the LED Indicators 529

    Catalyst 2900XL and 3500XL 532

Cisco Set-Based Switching Products 537

    SET IOS Software Features 538

    Catalyst 4000 Series 539

    Catalyst 5000 Family 541

    Catalyst 6000 Family 546

    Catalyst 8500CSR 550

    Exercise 10-2:   Evaluating Products for Use in a LAN
    Environment 552

  ✓ Two-Minute Drill 554

  Q&A Self Test 556

    Lab Question 559

    Self Test Answers 560

    Lab Answer 562

A About the CD **563**

Installing CertTrainer 564

    System Requirements 564

CertTrainer 564

ExamSim 564

    Saving Scores as Cookies 566

E-Book 566

DriveTime 566

Help 567

Upgrading 567

Glossary **569**

Index **613**

PREFACE

Welcome to the rapidly growing sector of the Information Technology (IT) industry of high speed Cisco switching! We have taken great care in writing this text to ensure that it is comprehensive, accurate, easy to read, and up to date.

For those seeking Cisco Certified Networking Professional (CCNP) or Cisco Certified Design Professional (CCDP) certification, this text is also designed to be the ideal study document for the BCMSN exam. This book also plays a critical role in the preparation for the Cisco Certified Internetworking Expert (CCIE) routing and switching certification as the technology contained within is inclusive within the CCIE lab.

We realize that there are many ways to learn any new subject. Texts such as this, instructor-lead training, on-the-job training, the "school of hard knocks," even asking questions are some of the many ways to learn. It's our job with this book to make the learning of this fast growing exciting technology as easy and effective as possible. We have spent a great deal of time ensuring that this has been accomplished.

I have personally been heavily involved in the IT industry since 1993, and in technical training since 1986. Over the years, I've learned a couple of critical principles in learning a new technical subject. They are essential to learning Cisco switching technology, but apply to all of life as well.

The first point is to have the technology immediately available while you learn it and continuously practice the steps and procedures contained within. For example, suppose you had never ridden a bicycle, and never seen one, and decided you wanted to learn all about bicycles and become a successful bicycle rider. Certainly there are many ways to accomplish the objective. Books, videos, classes, and perhaps the Internet would contain a plethora of valuable information. However, all the relevant data would be essentially rendered useless without one critical step in the learning process. You would obtain a bicycle, get on it and ride it. There is no substitute for action and use of the technology one is studying. As simple and obvious as this statement is, and as broad of a sphere of activities as it applies to, it is often left out.

Unfortunately, the IT technical training industry has been subjected to this approach and on occasion has omitted this critical step. For years various computer and networking vendors have been accused of their "paper certifications," obtained by individuals who have memorized text, passed certification exams, all without ever using or applying the technology in a real or even a lab environment.

Fortunately for the rest of us, Cisco has taken great care in the design of their certification and examination process to focus on actual use, application and troubleshooting of the technology, as well as the applicable theory and concepts. Often as an instructor I hear comments from students on the order of "the exam was too difficult," or "Why would they ask me questions like that?" The truth is that the thorough and challenging approach to examinations used by Cisco is really a blessing in disguise in that it's assurance that the CCNP certification won't be degraded in the industry to a mere "paper status."

The solution to this is for the student reading this text to have as much actual Cisco equipment as possible WHILE reading the text. We realize that this will be a challenge for these switching technologies, as the equipment is often costly. However, many resources and online auctions are available on the Internet for purchasing used Cisco equipment, which will totally suffice for use. The equipment can often be re-sold back in the same manner with a nominal depreciation.

For the purposes of this text the following is a suggested equipment list for the purpose of this subject matter.:

- One or more Switches with "SET based" switch operating system such as a Catalyst 5000, 6000, etc.

- One ore more Switch with IOS based OS such as 1900, 28xx, etc.

- One or more Router with IOS ideally with at least one Fast Ethernet interface. Ideally, this will be a Route Switch Module (RSM), a Route Switch Feature Card (RSFC) or a Multilayer Switch Module (MSM) in the Cat 5000 or CAT 6000 switch respectively. However, an external router with at least one 100BaseT connection will also suffice.

- Cabling to interconnect all devices, including Cat 5 twisted pair cable for the Ethernet connections and console cables for the switches. No Wide Area Networking (WAN) cable or devices are needed.

- One or more PC with a network interface card each to connect to the switches. Windows 95, 98, Windows NT, Windows 2000, Unix or Linux

PC's are all sufficient. The machines do not need to be high performance, support detailed graphics or high fidelity audio output, but instead, be functional, and support TCP/IP is a must. Laptops will work great.

If the student has access to a networking lab with multiple pieces of equipment, then the ideal list would include several (3-6) Set based switches, IOS based switches, and several routers as well. The text provides many opportunities for the student to actually implement the technologies in all of their capacities. Again, the equipment should be available to the student while reading. Another critical factor in learning a new subject is the meaning of words, definitions. This is often a grossly underestimated factor in learning. For example, consider the statement: "Increase the thermodynamic state of the air." Thermodynamic, in a common dictionary means "Physics that deals with the relationships of heat and other forms of energy." Therefore the statement simply above means "Turn up the heat." Failing to know one single word can completely alter the entire meaning.

This not only applies to technical words, but common English words as well. We have provided a comprehensive Glossary to aid the student with terms specific to BCMSN. However, it is critical that the student be disciplined to stop and look up every word not fully understood while reading the text, not later for another time. Many Internet sites also provide definitions to technical terms such as Cisco.com (Internetworking Glossary) and whatis.com.

We wish you the best of luck in your profession utilizing the technology contained within this text.

Please feel free to contact us with any comments, questions or suggestions you may have.

Chris M. Olsen
Technical Editor

In This Book

This book is organized around the topics covered within the CCNP Switching Exam administered at Sylvan Testing Centers. This book's primary objective is to help you prepare for and pass the CCNP Switching Exam 640-504. We believe that the only way to do this is to help you increase your knowledge and build your skills. After completing this book, you should feel confident that you have thoroughly reviewed all of the objectives that Cisco has established for the exam.

In Every Chapter

We've created a set of chapter components that call your attention to important items, reinforce important points, and provide helpful exam-taking hints. Take a look at what you'll find in the chapters:

- Each chapter begins with the **Certification Objectives**—what you need to know in order to pass the section on the exam dealing with the chapter topic. The Certification Objective headings identify the objectives within the chapter, so you'll always know an objective when you see it!

EXERCISE 1-1

- **Certification Exercises** are interspersed throughout the chapters. These are step-by-step exercises. They help you master skills that are likely to be an area of focus on the exam. Don't just read through the exercises; they are hands-on practice that you should be comfortable completing. Learning by doing is an effective way to increase your competency with the language.

- **From the Classroom** sidebars describe the issues that come up most often in the training classroom setting. These sidebars give you a valuable perspective into certification- and product-related topics. They point out common mistakes and address questions that have arisen from classroom discussions.

- **S & S** sections lay out specific scenario questions and solutions in a quick-to-read format.

SCENARIO & SOLUTION

You have just taken over as the network administrator and have no information on the password for one of your 3600 series routers. What is a possible solution?	Perform the password recovery process on the 3600 series router.
You have been informed that a new remote location needs connectivity. It will require ISDN access and a four-port hub. What model of router would provide a solution here?	The 803 and 804 both provide for ISDN with a four-port hub.?
An OC-1 connection is being installed at your central location that now employs a 2600 series router. What changes will need to be made at the central site to accommodate this connection?	A 3600 series with the HSSI port will be needed here.

- The **Certification Summary** is a succinct review of the chapter and a re-statement of salient points regarding the exam.

- The **Two-Minute Drill** at the end of every chapter is a checklist of the main points of the chapter. It can be used for last-minute review.

- The **Self Test** offers questions similar to those found on the certification exam. The answers to these questions, as well as explanations of the answers, can be found in Appendix A. By taking the Self Test after completing each chapter, you'll reinforce what you've learned from that chapter, while becoming familiar with the structure of the exam questions.

Some Pointers

Once you've finished reading this book, set aside some time to do a thorough review. You might want to return to the book several times and make use of all the methods it offers for reviewing the material:

1. *Re-read all the Two-Minute Drills*, or have someone quiz you. You also can use the drills as a way to do a quick cram before the exam.

2. *Review all the S & S scenarios* for quick problem solving.

3. *Re-take the Self Tests.* Taking the tests right after you've read the chapter is a good idea, because it helps reinforce what you've just learned. However, it's an even better idea to go back later and do all the questions in the book in one sitting. Pretend you're taking the exam. (For this reason, you should mark your answers on a separate piece of paper when you go through the questions the first time.)

4. *Complete the exercises.* Did you do the exercises when you read through each chapter? If not, do them! These exercises are designed to cover exam topics, and there's no better way to get to know this material than by practicing.

INTRODUCTION

How to Take a Cisco Certification Examination

This introduction covers the importance of your CCNP certification and prepares you for taking the actual examination. It gives you a few pointers on methods of preparing for the exam, including how to study and register, what to expect, and what to do on exam day.

Catch the Wave!

Congratulations on your pursuit of Cisco certification! In this fast-paced world of networking, few certification programs are as valuable as the one offered by Cisco.

The networking industry has virtually exploded in recent years, accelerated by nonstop innovation and the Internet's popularity. Cisco has stayed at the forefront of this tidal wave, maintaining a dominant role in the industry.

The networking industry is highly competitive, and evolving technology only increases in its complexity, so the rapid growth of the networking industry has created a vacuum of qualified people. There simply aren't enough skilled networking people to meet the demand. Even the most experienced professionals must keep current with the latest technology in order to provide the skills that the industry demands. That's where Cisco certification programs can help networking professionals succeed as they pursue their careers.

Cisco started its certification program many years ago, offering only the designation Cisco Certified Internetwork Expert (CCIE). Through the CCIE program, Cisco provided a means to meet the growing demand for experts in the field of networking. However, the CCIE tests are brutal, with a failure rate of over 80 percent. (Fewer than 5 percent of candidates pass on their first attempt.) As you might imagine, very few people ever attain CCIE status.

In early 1998, Cisco recognized the need for intermediate certifications, and several new programs were created. Four intermediate certifications were added: CCNA (Cisco Certified Network Associate), CCNP (Cisco Certified Network Professional), CCDA (Cisco Certified Design Associate), and CCDP (Cisco

Certified Design Professional)In addition, several specialties were added to the CCIE certifications; currently CCIE candidates can receive their CCIE in five areas: Routing and Switching, WAN Switching, ISP-Dial, SNA/IP Integration, and Design.

CCNP advice

I would encourage you to take beta tests when they are available. Not only are the beta exams less expensive than the final exams (some are even free!), but also, if you pass the beta, you will receive credit for passing the exam. If you don't pass the beta, you will have seen every question in the pool of available questions, and can use this information when you prepare to take the exam for the second time. Remember to jot down important information immediately after the exam, if you didn't pass. You will have to do this after leaving the exam area, since materials written during the exam are retained by the testing center. This information can be helpful when you need to determine which areas of the exam were most challenging for you as you study for the subsequent test.

Why Vendor Certification?

Over the years, vendors have created their own certification programs because of industry demand. This demand arises when the marketplace needs skilled professionals and an easy way to identify them. Vendors benefit because it promotes people skilled in their product. Professionals benefit because it boosts their careers. Employers benefit because it helps them identify qualified people.

In the networking industry, technology changes too often and too quickly to rely on traditional means of certification, such as universities and trade associations. Because of the investment and effort required to keep network certification programs current, vendors are the only organizations suited to keep pace with the changes. In general, such vendor certification programs are excellent, with most of them requiring a solid foundation in the essentials, as well as their particular product line.

Corporate America has come to appreciate these vendor certification programs and the value they provide. Employers recognize that certifications, like university degrees, do not guarantee a level of knowledge, experience, or performance; rather, they establish a baseline for comparison. By seeking to hire vendor-certified employees, a company can assure itself that not only has it found a person skilled in networking, but also it has hired a person skilled in the specific products the company uses.

Technical professionals have also begun to recognize the value of certification and the impact it can have on their careers. By completing a certification program, professionals gain an endorsement of their skills from a major industry source. This endorsement can boost their current position, and it makes finding the next job even easier. Often a certification determines whether a first interview is even granted.

Today a certification may place you ahead of the pack. Tomorrow it will be a necessity to keep from being left in the dust.

Signing up for an exam has become easier with the new Web-based test registration system. To sign up for the CCNP exams, access http://www.2test.com, and register for the Cisco Career Certification path. You will need to get an Internet account and password, if you do not already have one for 2test.com. Just select the option for first-time registration, and the Web site will walk you through that process. The registration wizard even provides maps to the testing centers, something that is not available when you call Sylvan Prometric on the telephone.

Cisco's Certification Program

Cisco now has a number of certifications for the Routing and Switching career track, as well as for the WAN Switching career track. While Cisco recommends a series of courses for each of these certifications, they are not required. Ultimately, certification is dependent upon a candidate's passing a series of exams. With the right experience and study materials, you can pass each of these exams without taking the associated class.

Table i-1 shows the Cisco CCNP 2.0 exam track.

The Foundation Routing and Switching exam (640-509) can be taken in place of the Routing, Switching, and Remote Access exams.

As you can see, the CCNA is the foundation of the Routing and Switching track, after which candidates can pursue the Network Support path to CCNP and CCIE, or the Network Design path to CCDA, CCDP, and to CCIE Design.

TABLE i-1	Exam Name	Exam #
CCNP 2.0 Track	CCNA 2.0	640-507
	Routing	640-503
	Switching	640-504
	Remote Access	640-505
	Support	640-506

Please note that if you have taken CCNP exams from the 1.0 track (Exam #'s 640-403, 640-404, 640-405, 640-440) you may take the remainder of your exams from the 2.0 track, but you will be certified as a CCNP 1.0.

CCNP Online

In addition to the technical objectives that are being tested for each exam, you will find much more useful information on Cisco's Web site at http://www.cisco.com/warp/public/10/wwtraining/certprog. You will find information on becoming certified, exam-specific information, sample test questions, and the latest news on Cisco certification. This is the most important site you will find on your journey to becoming Cisco certified.

CCNP Advice

When I find myself stumped answering multiple-choice questions, I use my scratch paper to write down the two or three answers I consider the strongest, and then underline the answer I feel is most likely correct. Here is an example of what my scratch paper looks like when I've gone through the test once:

21. B or C
33. A or C

It is extremely helpful to you mark the question and then continue. You can return to the question and immediately pick up your thought process where you left off. Use this technique to avoid having to reread and rethink questions.
You will also need to use your scratch paper during complex, text-based scenario questions to create visual images to help you understand the question. For example, during the CCNP exam you will need to draw multiple networks and the connections between them or calculate a subnet mask for a given network. By drawing the layout or working the calculation while you are interpreting the question, you may find a hint that you would not have found without your own visual aid. This technique is especially helpful if you are a visual learner.

Computer-Based Testing

In a perfect world, you would be assessed for your true knowledge of a subject, not simply how you respond to a series of test questions. But life isn't perfect, and it just isn't practical to evaluate everyone's knowledge on a one-to-one basis. (Cisco actually does have a one-to-one evaluation, but it's reserved for the CCIE Laboratory exam, and the waiting list is quite long.)

For the majority of its certifications, Cisco evaluates candidates using a computer-based testing service operated by Sylvan Prometric. This service is quite popular in the industry, and it is used for a number of vendor certification programs, including Novell's CNE and Microsoft's MCSE. Thanks to Sylvan Prometric's large number of facilities, exams can be administered worldwide, generally in the same town as a prospective candidate.

For the most part, Sylvan Prometric exams work similarly from vendor to vendor. However, there is an important fact to know about Cisco's exams: They use the traditional Sylvan Prometric test format, not the newer adaptive format. This gives the candidate an advantage, since the traditional format allows answers to be reviewed and revised during the test. (The adaptive format does not.)

CCNP advice

Many experienced test takers do not go back and change answers unless they have a good reason to do so. You should change an answer only when you feel you may have misread or misinterpreted the question the first time. Nervousness may make you second-guess every answer and talk yourself out of a correct one.

To discourage simple memorization, Cisco exams present a different set of questions every time the exam is administered. In the development of the exam, hundreds of questions are compiled and refined, using beta testers. From this large collection, a random sampling is drawn for each test.

Each Cisco exam has a specific number of questions and test duration. Testing time is typically generous, and the time remaining is always displayed in the corner of the testing screen, along with the number of remaining questions. If time expires during an exam, the test terminates, and incomplete answers are counted as incorrect.

CCNP advice

I have found it extremely helpful to put a check next to each objective as I find it is satisfied by the proposed solution. If the proposed solution does not satisfy an objective, you do not need to continue with the rest of the objectives. Once you have determined which objectives are fulfilled you can count your check marks and answer the question appropriately. This is a very effective testing technique!

At the end of the exam, your test is immediately graded, and the results are displayed on the screen. Scores for each subject area are also provided, but the system will not indicate which specific questions were missed. A report is automatically printed at the proctor's desk for your files. The test score is electronically transmitted back to Cisco.

In the end, this computer-based system of evaluation is reasonably fair. You might feel that one or two questions were poorly worded; this can certainly happen, but you shouldn't worry too much. Ultimately, it's all factored into the required passing score.

Question Types

Cisco exams pose questions in a variety of formats, most of which are discussed here. As candidates progress toward the more advanced certifications, the difficulty of the exams is intensified, through both the subject matter and the question formats.

In order to pass these challenging exams, you may want to talk with other test takers to determine what is being tested, and what to expect in terms of difficulty. The most helpful way to communicate with other CCNP hopefuls is the Cisco mailing list. With this mailing list, you will receive e-mail every day from other members, discussing everything imaginable concerning Cisco networking equipment and certification. Access http://www.cisco.com/warp/public/84/1.html to learn how to subscribe to this source of a wealth of information.

True/False

The classic true/false question format is not used in the Cisco exams, for the obvious reason that a simple guess has a 50 percent chance of being correct. Instead, true/false questions are posed in multiple-choice format, requiring the candidate to identify the true or false statement from a group of selections.

Multiple Choice

Multiple choice is the primary format for questions in Cisco exams. These questions may be posed in a variety of ways.

Select the Correct Answer   This is the classic multiple-choice question, in which the candidate selects a single answer from a minimum of four choices. In addition to the question's wording, the choices are presented in a Windows radio button format, in which only one answer can be selected at a time. The question will instruct you to "Select the best answer" when they are looking for just one answer.

Select the Three Correct Answers   The multiple-answer version is similar to the single-choice version, but multiple answers must be provided. This is an all-or-nothing format; all the correct answers must be selected, or the entire question is incorrect. In this format, the question specifies exactly how many answers must be selected. Choices are presented in a check box format, allowing more than one answer to be selected. In addition, the testing software prevents too many answers from being selected.

Select All That Apply   The open-ended version is the most difficult multiple-choice format, since the candidate does not know how many answers should be selected. As with the multiple-answer version, all the correct answers must be selected to gain credit for the question. If too many answers or not enough answers are selected, no credit is given. This format presents choices in check box format, but the testing software does not advise the candidates whether they've selected the correct number of answers.

Make it easy on yourself and find some "braindumps." These are notes about the exam from test takers, which indicate the most difficult concepts tested, what to look out for, and sometimes even what not to bother studying. Several of these can be found at http://www.dejanews.com. Simply do a search for CCNP and browse the recent postings. Another good resource is at http://www.groupstudy.com. Beware however of the person that posts a question reported to have been on the test and its answer. First, the question and its answer may be incorrect. Second, this is a violation of Cisco's confidentiality agreement, which you as a candidate must agree to prior to taking the exam. Giving out specific information regarding a test violates this agreement and could result in the revocation of your certification status.

Freeform Response

Freeform responses are prevalent in Cisco's advanced exams, particularly where the subject focuses on router configuration and commands. In the freeform format, no choices are provided. Instead, the test prompts for user input, and the candidate must type the correct answer. This format is similar to an essay question, except the response must be specific, allowing the computer to evaluate the answer.

For example, the question

Type the command for viewing routes learned via the EIGRP protocol.

requires the answer

show ip route eigrp

For safety's sake, you should completely spell out router commands, rather than using abbreviations. In this example, the abbreviated command **SH IP ROU EI** works on a real router, but is counted as wrong by the testing software. The freeform response questions almost always are answered by commands used in the Cisco IOS. As you progress in your track for your CCNP you will find these freeform response question increasingly prevalent.

Fill in the Blank

Fill-in-the-blank questions are less common in Cisco exams. They may be presented in multiple-choice or freeform response format.

Exhibits

Exhibits, usually showing a network diagram or a router configuration, accompany many exam questions. These exhibits are displayed in a separate window, which is opened by clicking the Exhibit button at the bottom of the screen. In some cases, the testing center may provide exhibits in printed format at the start of the exam.

Scenarios

While the normal line of questioning tests a candidate's "book knowledge," scenarios add a level of complexity. Rather than asking only technical questions, they apply the candidate's knowledge to real-world situations.

Scenarios generally consist of one or two paragraphs and an exhibit that describes a company's needs or network configuration. This description is followed by a series of questions and problems that challenge the candidate's ability to address the situation. Scenario-based questions are commonly found in exams relating to network design, but they appear to some degree in each of the Cisco exams.

You will know when you are coming to a series of scenario questions, because they are preceded by a blue screen, indicating that the following questions will have the same scenario, but different solutions. You must remember that the scenario will be the same during the series of questions, which means that you do not have to spend time reading the scenario again.

Studying Techniques

First and foremost, give yourself plenty of time to study. Networking is a complex field, and you can't expect to cram what you need to know into a single study session. It is a field best learned over time, by studying a subject and then applying your knowledge. Build yourself a study schedule and stick to it, but be reasonable about the pressure you put on yourself, especially if you're studying in addition to your regular duties at work.

One easy technique to use in studying for certification exams is the 30-minutes-per-day effort. Simply study for a minimum of 30 minutes every day. It is a small but significant commitment. On a day when you just can't focus, then give up at 30 minutes. On a day when it flows completely for you, study longer. As long as you have more of the flow days, your chances of succeeding are extremely high.

Second, practice and experiment. In networking, you need more than knowledge; you need understanding, too. You can't just memorize facts to be effective; you need to understand why events happen, how things work, and (most important) how and why they break.

The best way to gain deep understanding is to take your book knowledge to the lab. Try it out. Make it work. Change it a little. Break it. Fix it. Snoop around "under the hood." If you have access to a network analyzer, like Network Associate Sniffer, put it to use. You can gain amazing insight to the inner workings of a network by watching devices communicate with each other.

Unless you have a very understanding boss, don't experiment with router commands on a production router. A seemingly innocuous command can have a nasty side effect. If you don't have a lab, your local Cisco office or Cisco users' group may be able to help. Many training centers also allow students access to their lab equipment during off-hours.

Another excellent way to study is through case studies. Case studies are articles or interactive discussions that offer real-world examples of how technology is applied to meet a need. These examples can serve to cement your understanding of a technique or technology by seeing it put to use. Interactive discussions offer added value because you can also pose questions of your own. User groups are an excellent source of examples, since the purpose of these groups is to share information and learn from each other's experiences.

The Cisco Networkers conference is not to be missed. Although renowned for its wild party and crazy antics, this conference offers a wealth of information. Held every year in cities around the world, it includes three days of technical seminars and presentations on a variety of subjects. As you might imagine, it's very popular. You have to register early to get the classes you want.

Then, of course, there is the Cisco Web site. This little gem is loaded with collections of technical documents and white papers. As you progress to more advanced subjects, you will find great value in the large number of examples and reference materials available. But be warned: You need to do a lot of digging to find the really good stuff. Often your only option is to browse every document returned by the search engine to find exactly the one you need. This effort pays off. Most CCIEs I know have compiled six to ten binders of reference material from Cisco's site alone.

Scheduling Your Exam

The Cisco exams are scheduled by calling Sylvan Prometric directly at (800) 829-6387. For locations outside the United States, your local number can be found on Sylvan's Web site at http://www.prometric.com. Sylvan representatives can schedule your exam, but they don't have information about the certification programs. Questions about certifications should be directed to Cisco's training department.

This Sylvan telephone number is specific to Cisco exams, and it goes directly to the Cisco representatives inside Sylvan. These representatives are familiar enough with the exams to find them by name, but it's best if you have the specific exam number handy when you call. After all, you wouldn't want to be scheduled and charged for the wrong exam (for example, the instructor's version, which is significantly harder).

Exams can be scheduled up to a year in advance, although it's really not necessary. Generally, scheduling a week or two ahead is sufficient to reserve the day and time you prefer. When you call to schedule, operators will search for testing centers in your area. For convenience, they can also tell which testing centers you've used before.

Sylvan accepts a variety of payment methods, with credit cards being the most convenient. When you pay by credit card, you can even take tests the same day you call—provided, of course, that the testing center has room. (Quick scheduling can be handy, especially if you want to retake an exam immediately.) Sylvan will mail you a receipt and confirmation of your testing date, although this generally arrives after the test has been taken. If you need to cancel or reschedule an exam, remember to call at least one day before your exam, or you'll lose your test fee.

When you register for the exam, you will be asked for your ID number. This number is used to track your exam results back to Cisco. It's important that you use the same ID number each time you register, so that Cisco can follow your progress. Address information provided when you first register is also used by Cisco to ship certificates and other related material. In the United States, your Social Security number is commonly used as your ID number. However, Sylvan can assign you a unique ID number if you prefer not to use your Social Security number.

Table i-2 shows the available CCNP 2.0 exams and the number of questions and duration of each. This information is subject to change as Cisco revises the exams, so it's a good idea to verify the details when you register for an exam.

In addition to the regular Sylvan Prometric testing sites, Cisco also offers facilities for taking exams free of charge at each Networkers Conference in the United States. As you might imagine, this option is quite popular, so reserve your exam time as soon as you arrive at the conference.

TABLE i-2 Cisco Exam Lengths and Question Counts

Exam Title	Exam Number	Number of Questions	Duration (minutes)	Exam Fee (US$)
Routing 2.0	640-503	80	90	$100
Switching 2.0	640-504	80	90	$100
Remote Access 2.0	640-505	80	90	$100
Support 2.0	640-506	80	90	$100

Arriving at the Exam

As with any test, you'll be tempted to cram the night before. Resist that temptation. You should know the material by this point, and if you're too groggy in the morning, you won't remember what you studied anyway. Instead, get a good night's sleep.

Arrive early for your exam; it gives you time to relax and review key facts. Take the opportunity to review your notes. If you get burned out on studying, you can usually start your exam a few minutes early. On the other hand, I don't recommend arriving late. Your test could be canceled, or you might be left without enough time to complete the exam.

When you arrive at the testing center, you'll need to sign in with the exam administrator. In order to sign in, you need to provide two forms of identification. Acceptable forms include government-issued IDs (for example, passport or driver's license), credit cards, and company ID badge. One form of ID must include a photograph.

Aside from a brain full of facts, you don't need to bring anything else to the exam. In fact, your brain is about all you're allowed to take into the exam. All the tests are closed book, meaning that you don't get to bring any reference materials with you. You're also not allowed to take any notes out of the exam room. The test administrator will provide you with paper and a pencil. Some testing centers may provide a small marker board instead.

Calculators are not allowed, so be prepared to do any necessary math (such as hex-binary-decimal conversions or subnet masks) in your head or on paper. Additional paper is available if you need it.

Leave your pager and telephone in the car, or turn them off. They only add stress to the situation, since they are not allowed in the exam room, and can sometimes still be heard if they ring outside the room. Purses, books, and other materials must be left with the administrator before you enter. While you're in the exam room, it's important that you don't disturb other candidates; talking is not allowed during the exam.

In the exam room, the exam administrator logs onto your exam, and you have to verify that your ID number and the exam number are correct. If this is the first time you've taken a Cisco test, you can select a brief tutorial for the exam software. Before the test begins, you will be provided with facts about the exam, including the duration, the number of questions, and the score required for passing. Then the clock starts ticking, and the fun begins.

The testing software is Windows-based, but you won't have access to the main desktop or to any of the accessories. The exam is presented in full screen, with a single question per screen. Navigation buttons allow you to move forward and backward between questions. In the upper right corner of the screen, counters show the number of questions and time remaining. Most important, there is a Mark check box in the upper left corner of the screen—this will prove to be a critical tool in your testing technique.

Test-Taking Techniques

One of the most frequent excuses I hear for failing a Cisco exam is "poor time management." Without a plan of attack, candidates are overwhelmed by the exam or become sidetracked and run out of time. For the most part, if you are comfortable with the material, the allotted time is more than enough to complete the exam. The trick is to keep the time from slipping away when you work on any one particular problem.

Your obvious goal in taking an exam is to answer the questions effectively, although other aspects of the exam can distract from this goal. After taking a fair number of computer-based exams, I've developed a technique for tackling the problem, which I share with you here. Of course, you still need to learn the material. These steps just help you take the exam more efficiently.

Size Up the Challenge

First take a quick pass through all the questions in the exam. "Cherry-pick" the easy questions, answering them on the spot. Briefly read each question, noticing the type of question and the subject. As a guideline, try to spend less than 25 percent of your testing time in this pass.

This step lets you assess the scope and complexity of the exam, and it helps you determine how to pace your time. It also gives you an idea of where to find potential answers to some of the questions. Often the answer to one question is shown in the exhibit of another. Sometimes the wording of one question might lend clues or jog your thoughts for another question.

Imagine that the following questions are posed in this order:

Question 1: Review the router configurations and network diagram in exhibit XYZ (not shown here). Which devices should be able to ping each other?

Question 2: If RIP routing were added to exhibit XYZ, which devices would be able to ping each other?

The first question seems straightforward. Exhibit XYZ probably includes a diagram and a couple of router configurations. Everything looks normal, so you decide that all devices can ping each other.

Now consider the hint left by Question 2. When you answered Question 1, did you notice that the configurations were missing the routing protocol? Oops! Being alert to such clues can help you catch your own mistakes.

If you're not entirely confident with your answer to a question, answer it anyway, but check the Mark check box to flag it for later review. If you run out of time, at least you've provided a first-guess answer, rather than leaving it blank.

Take on the Scenario Questions

Second, go back through the entire test, using the insight you gained from the first go-through. For example, if the entire test looks difficult, you'll know better than to spend more than a minute or so on each question. Break down the pacing into small milestones; for example, "I need to answer 10 questions every 15 minutes."

At this stage, it's probably a good idea to skip past the time-consuming questions, marking them for the next pass. Try to finish this phase before you're 50 to 60 percent through the testing time.

By now, you probably have a good idea where the scenario questions are found. A single scenario tends to have several questions associated with it, but they aren't necessarily grouped together in the exam. Rather than rereading the scenario every time you encounter a related question, save some time by answering the questions as a group.

Tackle the Complex Problems

Third, go back through all the questions you marked for review, using the Review Marked button in the question review screen. This step includes taking a second look at all the questions you were unsure of in previous passes, as well as tackling the time-consuming ones you postponed until now. Chisel away at this group of questions until you've answered them all.

If you're more comfortable with a previously marked question, unmark it now. Otherwise, leave it marked. Work your way now through the time-consuming questions, especially those requiring manual calculations. Unmark them when you're satisfied with the answer.

By the end of this step, you've answered every question in the test, despite your reservations about some of your answers. If you run out of time in the next step, at least you won't lose points for lack of an answer. You're in great shape if you still have 10 to 20 percent of your time remaining.

Review Your Answers

Now you're cruising! You've answered all the questions, and you're ready to do a quality check. Take yet another pass (yes, one more) through the entire test, briefly rereading each question and your answer. Be cautious about revising answers at this point unless you're sure a change is warranted. If there's a doubt about changing the answer, I always trust my first instinct and leave the original answer intact.

Trick questions are rarely asked, so don't read too much into the questions. Again, if the wording of the question confuses you, leave the answer intact. Your first impression was probably right.

Be alert for last-minute clues. You're pretty familiar with nearly every question at this point, and you may find a few clues that you missed before.

The Grand Finale

When you're confident with all your answers, finish the exam by submitting it for grading. After what will seem like the longest ten seconds of your life, the testing software will respond with your score. This is usually displayed as a bar graph, showing the minimum passing score, your score, and a PASS/FAIL indicator.

If you're curious, you can review the statistics of your score at this time. Answers to specific questions are not presented; rather, questions are lumped into categories, and results are tallied for each category. This detail is also given on a report that has been automatically printed at the exam administrator's desk.

As you leave the exam, you'll need to leave your scratch paper behind or return it to the administrator. (Some testing centers track the number of sheets you've been given, so be sure to return them all.) In exchange, you'll receive a copy of the test report.

This report will be embossed with the testing center's seal, and you should keep it in a safe place. Normally, the results are automatically transmitted to Cisco, but occasionally you might need the paper report to prove that you passed the exam. Your personnel file is probably a good place to keep this report; the file tends to follow you everywhere, and it doesn't hurt to have favorable exam results turn up during a performance review.

Retesting

If you don't pass the exam, don't be discouraged—networking is complex stuff. Try to have a good attitude about the experience, and get ready to try again. Consider yourself a little more educated. You know the format of the test a little better, and the report shows which areas you need to strengthen.

If you bounce back quickly, you'll probably remember several of the questions you might have missed. This will help you focus your study efforts in the right area. Serious go-getters will reschedule the exam for a couple of days after the previous attempt, while the study material is still fresh in their minds.

Ultimately, remember that Cisco certifications are valuable because they're hard to get. After all, if anyone could get one, what value would it have? In the end, it takes a good attitude and a lot of studying, but you can do it!

1
Introduction to Emerging Switching Technologies and the Campus Network

CERTIFICATION OBJECTIVES

1.01	Origins and Directions of Switches/LAN Segmentation-Broadcast Issues
1.02	Introduction to VLANs
1.03	Switching at Different Layers of the OSI Model
1.04	Introduction to the Switch Block
✓	Two-Minute Drill
Q&A	Self Test

In order to design and build multilayer switched networks, it is important to first understand the demand for switches and what problems they solve. This chapter explains the problems the networking industry faces with existing technology, and the solution that switches provides.

The first sections of this chapter cover the origins of switching technology and explain in detail the problems facing businesses. The next sections introduce Virtual Local Area Networks (VLANs), and discuss where switching resides in the OSI model. The final section is an introduction to the switch block in Chapter 2, "Switch Block Concepts."

CERTIFICATION OBJECTIVE 1.01

Origins and Directions of Switches/LAN Segmentation-Broadcast Issues

About 15 years ago, LANs (local area networks) had little need for high-speed network connectivity. Networks usually consisted of a mainframe with "dumb" terminals or perhaps a few personal computers (PCs) connected to a central server for data storage and printing. Most business applications were installed on local desktop machines with very little data transmitted between the server and client. These "networks" were primarily used for storing and sharing data among small groups of users (workgroups).

This soon changed, and LANs quickly became the central point for all enterprise applications, data sharing, and storage. More and more applications were being staged from centralized servers. Companies soon were connecting all of their workgroups together into larger and larger organizations providing centralized data storage, workgroup collaboration (e-mail and scheduling software), accounting packages, and other enterprise applications. As the number of users located on these networks increased, so did the need to physically segment the users while logically connecting them to the core resources. Early networking devices were developed that allowed network administrators to geographically group centralized resources and link them with geographically disparate users.

These early networking devices were hubs, bridges, and routers. Each was responsible for a separate layer of communication. These devices worked very well during the first years of explosive growth. Technology soon caught up with these first- and second-generation networking devices. New applications were developed that pushed current technology beyond its capacity. Multimedia applications, networked voice applications, powerful engineering tools, and Enterprise Resource Planning packages took their toll on networks. It was time for data communication technology to catch up, and the answer was the *switch*. This new device combined the functionality of multiport bridges and sometimes routers into a single layer 2/3 device. The device allowed for reliable high-speed transmissions of data, while expanding port density and eliminating unnecessary networking devices.

> **New switches contain application-specific integrated chips (ASICs) that allow data to be switched several thousand times faster than predecessor switches, while allowing administrators more granularity and features.**

Broadcast Issues

The primary issue fueling the push for high-speed switching was the inherent nature of the primary transmission protocol used in the industry, Ethernet. While not the most efficient transport protocol, it's the most widely used. Due to inherent limitations in the protocol, steps had to be taken to design equipment that allowed Ethernet to work as efficiently as possible while scaling to thousands of users.

Ethernet Broadcasts

Look for a moment at Ethernet. Ethernet is a *broadcast* (contention) based media protocol. Ethernet technology states that, "each station must listen to the physical line for the absence of other traffic before transmitting." If no traffic is sensed, the transmitting station will broadcast its data over the wire. Each station on the Ethernet segment receives the packet and copies it to its buffer. The stations then check the packet's destination address against their own *Media Access Control* (MAC) address. If the destination address matches the receiving station's MAC address, the packet is processed; no match, the packet is dropped.

on the job

A MAC address is composed of a 48-bit hexadecimal address. Each address is unique. An International Committee assigns the first 12 bits to particular vendors; the remaining 36 bits are unique within the vendor's organization. The result is a unique hardware address assigned to each device. If duplicate MAC addresses (usually due to a manufacturing error) are located on the same network, the router's or switch's ARP cache will be corrupted. Tracking the machines down, isolating them from the network, and clearing the ARP cache on the router will solve the problem.

What if more than one station communicates at once? Take, for instance, two stations, both having data to pass. Both stations listen to the wire for a "quiet" period. The stations determine, at the same time, that the line is clear, so they send their packets. The packets collide! The stations receive a collision. Once the collision is received, the line is jammed (this notifies other stations of the collision) and a back-off algorithm is used to resend the packet. The back-off time is random and is calculated from the receipt of the collision. After the random back-off period, the stations will retransmit their data during the next available "quiet" period. This process of transmitting, experiencing collisions, and retransmitting is normal to Ethernet operation.

Now magnify this process a hundred times. Instead of two or three stations trying to pass data on the same physical link, we have a couple of hundred. Each of these stations listens to the line for a "quiet" period in order to transmit its data. Multiple stations sensing a quiet period transmit their data. This time, several of the stations transmit at the same time, causing collisions. The back-off period occurs for all of the stations. Most of the stations are able to retransmit without problems. Two of the stations have problems and manage to experience collisions the next 15 times they try to transmit. Typically, once the magic number of 16 collisions has been experienced on a network interface card (NIC), the packet is dropped. When a packet is dropped, it is purged from the NIC buffer.

Network Layer Broadcasts

Broadcasts also occur at other levels of communication. Depending on the network layer transport protocol, machines will broadcast for different services or reasons. The two primary network layer protocols are IP and IPX. Each of these protocols has a different methodology for broadcasts.

IP Broadcasts   Internet Protocol (IP) networks are probably the most popular in the world. IP is a very robust protocol. Its use as the protocol for the Internet has helped increase its popularity. IP uses broadcasts for a variety of reasons, the primary reason being to correlate a physical MAC address of a resource with a network address. This correlation is stored in an ARP (Address Resolution Protocol) cache or table. In order for a machine to properly address a packet, a destination MAC address is required.

ARP is a fairly simple protocol. When a machine first boots up and the IP "stack" is loaded, an ARP packet is broadcast out on the network. This ARP broadcast is initially for the machine's default gateway. This will be the first entry in the ARP cache. As the machine tries to access resources or send data to known network entities, the ARP cache will be checked for an entry. If there isn't an entry in the ARP cache for the network layer address, an ARP broadcast will be sent out. If the destination machine is on the local network, the response will be the MAC address of the appropriate machine. If the destination machine is on another network segment, the MAC address of the router interface (default gateway) will be used.

IPX Broadcasts   Internet Packet eXchange (IPX) is a Novell proprietary network protocol. Novell is currently one of the largest providers of network operating systems (NOS) in the world. The IPX protocol has similar broadcast issues that are focused in two primary areas: the server and the client.

The Novell server uses Service Advertisement Protocol (SAP) to broadcast out its services. These services can be anything from printers to file shares, and are typically rebroadcast every 30–90 seconds. The routers in an IPX network keep a SAP table of which network stations are advertising services. When a client sends a broadcast for a particular service, the router (or server if on the same segment) will answer with the appropriate network address.

The Novell client uses Get Nearest Server (GNS) broadcasts at boot-up to locate the closest Novell server with user authentication services running. This GNS request is only found during the initial login at boot-up time.

Increasing the number of workstations or resources on a flat IP or an IPX network can easily add unwanted broadcast traffic. Broadcast traffic, both network and physical layer, can add additional overhead to workstations and routers, and if not managed properly, can severely affect the network.

Internetworking Equipment

Networking equipment comes in all shapes, sizes, and functions, the core devices being hubs, bridges, routers, and switches. Each piece of equipment operates at a different layer of communication. These layers are identified in the Open System Interconnection (OSI) model.

OSI Model

The OSI model, seen in Figure 1-1, was designed to map current technologies and provide a method for future product development. It is comprised of the Physical layer, Data layer, Network layer, Transport layer, Session layer, and Application layer.

Physical Layer—Layer 1

The *physical layer* provides the "mechanical, electrical, functional, and procedural means" required for the transmission of data. This includes any form of transmission media (copper, fiber, microwave, wireless, etc.). It's at this layer that the basic network connections of devices are made.

Data Link Layer—Layer 2

The *data link* layer has "control of the physical layer detecting and correcting errors which may occur." This pertains to possible errors during physical layer transmission

FIGURE 1-1

The OSI reference model

The OSI Reference Model

Layer 7—Application
Layer 6—Presentation
Layer 4—Session
Layer 4—Transport
Layer 3—Network
Layer 2—Data Link
Layer 1—Physical

not produced by upper-level application layers. Hardware addresses are used to identify individual devices on the network. Bridges and switches are examples of layer 2 devices.

Network Layer—Layer 3
The *network layer* is responsible for receiving the data from the lower and upper layers and routing it to the appropriate destination networks. This path determination allows data to travel the most efficient path to its destination. Network addresses are used to identify source and destination networks. This is required for the routing protocols, which operate at this layer, to properly route packets.

Transport Layer—Layer 4
The *transport layer* is responsible for establishing, maintaining, and terminating communications between endstations. These communications are established on particular port numbers depending on the protocol being used. This layer is responsible for verifying that data sent is received properly. If errors are detected during the transport process, this layer will ensure that the stations know about the error and resend that piece of data.

Session Layer—Layer 5
The *session layer* arranges and orders data exchanges between application processes. This timing and flow control allows applications to communicate window sizes and error control mechanisms. It is important to note that the session layer handles upper-level applications as opposed to the transport layer, which handles system or physical connections.

Presentation Layer—Layer 6
The *presentation layer* is a type of universal translator. This layer takes data from the application in whatever format, and translates it into a universal format that the lower layers of the open system can understand and interpret. At this layer, file formats and data formats such as ASCII or EBCDIC are added or deleted as appropriate.

Application Layer—Layer 7
The *application layer is* the highest level of the OSI model and represents what the client views or inputs. In essence, it is the end-user's interface to the system.

Applications such as e-mail, newsreaders, or other applications' display modules reside here, providing the translation from code to something visual that the end user can understand. It's at this layer that user input is converted back into something the system can understand (i.e., ASCII or EBCDIC).

Hubs

Hubs were designed in order to connect multiple network devices together in an efficient manner. A hub, or concentrator as they're sometimes called, works at the basic level of network communication, the physical layer. It is a device that connects a set of network devices together on the same physical wire. In turn, the hub is linked to another hub, bridge, or router, depending on its location in the network.

Since hubs are fairly simple devices, operating at the physical layer, the devices connected to them must be on the same IP subnet. Hubs located on a single network segment share a single broadcast/collision domain. Hubs are capable of transmitting at 10/100 Mbps depending on the hub, and are used primarily in workgroup or SOHO (Small Office Home Office) situations where only a few devices need to be networked.

Since hubs are physical layer devices, sharing a common broadcast/collision domain over subscription can cause problems. The more devices plugged into hubs on a single network segment, the greater the chance of collisions and broadcast

FROM THE CLASSROOM

The Importance of Memorization

It's important to be able to memorize lists. The easiest way to do this is to create a funny saying or song about the list. Equate the words of the saying or song to the list. After repeating the saying a few times, you'll have no problem associating the list with the saying in the future. A good example for the OSI Reference model would be: Please Do Not Throw Sausage Pizza Away. Each of the words represents a layer of the reference model: Physical, Data link, Network, Transport, Session, Presentation, and Application.

—*James Ewing, CCNP, CCSE, CNE, MCSE*

storms. The increased number of stations effectively lowers the shared bandwidth. This decrease causes retransmissions, increased broadcasts, and collisions.

Bridges

Bridges are layer 2 devices that connect multiple network segments together for any number of reasons, including reduction of broadcast/collision domains, connecting dissimilar technologies together, or extending the effective range of a flat hub network. Since bridges are layer 2 devices, they don't perform layer 3 routing.

Bridges belong to the broadcast domains for each segment to which they're attached. This allows them to monitor all broadcasts and maintain a table of MAC addresses and which port they were heard on. This learning function helps the bridge determine which port to forward packets out.

The bridge maintains a list or table of which MAC addresses were learned on which bridge ports. When the bridge receives a packet, either a broadcast or directed, it first will look at the MAC address for the destination and check it against its table. If the address is found, the bridge forwards the packet to that port. If the address isn't found, the packet is flooded out all ports except for the port on which the packet was received.

There are several types of bridges: transparent, translational, source route, source route transparent, and source route translational. Each type of bridging has very distinct characteristics.

Transparent Bridging

Transparent bridging is found primarily on Ethernet networks and is one of the most common forms of bridging. This type of bridging is used to connect networks of the same type of transmission media together. This form of bridging passes frames along one hop or path at a time.

Source Route

IBM developed source route bridging for use in Token Ring networks. With source route bridging, the entire route (path) is included in the Routing Information Field (RIF), also known as the Routing Information Indicator (RII). This field has information of the destination MAC address, as well as whether the frame needs to be forwarded across the bridge to another ring (segment).

Translational Bridging

Translational bridging is used to bridge two different transmission media together that have dissimilar MAC formats. Examples of this include bridging Ethernet and FDDI, or Ethernet and Token Ring.

Source Route Transparent

Source route transparent bridging is the combination of transparent bridging and source route bridging, providing complete connectivity to all end devices. Token Ring stations and Ethernet stations can exist on the same device without having to perform translation.

Source Route Translational

Source route translational bridging bridges Token Ring and Ethernet together. The bridge converts the MAC addresses from the appropriate transmission media types in the forwarded media type. In other words, an Ethernet MAC address is converted to noncanonical, and a Token Ring address is converted to canonical where appropriate.

Routers

Routers are the "brains" of the network. These layer 3 devices are responsible for connecting multiple dissimilar networks together. Routers compare a packet's layer 3 network address to an internal routing table or database. This table is a list of all of the networks that the router "knows" about and the corresponding interface; either by a learning process, routing updates, or being directly connected. Once a packet is received, the destination network is looked up in the table, and the packet is forwarded to the appropriate next hop. If no correlation is found, the packet is either forwarded out the router's default gateway or dropped if no default route is defined.

Switches

Switches were developed in order to increase the number of stations on a network segment. Due to the broadcast and collision limitations of hubs and bridges, a new device needed to be designed that would address these issues while improving overall performance. Not only did the switch address these issues, it brought about a whole new way of thinking in the networking world.

Switches combined the best of both the hub and the bridge. The hub provided port density, while the bridge contributed layer 2 MAC address management and loop-free topology management. In addition to combining two networking devices into one, switch designers were able to greatly improve network performance by increasing back plane speeds and reducing retransmissions from broadcasts and collisions.

During the race to design switching platforms, two types of switching methods were developed: store-and-forward and cut-through. These methods describe how traffic is directed through the switch.

Store-and-Forward

Switches using the store-and-forward method store the entire frame in memory. Once the frame is in memory, the switch checks the destination address, source address, and the CRC (cyclical redundancy check). If no errors are present, the frame is forwarded to the appropriate port. While error checking ensures the validity of all frames prior to transmission, this process can add considerable delay to the switching process depending on the size of the frame. Currently, the Catalyst 1900, 2800, 3000, and 5000 series switches all support store-and-forward.

Cut-Through

Switches using the cut-through method check begin forwarding the frame as soon as the destination port is identified. This greatly reduces delays (or latency) because the frames are being forwarded as soon as they arrive. This is the standard switching method for the Catalyst 5000 series of switches.

Cut-through switching is the default for the Catalyst 5000 family of switches.

Take a few minutes and look at the following Scenario & Solution questions. If you have any problems answering the questions, re-read the appropriate section and try the question again.

SCENARIO & SOLUTION

A router operates at which OSI layer?	A router operates at layer 3, the network layer.
A hub operates at which OSI layer?	Layer 1, the physical layer.
What is considered a one-way bridge?	Half duplex is considered a one-way bridge, because only one party can talk at a time.
What are the main differences between store-and-forward and cut-through switching?	Store-and-forward receives the entire frame before forwarding it; cut-through starts forwarding as soon as the destination is identified.
Which type of bridging is the most common in Ethernet networks?	Transparent bridging.
What is a MAC address?	A MAC, Media Access Control, address is the hardware address of a network card or device.

EXERCISE 1-1

OSI Layer Matching

It is very important to understand the OSI model and the networking equipment associated with the various layers. In this exercise, fill in the layer number, the description, and the appropriate networking device (if any) in Table 1-1.

TABLE 1-1 OSI Layer Matching

OSI Layer	Layer Number	Description	Networking Device
Transport			
Presentation			
Network			
Physical			
Application			
Data Link			
Session			

CERTIFICATION OBJECTIVE 1.02

Introduction to VLANs

In order to understand VLANs, we must first understand their predecessor: the LAN. As stated in the beginning of the chapter, a LAN is primarily a group of computers or resources that are physically grouped together. These resources had to be in close proximity to each other primarily due to the limiting technology of the day. As newer technology came to light, the ideas surrounding LANs changed. A new concept known as a virtual local area network (VLAN) was born. VLANs allowed users and resources to exist virtually anywhere.

The push behind this new technology was that users and resources weren't always located in close proximity to each other. The current technology (LANs) required connections to each other using routers. Since routers are layer 3 devices, they look farther into the packet for additional information regarding the source and destination networks. This additional "look" adds latency to the transmission or forwarding of the packet; in some instances, it's 40 percent higher. With the addition of high-speed LAN switches, and subsequently VLANs, resources and users could now be grouped logically.

Additionally, the advent of Asynchronous Transfer Mode (ATM) added the capability to extend VLANs over distances never before possible. Suddenly, large campus networks had a high-speed solution to their networking needs.

These resources could be grouped at two different layers: layer 2 or layer 3.

Layer 2 VLANs

A layer 2 VLAN is called a *switched* VLAN. The VLAN is set up on a switch and is considered one distinct broadcast domain. Within this segment are all of the machines on the network (same network address range). A layer 2 VLAN doesn't have connectivity to other VLANs unless directly attached to a router.

Layer 3 VLANs

A layer 3 VLAN is called a *routed* VLAN. This VLAN type is set up on both a switch and a router or route switch module (RSM). This router has the ability to *switch* packets between VLANs at higher speeds than merely routing them.

University West, pictured in Figure 1-2, is a large university campus consisting of several buildings spread across several hundred acres of property. On the far northern end of the campus is the Administration building. This building has individual point-to-point router links to each outlying campus building. Each building consists of a LAN connected to the central office via a serial router connection. These connections were usually no more than T1 speeds (1.544Mbps), due to the high cost of the connections. Each building has a number of workgroup hubs connected to the router.

Each building currently exists as a separate broadcast domain. The broadcast domains are terminated on the routers located in the individual buildings. As more

FIGURE 1-2 University West Campus—before VLANs

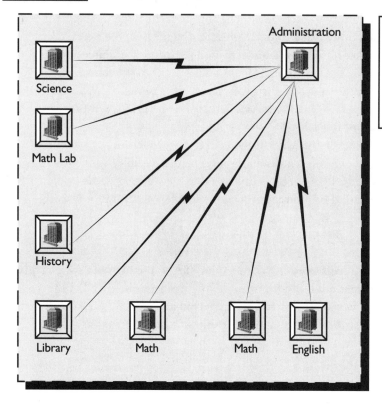

and more users are added, broadcasts rapidly increase. Increased broadcasts cause *broadcast storms*. Broadcast storms are events on a (usually a flat unsegmented) network. These events are caused by an overload of broadcasts on a segment (network). The more retransmits or broadcasts on a network, the larger a broadcast storm grows. Sometimes these events can last for hours, causing severe degradation in performance.

Several of these buildings, belonging to the math department, need to be connected together to share a graphics server laboratory in one of the buildings. The files on the graphics server are very large, and the computing power is enormous. The students are using the server to do experimental research. Since the current LAN/WAN technology will only allow 10/100 Mbps connection to a router with a 1.544 Mbps connection to another building, the only feasible solution is to require students to physically visit the graphics lab.

Now take a look at the design after the introduction to switching and VLANs. University West, Figure 1-3, is a large campus consisting of several buildings spread across several hundred acres of property. In the far northern end of the campus is the Administration building. This building is connected to the other buildings via fiber optic ATM link. These links are OC-3 (155 Mbps) connections. Each building has a Cisco 5500 with ATM processor and OC-3 card in it. This technology allows for the introduction of VLANs. VLANs provide the ability to separate workgroups logically as opposed to physically. No longer is each building required to work as a separate entity. Now, VLANs can be created to support the administrative branch, math departments, science departments, and so forth. Extending the VLANs over ATM to the appropriate buildings can extend individual networks to multiple buildings on campus.

An additional benefit from the introduction of VLANs is the reduction of the broadcast domains. Before the redesign, each building consisted of its own broadcast domain. These broadcast domains were growing beyond acceptable limits, causing severe problems. Now each building has effectively been divided into at least two broadcast domains that terminate on a switch/router in a centralized location.

Now, students located in any of the math buildings can have direct access to the graphics lab without physically visiting the lab. Likewise, administrative users will have access to the administration systems, and other buildings will have access to the library computer systems. This method of design allows for resources to be shared and distributed at any location in the campus while providing access to end users.

FIGURE 1-3 University West campus—with VLANs

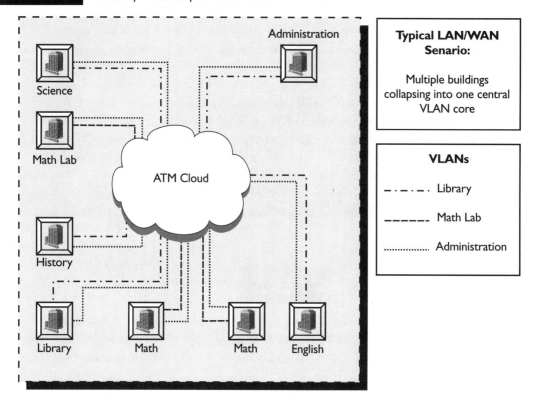

EXERCISE 1-2

Examples of VLANs

Read the following scenario. Then propose a solution using the preceding case study as a reference.

Scenario:

A local hospital has a very large campus network. This campus contains the main hospital, a burn unit, a medical college (classrooms), and a separate lab facility. Currently, all buildings are connected to the central hospital Administration building. The new hospital administrator wants to connect the buildings with a high-speed network, digitize x-ray pictures, and centralize patient and student

records, making them accessible to each building. Describe in detail how the hospital could redesign their network to facilitate the new director's vision.
Answer:
A high-speed network will be designed using a combination of ATM and VLANs. The central hospital administration office will house the servers that contain patients' records and x-rays. These resources will reside on a VLAN that will be accessible by all of the buildings except the medical college. The medical college will house the students' records. These will be accessible from anywhere on the campus. The lab facility will contain the lab results for the patients. Since these are restricted to being viewed by doctors and nurses only, special care will need to be taken to safeguard this data. One way to accomplish this would be to have a select few workstations in a protected VLAN with access to the lab network.

CERTIFICATION OBJECTIVE 1.03

Switching at Different Layers of the OSI Model

Switching can occur at four different levels: layer 2, layer 3, layer 4, and multilayer. Each of these layers of switching can be used in different scenarios, depending on the requirements. Layer 2 switching allows for security and micro-segmentation of the network, layer 3 allows inter-VLAN switching to occur with the use of a router, layer 4 switching combines layer 3 switching and network address translation (NAT) to switch traffic destined to one server to multiple servers hidden behind one IP address, and multilayer switching takes layer 4 switching to the next level by utilizing session tracking and server monitoring to provide "intelligent" load-balanced switching.

Layer 2

Layer 2 switching is hardware-based switching that provides wire-speed performance, bridging, high throughput, and higher port densities, all at lower prices than traditional bridges. The way it works is pretty simple: When a switch comes online (is powered up), it sets its ports into a "listening/learning" state. In this state, the ports record in Content Addressable Memory (CAM) which MAC addresses are heard on which ports; future-forwarding decisions made by the switch will use this CAM table. Once the port has finished its "listening/learning" period, it will most likely go to a "forwarding" state (additional port states will be explained in later chapters).

Once the switch has initialized, built its CAM table, and set its ports to the forwarding state, it's ready to switch frames. When a switch receives a frame, it first examines the destination MAC address. This address is checked against the current CAM table to determine if the switch "knows" where to forward the frame. If the destination address is in the CAM table, the switch forwards the frame to the appropriate port. If no entry exists in the table for the destination address, then the switch will broadcast the frame out all ports in the same layer 2 VLAN as the source port *except* the source port itself.

Layer 3

Layer 3 switching occurs at the routing level. There are several benefits to layer 3 switching. Since a router is added to the switching picture, network administrators can perform optimal route selection, and limit broadcast/multicast domains. Additionally, routers can add security through the addition of *access control lists* (ACLs). In order for a router to be able to switch traffic, it has to have a way to identify VLANs.

This method is called *frame tagging*, and is implemented with Cisco's proprietary inter-switch link (ISL) protocol. This protocol links Ethernet or Token Ring frames with a "color" tag that identifies the pertinent VLAN information.

ISL is a trunking protocol, meaning that it's used to link switches to other switches or routers in order to carry multiple VLAN traffic to those other devices. It can only be implemented on high-speed interfaces (100-Mbps full-duplex or higher). As traffic from multiple VLANs enters the switch, it's immediately forwarded out all trunk ports. This propagation of traffic allows the routers or other switches to see all of the trunked traffic and determine if any of the traffic is destined for that device's ports.

A layer 3 VLAN is set up either on a separate router attached to the switch (router on a stick) with the Fast Ethernet port of the router set up as an ISL trunk to the switch, or on an integrated Route Switch Module (RSM) inserted into the Cisco Catalyst 5000 series switches. Using an RSM is preferred, due to higher throughput capabilities of transferring the frames through the gigabit back plane of Catalyst 5000 series switches.

The layer 3 VLAN contains the IP network information for a VLAN that needs to have access via routing to other VLANs. Once again, the switch will receive a frame from an endstation. This time, the destination MAC address will be that of the router or RSM. The switch will forward the frame to the appropriate trunk port. Once the frame reaches the trunk port, ISL applies a frame tag, which identifies the frame's VLAN information. When the router receives the tagged frame, it strips off the tag and the framing information. At this point, the frame becomes a packet. The router will look at the packet's IP information and compare it against its routing table. If the packet needs to be forwarded (switched) to another VLAN, the router will put a new tag (the tag of the destination VLAN) on the packet (changing it back into a frame) and forward it back to the switch. Once the switch receives the retagged frame, it'll be processed like any other layer 2 frame.

exam
Watch   ***Layer 3 switching requires a router to perform inter-VLAN switching.***

Take a few minutes and look at the following Scenario & Solution questions before going to the next section.

Layer 4

What if you could take switching to the application layers? Until now, we could only separate networks into switched and routed VLANs. With layer 4 switching,

SCENARIO & SOLUTION	
What is a LAN?	A LAN is a group of computers or resources on the same physical segment or "wire."
What is a VLAN?	A VLAN is a virtual LAN, and allows multiple LANs to reside in a switch separated by software.
Can users on a particular VLAN reside anywhere on the network?	Yes, users can reside anywhere on the network and belong to a particular VLAN, providing the VLAN has been properly extended (ATM or ISL).
What is ISL?	Inter-Switch Link protocol is a frame tagging/trunking protocol.
What is a router attached to a switch called?	"Router on a stick."

we can now perform some interesting "magic" in the network. Layer 4 switching uses the transport layer port information in conjunction with the layer 3 network address. Switch vendors have taken different approaches to implementing layer 4 switching in their equipment, but essentially offer the same service from layer 4 switching. These include server farm load balancing, quality of service (QoS), and traffic shaping.

Server Farm Load Balancing

Layer 3 switching and network address translation (NAT) are combined to provide load balancing across a server farm. The layer 4 VLAN is set up with the servers to be accessed with one range of network addresses "hidden" (NAT'd) behind a single address. This form of layer 4 switching allows network administrators to add or remove servers from the farm without interruption of service to the end user, while providing additional security by "hiding" the servers behind a NAT'd address.

Quality of Service (QoS)

Layer 4 switching also provides quality of service. Layer 4 VLANs can be created using a combination of layer 3 VLANs and queuing strategies. Queuing strategies give network administrators the ability to identify queues by transport layer protocol (i.e., FTP, SMTP) and assign delivery priorities to these queues. In the case of FTP and SMTP (File Transfer Protocol, and Simple Mail Transport Protocol), a network administrator could set up an FTP queue to have a higher priority than SMTP, allowing FTP users to experience a higher quality of service than SMTP users.

Traffic Shaping

The concepts of traffic shaping are very close to those of quality of service. Using a combination of layer 3 VLANs and queuing, network administrators can create a layer 4 VLAN capable of assigning specific maximum transmission rates by specific transport protocol, TCP port, or UDP port. This gives them the flexibility to provide maximum bandwidth to mission-critical applications, while allowing not so important applications lower bandwidth pipes.

Layer 4 switching is based on conversations between specific machines.

SCENARIO & SOLUTION

What is layer 4 switching?	Layer 4 switching is based on conversation pairs.
What is multilayer switching?	Switching that is performed at layers 2, 3, and 4.
What are some of the benefits to layer 4 switching?	Quality of Service (QoS), traffic shaping, load balancing.
Does layer 4 rely on IP addresses only to make switching decisions?	No, it uses a combination of IP addresses and protocol port numbers.

Multilayer Switching

Multilayer switching, according to Cisco, is the ability to perform switching at layers 2, 3, and 4. In order for switching to be done at so many different layers, the switches have to have large amounts of memory to manage the switching tables for each of the layers. Additionally, specifically designed ASICs are required to perform various switching and routing functions on the line cards where available. The whole concept is to switch whenever possible, routing only when needed.

Use the Scenario & Solution questions on the top of this page to review the last couple of switching types. If you have any problems, review the individual sections.

EXERCISE 1-3

Benefits of Switching at Different Layers

In the Table 1-2, you'll find a switching layer on the left-hand side. On the right-hand side, list as many characteristics for switching at that layer as possible.

The immediate characteristics that come to mind for this exercise are:

- **Layer 2** Single broadcast domain, one physical segment, and layer 2 security.
- **Layer 3** Optimal Route Selection, security (access lists), high-speed packet forwarding.
- **Layer 4** Switching based on conversations.
- **Multilayer** All three switching layers at wire speed.

TABLE 1-2

Switching Layer Characteristics

Switching Layer	Characteristics
Layer 2	
Layer 3	
Layer 4	
Multilayer	

CERTIFICATION OBJECTIVE 1.04

Introduction to the Switch Block

Within the last few years, network design has taken on the building-block approach for designing switched networks. This building-block approach takes the network and breaks it into three distinct layers: the access layer, the distribution layer, and the core layer. These layers, shown in Table 1-3, are combined to form switch blocks. These modular blocks are then used to design the switched network.

Design Layers

As campus networks became increasingly complex, network designers began using specific design layers to describe and define their networks. These layers correlate the position of the network with the type of access and equipment used.

Access Layer

The access layer is the layer that the client connects to the network. This layer is usually made up of small to medium-sized workgroup switches or hubs. The

TABLE 1-3

Design Layer Characteristics

Design Layer	Characteristics
Access layer	Entry point for end users into the switched network
Distribution layer	Aggregation point for access layer switches
Core layer	Aggregation point for multiple distribution layers

switches operate at layer 2 and are connected to the next layer via an uplink connection or a trunk port. The primary function of this layer is to connect end users to core resources.

Access layer switches and equipment include hubs, Cisco Catalyst 1900, 2820, 2900, 4000, and even the 5000 series switches. Any of these may be used, depending on the number of users that need to connect to the distribution layer.

Distribution Layer

The distribution layer is the aggregation point for access layer switches. Access layer switches and/or hubs are connected to each other at this layer. This layer terminates VLANs and broadcast domains, while providing inter-VLAN routing and security to the core.

Since the distribution layer must handle routing and high-speed switching between multiple access layer points, only the larger switches should be used. These switches include the Catalyst 8500, 6000, or 5000 series of switches.

Core Layer

The core is the backbone of the campus, tying all of the distribution layers into one backbone. This layer is responsible for performing high-speed switching and routing. The core layer should be the most fault tolerant and robust of all network layers. For this reason, the Catalyst 6500 or 8500 series switch, or the Cisco 12000 GSR (Gigabit Switch Router), should be used. These switches/routers are capable of performing wire-speed multilayer switching.

Types of Blocks

There are a couple of different types of blocks to consider. The primary blocks are the switch block and the core block. Secondary blocks include WAN, server, and legacy equipment. These blocks all have specific requirements for design.

Switch Blocks

Switch blocks are comprised of access-layer and distribution-layer aggregation. The primary goal of a switch block is to maximize the use of scalable layer 2 and layer 3 switching. Additionally, the switch block is used to define a single broadcast domain. This "segmentation" protects other parts of the network from being adversely affected by problems within the switch block. Likewise, the switch block is protected from problems experienced outside of the switch block.

The primary goal is to maximize the use of scalable layer 2 and layer 3 switching.

Core Block

A core block is used as an aggregation point for two or more switch blocks. As a centralized campus backbone, the core must be capable of rapidly switching traffic to other switch blocks as quickly as possible. The switches in the core must be very high-end switches such as the Cisco Gigabit Switch Router (GSR12000) capable of ATM cell, frame, or packet switching.

There are several ways to design the core. The main thing to remember, however, is to make the core as robust and redundant as possible.

WAN Block

The wide area networking (WAN) block provides access to remote offices and Internet connectivity. These connections can include T-1, T-3, or high-speed ATM connectivity. This block can be connected directly to the core, or connected to a distribution layer switch block and then into the core.

Server Block

The server block, or *farm* as it's sometimes called, houses the server resources for the campus. These resources can exist in one or more server blocks, and are connected to the core. Connecting these directly to the core provides high-speed access to resources as needed.

Legacy Equipment Block

The legacy equipment block includes mainframes, printers, and other SNA-style devices that wouldn't normally fit into one of the other blocks. These blocks will usually have to be bridged or routed into the core at some point. By keeping legacy equipment in one or two general blocks, faults can be rapidly isolated if necessary.

TABLE 1-4	Component	Block
Blocks and Their Components	A mainframe, 3270 Emulator, SNA printers	
	Serial connections to the Internet and remote offices	
	Multiple access layers and a distribution layer	
	Multiple distribution layers	
	A room full of servers	

EXERCISE 1-4

Blocks and Their Components

Write the appropriate block next to the following components in Table 1-4.
The answers are Legacy, WAN, Switch, Core, and Server, respectively.

CERTIFICATION SUMMARY

The first networks were simple networks providing access for small groups of people to a centralized resource. As newer technology developed, network designers were able to extend these networks to people more geographically dispersed than before. The primary device used was the LAN switch.

The LAN switch added the new term *VLAN* to networking. Virtual LANs (VLAN) were configured using a combination of software and hardware. VLANs enabled users to be grouped together functionally as opposed to geographically.

Switching evolved beyond layers 2 and 3 of the OSI model. Newer switching platforms allowed switching at layer 4 and higher, providing quality of service (QoS), traffic shaping, load balancing, and policy-based switching. This flexibility gave network administrators the ability to better define their switched environments around specific applications (voice networks, multimedia, video, and data).

Network designers have developed a simple methodology for designing switched networks. They have broken down the methodology into three layers: the access layer, the distribution layer, and the core. Within these layers exist switch blocks and core blocks. Switch blocks are composed of switches from the access and distribution layers, while the core block aggregates two or more switch blocks into a high-speed campus backbone.

TWO-MINUTE DRILL

Here are some of the key points from each certification objective in Chapter 1.

Origins and Directions of Switches/LAN Segmentation-Broadcast Issues

- ❑ Ethernet is a broadcast medium.
- ❑ MAC addresses are unique data link addresses; each network device has one.
- ❑ The OSI model is used to map computer systems against an open system.
- ❑ Routers operate at the network layer.
- ❑ A CAM table correlates MAC addresses to physical ports.

Introduction to VLANs

- ❑ VLANs are virtual LANs that allow users to be geographically discrete from resources.
- ❑ Layer 2 VLANs are called *switched* VLANs.
- ❑ Layer 3 VLANs are called *routed* VLANs.
- ❑ VLANs help reduce broadcast domains.

Switching at Different Layers of the OSI Model

- ❑ ISL is a frame tagging/trunking protocol used to identify and transport traffic from multiple VLANs.
- ❑ Layer 3 VLAN traffic can be routed to other networks.
- ❑ Layer 4 switching provides server load balancing, QoS, and traffic shaping.
- ❑ Multilayer switching combines layers 2, 3, and 4.

Introduction to Switch Block

- ❑ Design layers are access, distribution, and core.
- ❑ A switch block is comprised of network resources from the access and distribution layers.
- ❑ A core block is comprised of two or more switch blocks.

SELF TEST

The following questions will help you measure your understanding of the material presented in this chapter. Read all the choices carefully because there might be more than one correct answer. Choose all correct answers for each question.

Origins and Directions of Switches/LAN Segmentation-Broadcast Issues

1. Early networks had little need for high-speed networking. Which of the following new technologies helped push switching technology? (Choose all that apply.)

    A. Voice over IP
    B. Mainframes
    C. Video conferencing
    D. Dumb terminals
    E. Enterprise Resource Planning applications

2. Which of the following are examples of early networking equipment? (Choose all that apply.)

    A. Firewall
    B. Hubs
    C. Windows NT server
    D. Bridges
    E. Routers

3. The _____ combined the functionality of multiport bridges and sometimes routers into a single layer 2/3 device. (Fill in the blank.)

    A. Router
    B. Firewall
    C. Hub
    D. Switch

4. Ethernet is a layer 1 protocol. Which of the following characteristics best describe Ethernet transmissions?

    A. Broadcast
    B. Unicast

C. Multicast
D. Telecast

5. Which of the following belong to the OSI model? (Choose all that apply.)
   A. Physical
   B. Data communication
   C. Network
   D. API
   E. Session
   F. Transparent

6. The physical layer of the OSI model provides which of the following?
   A. Session control function
   B. Password encryption at the hardware level
   C. Mechanical, electrical, and procedural means for transmission
   D. Defines the connection of computers to electrical outlets

7. Which of the following equipment operates at layer 2 of the OSI model? (Choose all that apply.)
   A. Firewall
   B. Hubs
   C. Bridges
   D. Switches
   E. Routers

8. What are the two types of switching? (Choose all that apply.)
   A. Cut-through
   B. Store-and-forward
   C. Forward-and-forget
   D. Pass through

Introduction to VLANs

9. Which of the following best describes the term VLAN?
   A. A group of computers on the same physical network

B. A group of computers in different cities connected together

C. A group of computers on the same logical network

D. A group of computers on the same network in the same city

10. Your company wants to physically separate a group of accounting servers from the network with a firewall. Which of the following types of VLANs would be the best for this scenario?

    A. Layer 2 VLAN
    B. Layer 3 VLAN
    C. ISL trunked VLAN
    D. Secure VLAN

11. Each VLAN consists of how many distinct broadcast domains?

    A. Four
    B. Three
    C. One
    D. Two

Switching at Different Layers of the OSI Model

12. You have proposed to your management team that your company should perform layer 4 switching. Which of the following are benefits of layer 4 switching? (Choose all that apply.)

    A. Unique session control
    B. Server load balancing
    C. Faster application to data encoding
    D. QoS
    E. Traffic shaping

13. The network administrator in your office needs to connect multiple switches together to upload traffic to the distribution layer. Which of the following protocols is used to trunk Cisco routers and switches together?

    A. BGP
    B. ISL
    C. RIP V2

30 Chapter 1: Introduction to Emerging Switching Technologies and the Campus Network

   D. STP
   E. OSPF

14. What is frame tagging?
    A. A process of identifying frames from a particular VLAN
    B. A process involving spray paint and bridges
    C. A process of identifying damaged frames that need to be dropped

15. At what point in the network does a frame become a packet?
    A. Any time the frame is forwarded to a layer 3 VLAN.
    B. Any time the frame is forwarded to layer 1 for physical distribution.
    C. Any time the frame is tagged and passed to another switching device.
    D. Any time the frame is placed in a QoS queue for transport.

Introduction to Switch Block

16. Which of the following are *not* layers used for designing switched networks? (Choose all that apply.)
    A. Access layer
    B. Routed layer
    C. PNNI layer
    D. Core layer

17. As the network administrator for a very large corporation, you've been put in charge of designing the access layer of a new network. Which of the following switches would you recommend? (Choose all that apply.)
    A. 2900
    B. 5000
    C. 8500
    D. 6500

18. The following are the layers used for designing switched networks. Place them in order, with number one being the layer closest to the user.
    A. Distribution layer, Access layer, Core layer

B. Access layer, Core layer, Distribution layer

   C. Core Layer, Distribution layer

19. A core block is comprised of two or more _____ blocks.

   A. WAN

   B. Switch

   C. Server

   D. Distribution

20. Your company has recently purchased another company. Until now, you haven't required connectivity to other offices. Which block could you add to your network to provide connectivity to the newly acquired offices?

   A. Switch

   B. Legacy

   C. Server

   D. WAN

21. Switch blocks are comprised of which of the following? (Choose all that apply.)

   A. Access layer

   B. Legacy blocks

   C. Core layer

   D. Distribution layer

LAB QUESTION

Your company is trying to move from a flat hub/router-centric network to a completely layer 3 switched network. There are three distinct user groups within your company: sales, marketing, and product engineering. All of the groups need access to specific resources, shared resources (e-mail, applications, and accounting packages), and the Internet. The product engineering department needs to have a secure network due to the R&D it performs. While the company will be moving away from its mainframe within the next two years, connectivity needs to be maintained to all legacy equipment.

With this information, design a network for your new company. Explain which design blocks you will use, and what equipment will be used in each block. Additionally, describe the VLAN structures and your reasons for implementing the VLANs you have chosen to create.

SELF TEST ANSWERS

Origins and Directions of Switches/LAN Segmentation-Broadcast Issues

1. ☑ A, C, E. These applications all require large amounts of bandwidth and a certain quality of service.
   ☒ B and D are incorrect because these are legacy applications have very low bandwidth requirements.

2. ☑ B, D, E. These are all listed in the chapter as examples of early networking equipment (before switches).
   ☒ A and C are incorrect because a firewall is a layer 4 device and is not listed as a predecessor to the switch. A Windows NT server is an example of a network resource, not networking equipment.

3. ☑ D. A switch combines the functionality of a multiport bridge and a router into a single layer 2/3 device.
   ☒ A, B, and C are incorrect because a router is a layer 3 device; a firewall is a layer 3 and 4 device; and a hub is a layer 1 device.

4. ☑ A. Ethernet is a broadcast-based media protocol; its transmissions are to all stations.
   ☒ B, C, and D are incorrect because a unicast is a one-way transmission (one to one); multicast is one to a group; and a telecast is not related at all.

5. ☑ A, C, E. Physical (layer 1), network (layer 3), and session (layer 5).
   ☒ B, D, and F are incorrect because Data link is the correct answer, not data communication; and transparent is a form of bridging.

6. ☑ C. This definition was taken directly from the chapter.
   ☒ A, B, and D are incorrect. A is the function of another layer of the OSI model. B is not possible, and D is unrelated.

7. ☑ C, D. Both of these devices correlate layer 2 addresses with physical ports for traffic forwarding decisions.
   ☒ A and B are incorrect because a firewall is a layer 4 device, and a hub is a layer 1 device.

8. ☑ A, B. Cut-through switching starts forwarding the frame as soon as it's received; store-and-forward stores the entire frame before forwarding it to its final destination.
   ☒ C and D are incorrect because neither of these answers relate to the material at hand.

Introduction to VLANs

9. ☑ **C.** A VLAN is a group of computers or resources on the same logical network.
   ☒ **A**, **B**, and **D** are incorrect. **A** is considered the definition for LAN. **B** is the definition for a WAN, and **D** is the definition for a MAN.

10. ☑ **A.** The firewall can be used as a router. Place one interface of the firewall in the layer 2 VLAN with the servers. This will be the server's default gateway. Use the firewall to route traffic to and from the unsecured network.
    ☒ **B**, **C**, and **D** are incorrect because they don't provide security as required. The servers could still be compromised due to the router's inability to completely secure the network.

11. ☑ **C.** A single VLAN by definition contains one distinct broadcast domain.
    ☒ **A**, **B**, and **D** are incorrect by virtue of the definition of a VLAN.

Switching at Different Layers of the OSI Model

12. ☑ **B, D, E.** Server load balancing, QoS, and traffic shaping are benefits of layer 4 switching. This form of switching combines layer 3 switching with layer 4 ports.
    ☒ **A** and **C** are incorrect. Unique session control would be layer 5 switching and faster application to data encoding would be a function of layers 6 and 7.

13. ☑ **B.** ISL (Inter-Switch Link) protocol is the protocol used to trunk switches together. This protocol adds frame-tagging information, identifying which VLAN a frame came from.
    ☒ **A, C, D,** and **E** are incorrect. BGP (Border Gateway Protocol), OSPF (Open Shortest Path First), and RIP V2 (Routed Internet Protocol) are routing protocols. STP (Spanning Tree Protocol) is used to determine a loop-free bridging environment.

14. ☑ **A.** Frame tagging is the process of identifying frames with a particular VLAN.
    ☒ **B** and **C** are incorrect definitions of frame tagging.

15. ☑ **A.** A packet is formed at layer 3.
    ☒ **B, C,** and **D** are incorrect. Layer 1 is the electrical transfer layer; passing it to another switching device is ISL (layer 2); and QoS occurs at layer 4 of the OSI model.

Introduction to Switch Block

16. ☑ **B, C.** The routed layer isn't a layer used in designing switched networks. PNNI is a term related to ATM switching.
    ☒ **A** and **D** are incorrect. Both of these layers are used in designing switched networks.

17. ☑ **A, B.** The Catalyst 2900 is a 24-port workgroup switch ideal for access layer connection. The Catalyst 5000 series switches are great access layer switches for closets, which include a large user population.
    ☒ **C and D** are incorrect because both the 6500 and the 8500 switches are primarily used for high-density distribution and core placement.

18. ☑ **B.** The correct order is: (1) Access layer, (2) Distribution layer, and (3) Core layer.
    ☒ **A and C** are the incorrect order.

19. ☑ **B.** By definition, a core block is comprised of two or more switch blocks.
    ☒ **A, C, and D** are incorrect because they are not the definition of a core block.

20. ☑ **D.** The WAN block provides connectivity from the core to remote offices or the Internet.
    ☒ **A, B, and C** are incorrect. A switch block is for local connectivity; a legacy block is for mainframes and older equipment; and a server block is also for local resources.

21. ☑ **A, D.** Switch blocks are comprised of access layer switches and distribution layer switches.
    ☒ **B and C** are incorrect. The legacy block is its own block, and the core layer aggregates switch blocks.

LAB ANSWER

The first step is to write down all of the requirements and then form them into specific design blocks.

- **Core block**   The core block will consist of a pair of 6000 series switches and a pair of 7200 routers. This will be the central point of the network.
- **Server block**   The server block will consist of shared resources. The servers will be connected to a pair of 6000 series switches that have connectivity to the core block.
- **WAN block**   The WAN block will consist of a single 2600 router with a T-1 to the Internet. The WAN block will be connected to the core block.
- **Legacy block**   The Legacy block will contain all of the legacy equipment and connectivity to the core block.
- **Switch blocks**   There will be three switch blocks. The engineering switch block will need to be separated from the other blocks by a firewall. The other two switch blocks will be connected to the core blocks. The switch blocks will contain 2948G switches that are uplinked to Catalyst 6000 series switches. These 6000s will serve as the distribution point and have connections to the core block.

This design follows the basic design premise of having an access layer, a distribution layer, and a core layer.

The VLANs will be laid out as follows: Each of the blocks will have an individual Layer 3 VLAN. These VLANs will be terminated on the distribution switch located within their block. The distribution blocks will each have uplinks to the core that will be in the same VLAN. Having the uplinks in the same VLAN will ensure wire-speed switching in the core block.

This isn't the only possible design, merely a recommended approach to the case study.

2
Switch Block Concepts

CERTIFICATION OBJECTIVES

2.01	Switch Block
2.02	Fast Ethernet Implementations
2.03	Duplex Settings
2.04	Gigabit Ethernet
2.05	Connections
2.06	Fundamental Switching Commands
✓	Two-Minute Drill
Q&A	Self Test

Today's growing campus networks consist of a variety of different applications; for example, streaming audio and video, large database access, and Internet and intranet traffic. These factors have the potential to bog down your campus network. Additionally, most companies are near the 10 Mbps barrier at the access layer.

This chapter discusses how to configure the connections within the switch block at the Access layer. We will also be touching on different types of Ethernet that can be used in campus networks today.

CERTIFICATION OBJECTIVE 2.01

Switch Block

Before we configure our switch block, it is important to take into consideration what type of media we will be using, for example, 10BaseT, Fast Ethernet, etc. We will make our selection based on what type of applications our users will be using. Some things to consider: are they using a Web browser to browse simple text-based Web pages on your company intranet, or using some high-end graphics program to print huge posters? In Figure 2-1, the user browsing the Web is not going to generate as much traffic as the Mac user printing a large graphical poster.

Another comparison might be a user running a huge query on a large database versus a user checking e-mail on his palm device. The user checking the database is going to generate more traffic than the user who is using the palm device. Determining how much bandwidth will be required for the present and future will help in the configuration of your switch block. The modular approach to configuring your campus network allows configuring bandwidth correctly at each level. This will allow an administrator to determine if a user requires a 10 Mbps connection or 100 Mbps connection. Poor planning can result in bottlenecks and network slowdown.

It's time to describe the basic characteristics of Ethernet, Fast Ethernet, and Gigabit. Ethernet is 10 Mbps, Fast Ethernet (FE) is 100 Mbps, and Gigabit supports up to 1000 Mbps.

Let's compare the differences between the 10BaseT hub and the 10BaseT switch. Suppose we change Figure 2-1 by removing the switch and replacing it with a

FIGURE 2-1 Problem: Need for more bandwidth

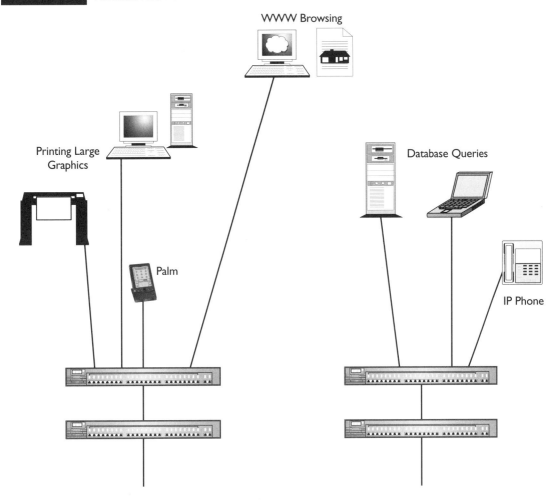

10BaseT hub (Figure 2-2)—how will this affect this network? All of the users connected to the hub will now be sharing 10 Mbps, whereas when we used the switch, each port had a dedicated 10 Mbps connection for each user. Today's networks often consist of multimedia, database, and imaging programs, which can easily saturate this 10 Mbps network. For this reason, companies today are replacing hubs with switches to increase performance, thereby allowing for dedicated connections and full-duplex support. Full duplex allows you to send and receive at

40 Chapter 2: Switch Block Concepts

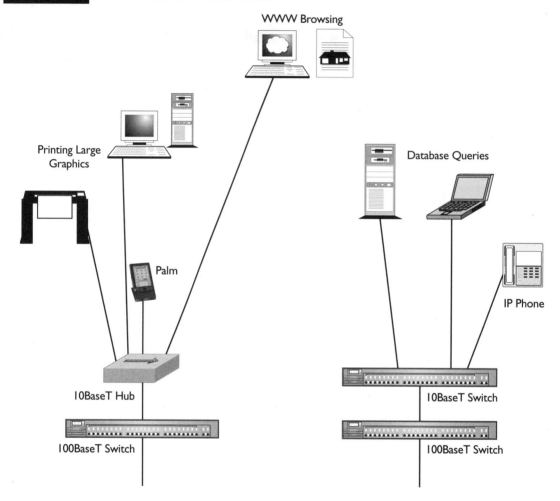

FIGURE 2-2   A 10BaseT hub and a 10BaseT switch

the same time, which also reduces collisions. See Table 2-1 for usage and distance for Ethernet.

exam
ⓦatch

Notice in Table 2-1 that your Access layer is the only layer where we typically see 10 Mbps. You should not implement 10 Mbps at the Distribution layer or the Core layer.

Fast Ethernet Implementations

| TABLE 2-1 | Usage and Distance for Ethernet |

Hierarchical Model	Usage
Access layer	Connect your switch to your end-users' computers, servers, and devices such as printers and IP telephones.
Distribution layer	Because of 100Base and 1000Base technology, we usually don't use 10 Mbps at the Distribution layer—10 Mbps is too slow.
Core layer	Because of 100Base and 1000Base technology, we usually don't use 10 Mbps at the Core layer. 10 Mbps is too slow.

Ethernet Rules	Distance
Unshielded twisted-pair (UTP)	100 meters total: 5 meters from switch to path panel, 90 meters from patch panel to punch-down block, and 5 meters from the punch-down block to the desktop.

CERTIFICATION OBJECTIVE 2.02

Fast Ethernet Implementations

You can deploy Fast Ethernet in today's Ethernet networks (Figure 2-3), and you can increase the speed to 100 Mbps without making a ton of changes to your existing cabling, if you installed category-five (CAT 5) cable. You can usually take advantage of the CAT 5 cable that may already be in your network. You can update your hubs, switches, and network cards on your workstations without having to run new cable to each workstation. This cost-effective solution will also enhance client/server performance across your enterprise.

Notice in Figure 2-3 that we added 100 Mbps switches to our old 10 Mbps network. We were able to take advantage of our existing cable as long as that cable is CAT 5 or better. In addition, we did not have to upgrade all our equipment at the same time; we can still use some of our 10 Mbps hubs until our budget allows us to replace them with 100-Mbs hubs or switches. Even though the price of 100 Mbps network cards for notebooks has decreased to around $120.00, they are still expensive when compared to the 10/100 Mbps cards we can purchase for our desktop PCs for

FIGURE 2-3 Upgrading to 100 Mbps

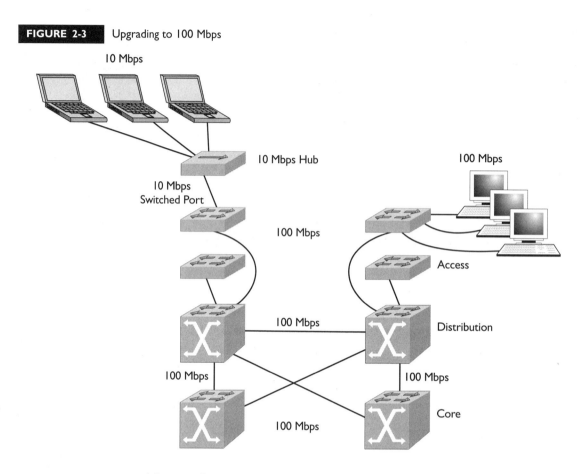

around $20.00–$30.00. So, we can wait until next year's budget to purchase those or, if our budget allows, we can replace them with 100 Mbps cards, pull that hub out, and replace it with a 100 Mbps hub or switch. That is the benefit of Ethernet mixed with Fast Ethernet: we don't have to upgrade everything all at once.

Of course, we can use Fast Ethernet in the entire switch block, among all of our layers (Figure 2-4). We have used 100 Mbps between our devices, which supports a greater amount of traffic between switches and our workstations and servers. Many computers trying to connect to the same server simultaneously will create a bottleneck. Using Fast Ethernet between our switches will help to avoid this problem in your campus network. As we discussed earlier, increasing that 10 Mbps pipe to a 100 Mbps is 10 times faster.

Fast Ethernet Implementations 43

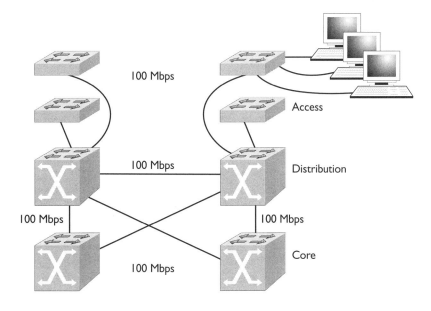

FIGURE 2-4

100 Mbps among all of our layers

Notice that our entire switch block is using 100 Mbps to increase the speed between our links. Remember that Fast Ethernet is based on CSMA/CD, which can use your existing 10BaseT cabling. It also uses the same frame types, lengths, and formats. We can now transfer data from 10 Mbps to 100 Mbps with no problems and increase our speed 10 times. Fast Ethernet can run over unshielded twisted-pair (UTP) or fiber (Table 2-2).

TABLE 2-2 Specifications for 100BaseT

100Base Technology	Wiring	Length
100BaseTX	EIA/TIA Category 5 (UTP) Unshielded twisted-pair, 2 pair	100 meters
100BaseT4	EIA/TIA Category 3, 4, 5 (UTP) Unshielded twisted-pair, 4 pair	100 meters
100BaseFX	MMF cable, with a 62.5-micron fiber-optic core and 125-micron outer cladding (62.5/125)	400 meters

EXERCISE 2-1

Choosing the Correct Media Type

Scenario: Your company is setting up a small campus network in one building to provide e-mail services and SQL database services to internal employees. The users will also be connecting to the corporate office through the router. You have already confirmed that five of the 30 users do not have 100 Mbps cards. The e-mail server and SQL database server have 100 Mbps cards that support full duplex. The computers currently have network cards, but the company does not have the media installed.

Solution: Because your company does not have the media installed, recommend CAT 5 cabling, which will support 10/100 Mbps. Connect the 15 users to a 10/100 Mbps switch like the 2900 series switch, and connect that switch to both of your distribution switches for fault tolerance. Cisco recommends that you use Catalyst 55xx series switches at the Core and Distribution layers, so you should use Fast Ethernet in your switch block to get the best performance. Upgrade those five users to 100 Mbps cards so that your entire network is using Fast Ethernet.

CERTIFICATION OBJECTIVE 2.03

Duplex Settings

There are two types of duplex: *half duplex* and *full duplex*. Let's compare the two.

Half duplex allows for data transmission in only one direction at a time, between a sending device and a receiving device. Think of a walkie-talkie or a CB radio where only one person can communicate at a time.

Full duplex allows for bi-directional traffic between devices. For this reason, full duplex is faster than half duplex. Think of a telephone call, where you have the ability to talk at the same time as the other person—this is an example of full duplex. You speed up the transfer because data can be sent and received at the same time. This can occur if you are using resources that can both send and receive data simultaneously. Switches offer full duplex to their directly connected workstations and servers, providing both with the asymmetrical data transfer they require.

FIGURE 2-5

Increasing performance with full duplex

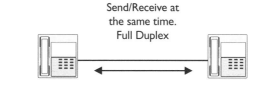

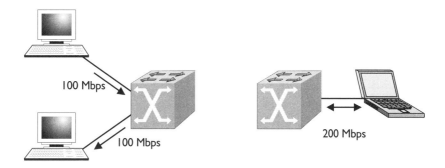

Because we have separate paths for sending and receiving data, we can disable collision detection and loopback functions. Switches are required to use full duplex. Ethernet is traditionally half duplex. Hubs do not support this type of technology. See Figure 2-5.

Now that we know the differences between full duplex and half duplex, here is a quick reference for possible scenarios and the appropriate solution:

SCENARIO & SOLUTION	
All of the end-user devices support full duplex.	Install a switch on your network, and configure it for full duplex.
I am connecting my distribution switches together.	Configure them for full duplex to increase performance.
My high-end server supports full duplex.	Install a switch on your network, and configure it for full duplex.

EXERCISE 2-2

Selecting the Correct Duplex

Scenario: You need to configure your company's switch block, which consists of the following equipment:

- Four 2900 series switches
- Four 5505 series switches, two of which have RSFCs
- Two 100 Mbps hubs

How would you cable the configuration, and what duplex setting would you configure on these devices?

Solution: Use the 2900 series switches as your Access layer devices, and connect the 100 Mbps hubs to them. Use the two 5505s that have the RSFCs at the Distribution layer because they support Layer 3. Use the remaining two 5505s at the Core layer. Connect your Access layer devices to both distribution switches, and then connect both of your distribution switches to the Core layer. Set up full duplex between all of the devices in your switch block to deliver maximum performance and bandwidth. Remember that hubs do not support full duplex.

CERTIFICATION OBJECTIVE 2.04

Gigabit Ethernet

Now let's discuss the interaction and efficiency of Gigabit Ethernet as present in the switch block, the core block, and the server block. Gigabit Ethernet improves client/server performance across the enterprise, and is used similarly in each of the three areas. In the switch block, Gigabit Ethernet is implemented in situations where a link connects centrally located aggregation switches to an access switch. From the access switch, we connect to the distribution switch through a Gigabit Ethernet uplink. Once we connect to the Distribution layer, we move to the core block. Here, Gigabit Ethernet links are used from the Distribution layer switches to each location with a central campus core. Good placement of a Gigabit Ethernet switch is typically central to the server block. In some environments, high-performance servers need the connectivity that

TABLE 2-3 Gigabit Deployment

Layer	Used
Access	Gigabit is not normally used between end-user devices and the access switches. In the near future, once the cost of gigabit networks cards drops, we should see Gigabit become the standard way to connect your computers in your network to the switches in your switch block.
Distribution	Gigabit supports high-speed connections between the Access and Distribution layer devices.
Core	Gigabit supports high-speed connections to the Distribution layer, to the server blocks, and between core devices.

Gigabit Ethernet switches can provide. A high-end audio/video server has the potential to overwhelm multiple Fast Ethernet connections easily. A possible solution to keeping up with swift growth in server speed and throughput is Gigabit Ethernet. By connecting directly to a Gbps interface on LAN switches, Gigabit Ethernet provides for a scalable solution. Table 2-3 lists the layers where Gigabit should be deployed.

Gigabit Ethernet increases speeds from 100 Mbps to up to 1 Gbps. In large Fortune 500 companies, Gigabit is as popular as Fast Ethernet was a few years ago. This speed is crucial to the way these companies are now doing business. Gigabit allows large amounts of traffic to be switched between devices—it's like Ethernet on steroids. In order for this to work, several changes need to be made to the physical interface. To push the bandwidth up to 1 Gbps, two technologies are merged together: American Standards Institute (ANSI) X3T11 FiberChannel and IEEE 802.3 Ethernet. See Table 2-4 for the distance of Gigabit.

TABLE 2-4 Gigabit Distance

1000Base Technology	Wiring	Length
1000BaseCX	Copper shielded twisted-pair	25 meters
1000BaseT	Copper EIA/TIA Category 5 (UTP) Unshielded twisted-pair, 4 pair	100 meters
1000BaseSX	Multimode fiber cable, with a 62.5-micron fiber-optic core and 50-micron fiber-optic core; 780 nanometer laser	260 meters
1000BaseLX	Single-mode fiber cable, 9-micron core, 1300-nanometer laser	3 km (Cisco supports up to 10 km)

48 Chapter 2: Switch Block Concepts

CERTIFICATION OBJECTIVE 2.05

Connections

Let's take a closer look at how we can connect to our switches to configure them. First, we must establish a physical connection by using the Ethernet port or the console port. We will discuss both.

Cabling

Normally, we use the console port to first configure the switch; once we have the Ethernet port configured, we can use Telnet to make future configuration changes. Figure 2-6 shows the 1900 series console port connection.

You will use your rollover cable to connect to the 1900 series switch. This is not the same as a straight through patch cable. Rollover cables have a RJ-45 connector on both sides. One end of this rollover cable will plug directly into your switch as pictured in Figure 2-6. Depending on what type of serial port your machine has, you need to use either RJ-45 to DB-9 or RJ-45 to DB-25 adapters on the other end of the cable. The new switches and routers are color-coded, and the rollover cable is usually light blue to match the color on the switch. This cable is black if you have an older router or switch. This is the same for the 1900/2800 or 2900 XL switches.

To connect to a 5000, we have a few different types of connections depending on which Supervisor Engine your switch has (Figure 2-7).

FIGURE 2-6

1900 series console port connection

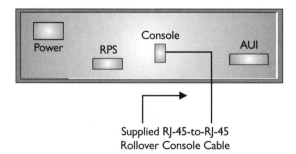

FIGURE 2-7 5000 series switch

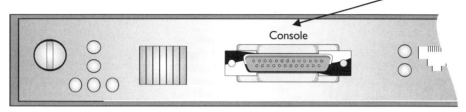

Connecting a Terminal to the Supervisor Engine I and II Console Port

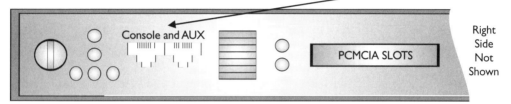

Connecting a Terminal to the Supervisor Engine III Console Port

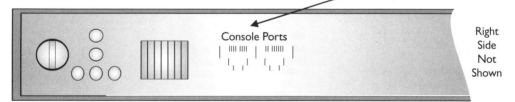

Connecting a Terminal to the Supervisor Engine II G and III G Console and RSFC Ports

Cisco has several different types of Supervisor Engines that can work in the 5000 series switch. Supervisor Engines I and II use a Cisco 25-pin female connector that usually comes with the switch. This adapter consists of a 25-pin male connector plugged into an RJ-45 connector. Then you connect the rollover cable supplied by Cisco to the RJ-45 connector on the switch to either a female DB-25/or a female DB-9 connector. This connector will then connect to your PC. See Table 2-5 for console port pinouts (RJ-45).

You can detect a rollover cable by comparing the two modular ends of the cable (Figure 2-8). Hold the cables in your hand, side by side, with the tab at the back. The wire connected to the pin on the outside of the left plug should be the same

Chapter 2: Switch Block Concepts

TABLE 2-5 Console Port (DTE) Pinouts (RJ-45)

Pin	1	2	3	4	5	6	7	8
Signal	—	DTR	TxD	GND	GND	RxD	DSR	—
Input/Output	—	Output	Output	—	—	Input	Input	—

color as the pin on the outside of the right plug (a rollover cable reverses pins 1 and 8, 2 and 7, 3 and 6, and 4 and 5).

on the job

Connecting an actual telephone line, live ISDN line, or an Ethernet cable to the console port can damage your switch. Make sure you use a rollover cable.

When you are finished cabling your console port on your 1900/2800/2900 XL series switch, your cables should look like Figure 2-9. Connecting your PC/workstation to a 5000 series switch will be the same, with one exception: you will need the adapter we discussed earlier on your switch, which will again depend on what type of supervisor module you are using.

FIGURE 2-8 Identifying a rollover cable

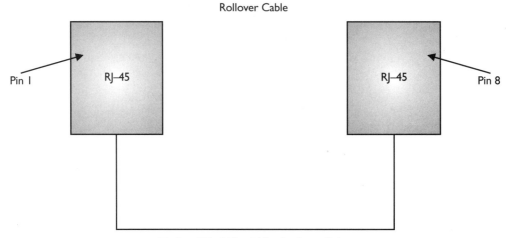

FIGURE 2-9 Connect the console cable to the PC/UNIX workstation

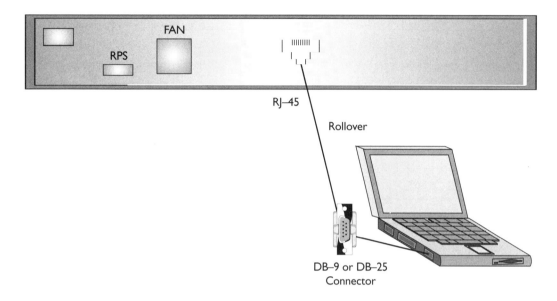

EXERCISE 2-3

Console Connection to Your 1900/2800 Or 2900XL Switches

Perform the following steps to cable and connect to your 1900/2800 or 2900 XL switch through the serial console:

1. Connect one end of your rollover cable to the console port.
2. Attach one of the following adapters to your PC/UNIX workstation or modem: RJ-45 to DB-9 female (labeled Terminal) to connect to a PC, RJ-45 to DB-25 female (labeled Terminal) to connect to a UNIX workstation, or RJ-45 to DB-25 male (labeled Modem) to connect to a modem. You can also use the RJ-45 to DB-25 female connector to connect to your PC if you only have a 25-pin serial connection on your PC.
3. Connect the other end of the rollover cable to the adapter.
4. Connect an AC power cable to each power supply. Remember, some models can have more than one power supply.

5. Attach each power cable to a grounded outlet. If possible, connect each cable to an outlet on a separate circuit. Make sure that the power source is within range.

6. Turn the power supplies ON (I). The switch begins the boot process. The LEDs on the power supplies should be green.

7. From your PC/UNIX workstation, start your emulation program.

8. Configure your emulation program. To configure HyperTerminal for Windows, the default settings of the console port are 9600 baud, 8 data bits, 1 stop bit, no parity, and no flow control. Make sure you configure the port your adapter is plugged in to. See Figure 2-10.

9. Press ENTER/RETURN to connect to your switch

FIGURE 2-10

HyperTerminal settings for Windows users

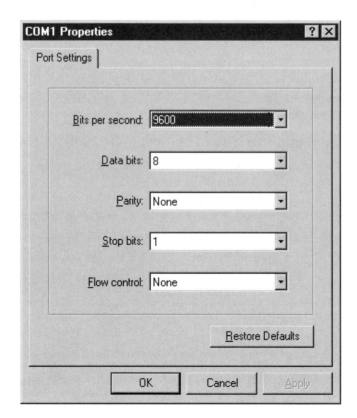

EXERCISE 2-4

Console Connection to Your 5000 Series Switches

Perform the following steps to cable and connect to your 5000 series switch through the serial console:

1. Connect one end of your rollover cable to the console port.

2. Attach one of the following adapters to your PC/UNIX workstation or modem: RJ-45 to DB-9 female (labeled Terminal) to connect to a PC, RJ-45 to D-subminiature female (labeled Terminal) to connect to a UNIX workstation, or RJ-45 to D-subminiature male (labeled Modem) to connect to a modem. You can also use the RJ-45 to DB-25 female connector to connect to your PC if you only have a 25-pin serial connection on your PC.

3. Connect the other end of the rollover cable to the adapter.

4. Connect an AC power cable to each power supply. Remember, some models can have more than one power supply.

5. Attach each power cable to a grounded outlet. If possible, connect each cable to an outlet on a separate circuit. Make sure that the power source is within range.

6. Turn the power supplies ON (I). The switch begins the boot process. The LEDs on the power supplies should be green.

7. From your PC/UNIX workstation, start your emulation program.

8. Configure your emulation program. The default settings of the console port are 9600 baud, 8 data bits, 1 stop bit, no parity, and no flow control. Keep all other settings the same. Make sure you configure the port your adapter is plugged in to. See Figure 2-10.

9. Press ENTER/RETURN to connect to your switch

---

exam
ⓌatCh

Notice that the settings for HyperTerminal are 9600 baud, 8 data bits, and 1 stop bit, no parity, and no flow control. You only have to adjust two settings: baud and flow control; you can leave the others at the default settings.

FIGURE 2-11

Wiring diagram for a straight-through cable

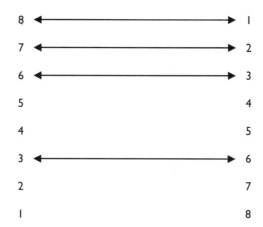

Ethernet Connection to Both Switch Types

Cisco's 1900/2800 series switches have fixed port types, either 10BaseT or 100BaseT. This means you can't switch a port from 10BaseT to 100BaseT. However, Cisco's 5000 series switches have ports that you can configure for either 10BaseT or 100BaseT. Remember that all UTP connections between the device and the switch must be within 100 meters. When you connect your routers, workstations, and servers to the switch, you must use a straight-through cable (Figure 2-11 and Table 2-6). When you connect your switch to other repeaters or switches, make sure you use a crossover cable (Figure 2-12 and Table 2-7). Once a connection is made between the device and the switch, you should see the port status LED come on. If

TABLE 2-6 Pin Layout for a Straight-Through Cable

Pins 1 and 2 must be a twisted pair.
Pins 3 and 6 must be a twisted pair.
Pins 4, 5, 7, and 8 are not used in this application, although they may be wired in the cable.

FIGURE 2-12

Wiring diagram for a crossover cable

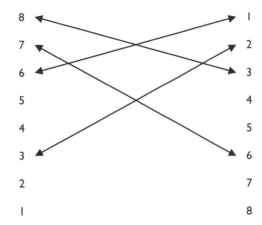

it does not, you might have the wrong cable, or your device at the other end is not on. Figure 2-13 shows the Ethernet ports on a switch. This book does not discuss cabling to a Gigabit Ethernet port.

As we pointed out earlier, the ports on the 1900 and 2800 series switches are fixed. Notice that ports 1x through 24x are 10BaseT, and the two ports at the right-hand side are 100BaseTX ports.

Notice that the ports for a 5000 series switch (Figure 2-14) are not fixed and can be configured for either 10BaseT or 100BaseT.

Now that we have discussed the various ways to cable your switches together and to the endstations, refer to the following Scenario & Solution as a quick reference for possible scenarios and the appropriate solution.

TABLE 2-7 Crossover Cable Pin Out

Pins 1 and 2 at B must be a twisted pair wired through to pins 6 and 3, respectively, at A.
Pins 3 and 6 at A must be a twisted pair wired through to pins 2 and 1, respectively, at B.
Pins 1 and 2 at B must be a twisted pair wired through to pins 6 and 3, respectively, at A.

FIGURE 2-13 Ethernet ports on a 1900 series switch

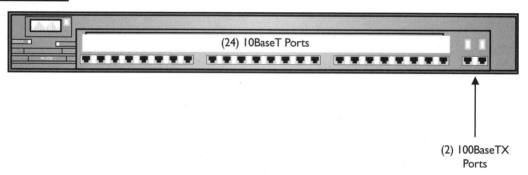

SCENARIO & SOLUTION

You are connecting a switch to another switch.	Install a crossover cable between them.
You are connecting a PC to your Access layer switch.	Use a regular straight-through cable from your PC to the switch.
When configuring your 1900s from the console port, what is the name of the cable that connects to your serial port on the PC?	The correct answer is rollover cable.
What default settings must change when you configure HyperTerminal for a Windows-based OS?	Bits per second, and flow control.

FIGURE 2-14 Ethernet module for a 5000 series switch. This is not a complete picture of a 5000 series switch, just one module that goes inside the switch.

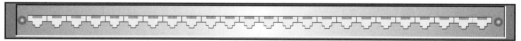

EXERCISE 2-5

Cabling Switch Block Devices

Scenario: Your company has decided to use 1900 series switches at the Access layer, and you have been selected to cable these five devices to the Distribution layer 5505 switches. You have received the switches and now need to install them. You have the following equipment:

- Five light-blue rollover cables
- Five power cables
- Twenty-five green straight-through cables
- Five crossover cables
- Five 9-pin RJ-45 to RJ-45 adapters

How should you cable these devices?

Solution: Cable each of the light-blue cables from the back of your switch to the port labeled "Console Port," and at the other end of the cable, connect each 9-pin RJ-45 to RJ-45 adapter. Then connect that adapter to the back of your serial port on the back of your PC. This will allow you to configure this device. In this case, use crossover cables to connect your switches to your distribution switches. You should connect each Access layer device to both distribution switches. Connect your desktops to your Access layer switches. This connection will be from your patch panel to your Access layer device. You will use the straight-through cables for this connection. Plug the power adapters into the back of each switch. These switches do not have a power switch. They should automatically power up, and you should notice the lights flashing green. One of the ports will then turn amber; this is due to Spanning Tree. This is normal, and you will learn more about Spanning Tree later in this book. The green LED lights on those connections will confirm that the devices are ready for access.

CERTIFICATION OBJECTIVE 2.06

Fundamental Switching Commands

Now that we looked at connecting the cables to the switch, let's discuss configuring the switch. Before we can configure our switches, we need to keep in mind that some of Cisco's switches are IOS based, and some are set based. This is because Cisco purchased some of these switches from other companies. See Table 2-8 to see which switch is IOS based, and which switch is set based. In this section, we will show the commands for both switches.

Once we have determined our OS type, we can start looking at the commands to configure our switch.

IP Address

Before we can manage our switch with telnet, we need to configure an IP address and associate it with a virtual LAN (VLAN). VLANs are discussed in complete detail in the next chapter. Even though switches are Layer 2 devices, we still need an IP address so that we can telnet into the switch to manage and ping the device (Figure 2-15).

TABLE 2-8   Cisco Switches IOS Or Set-Based Interface

Switch	OS	Notes
1900	IOS based	Enterprise version adds IOS-like interface. Similar to a router.
2800	IOS based	Enterprise version adds IOS-like interface. Similar to a router.
1948G	Set based	
2900XL	IOS based	Similar to a router.
2926	Set based	
2926G	Set based	
3000	Set based	No longer used.
3500 XL	IOS based	Similar to a router.
4000–6000	Set based	
8500	IOS based	Similar to a router.

Fundamental Switching Commands

FIGURE 2-15

An IP address associates a switch with a management VLAN

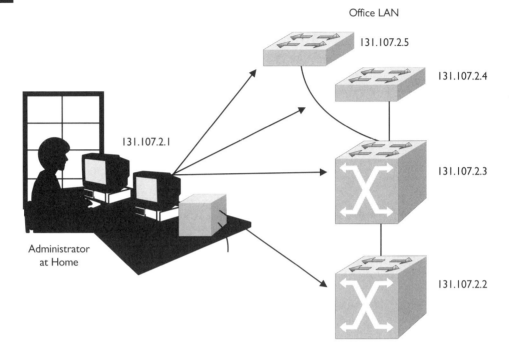

An IP Address Associates a Switch with a Management VLAN

To assign an IP address to an IOS-based device, enter the following command in global configuration mode:

```
Switch(config)# ip address ip address netmask
```

Now that we have configured our IP address, we will use the "show ip" command to view those changes.

```
Switch# show ip
 IP Address:  131.107.2.200
 Subnet Mask:  255.255.255.0
 Default Gateway: 0.0.0.0
 Management VLAN: 1
 Domain name:
 Name server 1:  0.0.0.0
 Name server 2: 0.0.0.0
 HTTP server: Enabled
 HTTP port: 80
 RIP: Enabled
```

Notice that the management interface is on VLAN 1. If you made an error configuring your IP address, you can remove the IP address and subnet mask by typing **no ip address** in global configuration mode.

```
Switch(config)no ip address ip address netmask
```

Notice in the previous code that the default management VLAN is VLAN 1. You must remember that every port is a member of VLAN 1 by default. You can adjust this later if you want to change the default.

sc0

Configure the in-band logical interface to assign an IP address to a set-based device.

```
Switch(enable)set interface sc0   ip address netmask broadcast address
```

Once you have configured the management IP address, you need to match this address to the management VLAN. The VLAN must match the subnet of the IP address.

```
Switch(enable)set interface sc0   vlan
```

Cisco switches will automatically default to VLAN 1 if you do not configure them otherwise.

Now that our switch is configured, let's look at it with the "show interface" command.

```
Switch(enable)show interface
S10:flags=51<UP,POINTPOINT,RUNNING>
    Slip 0.0.0.0 dest 0.0.0.0
Sc0:flags=63<UP,BROADCAST,RUNNING>
    Vlan 1 inet 131.107.2.200 netmask 255.255.255.0 broadcast 131.107.2.255
```

Description

Now that we have our IP address configured, it's a good idea to configure a description on your switch. The switch does not require this field to function, but this description helps administrators know what ports on the switch are configured to your devices. The term *devices* refers to routers, workstations, servers, and switches. These descriptions will show up when you display the configuration of your switch (Figure 2-16). Even if you are the only administrator, descriptions can be helpful. Let's suppose you configured your switches eight months ago. Now you connect via Telnet to look at your configuration, and you can't remember which port is connected to your accounting servers. If you had taken the extra few minutes to put a description on your ports, you would be able to figure it out within minutes. If you choose not to add a description, you should have a good network diagram.

To assign a description to an IOS-based interface, enter the following command in interface configuration mode. The reason we do not enter this command in global configuration is that we want to be able to have different descriptions for different ports. For example, you might have one port going to the marketing department hub and another port going to the sales department. Therefore, on one port you list marketing, and on the other you list sales.

FIGURE 2-16 Descriptions on ports. We could have used longer names on our ports, but in this case, our company has standardized on three-digit codes.

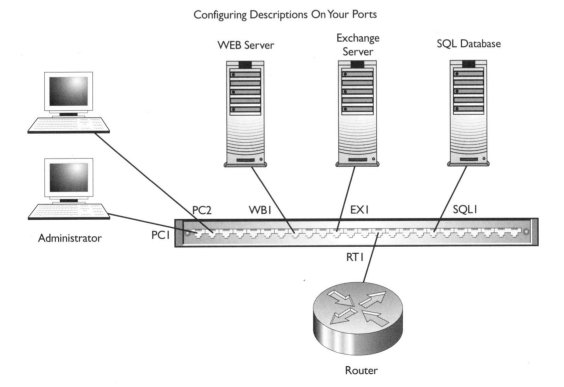

62 Chapter 2: Switch Block Concepts

```
Switch(config-if)# description description string
```

If you want to use spaces in your description, you must use quotation marks; for example, Switch(config-if)#description "Accounting Server Building 3"

To assign a description to a set-based device, enter the following command in privileged mode:

```
Switch(enable)set port name mod/number description
```

In the preceding command, we have a few variables we need to define: mod specifies the target module on which the port resides, the number identifies the specific port, and "description" is your description.

We also have a 21 alphanumeric character limit in our descriptions. If you type the command "set port name *mod/num*", followed by an ENTER/RETURN, the description will be cleared.

Cisco's recommends that you have a description on every interface. Make your descriptions as descriptive as possible. Notice in Figure 2-16 that we have provided descriptions on the ports that have physical connections.

Because the administrator took the time to configure the descriptions on each port on the switch, he can easily identify what port is connected to the Web server or the exchange server. This is helpful if the administrator needs to troubleshoot a port, or bring a port up or down. He can accomplish all of this remotely with Telnet.

Defining Link Speed

Remember, the speed on the 1900/2800 series routers are fixed; they can't be configured. For example: if you type the command:

```
Switch#show interface Ethernet 0/3
```

You will see the following:

```
Ethernet 0/3 is Enabled
Hardware is Built-in 10Base-T
```

Remember that we can configure the 2900/4000/5000/6000 series switch. To change the port speed, enter the following command:

```
Switch(enable)set port speed mod_num/port_num 10|100|auto
```

If you set the speed to auto, both the port speed and duplex will be detected. You might want to set each port manually. Some network cards have problems with autodetection. Cisco recommends configuring this manually. You can also enter the command "show" port to verify your speed.

Now that we have discussed defining link speed, refer to the following Scenario & Solution questions as a quick reference for possible questions relating to link speed.

Full Duplex

Now we will configure your switch with Full duplex, which will allow two devices to send and receive data at the same time. Full-duplex Ethernet and Fast Ethernet links are useful for connecting server-to-server, server-to-switch, and switch-to-switch, because reads and writes are symmetric. This will also decrease collision traffic. Remember that both devices have to support Full duplex (Figure 2-17).

To configure full duplex on your 1900/2800 or 2900 XL series switch, enter the following command in interface configuration mode. See Table 2-9 for the different configurations.

```
Switch(config-if)#duplex {auto|full|full-flow-control|half}
```

To configure full duplex on a set-based switch, enter the following command. You cannot manually change the duplex mode of ports configured for auto.

```
Switch(enable)set port duplex mod num/port num {full|half}
10 Mbps - half
100 Mbps - full
```

SCENARIO & SOLUTION

If the port speed is set to auto on a 10/100 Mbps Fast Ethernet port	Both duplex and speed are autonegotiated.
The 1900 series switch	Has 12 or 24 10BaseT ports and two Fast Ethernet fixed ports.
The Catalyst 2900/4000/5000/6000 series switch has	Ports that can be configured as either 10/100/auto.

TABLE 2-9	Parameters for the Duplex Command
Auto	Sets the 100BaseTX port into autonegotiation mode. This is the default for the 100BaseTX port. This argument is only on the 100BaseT ports. You should not set this value to auto, because some vendor's NICs will not be detected correctly.
Full	Forces the 10BaseT or 100Base port into full duplex.
Full-flow-control	Forces the 100BaseTX port into full-duplex mode with flow control. This argument is only on the 100BaseTX ports.
Half	Forces the 10BaseT or 100BaseTX port into half-duplex mode. This is the default for the 10BaseT port.

Once we have the port configured, we can use the "show port" command to check our configuration. For example:

```
Switch(enable)show port 2/3
Port Name    Status     Vlan   Level    Duplex   Speed   Type
2/3          connected  1      normal   full     100     10/100BaseTX
```

Cisco's 29XX, 4000, 5000, and 6000 series switches may or may not be automatically enabled. To enable a port, use the "set port enable" command in privileged mode.

Notice in Figure 2-17 that these devices are able to send and receive at the same time, for potentially double the throughput.

Ping

Now that we have configured our switch correctly with an IP address, we should make sure that our switch can see other devices on our network. We use the ping utility for this. Ping sends a specified number of ICMP echo requests, and measures the time the destination device takes to respond to each echo request. This is probably one of the most effect troubleshooting commands. To test your switch with the ping command, enter the following:

```
Switch(enable)ping destination IP address
```

After you enter the ping command, you should see something like this:

```
Switch(enable)ping 131.107.2.200
Sending 5, 100-byte ICMP Echos to 131.107.2.200, time out is 2 seconds:
!!!!!
Success rate is 100 percent (5/5), round-trip min/avg/max 0/2/10/ ms
```

FIGURE 2-17 Full duplex

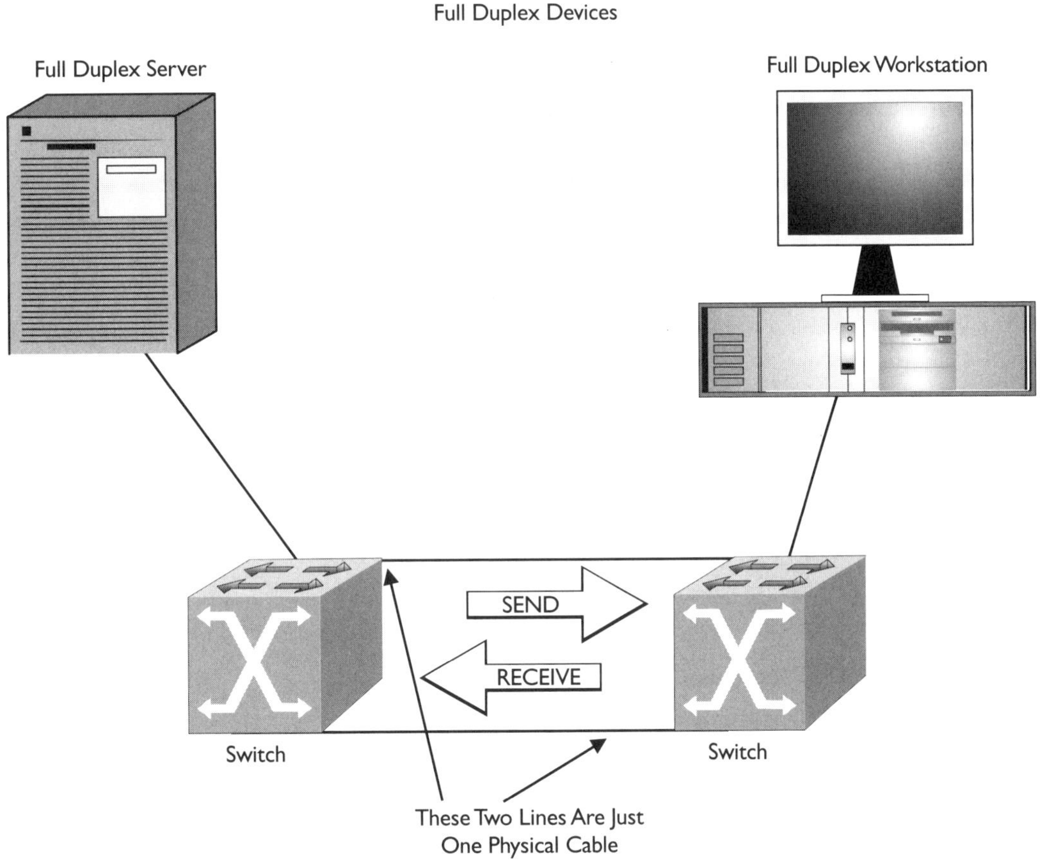

Full Duplex Devices

Full Duplex Server

Full Duplex Workstation

SEND
RECEIVE

Switch   Switch

These Two Lines Are Just One Physical Cable

This lets you know that the ping was successful and your device can communicate with 131.107.2.200. Table 2-10 lists a few other responses that you can get to inform you of a problem.

Notice in Figure 2-18 that our administrator is trying to verify that the 100BaseT switch 131.107.2.200 is working. She uses the ping utility to see if she can communicate with the switch. After she pinged the switch and received the success ICMP responses, she can now inform her boss that the switch is back online. Internet Control Message Protocol (ICMP) reports errors and control messages on behalf of IP (documented in RFC 792).

TABLE 2-10 Ping Responses

Destination does not respond	No answer is returned if the destination host does not respond.
Unknown host	This happens if the destination host does not exist.
Destination unreachable	This happens if the router/default gateway can't reach the specified network.
Network or host unreachable	This happens if there is no entry in the router table for the destination host or network.

FIGURE 2-18 Ping utility

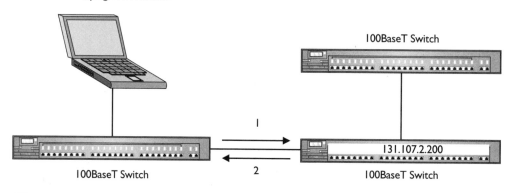

Sending 5, 100-byte ICMP Echos to 131.107.2.200, Time Out Is 2 Seconds:
|||||
Success Rate Is 100 Percent (5/5), Roundtrip min/avg/max 0/2 10/ms

Traceroute

If you are using Cisco's 2926/2926G/2948G/4000/5000 series switches, you can use the "trace route" command. This command will show you a hop-by-hop path from your source to your destination. This is useful if you are trying to determine where the problem is in your path. You must be in privileged mode to use the "trace route" command.

```
Switch(enable)traceroute destination IP address
```

After you enter the "trace route" command, you should see something like this:

```
Switch(enable)traceroute 131.107.1.1
Console> (enable) traceroute 131.107.1.1
traceroute to 131.107.1.1 (131.107.1.1), 30 hops max, 40 byte packets
 1 131.107.2.2 (131.107.2.2)   2 ms   * 2 ms
Console> (enable)
```

Notice that we can trace the route to 131.107.1.1, and that we were successful.

exam Watch *In the previous two paragraphs, we mentioned two troubleshooting tools: ping and traceroute. These two tools are used most often to verify that your connections and routes are functioning correctly. You also can use a packet analyzer such as Microsoft's Network Monitor or a sniffer product to look at the packets.*

FROM THE CLASSROOM

Third-Party Tools to Trace Your Wide Area Network

There are plenty of good third-party tools that your can use to trace your wide area network; for example:

- NeoTrace (www.neotrace.com)
- Visual Route (www.visualroute.com)

Both of these programs use graphics instead of just text, making your traces easier to read and troubleshoot. Both of these companies offer trail versions that you can download and use.

—*John Friedrich (CCNA, CCI, CCA, MCSE+I, MCT, CNE)*

Hostnames/Prompts

Did you notice that in that last couple of command examples, the name of our switches is "Switch?" This is because your switch comes with factory default settings. To be able to distinguish one switch from another, we can assign a hostname on the IOS-based switches, or change the prompt on the set-based switches (Figure 2-19). To set a hostname on a 1900/2800/2900XL series switch, enter the following command in global configuration mode:

```
Switch(config)hostname name (where name can be 1 to 255 alphanumeric characters.)
```

For example:

```
Switch(config)hostname spiderman
```

Once you enter the preceding command, you will see the hostname change from "switch" to "spiderman."

If you are using a set-based switch, the name you assign as your system name is used to define the system prompt. You can assign a name that will be visible through the CLI; this can be different from the system name. You have to be in privileged mode to set a prompt in a set-based switch. Enter the following command to change the prompt:

```
Switch(enable)set prompt name
```

Notice in Figure 2-19 that we will have no problem determining which switch we are connected to. We used superhero names to show you that you can choose any name. This will help you to determine which device you are connected to. Pick a name that you and your team of administrators will be able to easily identify.

Passwords

Now that we have configured our switch with an IP address, description, speed, duplex, and so forth, we want to make sure that we secure our switches with password protection to limit access to our devices. Security is discussed in detail later in this book. We have two different types of login passwords: a login password, and an enable password. The login password requires users to enter a password before accessing any line, even the console. The enable password is used to make any configuration changes. You should use both to secure your device. The login

Fundamental Switching Commands **69**

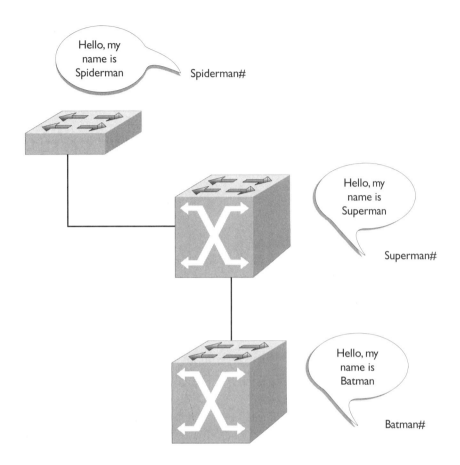

FIGURE 2-19

Hostname and prompt example

password is like window-shopping: you can view your configuration, but you cannot make any changes. When making configuration changes, we use the enable password to protect your devices from unauthorized use. For total protection, you should use both. Cisco also has levels of authority that you can configure. A privilege level of "1" allows the user normal EXEC-mode user privileges, and a level of "15" allows the same access as the enable password. This way, you can let some users window-shop, and allow other users complete control of the switch.

Enter the following command in global configuration to configure passwords on an IOS-based switch:

```
Switch(config)enable password level 1 password
Switch(config)enable password level 15 password
```

The passwords must be alphanumeric characters, and more than four characters but less than eight characters. Passwords on these switches are not case sensitive.

To configure passwords on a set-based switch, enter the following command in privileged mode:

```
Switch(enable)set password
Enter old password:  old password
Enter new password:  new password
Retype new password: new password
Password changed.
Switch (enable)set enablepass
Enter old password:  old password
Enter new password:  new password
Retype new password: new password
Password changed.
```

Passwords can be any set of alphanumeric characters, and passwords on these switches are case sensitive.

EXERCISE 2-6

2900 Fundamental Switching Commands

Follow these steps to view the default settings for your 2900 series switch. Note: these are not all the commands that you have available on the 2900 series switch; this exercise is just introducing the basics.

1. Connect your console cable to the back of the switch, and configure Hyper-Terminal to connect to it.
2. The 2900 is IOS based, and commands are very similar to router IOS commands. Go to privileged mode.
3. Switch>**enable**
4. Switch#
5. Type **show flash** and record the IOS version of your switch.
6. Type **show run** and record the default settings on your switch.
7. Type **show int vlan1** and record the status of the interface.
8. From privileged mode, type **config t** to go to global configuration mode.

9. Switch(config)#
10. Type **int vlan1**
11. Switch(config-if)#
12. Type **ip address 10.1.0.1 255.255.0.0**
13. Type **exit** to return to global configuration mode.
14. Type **hostname Spiderman** to configure a hostname for the switch.
15. Type **int f0/1**
16. Switch(config-if)#
17. Type **description Port_to_Marvel**
18. Type **speed 100**
19. Type **duplex full**
20. Type **end**
21. Type **show run** to view changes.
22. Type **copy run start** to save those changes.
23. Type **show start** to view saved changes.

CERTIFICATION SUMMARY

In this chapter, we discussed that the number of users, and applications those users are using, will impact network bandwidth performance. We covered the Access, Distribution, and Core layers. We learned that Ethernet operates at 10 Mbps, Fast Ethernet at 100Mbps, and Gigabit at 1000Mbps. We also discussed where and when to use each, and the distance required. We looked at Full duplex and how to use it to increase performance. We examined the physical connections of IOS-based switches and set-based switches.

Finally, we looked at the basic commands to start configuring and test our switches.

TWO-MINUTE DRILL

Please take a few minutes to review this section carefully. The *Two-Minute Drill* is a quick review of exam objectives to help you review for the exam.

Switch Block

- ❏ Module design of your campus network topology allows for scaling bandwidth at each level.
- ❏ Cisco uses three levels: Access, Distribution, and Core.
- ❏ The Access layer provides connectivity between your access switches and your end-user stations.
- ❏ The Distribution layer provides connectivity between your Distribution layer and Access layer. It also provides connectivity from your Core layer to your Distribution layer.
- ❏ The Core layer provides inter-switch connectivity.
- ❏ The number of users and the types of applications will affect your bandwidth requirements, and will help you decide what cable media to use.
- ❏ Switching is a solution to your Ethernet bandwidth bottlenecks.

Fast Ethernet Implementations

- ❏ Fast Ethernet functions at 100 Mbps.
- ❏ Fast Ethernet is also known as FE.
- ❏ Fast Ethernet is 10 times faster than Ethernet.
- ❏ Fast Ethernet is used between Access-layer devices and Core-layer devices.
- ❏ Fast Ethernet uses CSMA/CD.

Duplex

- ❏ 100 Mbps is available in each direction.
- ❏ Duplex allows transmission of data in both directions.
- ❏ There are separate paths for transmitting and receiving data.

❑ Full duplex increases performance at the Distribution layer.

Gigabit Ethernet
❑ Gigabit is effective in the switch, core, and server block.
❑ Gigabit operates at 1000 Mbps.
❑ Gigabit offers high-speed performance.
❑ Gigabit allows servers high throughput.

Connections
❑ IOS-based switch 1900/2800/2900 XL/5000 uses RJ-45 to RJ-45 rollover cable to connect to the console port.
❑ Do not connect an actual telephone line, ISDN, or Ethernet cable to the console port.
❑ 1900/2800 series switch Ethernet ports are fixed.
❑ 5000 series switch can be set for 10BaseT or 100BaseT.
❑ All connections between the end devices and your switch cannot exceed 100 meters.

Fundamental Switching Commands
❑ IOS-based switch: **enable password level 1** *password* (sets the log-on password).
❑ IOS-based switch: **enable password level 15** *password* (sets the enable password).
❑ IOS-based switch: Passwords are not case sensitive.
❑ IOS-based switch: **hostname** *name* (sets the hostname).
❑ IOS-based switch: **ip address** *ip address netmask* (sets the IP address).
❑ IOS-based switch: **show IP** (shows the IP configuration).
❑ IOS-based switch: **description** *description string* (sets a description on an interface).
❑ IOS-based switch: **duplex** *{auto|full|full-flow-control|half}* (sets the duplex).

- Set-based switch: **set password** (sets the log-on password).
- Set-based switch: **set enablepass** (sets the enable password).
- Passwords on a set-based switch are case sensitive.
- Set-based switch: **set prompt** *name* (sets the name to the CLI).
- Set-based switch: **set interface sc0** *ip address netmask broadcast address* (assigns your IP address to your in-band logical interface.
- Set-based switch: **set interface sc0** *vlan* (assigns the IP address to a management VLAN).
- Set-based switch: **show interface** (show interface configuration).
- Set-based switch: **set port name** *mod/number description* (sets the description on an interface).
- Set-based switch: **set port speed** *mod_num/port_num 10|100|auto* (sets the port speed).
- Set-based switch: **set port duplex mod num/port num {full|half}** (sets the duplex).

SELF TEST

The Self Test questions will help you measure your understanding of the material presented in this chapter. Read all of the choices carefully, as there may be more than one correct answer. Choose all correct answers for each question.

Switch Block

1. Which layer provides connectivity between the access switch and the end-user devices?

    A. Access layer
    B. Distribution layer
    C. Core layer
    D. End-user layer

2. The 100-meter rule is broken down into which of the following? (Choose all that apply.)

    A. 5 meters from the switch to the patch panel.
    B. 100 meters from the patch panel to the office punch-down block.
    C. 5 meters from the punch-down block to the desktop connection.
    D. 90 meters from the patch panel to the office punch-down block.

3. Gail has been hired to configure the company's new switch block. She is configuring the specifications for her switch. She has one Catalyst 5000 series switch for her Core layer, one Catalyst 2900 series switch for her Distribution layer, and one 1900 series switch for her Access layer. She is not using fiber. Which type of cabling should Gail purchase?

    A. Thinnet
    B. Thicknet
    C. Token Ring
    D. Fast Ethernet

Fast Ethernet Implementations

4. Fast Ethernet is based on _____ technology.

    A. CSMA/CD
    B. CSMA/CA
    C. CMSA/CD
    D. CD/CSAM

5. John is a Cisco network consultant who has been hired by Dynacomp Systems to migrate the company 10 Mbps to 100 Mbps. What items should John include in his proposal? (Choose all that apply.)

    A. Examine the existing cable to determine if it can be used.
    B. Check the network cards in workstations to see if they already support 100 Mbps.
    C. Check to see if they already have 100 Mbps hubs and switches.
    D. Check the servers and all other devices to see if they support 100 Mbps.

6. Which 100BaseT technology uses MMF cable with a 62.5-micron fiber-optic core and 125-micron outer cladding (62.5/125)? (Choose all that apply.)

    A. 100BaseT4
    B. 100BaseTX
    C. 100BaseFX
    D. 100BaseT2

7. Christopher has been hired to connect building A to building B. The distance between the two buildings is 300 meters. He also wants to make sure that EMI is not an issue. Which 100BaseT specification supports this?

    A. 100BaseT4
    B. 100BaseTX
    C. 100BaseFX
    D. 10BaseT

Duplex

8. Which of the following are related to Full duplex? (Choose all that apply.)

    A. Separate paths for sending and receiving data.
    B. Disable collision detection and loopback functions.
    C. Single path for sending and receiving data.
    D. Enable collision detection and loopback functions.

9. Which of the following are the differences between Full duplex and half duplex? Assume that all devices support both Full and half duplex.

    A. Half duplex uses separate paths for sending and receiving data.

B. Half duplex is faster than Full duplex between switches, because you are only using one path for sending and receiving data.
  C. Full duplex is faster than half duplex between switches, because you are using two separate paths for sending and receiving data.
  D. Full duplex uses separate paths for sending and receiving data.

Gigabit Ethernet

10. Which of the following are true about Gigabit Ethernet?
    A. Gigabit is 10 times faster than 10 Mbps.
    B. Gigabit is 10 times faster than 100 Mbps.
    C. Gigabit is 10,000 times faster than 100 Mbps.
    D. Gigabit is faster than 100 Mbps.

11. Which of the following 1000Base specifications use copper cabling?
    A. 1000BaseCX
    B. 1000BaseT
    C. 1000BaseSX
    D. 1000BaseLX

12. Which of the following 1000BaseSX specifications are true?
    A. Multimode fiber cable, with a 102.5-micron fiber-optic core and 50-micron fiber-optic core; 780 nanometer laser.
    B. Multimode fiber cable, with a 82.5-micron fiber-optic core and 50-micron fiber-optic core; 780 nanometer laser.
    C. Multimode fiber cable, with a 62.5-micron fiber-optic core and 50-micron fiber-optic core; 780 nanometer laser.
    D. Multimode fiber cable, with a 75.5-micron fiber-optic core and 50-micron fiber-optic core; 780 nanometer laser.

13. Julia just received some multimode fiber cable, with a 62.5-micron fiber-optic core and 50-micron fiber-optic core; 780 nanometer laser. She has installed this cable between the accounting building and the marketing building switches. The distance between the two building is 400 meters. She is unable to connect from one switch to the other. What did Julia do wrong?
    A. She used fiber-optic cabling; she should have used twisted-pair.
    B. She should have used fiber-optic cable with a 10.5 micron fiber-optic core.

C. The cable she used should have had a 900 nanometer laser.

D. She should have used single-mode fiber cable, 9-micron core, 1300-nanometer laser; this cable will go over the 400 meters.

Connections

14. Amy just purchased a 2900 series switch from an online auction. The switch didn't come with any cables or documentation; however, did come with one RJ-45 to DB-9 connector labeled terminal. She is trying to connect to the console port of the switch. She used a standard RJ-45 patch cable that she bought at the local computer store. Her PC has a 9-pin serial connector labeled "com2." She has configured hyperterm to look at com2. Why can't Amy make the connection?

    A. Amy should be using a rollover cable to connect to the 2900.

    B. Amy should be using the DB-25 connector from Cisco.

    C. The 2900 console port should be used with a fiber cable.

    D. Amy should be using an ISDN cable to connect to the 2900.

15. Bill, a network administrator of a local graphics arts company, just purchased a 5505 series switch. Bill bought the top-of-the-line Supervisor III Engine. The switch was missing the console cable. Bill is planning to use the light-blue console cable that came with his 2900 switch. Bill is able to make a connection to the 2900 series switch but not the 5505 series switch using the same PC. What did Bill do wrong?

    A. Bill did nothing wrong; his 5505 switch is not working.

    B. Bill has the wrong Supervisor III Engine installed in the 5505.

    C. Bill should have used the red, white, and blue cable that comes from Cisco.

    D. Bill needs to use a regular patch cable to connect to the console port.

16. John is working on a new project called Project Snowball. His job is to connect his notebook to the company's Cisco devices and configure them. How should John configure Hyper-Terminal on his PC? The order is Bits per second, Data bits, Parity, Stop bits, Flow control.

    A. 8,9600,None,2,None

    B. 9600,8,1,1,None

    C. None,8,None,1,None

    D. 9600,8,None,1,None

Fundamental Switching Commands

17. What is the command to set the host or system name to Pembroke Pines on a 1900/2800 or 2900 XL series switch? You are already in global configuration mode.

  A. Switch(config)#hostname Pembroke Pines, ENTER/RETURN
  B. Switch(config)#hostname "Pembroke Pines", ENTER/RETURN
  C. Switch(config)#host Pembroke Pines, ENTER/RETURN
  D. Switch(config)#name Pembroke Pines, ENTER/RETURN

18. What command can be used to view the IP address and the subnet mask for an IOS-based switch? You are already in global configuration mode.

  A. **Switch**#show ip
  B. **Switch**#ip address ?
  C. **Switch**#ip address /?
  D. Switch#ip address help

19. What command do you use to configure the port speed on a set-based switch? You are already in privileged mode.

  A. Switch(enable)set port speed mod_num/port_num 10/100/auto
  B. Switch(enable)set port speed port_num/mod_num 10/100/auto
  C. Switch(enable)set port speed mod_num/port_name 10/100/auto
  D. Switch(enable)set port mod_name/port_name 10/100/auto

20. Which command do you use to configure the duplex on a IOS-based switch? You are already in interface mode.

  A. Switch(config-if)duplex (auto|full|full-flow-control|half)
  B. Switch(config-if)set duplex(auto|full|full-flow-control|half)
  C. Switch(config-if)duplex set(auto|full|full-flow-control|half)
  D. Switch(config-if)set duplex full

21. Which command is used on a set-based switch to assign an IP address to the in-band logical interface from privileged mode?

  A. Switch(enable)**set sc0 interface** ip address netmask broadcast address
  B. Switch(enable)**interface set sc0** ip address netmask broadcast address
  C. Switch(enable)**set interface sc0** ip address netmask broadcast address
  D. Switch(enable)**sc0 interface set** ip address netmask broadcast address

LAB QUESTION

You have been hired to work for a consulting company called Dynacomp Systems, Inc. Dynacomp Systems has started a new Web site called www.dynacomp.com/vlabs. This Web site offers virtual labs for individuals studying for the Certified Cisco Network Professional (CCNP) exams. Students will be able to connect to the site and click on a link that will directly connect them to the console ports on all of the Cisco devices. Dynacomp is not using a software-based solution for the equipment; the students will be connecting directly into real Cisco switches and routers to use during their labs. The owner has already preconfigured the core devices, the routers, and the server that will let the students connect directly into the Cisco switches and routers. Your job is to configure one of the two switch blocks and connect that switch block to the core devices.

All of these devices are going to be on the same VLAN.

Switch Block Equipment List:

- One PC running Windows NT Professional
- One 1912 access switch
- Two Catalyst 5505 switches with:
    - 4.3(1a) software or higher
    - Supervisor Engine III Base Module
    - 24-port 10/100TX card

Visual Objective:
Use Figure 2-20 as a guideline during this lab.

Objectives:

- Physically cable your switch block.
- Configure a Fast Ethernet connection between your distribution switch and your Access layer switch.
- Configure a Fast Ethernet connection between your distribution switches.
- Configure a Fast Ethernet connection between your core switches and your distribution switches.
- Connect your personal computer to an Ethernet port on your Access layer switch 1.

Task 1: Identifying IP addresses and names for your devices.
Use Tables 2-11, 2-12, and 2-13 to configure your IP addresses, names, and cable port assignments of the devices you are installing.

FIGURE 2-20   Visual switch block diagram

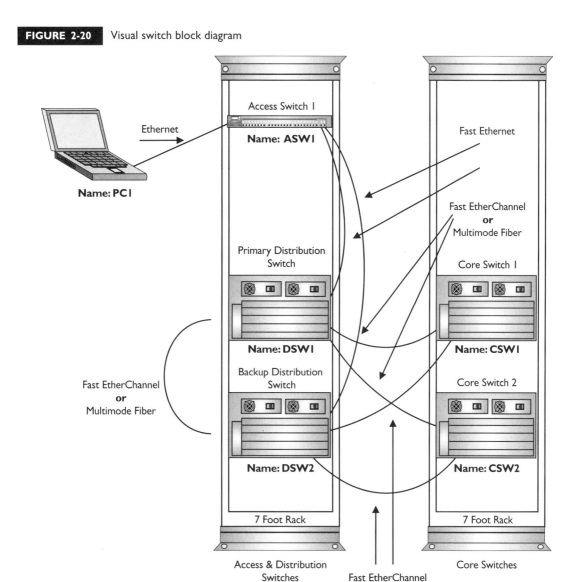

Using Tables 2-11, 2-12, and 2-13, fill in the network topology diagram in Figure 2-21.

Chapter 2: Switch Block Concepts

TABLE 2-11 PC and Access Switch Device Names and IP Addresses, Distribution Switch Device Names and IP Address, and Access and Distribution Switch Mod/Port Assignments

PC Name	PC IP Address	Access Switch Name	Access Switch IP Address	Primary Distribution Switch Name	Backup Distribution Switch Name
PC1	131.107.1.1	ASW1	131.107.2.1	DSW1	DSW2

Distribution Switch Name	Distribution IP Address
DSW1	131.107.2.11
DSW2	131.107.2.12

Access Switch Name	Access Switch/Mod for PC	Primary Access FE Mod/Port	Primary Distribution Mod/Port	Backup Access FE Mod/Port	Backup Distribution Mod/Port
ASW1	0/3	0/26	2/1	0/27	2/1

Task 2: Physically cabling the devices in the switch block.

1. Connect your PC to the access switch.
2. Connect your access switch to both the primary and backup distribution switches.
3. Connect your distribution switches to the core switches.

Table 2-14 lists the steps to complete your task.

TABLE 2-12 Distribution and Core Switch Mod/Port Assignments

Distr. Switch Name	Distr. Port	Core Switch Name	Core Port	Core Switch 1 IP Address	Distr. Port	Core Switch Name	Core Port	Core Switch 2 IP Address
DSW1	2/5-6	CSW1	2/1-2	131.107.100.1	2/7-8	CSW2	2/1-2	131.107.101.1
DSW2	2/5-6	CSW1	2/3-4	131.107.100.1	2/7-8	CSW2	2/3-4	131.107.101.1

Lab Question

TABLE 2-13 Distribution-to-Distribution Switch Mod/Port Assignment

Distribution Switch Name	Distribution Port	Distribution Switch Name	Distriburion Port
DSW1	2/9-12	DSW2	2/9-12

FIGURE 2-21 Fill in the information using Tables 2-11, 2-12, and 2-13

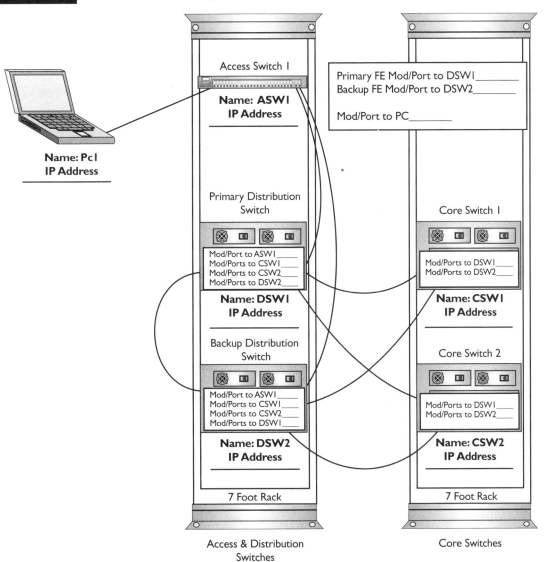

Chapter 2: Switch Block Concepts

TABLE 2-14 Complete Task 2 Table

Number	Task	Completed
1.	Cable connections between DSW1 ports 2/5–6 to ports 2/1–2 on CSW1, using two crossover cables.	
2.	Cable connections between DSW1 ports 2/7–8 to ports 2/1–2 on CSW2, using two crossover cables.	
3.	Cable connections from DSW1 ports 2/9–12 to ports 2/9–12 on DSW2, using four crossover cables.	
4.	Cable a connection between PC1's Ethernet port to 0/3 on ASW1, using a straight-through cable.	
5.	Cable a connection between ASW1 port 0/26 to port 2/1 on DSW1, using a crossover cable.	
6.	Cable a connection between ASW1 port 0/27 to port 2/1 on DSW2, using a crossover cable.	
7.	Cable connections between DSW1 ports 2/5–6 to ports 2/1–2 on CSW1, using two crossover cables.	
8.	Cable connections between DSW1 ports 2/7–8 to ports 2/1–2 on CSW2, using two crossover cables.	
9.	We are not going to connect crossover cables from DSW2 to CSW1 at this time. This will be done in a future lab in this book.	NA
10.	Connect one rollover cable between ASW1's console port and your PC's serial port. You will need to add the appropriate adapter to the side of the cable that connects to your serial port on your PC—either the 9-pin to RJ-45 or 25-pin to RJ-45.	
11.	Configure HyperTerminal Settings on your Windows-based PC. Connection using: Direct to Com1 or Com2 (whichever port you connected the rollover cable to) Bits per second: 9600 Data bits: 8 Stop bits: 1 Flow control: None	
12.	In your HyperTerminal session, enter a Return/Enter.	
13.	You should see a Switching menu in your session.	
14.	Now that you have connected all of the cables except for the ones noted in step 9, you should see the status lights turn green on all of your connected ports. This will confirm that you have cabled everything correctly.	

Required Equipment:

- 10 crossover cables (to connect between your switches)
- 1 straight-through patch cable (to connect from your PC's Ethernet port to your access switch)
- 1 rollover cable (to connect from your PC to your switches)
- 1 RJ-45-to-DB-9 or RJ45-DB-25 (depending on which type of connector you have on your PC)

Task 3: Configuring an Ethernet connection between your PC and the Access layer switch.

Objectives:

- Configure your network properties on your PC.
- Configure your password on the access switch.
- Configure a hostname on your access switch.
- Configure the IP address and subnet mask on your access switch.
- Enter a description for the Ethernet port on your access switch.
- Set the port to Full duplex on the access switch.

Table 2-15 lists the steps you should follow to complete this task.

TABLE 2-15 Complete Task 3 Table

Number	Task	Completed
1.	On your Windows-based PC right-click on My Network Places, select Properties, and then right-click again on Local Area Connection, properties. Configure your settings the same as Figure 2-22.	
2.	Open a HyperTerminal session to your access switch.	
3.	Select option **K** to enter CLI mode.	
4.	From the global configuration, enter **enable password level 1 cisco**. This will set the enable password to cisco.	
5.	From the global configuration, enter **enable password level 15 password**. This will set the privileged password to password.	
6.	From the global configuration, enter **hostname PC1**. This will configure your hostname.	
7.	From the global configuration, enter **ip address 131.107.2.1 255.255.0.0**. This will assign your IP address to your access switch.	

Chapter 2: Switch Block Concepts

TABLE 2-15 Complete Task 3 Table

Number	Task	Completed
8.	From the global configuration, enter **interface ethernet 0/3**. This will allow you to configure this port.	
9.	From the interface mode, enter the description **To PC1**. This will set the description to To PC1.	
10.	From the interface mode, enter **duplex full**. This will set the port to Full duplex.	
11.	From privileged mode, enter the **show run** command to verify the configuration.	
12.	Enter **show interface ethernet 0/3** to look for the duplex setting. Make sure it is set for full duplex.	
13.	From your PC, ping your access switch. In this case, type **ping 131.107.2.1** at a command prompt. This will verify connectivity from your PC to your access switch.	

FIGURE 2-22

Windows network properties

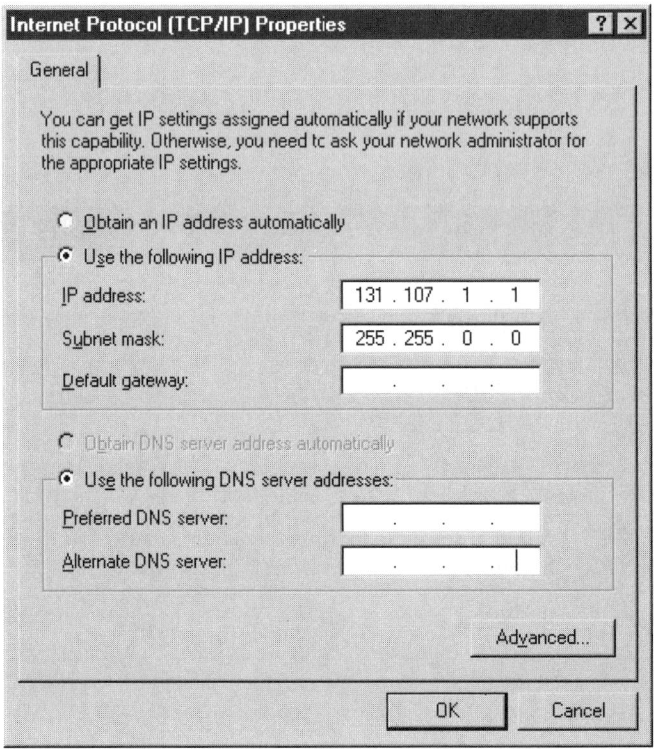

Task 4: Configuring a Fast Ethernet connection between your Access layer switch and your primary distribution switch.

Objectives:

- Create a port description for the primary Fast Ethernet port on your access switch.
- Set the port duplex for the Fast Ethernet port.
- Configure your primary distribution switch.

Table 2-16 lists the steps you should follow to complete this task.

Task 5: Repeat the same steps in Task 4 to configure your Fast Ethernet connection between your Access layer switch and your backup distribution switch. Make sure you use the correct names and IP addresses that you entered in Figure 2-22.

Objectives:

- Create a port description for the backup Fast Ethernet port on your access switch.
- Set the port duplex for the Fast Ethernet port.
- Configure your backup distribution switch.
- You should be able to ping between your access switch and your backup distribution switch.

Task 6: Repeat the same steps in Task 4 to configure a Fast Ethernet connection between your distribution switches and your core switches. Make sure you use the correct names and IP addresses that you entered in Figure 2-22.

Objectives:

- Configure your distribution-to-core connections.
- Configure your distribution-to-distribution connections.
- You should be able to ping between distribution switches.

TABLE 2-16 Complete Task 4 Table

Number	Task	Completed
1.	Complete the next couple of steps from your access switch. From the global configuration, enter interface fastethernet 0/26. This will allow you to configure the port that is connecting to your primary distribution switch.	
2.	From the interface configuration mode, enter duplex full to set the port to full duplex.	
3.	From the interface configuration mode, enter description "Link to DSW1". This will set the description to "Link to DSW1."	
4.	You must administratively disable your link to your backup distribution switch to prevent Spanning Tree from possibly disabling your primary link. This will be discussed later in this book.	NA
5.	From the interface configuration mode, enter the interface fastethernet 0/27 command so we can configure this port.	
6.	From the interface configuration mode, enter the shutdown command to administratively disable the port.	
7.	Complete the remaining steps on your distribution switch. Connect your patch cable from the serial port of your PC to the console port on your distribution switch. From privileged mode, enter set password to enter the old password, and then for the new password enter cisco. This will set the login password to cisco.	
8.	From privileged mode, enter set prompt DSW1. This will configure your unique name for your distribution switch.	
9.	From privileged mode, enter set interface sc0 131.107.2.11 255.255.0.0 131.107.255.255. This will assign an IP address to your distribution switch.	
10.	From privileged mode, enter set port speed 2/1 100. This will set your port speed to 100 Mbps.	
11.	From privileged mode, enter set port duplex 2/1 full. This will set your duplex to full.	
12.	From privileged mode, enter set port name 2/1 "FE to Access Switch". This will set your description on this port to "FE Access Switch."	
13.	From privileged mode, enter set port disable 2/5-8 to disable the ports to the core. We will active these in a later lab.	
14.	From privileged mode, enter show config to see the changes.	
15.	From privileged mode, enter ping 131.107.2.1 to test connectivity between your access switch and your distribution switch.	
16.	If you were successful in step 15, you have correctly configured your distribution switch.	

SELF TEST ANSWERS

Switch Block

1. ☑ **A.** Access layer is the correct answer.
   ☒ **B** and **C** are incorrect because they are typically not used to connect to your end-user devices. **D** is incorrect because the end-user layer does not exist.

2. ☑ **A, C, D.** The 100-meter rule states 5 meters from the switch to the patch panel, 5 meters from the punch-down block to the desktop connection, and 90 meters from the patch panel to the office punch-down block.
   ☒ **B** is an incorrect distance.

3. ☑ **D.** All of her switches support Fast Ethernet, and this would be 100 Mbps.
   ☒ **A, B,** and **C** are incorrect because Thinnet is 10 Mbps, Thicknet is 10 Mbps, and Token Ring is 16 Mbps. Therefore, the fastest and most cost-effective solution would be Fast Ethernet.

Fast Ethernet Implementations

4. ☑ **A.** Carrier-Sense-Multiple-Access/Collision Detection is the correct answer.
   ☒ **B** is incorrect because it is Carrier-Sense-Multiple Access/Collision Avoidance. **C** and **D** are fictional, and are therefore incorrect.

5. ☑ **A, B, C, D. A** is correct because you should check to see if you already have Category 5 (CAT 5) cabling installed, which will support 100 Mbps. This will prevent you from having to waste money installing new cable to support 100 Mbps. **B** is correct because most network cards today support both 10 and 100 Mbps. This again will save you money if you can use your existing cards. **C** is correct for the same reason: your hubs may already support 100 Mbps. **D** is the same.
   ☒ There are no incorrect choices.

6. ☑ **C.** 100BaseFX meets the specifications.
   ☒ **A** and **B** are incorrect because they do not use fiber cable. **D** is incorrect because there is no such thing as 100BaseT2.

7. ☑ **C.** The maximum distance is 400 meters, and because this uses fiber-optic cable, EMI interface is not a factor.
   ☒ **A** and **B** are incorrect because they do not support 300 meters. **D** is incorrect because it is not a 100BaseT specification.

Duplex

8. ☑ **A, B.** Full duplex supports separate paths for sending and receiving data, and because you are a point-to-point connection, you can disable collision detection and loopback functions.
   ☒ **C** is incorrect because Full duplex uses separate paths for sending and receiving data. **D** is incorrect because collision detection and loopback functions should be disabled.

9. ☑ **C, D.** Full duplex supports separate paths for sending and receiving data, and is faster between switches.
   ☒ **A** and **B** are incorrect because half duplex does not use separate paths for sending and receiving data, and half duplex is slower than Full duplex.

Gigabit Ethernet

10. ☑ **B, D.** Gigabit is 10 times faster than 100 Mbps, and is a lot faster than 100 Mbps.
    ☒ **A** and **C** are incorrect because Gigabit is not 10 times faster than 10 Mbps and is not faster than 100 Mbps.

11. ☑ **A, B.** 1000BaseCX and 1000BaseT use copper cabling.
    ☒ **C** and **D** are incorrect because they use fiber cabling.

12. ☑ **C.** Multimode fiber cable, with a 62.5-micron fiber-optic core and 50-micron fiber-optic core; 780 nanometer laser.
    ☒ **A, B,** and **D** are false statements.

13. ☑ **D.** This cable can go 3 km, and even farther with Cisco equipment.
    ☒ **A** is incorrect because it would never go that distance. **B** and **C** are incorrect because they contain false information.

Connections

14. ☑ **A.** The 2900 uses a light-blue rollover cable for the console port.
    ☒ **B** is incorrect because it is the wrong connector for her PC; in addition, she is still using the wrong cable. **C** is incorrect because it is the wrong cable. **D** is incorrect because you do not use an ISDN cable; in fact, you can damage the switch by connecting it to your ISDN connection.

15. ☑ **D.** For this series switch, you use just a regular RJ-45 patch cable, not a rollover cable.
    ☒ **A** is incorrect because his switch does work. **B** is incorrect because the Supervisor III will

work in a 5505. C is incorrect because red, white, and blue are the colors of the American flag, not a cable from Cisco.

16. ☑ **D.** Cisco recommends 9600 Bits per second, 8 Data bits, None for Parity, 1 Stop bit, None for Flow control.
    ☒ **A, B,** and **C** are the wrong configuration.

Fundamental Switching Commands

17. ☑ **B.** You have to use "" to include the space between Pembroke and Pines.
    ☒ **A** is incorrect because the space would be treated as a mistake. **C** and **D** are incorrect because they are using the wrong command; in addition, they are missing the "" around Pembroke Pines.

18. ☑ **A. Switch#**show ip will show you the IP address, subnet mask, default gateway, management VLAN, domain name, etc.
    ☒ **B, C,** and **D** are the incorrect commands.

19. ☑ **A.** mod_num is the module number of the port, port_num is the port number, and 10/100/auto is the speed of the port.
    ☒ **B, C,** and **D** are incorrect because they contain the wrong syntax or the wrong commands.

20. ☑ **A.** Auto sets the port into auto-negotiation mode, full sets the port to full duplex, full-flow-control sets the port to Full duplex with flow control, and half sets the port to half duplex.
    ☒ **B, C,** and **D** are incorrect because they contain the incorrect command or syntax.

21. ☑ **C. This command** is used on a set-based switch to assign an IP address to the in-band logical interface from privileged mode.
    ☒ **A, B,** and **D** are incorrect because they contain the wrong syntax.

LAB ANSWERS

The answers to the Lab are shown in Figure 2-23.

92 Chapter 2: Switch Block Concepts

FIGURE 2-23 Lab answers to Figure 2-22

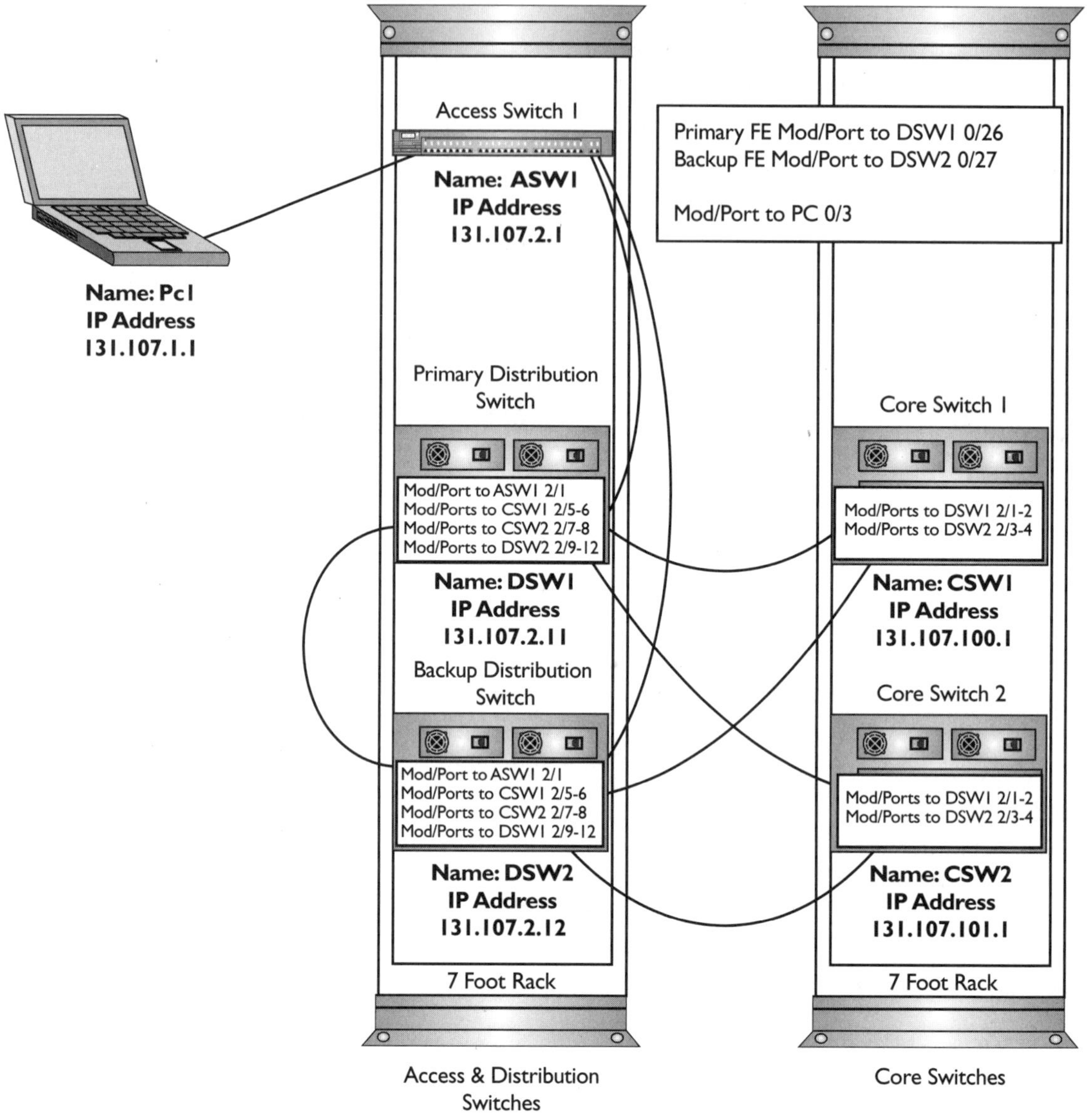

Name: Pc1
IP Address
131.107.1.1

Access Switch 1
Name: ASW1
IP Address
131.107.2.1

Primary FE Mod/Port to DSW1 0/26
Backup FE Mod/Port to DSW2 0/27

Mod/Port to PC 0/3

Primary Distribution Switch

Mod/Port to ASW1 2/1
Mod/Ports to CSW1 2/5-6
Mod/Ports to CSW2 2/7-8
Mod/Ports to DSW2 2/9-12

Name: DSW1
IP Address
131.107.2.11

Backup Distribution Switch

Mod/Port to ASW1 2/1
Mod/Ports to CSW1 2/5-6
Mod/Ports to CSW2 2/7-8
Mod/Ports to DSW1 2/9-12

Name: DSW2
IP Address
131.107.2.12

7 Foot Rack

Access & Distribution
Switches

Core Switch 1

Mod/Ports to DSW1 2/1-2
Mod/Ports to DSW2 2/3-4

Name: CSW1
IP Address
131.107.100.1

Core Switch 2

Mod/Ports to DSW1 2/1-2
Mod/Ports to DSW2 2/3-4

Name: CSW2
IP Address
131.107.101.1

7 Foot Rack

Core Switches

3
Virtual Local Area Networks (VLANs)

CERTIFICATION OBJECTIVES

3.01   VLAN Overview
✓   Two-Minute Drill
Q&A   Self Test

You have seen how switches can be used to direct unicast traffic to appropriate ports using a MAC address table or a content addressable memory (CAM) table. Switches offer better throughput in such conditions, but do not address the issue of broadcast. Switches by default propagate broadcasts out of every interface except the interface on which the broadcast was received. In a large single-segment environment, the amount of broadcast frames generated by all of the endstations connected to the switched network can significantly negatively impact network performance. Broadcasts can consume an excessive percentage of the total bandwidth available, reducing the effective throughput of information at an exponential rate. The method of dealing with broadcast issues is to segment large broadcast domains into smaller networks, and to use routers to route between them. Since broadcasts are not propagated beyond a router boundary, they are restricted to the physical segment on which they originated. Virtual Local Area Networks, or VLANs, provide the means to create a large number of micro-segmented networks while maximizing the flexibility of assigning any port in a switched network to any VLAN recognized by the management domain. A management domain is a group of switches that exchange information about the VLANs they carry, and build a consistent view of all the VLANs across all the switches in the domain. Every switch in a management domain will have the exact same list of VLANs in its VLAN database.

In today's world, companies continuously reorganize in an effort to maximize their productivity. This results in frequent moves and the creation of workgroups that may end up in disparate locations throughout that company. The location of these workgroups rarely coincides with the physical topology of the network. VLANs offer the flexibility required to accommodate these changes while retaining solid control over network security, management, and performance.

CERTIFICATION OBJECTIVE 3.01

VLAN Overview

What is a VLAN? In a switched network, a VLAN is a logical representation of a normal physical network segment. This virtual segment can be localized on a single switch, or can have a presence on any number of switches within a management domain. Ports on a switch are assigned to a VLAN, making those ports part of a common segment or broadcast domain. These ports are not physically limited to a single switch. Imagine the management domain depicted in Figure 3-1. The domain contains three Cisco Catalyst 1900 switches, all exchanging information about VLANs 1, 2, and 3. You, as the network administrator, assign ports 1 through 8 of each switch to be members of VLAN 1, ports 9 through 16 as members of VLAN 2, and ports 17 through 24 to VLAN 3. In this scenario, a broadcast from an endstation connected to port #1 of the first switch would be forwarded to all the ports in the same VLAN; in this case, ports 1 through 8 of every switch in the management domain. VLANs are often referred to with colors. On network diagrams, the colors represent the reach of each VLAN across the entire network. In Figure 3-1, broadcasts from the green VLAN (VLAN 1) would not propagate to the red (VLAN 2) or blue VLAN (VLAN 3). The broadcasts are restricted to the VLAN they are on.

VLANs provide network administrators with additional flexibility in that any port of a switch can be mapped to any VLAN that is part of its management domain. Imagine, for example, a company that is operating in a two-story building. Each floor has a separate wiring closet with Cisco Catalyst switches interconnected via a fiber-optic backbone. The marketing group operates on the first floor, and the

FIGURE 3-1

VLANs and broadcast domains

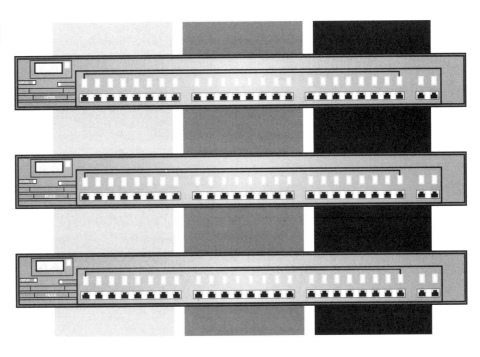

development group is on the second floor. One of the requirements of the development group is that all of their endstations be isolated from the production network by operating on a different physical segment. This is because the development group often simulates various network conditions in the testing of their product, which could negatively impact the network performance for the rest of the company. So far, there is no networking issue. The development group is located solely on the second floor, so it is easy to interconnect all the endstations on that floor, since they are all on the same network, in a common physical location. In this situation, traditional hubs could be used to provide this level of isolation. A router in the first-floor wiring closet would route between each network and provide connectivity between the two floors.

Now suppose that months later, following a lengthy reorganization study, it was decided that a small branch of the development team would now be called "technical marketing" and would assist the regular marketing group with setting up trade shows and customer demonstrations. These people, although situated on the second floor, must be connected to the marketing segment located on the first floor. On top of this, the VP of development wishes to relocate to the first-floor corner office where the view is much nicer. Of course, he must remain connected to the second-floor development network. These seem like trivial changes, but they represent very real examples of where a network lacking the flexibility of VLAN technology can start to collapse. Without VLANs, the network administrator would have to run separate hubs to each floor and connect them through additional wiring between the floors. The hub connecting the VP on the first floor would have only one of its ports in use, resulting in a waste of hardware and additional wiring costs. The same is true for the technical marketing group located on the second floor. A switched network using VLANs can solve these issues by mapping specific ports on different switches as members of any desired VLAN. It is important to realize that VLANs are created through software only. Switches do not need additional hardware whenever a VLAN is added. The VLAN is simply created in the switch software and can be allocated ports through the configuration interface. Each switch is aware of all the VLANs available, and the network administrator needs only to select which VLAN will be used on any specific port of a switch. Figure 3-2 describes the preceding scenario with and without VLAN technology. Notice how the VLAN topology makes use of a special link called a trunk. A trunk is a connection between two switches that can carry multiple VLANs on the same cable. Trunks are described in detail later in this chapter.

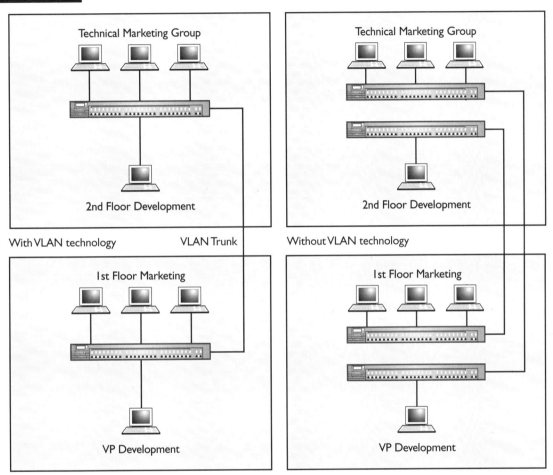

FIGURE 3-2 The advantage of VLAN flexibility in a network topology

VLANs can be incorporated into most existing network topologies. There are five types of VLANs defined in the Catalyst 5000 series:

- Ethernet
- FDDI
- Token Ring/802.5
- FDDI-net
- Token Ring-net

The Token Ring and FDDI VLAN types represent a single logical ring across the entire management domain. This means that the ring number for every member of that VLAN will be the same throughout the entire network. In a source-route bridging environment, it is possible to separate those VLANs into separate rings connected by source-route bridges. This is accomplished using the Token Ring-net and FDDI-net VLAN types.

How does a switch know what VLAN a certain frame belongs to? When processing VLAN frames, switches add an additional header to the frame. Part of this new header is a field called the VLAN ID that identifies which VLAN a frame belongs to. These VLAN IDs remain attached to the frames as they travel across the switched network. At the destination, the switch examines the list of ports that are part of the VLAN identified by the incoming frame. If the frame is a broadcast frame (destination MAC address ffff.ffff.ffff), the switch strips the header and floods the frame in its original state to every port in the list. For a unicast frame (destination MAC of a specific endstation), the switch strips the header, looks up the destination MAC address of the frame in its MAC address table or content addressable memory (CAM) table, and sends the frame to the appropriate port in that VLAN. The CAM table maintains an association between MAC addresses and ports.

Creating Virtual LANs

The "set-based" commands used to create and manage VLANs on switches like the Catalyst 5000 series differ from those used on "IOS-based" switches like the Catalyst 2900XL series. The process, however, is similar for either platform and is separated into two distinct tasks:

- Creating VLANs in a management domain
- Grouping switch ports into the VLANs

Set-Based and IOS-Based Platforms

Throughout this chapter, we make use of the terms *set-based* and *IOS-based* switches. As a reference, Table 3-1 is a comprehensive list of which Cisco Catalyst hardware is set-based and which is IOS-based.

TABLE 3-1	Switch Platform	Set-Based	IOS-Based
Software Platform of Catalyst Switches	8500 series	X	
	6000 series	X	
	5000 series	X	
	4912G Gigabit switch	X	
	4000 series	X	
	3500 series		X
	2948G Gigabit switch	X	
	2926 series	X	
	2900XL series		X
	1200 series	X	

EXERCISE 3-1

Unpacking and Installing a Core Catalyst Switch

Most Catalyst switches can be used right out of the box without any configuration. This provides you with a switch configured to use VLAN 1 on all ports. In most cases, you will want to configure the switch to provide you with more functionality. In this exercise, you are provided with a brand-new set-based Catalyst 5509 switch with the following modules on board:

- Slot 1   Supervisory Module III
- Slot 2   Supervisory Module III (redundant backup)
- Slot 3   24-port 10/100 Mbps Ethernet module
- Slot 4   24-port 10/100 Mbps Ethernet module
- Slot 5   24-port 10/100 Mbps Ethernet module

Your task is to configure the switch to operate in an existing management domain without interacting with other switches. The existing domain is called "company-domain." You are to use "my-domain" as VTP domain name for your switch. Next, you need to create VLAN 30 and make all the ports of module 3 static members of that VLAN. Do the same for VLANs 40 and 50 for the modules in slots 4 and 5. Finally, make port 24 on each Ethernet module an ISL trunk that will carry *only* the VLANs listed previously.

1. The first step is to establish a proper management domain. To accomplish this, issue the command "set vtp domain company-domain". This will enable you to create VLANs on your switch.

2. Now create VLANs 30, 40, and 50. You do not need to create VLAN 1 since it is present by default. To do this, you need to issue the following commands: "set vlan 30", "set vlan 40" and "set vlan 50".

3. Now that you have created the VLANs, set the Ethernet ports as static members in their appropriate VLANs. To do this, issue the following commands: "set vlan 30 3/1-24", "set vlan 40 4/1-24", and "set vlan 50 5/1-24".

4. Next, make port 24 of modules 3, 4, and 5 ISL trunks for VLANs 1, 30, 40, and 50 only. In order to do this, you must first clear the VLAN list from each trunk. To do so, issue the following commands: "clear trunk 3/24 1-1005", "clear trunk 4/24 1-1005", and "clear trunk 5/24 1-1005". At this point, the list of allowable VLANs for these ports is cleared.

5. Add the required VLANs to the trunk list, and create the trunks themselves on the ports. To do so, issue the following commands: "set trunk 3/24 on isl 1,30,40,50", "set trunk 4/24 on isl 1,30,40,50", and "set trunk 5/24 on isl 1,30,40,50".

6. Finally, change the VTP operating mode of your switch from server mode to transparent mode. This way, the switch will operate transparently without impacting the existing management domain around it. To do so, issue the following command: "set vtp mode client". Notice how the domain name "company-domain" was superfluous information. Since the switch operates in transparent mode, it does not need any information about the domain surrounding it.

Creating VLANs in a Management Domain
This assumes that you are operating in a preexisting management domain. Later in this chapter, we will cover how to establish a proper domain prior to creating VLANs. The default settings when creating VLANs are aimed toward Ethernet. The VLAN type is set to Ethernet and the maximum transfer unit (MTU) is set to 1500 bytes, which is the standard MTU for Ethernet segments. These parameters can all

be specified during the creation of VLANs or changed later if required. The following covers the procedures for creating VLANs in set-based and IOS-based Catalyst switches.

Creating VLANs on a Set-Based Switch The command "set vlan" with the appropriate parameters is used to create VLANs on a set-based switch. By simply typing set vlan <vlan_number>, this will create an Ethernet VLAN with the default parameters. The following code example shows the various parameters used with the "set vlan" command and the successful creation of a default Ethernet VLAN.

```
Cat-5500% (enable) set vlan ?
Usage: set vlan <vlan_num> <mod/ports...>
       (An example of mod/ports is 1/1,2/1-12,3/1-2,4/1-12)
Usage: set vlan <vlan_num> [name <name>] [type <type>] [state <state>]
                           [said <said>] [mtu <mtu>] [ring hex_ring_number>]
                           [decring <decimal_ring_number>]
                           [bridge <bridge_number>] [parent <vlan_num>]
                           [mode <bridge_mode>] [stp <stp_type>]
                           [translation <vlan_num>] [backupcrf <off|on>]
                           [aremaxhop <hopcount>] [stemaxhop <hopcount>]
       (name = 1..32 characters, state = (active, suspend)
        type = (ethernet, fddi, fddinet, trcrf, trbrf)
        said = 1..4294967294, mtu = 576..18190
        hex_ring_number = 0x1..0xffff, decimal_ring_number = 1..4095
        bridge_number = 0x1..0xf, parent = 2..1005, mode = (srt, srb)
        stp = (ieee, ibm, auto), translation = 1..1005
        hopcount = 1..13)
Cat-5500% (enable)
Cat-5500% (enable) set vlan 600
Vlan 600 configuration successful
Cat-5500% (enable) show vlan 600
VLAN Name                             Status    IfIndex Mod/Ports, Vlans
---- -------------------------------- --------- ------- --------------------
600  VLAN0600                         active    1907    5/1-2
                                                        7/7
                                                        9/5-6
                                                        11/1,11/8

VLAN Type  SAID       MTU   Parent RingNo BrdgNo Stp  BrdgMode Trans1 Trans2
---- ----- ---------- ----- ------ ------ ------ ---- -------- ------ ------
600  enet  100600     1500  -      -      -      -             0      0

VLAN AREHops STEHops Backup CRF
---- ------- ------- ----------
Cat-5500% (enable)
```

exam watch

Notice in the previous example that the Catalyst switch created a default Security Association Identifier (SAID) value of 100600 for VLAN 600. If not specified during the creation of a VLAN, the switch allocates a SAID value of 100000 + VLAN #. SAIDs are used in FDDI VLANs, and their use is covered later in this chapter.

Creating VLANs on an IOS Switch VLAN creation on an IOS switch is done differently than on a set-based switch. It involves placing the switch in vlan configuration mode, which is different from the regular IOS configuration mode. To enter the vlan configuration mode, the command "vlan database" must be entered from the privileged exec mode. The switch prompt will then display "switch(vlan)", indicating that the switch has entered the vlan configuration mode. From this prompt, the command "vlan" is used to configure and modify VLAN parameters. The following code shows the options for the vlan command on an IOS switch. Like the set-based switches, entering "vlan <vlan_number>" will create a VLAN with the default settings. In this case, VLAN 700 is created as an Ethernet VLAN. The default parameters created for the VLAN are the same as for a set-based switch.

```
sw-2924XL#vlan database

sw-2924XL(vlan)#vlan 700 ?
  are         Maximum number of All Route Explorer hops for this VLAN
  backupcrf   Backup CRF mode of the VLAN
  bridge      Bridging characteristics of the VLAN
  media       Media type of the VLAN
  mtu         VLAN Maximum Transmission Unit
  name        ASCII name of the VLAN
  parent      ID number of the Parent VLAN of FDDI or Token Ring type VLANs
  ring        Ring number of FDDI or Token Ring type VLANs
  said        IEEE 802.10 SAID
  state       Operational state of the VLAN
  ste         Maximum number of Spanning Tree Explorer hops for this VLAN
  stp         Spanning tree characteristics of the VLAN
  tb-vlan1    ID number of the first translational VLAN for this VLAN
  tb-vlan2    ID number of the second translational VLAN for this VLAN

sw-2924XL(vlan)#vlan 700
VLAN 700 added:
    Name: VLAN0700
```

```
sw-2924XL(vlan)#exit
Exiting....
sw-2924XL#
sw-2924XL#show vlan id 700
VLAN Name                             Status    Ports
---- -------------------------------- --------- -------------------------------
700  VLAN0700                         active

VLAN Type  SAID       MTU   Parent RingNo BridgeNo Stp  BrdgMode Trans1 Trans2
---- ----- ---------- ----- ------ ------ -------- ---- -------- ------ ------
700  enet  100700     1500  -      -      -        -    -        0      0
sw-2924XL#
```

Static vs. Dynamic VLANs

We have seen how VLANs can be propagated to every switch within a management domain. When a switch receives a frame with a specific VLAN ID, it needs to know which port or ports to send this frame to. The switch uses its own port mapping database to determine the membership of each VLAN. Switch port allocation into this database is done in one of two ways: static or dynamic port allocation. You can view this database by using the switch command "show vlan". The output of this command lists the VLANs known to that switch, along with the switch ports associated with each VLAN. This command is identical in set-based and IOS-based switches. The following code example shows the output of the "show vlan" command on a set-based Cisco Catalyst 5509 switch. The output format of an IOS based 2924XL is identical.

```
VLAN Name                             Status    IfIndex Mod/Ports, Vlans
---- -------------------------------- --------- ------- ------------------------
1    default                          active    5       8/2
128  VLAN0128                         active    156     1/1-2
                                                        3/1-24
                                                        4/1-24
                                                        5/1-24
                                                        6/1-24
                                                        7/1-24
                                                        8/3-21,8/23-24
1002 fddi-default                     active    6
1003 token-ring-default               active    9
1004 fddinet-default                  active    7
1005 trnet-default                    active    8
```

```
VLAN Type  SAID       MTU   Parent RingNo BrdgNo Stp  BrdgMode Trans1 Trans2
---- ----- ---------- ----- ------ ------ ------ ---- -------- ------ ------
1    enet  100001     1500  -      -      -      -    -        0      0
128  enet  100128     1500  -      -      -      -    -        0      0
1002 fddi  101002     1500  -      -      -      -    -        0      0
1003 trcrf 101003     1500  0      0x0    -      -    -        0      0
1004 fdnet 101004     1500  -      -      0x0    ieee -        0      0
1005 trbrf 101005     1500  -      -      0x0    ibm  -        0      0

VLAN AREHops STEHops Backup CRF
---- ------- ------- ----------
1003 7       7       off
Cat-5509 (enable)
```

Static VLANs

Static allocation is the most simple and widely used method of allocating switch ports to VLANs. The most common way to statically assign a port to a VLAN is through the command-line interface of the switch. The interface command "set vlan <vlan> <mod/port>" on a Catalyst 5000 series switch or the interface command "switchport access vlan <vlan>" on an IOS-based switch are used for this purpose. The output of these commands is shown in the following code.

```
Set-based switch. Catalyst 5509.
Cat-5509> (enable) set vlan 128 7/2
VLAN Mod/Ports
---- -----------------------
128  1/1-2
     3/1-24
     4/1-24
     5/1-24
     6/1-24
     7/1-24
     8/1,8/3-21,8/23-24

Cat-5509> (enable)

IOS-based switch. Catalyst 2924XL-EN.
sw-2924XL#conf t
Enter configuration commands, one per line.  End with CNTL/Z.
sw-2924XL(config)#interface fastethernet 0/9
sw-2924XL(config-if)#switchport access vlan 128
sw-2924XL(config-if)#end
sw-2924XL#
```

Static VLAN allocation can also be done using SNMP-based tools. Graphical network management software such as HP OpenView, Tivoli NetView, or Cisco's CiscoView provide network managers with the ability to configure static VLAN membership through the switch's Simple Network Management Protocol interface. Figure 3-3 shows the use of CiscoView to allocate a switch port of a Catalyst 5509 switch to a specific VLAN.

Dynamic VLANs

The second method of allocating ports to VLANs is called dynamic membership. With dynamic membership, a switch port is not placed into any specific VLAN. Instead, the switch decides what VLAN to place the port depending on the MAC address of the endstation connecting to the switch. A database mapping MAC addresses to specific VLANs is used by all the switches in a management domain to provide the VLAN connection required by the endstation connecting to a switched

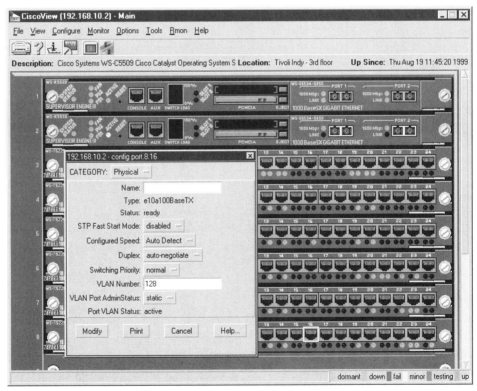

FIGURE 3-3

Static VLAN membership using CiscoView

port. This method of port allocation is normally used when user mobility and flexibility are important factors in a network design. The switches make use of an external Virtual Management Policy Server (VMPS) to handle the MAC address to switched port database. The database itself resides as a text file on a tftp server, to be accessed by the VPMS when required. When an endstation connects to a switch port that has been configured for dynamic VLAN allocation, the switch sends a request to the VMPS with the MAC address of the newly connected endstation. The VMPS looks up the MAC address in its database and replies to the requesting switch with a valid VLAN number for that MAC address, or an error message reporting that the MAC address was not found. The database file itself is an ASCII file that must manually be created by the network administrator and uploaded to the tftp server before starting the VMPS process. The following example shows a basic sample of a VMPS database file. Lines starting with an exclamation point denote a comment line that is not interpreted as a command by the VMPS.

```
!vmps domain <domain-name>
! The VMPS domain must be defined.
!vmps mode { open | secure }
! The default mode is open.
!vmps fallback <vlan-name>
!vmps no-domain-req { allow | deny }
!
! The default value is allow.
vmps domain MyDomain
vmps mode open
vmps fallback default
vmps no-domain-req deny
!
!MAC Addresses
!
vmps-mac-addrs
!
! address <addr> vlan-name <vlan_name>
!
address 00a0.ccf4.0445 vlan-name engineering
address 00c9.abaa.cafe vlan-name marketing
address 0013.4634.0ca3 vlan-name marketing
address 10c4.044d.0c0a vlan-name development
address ffa0.0fb3.000d vlan-name engineering
!
```

If a valid VLAN is returned to the switch, the port is placed in the appropriate VLAN, and an entry for that MAC address is entered in the CAM table of that switch.

If the VPMS returns a message saying that the requested MAC address was not found in the database, the switch places the port in a fallback VLAN. Note that only one fallback VLAN can be configured on a switch. This can be very restrictive, depending on the topology of the network in a multi-VLAN environment. For example, imagine a company that occupies a four-story building. Each floor operates on separate VLANs that connect to a single Catalyst 5500 switch controlling the entire building. It would be very useful if the ports for each floor could be assigned their native VLAN as fallback VLAN for that floor. Every port could be placed in dynamic allocation, with every endstation defaulting to the appropriate floor VLAN should their MAC address not be in the VMPS database. Unfortunately, this is not the case. Since only one VLAN can be selected as the fallback VLAN, anyone not in the VMPS database will default to the fallback VLAN no matter where they are located in the building.

> **exam**
> **⊕atch**
>
> *The switches use VMPS Query Protocol (VQP), which is a UDP protocol frame running on port 1589. VMPS queries are sent on the management VLAN of a switch. This is the VLAN that the sc0 interface of the switch is configured to use. It is therefore important for dynamic allocation to work properly to configure the management interfaces of all the switches to operate on the same VLAN. Furthermore, the port security feature of the Catalyst switch will prevent dynamic allocation from working properly. Make sure that this feature is disabled when using VMPS.*

The command "set vmps" is used to configure the VMPS and its clients. The following code demonstrates how to configure the VMPS and a client switch with port 4/1 in dynamic membership mode.

```
On the VMPS
Cat-5509-Server> (enable) set vmps tftpserver 10.1.1.1 vmps-database.txt
IP address of the TFTP server set to 10.1.1.1
VMPS configuration filename set to vmps-database.txt
Cat-5509-Server> (enable) set vmps state enable
Vlan Membership Policy Server enable is in progress.
On the Client switch:
Cat-5509-Client> (enable) set vmps server 10.1.1.10
10.1.1.10 added to VMPS table as primary domain server.
Cat-5509-Client> (enable) set port membership 4/1 dynamic
Port 4/1 vlan assignment set to dynamic.
Spantree port fast start option enabled for ports 4/1.
Cat-5509-Client> (enable)
```

Note that in this example, one switch serves as VMPS, and the other switch operates as a client. Should the VMPS switch itself also need to operate as a client, it would to declare itself as client to its own VMPS service by issuing the command "set vmps server 10.1.1.10".

Trunking

Trunking is at the core of VLAN technology. Simply put, it allows for a single link to carry frames belonging to multiple VLANs from switch to switch, or to any other device capable of doing trunking. Trunking is normally used between switches, but a new generation of network interface cards for high-end servers now harnesses the power of VLAN trunking, allowing these servers to have a logical presence on any number of VLANs without the need of individual NICs or additional cabling. Intel's EtherExpress Pro/100 and 3Com's Fast EtherLink Server NIC, for example, are two NICs that provide end-system level trunking support, allowing high-end servers to have a presence in multiple VLANs.

A VLAN trunk can be configured to carry any number of VLANs belonging to a management domain. This level of flexibility enables network administrators to use trunking as a mean of load sharing within their network topology. Imagine, for example, two 100BaseT connections linking two switches together in an environment containing 10 VLANs. Before the introduction of trunking, only two VLANs could have been shared between these switches, one carried by each connection. With trunking technology, each of these connections can carry all the packets of every VLAN between each switch. If we simply declare both connections to be VLAN trunks, the switch will see these connections as dual paths to the same VLANs. Connection A will carry frames for VLAN 1, and so will connection B. The switch will therefore run the Spanning Tree algorithm and put one of the connections in blocking state. This can result in connection A being the active link in every VLAN, while connection B is blocked in every VLAN. This represents a bad networking design leading to a waste of bandwidth. The advantage is that if connection A fails, Spanning-Tree will recompute and place connection B in forwarding state in every VLAN. There are two solutions to this problem. The first is a brute-force approach using trunking parameters only. Since we can select exactly which VLANs a trunk can carry, we can easily configure connection A to carry VLANs 1–5, and connection B to carry VLANs 6–10. In this case, we make better use of the bandwidth by distributing the load of VLANs between the two links. There is a flaw to this method, however: Should one of the connections fail, half of the VLANs would not be able to flow between the two switches, since the other connection is not configured to support them. The solution to this problem is the judicious manipulation of the Spanning Tree algorithm in conjunction with VLAN trunking. Remember that the Catalyst switches run a separate instance of the Spanning Tree algorithm for each VLAN. This means that we can manipulate the Spanning Tree attributes of our trunking ports for every VLAN they carry. We first need to make both connections carry all 10 VLANs. Then, by manipulating the priority of the trunk ports in each VLAN, we configure connection A to have a higher priority for VLANs 1–5, and connection B a higher priority for VLANs 6–10. This places VLANs 1–5 on connection A in forwarding state, and VLANs 6–10 of connection B in forwarding state. This produces the same type of load balancing provided by VLAN selection alone. The advantage is that should one of the two connections fail, Spanning Tree would detect this break and move the state of the other connection from blocking state to forwarding state in the remaining VLANs. This method provides for both load sharing and link redundancy.

Trunking can be accomplished in various ways, depending on the media used or the vendor compatibility required. The following describes the various trunking technologies available, and explains when and where they should be used.

ISL

Inter-Switch Link (ISL) is Cisco Systems' proprietary solution for VLAN trunking. Cisco has licensed its ISL technology to most high-end systems companies such as SUN or Compaq, so many ISL-capable network interface cards (NIC) are available on the market today. ISL, however, has not been licensed to other switching vendors, so interconnectivity between switches in a multivendor environment cannot be achieved by using ISL. An ISL frame is composed of a 26-byte ISL header, an encapsulated data frame of 1 to 24.5 kb of information, followed by a 4-byte Cyclic Redundancy Check (CRC). Figure 3-4 shows the ISL frame header itself. The definitions for each field are as follows:

- **DA** A 40-bit multicast destination address.
- **Type** A 4-bit field identifying the type of frame being carried. The most common values are 0000 for Ethernet, 0001 for Token Ring, and 0011 for ATM.

FIGURE 3-4 ISL frame header

DA	Type	User	SA	LEN	AAAA03	HSA	VLAN	BPDU	Index	Res

- **User** A 4-bit field extending the definition of each frame type. For Ethernet, the values are as follows:

Field	Definition
0000	Normal Priority frame
0001	Priority 1 frame
0010	Priority 2 frame
0011	Highest Priority frame

- **SA** A 48-bit source MAC address of the transmitting ISL device.
- **LEN** A 16-bit field reflecting the length of the ISL frame minus DA, SA, LEN, and CRC.
- **AAAA03** 802.2 LLC header.
- **HAS** Manufacturer's vendor code (first 3 bytes of the source MAC address).
- **VLAN** 15-bit VLAN ID. Only the first 10 bits of this field are used, yielding a possibility of 1024 VLANs.
- **BPDU** 1-bit field indicating if the frame is a Spanning Tree bridge protocol data unit or a Cisco Discovery Protocol frame.
- **Index** A 16-bit field identifying the port identifier of the sending port. This field is not used in the operation of ISL, but instead used for troubleshooting purposes.
- **Res** A 16-bit field reserved for additional information.

> *exam* 🕅 *atch*
>
> *The VLAN ID tag is a 15-bit field, providing 32,768 possible VLAN numbers. The switches themselves, however, do not all support 1024 simultaneous VLANs. For example, the Catalyst 5000 series switch can only support 250 simultaneous VLANs per switch. Furthermore, the valid range of VLAN numbers used by ISL is 1–1000.*

This added frame can be readily seen when examining the trace of a network analyzer. Figure 3-5 shows the decoded output of a captured ISL frame. Notice how each field appears in the frame header.

The advantage of using ISL in a Cisco Catalyst environment is that ISL trunking is an extension of the frame format used on the backplane of the Catalyst switch itself. Some fields are dropped while traveling on the switching fabric, reducing the

VLAN Overview

FIGURE 3-5

ISL frame decoded using a network analyzer

ISL header to 12 bytes only, but essentially the ISL frame format remains. This direct compatibility between the switching fabric and the trunking protocol leads to accurate transmission and very low latency by the switch in processing each frame. The default trunk port configuration of set-based switches is "auto." This means that upon detecting a new connection, the switch will not itself attempt to trunk, but will accept an ISL trunking request from the remote device and start the trunking process. The command "set trunk" on set-based switches and the interface command "switchport mode trunk" on IOS-based switches are used to specifically place switch ports in ISL trunking mode. In turn, the "clear trunk" command and "no switchport mode trunk" interface command are used to remove a port from performing trunking functions. The following code shows the various parameters of these commands and the successful creation of trunk ports on a set-based Catalyst 5509 switch and an IOS-based Catalyst 2924XL switch. These commands are applicable to every switch in the set-based and IOS-based families listed in Table 3-1.

On a set-based switch:

```
Cat-5509> (enable) set trunk
Usage: set trunk <mod/port> [on|off|desirable|auto|nonegotiate] [vlans]
[trunk_type]
       (vlans = 1..1005
        An example of vlans is 2-10,1005)
       (trunk_type = isl,dot1q,dot10,lane,negotiate)
Cat-5509> (enable)
Cat-5509> (enable) set trunk 4/1 on 1-1005 isl
Adding vlans 1-1005 to allowed list.
Port(s)  4/1 allowed vlans modified to 1-1005.
Port(s)  4/1 trunk mode set to on.
Port(s)  4/1 trunk type set to isl.
Cat-5509> (enable)
Cat-5509> (enable) show trunk
* - indicates vtp domain mismatch
Port      Mode          Encapsulation  Status        Native vlan
--------  ------------  -------------  ------------  -----------
 4/1      on            isl            trunking      1

Port      Vlans allowed on trunk
--------  ---------------------------------------------------------------
 4/1      1-1005

Port      Vlans allowed and active in management domain
--------  ---------------------------------------------------------------
 4/1      1

Port      Vlans in spanning tree forwarding state and not pruned
--------  ---------------------------------------------------------------
 4/1      1
Cat-5509> (enable)
On an IOS-based switch:
sw-2924XL#conf t
Enter configuration commands, one per line.  End with CNTL/Z.
sw-2924XL(config)#int fastethernet 0/14
sw-2924XL(config-if)#switchport mode ?
```

```
  access  Set trunking mode to ACCESS unconditionally
  trunk   Set trunking mode to TRUNK unconditionally
sw-2924XL(config-if)#switchport mode trunk
sw-2924XL(config-if)#switchport trunk ?
  allowed  Set allowed VLAN characteristics when interface is in trunking mode

sw-2924XL(config-if)#switchport trunk allowed ?
  vlan  Set allowed VLANs when interface is in trunking mode

sw-2924XL(config-if)#switchport trunk allowed vlan ?
  WORD    VLAN IDs of the allowed VLANs when this port is in trunking mode
  add     add VLANs to the current list
  all     all VLANs
  except  all VLANs except the following
  remove  remove VLANs from the current list

sw-2924XL(config-if)#switchport trunk allowed vlan all
sw-2924XL(config-if)#end
sw-2924XL#
```

You will notice that one of the key parameters in configuring VLAN trunks is the list of VLANs to be carried. This is the parameter used in the load-balancing example at the beginning of this section.

FROM THE CLASSROOM

Controlling VLAN Presence on a Trunk

Setting up trunks to operate with specific VLANs is a common task in the classroom. One would assume that by issuing the command "set trunk 4/1 on 1-10 isl", only VLANs 1 through 10 would be carried by this newly defined trunk. Whenever this command is processed, however, the switch gives the following message: "Port(s) 4/1 allowed vlans modified to 1-1005." This is because the default setting for trunk ports is to carry all VLANs on the switch. By specifying VLANs 1–10, the command simply adds those VLANs to the already existing list of possible VLANs for that trunk. The original 1–1005 VLAN list remains intact. In order for a port to carry only VLANs 1 through 10, the command "clear trunk 4/1 1-1005" must first be issued to clear the default VLAN list for that trunk. Following this, the command "set trunk 4/1 on 1-10 isl" will successfully create an ISL trunk carrying only VLANs 1 through 10.

— *Benoit Durand, CCIE #5754*

802.1Q

802.1Q is the Institute of Electrical and Electronics Engineers' answer to Cisco's proprietary ISL encapsulation. Structured similarly to ISL, 802.1q provides vendors with a standard VLAN trunking protocol to be used in a multivendor environment. It is important to note that not all Cisco Catalyst switch platforms support 802.1Q trunking. Smaller trunking-capable workgroup switches such as the 2900XL-EN series only support ISL as trunking protocol. Others, such as the 2948G Gigabit switch, only support 802.1q. Table 3-2 shows the trunking capabilities of the various Cisco Catalyst platforms.

Make sure you remember the trunking capabilities of each switch model. It is very likely that you will be asked to identify which models are capable of ISL trunking, and which are capable of 802.1q.

The specifications for 802.1q are copyrighted and available at the IEEE Web site for a nominal fee. The use of 802.1q becomes a necessity when trunking VLANs to a non-Cisco switch. Many vendors employ proprietary trunking solutions within their own product lines, but most now support 802.1q to provide multivendor support. Within a Cisco switching environment, 802.1q induces an additional level of latency from the conversion of 802.1q trunking frames. Cisco Catalyst switches use an ISL-based frame format on their backplane. Carrying 802.1q trunks between many Cisco Catalyst switches will introduce multiple conversions along the way and lead to reduced switching speeds throughout the management domain.

TABLE 3-2 Trunking Capabilities of the Catalyst Family

Switch Platform	ISL	802.1q
8500 series	X	X
6000 series	X	X
5000 series	X	X
4912G Gigabit switch		X
4000 series	X	X
3500 series	X	X
2948G Gigabit switch		X
2926 series	X	
2900XL series	X	X (with IOS version 12)

VLAN Overview

on the job

When trunking between Cisco Catalyst switches, use ISL encapsulation whenever possible. Identify the trunking points where the Catalyst switches will need to connect to a non-Cisco switch, and limit 802.1q to these links only. This will limit the latency of the frame switching within your management domain.

The following code shows the successful creation of an 802.1q trunk on a set-based Catalyst 5509 switch.

```
Cat-5509> (enable) set trunk
Usage: set trunk <mod/port> [on|off|desirable|auto|nonegotiate] [vlans]
[trunk_type]
        (vlans = 1..1005
         An example of vlans is 2-10,1005)
        (trunk_type = isl,dot1q,dot10,lane,negotiate)
Cat-5509> (enable) set trunk 4/1 on 1-1005 dot1q
Adding vlans 1-1005 to allowed list.
Please use the 'clear trunk' command to remove vlans from allowed list.
Port(s)  4/1 allowed vlans modified to 1-1005.
Port(s)  4/1 trunk mode set to on.
Port(s)  4/1 trunk type set to dot1q.
Cat-5509> (enable) show trunk
* - indicates vtp domain mismatch
Port      Mode         Encapsulation  Status        Native vlan
--------  -----------  -------------  ------------  -----------
 4/1      on           dot1q          trunking      1

Port      Vlans allowed on trunk
--------  ---------------------------------------------------------------
 4/1      1-1005

Port      Vlans allowed and active in management domain
--------  ---------------------------------------------------------------
 4/1      1

Port      Vlans in spanning tree forwarding state and not pruned
--------  ---------------------------------------------------------------
 4/1      1
Cat-5509> (enable)
```

For an IOS-based switch, trunk encapsulation is assumed to be ISL unless otherwise specified. The interface command "switchport trunk encapsulation <encaps_type>" is used to specify 802.1q encapsulation. The following code shows the successful configuration of an 802.1q trunk port on an IOS-based switch.

```
Cat-2900#conf t
Enter configuration commands, one per line.  End with CNTL/Z.
Cat-2900(config)#interface fastEthernet 0/8
Cat-2900(config-if)#switchport mode trunk
Cat-2900(config-if)#switchport trunk ?
  allowed        Set allowed VLANs when interface is in trunking mode
  encapsulation  Set trunking encaps when interface is in trunking mode
  native         Set trunking native characteristics when interface is in
                 trunking mode
  pruning        Set pruning VLAN characteristics when interface is in
                 trunking mode

Cat-2900(config-if)#switchport trunk encapsulation ?
   dot1q  Interface uses only 801.1q trunking encapsulation when trunking
   isl    Interface uses only ISL trunking encapsulation when trunking

Cat-2900(config-if)#switchport trunk encapsulation dot1q
Cat-2900(config-if)#end
Cat-2900#
```

The valid range of VLAN numbers in 802.1q is 0–4096. This can cause a conflict when using ISL trunking in the same network, since ISL VLANs range from 1–1000 only. ISL is incapable of transporting VLANs having an ID greater than 1000. A special VLAN mapping can be configured to handle this situation. The command "set vlan mapping dot1q <dot1q_vlan> isl <isl_vlan>" is used on set-based switches to manually convert 802.1q VLANs greater than 1000 to an ISL VLAN. The command "show vlan mapping" is used to verify the 802.1q to ISL configuration. The following shows the mapping of 802.1q to ISL VLANs on a Catalyst 5500 switch.

```
Cat-5500> (enable) set vlan mapping dot1q 2000 isl 200
Vlan mapping successful
Cat-5500> (enable) set vlan mapping dot1q 3000 isl 300
Vlan mapping successful
Cat-5500> (enable) show vlan mapping
802.1q vlan     ISL vlan        Effective
----------------------------------------
2000            200             true
3000            300             true
Cat-5500> (enable)
```

IEEE 802.10

FDDI uses a completely different encapsulation method to carry VLANs across its rings. 802.10 encapsulation is used to link FDDI VLANs to existing VLANs within the switching domain. Unlike ISL and 802.1q where the switch can simply convert frame types, 802.10 VLANs must be translated into an existing Ethernet or Token Ring VLAN. This can be an issue if your management domain approaches the VLAN limit of switch. For example, if 150 VLANs were active on a Catalyst 5000 switch, adding an FDDI trunk to link two switches would not be possible. The one-for-one requirement of FDDI translation would bring the total VLAN count to 300, which is beyond the 250 VLAN capabilities of the Catalyst 5000 switch. The header of an 802.10 frame format is shown in Figure 3-6.

In order to address concerns with security and authentication in shared Metropolitan Area Networks (MANs), 802.10 was developed with mechanisms that include optional encryption and authentication. The protected header, data field, and ICV have the option of being encrypted, therefore providing end-to-end security as the 802.10 frame travels shared public networks. The Integrity Check Value (ICV) field uses a security algorithm to ensure the authenticity of the 802.10 frame at its destination.

exam
👁atch

802.10 frames do not use a VLAN ID tag like ISL or 802.1q do. Instead, the SAID field, carried in the clear header, is used to identify the VLAN while the frame is traveling on the FDDI ring.

Since the translation definition of FDDI VLANs to Ethernet or Token Ring VLANs is done through the VLAN number and not the SAID value, you can effectively ignore the SAID value and let the Catalyst switch assign the default value. A completely separate set of VLANs must be created to run on the FDDI ring. Existing Ethernet and Token Ring VLANs cannot be carried directly onto FDDI. Instead, they are translated into 802.10 frames by mapping them against a partner FDDI VLAN. While designing your network and your VLAN numbering scheme, it is a good idea to keep in mind the purpose of FDDI VLANs, and to number your VLANs in a manner that will make network configuration and troubleshooting an easier task. Take, for example, the network depicted in Figure 3-7. Ethernet VLANs 1 and 2 need to be trunked between two Catalyst 5500 switches through an FDDI ring. In this example, we chose to create FDDI VLANs 110 and 120 to handle

FIGURE 3-6 IEEE 802.10 frame header

| Mac Header | Clear Header | Protected Header | Data | ICV |

FIGURE 3-7 Ethernet to FDDI VLAN mapping

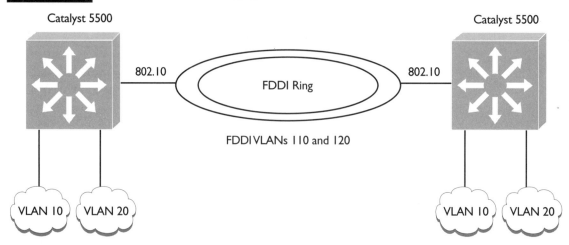

Ethernet VLANs 10 and 20, respectively. This simple numbering scheme makes it easier to understand the network topology and troubleshoot possible problems.

The first task in mapping Ethernet VLANs across FDDI is to create the partner FDDI VLANs that will be carried by the 802.10 trunk. As for Ethernet VLANs, the "set vlan" command is used for that purpose. The following code shows the successful creation of FDDI VLAN 110.

```
Cat-5509> (enable) set vlan 110 type fddi said 100110

Vlan 110 configuration successful
Cat-5509> (enable) show vlan 110
VLAN Name                             Status    IfIndex Mod/Ports, Vlans
---- -------------------------------- --------- ------- --------------------
110  VLAN0110                         active    64

VLAN Type  SAID       MTU   Parent RingNo BrdgNo Stp  BrdgMode Trans1 Trans2
---- ----- ---------- ----- ------ ------ ------ ---- -------- ------ ------
110  fddi  100110     1500  -      -      -      -    -        0      0

VLAN DynCreated  RSPAN
---- ---------- --------
110  static     disabled

VLAN AREHops STEHops Backup CRF 1q VLAN
---- ------- ------- ---------- -------
Cat-5509> (enable)
```

The next task following the creation of the partner FDDI VLANs is to map the Ethernet or Token Ring VLANs against their partner FDDI VLANs. Again, the "set vlan" command is used for this purpose. In this case, however, the "translation" keyword is used to map the translation between Ethernet and FDDI. The syntax of the command is as follows: set vlan <ethernet_vlan> translation <fddi_vlan>. The following code example shows the translation of Ethernet VLANs 10 and 20 to their partner FDDI VLANs 110 and 120. Notice how the output of the command "show vlan" now reflects the VLAN translation function.

```
Cat-5509> (enable) set vlan 10 translation 110
Vlan 200 configuration successful
Cat-5509> (enable) set vlan 20 translation 120
Vlan 200 configuration successful
Cat-5509> (enable) show vlan
VLAN Name                             Status    IfIndex Mod/Ports, Vlans
---- -------------------------------- --------- ------- --------------------
1    default                          active    5       1/1-2
                                                        3/1-24
                                                        4/1-24
10   VLAN0010                         active    59
20   VLAN0020                         active    60
110  VLAN0110                         active    61
120  VLAN0120                         active    62
1002 fddi-default                     active    6
1003 trcrf-default                    active    9
1004 fddinet-default                  active    7
1005 trbrf-default                    active    8       1003

VLAN Type  SAID       MTU   Parent RingNo BrdgNo Stp  BrdgMode Trans1 Trans2
---- ----- ---------- ----- ------ ------ ------ ---- -------- ------ ------
1    enet  100001     1500  -      -      -      -    -        0      0
10   enet  100010     1500  -      -      -      -    -        110    0
20   enet  100020     1500  -      -      -      -    -        120    0
110  fddi  100110     1500  -      -      -      -    -        10     0
120  enet  100120     1500  -      -      -      -    -        20     0
1002 fddi  101002     1500  -      -      -      -    -        0      0
1003 trcrf 101003     4472  1005   0xccc  -      -    srb      0      0
1004 fdnet 101004     1500  -      -      -      ieee -        0      0
1005 trbrf 101005     4472  -      -      0xf    ibm  -        0      0
```

The last task is to configure the 802.10 trunk across the FDDI ring. The Catalyst switch obviously requires that an FDDI module be installed in order for this configuration to operate properly. Let us assume that ports 2/1 and 2/2 of a Catalyst

5509 are FDDI ports. To configure 802.10 trunking on these ports, the command "set trunk" is used. Although the switch will only trunk FDDI-type VLANs over an 802.10 trunk, it is a good idea to specify the VLANs to be supported when configuring the trunk. The following code shows the successful creation of an 802.10 trunk on port 2/1 to support VLANs 110 and 120 created in our previous example.

```
Cat-5509> (enable) clear trunk 2/1 1-1005
Removing Vlan(s) 1-1005 from allowed list.
Port  2/1 allowed vlans modified to .
Cat-5509> (enable) set trunk 2/1 on 110,120 dot10
Adding vlans 110,120 to allowed list.
Port(s)  2/1 allowed vlans modified to 110,120.
Port(s)  2/1 trunk mode set to on.
Port(s)  2/1 trunk type set to dot10.
Cat-5509> (enable)
```

In our example, once these steps are mirrored on the second Catalyst 5500, the flow of frames between two endstations connected to Ethernet VLAN 10 on each switch would be as follows:

1. The sending Catalyst switch translates VLAN 10 Ethernet frames into VLAN 110 FDDI frames.

2. VLAN 110 FDDI frames are encapsulated using the 802.10 trunking protocol and placed on the FDDI ring through port 2/1.

3. The receiving Catalyst switch retrieves the FDDI VLAN 110 frames and translates them back into VLAN 10 Ethernet frames for normal transmission across its switching fabric.

LANE

LAN Emulation (LANE) is the technology used to propagate VLANs over an Asynchronous Transfer Mode (ATM) network. It hides the ATM network by making it appear like an extension of the local area network. This allows network administrators to extend the reach of VLANs to wide area network (WAN) links. Using LANE, VLANs can now span multiple remote locations, allowing companies to continue to support workgroup connectivity, even though the physical location of these workgroups may have expanded beyond the scope of their original LAN. The use of LANE across a WAN has to be done cautiously. Like regular Ethernet and Token Ring VLANs, LANE must carry all the broadcast traffic to every LANE destination across the WAN that belongs to that VLAN. This consumes costly

WAN bandwidth and can actually bring the network to a halt in broadcast-intensive environments. The operation of ATM is beyond the scope of this text. However, in order to properly understand LANE and its operation, it is important to be aware of some key elements of ATM.

ATM Key Elements   ATM operates using two different types of connections: Permanent Virtual Circuits (PVCs) and Switched Virtual Circuits (SVCs). ATM PVCs operate very similarly to a Frame Relay data-link channel. They can operate in a point-to-point or point-to-multipoint topology. Like the Data Link Channel Identifier (DLCI) of a Frame Relay connection, ATM uses two parameters to identify a connection: a Virtual Path Identifier (VPI) and a Virtual Channel Identifier (VCI). This pair of numbers identifies a single permanent connection across an ATM network. Like DLCIs, the VPI/VCI pair is locally significant to an ATM device. This means that it does not represent the final address of the destination, but merely identifies the first leg between the ATM device and the ATM switch it is connected to. Preconfigured switching routes in the ATM network are then used to switch the inbound cells to their destination, based on their VPI/VCI pair. ATM switches do not know the final destination of the cells; they simply know which neighboring ATM switch to send the cells to.

Contrary to PVCs, switched virtual circuits are created on demand and are torn down when no longer in use. LANE makes extensive use of SVCs in its operation. Unlike PVCs, where the path of all cells follows a preset route across the ATM network, the path used by cells on SVCs can be reconfigured on-the-fly by the ATM switches. This is made possible by the fact that SVCs use the address of the destination ATM device to make a switching decision. Network Service Access Point (NSAP) addresses are 20-byte sequences used to identify ATM devices. In a public network, where the selection of addresses needs to respect a specific convention, the address itself is a complex construct of parameters, some selected by the users, some preselected by the geographical location, and others assigned by regulating bodies such as the IEEE. In private networks, any NSAP address can be used. There are methods to simplify the NSAP address plan of an ATM network, while providing a certain degree of summarization that will enable the ATM to operate more smoothly. Like routers, ATM switches exchange information about the ATM devices they support. This is done through the advertisement of NSAP addresses through the Private Network-Node Interface (PNNI) protocol used by the ATM switches. It is through this protocol that the switch can determine the best path possible for a connection's destination NSAP address. ATM switches like Cisco's LightStream 1010 come preprogrammed with an ATM prefix. The switch uses this unique identifier by default as the first 13 bytes for its NSAP addresses. The remaining 7-byte block, called the End System Identifier (ESI), is used to identify the individual ATM devices connected directly to that switch. It is therefore possible for the ATM switch to advertise only its prefix to other ATM switches. Any destination NSAP matching that prefix would be sent to that switch. In turn, that switch would examine the ESI portion of the destination NSAP to decide which directly connected ATM device to send the cells to.

In order for SVCs to be properly created on an ATM network, a few important well-known PVCs need to be defined to support SVC operations. The Interim Local Management Interface (ILMI) PVC is a well-known PVC that operates on VPI 0/VCI 16. ILMI is used between ATM peers to provide management and health information. The second mandatory channel is the signaling PVC. The International Telecommunications Union's specifications for signaling protocols are called "series Q." The signaling protocol for ATM is called Q. Signaling ATM Adaptation Layer, or Q.SAAL. The well-known VPI and VCI for Q.SAAL are 0 and 5, respectively. These mandatory PVCs must be defined on ATM devices before any SVC can be created. The following shows the output of the command "show atm vc" on a Cisco 7206 router using an ATM port adapter module. Notice the ilmi and qsaal PVCs.

```
ATM-7204#show atm vc
            VCD /                                   Peak Avg/Min Burst
Interface   Name      VPI   VCI   Type   Encaps    Kbps   Kbps  Cells  Sts
1/0         1         0     5     PVC    SAAL      149760    0      0  UP
1/0         2         0     16    PVC    ILMI      149760    0      0  UP
1/0.2       10        5     69    PVC    SNAP      149760    0      0  UP
ATM-7204#
```

LANE Concepts Similarly to FDDI, LANE does not map Ethernet and Token Ring VLANs directly across the ATM network. It maps the VLANs to an Emulated LAN (ELAN), which is the representation of a VLAN in LANE. ELANs represent individual broadcast domains across ATM and offer data-link layer connectivity to LANE clients throughout the network. They are the extension of Ethernet and Token Ring VLANs across ATM. There are multiple components required in order to establish an operational LANE network. The following is a short description of each component.

- **LAN Emulation Client (LEC)** A LEC is any end system that operates as a client to LANE. It can be a Catalyst switch equipped with a LANE module, a router, or even a computer with an ATM interface directly attached to the ATM network. A LEC normally serves as a connectivity point for stations connected to a regular Ethernet or Token Ring segment. The LEC has four distinct responsibilities in LANE:
    - Forwarding data
    - NSAP to MAC address resolution
    - LANE control
    - Layer 2 emulation of Ethernet services to upper-layer protocols
- **LAN Emulation Configuration Server (LECS)** Like with VLANs in a management domain, there is normally more than one ELAN in a LANE topology. When a LEC tries to join an ELAN, it first goes to the LECS to get information about the ELAN it wishes to join. The LECS contains configuration information about every ELAN in the LANE topology. When it receives a request for a specific ELAN, the LECS returns the NSAP address of the LAN Emulation Server (LES) for that ELAN. There is a single active LECS in a LANE topology, with a single active LES per ELAN. When the LEC first connects to the ATM network, it receives the NSAP address of the LECS from the ATM switch. This enables the LEC to quickly find the LECS and gather the required information to connect to the desired ELAN. LECS functions can be configured on a Cisco router, Catalyst LANE module, or on a Cisco LS-1010 ATM switch.
- **LAN Emulation Server (LES)** The function of the LES is to manage the LECs (multiple LAN Emulation Clients, not to be confused with the LECS) that make up the ELAN. It manages and handles NSAP-to-MAC address resolution through a process called LAN Emulation Address Resolution Protocol (LE-ARP). When a LEC first joins an ELAN, it registers its MAC address and NSAP address with the LES. When that station needs to forward data to another LEC in the ELAN, it sends an LE-ARP request to the LES with the MAC address of the destination LEC. The LES performs a lookup in its ELAN database and responds to the LEC with the appropriate NSAP address. LES functions can be performed by a Cisco router, Catalyst LANE module, or LS-1010 ATM switch.

on the Job

Although the LS-1010 can serve as LES, Cisco recommends that LES services be configured on a different device. The high-speed switching nature of the LS-1010 does not make it the ideal platform for this task. Sporadic requests from LECs interrupt the cell switching process of the LS-1010. It is best to configure the LES service on a router or a Catalyst LANE module.

Broadcast Unknown Server (BUS) We have already mentioned how an ELAN, like a VLAN, represents a broadcast domain. When a LEC needs to forward data to another LEC, it queries the LES about the NSAP address of the destination LEC. However, when a LEC needs to broadcast a frame to the entire ELAN, a new component of LANE is introduced. When the LES receives an LE-ARP request with a destination MAC address of ffff.ffff.ffff, it returns to the LEC the NSAP address of the BUS. As with the LES, there is only one active BUS per ELAN. In Cisco's implementation of LANE, the BUS service is performed on the same platform as the LES service, thus referring to this device as the LES/BUS pair. The BUS handles all broadcasts and multicasts for its ELAN. When it receives a broadcast to be sent, it forwards the frame to every LEC in the ELAN over a point-to-multipoint SVC. In phase 1 of LANE implementation, there are no provisions for a backup LES or BUS within each ELAN. The LANE Network-Node Interface (LNNI) protocol, part of the next release of LANE, will enable two or more devices to operate as an active and backup LES/BUS pair for an ELAN.

LANE Operation We have covered the basic components of LANE and their functions. The following describes the sequence of events when a LEC joins an ELAN and starts forwarding information to another LEC.

1. The first step happens when the LEC connects to the ATM network. The LEC already knows which ELAN it wishes to use, but it does not know where to go to connect to that ELAN. For the purpose of this example, we will assume that the LEC wishes to become a member of ELAN 1. Upon connecting to the ATM switch, the LEC receives the NSAP address of the LECS for the LANE network.

2. The LEC then contacts the LECS to get the NSAP address for the LES of ELAN 1. This communication is accomplished through a Configuration Direct SVC, which is a temporary bidirectional conduit between the LEC and the LECS.

3. Once the LEC has obtained the NSAP address of its LES, it contacts the LES using a Control Direct SVC, which is a temporary bidirectional conduit between the LEC and the LES. Once the LES has identified the LEC as a valid member of its ELAN, it enters that LEC's MAC and NSAP address in its ELAN table for future resolution. It also creates a Control Distribute SVC, which is a point-to-multipoint conduit between the LES and all the LECs in its ELAN. This SVC is used by the LES to send control information to the LECs.

4. At this point, the LEC is a member of ELAN 1. It must now resolve the NSAP address of the BUS for ELAN 1. It does this by sending an LE-ARP request to the LES to resolve the NSAP address for the broadcast MAC address (ffff.ffff.ffff). The LES recognizes this special MAC address and returns the NSAP address of the BUS to the LEC.

5. The LEC then establishes a Multicast Send SVC to the BUS, which is a bidirectional conduit between the LEC and the BUS. The BUS recognizes the new member of the ELAN and creates a Multicast Forward SVC, which is a point-to-multipoint SVC used by the BUS to forward broadcast frames to every LEC in the ELAN.

6. The LEC is now aware of every LANE component in its ELAN. In order for the LEC to transmit information to another LEC, it must first resolve an NSAP address for the destination MAC address of the frame it needs to forward. The LEC sends an LE-ARP request to the LES, and simultaneously starts forwarding the frames to the BUS.

7. While the LE-ARP process takes place, the BUS forwards the frames to every LEC in the ELAN. This is done in order to avoid timeouts and dropped packets at upper layers while LE-ARP is taking place. Once the LES receives the NSAP address of the target LEC, it stops sending frames to the BUS. The LEC then initiates a Data Direct SVC to the target LEC and waits until the BUS is done transmitting the frames it received from the sending LEC. Once the BUS is done transmitting the frames, the LEC takes over by sending the frames directly to the target LEC through the Data Direct SVC.

LANE Configuration There are no special configurations required on the Catalyst switch engine itself. Instead, all of the LANE configurations occur on the Catalyst LANE module residing in the Catalyst switch chassis. The LANE module can be accessed via console connection or through the command "session

<module_number>". The LANE module is IOS-based and is configured similarly to an ATM router. There are no set-based commands pertaining to LANE. The IOS-based LANE module itself interfaces directly with the backplane of the Catalyst switch to provide LANE services. ATM routers and switches are also strictly IOS-based. The commands listed in this section are therefore all IOS-based commands. The first step is to configure the basic ATM parameters so that the LANE module can create SVCs on the ATM network. It is best to let the ATM switch assign an NSAP prefix to the LANE module and only specify the ESI address if required. If not specified, the NSAP address of the LANE module will be based on default values. These ATM configurations are done at the major interface level of the ATM interface. All other LANE configurations, except for LECS services, must be configured on an ATM subinterface. The following code displays the configuration of the major ATM interface of a LANE module.

```
lane# conf t
Enter configuration commands, one per line.  End with CNTL/Z.
lane(config)# interface ATM1/0
lane(config)# no ip address
lane(config)# atm pvc 1 0 5 qsaal
lane(config)# atm pvc 2 0 16 ilmi
lane(config)# end
4w6d: %SYS-5-CONFIG_I: Configured from console by vty0 (172.21.1.5)
lane#
```

At this point, the LANE module is ready to start providing LANE services. The command "show lane default-atm-addresses" gives the default NSAP addresses for LANE services. Notice the "**" in the selector byte position of the NSAP addresses shown in the following code. This byte represents the ATM subinterface number on which a service is configured. The LECS selector byte is automatically set to 00 since the service cannot run on a subinterface.

```
lane#show lane default-atm-addresses
interface ATM0:
LANE Client:         47.00918100000000009254C301.00D0C01DB81C.**
LANE Server:         47.00918100000000009254C301.00D0C01DB81D.**
LANE Bus:            47.00918100000000009254C301.00D0C01DB81E.**
LANE Config Server:  47.00918100000000009254C301.00D0C01DB81F.00
note: ** is the subinterface number byte in hex
lane#
```

For the purpose of this example, we will configure all of the LANE services on the same LANE module. In order for the LECS service to operate properly, the LANE database must first be configured with the NSAP address of the LES for each ELAN.

This involves placing the LANE module in a LANE database configuration mode, which differs from the regular IOS configuration. To place the module in LANE database configuration, the command "lane database" is issued from privileged exec mode. The following shows the successful creation of a LANE database on a Catalyst 5500 LANE module serving as LECS. Notice the selector bytes of the NSAP addresses are set to 01 for elan1 and 02 for elan2. This means that when the LES services on the LANE module are configured, they must remain consistent and be configured on subinterfaces atm 0.1 and atm 0.2.

```
lane(config)#lane database My_Database
lane(lane-config-da)#name elan1 server-atm-address
47.00918100000000009254C301.00D0C01DB81D.01
lane(lane-config-da)#name elan2 server-atm-address
47.00918100000000009254C301.00D0C01DB81D.02
lane(lane-config-da)#end
lane#
```

Another element that needs to be configured is the NSAP address of the LECS. Remember that when a LEC first connects to the ATM network, it is provided with the NSAP address of the LECS of the entire LANE topology. This address is provided to the LEC by the ATM switch. On an IOS-based LS-1010 switch, this is done through the global configuration command "atm lecs-address-default". The following shows the successful configuration of the LECS NSAP address. Notice how the NSAP address configured on the LS-1010 is an exact match of the LECS NSAP address reported by the command "show lane default-atm-addresses" on the LANE module previously shown.

```
ls1010#
ls1010#conf t
Enter configuration commands, one per line.  End with CNTL/Z.
ls1010(config)#atm lecs-address-default 47.00918100000000009254C301.00D0C01DB81F.00
ls1010(config)#end
ls1010#
```

NSAP addresses are unusually awkward to work with. Their format and length make them easy targets for typos and omissions. When configuring NSAP addresses on ATM devices, it is highly recommended to use the cut-and-paste features of your operating system. This will remove any possibility of a mistyped digit, and remove one variable from the equation when troubleshooting LANE.

We are now ready to start the LANE services. For this purpose, the interface command "lane" is used. The following code starts LECS, LES/BUS, and LEC services on the LANE module. Three important factors to note: First, the LECS service is the only service not running on a subinterface. Secondly, the subinterfaces used for the LES services match the selector bytes declared in the LANE database of the LECS. Finally, notice how the LEC configuration maps a VLAN carried by the Catalyst switch to the ELAN carried by the ATM network. This is the location where the two technologies meet. In this example, VLAN 1 maps onto elan1 and VLAN 2 onto elan2.

```
lane#conf t
Enter configuration commands, one per line.  End with CNTL/Z.
lane(config)#int atm 1/0
lane(config-if)#description LECS services
lane(config-if)#lane config My_Database
lane(config-if)#lane config auto-config-atm-address
lane(config-if)#exit
lane(config)#interface atm 1/0.1 multipoint
lane(config-if)#description LES service for ELAN 1
lane(config-subif)#lane server-bus ethernet elan1
lane(config-subif)#exit
lane(config)#interface atm 1/0.2 multipoint
lane(config-if)#description LES service for ELAN 2
lane(config-subif)#lane server-bus ethernet elan2
lane(config-subif)#exit
lane(config)#interface atm 1/0.3 multipoint
lane(config-if)#description LEC on ELAN 1
lane(config-subif)#lane client ethernet 1 elan1
lane(config-subif)#ip address 192.168.15.1 255.255.255.0
lane(config-subif)#end
lane#
lane#ping 192.168.15.10

Type escape sequence to abort.
Sending 5, 100-byte ICMP Echos to 192.168.15.10, timeout is 2 seconds:
!!!!!
Success rate is 80 percent (5/5), round-trip min/avg/max = 1/1/4 ms
lane#
```

At this point, we have an operational LANE configuration. The command "show lane" can be used to view the operational status of each LANE component. The following shows the output of the "show lane" command for each major LANE component of the preceding example.

```
lane#show lane config
LE Config Server ATM1/0 config table: My_Database
Admin: up   State: operational
LECS Mastership State: active master
list of global LECS addresses (22 seconds to update):
47.00918100000000009254C301.00D0C01DB81F.00  <-------- me
ATM Address of this LECS: 47.00918100000000009254C301.00D0C01DB81F.00 (auto)
 vcd  rxCnt  txCnt  callingParty
   5    0      0    47.00918100000000009254C301.00D0C01DB81D.03 LEC
cumulative total number of unrecognized packets received so far: 0
cumulative total number of config requests received so far: 1
cumulative total number of config failures so far: 0

lane#
lane#show lane server
LE Server ATM1/0.1, Elan name: elan1, Admin: up, State: operational
Type: ethernet, Max Frame Size: 1516
locally set elan-id: not set
elan-id obtained from LECS: not set
ATM address: 47.00918100000000009254C301.00D0C01DB81D.01
LECS used: 47.00918100000000009254C301.00D0C01DB81F.00 connected, vcd 6
control distribute: vcd 57, 1 members, 1 packets
proxy/ (ST: Init, Conn, Waiting, Adding, Joined, Operational, Reject, Term)
lecid ST vcd   pkts Hardware Addr   ATM Address
   1  O  54     1  00d0.c01d.b81c  47.00918100000000009254C301.00D0C01DB81C.03
lane#
lane#show lane client
LE Client ATM1/0.3  ELAN name: elan1  Admin: up   State: operational
Client ID: 1                 LEC up for 2 minutes  37 seconds
Join Attempt: 13
Last Fail Reason: Control Direct VC being released
HW Address: 00d0.c01d.b81c   Type: ethernet         Max Frame Size: 1516
ATM Address: 47.00918100000000009254C301.00D0C01DB81C.03

VCD  rxFrames  txFrames  Type        ATM Address
  0      0         0     configure   47.00918100000000009254C301.00D0C01DB81F.00
  0      0         0     direct      47.00918100000000009254C301.00D0C01DB81D.01
  0      0         0     distribute  47.00918100000000009254C301.00D0C01DB81D.01
  0      0         0     send        47.00918100000000009254C301.00D0C01DB81D.01
  0      0         0     forward     47.00918100000000009254C301.00D0C01DB81D.01
lane#
```

Notice how in the selector byte of the NSAP address of each LANE service matches the number of the subinterface under which they run. For example, the command "show lane server", which displays information about the LES service, shows the NSAP address of the LES service running on interface ATM 1/0.**1** as 47.00918100000000009254C301.00D0C01DB81D.**01**.

Now that you know more about LANE, here are some possible scenarios that you might encounter, and the appropriate answers.

DTP

We have seen how to configure trunking between two switches. The process involved forcing a certain port into trunking mode. There is a dynamic counterpart to these configurations called Dynamic Trunking Protocol (DTP). DTP enables switches to automatically negotiate whether a port should perform trunking functions, the trunking protocol to be used, and the VLANs to be carried. DTP is a more recent version of Cisco's Dynamic ISL (DISL) protocol in that it can also accommodate 802.1q trunking, while DISL only worked with Cisco's proprietary ISL protocol. Dynamic trunking is accomplished through an exchange of information upon linkup. By default, all trunk ports are in a state called "auto." The trunking configuration of a switch port can be in one of five different states:

- **Auto** In this state, the switch port listens for DTP messages from its peer switch. If the peer switch announces that it wishes that link to operate as a

SCENARIO & SOLUTION

You configured LANE on your company's 128 kbps fractional T1 link, and now everyone is complaining about network performance.	ELANs are the extension of VLANs. They must carry the broadcast traffic from the VLANs across the 128 kbps link. Considering the slow speed of the connection, the broadcasts are the likely cause of the lack of performance.
I have two Cisco routers and an LS-1010 switch, and need to configure LANE on them. Which platform should I use to provide LES/BUS services?	Use one of the Cisco routers. The LS-1010, although capable of performing LES/BUS functions, is not the optimal choice.
I do not have a Cisco router or a LANE module to connect to the LANE network. Can my server still access ELANs on the ATM network?	Yes. High-end server vendors now offer ATM NICs that have the appropriate software to connect that server directly to the LANE network. This provides the server with high-speed ATM access of multiple ELANs.

VLAN Overview

trunk, then the switch creates a trunk with its peer. A switch in "auto" mode does not advertise any desire to become a trunk. Therefore, two switches in "auto" mode will not create a trunk between them.

- **On** A port in "on" state will initiate DTP messages to peer switches. The port will be in trunking mode independently of the state of the peer switch, but keeps advertising its state through DTP so that peers in "auto" mode can create an appropriate trunk on their end.

- **Off** A port in "off" state will not permit trunking to be established with a peer switch, no matter what the DTP state of the peer is.

- **Desirable** A switch port in "desirable" state initiates DTP messages to its peers, trying to establish a trunk on these ports.

- **Nonegotiate** A port in "nonegotiate" state does not originate listen to any DTP advertisement. Instead, the switch port is placed in trunking mode and will operate as such independently of the peer switch.

As you can see, many possible combinations of states are possible. Table 3-3 shows DTP combinations and their trunking outcome.

The recommended trunking state for trunk ports is to configure switch ports closest to the core of the network in "desirable" state, and the outer switch ports in "auto" state. It is also possible to set both sides to state "on," but in this case, care must be taken to ensure that all trunking parameters are consistent on both sides of the link.

TABLE 3-3 DTP Trunking State Combination

Switch/peer	Auto	Desirable	On	Off	Nonegotiate
Auto	No trunk	Trunk	Trunk	No Trunk	No Trunk
Desirable	Trunk	Trunk	Trunk	No Trunk	No Trunk
On	Trunk	Trunk	Trunk	No Trunk	Trunk
Off	No Trunk	No Trunk	No Trunk	No Trunk	No Trunk
Nonegotiate	No Trunk	No Trunk	Trunk	No Trunk	Trunk

exam Watch — *The default trunking state for switch ports is "auto." If presented with a command "set trunk 4/1 isl", remember that the port will be in "auto" state unless otherwise specified. Two switch ports in "auto" state will not create a trunk port between them.*

DTP also includes detailed messages to report on the state of trunking ports. The following is a list of the most common DTP messages encountered:

- **DTP-1-ILGLCFG: Illegal config (on, isl—on,dot1q) on Port 1/1**   This occurs when two switches are configured in state "on," but one switch is configured to operate using ISL, while the peer switch is configured to use 802.1q.
- **DTP-3-TRUNKPORTFAIL: Port 1/1 failed to become trunk**   This occurs when a switch port in state "on" or "desirable" fails to create a trunk with its peer.
- **DTP-5-TRUNKPORTON: Port 1/1 has become trunk**   This is an informational message indicating that a switch port has successfully started trunking functions with its peer switch.
- **DTP-5-NONTRUNKPORTON: Port 1/1 has become non-trunk**   This is an informational message indicating that a switch port is in nontrunking mode.

Now that you have seen the various trunking methods, here is a quick reference for possible scenarios where trunking is required, and the appropriate answers.

VTP

So far, we have seen how VLANs can be deployed throughout a management domain, how trunks can be configured to carry multiple VLANs across a single connection, and how LANE can propagate VLAN communication across a wide area network. When two switches communicate with each other, we have assumed that they both had identical knowledge of the VLANs they share. Indeed, if a VLAN is statically created on two different switches and given identical parameters, these two switches can be trunked together and exchange frames for that VLAN. In a large management domain, it would be a cumbersome to create all these VLANs on each

SCENARIO & SOLUTION

I need to extend VLANs across a wide area network.	Use ATM LANE. This is the only VLAN-capable WAN technology.
I am connecting to a Nortel switch and wish to do trunking.	Use 802.1q. ISL is a Cisco proprietary protocol that does not operate with non-Cisco hardware.
My Ethernet VLANs are not communicating through my FDDI link.	Use 802.10 and map your Ethernet VLANs to your FDDI VLANs. FDDI does not natively carry ISL or 802.1q VLANs.
I want the best-performing trunking protocol in a Cisco-only environment.	Use ISL. The Catalyst switches use an ISL derivative on the backplane, making ISL trunks an extension of their switching fabric. Using other trunking protocols such as 802.1q induces latency due to conversion.

switch. VLAN Trunk Protocol (VTP) is used by switches to alleviate this burden. VTP is advertised on trunked ports to announce the following information:

- Management domain
- Configuration revision number
- Known VLANs and associated parameters

Switches running VTP will build a consistent database of every VLAN in the management domain by exchanging information between them. This allows for the management of the domain to be maintained from a single switch. If a VLAN is created or deleted on one of the switches in the management domain, this change is carried across to every switch in the domain, updating their VLAN database to reflect the changes. This is accomplished using the configuration revision number. When a VLAN change is made on a switch, that switch increments the configuration revision number for the domain and sends VTP updates to every other switch in the domain. When receiving this update, the remote switch compares the configuration revision to its own. Since the new update contains a higher revision number, the remote switch adopts the new VLAN configuration received through VTP.

The use of VTP can lead to one of the most monstrous problems in a switching environment. Imagine an established production network running 100 VLANs across a management domain containing over 50 Catalyst switches. The management domain uses VTP to keep the VLAN databases consistent and up to date on every switch. Assume that the configuration revision for the domain is version 5. A new switch now needs to be added to the domain. The network administrator, wanting to make sure that the new hardware works properly, sets up the switch on an isolated network for tests and burn-in period. Multiple VLANs are created and deleted to verify the proper operation of the switch. Each of these changes increases the configuration revision, resulting in a final revision number of 9. The network administrator, satisfied with the testing, deletes all the VLANs on the new switch in preparation for its inclusion into the production domain. This last operation increases the revision number to 10. We now have a switch with no programmed VLANs and a revision number higher than the one running on the production network. When the network administrator finally connects the new switch to the production network, a major catastrophe happens. All of a sudden, the network ceases to operate, and that network administrator's pager starts glowing bright red. What happened? The network succumbed to the pitfall of VTP. When connecting to the production network, the new switch started to exchange VTP information with the other switches in the management domain. Since the new switch had a higher revision number, all the other switches in the domain adopted the new VLAN database configuration propagated by the new switch. Since that switch had no VLANs configured, all the VLANs on the production network were deleted, and every port was placed into inactive state.

VTP advertisements are classified into two different categories:

- **Summary advertisements** These messages are sent on VLAN 1 every 300 seconds to keep the management domain up to date. The advertisement includes a list of the VLANs in the domain and the revision number of the current VTP configuration. VLAN trunks must therefore include VLAN 1 as part of the VLANs they carry in order for VTP to operate properly.

- **Subset advertisements** These messages contain parameter information about the VLANs themselves, such as VLAN ID, type, MTU, SAID, and VLAN name.

Before any VTP exchange can occur, a valid management domain must be created. This is done through VTP configurations. On a Catalyst switch, the basic VTP parameter required to create a valid management domain is the VTP domain name. Switches with different domain names will not exchange VTP information. It is therefore important to have a consistent domain name entry on every switch. Since there can be drastic effects to using VTP, an optional authentication mechanism is also included in the configuration of VTP. The command "set vtp" is used to configure a valid management domain on a set-based switch. The following shows the creation of a management domain called "switch-domain" on a set-based switch.

```
Cat-5509> (enable) set vtp ?
  domain                    Set VTP domain
  mode                      Set VTP mode
  passwd                    Set VTP password
  pruneeligible             Set VTP pruning
  pruning                   Set VTP pruning
  v2                        Set VTP version 2
Cat-5509> (enable) set vtp domain switch-domain
VTP domain switch-domain modified
Cat-5509> (enable)
```

Following the configuration of the management domain, you can examine the vtp parameters using the command "show vtp domain". Following is the output of that command. Notice the revision number is set to 0. The revision number is reset whenever the VTP domain name changes. When connecting a new switch to an existing domain, changing the VTP domain name to an arbitrary value and then back to the valid domain name is an excellent method of ensuring that the new switch will not overwrite the existing VLAN database. It will instead be provided with a VLAN database by the existing management domain.

```
Cat-5509> (enable) show vtp
Show vtp commands:
-----------------------------------------------------------------------
show vtp domain               Show VTP domain information
show vtp statistics           Show VTP statistic information
Cat-5509> (enable) show vtp domain
Domain Name                         Domain Index VTP Version Local Mode  Password
------------------------------      ------------ ----------- ----------- ----------
switch-domain                           1            2        server        -
```

```
Vlan-count Max-vlan-storage Config Revision Notifications
---------- ---------------- --------------- -------------
11         1023             0               enabled

Last Updater     V2 Mode  Pruning  PruneEligible on Vlans
--------------   -------- -------- ------------------------
69.144.0.252     disabled disabled 2-1000
Cat-5509> (enable)
```

On an IOS-based switch, the configuration of a management domain is accomplished in VLAN configuration mode. The following shows the successful creation of a management domain on an IOS-based switch.

```
Cat-2900#vlan database
Cat-2900(vlan)#vtp ?
  client       Set the device to client mode.
  domain       Set the name of the VTP administrative domain.
  password     Set the password for the VTP administrative domain.
  pruning      Set the administrative domain to permit pruning.
  server       Set the device to server mode.
  transparent  Set the device to transparent mode.
  v2-mode      Set the administrative domain to V2 mode.

Cat-2900(vlan)#vtp domain switch-domain
Changing VTP domain name from null to switch-domain
Cat-2900(vlan)#
```

Like on the set-based switch, the command "show vtp status" displays the pertinent VTP information. The same parameters are displayed, but in a different format.

```
Cat-2900# show vtp status
VTP Version                     : 2
Configuration Revision          : 0
Maximum VLANs supported locally : 68
Number of existing VLANs        : 11
VTP Operating Mode              : Server
VTP Domain Name                 : switch-domain
VTP Pruning Mode                : Disabled
VTP V2 Mode                     : Disabled
VTP Traps Generation            : Disabled
MD5 digest                      : 0x29 0x8E 0x5B 0xC5 0xD1 0x2D 0x82 0xFF
Configuration last modified by 69.144.0.252 at 3-18-01 23:30:55
Cat-2900#
```

There are three different modes of operation for VTP capable switches. This defines their role and interaction in the management domain. For example, not every switch should have the ability of creating or deleting VLANs. There rarely is any requirement for a workgroup switch, isolated somewhere in a user's office, to be able to delete VLANs. Network administrators usually limit these functions to core switches located in a protected environment. For this purpose, VTP includes mechanisms to restrict this functionality to select switches. This involves placing the switch in server, client, or transparent mode. Each mode is described next. To configure a set-based switch into these modes, the command "set vtp mode" is used. The following example shows the successful configuration of a Catalyst 5509 to operate as a VTP server.

```
Cat-5509> (enable) set vtp mode ?
  client                VTP client mode
  server                VTP server mode
  transparent           VTP transparent mode
Cat-5509> (enable) set vtp mode server
VTP domain switch-domain modified
Cat-5509> (enable)
```

On IOS-based switches, the VTP mode configuration is performed from the "vlan database" configuration mode. The following example shows the successful configuration of a Catalyst 2924XL-EN to operate as a VTP server.

```
Cat-2900# vlan database
Cat-2900(vlan)# vtp ?
  client        Set the device to client mode.
  domain        Set the name of the VTP administrative domain.
  password      Set the password for the VTP administrative domain.
  pruning       Set the administrative domain to permit pruning.
  server        Set the device to server mode.
  transparent   Set the device to transparent mode.
  v2-mode       Set the administrative domain to V2 mode.

Cat-2900(vlan)# vtp server
Setting device to VTP SERVER mode.
Cat-2900(vlan)# exit
APPLY completed.
Exiting....
Cat-2900#
```

Server

A switch in server mode has the capability of creating or deleting VLANs in the management domain. It is responsible for the transmission of VTP advertisements to other switches connected to them via trunks. This keeps the VTP domain up to date. Switches in server mode also store the VLAN database in their nonvolatile memory.

Client

A switch in client mode operates very similarly to a switch in server mode. It receives and transmits VTP advertisements to connected switches, but cannot modify the management domain. This means that VLANs cannot be created or deleted from a client switch. Also, a switch in client mode will not save the VLAN database to its nonvolatile memory; instead, the switch requests a VTP update upon boot-up. Simply setting a switch to operate in client mode after being in server mode does not solve the problem of adding a new switch to an existing management domain. For example, if the new switch was in server mode during its burn-in test period and had all of its VLANs deleted, and then was placed in client mode, the VTP revision number of that switch, if higher than the revision number of the production network, will still cause the production network to adopt the VLAN database of the new switch, even though that switch is in client mode.

Transparent Mode

Transparent mode allows the switch to operate independently of the management domains around it. That switch will be able to create or delete VLANs within its own platform, but will not originate or listen to any VTP advertisements. It will, however, relay received VTP advertisements to other switches it is connected to. This ensures the continued operation of the VTP domains around the switch in transparent mode. To the rest of the management domain, the transparent switch appears as a bridge that has no impact on VTP.

Pruning

Pruning is a method used by VTP to conserve trunk bandwidth by eliminating traffic belonging to unused VLANs. In a large management domain, information about every VLAN is propagated through VTP to each switch. In turn, VLAN trunks carry all the broadcast and multicast traffic of every VLAN to each switch. In

VLAN Overview

the case of unicasts, the MAC address tables of the switch ensure that the path of a frame is optimized and sent only to the necessary ports. Only switch ports that form the path from source to destination need to carry that frame. There is no waste of bandwidth in this situation. In the case of broadcasts and multicasts, however, the situation is much different. Since there is no specific destination, these frames must be flooded throughout the VLAN. Unfortunately, not every switch in the management domain has member ports that VLAN. In those cases, broadcast floods for VLANs that are not used on that switch constitute a waste of bandwidth on that trunk. Figure 3-8 shows an example where switch A does not need to receive frames for VLAN 2 since it has no ports that are members of that VLAN. In order to conserve that bandwidth, VTP uses pruning to "prune" those unused VLANs from the trunk. The switch is still aware of the existence of that VLAN, but it will no longer receive the broadcasts and multicasts associated with that VLAN. In order for that VLAN to be pruned, it must first be identified as "prune eligible" and have the

FIGURE 3-8

VTP pruning

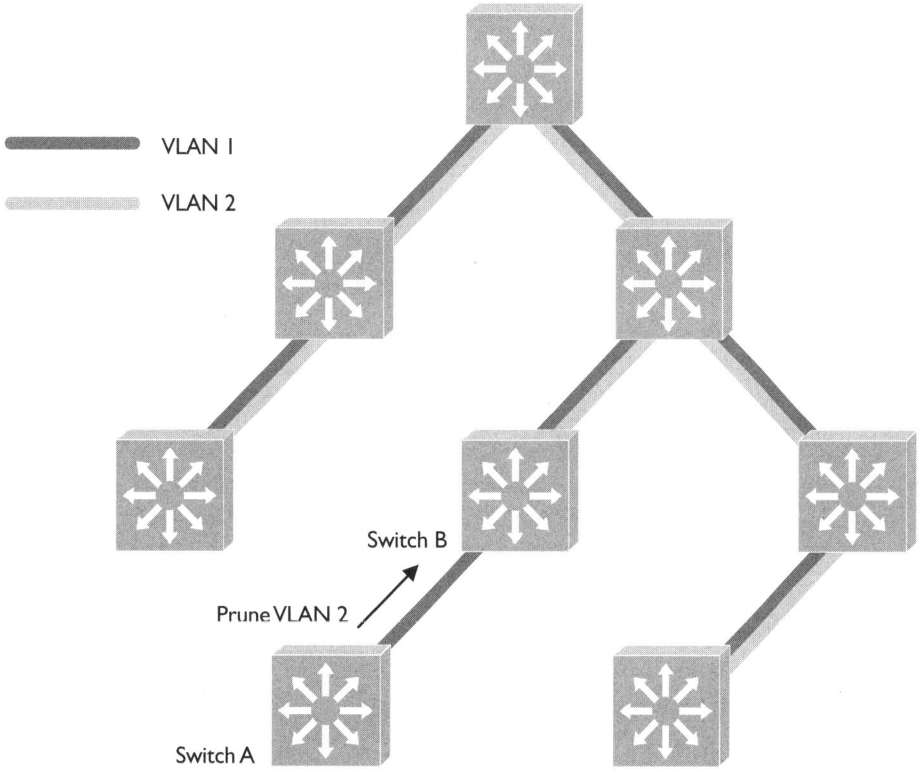

pruning option enabled on the switch. By default, the pruning process is disabled, and all VLANs except for VLAN 1 are marked as prune eligible. In Figure 3-8, switch A would send a prune message to switch B for VLAN 2, requesting that switch B stop sending broadcasts and multicasts for VLAN 2.

Using pruning means that the VLAN trunk must now keep track of the pruning state of each VLAN. There are two states possible for each VLAN:

- **Joined**   In this state, the trunk will carry broadcast and multicast frames for that VLAN.

- **Pruned**   Broadcast and multicast frames will not be carried propagated for that VLAN, except for Spanning Tree Protocol frames, Cisco Discovery Protocol frames, and VTP frames.

Once a VLAN is pruned from a switch, that switch is not prevented from using that VLAN later. In Figure 3-8, should a port on switch A later be allocated as a member of VLAN 2, the switch would send a join message to switch B, which would resume sending VLAN 2 broadcasts and multicasts on that trunk. Join messages are sent on VLAN 1.

The following example shows the configuration of VTP pruning on a set-based and an IOS-based switch.

```
Cat-5509> (enable) set vtp pruning ?
  disable                 Disable VTP pruning
  enable                  Enable VTP pruning
Cat-5509> (enable) set vtp pruning enable
This command will enable the pruning function in the entire management domain.
All devices in the management domain should be pruning-capable before enabling.
Do you want to continue (y/n) [n]? y
VTP domain switch-domain modified
Cat-5509> (enable)

Cat-5509> (enable) set vtp pruneeligible ?
  <vlan>                  VLAN number
Cat-5509> (enable) set vtp pruneeligible 2-1000
Vlans 2-1000 eligible for pruning on this device.
VTP domain switch-domain modified.
Cat-5509> (enable)
```

VLAN Overview

For IOS-based switches, the configuration of VTP pruning is accomplished from the "vlan database" configuration mode to enable pruning, and at the interface level to manipulate pruning eligibility.

```
Cat-2900# vlan database
Cat-2900(vlan)# vtp pruning
Pruning switched ON
Cat-2900(vlan)# exit
APPLY completed.
Exiting....
Cat-2900# conf t
Cat-2900(config)#int fa 0/8
Cat-2900(config-if)#switchport trunk pruning ?
  vlan  Set VLANs enabled for pruning when interface is in trunking mode

Cat-2900(config-if)#switchport trunk pruning vlan ?
  add     add VLANs to the current list
  except  all VLANs except the following
  none    no VLANs
  remove  remove VLANs from the current list

Cat-2900(config-if)#switchport trunk pruning vlan add 600
Cat-2900(config-if)#end
Cat-2900#
```

Here are a few scenarios involving VTP, and the appropriate answers.

SCENARIO & SOLUTION

I am concerned that the workgroup switches can be used to hack my VTP management domain.	Configure the workgroup switch to operate as a VTP client. VTP clients cannot modify the management domain.
All my VLANs are configured to be eligible for pruning, but none of them are actually being pruned. What's wrong?	The pruning process itself is disabled by default. Even though VLANs are identified as being prune eligible, the pruning process needs to be enabled before any pruning can occur.
I connected two switches together and made their ports members of VLAN 1, which is the VLAN on which VTP operates. The list of VLANs does not get propagated between the switches. Why?	VTP operates on trunk ports only. Setting the two ports as static members of VLAN 1 will not cause VTP to operate between the two switches.

Command Details

This chapter covered many commands to configure VLANs, VTP, and other VLAN functionality. This section describes in detail the use and syntax of each of these commands as they are applied in this chapter. It can be used as a reference tool when configuring VLANs in your network topology. It is divided into two sections: set-based commands and IOS-based commands.

Set-Based Commands

This section describes the commands used by set-based switches to properly configure VLANs and related components.

set vtp   The "set vtp" command is the first step in configuring VLANs. It is used to establish a proper management domain prior to creating any VLAN. Table 3-4 gives the details of how to use this command.

set vlan   Once a proper management VLAN has been established, VLANs can now be created on that domain. In order for the "set vlan" command to be successful, the switch must be operating in server mode. Table 3-5 gives the details of how to use this command.

Set Trunk   The set trunk is used to configure and establish a trunking connection between two switches. This can also be used to create trunks to

TABLE 3-4   The "set vtp" Command

set vtp domain domain_name	Creates a management domain named "domain_name."
set vtp mode server	Configures the switch as a VTP server.
set vtp mode client	Configures the switch as a VTP client.
set vtp pruning enable	Enables the pruning process on the switch.
set vtp pruning disable	Disables the pruning process on the switch.
set vtp pruneeligible 1-100	Declares a particular VLAN range as eligible for pruning. Requires the pruning process to be enabled globally.
set vtp password my_password	Sets an authentication password for the management domain.

VLAN Overview

TABLE 3-5 The "set vlan" Command

set vlan <vlan_number>	Creates an Ethernet VLAN using default values.
set vlan <vlan_number> <mod/port>	Adds a range of switch ports to the specified VLAN. The switch port format is Module #/Port #. A list of ports can be built with a comma "," as separator or a dash "-" to mark a range. For example: 5/6, 5/7, 5/10–12. This range would cover ports 6,7,10,11,12 of module number 5.
set vlan <isl_vlan> translation <d10_vlan>	Sets the mapping of an ISL VLAN to an FDDI 802.10 VLAN.
set vlan <vlan_number> name My_Name	Sets the name of a VLAN.
set vlan <vlan_number> said <said_num>	Sets the SAID value of a VLAN. This is used as VLAN ID in 802.10 frames.
set vlan <vlan_number> type <vlan_type>	Sets the type for that VLAN. Valid types are ethernet, fddi, fddinet, trcrf, and trbrf.

ISL-capable devices such as high-end servers requiring a presence in multiple segments. Table 3-6 gives the details of how to use this command.

set vmps The configuration of a virtual management policy server allows the management domain to configure dynamic VLAN membership for the switch ports they control. The following are the commands required to establish this service. One last command, "set port", is required to place the actual ports in dynamic membership mode. Table 3-7 gives the details of how to use this command.

TABLE 3-6 The "set trunk" Command

set trunk <mod/port> mode <mode>	Sets the mode of operation. Valid modes are on, off, desirable, auto, nonegotiate.
set trunk <mod/port> type <type>	Sets the type for this trunk. Valid types are isl, dot1q, dot10, lane, negotiate
set trunk <mod/port> vlan <vlan_range>	Sets the range of VLANs to be carried on the trunk. A VLAN range can be built with a comma "," as separator or a dash "-" to mark a range. For example: 6, 7, 10–12. This range would cover VLANs 6, 7, 10, 11, and 12.

TABLE 3-7 The "set vmps" Command

set vmps server <ip_address>	Declares the IP address of the VMPS server.
set vmps state <enable/disable>	Enables or disables the vmps client process on the switch.
set vmps tftpserver <ip_address> <dbase>	Starts the vmps server process on the switch, and instructs the vmps to download a configuration file named "dbase" from a tftp server at the specified IP address.

set port The "set port" command has an extensive range of options, controlling many aspects of switch port operations such as speed, duplex, and other parameters. The "membership" parameter is used to specify the type of VLAN membership for that port.

set port membership <mod/port> <type>	Sets the port membership type. Valid types are static and dynamic. For VMPS operation, dynamic port membership is used.

clear vtp The command "clear vtp" is used to clear VTP statistics and VLANs from the prune eligibility table.

clear vtp statistics	Clears VTP statistics.
clear vtp pruning <vlan_range>	Removes a VLAN range from pruning eligibility.

clear vlan The "clear vlan" command is used to remove a VLAN range from the entire management domain. It is also used to remove ISL-to-802.1q VLAN mappings from the switch configuration.

clear vlan <vlan_number>	Removes a VLAN or VLAN range from the entire management domain. A VLAN range can be built with a comma "," as separator or a dash "-" to mark a range. For example: 6, 7,10–12. This range would cover VLANs 6, 7, 10, 11, and 12.
clear vlan mapping dot1q <vlan_number>	Removes the ISL-to_802.1q VLAN mapping for 802.1q VLAN number "vlan_number."

clear vmps The "clear vmps" command is used to clear VMPS statistics and remove servers from the list of VMPS servers to be used by a client switch.

| clear vmps statistics | Resets all VMPS statistics. |
| clear vmps server <ip_address> | Removes a specified server from the list of VMPS servers to be used by a client switch. |

clear trunk The clear trunk is used to reset a trunk to default values, or remove VLANs from an existing trunk.

| clear trunk <mod/port> | Resets a trunk port to default values. This sets the operating mode to "auto" and the trunk type to "negotiate." |
| clear trunk <mod/port> <vlan_range> | Removes a VLAN range from an existing trunk. |

show vlan The "show vlan" command is used to display the characteristics of specific VLANs, 802.1q mappings, and trunking information. Table 3-8 gives the details of how to use this command.

show vtp The "show vtp" command displays information about the management domain and its operation. One of the most important parameters is the VTP revision number.

| show vtp domain | Displays information about the management domain. |
| show vtp statistics | Displays the number of VTP join messages transmitted and received. |

TABLE 3-8 The "show vlan" Command

show vlan	Displays information about every known VLAN in the management domain.
show vlan <vlan_number>	Displays information about a specific VLAN number.
show vlan mapping	Displays ISL-to-802.1q mapping information.
show vlan trunking	Displays VLAN trunking information.

show vmps The "show vmps" command is used to display the operating parameters of VMPS. This includes the VMPS server list, MAC addresses in use and their VLAN association, and VMPS statistics. Table 3-9 gives the details of how to use this command.

IOS-Based Commands

This section describes the commands used by IOS-based switches to properly configure VLANs and related components.

vlan database This command is issued from privileged exec mode to enter the VLAN configuration mode. This includes the configuration of all VLAN and VTP parameters.

| switch# vlan database | Enters VLAN configuration mode. |

vlan This command is issued from VLAN configuration mode. It controls the creation and deletion of VLANs along with associated VLAN parameters. The switch must be operating in VTP server mode in order for this command to be successful. Table 3-10 gives the details of how to use this command.

vtp The "vtp" command is issued from VLAN configuration mode. It controls all aspects of VTP for the switch and its interaction with the management domain. Table 3-11 gives the details of how to use this command.

switchport This command is issued from interface configuration mode. It is used to select the mode of operation of VLAN capable ports. A port can either be in trunking mode or have a specific VLAN selected for its operation. By default, a

TABLE 3-9 The "show vmps" Command

show vmps mac <mac_address>	Displays the dynamic VLAN mapping of a specific MAC address.
show vmps statistics	Displays statistics on the VMPS process. This includes the number of VMPS queries and errors.
show vmps vlan <vlan_name>	Displays the list of MAC addresses assigned to a specific VLAN.

VLAN Overview

TABLE 3-10 The "vlan" Configuration Command

Command	Description
sw(vlan)# vlan <vlan_num>	Creates a VLAN with default parameters.
sw(vlan)# no vlan <vlan_num>	Deletes a VLAN from the entire management domain.
sw(vlan)# vlan <vlan_num> said <said>	Sets the SAID value for a VLAN.
sw(vlan)# vlan <vlan_num> state <state>	Sets the operational mode of a VLAN. Valid states are "active" and "suspend."
sw(vlan)# vlan <vlan_num> name <name>	Sets the name for a particular VLAN.
sw(vlan)# vlan <vlan_num> media <type>	Sets the media type for a specific VLAN. Valid types are "ethernet," "tokenring," "fddi," "fd-net," and "tr-net."

switch port will be set as a member of VLAN 1. Table 3-12 gives the details of how to use this command.

TABLE 3-11 The "vtp" Configuration Command

Command	Description
sw(vlan)# vtp domain <domain_name>	Sets the VTP domain name to be used by the switch. This establishes a valid management domain for that switch.
sw(vlan)# vtp password <password>	Sets the authentication password for the VTP domain if one is required.
sw(vlan)# vtp client	Sets the switch to operate as a VTP client. In this mode, the switch cannot create or delete VLANs in the management domain. It also does not save the VLAN database to its nonvolatile memory.
sw(vlan)# vtp server	Sets the switch to operate as a VTP server. In this mode, the switch can create or delete VLANs in the management domain. The switch also saves a copy of the VLAN database to its nonvolatile memory.
sw(vlan)# vtp pruning	Enables the pruning process on that switch.
sw(vlan)# vtp transparent	Sets the switch to operate in transparent mode. In this mode, the switch will not process any VTP advertisement. It operates in a stand-alone fashion and is transparent to any surrounding management domain.
sw(vlan)# no vtp password	Removes the optional password feature for VTP authentication.
sw(vlan)# no vtp pruning	Disables the pruning feature of VTP for that switch.

TABLE 3-12 The "switchport" Interface Command

sw(config-if)# switchport mode trunk	Sets the mode of operation of a switch port to be a trunk.
sw(config-if)# switchport mode access	Sets the mode of operation of a switch port for static VLAN membership.
sw(config-if)# switchport trunk allows vlan <vlan-id>	Specifies the VLANs allowed to be carried by a trunk. The default value is "all."
sw(config-if)# switchport access vlan <vlan-id>	Sets the switch port to be a static member of a specific VLAN.
sw(config-if)# switchport access vlan dynamic	Sets the switch port to operate in dynamic VLAN membership using an external VMPS.

vmps This global configuration command is used to specify the IP address of the VMPS to be used when dynamic VLAN membership is configured on at least one switch port.

sw(config)# vmps server <ip_address>	Specifies a VMPS to be accessed when using dynamic VLAN membership.

show vlan The "show vlan" command is used to display the VLAN database and the parameters associated with each VLAN.

sw# show vlan	Shows the entire VLAN database, including all the parameters associated with each VLAN.
sw# show vlan <vlan_id>	Shows all the parameters for a specific VLAN.

show vtp This command display domain statistics and packet counters for the VTP domain. One of the most important parameters is the VTP revision number.

sw# show vtp counters	Shows the number of VTP join messages transmitted and received.
sw# show vtp statistics	Shows the statistics for the management domain, including domain name, revision number, operating mode, and authentication information.

show vmps This command displays the number of transmitted and received VQP packets. It is a useful command when troubleshooting VMPS operation.

sw# show mps statistics	Displays the number and types of VQP packets transmitted and received.

CERTIFICATION SUMMARY

You now know how VLAN technology permits network managers to extend the reach of networking segments throughout the LAN and WAN. Mechanisms such as trunking, VTP, and dynamic VLAN membership are used to simplify the operation and management of VLANs. You should now have the knowledge and tools required to set up a valid management domain and start creating VLANs to satisfy the networking demands of your users.

Knowledge of multiple underlying technologies is important for the successful implementation of VLANs. A basic knowledge of ATM, for example, is essential when setting up LANE. Be aware of the VLAN requirements when setting up 802.10 on FDDI. The additional VLAN requirement could have an impact on your management domain. When used properly, VLANs provide network environments with the flexibility required to meet the demands of evolving networks.

✓ TWO-MINUTE DRILL

Here are some of the key points in Chapter 3.

VLAN Overview

- Virtual Local Area Networks (VLANs) represent individual broadcast segments that can be extended throughout the LAN, MAN, and WAN topology.
- The five types of VLANs are Ethernet, Token Ring, FDDI, Token Ring-Net, and FDDI-Net.
- FDDI and Token Ring VLANs appear as a single ring throughout the management domain. In a source-route bridging environment, in order for each VLAN to appear as a separate ring connected via a source-route bridge, FDDI-net and Token Ring-Net VLAN types must be used.
- In order to create VLANs on a switch, a proper management domain must first be established through VLAN Trunking Protocol (VTP), and the switch must be operating as a VTP server.
- There are two ways to allocate a switch port to a VLAN: static membership, which requires manual configuration by a network administrator, and dynamic membership, which makes use of a VLAN Management Policy Server VMPS.
- The VMPS uses a MAC address-to-VLAN database to respond to VMPS Query Protocol (VQP) requests from client switches. This database is stored externally on a tftp server.
- In VMPS, there is a single "fallback" VLAN for any MAC address not found in the VMPS database. All unknown MACs are placed in that VLAN upon connecting to the switch.
- Trunking allows one connection to carry frames from multiple VLANs between switches. There are five operating trunk types possible: ISL, 802.1q, 802.10, LANE, and Negotiate. When using the "Negotiate" trunk type, the switch makes use of Dynamic Trunking Protocol (DTP) to negotiate the trunk parameters.

- There are five different trunk operating modes: on, off, auto, desirable, and nonegotiate. Be aware of the resulting combination of each mode.
- 802.10 FDDI trunks require a one-to-one mapping to an Ethernet or Token Ring VLAN. ISL frames cannot natively be carried onto FDDI. This doubles the VLAN count in a management domain and can be an impact on VLAN design.
- Local Area Network Emulation (LANE) is the technology used to extend VLANs onto an ATM network. LANE creates Emulated LANs (ELAN), which are mapped one-to-one to an Ethernet or Token Ring VLAN. Since ELANs also represent a broadcast domain, broadcast traffic over ATM can become a concern and use substantial WAN bandwidth.
- There are four main components for LANE: the LAN Emulation Client (LEC), the LAN Emulation Server (LES), the Broadcast Unknown Server (BUS), and the LAN Emulation Configuration Server (LECS). In Cisco's implementation of LANE, the LES and BUS service are performed on the same platform.
- LANE makes extensive use of ATM Switched Virtual Channels (SVCs). For SVCs to operate properly, Permanent Virtual Circuits (PVCs) must be configured to support two important ATM services: Q.Signaling ATM Adaptation Layer (Q.SAAL), which runs on Virtual Path Identifier (VPI) 0 and Virtual Channel Identifier (VCI) 5, and Interim Local Management Interface (ILMI), which runs on VPI 0 and VCI 16.
- VTP is a protocol used by switches in a management domain to exchange information about the VLANs present in the domain. The switches use a revision number to decide which VLAN database is the most up to date. Be aware of the pitfalls of VTP when it comes to installing new switches in a management domain. There are three modes of operation for a switch running VTP: server, client, and transparent.
- Since not all switches need to receive broadcast frames from every VLAN, they use a method call "pruning" to inform upstream switches to stop sending broadcast and multicast traffic for those VLANs, except for Spanning Tree Protocol (STP), Cisco Discovery Protocol (CDP), and VTP frames. They can later send join messages to reenable full connectivity.

SELF TEST

The following questions will help you measure your understanding of the material presented in this chapter. Read all the choices carefully, as there might be more than one correct answer. Choose all correct answers for each question.

VLAN Overview

1. Your company's development group has a team of power users who developed a set of broadcast-based applications. Other users in the development group complain of poor network performance. After monitoring the network usage in the development VLAN, you notice that the high level of broadcasts are the cause of the poor network response in that VLAN. What should you do?

    A. Combine the development VLAN with all other VLANs so that the broadcasts have a larger segment on which to propagate, thus reducing the broadcast density.

    B. Put the power users on their own switch, so that the MAC address table of that switch can forward the broadcasts only to the required ports.

    C. Segment the development VLAN into two VLANs, one of which will service only the power users, restricting broadcasts to that segment.

    D. Use VTP pruning on the development VLAN in order to stop receiving all the broadcasts.

2. A VLAN can be best compared to:

    A. A collision domain
    B. A broadcast domain
    C. A management domain
    D. A public domain

3. Which one of the following is NOT a valid VLAN type?

    A. Ethernet
    B. Ethernet-net
    C. Token Ring
    D. Token Ring-net
    E. FDDI
    F. FDDI-net

4. You are using dynamic VLAN allocation in your network and everything is working properly. A visiting employee from another location complains that he cannot connect properly to the rest of the network. He has set his IP address to match those of your subnet and gets a valid link light on his networking card, but he still cannot communicate with the rest of the network. What is the most probable reason for his connection to fail?

   A. His networking configuration is probably wrong or has an overlapping IP address with another machine on the same subnet.
   B. Since he is a visiting user, his MAC address is not properly entered in the MAC address table of the switch.
   C. The switch he is connecting to is in client mode, which prevents the addition of new MAC addresses to the VTP table. The switch must first be reconfigured for server mode.
   D. Since he is a visiting user, the MAC address of that endstation is not entered in the VMPS database. This results in this port being placed in the fallback VLAN, which is a different segment from the rest of the people in the building.

5. What is the range of VLANs handled by Cisco's ISL?

   A. 1–32768 VLANs
   B. 1–1000 VLANs
   C. 1–4096 VLANs
   D. 1–250 VLANs

6. You have five VLANs in your network, VLANs 1, 2, 3, 4, and 5. A broadcast-intensive VLAN, VLAN 5, causes problems on trunks because it consumes much of the available bandwidth. One of the trunks connects to a non-Cisco switch that does not understand pruning. You decide to manually remove this VLAN from the trunk by issuing the following command: "set trunk 4/1 1-4" to select only VLANs 1 through 4 for this trunk. This does not solve the problem. Why?

   A. 802.1q trunks carry all VLANs. Unlike ISL, individual VLANs cannot be disabled.
   B. Broadcast traffic is carried across all VLANs in order to reach every possible destination.
   C. Disabling VLANs require pruning support. This cannot be accomplished.
   D. The command "clear trunk 4/1 5" must be issued to remove VLAN 5 from the trunk.

7. Which of the following is NOT a trunk type?

   A. 802.5
   B. 802.1q

C. ISL

D. 802.10

8. When configuring a trunk port on a Cisco switch, when are you likely to use 802.1q?

   A. In an FDDI environment. FDDI requires a different encapsulation than Ethernet and Token Ring networks.

   B. Whenever possible. 802.1q is the latest encapsulation standard and it offers greater performance over ISL

   C. When connecting to a non-Cisco switch.

   D. When authentication and encryption are required on the trunk.

9. Which of the following statement is true about FDDI trunks?

   A. FDDI VLANs cannot use ISL. They must use 802.1q.

   B. The FDDI trunk identifies trunked frames by their VLAN ID.

   C. FDDI trunks are secure since they use mandatory encryption.

   D. FDDI VLANs carried by the trunk must be translated to an ISL VLAN.

10. What is the default SAID value for VLAN 100?

    A. 100

    B. 1100

    C. 10100

    D. 100100

11. You have configured LANE on your network. You think you have covered all the bases, yet your LEC cannot seem to connect to the network. Upon further inspection, it appears that the LEC does not know how to reach the LECS. What is the likely cause of the problem?

    A. The NSAP address of the LECS has not been configured on the ATM switch.

    B. ILMI and Q.SAAL, the two mandatory PVCs, have not been defined on the LEC.

    C. The LECS cannot establish a communication with the LES.

    D. The BUS does not process the LEC's request for the address of the LECS.

12. What primary function does LE-ARP process in LANE?

    A. Resolves a MAC address for a given IP address.

    B. Resolves an NSAP address for a given IP address.

C. Resolves an NSAP address for a given MAC address.

D. Resolves an IP address for a given domain name.

13. In a Cisco LANE environment, which service is likely to run the following NSAP address: 47.00918100000000009254C301.00D0C01DB81F.00?

    A. The LECS
    B. The LES
    C. The BUS
    D. The LEC

14. You wish to configure a new ISL trunk between two Catalyst 5000 switches. One switch is connected to the rest of the network and has a valid list of VLANs. The new switch is configured with the valid VTP domain information, but does not yet have any VLANs in its database. You plan for VTP to provide this information to the new switch once the switches are connected. Both switches have their sc0 interface up and active in VLAN 1. You issue the following command on both switches: "set trunk 4/1 isl 1-1005 auto." The switch reports that the commands have been successfully accepted. You attempt to ping the other switch, and your pings are successful. VTP, however, does not seem to be working since no VLANs appear in your VLAN database. You verify the VTP information and find it accurate. What is the likely cause of the problem?

    A. VTP requires a password for authentication. Without it, it would be vulnerable to malicious attacks through the VTP revision number. A password must be configured in order for VTP to operate properly.
    B. The trunk is operating since pings are going across. The problem must be with VTP parameters. Something must be wrong, check them again.
    C. The combination "auto-auto" for the modes of operation of the trunk configuration will not create a trunk between the switches. A different combination must be used.
    D. VTP does not have the proper connectivity to exchange information about the VLANs in the network.

15. In a VTP environment, where is the VLAN database stored?

    A. A VTP switch in client mode
    B. A VTP switch in server mode
    C. A VTP switch in transparent mode
    D. A tftp server

16. You are about to connect a new switch to an active VTP environment. The live network contains over 100 active VLANs, and you are worried that connecting the new switch may have a negative impact on the management domain. What is the best method of ensuring that the new switch will not overwrite the active VLAN database?

   A. Change the new switch from VTP server mode to VTP client mode. In client mode, the new switch cannot make any changes to the VTP domain.

   B. Delete all VLANs from the new switch prior to connecting it to the existing management domain. This will force the existing management domain to populate the new switch with the list of VLANs in their database.

   C. Configure a VTP password on the switches in the existing management domain, but do not configure it on the new switch. Without the VTP password, the new switch will not be allowed to make any modifications to the management domain.

   D. Change the VTP domain name to a new name and change it back to its proper value. Changing the domain name will reset the VTP revision number to 0, ensuring that the new switch will have a lower revision value than the existing management domain.

17. Which of the following is NOT a requirement for a management domain to operate properly?

   A. The management must contain at least one VTP server.
   B. Trunk ports must be configured to carry VTP information.
   C. VTP passwords must match across the management domain if authentication is used.
   D. The domain name must be consistent across all switches.

18. You have two switches connected together via a nontrunk connection. You have the following static allocation of ports on each switch:

   Switch A: VLAN 10   Ports 1 and 2
   Switch B: VLAN 20   Ports 1 and 2

   Ports 2 of switch A is connected to port 2 of switch B. Port 1 of switches A and B has an endstation connected to it. Will a broadcast from the endstation on switch A reach the endstation on switch B? Why?

   A. Yes it will. The switches don't care that the VLANs are different.
   B. No it will not. There is a VLAN mismatch between the switches, so no communication can happen.
   C. Yes it will. The switch will recognize the VLAN mismatch and perform translation between VLANs

D. No it won't. The broadcast will reach switch B, but since the frame is from VLAN 10, it will not forward it to port 1 since it is in VLAN 20.

19. Which of the following information is NOT carried on a pruned VLAN?
    A. STP frames
    B. VTP frames
    C. VQP frames
    D. CDP frames

20. By default, which VLANs are eligible for pruning?
    A. None. Pruning eligibility must be enabled before any pruning can occur.
    B. All VLANs are pruning eligible by default.
    C. All VLANs except VLAN 1 are eligible by default.
    D. All VLANs except FDDI VLANs are eligible by default.

LAB QUESTION

Congratulations! You have just been hired as a high-priced engineer to redesign and optimize the network infrastructure of Widgets Inc. Widgets Inc. produces specialized software, and as such, has greater network requirements than most companies. Widgets recently acquired a smaller company in another city and must now integrate this new facility into its existing network. For the time being, each site operates on a flat network. Each floor has a wiring closet connecting all the ports on that floor. These wiring closets are connected through a daisy-chaining hubs from floor to floor. A T1 connection has been installed between the sites, providing routed connectivity across the wide area network. The present networking topology is shown in Figure 3-9.

The network administrator of Widgets informs you that the company is willing to redo the wiring between the floors to a data center on the first floor of each building, should it be required. He also informs you that they will move the departments internally so that each department operates on the same floor of either building. This arrangement is also shown in Figure 3-9. The people at Widgets do not know how to accomplish their networking goals, but they provide you with the following requirements:

   A. The speed of the link between the two facilities must increase from T-11 to DS-3, which is 45 Mbps.
   B. Each department must operate within the same network independently of what building the employees are located in. Widgets plan to use four different IP subnets, one for each department.

158 Chapter 3: Virtual Local Area Networks (VLANs)

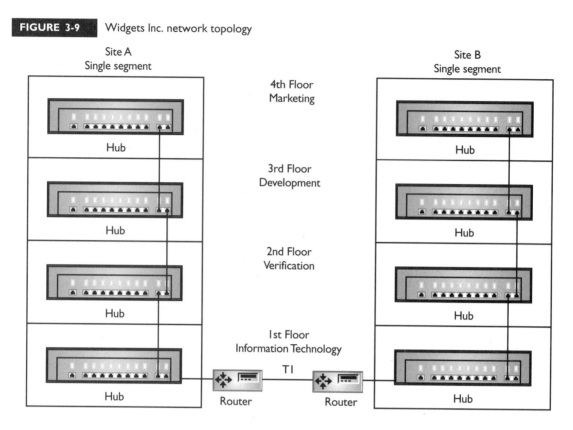

FIGURE 3-9 Widgets Inc. network topology

C. The IT folks are called to repair computers from the other departments. As such, they must be able to connect computers belonging to other departments on the IT floor but still operate in the appropriate networks.

D. The management of all these new segments must be simplified by automatic mechanisms. Widgets does not want to have to reconfigure every device every time a new segment is added to the network.

E. Broadcast traffic must be reduced wherever possible.

Write down in bullet points the list of changes you would propose.

SELF TEST ANSWERS

VLAN Overview

1. ☑ **C.** By segmenting the power users to their own VLAN, their broadcasts will not be propagated beyond their segment. Other VLANs, including the VLAN for the rest of the development team, will no longer be affected by the broadcasts of the power users group.
   ☒ **A** is incorrect because by joining VLANs together, you are creating a larger broadcast domain. This means that the broadcasts from the power users group will now affect everyone in the network. **B** is incorrect because a switch will forward broadcasts out of every interface except the one on which it received the broadcast. The MAC address table does not come into play for broadcasts or multicasts. **D** is incorrect because the rest of the development group will need to be connected to the network, so no pruning message would ever be sent upstream to stop receiving broadcasts from that segment.

2. ☑ **B.** VLANs extend the connectivity of Ethernet and Token Ring segments. These segments carry broadcasts to every endstation member of that segment.
   ☒ **A** is incorrect because switches limit the collision domain to individual ports through the use of their MAC address table. Collision domains are more prevalent in networking environments that use hubs instead of switches. **C** is incorrect because it refers to the domain encompassing all VTP speaking switches. A management domain maintains a list of VLANs and their parameters. It does not impact broadcasts themselves. **D** is incorrect because it has nothing to do with computer networking. It refers to publicly available software, text, and other materials.

3. ☑ **B.** There is no such VLAN type. The "–net" VLAN types are used by token-passing technologies like Token Ring and FDDI. Ethernet is not a token-passing technology, it is a Carrier-Sense Multiple Access/Collision Detection (CSMA/CD) technology.
   ☒ **A, C, D, E,** and **F** are incorrect because they are all examples of valid VLAN types.

4. ☑ **D.** When a VMPS receives a MAC address through VQP, it looks up that MAC address in its MAC address-to-VLAN table. If the MAC address is not found, that port is placed in a fallback VLAN. This placed the user in a different segment than the rest of the employees, preventing him from communicating with them via the network.
   ☒ **B** is incorrect since the switch automatically enters MAC addresses into the MAC address table when an endstation connects to one of its ports. A new MAC address would simply be entered as a new entry in that table. **C** is incorrect because the VTP server and client modes of operation refer to the ability of a switch to create and delete VLANs within a management

domain. It has nothing to do with MAC addresses. **A** is a possibility, but is not the likely cause of difficulties, considering that he is a visiting user and that dynamic VLAN allocation is used in the network.

5. ☑ **B.** 1–1000 VLANs is the range of VLANs handled by Cisco's ISL.
   ☒ **A** is incorrect because it refers to the range possible using the VLAN ID field, which is a 15-bit field resulting in 32,768 possible combinations. **C** is incorrect because it is the VLAN range of 802.1q. **D** is incorrect because it is the number of VLANs possible on a Catalyst 5000 platform.

6. ☑ **D.** The command "set trunk 4/1 1-4" adds VLANs 1–4 to the existing list of VLANs to be carried. Since the trunk already carries 1–5, adding 1–4 does not solve the problem. The command "clear trunk 4/1 5" will purge VLAN 5 from the list of supported VLANs.
   ☒ **A** is incorrect because 802.1q provides VLAN selection on the trunks. **B** is incorrect because VLANs are individual broadcast domains. Broadcasts from VLAN 5 would not propagate to other VLANs. **C** is incorrect because pruning works with operating VLANs. If a VLAN is not present on the trunk, it will not exchange VTP pruning information about that VLAN.

7. ☑ **A.** IEEE 802.5 specification describes the Token Ring standard.
   ☒ **B, C,** and **D** are incorrect because they represent valid trunk types.

8. ☑ **C.** ISL is a Cisco proprietary trunking protocol. When configuring a trunk to a non-Cisco switch over Ethernet or Token Ring, it is necessary to use 802.1q.
   ☒ **A** is incorrect because FDDI uses 802.10. **B** is also incorrect. In a Cisco environment, ISL outperforms 802.1q because the backplane of the Catalyst switch uses an ISL-based format. Less processing is required, leading to greater performance. There are no mechanisms to perform authentication or encryption in either ISL or 802.1q; therefore, **D** is incorrect.

9. ☑ **D.** FDDI VLANs need to be translated from an ISL VLAN to an FDDI VLAN.
   ☒ **A** is incorrect. FDDI VLANs use 802.10. **B** is also incorrect because 802.10 uses the SAID field to identify trunked frames. **C** is incorrect. Although 802.10 includes mechanisms for authentication and encryption, these features are optional and disabled by default.

10. ☑ **D.** The default SAID value is 100,000 + the VLAN ID; in this case, 100,000 + 100 = 100100.
    ☒ **A, B,** and **C** are incorrect because they do not follow the default VLAN calculation formula.

11. ☑ **A.** The ATM switch provides the LEC with the NSAP address of the LECS. This is the first part of LANE communication. If the LEC does not know the NSAP address of the LECS, LANE connectivity cannot progress any further. The NSAP address of the LECS must therefore be configured on the ATM switch.

☒ **B** is incorrect. Although these PVCs will be required to create channels for LANE to operate, the LEC won't attempt to create those conduits since it does not know where to go to reach the LECS. **C** is incorrect because the LECS does not communicate directly with the LES. **D** is incorrect because the LEC does not use the BUS to find the address of the LES.

12. ☑ **C.** LE-ARP resolves an NSAP address for a given MAC address. LANE works at layer 2, which is the MAC address layer.
    ☒ **A** is incorrect because it is the ARP process of TCP/IP. **B** is incorrect because there is no process that resolves an IP address to an NSAP address. **D** is incorrect because it describes the Domain Name Server (DNS) resolution process.

13. ☑ **A.** In ATM LANE, the value of the selector byte represents the ATM subinterface under which a service is running. The LECS is the only LANE service that can run on a major interface. As such, it is the only service that can have a selector byte of 00. All other services will have selector byte values greater than 0.
    ☒ **B, C,** and **D** are incorrect because the selector byte would have a nonzero value representing the subinterface under which the service is running.

14. ☑ **C.** The mode "auto" accepts trunking requests but does not send trunking requests. By having both switches in the "auto" mode means that neither switch will attempt to start a trunk between them.
    ☒ **A** is incorrect because authentication is not a mandatory parameter of VTP. It is, however, a good idea to specify a VTP password in insecure environments. **B** is also incorrect because VTP needs a valid trunk in order to operate properly. Since the trunk is not operational, VTP parameters are not yet exchanged between the two switches. **D** is incorrect because the pings show that VLAN 1 and the sc0 interfaces can communicate with each other. By default, switch ports are members of VLAN 1. Since the trunk did not successfully negotiate, the ports were still statically assigned to VLAN 1, which allowed the switches to communicate together.

15. ☑ **B.** A VTP server saves the VLAN database to its nonvolatile memory. VTP does not make the use of a tftp server. Upon power-up, VTP servers will feed VTP clients with the saved VLAN database.
    ☒ **A** and **C** are incorrect because these VTP modes do not save a copy of the VLAN database. **D** is incorrect because switches do not store their VLAN database on tftp servers.

16. ☑ **D.** The issue of overwriting a VLAN database occurs when a switch with an invalid VLAN database but higher revision number connects to a VTP management domain.
    ☒ **A** is incorrect. A VTP client will not be able to impact the management domain once synchronized with the other switches, but will still overwrite a VLAN database when connecting to the domain if its revision number is higher than the domain's. **B** is incorrect

because VTP does not treat a blank VLAN database any differently. It would simply overwrite every switch in the management domain with a blank VLAN database. C is also incorrect. Not giving the new switch a VTP password would prevent it from participating in the VTP process altogether.

17. ☑ **A.** A VTP server is not required in order for the management domain to operate properly. Switches in client mode will receive and transmit VTP packets across the domain, keeping the domain up to date with the latest revision of the database. This is not a recommended scenario, however, since only VTP servers can save the VLAN database to nonvolatile memory. Should a power failure occur, a management domain with switches in VTP client mode only would not have the means to recover, since the VLAN database would not have been saved anywhere. All other answers are required for VTP to operate properly.
☒ **B, C,** and **D** are incorrect because they are all essential for VTP to operate properly.

18. ☑ **A.** Since trunking is not enabled on that link, frames carried on that link do not carry a VLAN ID tag. As such, switch B does not know what VLAN the broadcast originated from on switch A. Since it received the broadcast on a port that is a static member of VLAN 20, it simply forwards the frame to all the ports that are members of VLAN 20; in this case, to the endstation on port 1.
☒ **B** is incorrect because trunking is not enabled, and the switches do not care about the VLAN number. In fact, the VLAN ID is not attached to the frames at all. **C** is also incorrect because the switches are not operating in trunking mode, and the VLAN ID is not sent with the frame. The receiving switch has no way to detect a misconfiguration and simply treats the frame as if it was for VLAN 20. **D** is also incorrect for the same reason. Switch B has no way to determine that the frame came from VLAN 10. It simply forwards it to all the members of VLAN 20.

19. ☑ **A.** VQP frames are used by the VMPS process to manage dynamic port allocation. They are of no use if the VLAN is pruned. STP frames are necessary to ensure a loop-free topology should the VLAN be reactivated. VTP frames are required to exchange information about the VLANs present in the domain, even if they are not being used. CDP provides information about the Cisco hardware connected to a specific link. It remains active to provide managerial information.
☒ **B, C,** and **D** are incorrect because they are all frames that are carried on a pruned VLAN.

20. ☑ **C.** All VLANs except for VLAN 1 are eligible. VLAN 1 is precluded from participating in the pruning process since VTP join messages are carried on VLAN 1. Every other VLAN will be eligible for pruning. Note that the pruning process itself must first be activated before any pruning activity can occur. This process is disabled by default.

☒ **A**, **B**, and **D** are incorrect because they do not represent the default settings for pruning eligibility.

LAB ANSWER

- The four new segments must be present in each building. VLAN technology is required.
- Convert the wide area link to ATM to accommodate the DS-3 link speed. This satisfies requirement A.
- Configure LANE over the ATM wide area link in order to extend the VLANs between the buildings.
- Replace the daisy-chained hubs with workgroup switches, and connect them individually to a core switch located in the data center on the IT floor. Each floor switch will handle an individual segment for that floor. This, in conjunction with LANE, will satisfy requirement B.
- Configure VMPS in each building and configure the first floors for dynamic port membership. Program the MAC addresses of all the endstations into the VMPS database. When connecting any endstation to the IT segment, VMPS will place this endstation into the appropriate VLAN, satisfying requirement C.
- Configure VTP across the entire network. Configure the core switches in each building as VTP servers and the workgroup switches as VTP clients. Any change to the VLAN database will be propagated to every switch in the entire network, satisfying requirement D.
- Enable VTP pruning across the management domain. The workgroup switches will send the appropriate prune messages to the core switches in order to stop receiving unnecessary broadcasts from unused VLANs. This satisfies requirement E.

The resulting network topology is shown in Figure 3-10.

FIGURE 3-10 Improved network topology

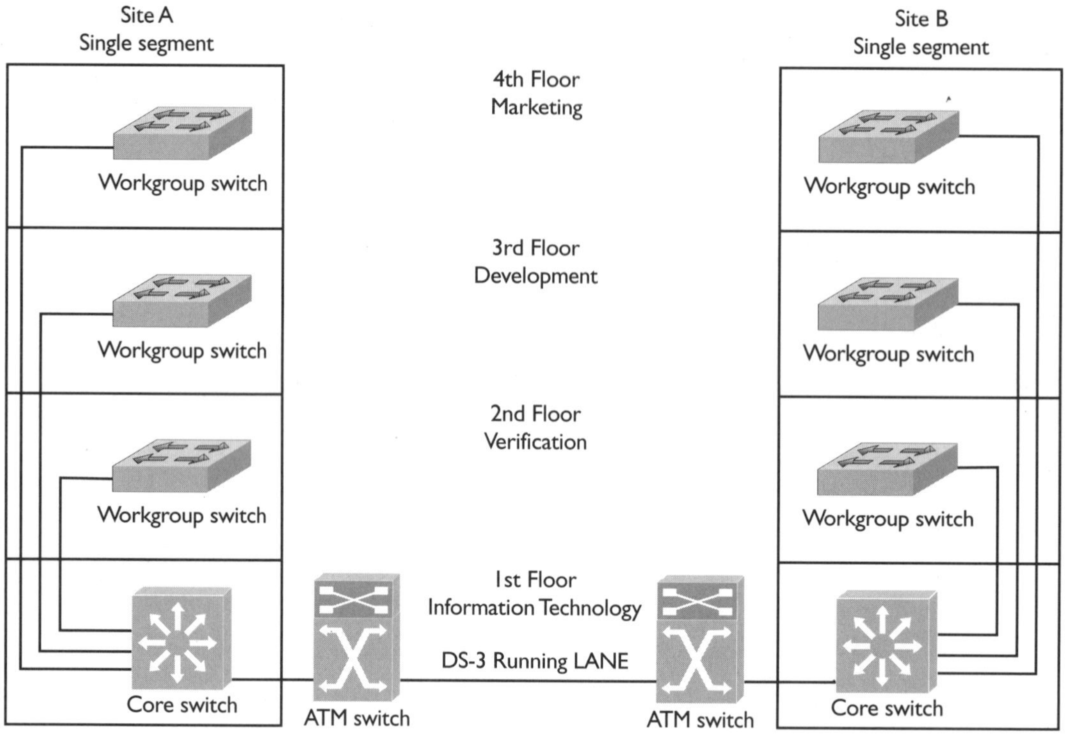
Site A
Single segment
Site B
Single segment
4th Floor
Marketing
Workgroup switch
Workgroup switch
3rd Floor
Development
Workgroup switch
Workgroup switch
2nd Floor
Verification
Workgroup switch
Workgroup switch
1st Floor
Information Technology
DS-3 Running LANE
Core switch
ATM switch
ATM switch
Core switch

4

Redundant Links and the Spanning Tree Protocol

CERTIFICATION OBJECTIVES

4.01	Redundant Links
4.02	Bridging Loops, Spanning Tree, BPDUs
4.03	Fast EtherChannel
4.04	PortFast, UplinkFast, BackboneFast
4.05	Commands
✓	Two-Minute Drill
Q&A	Self Test

If there is one thing we can all identify with, it's traffic. We spend so much of our time sitting in it trying to get to our various destinations throughout the day. If you are anything like me, you probably take the same roads to work day in and day out. However, I have a question for you. What happens when an accident or road construction closes that familiar road for the day? Does it cut us off completely from our destination? Not likely. Most of us have an alternate route in mind for when such a situation presents itself. Taking this alternate route allows us to arrive at our intended destination despite the fact that our normal path is unavailable. This is the basic concept of multiple path redundancy: Having more than one path to a given destination.

With computer networks, we must be able to plan ahead and provide that same kind of multiple path redundancy for data to arrive at its intended destination in the event that the normal path is unavailable. Providing this redundancy, though, does come with some complications. If you do not plan carefully, your good intentions can do much more harm to your network than good.

In this chapter, we are going to discuss the methods, protocols, utilities, and commands that allow us to provide redundancy on a bridged/switched network, and address the issues and complications that this kind of redundancy will present.

CERTIFICATION OBJECTIVE 4.01

Redundant Links

Most networks nowadays require some form of fault tolerance/redundancy. A failure in a critical component on the network can disrupt the availability of important resources on a network.

Some mission-critical applications need to be available to users 24 hours a day, 7 days a week. The only way to ensure this kind of availability is to eliminate any single points of failure on the network.

The primary goal of network link redundancy is to eliminate the possibility of any single component failure disrupting the end users' ability to reach their intended destination.

There are many components on a network link that represent a single point of failure; Power supplies, routers, switches, CSU DSUs, physical layer cabling, and network interface cards (NICs) are just a few examples. When building redundancy into your network designs, you need to consider all of the possible vulnerabilities.

For example, look at Figure 4-1.

This is a very basic example of the need for redundancy. There are many single points of failure here. Notice that users A, B, and C all connect to the Closet 1 switch. The drawing only represents three users, but in reality there are probably many more connected to the Closet 1 switch.

The Closet 1 switch connects to Core 1. Core 1 houses the Server resources, Server 1 and Server 2, that users A, B, and C need access to. If the link between Closet 1 and Core 1 fails for any reason, it will cut off access to the servers for all users connected to Closet 1.

Now look at Figure 4-2.

With this redundant design in place, the link failure between Closet 1 and Core 1 does not cut off all of the users connected to the Closet 1 switch from the server resources. An alternate path exists through Core 2. With a transparent fail over to the alternate path, chances are that the end users will not even notice the failure.

FIGURE 4-1

Single point of failure

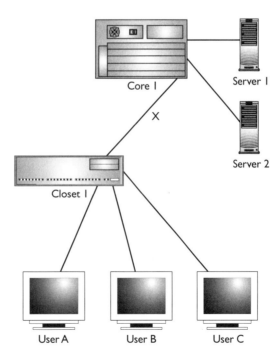

X=Link Failure

168 Chapter 4: Redundant Links and the Spanning Tree Protocol

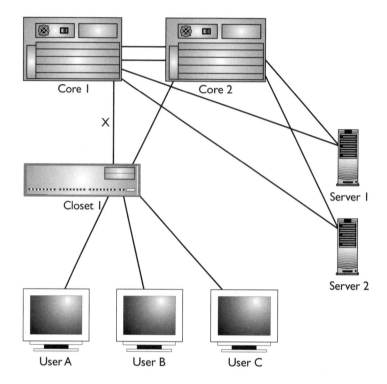

FIGURE 4-2

Redundant network design

X=Link Failure

This design will also protect against a failure of the Core 1 switch; a failure of the Core 2 switch; a physical cable problem between Closet 1 and the Core switches; a NIC failure in any one of the servers; or a link problem between the Core switches.

There is still a single point of failure, though. Can you see it? If the Closet 1 switch fails, all users connected to it will still be cut off from the server resources. We could further complicate this design to provide protection against that type of failure as well.

There are many ways to provide redundancy; it really just becomes a matter of how much redundancy is required. The best rule here is to find out what the uptime requirements are for a particular network and approach it realistically, trying to eliminate as many of the single points of failure as possible within the constraints (budget and political) you've been given.

exam
ⓦatch

The primary goal of network link redundancy is to eliminate the possibility of any single component failure disrupting the end users' ability to reach their intended destination.

Redundant Links **169**

Pros/Cons

As with anything else in the world, network redundancy has its good, and it has its bad. Let's look at the pros and cons of implementing network redundancy.

Pros

Some of the positive impacts of implementing network redundancy include:

- Eliminates single points of failure on the network
- Provides auto recovery (transparent to end users) when failures do occur
- Provides improved network availability and uptime for mission-critical applications

Cons

Some of the negative impacts of implementing network redundancy include:

- Can be cost prohibitive (requires more hardware)
- Requires good planning
- Adds a lot of complexity to the network topology
- Can make network troubleshooting more difficult
- Can create loops

EXERCISE 4-1

Redundant Links

In this exercise, we will apply what we have learned in this section and decide if the following statements are positive (P) or negative (N) impacts of implementing network redundancy.

Place a P or an N on the line next to the statement.
__Adds a lot of complexity to the network topology
__Can be cost prohibitive
__Eliminates single points of failure on a network
__Can create loops
__Provides improved uptime and availability of mission-critical applications

___Provides auto recovery when failures do occur
___Requires good planning
Answer:
N, N, P, N, P, P, N, respectively.
Fill in the blank contained in the following statement:
Some mission-critical applications need to be available to users 24 hours a day, 7 days a week. The only way to ensure this kind of availability is to eliminate any _____ on the network.
Answer: Single points of failure.

CERTIFICATION OBJECTIVE 4.02

Bridging Loops, Spanning Tree, BPDUs

In this section, we will take a look at the issues associated with providing multiple paths on a bridged or switched network. We will discuss what bridging loops are, what causes them, and how we can prevent them by using the Spanning Tree Protocol. After that, we will take a deep look at the inner workings of the Spanning Tree Protocol.

We will look at Bridge Protocol Data Units (BPDUs), which are special frames broadcast by all bridges/switches to provide the network topology information needed to build the Spanning Tree. We will also cover the various states that a bridge port can be placed in by the Spanning Tree. Finally, we will discuss the Per VLAN Spanning Tree, or PVST.

Keep in mind as you read this chapter that I will use the terms *bridge* and *switch* interchangeably throughout the text. Remember, a switch is essentially nothing more than a multiport bridge; therefore, any of the discussions in this chapter can be applied to a bridged or switched network.

Bridging Loops

Earlier we talked about providing our host's data transmissions with multiple physical paths through the network in order to ensure that if one path is unavailable, the data can use the alternate path to get to its destination. Multiple paths on a bridged or switched network, however, will create havoc in the form of *loops*.

Loops are the result of the basic function of transparent bridges with redundant paths. Remember:

- Bridges forward all broadcasts out of every port except for the port on which the broadcast was received.

- Bridges forward all frames with a destination address that is unknown (not in the bridge table) out of every port except the port on which the frame was received.

Therefore, if multiple paths to a destination exist, it is possible for two bridges in parallel to forward a single broadcast or frame back and forth to each other, essentially populating both bridge tables with inaccurate information and resulting in an endless loop, many headaches, and utter chaos on the network.

Let's take a closer look. Refer to Figure 4-3.

Figure 4-3 illustrates a bridging loop. Let's step through the process of a loop in the making:

Host 1 on Network A transmits a unicast frame destined to the hardware address of Host 2 on Network B. Both Bridge Y and Bridge Z receive the frame and update their table to reflect the fact that Host 1 resides on Network A. The tables on bridge Y and bridge Z do not yet contain an entry for Host 2 (the host for which the frame is destined), so the bridges then, by the nature of their operation, forward the packet out all ports except the port they received the frame on. Each bridge then forwards the frame out of its respective Network B interface. Two copies of this frame actually wind up being broadcast on Network B where Host 2 receives them, but something else happens here, and this is the kicker. Because both bridges on Network B broadcast the frame, bridge Y will receive the broadcast frame from bridge Z, and bridge Z will receive the broadcast frame from bridge Y. Both bridges will then incorrectly surmise that Host 1 has moved to Network B, and update their tables to reflect this change.

Both bridges still do not have an entry for Host 2 in their tables. This means that both bridges will then broadcast the frame out all ports except the port that they received the frame on, so this same frame is then broadcast back out of the Network A port on both bridges. If Host 2 cannot respond for any reason, this process will repeat over and over, creating the bridging loop. If Host 1 had originally sent out a broadcast frame as opposed to the unicast frame, the situation would be even worse.

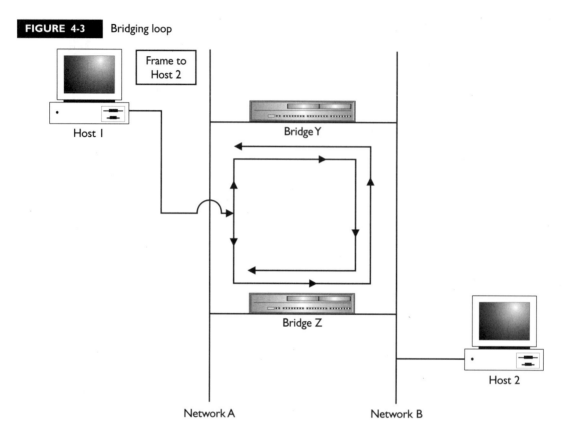

FIGURE 4-3 Bridging loop

If a bridging loop occurs on a broadcast-intensive network, the number of frame copies will multiply exponentially with each pass through the loop. As you can guess, it doesn't take very long before the entire network is brought to its knees, and communication over the network is impossible. This is known as a *broadcast storm.*

Hmmm, well then how can we prevent these loops and provide redundancy in the form of multiple physical paths between network hosts? This is the very reason the Spanning Tree Protocol was developed.

What Is the Spanning Tree Protocol?

The Spanning Tree Protocol, sometimes referred to as STP, is implemented between network devices (bridges and switches) to provide a stable, fault-tolerant, loop-free network environment. STP achieves this by running the Spanning Tree algorithm, detecting the presence of multiple physical paths and logically disabling (blocking-stand by mode) one or more of the redundant links. This guarantees that only one path between network devices will be active at a given time.

STP was originally developed by DEC, and eventually the DEC implementation of STP evolved into the IEEE 802.1d standard. Cisco devices support both versions of the Spanning Tree Protocol. It is important to note, however, that the DEC version and the 802.1d version of the Spanning Tree Protocol are not compatible or interchangeable. You must make certain that all bridges and switches on the entire network are running the same version of STP in order to ensure proper functionality of the protocol.

Luckily, on Cisco devices, STP is on by default—you don't have to turn it on. This will help prevent some headaches for an administrator who wishes to just drop a new switch into the network and not have the worry of inadvertently creating a redundant link that might result in a loop.

Although STP is enabled by default, there are configurable settings that can be set to optimize and customize your specific configuration. We'll cover those settings later in the chapter.

Understanding How STP Works

To understand how the Spanning Tree Protocol works, we must first understand some of the components and concepts of the protocol. There are many pieces to this puzzle, so let's look at each one individually and then we will tie it all together when we look at STP in action. First, an overview of Spanning Tree functionality and terminology.

In its most simple sense, there are basically just four steps involved in building a Spanning Tree for a given network:

1. Election of the root bridge
2. Election of root ports
3. Election of designated ports
4. Changing of the port states

The Spanning Tree algorithm runs initially when the network is first started up. It selects a bridge to act as the root bridge of the tree. It makes this selection based on several elements that will be discussed later.

The root bridge is more or less the center of STP's universe. It acts as the anchor for the Spanning Tree. All ports on all other bridges in the tree are automatically configured with respect to their logical distance (Cost) from the root bridge.

Once the root bridge has been selected, all of the other bridges in the network then must determine which ports are root ports and which ports are designated ports.

- **Root port** A port on a bridge that is the closest, in terms of cost, to the root bridge.
- **Designated port** Each individual network segment must have a port on one of the bridges connected to the segment that is designated as the closest port, again, in terms of cost, to the root bridge.

It is possible for a port to be both a root port for the bridge and a designated port for a particular network segment. If a port is neither a root port nor a designated port, Spanning Tree sees it as a redundant link (the odd man out). Redundant link ports are then put into a blocking state A port in the blocking state will not allow any user data frames to pass. A blocked state port is able to receive BPDUs (it can also receive CDP frames on Cisco switches). All other ports are put in a forwarding state (allows all network traffic to flow). This action ensures that only one of the parallel (redundant) links on the network will be active at any given time. This tree will remain stable and intact until a network topology change is detected on the network. If an active link in the forwarding state goes down, causing a topology change, STP will rerun the Spanning Tree algorithm and reconverge. The blocked state port will automatically become active after the Spanning Tree reconvergence takes place, ensuring that a path through the network is always available. If the downed link does come back up, another topology change is detected, and STP reruns the algorithm again, reconverging and settling on a new topology.

How is this change in topology detected? Or, for that matter, how does the algorithm make the determinations about who will be the root bridge, which ports get blocked, and which ones don't?

This information is gathered through the use of Bridge Protocol Data Units (BPDUs), which we will cover next.

BPDUs

BPDUs are special multicast frames that are broadcast out by all of the bridges and switches on the network. These frames contain all of the vital topology information about each sender that is needed by the bridges to build and maintain the Spanning Tree. They are the lifeblood of the protocol. Keep in mind that BPDUs are only exchanged between switches and bridges, not servers, routers, or workstations. Also, there is no such thing as a *Switch* Protocol Data Unit. Bridge Protocol Data Units are used by both bridges and switches.

Each port on a bridge will transmit a BPDU out of each port every two seconds by default (Hello Time). Each bridge will examine all of the BPDUs it receives, and sends, on each port to find the best (lowest value) BPDU. It will then save a copy of that BPDU for the port. If the saved BPDU originated from another bridge, the receiving bridge will then stop transmitting BPDUs out of that port. If the receiving bridge stops receiving the "best" BPDU (perhaps due to a link failure), the saved copy will expire in 20 seconds by default (Max Age), and the bridge will begin sending BPDUs out of that port once again (topology change).

There are two types of BPDUs:

- **Configuration BPDUs** The majority of the BPDUs on a healthy network will be of this variety. These BPDUs are exchanged by all bridges on the network, flooding the network with the topology information needed by STP.

- **Topology Change Notification (TCN) BPDUs** When a topology change occurs—for example, an active link goes down—this type of BPDU alerts the root that the active topology has changed, triggering a recalculation of the Spanning Tree algorithm and reconvergence. This type of BPDU will originate from the bridge that experiences a change in the state of one of its ports.

Let's dissect a BPDU frame and have a closer look (Figure 4-4).

BPDUs exist only at layers 1(physical) and 2 (data link) of the OSI model. You'll notice that there is no routing information contained in the BPDU frame.

The following fields are contained in a configuration BPDU:

- **Protocol ID** Always contains the value of 0.

FIGURE 4-4 A BPDU configuration frame

Protocol ID	Version	Type	Flags	Root BID	Root Path Cost	Sender Bid	Port ID	Message Age	Message Age	Hello Time	Forward Delay
2-Bytes	1-Byte	1-Byte	1-Byte	8-Bytes	4-Bytes	8-Bytes	2-Bytes	2-Bytes	2-Bytes	2-Bytes	2-Bytes

- **Version**   Always contains the value of 0.
- **Type**   Determines the type of BPDU, configuration, or TCN (Topology Change Notification).
- **Flags**   Used in conjunction with the TCN BPDU type. Indicates either a topology change or a topology change acknowledgment.
- **Root BID**   Contains the bridge identifier of the bridge that has been designated as the root bridge.
- **Root Path Cost**   Defines the cumulative cost from the bridge that originated the BPDU, across all links to the root bridge.
- **Sender BID**   Contains the bridge identifier of the bridge that generated the BPDU.
- **Port ID**   Identifies which port the BPDU left the transmitting bridge on.
- **Message Age**   The amount of time since the root bridge advertised a BPDU based on the current topology information.
- **Max Age**   Defines the maximum time that a BPDU will be saved for a port.
- **Hello Time**   The amount of time between BPDU broadcasts.
- **Forward Delay**   The amount of time that a port will spend in the listening and learning STP port state.

Now that we know what kind of information a BPDU contains, let's look at how Spanning Tree uses the fields in these frames to determine the selection of the root bridge, root ports, and designated ports in a bridged network.

Bridge Identifier (BID) and the Election of the Root Bridge

Spanning Tree looks at the sender BID field of every BPDU on the network in order to elect the root bridge. The BID is an 8-byte field comprised of the bridge priority (2 bytes) and the sending bridge's MAC address (6 bytes). The bridge with the lowest bridge priority will become the root bridge for the Spanning Tree. The bridge priority defaults to 32768, but it can be changed if an administrator wishes to force a bridge to become the root.

In the event of a tie in the bridge priority, the MAC addresses of the bridges will be used to determine which one will be the root bridge. The bridge with the lowest MAC address wins the election and becomes the root bridge.

exam Watch

The bridge with the lowest BID bridge priority wins the election to become the root bridge. In the case of a tie, the MAC address of the bridges will be used to determine the root bridge. The MAC address will act as the tiebreaker. The bridge with the lowest MAC address will win.

For example, if Bridge 1 has a low bridge priority and a high MAC address, and Bridge 2 has a low MAC address and a high bridge priority, Bridge 1 will win the election. This is because the bridge priority is looked at first to determine the root bridge. The MAC address plays no part in the election unless the bridge priorities are the same for all bridges on the network.

on the Job

If you find yourself designing an implementation of the Spanning Tree Protocol, it is usually considered good practice to manually select your root bridge by changing the bridge priority to a lower number on the selected bridge when you are configuring it. This way, you are not at the mercy of whichever bridge happens to have the lowest MAC address, as would be the case if all BIDs are left at default.

As a rule, you want to keep the root bridge near the physical center of your network. Also, you generally want to make your fastest switch on the network the root bridge. For example, a Catalyst 6000 would make a better choice as a root bridge than a Catalyst 19xx. This is because the root bridge will always be forwarding. This will ensure that your faster switch is forwarding, and one of the slower switches will be blocking. These two actions will help to speed up STP convergence, provide for more efficient operation of the protocol, and improve network performance.

Path Cost and the Election of Root Ports

Every bridge on the network that is not a root bridge must elect a port to be the root port for the bridge.

Cost, as we said earlier, is used to determine which port will be the root port. Each port on a bridge has a cost associated to it. This cost is the inverse of the link speed (bandwidth). That is to say that the faster the link, the lower the port cost.

The IEEE has assigned the following cost values; however, an administrator who wishes to customize his or her implementation of Spanning Tree can tune these values. See Table 4-1 (chart in Figure 4-5).

As a bridge receives a BPDU on a port, it adds the cost to the root path cost field of the BPDU and passes the BPDU on to the next bridge. The next bridge will do

TABLE 4-1	Bandwidth (Link Speed)	STP Cost
IEEE STP Cost Values Related to Bandwidth	4 Mbps	250
	10 Mbps	100
	16 Mbps	62
	45 Mbps	39
	100 Mbps	19
	155 Mbps	14
	622 Mbps	6
	1 Gbps	4
	10 Gbps	2
	Greater then 10 Gbps	1

the same. The root path cost field contains the cumulative path costs that the BPDU encountered on its way from the root bridge to the receiving bridge. The root path cost field is only incremented upon receipt on a port.

The receiving bridge examines all of the BPDUs it receives on each port to find the port that has the lowest root path cost (total cost to get to the root bridge). That port will be elected the root port for the bridge.

Path Cost and the Election of Designated Ports

As with root ports, designated ports are determined by cost also. Each individual segment on the network must have one, and only one, designated port. That is, one port designated for the network segment that will forward all of the traffic for that particular segment.

The port with the lowest root path cost—that is, the lowest cumulative cost to reach the root bridge—on a network segment will become the designated port. In the event that two paths have an equal root path cost, the bridges will look to the BID field to determine the designated bridge. The lowest bridge priority will win out. If the bridge priorities are equal, it resorts to the MAC address once again to be the tiebreaker.

The bridge that houses the designated port for a particular network segment is also referred to as the designated bridge for that segment.

This is where the loop-breaking mechanism of STP becomes obvious. With only one port for each network segment having the ability to forward traffic, the possibility of a loop is eliminated.

Convergence

Once the root ports and the designated ports have been determined, STP will put any port that is neither a root port nor a designated port into a blocking state. In the blocking state, a port cannot forward any traffic (except BPDU and CDP); thus, the redundant link, and any possibility of a loop, has been eliminated. STP will block only one port per loop. It is possible in a more complex topology to have a loop within a loop. In this situation, STP still only blocks one port per loop. Root ports and designated ports will then transition into a forwarding state, and user data can begin to flow in a stable, redundant, loop-free Spanning Tree topology.

STP Port States

We already discussed briefly a couple of the STP port states. Let's now look at each of these states in more detail.

There are five STP port states:

- **Disabled**   A port on a bridge that is disabled means that the port has been manually shut down by an administrator (administratively down) and will not participate in Spanning Tree or, for that matter, participate at all on the network. No traffic of any kind will be passed through a disabled port.

- **Blocking**   When the network initializes, all of the bridge ports on the network will be in the blocking state. In this state, each bridge is listening for and exchanging BPDUs (and CDP frames on Cisco switches). Until a bridge hears otherwise (from a BPDU), it will assume it is the root bridge for the Spanning Tree. It is during this state that the actual root bridge will be determined. No user data is able to pass during this state. The bridge ports then transition into the listening state. (Keep in mind that this transition from the blocking state into the listening state only occurs during network initialization or a topology change. If a port is in the blocking state after STP has converged, it will stay in that state unless a topology change is detected. Only then can a blocked port transition into a listening state.)

- **Listening**   During this state, the bridges continue to exchange BPDUs attempting to settle on the active topology. This is the state where root ports and designated ports are elected for each bridge. After the root ports and designated ports have been assigned, any port that is neither a root port nor a designated port will be forced back to the blocking state. No user data is able to pass during this state. From here, the root and designated bridge ports then transition into the learning state.

- **Learning**   In the learning state, the bridge is receiving frames and beginning to build its bridging table, associating each received frame's source MAC address with a particular bridge port. No user data is able to pass during this state. After this state, the ports all transition into the forwarding state.
- **Forwarding**   This is the state where the ports can finally begin both sending (forwarding) and receiving user data (frames).

STP Timers

If you look back at the BPDU frame in Figure 4-2, you will notice that there are three timers that STP uses:

- **Hello Time**   Defines the time interval between transmissions of configuration BPDU frames. It defaults to 2 seconds. That means that every 2 seconds, the bridge will send out a configuration BPDU.
- **Forward Delay**   This timer defines the amount of time that a port will spend in the listening and learning states. Its default setting is 15 seconds; that is to say, 15 seconds for each state. It means that it will spend a total of 30 seconds transitioning through both states.
- **Max Age**   This defines the maximum amount of time a BPDU will be saved for a port. This timer defaults to 20 seconds. Remember, the "best BPDU" is saved for each port, and each port will receive that "best BPDU" every 2 seconds (Hello Time). The Max Age timer allows a BPDU to time out in the event of a link failure. For example, if a port stops receiving the "best BPDU" for 20 seconds (default Max Age), the BPDU ages out, forcing a recalculation of Spanning Tree. If not for the Max Age timer, STP would not be able to detect link failures.

Keep in mind that all of these timers can be modified and tuned using set commands. It is best, however, to leave the timers at the defaults unless you are very comfortable tuning Spanning Tree. Playing with these timers can really open up a can of worms if you are not careful.

Refer to Figure 4-5. This is an actual configuration BPDU packet decode captured from a network. See if you can apply what we have discussed to decipher all of the information contained in the fields of this packet.

Bridging Loops, Spanning Tree, BPDUs 181

FIGURE 4-5

A configuration BPDU packet decode

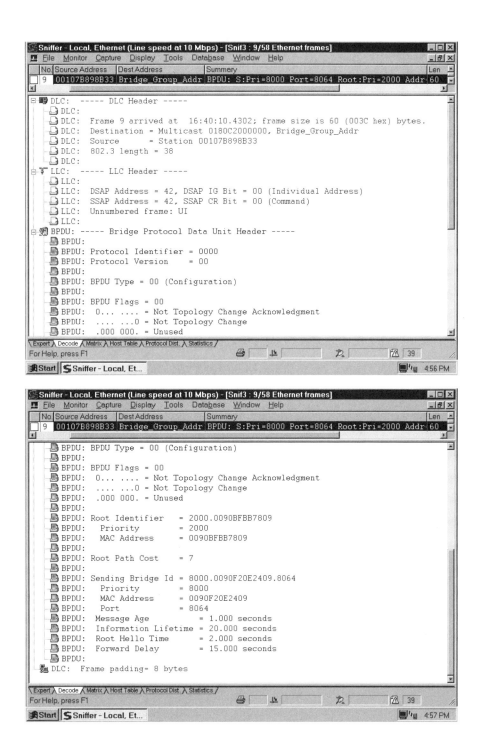

FROM THE CLASSROOM

How the Root Bridge is Selected

The concept of how the root bridge is selected is an important one. It is made somewhat difficult to understand due to the terminology involved.

Remember, the bridge priority portion of the BID (bridge identifier) field in the BPDU is first examined to make the root bridge determination. The part that most people have trouble grasping is that the lowest bridge priority wins. I think this is due in part because we all tend to associate priority to automatically mean higher. *High priority* is a term we commonly hear; therefore, we tend to think that the higher number should win out since, after all, STP is looking at the bridge's "priority." To add to the confusion, routing tends to use the highest address when performing such tasks as OSPF router ID elections; in that case, the highest address wins.

Just as these strong associations can hinder our understanding, I hope that the following association can clear it up in your mind.

It helps to think of the root bridge election as sort of a wacky auction. STP is auctioning off to all of the bridges on the network the dubious title of "root bridge." All of the bridges on the network are BIDding (sorry, I couldn't resist) on this item. Unlike a normal auction, though, the bids in this auction start out high but go lower. Finally, the gavel sounds and STP announces, "Sold to the **lowest** BIDder!" and the winning bridge becomes the root bridge.

Remember, if all of the bridges remain at the default BID of 32,768, and there is a tie, STP will examine the MAC address portion of the BID in the BPDU. In this case, the bridge with the **lowest** MAC address will win the "wacky auction" and become the root bridge.

—*David Bennett, CCNA, CCNP, CCDA, CNE, MCNE, MCSE, ASE*

Spanning Tree per VLAN

The IEEE 802.1Q standard specifies only one instance of Spanning Tree to cover all VLANs. This is referred to as *Common* or *Mono Spanning Tree*.

Only running one instance of Spanning Tree for all of the VLANs on the network is not a really efficient way to utilize the Spanning Tree Protocol. It does not allow the administrator any granular control over each VLAN.

Suppose as an administrator, you wanted a different active topology, different path costs, different timers, or a different root bridge for each VLAN. With only one instance of STP for all of the VLANs on your network, you are locked into a single configuration of STP to suit all of the VLANs on your network. That is where Cisco comes to the rescue!

Cisco switches are capable of running one instance of the Spanning Tree Protocol per each VLAN. This feature is referred to as the Per VLAN Spanning Tree, or PVST.

> **exam**
> **Watch**
>
> *A requirement for running PVST is that Cisco Inter-Switch Link encapsulation (ISL) must be enabled.*

PVST will afford an administrator much greater control and flexibility in customizing Spanning Tree for his particular network. With PVST, you can customize each VLAN's Spanning Tree implementation independent of one another. This means that you can have one particular root bridge for VLAN A, and a different root bridge for VLAN B. You can also customize any of the other tunable STP settings on a per VLAN basis. PVST can also be used to provide load balancing on your network.

You can probably see how this can be a powerful feature—but Cisco doesn't stop there. If you want the best of both worlds, and for some ungodly reason find yourself with a network that has both Common and Per VLAN STP running, you can use Cisco's PVST+ (PVST Plus). PVST+ was developed to allow Cisco devices to support the 802.1Q standard. It provides all of the good stuff that PVST provides, but PVST+ adds interoperability between a Common Spanning Tree region and a PVST Spanning Tree region on a given network.

> **exam**
> **Watch**
>
> *Cisco switches are capable oft running one instance of the Spanning Tree Protocol per VLAN. This feature is referred to as PVST, or Per VLAN Spanning Tree.*

Spanning Tree Protocol in Action

Now that we understand the theory, let's take a deeper look at the Spanning Tree Protocol in action on a simple three-segment, bridged network. Refer back to the four steps involved in building a Spanning Tree:

1. Election of the root bridge
2. Election of root ports
3. Election of designated ports
4. Changing of the port states

184 Chapter 4: Redundant Links and the Spanning Tree Protocol

Refer to Figure 4-6.

Step 1: The network has just started up. All of the ports on the bridges are currently in a blocking state. Each port is listening for and sending out BPDUs. Each port on each bridge processes and analyzes the BPDUs, and the root bridge election takes place. It is determined that bridge A will act as the root bridge; it won the election because it had the lowest MAC address. If you'll notice, bridges A, B, and C all have the default setting for bridge priority of 32,768; therefore, the MAC address portion of the BID field in the BPDU was used to elect the root bridge. The bridges now transition into the listening state.

Step 2: In the listening state, each bridge is examining the root path cost field of the BPDUs to determine which ports to elect as root ports and designated ports. The root bridge is sending BPDUs out of both port 1 and port 2 with a root path cost of 0. Port 1 on bridge B receives the BPDU from the root. Bridge B adds the cost of 19 to the BPDU field and transmits the BPDU out of port 2. Port 1 on bridge C receives the BPDU from bridge B. Bridge C adds the cost of 19 to the

FIGURE 4-6 The Spanning Tree Protocol in action

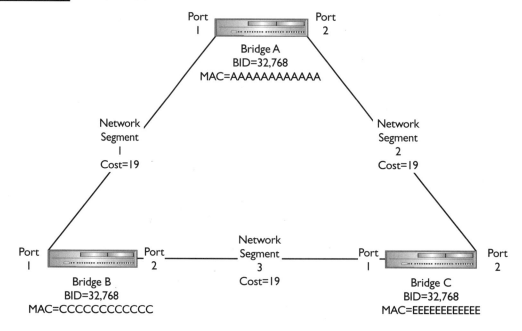

BPDU. Bridge C now knows that its port 1 root path cost is 38 (19+19). Notice, though, that bridge C will have also received one of the BPDUs from the root bridge on port 2 with a cost of 0. It will add the cost of 19 to that BPDU. Bridge C now knows now that the root path cost on port 2 is 19. Thus, port 2 is elected the root port (lowest root path cost) for bridge C. The same exact process takes place on bridge B, and port 1 on bridge B is elected root port.

Step 3: While still in the listening state, each network segment must elect a designated port to forward traffic for the segment. The process is very similar to the root port elections. Let's look at segment 1. What ports are directly connected to segment 1? Port 1 of the root bridge and port 1 of bridge B. Next, what is the cost associated with each of these ports. Remember, the root bridge (bridge A) is transmitting BPDUs with a root path cost of 0 (obviously, being the root bridge, there is no cost to get there), so port 1 on the root bridge (bridge A) has a root path cost of 0. We said earlier that port 1 on bridge B has a cost of 19. Which port will be the designated port for segment 1? That's right, port 1 on the root bridge. You are starting to get the hang of this.

The same circumstance is true for network segment 2. Port 2 on the root bridge (bridge A) with a cost of 0 will be the designated port for that segment.

Network segment 3 is where this gets a little interesting. What bridge ports are directly connected to segment 3? Port 2 of bridge B, and port 1 of bridge C. What are the costs associated with these ports? Well, both ports have a root path cost of 19. It's a tie. Does STP just give up and call it quits when faced with a tie? Of course not; it uses the same method it always uses to break a tie: It looks at the BID field to find the lowest bridge identifier, or MAC address (if the bridge identifiers are equal). In our case, port 2 on bridge B will win because of its lower MAC address. That leaves port 1 on bridge C as the odd man out, a redundant link, neither a root port nor a designated port. See Figure 4-7 for our modified port designations.

Step 4: While still in the listening state, STP will force port 1 of bridge C back into the blocking state because it represents a redundant link (a loop waiting to happen). All of the remaining ports (root ports and designated ports) now transition into the learning state and begin building their bridge tables. Also note that it is not possible for a root bridge to have a port in the blocked state. A root bridge port will always be in a forwarding state once the STP process concludes.

The process concludes when the ports then transition into the forwarding state and begin forwarding user frames over the network in a stable, loop-free Spanning Tree topology.

FIGURE 4-7 Port designations

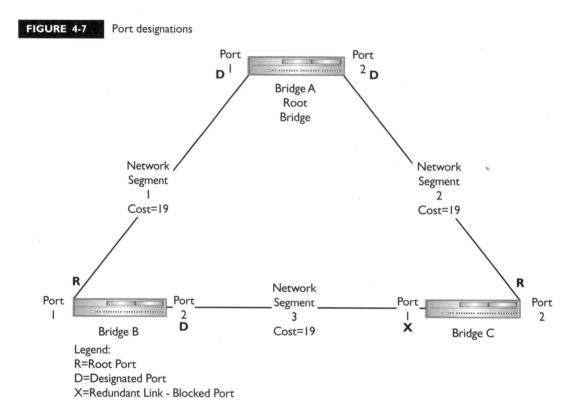

Enabling Spanning Tree

By default, Spanning Tree Protocol is enabled on every port on a Cisco switch. If, for some reason, you need to enable or disable it, use the following commands (Be careful when disabling Spanning Tree. Make sure that no loops exists on your network before you execute the disable command):

On a set command-based switch, the commands would be:

```
Switch1(enable)> set spantree enable module #/port #
Switch1(enable)> set spantree disable module #/port #
```

On a Cisco IOS command-based switch, enter the following commands in global configuration mode:

```
Switch1(config)#spantree vlan-list
```

Bridging Loops, Spanning Tree, BPDUs

SCENARIO & SOLUTION

Your boss has stated that providing redundancy in the form of redundant links on the network is critical. He realizes that this will cause loops on the network, and asks you to submit a plan to eliminate the loops and provide the redundancy.	You would submit a plan to implement the Spanning Tree Protocol on all of the switches on the network. This will assure a stable, loop-free, fault-tolerant network.
You are implementing the Spanning Tree Protocol on your network and you want to make sure that a specific switch will become the root bridge for the Spanning Tree. How can this be accomplished?	This can be accomplished by altering the bridge priority of the switch that you want to make the root bridge for Spanning Tree. You would have to make sure that the bridge priority you specify is the lowest bridge priority on the network.
You want to specify a different root bridge for each VLAN on the network. How can you accomplish this?	Cisco switches allow you to run one instance of Spanning Tree per VLAN. This will allow you to change the Spanning Tree settings on a VLAN-to-VLAN basis.

This command enables Spanning Tree on a specific VLAN. The vlan-list argument is referring to the specific VLAN that you want Spanning Tree to be enabled for.

```
Switch1(config)#no spantree vlan-list
```

This command will disable Spanning Tree on a specified VLAN. Now that you understand how the Spanning Tree Protocol works, here are some possible scenario questions and their answers.

EXERCISE 4-2

Enabling Spanning Tree

In this exercise, we will apply what we have learned in this section and enable Spanning Tree on a switch. This lab assumes you have access to a Catalyst 5000 switch (the CAT 5000 is a set-based switch; remember, the commands are different for IOS based switches) and that you have a VLAN configured as VLAN 10. To complete the exercise, perform the following steps:

1. Log in to the switch and enter the privileged mode.
2. Enter the following command to enable Spanning Tree on VLAN 10:

   ```
   Switch1(enable)set spantree enable 10
   ```

   This command will produce the following output:

   ```
   Spantree 10 enabled.
   ```

3. Spanning Tree should now be enabled for VLAN 10. To confirm this, type the following command:

   ```
   Switch1(enable)show spantree 10
   ```

   This command should produce an output similar to the following:

   ```
   VLAN 10
   Spanning tree enabled
   Spanning tree type          ieee
   Designated Root             00-10-0d-4a-76-21
   Designated Root Priority    32768
   Designated Root Cost        19
   Designated Root Port        1/2
   Root Max Age   20 sec    Hello Time 2 sec    Forward Delay 15 sec
   Bridge ID MAC ADDR          00-10-0d-cc-3a-b6
   Bridge ID Priority          32768
   Bridge Max Age 20 sec    Hello Time 2 sec    Forward Delay 15 sec
   Port      Vlan  Port-State     Cost    Priority  Fast-Start  Group-Method
   --------- ----  -------------  -----   --------  ----------  -----------
   1/2       10    forwarding     19      32        disabled
   ```

   This exercise is complete.

CERTIFICATION OBJECTIVE 4.03

Fast EtherChannel

Fast EtherChannel is a Cisco proprietary feature that provides for increased bandwidth, load balancing, and redundancy between network devices. It is able to achieve this by allowing you to group (bundle) multiple fast Ethernet ports together.

Fast EtherChannel will then treat this multiport grouping as one single physical port (Figure 4-8).

Let's look at the features of Fast EtherChannel in a little more detail:

- **Increased bandwidth**   EtherChannel provides an incremental increase in bandwidth. When bundling ports, you must combine them in groups of two or four. Bundling two fast Ethernet ports would result in 400 Mbps (in full-duplex mode) of aggregate bandwidth..
- **Load balancing**   Because there are multiple ports, traffic can be distributed evenly across the channel, resulting in a more robust and efficient use of the bandwidth.
- **Redundancy**   If one link in the bundle fails, the traffic from the failed link is rerouted to one of the other links in the EtherChannel. The link failure and rerouting is transparent to the end users on the network.

Normally, these grouped parallel links would cause loops on your network. However, with Fast EtherChannel, the Spanning Tree Protocol will treat these multiple ports as one single physical port. When the STP port state changes on the EtherChannel, the port state changes for all of the links in the bundle, maintaining a stable, loop-free network.

exam
Watch

Despite the fact that multiple physical ports form an EtherChannel bundle, the Spanning Tree Protocol will treat any Fast EtherChannel bundle as one single physical port. No loop is possible within a single EtherChannel bundle.

Fast EtherChannel is starting to be supported by NIC (network interface card) vendors. This allows you to connect multiport NIC cards on your network servers to multiple ports on the Ethernet switch, leveraging the benefits of Fast

FIGURE 4-8   Fast EtherChannel implementation between two switches using four Fast Ethernet ports on each switch for a total (maximum) of 800 Mbps full duplex (able to transmit and receive at the same time), redundancy, and load balancing.

EtherChannel: increased bandwidth, load balancing, and redundancy on a server-to-switch basis (Figure 4-9).

Fast EtherChannel port groupings are referred to as a *bundle*. The Fast EtherChannel bundles are managed by the EBC (Ethernet Bundle Controller). The EBC works in conjunction with the EARL (Early Address Recognition Logic) chip to manage link failures and load distribution.

When enabling Fast EtherChannel, certain specifications must be adhered to, or the ports will automatically become disabled. The specifications follow:

- All ports assigned to the channel must belong to the same VLAN, or be configured as trunk ports (do not set the ports for dynamic VLAN). If they are configured as trunk ports, be sure to have the same trunk mode and VLAN range set for all ports at both ends of the connection.

- All ports involved in the EtherChannel at both ends of the connection must be configured for the same speed and duplex setting.

- You must disable port security on EtherChannel ports.

Other rules may apply, and vary from switch model to switch model. For instance, some models require that the ports assigned to the EtherChannel be contiguous ports on the switch. You cannot arbitrarily pick any port to belong to a bundle. With some of the newer models, that is no longer the case.

Another item to be aware of is that the number of links you may have in a bundle can also vary from switch to switch.

The best rule of thumb here is to just be aware of these variations and make sure you understand the Fast EtherChannel particulars for any switch you are working with.

FIGURE 4-9 Fast EtherChannel implementation between a file server and a switch using two Fast Ethernet ports for a total of 400 Mbps full duplex, redundancy, and load balancing.

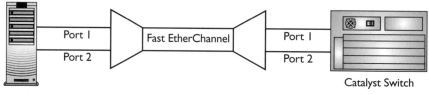

PAgP Functionality

The Port Aggregation Protocol (PAgP) was developed by Cisco as an enhancement to Fast EtherChannel technology. It is sometimes referred to as Fast EtherChannel Phase II.

PAgP complements Fast EtherChannel by automating the creation of Fast EtherChannel bundles between Catalyst switches. The protocol achieves this by sending PAgP packets out of the Fast EtherChannel capable ports on a switch. The purpose of these packets is to discover if any of the neighboring connected switches ports have Fast EtherChannel capabilities. If PAgP finds multiple ports connected between two switches that are Fast EtherChannel capable, it will negotiate the creation of a Fast EtherChannel bundle between the two switches. Keep in mind that all of the earlier stated specifications about the creation of a Fast EtherChannel bundle still apply.

Fast EtherChannel capable ports on a switch can be configured to one of four PAgP states:

- **On**   The port sends out PAgP packets and will become part of the Fast EtherChannel bundle.
- **Off**   The port will not become part of the Fast EtherChannel bundle.
- **Desirable**   The port sends out PAgP packets and will become part of the Fast EtherChannel bundle, only if the other end agrees to form the Fast EtherChannel bundle.
- **Auto**   (This is the default setting.) Tells the switch to enable Fast EtherChannel only if the other end of the connection is set to On or Desirable. Basically, a port set to auto will become part of the Fast EtherChannel bundle only if the other end of the link initiates the bundle creation. If two sets of ports have both ends of the link configured for auto mode, a bundle will not be formed.

Commands Related to Fast EtherChannel

If you need to find out if a particular port can support Fast EtherChannel on a set command-based switch, you could enter the following command:

```
Switch1(enable) show port capabilities module #/port #
```

To configure a group of ports for EtherChannel on a set command-based switch, enter the following command:

```
Switch1(enable) set port channel module #/port #'s
{on|off|auto|desirable}
```

If the switch that you are working on is a Cisco IOS command-based switch, you would enter the following command in global configuration mode to create a virtual port channel interface on the switch:

```
Switch1(config)#port-channel mode {on|off|auto|desirable}
```

Now that you understand how the Fast EtherChannel works, here are some possible scenario questions and their answers:

SCENARIO & SOLUTION

You are asked for a solution that would allow greater bandwidth between the two core switches in your network. They are currently connected via one Fast Ethernet port.	You would submit a plan to implement Fast EtherChannel between the core switches, bundling four Fast Ethernet ports on each switch to create a 800 Mbps (full duplex) EtherChannel.
Your boss accepts your plan for the Fast EtherChannel implementation, but he is very concerned that the multiple port configuration will result in loops on the network.	You explain to your boss that the Spanning Tree Protocol will see and treat these multiple ports as a single port because they are bundled as a channel.
Your boss also raises concerns over fault tolerance. "What if one of the bundled links dies?" he asks.	You explain to him that in the event that an individual link fails in the bundle, the traffic associated with that link will be rerouted to one of the other links in the bundle, and that the bundle does provide excellent fault tolerance protection from individual link failures. Of course, the link speed will be reduced in this case.

EXERCISE 4-3

Enabling Fast EtherChannel

In this exercise, we will apply what we have learned in this section and enable Fast EtherChannel bundle on two ports on each switch. This lab assumes you have access to two Catalyst 5000 switches, and that all of the requirements for Fast EtherChannel have been met. (The CAT 5000 is a set-based switch; remember, the commands are different for IOS-based switches.) It also assumes that ports 5 and 6 on module 2 are connected between the two switches. To complete the exercise, perform the following steps:

1. Log in to switch 1 and enter the privileged mode.
2. Enter the following command to enable Fast EtherChannel on module 2, ports 5 and 6:

   `Switch1(enable)`**`set port channel 2/5-6 on`**

3. Log in to switch 2 and enter the privileged mode.
4. Enter the following command to enable Fast EtherChannel on module 2, ports 5 and 6:

   `Switch2(enable)`**`set port channel 2/5-6 on`**

5. You should see the following output after entering this command on either switch:

   `Port(s) 2/5-6 channel mode set to on`

6. To confirm the channel configuration, you can enter the following command:

   `Switch1(enable)`**`show port channel`**

   This command should produce an output similar to the following:

Port	Status	Channel Mode	Channel status	Neighbor device	Neighbor port
----	-----	-------	-------	----------------	--------
2/5	connected	on	channel	WS-C4545 053678271	2/5
2/6	connected	on	channel	WS-C4545 053678271	2/6

   This exercise is complete.

CERTIFICATION OBJECTIVE 4.04

PortFast, UplinkFast, BackboneFast

In this section, we will examine three of Cisco's enhancements to the Spanning Tree Protocol that allow for greater control over the behavior of the protocol.

PortFast

Refer back to earlier in the chapter when we discussed the various port states that STP employs. A port starts out in the blocking state and progresses through listening, learning, and finally to the forwarding state. The forwarding state is the state in which user data packets can be transmitted. Prior to the forwarding state, no user data packets can traverse the network. We also know that a port running Spanning Tree will take 30 seconds (using the default timers) before it reaches the forwarding state. On certain links, primarily links that are connected to end-station devices (servers and workstations), this is not desirable. Some protocols and applications will not function properly given this delay.

When PortFast is enabled on a particular port, that port will essentially bypass the blocking, listening, and learning states, and jump right to forwarding. That's right, as soon as the switch senses the link, it is immediately able to forward user data.

This "bypassing" of the port states is only true during the initial startup of the PortFast-enabled link. If an STP recalculation occurs due to a link failure somewhere on the network, all ports on the switch, including PortFast ports, will go through all states before STP stabilizes once again.

on the job

One situation in which PortFast is very useful is when you have a workstation computer on your network that completes its boot-up sequence in less than 30 seconds. "Why?" you might ask. Well, think about the boot-up sequence of a typical PC. During the boot process, the network interface card in the PC will initialize. This initialization will activate the link on the switch port. That port will then go through the Spanning Tree process and transition through the listening and learning states of STP (30 seconds total—forward delay). It will then finally proceed to the forwarding state.

This is no problem if your workstation does not need access to the network prior to the 30-second forward delay. Nowadays, though, more often than not, the workstation will need the network to be available almost immediately after the NIC initializes (DHCP requests, for example).

With PCs getting faster and faster all the time, it is not uncommon to find a workstation completing its boot-up process in under 30 seconds.

This can be a tricky problem to troubleshoot, especially if the people responsible for connecting the workstation aren't aware of the Spanning Tree process. This problem could appear to be a physical connectivity issue.

Rather than guessing which PCs will boot quickly and which ones will not, it is good practice to enable PortFast on all ports that are connected to end-user workstations or servers. This way, you can avoid ever having to deal with this problem. Do not enable PortFast on switch-to-switch connections, as this will cause problems with the STP process.

Commands to Enable PortFast

To enable PortFast on a set command-based switch, enter the following command:

```
Switch1(enable)set spantree portfast module #/port # {enable|disable}
```

To enable PortFast on a Cisco IOS command-based switch, enter the following command in interface configuration mode:

```
Switch1(config-if)#spantree start-forwarding
```

To avoid any problems, you should make sure that PortFast is only enabled on ports that connect to a single end station such as a server, or a user workstation.

UplinkFast

After a link failure, the time that STP takes to recalculate and reconverge can cause disruptions and instability on the network. UplinkFast is a patented Cisco technology that reduces the STP convergence time when a topology change occurs on a network.

UplinkFast achieves this by allowing a port that is in the blocking state (standby) to immediately jump to the forwarding state when the switch senses a link failure on the its root port, bypassing the listening and learning states. With UplinkFast enabled, the switch does not have to wait for the Max Age timer to expire to trigger this reconfiguration. This greatly reduces the amount of time involved in cutting over to the standby port (port in the blocking state) on a bridge.

UplinkFast is designed to be used only on access-layer (leaf-node) switches. It is not meant to be enabled on all switches on a network. Do not use the UplinkFast feature on core-layer switches, or root bridges. For UplinkFast to function properly, three conditions must be true:

- UplinkFast must be enabled on the switch.
- One of the switch ports must be in the blocked state (standby).
- The link failure must occur on the root port (forwarding port) of the switch.

Basically, this means that for UplinkFast to be useful, the failure must occur on a link that is directly connected to the switch that has UplinkFast enabled.

exam
Watch *The UplinkFast feature is designed to be used with access-layer switches. Do not enable UplinkFast on switches in the core of a network.*

Commands to Enable UplinkFast

Two things to keep in mind when you enable UplinkFast on a switch:

- It is enabled for all VLANs on the switch; you cannot enable UplinkFast on a single VLAN.
- It increases bridge priority on the switch. This makes the switch less likely to become the root switch for the Spanning Tree. UplinkFast also increases the costs associated with all of the ports on that switch. This reduces the possibility that one of the ports on the switch will become a designated port. The goal of these actions is to satisfy the three required conditions of UplinkFast that were stated in the previous section

To enable UplinkFast on a set command-based switch, enter the following command:

```
Switch1(enable)set spantree uplinkfast {enable|disable}
[rate station-update-rate] [all-protocols off|on]
```

The rate station-update-rate value refers to the number of multicast packets that will be transmitted every 100 milliseconds. It defaults to 15, but can be configured on the command line.

To enable UplinkFast on an IOS command-based switch, enter the following command in global configuration mode:

```
Switch1(config)#spanning-tree uplinkfast
```

BackboneFast

UplinkFast may be useful in situations where a link that is directly connected to the UplinkFast switch fails. However, it is not very useful in a situation where a link on the backbone, which is not directly connected, fails (Figure 4-10).

Notice that Cat1 is the root switch. Prior to the link failure, Cat2 and Cat3's root ports are in the forwarding state. Cat2's port on link 3 is in the blocking state. This is a pretty straightforward Spanning Tree.

When link 2 fails, Cat 2, because it is not directly connected to link 2, has no direct knowledge of the link failure. Cat2 will begin receiving inferior BPDUs from Cat3. With normal STP, Cat2 will keep its "best" BPDU until the max-age timer

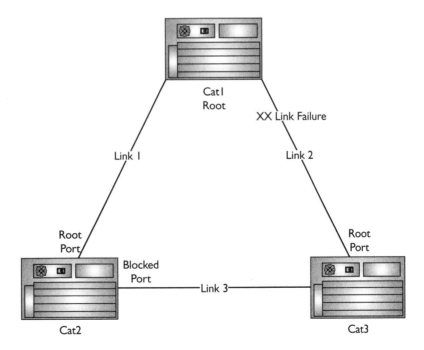

FIGURE 4-10

BackboneFast example

expires (20 seconds by default). At that point, an STP recalculation will take place, and Cat2's blocked port will transition through the listening, learning, and forwarding states. For the time it takes for this reconvergence, Cat3 will have no link to the root bridge.

BackboneFast speeds up this process by forcing the Max Age timer on Cat2 to immediately expire.

BackboneFast specifies that when a root port or blocked port on a switch receives an inferior BPDU from the network segment's designated switch, this "inferior BPDU" indicates an indirect link failure and that the designated switch has lost its connection to the root switch. This causes the receiving blocked port or root port to immediately expire its Max Age timer and force a recalculation, thus reducing that waiting time.

Refer back to our example. With BackboneFast enabled on all switches on the network, as soon as the link failure occurs, Cat3 will begin sending inferior BPDUs to Cat2. Cat2's Max Age timer will immediately expire. At that point, STP recalculation will take place, and Cat2's blocked port will transition through the listening, learning, and forwarding states, providing Cat 3 with a new path to the root switch (Cat1).

Commands to Enable BackboneFast

To enable BackboneFast on a set command-based switch, enter the following command:

```
Switch1(enable)set spantree backbonefast {enable|disable}
```

To enable BackboneFast on an IOS command-based switch, enter the following command in global configuration mode:

```
Switch1(config)#spanning-tree backbonefast
```

on the job **We said earlier that UplinkFast should only be enabled on access layer (leaf-node) stations, and that it should not be enabled on all switches on a network. BackboneFast, on the other hand, Should be enabled on all switches on a network in order to work properly.**

As you can see, enabling BackboneFast on all switches on your network involves only one relatively simple configuration step, and it will benefit your network greatly by allowing indirect link failure information to propagate through the network much more quickly than if it were left disabled.

Now that you understand how PortFast, UplinkFast, and BackboneFast work, here are some possible scenario questions and their answers.

SCENARIO & SOLUTION

Some of the new workstations on your network do not seem to be able to connect to the network properly. Everything appears to be configured properly. What is one possible way to resolve this problem?	Enable PortFast on all ports that are connected to end-user workstations. These stations may be attempting to communicate on the network before the port is in the forwarding state and the SpanningTree process has completed. PortFast will bypass the blocking, listening, and learning states and put the port in the forwarding state immediately upon initialization of the link.
You want your switches to be able to sense a directly connected link failure and have the blocked port immediately transition to forwarding state, bypassing the delays involved in passing through the listening and learning states. How can you achieve this?	Enable UplinkFast on the switch that houses the blocked port. With UplinkFast enabled on a switch, a link failure on the root port of that switch will trigger the blocked port to transition immediately into forwarding state.
You want your switches to be able to sense an indirect link failure and have the blocked port immediately expire its Max Age timer and begin transitioning through listening, learning, and forwarding states. How can you achieve this?	Enable BackboneFast on all of the switches on your network. This will ensure that any indirect link failure on the network will propagate through the network quickly, resulting in faster Spanning Tree convergence.

EXERCISE 4-4

Enabling PortFast, BackboneFast, and UplinkFast

In this exercise, we will apply what we have learned in this section and enable PortFast, UplinkFast, and BackboneFast on a switch. This lab assumes you have access to a Catalyst 5000 switch. (The CAT 5000 is a set-based switch; remember, the commands are different for IOS-based switches.) To complete the exercise, perform the following steps:

1. Log in to the switch and enter the privileged mode.

2. Enter the following command to enable PortFast on module 2 port 5 (you may use whatever module and port you have available):

```
Switch1(enable)set spantree portfast 2/5 enable
```

This command will produce the following output:

```
Warning: Spantree port fast start should only be enabled on ports connected
to a single host. Connecting hubs, concentrators, switches, bridges, etc.
to a fast start port can cause temporary spanning tree loops. Use with caution.
Spantree port 2/5 fast start enabled.
```

3. Now we will enable UplinkFast on the switch. Remember, UplinkFast should only be enabled on access layer switches, but we can overlook that for the purpose of this exercise. Enter the following command to enable UplinkFast:

```
Switch1(enable)set spantree uplinkfast enable
```

This command should produce an output similar to the following:

```
VLANs 1-1005 bridge priority set to 49152.
The port cost and portvlancost of all ports set to above 3000.
Station update rate set to 15 packets/100ms.
uplinkfast all-protocols field set to off.
uplinkfast enabled for bridge.
```

Notice the increased bridge priority and port costs.

4. Now we will enable BackboneFast on the switch. Enter the following command to enable BackboneFast:

```
Switch1(enable)set spantree backbonefast enable
```

This command should produce the following output:

```
Backbonefast enabled for all VLANs
```

This exercise is complete.

CERTIFICATION OBJECTIVE 4.05

Commands

In this section, we will discuss in more detail some of the commands for configuring, verifying, and troubleshooting some of the various features discussed in this chapter.

exam 🕲 *atch*

Make sure you know the different commands for both the set command-based switches and the IOS command-based switches. This is true for any command that is presented in this chapter.

set spantree (All of the Variables to the Command; Timers, Cost, etc.)

We have already seen how we can use the set spantree command to enable and disable the Spanning Tree Protocol on a switch. Now let's look at how we can use the variations of this command to tune some of the different parameters of Spanning Tree that were discussed earlier in the chapter.

set spantree and the Selection of the Root Bridge

You can designate a switch to become a root or a secondary root (backup root) switch for a specific set of VLANs or for all VLANs on the network. To do this, enter the following command:

```
Switch1(enable) set spantree root [secondary] vlans [dia network_diameter] [hello hello_time]
```

The vlans optional parameter allows you to specify certain VLANs or all VLANs. If you do not specify any VLANs, it will default to VLAN 1.

The diameter optional parameter allows you to specify the maximum number of bridges between two endstations.

The hello time optional parameter allows you to specify the number of seconds between BPDUs generated by the root bridge.

The set spantree root command reduces the bridge priority of the switch from the default of 32,768 to 8,192. Remember, the bridge priority is the value that is used to select the root bridge for the Spanning Tree. The lowest bridge priority wins.

Another way to modify the bridge priority setting for a switch on a particular VLAN would be to enter the following command:

```
Switch1(enable) set spantree priority bridge_priority [vlan]
```

With this command, you can set the bridge priority value to any number between 0 and 65,535.

set spantree and Cost

Remember that path cost is used by the Spanning Tree to determine which ports will forward and which ports will block. Path cost is the cumulative amount of cost that a BPDU encounters crossing over switch ports on its travels around the network.

To modify a port cost, which will influence the Spanning Tree port selections, enter the following command:

```
Switch1(enable) set spantree portcost module #/port # cost
```

The cost value you specify can range from 1 to 65,535.

Another setting that can influence Spanning Tree's selection of which ports forward or block is the port priority setting. The port that has the lowest port priority setting will forward frames for all VLANs.

To modify a particular port's port priority setting, enter the following command:

```
Switch1(enable) set spantree portpri module #/port # priority
```

You can set the priority to any number between 0 and 63. By default, port priority is set to 32.

set spantree and the STP Timers

To modify the setting for the forward delay on a VLAN, enter the following command:

```
Switch1(enable) set spantree fwddelay delay [vlan]
```

Recall that the forward delay is the amount of time that a port will spend in the listening and the learning states. It defaults to 15 seconds.

To modify the setting for the hello time on a VLAN, enter the following command:

```
Switch1(enable) set spantree hello interval
```

The hello timer affects the amount of time between BPDUs that are generated by the root bridge. It defaults to 2 seconds.

To modify the setting for the max-age timer on a VLAN, enter the following command:

```
Switch1(enable)set spantree maxage agingtime [vlan]
```

The Max Age timer affects the maximum amount of time that the best BPDU will be saved for a port. It defaults to 20 seconds.

show spantree

You can gain a lot of valuable information about your Spanning Tree configuration by using the show spantree command. The following is a sample output of the command. Notice that everything we have talked about in this chapter regarding the information contained in a Spanning Tree BPDU shows up in this output.

```
Switch1> (enable) show spantree
VLAN 1
Spanning tree enabled
Spanning tree type          ieee

Designated Root             00-90-0c-6e-f0-00
Designated Root Priority    49152
Designated Root Cost        0
Designated Root Port        1/0
Root Max Age    20 sec    Hello Time 2 sec    Forward Delay 15 sec

Bridge ID MAC ADDR          00-90-0c-6e-f0-00
Bridge ID Priority          49152
Bridge Max Age 20 sec    Hello Time 2 sec    Forward Delay 15 sec

Port      Vlan  Port-State       Cost   Priority  Fast-Start  Group-Method
--------- ----  ---------------  -----  --------  ----------  ------------
  1/1      1    not-connected    3019      32     disabled
  1/2      1    not-connected    3019      32     disabled
  4/1      1    not-connected    3100      32     disabled
  4/2      1    not-connected    3100      32     disabled
  4/3      1    forwarding       3100      32     disabled
  4/4      1    forwarding       3100      32     disabled
  4/5      1    not-connected    3100      32     enabled
```

```
4/6       1       not-connected    3100      32     enabled
4/7       1       not-connected    3100      32     disabled
4/8       1       not-connected    3100      32     disabled
4/9       1       forwarding       3100      32     disabled
4/10      1       forwarding       3100      32     disabled
4/11      1       not-connected    3100      32     disabled
4/12      1       not-connected    3100      32     disabled
```

Notice that this switch is the root switch for Spanning Tree.

show port

Show port is a wonderful command to use when troubleshooting a particular port's status. The following sample is showing the stats for slot 4 port 4. show port by itself will show the stats for all ports. Look at some of the valuable information that can be gained by using this command.

```
Switch1> (enable) show port 4/4
Port  Name              Status       Vlan       Level   Duplex Speed Type
----- ----------------- ------------ ---------- ------- ------ ----- ------------
 4/4                    connected    1          normal  a-half a-10  10/100BaseTX

Port  Security Secure-Src-Addr  Last-Src-Addr    Shutdown Trap     IfIndex
----- -------- ---------------- ---------------- -------- -------- -------
 4/4  disabled                                   No       disabled 8

Port     Broadcast-Limit Broadcast-Drop
-------- --------------- --------------
 4/4           -               0

Port  Align-Err  FCS-Err    Xmit-Err   Rcv-Err    UnderSize
----- ---------- ---------- ---------- ---------- ---------
 4/4           0          0          0          0         0

Port  Single-Col Multi-Coll Late-Coll  Excess-Col Carri-Sen Runts     Giants
----- ---------- ---------- ---------- ---------- --------- --------- ---------
 4/4           0          0          0          0         0         0         0

Last-Time-Cleared
--------------------------
Fri Apr 28 2000, 14:20:46
```

show spantree uplinkfast

You can use the show spantree uplinkfast command to check the status of UplinkFast on your set command-based switch. The following is a sample output from the command:

```
Switch1> (enable) show spantree uplinkfast
Station update rate set to 15 packets/100ms.
uplinkfast update packets enabled for all protocols.
VLAN         port list
```

If this were an IOS command-based switch, you could enter the following command to check the status of UplinkFast, which would produce the following output:

```
Switch1# show uplink-fast
Uplink fast enabled
Uplink fast frame generation rate 15
```

EXERCISE 4-5

Using Set and Show Commands

In this exercise, we will apply what we have learned in this section and use some of the set and show commands that were discussed. This lab assumes you have access to a Catalyst 5000 switch. (The CAT 5000 is a set-based switch; remember, the commands are different for IOS-based switches.) To complete the exercise, perform the following steps:

1. Log in to the switch and enter the privileged mode.

2. Let's ensure that this switch will become the root for VLAN 1 by typing the following command:

   `Switch1(enable)`**`set spantree root 1`**

   This command should produce the following output:

   ```
   VLAN 1 bridge priority set to 8192.
   VLAN 1 bridge max aging time set to 20.
   VLAN 1 bridge hello time set to 2.
   VLAN 1 bridge forward delay set to 15.
   Switch is now the root switch for active VLAN 1.
   ```

3. Let's modify a particular port's cost. Enter the following command to set the port cost for port 3 on module 4 to a cost value of 7:

   `Switch1(enable)`**`set spantree portcost 4/3 7`**

This command should produce the following output:

```
Spantree port 4/3 path cost set to 7.
```

4. Now let's change the forward delay timer to a value of 10 seconds instead of the default of 15 seconds for VLAN1. Enter the following command:

   Switch1(enable)**set spantree fwddelay 10 1**

   The 10 on the command line represents the number of seconds we would like to change the delay to. The 1 on the command line specifies that we will make this change for VLAN 1. This command should produce the following output:

   ```
   Spantree 1 forward delay set to 10 seconds.
   ```

5. Let's also modify the hello interval, increasing it from the default of 2 seconds to 3 seconds. Enter the following command:

   Switch1(enable)**set spantree hello 3**

   This command should produce the following output:

   ```
   Spantree 1 hello time set to 3 seconds.
   ```

6. Finally, let's modify the max-age timer for VLAN 1, decreasing it from the default of 20 seconds to 15 seconds. Enter the following command:

   Switch1(enable)**set spantree maxage 15 1**

   This command should produce the following output:

   ```
   Spantree 1 max aging time set to 15 seconds.
   ```

7. To confirm all of our changes, execute the following command:

   Switch1(enable)**show spantree**

You should see an output similar to the following. Check out all of the parameters that were changed.

```
VLAN 1
Spanning tree enabled
Spanning tree type        ieee

Designated Root           00-90-0c-6e-f0-00
Designated Root Priority  8192
Designated Root Cost      0
Designated Root Port      1/0
```

```
Root Max Age    15 sec     Hello Time 3 sec    Forward Delay 10 sec

Bridge ID MAC ADDR          00-90-0c-6e-f0-00
Bridge ID Priority          8192
Bridge Max Age 15 sec    Hello Time 3 sec    Forward Delay 10 sec

Port     Vlan  Port-State       Cost    Priority  Fast-Start  Group-Method
-------- ----  ---------------  -----   --------  ----------  ------------
 1/1      1    not-connected    3019       32     disabled
 1/2      1    not-connected    3019       32     disabled
 4/1      1    not-connected    3100       32     disabled
 4/2      1    not-connected    3100       32     disabled
 4/3      1    forwarding          7       32     disabled
 4/4      1    forwarding       3100       32     disabled
 4/5      1    not-connected    3100       32     enabled
 4/6      1    not-connected    3100       32     enabled
 4/7      1    not-connected    3100       32     disabled
 4/8      1    not-connected    3100       32     disabled
 4/9      1    forwarding       3100       32     disabled
 4/10     1    forwarding       3100       32     disabled
 4/11     1    not-connected    3100       32     disabled
 4/12     1    not-connected    3100       32     disabled
```

The exercise is complete.

CERTIFICATION SUMMARY

We sure did cover a lot of ground in this chapter.

First, we looked at what redundancy is, and why we need redundant links on a network.

After that, we discussed bridging loops, what causes them, and how we can prevent them with the Spanning Tree Protocol. We also took an in-depth look at how the Spanning Tree protocol functions. Remember the four steps of the Spanning Tree protocol?

1. Election of the root bridge
2. Election of root ports
3. Election of designated ports

4. Changing of the port states

We looked at each step in detail and actually saw how this process happens in action. We discussed the role of the BPDU (Bridge Protocol Data Unit) in this process.

We talked about the various states that a port can be in when running Spanning Tree Protocol:

- Disabled
- Blocking
- Listening
- Learning
- Forwarding

We also covered Spanning Tree Per VLAN, or PVST. This allows one instance of Spanning Tree per each VLAN.

Next, we looked at Fast EtherChannel and how it can provide us with better throughput, and load balancing and redundancy. It does this by creating a bundle out of multiple Ethernet links and treating them as a single link. Spanning Tree also treats a Fast EtherChannel bundle as a single link.

After that, we looked at PortFast, which allows a port to bypass the listening and learning states and jump right into the forwarding state. PortFast is best enabled on ports that connect to user endstations.

UplinkFast was also covered. UplinkFast allows a switch that has both a root port in forwarding state and a blocked port to immediately sense a failure on the root port and transition the blocked port immediately into forwarding state, cutting down on the delay of waiting for the Max Age timer to expire. UplinkFast should only be enabled on access-layer switches.

BackboneFast is similar to UplinkFast, except that it is able to sense indirect (not directly connected) link failures and quickly transition a blocked port into forwarding state. BackboneFast should be enabled on all of the switches on a network.

Finally, we covered some of the commands to fine-tune a Spanning Tree implementation, as well as some of the commands to verify and troubleshoot the switches.

TWO-MINUTE DRILL

Here are some of the key points from each certification objective in Chapter 4.

Redundant Links

- Redundant links are needed on a network to provide multiple paths to a given destination.
- The primary goal of redundancy is to eliminate as many single points of failure as possible.

Bridging Loops, Spanning Tree, BPDUs

- Bridging loops are caused by having multiple paths to a destination with a bridge on each of the parallel network segments.
- The Spanning Tree Protocol prevents bridging loops by logically disabling (blocking) one of the multiple paths.
- The four steps of Spanning Tree are:
    1. Election of the root bridge
    2. Election of the root ports
    3. Election of the designated ports
    4. Change of the port states
- A root port is a port on a bridge that is closest, in terms of cost, to the root bridge.
- A designated port is a port on a bridge that is designated to forward all traffic for a network segment that the bridge is attached to. It will be the closest, in terms of cost, to the root bridge.
- A BPDU is a multicast frame that contains all of the vital topology information about each sender that the bridges need to build and maintain the Spanning Tree.
- There are two types of BPDUs: Configuration BPDUs, and Topology change BPDUs.

- ❏ The bridge with the lowest bridge priority will become the root bridge. The bridge priority is part of the BID. The other part of the BID is the bridge's MAC address.
- ❏ The port with the lowest cost will become the root port.
- ❏ One port on a connected bridge will be elected the designated port for that network segment. The bridge that houses the designated port is also referred to as the designated bridge.
- ❏ There are five STP port states:
    1. Disabled
    2. Blocking
    3. Listening
    4. Learning
    5. Forwarding
- ❏ There are three STP timers:
    1. Hello Time
    2. Forward Delay
    3. Max Age
- ❏ Cisco switches allow you to run one instance of Spanning Tree per VLAN. This is referred to as PVST (Per VLAN Spanning Tree).

Fast EtherChannel

- ❏ Fast EtherChannel provides increased bandwidth, load balancing, and redundancy between network devices by allowing you to bundle multiple fast Ethernet ports together and treat them as a single link. Spanning Tree also treats the bundle as a single link.
- ❏ PAgP (Port Aggregation Protocol) complements Fast EtherChannel by automating the creation of Fast EtherChannel bundles.

PortFast, UplinkFast, BackboneFast

- ❏ PortFast should be enabled on ports that connect endstation devices (servers and workstations). It allows the port to essentially bypass the blocking, listening, and learning states, and immediately jump to the forwarding state.
- ❏ UplinkFast is a technology that allows a switch to detect and adjust to a directly connected link failure.
- ❏ BackboneFast is a technology that allows a switch to detect and adjust to an indirect (not directly connected) link failure.

Commands

- ❏ The set spantree command can be used to tune the Spanning Tree BID, cost, and timers settings.
- ❏ The show spantree command can be used to gain valuable information about your Spanning Tree configuration.
- ❏ The show port command is an excellent command to use to troubleshoot port status.

SELF TEST

The following questions will help you gauge your understanding of the material presented in this chapter. Read all the choices carefully, as there may be more than one correct answer. Choose all correct answers for each question.

Redundant Links

1. The primary goal of network link redundancy is to:
   A. Prevent network loops from occurring in situations where multiple paths exist on the network.
   B. Allow devices to sense link failures and alert the network administrators.
   C. Eliminate the possibility of any single component failure disrupting the end-users' ability to reach their intended destination.
   D. None of the above.

2. Which of the following are negative impacts of implementing network link redundancy? (Choose all that apply.)
   A. Adds a lot of complexity to network topology.
   B. Eliminates single points of failure on the network.
   C. Provides no fault tolerance.
   D. Can be cost prohibitive.

Bridging Loops, Spanning Tree, BPDUs

3. Which following BPDU field is the determining factor for STP's selection of the root bridge?
   A. Root path cost
   B. Port ID
   C. Sender BID
   D. Max Age

4. Which of the following is not one of the four steps involved in building a Spanning Tree?
   A. Election of designated ports
   B. Election of the root ports

C. Changing of the port states
D. Manually setting the STP timers
E. Election of the root bridge

5. Which of the following are STP port states? (Choose all that apply.)

   A. Learning
   B. Listening
   C. Flowing
   D. Forwarding
   E. Blocking

6. You attach a sniffer to your network and notice that every two seconds, a configuration BPDU is being transmitted from the root bridge of the Spanning Tree. What can you conclude from this?

   A. Spanning Tree is recalculating and reconverging every two seconds due to topology changes. This is causing major network problems.
   B. You will need more information than this in order to figure out the problem.
   C. There is a loop condition on the network.
   D. This is an indication that the network is perfectly healthy and that Spanning Tree is doing its job.

7. Which of the following definitions refers to a designated port?

   A. A port designated to be in the blocking state, eliminating the possibility of a loop.
   B. A port identified as the forwarding port for an individual network segment. It will be the closest port on the segment, in terms of cost, to the root bridge.
   C. A port on a bridge that is the closest, in terms of cost, to the root bridge.
   D. None of the above.

8. What is the main factor used to determine which port on a bridge will become the root port?

   A. BID
   B. The port's MAC address
   C. Root path cost
   D. Port ID

9. Which of the following can be considered contributing factors in the creation of network loops? (Choose all that apply.)
    A. Multiple links connected by bridges in parallel.
    B. The fact that bridges forward all broadcasts out of every port except for the port on which the broadcast was received.
    C. The fact that bridges forward all frames with a destination address that is unknown (not in the bridge table) out of every port except the port on which the frame was received.
    D. All of the above.

10. A new department has requested its own VLAN. You are asked if the new VLAN, VLAN 10, can have a customized STP topology separate from the other VLANS on the network. What should your reply be?
    A. No. We can only run one instance of Spanning Tree for all VLANs on the network.
    B. Yes. Cisco switches will allow us to create one instance of Spanning Tree per each individual VLAN (PVST). Each instance of Spanning Tree can have its own custom settings.
    C. There are no settings in Spanning Tree that can be customized.
    D. None of the above.

11. During which STP port state are the root ports and designated ports on the bridges elected?
    A. Blocking
    B. Learning
    C. Forwarding
    D. Listening

12. Which of the following statements about the Spanning Tree Protocol are true? (Choose all that apply.)
    A. STP was originally developed by DEC.
    B. STP is defined in the IEEE 802.1d standard.
    C. The DEC version of STP and the IEEE version are fully compatible.
    D. STP guarantees multiple active physical paths between network devices.

Fast EtherChannel

13. Your boss wants to increase the amount of bandwidth between the two main switches on your network. There is currently one 100-Mbps port on each switch connecting the two switches. He would also like to provide redundancy on this link. What would your suggestion be?

    A. Configure the switch for BackboneFast.
    B. Configure a multilink Fast EtherChannel bundle between the two switches.
    C. Configure the switch for UplinkFast.
    D. It can't be done; make due with what you have.

14. What two devices are responsible for managing link failures and load distribution on a Fast EtherChannel bundle?

    A. EARL (Early AdSdress Recognition Logic).
    B. RSM (Route Switch Module).
    C. EBC (Ethernet Bundle Controller).
    D. FEC (Fast EtherChannel Controller).

PortFast, UplinkFast, BackboneFast

15. It is brought to your attention that a new workstation on your network cannot seem to connect. Spanning Tree is enabled on your network. You have determined that the port for the workstation is enabled, and the workstation's network configuration is correct. What next step would you take to allow this new workstation to connect?

    A. Enable PortFast on the port that the workstation is connected to.
    B. Enable UplinkFast on the port that the workstation is connected to.
    C. Replace the network interface card in the workstation.
    D. Disable Spanning Tree.

16. You are asked if there is a way to speed up the Spanning Tree recalculation and reconvergence process in the event of indirect link failures, for all of the switches on the network. What would be the best way to accomplish this?

    A. Enable BackboneFast on all of the switches.
    B. Enable PortFast on every port on every switch on the network.
    C. Enable UplinkFast on all of the switches on the network.
    D. Configure Fast EtherChannel bundles between all the switches on the network.

Commands

17. You want to specify that a certain switch will become the Spanning Tree root switch for VLAN 10. What command would you type on the switch to make this happen?

   A. Spantree root

   B. Set spantree root 10

   C. Set spantree root

   D. Set switch root 10

18. What command can be used to aid in troubleshooting a particular port's status on a set command-based switch (IOS or SET based)?

   A. Show port *mod #/port #*

   B. Show port status

   C. Show spantree port

   D. Show spantree

19. You are asked to check the status of UplinkFast on the switches that have UplinkFast enabled. Your switch is a set command-based switch. What command can you use to accomplish this?

   A. Show spantree uplinkfast

   B. Show uplinkfast status

   C. Show uplinkfast

   D. Show spantree

20. You need to find out which switch is the designated root switch for the Spanning Tree. What would be the best command to use to make this determination on a set command-based switch?

   A. Show Spantree Config

   B. Show Root

   C. Show Port

   D. Show Spantree

LAB EXERCISE

Refer to the sample network in Figure 4-11.

FIGURE 4-11 Sample network

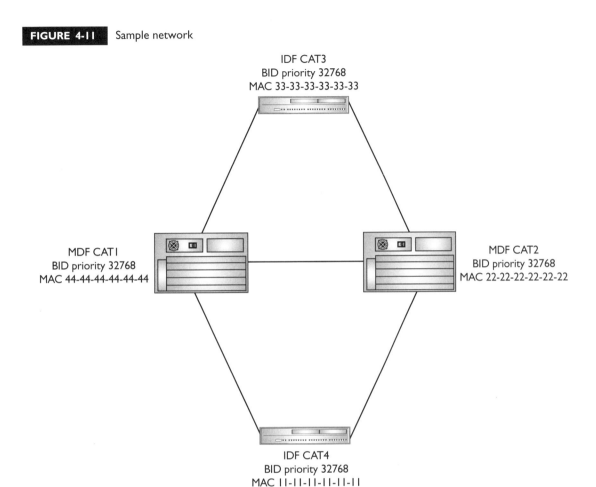

The two MDF (Main Distribution Facility) switches are in the primary communications room of the building. MDFs are typically the central point of a star network topology.

The two IDF (Intermediate Distribution Facility) switches are located in two separate closets on different floors in the building. An IDF is typically a secondary communications room or closet in a star network topology.

Assume that all links are Fast Ethernet.

Based on the information provided, label the root bridge, root ports, designated ports, forwarding ports, and blocked ports for Spanning Tree.

After you are finished labeling, try to think of some ways that this STP implementation could be optimized. Think about what was discussed in the chapter, and jot down some ideas.

SELF TEST ANSWERS

Redundant Links

1. ☑ **C.** The primary goal of network link redundancy is to eliminate the possibility that a single component failure will disrupt the end-users' ability to reach their intended destination.
   ☒ **A** is incorrect because preventing network loops is the job of the Spanning Tree Protocol. **B** is incorrect because devices sensing link failures and alerting network administrators is not the primary goal of network link redundancy. **D**, none of the above, is incorrect because there is a correct choice.

2. ☑ **A, D.** Network link redundancy adds a lot of complexity to the network topology and can be cost prohibitive.
   ☒ **B** is incorrect because eliminating single points of failure is one of the positive impacts of implementing network link redundancy. **C** is incorrect because network link redundancy does provide fault tolerance.

Bridging Loops, Spanning Tree, BPDUs

3. ☑ **C.** Spanning Tree looks at the sender BID field of every BPDU on the network in order to elect the root bridge. The BID field is actually comprised of the sending bridge's priority and the sending bridge's MAC address. The bridge with the lowest priority will become the root bridge. In the event of a tie, the bridge with the lowest MAC address will be used to determine the root.
   ☒ **A** is incorrect because the root path cost field is used to elect root ports and designated ports. **B** is incorrect because the port ID field simply identifies the port on which the BPDU left the transmitting bridge. **D** is incorrect because the Max Age field defines the maximum time that a BPDU will be saved for a port.

4. ☑ **D.** You can manually set the STP timers if you wish to tune your Spanning Tree implementation; however, it is not one of the four steps involved in building the Spanning Tree.
   ☒ **A, B, C,** and **E** are incorrect because they are the four steps involved in building the Spanning Tree

5. ☑ **A, B, D, E** are all STP port states.
   ☒ **C** is incorrect because flowing is not an STP port state.

6. ☑ **D.** Once Spanning Tree has converged, you will see BPDUs from the root bridge every two seconds (default hello time). This is a healthy network.
   ☒ **A** is incorrect because a configuration BPDU does not indicate topology changes or recalculation and reconvergence. That is the job of the TCN (Topology Change Notification)

Self Test Answers **219**

BPDU. **B** is incorrect because you have all of the information you need to deduce that there is no problem. **C** is incorrect because BPDUs will not indicate a loop condition.

7. ☑ **B.** A designated port is a port assigned to forward traffic for a particular network segment.
   ☒ **A** is incorrect because the port in blocking state is simply referred to as the blocked port. **C** is incorrect because it defines a root port on a bridge. **D** is incorrect.

8. ☑ **C.** The port with the lowest root path cost will become the root port for the bridge.
   ☒ **A** is incorrect because the BID is the main determining factor for the selection of the root bridge. **B** is incorrect because the port's MAC address is not used to determine root port assignments. **D** is incorrect because the port ID simply identifies the port.

9. ☑ **D. A, B,** and **C** can all be considered contributing factors in the creation of network loops.
   ☒ There are no incorrect choices.

10. ☑ **B.** Running Per VLAN Spanning Tree (PVST) will allow you to satisfy the request.
    ☒ **A** is incorrect because Cisco switches are capable of running one instance of STP per VLAN. **C** is incorrect because there are many tunable settings in Spanning Tree. **D** is incorrect.

11. ☑ **D.** During the listening state, the root ports and designated ports are identified and elected.
    ☒ **A, B,** and **C** are incorrect; they are simply three other STP port states.

12. ☑ **A, B.** STP was originally developed by DEC, and evolved into the IEEE 802.1d standard.
    ☒ **C** is incorrect because the DEC version and the IEEE version of STP are not compatible with one another. **D** is incorrect because STP guarantees that only one physical path between network devices will be active.

Fast EtherChannel

13. ☑ **B.** Configuring a multilink Fast EtherChannel bundle between the two switches will satisfy both requirements. It will provide increased bandwidth and fault tolerance on the link.
    ☒ **A** is incorrect because BackboneFast is enabled on a switch to allow the switch to sense and adjust to indirect link failures. **C** is incorrect because UplinkFast is enabled on a switch to allow the switch to sense and adjust to directly connected link failures. **D** is incorrect, and probably not the answer your boss would want to hear.

14. ☑ **A, C.** The EARL and EBC are responsible for managing link failures and load distribution on the Fast EtherChannel bundle.
    ☒ **B** is incorrect because the RSM is responsible for routing between VLANs on a switch. **D** is incorrect because no such device exists.

PortFast, UplinkFast, BackboneFast

15. ☑ **A.** Enabling PortFast on the workstation's port will resolve the issue. The workstation needs access to the network before the STP port is placed into the forwarding state. PortFast will allow the port to bypass the blocking, listening, and learning states, and jump right to the forwarding state so the workstation will be able to communicate on the network.
    ☒ **B** is incorrect because UplinkFast is enabled on a switch to allow the switch to sense and adjust to a directly connected link failure. **C** is incorrect because you had already determined that the workstation's network configuration is correct. **D** is incorrect because disabling Spanning Tree on your network will result in creating loop conditions on the network, which would prevent all workstations and servers from communicating.

16. ☑ **A.** BackboneFast will allow indirect link failure information to propagate through the network much more quickly. BackboneFast can be enabled on all switches on the network.
    ☒ **B** is incorrect. PortFast allows a port to bypass the blocking, listening, and learning states, and should only be enabled on ports that are connected to end-user devices. **C** is incorrect because UplinkFast can only detect directly connected link failures. It should only be enabled on access layer devices. **D** is incorrect. Although this may speed up the network overall, it is not the best way to approach the problem.

Commands

17. ☑ **B.** Set spantree root 10 will designate the switch to be the root bridge for VLAN 10.
    ☒ **A** is incorrect because it is an invalid command. **C** is incorrect because the command would set the switch to be the root for VLAN 1, because if no VLAN is specified, it defaults to VLAN 1. **D** is incorrect because it is an invalid command.

18. ☑ **A.** Show port specifying the module and port number will help in troubleshooting a particular port's status on a set command-based switch.
    ☒ **B** and **C** are incorrect because they are invalid commands. **D** is incorrect; although show spantree will return some port information, show port is much more detailed.

19. ☑ **A.** Show spantree uplinkfast will display the status of UplinkFast on a set command-based switch.
    ☒ **B** and **C** are incorrect because they are invalid commands. **D** is incorrect because show spantree will not display any UplinkFast information.

20. ☑ **D.** The show spantree command will return a lot of information about the Spanning Tree configuration, including the designated root MAC address.

☒ **A** and **B** are incorrect because they are not valid commands. **C** is incorrect because the show port command returns information about a specified port or all ports on a switch.

LAB ANSWER

Refer to Figure 4-12.

Notice first that because all links are Fast Ethernet, I've labeled the cost of 19 to each network segment. Now let's step through the STP process.

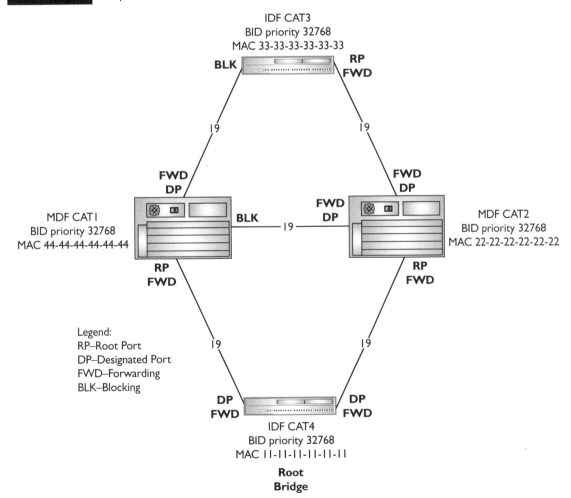

FIGURE 4-12 Sample network

1. **Elect a root bridge.** Look at the BID priority of each switch. They have all been left at the default; therefore, the MAC address is used to determine the root bridge. IDF CAT 4 has the lowest MAC address. It becomes the root bridge for the Spanning Tree.

2. **Election of root ports.** Every bridge that is not the root bridge must elect one port to be the root port for the bridge. Cost is the determining factor. MDF Cat1 and MDF Cat2 are pretty straightforward. Both root ports have a cost of 19. If you look at the other ports on Cat1 and Cat2, you'll notice that the costs are higher.

   IDF Cat3 is where this gets interesting. Notice that both of its ports receive a BPDU with a cost of 38 (19+19). It will look at the sender's BID field of each BPDU to make that determination. The sending bridge's priorities are the same, so it resorts to the MAC address. In that case, the BPDU that came from MDF Cat2 wins out (lowest MAC) and the port on IDF Cat3 that is attached to MDF Cat2 becomes the root port.

3. **Election of designated ports.** Each network segment must designate a port to forward all traffic for that segment. Look at each segment. What ports are directly connected to the segment? Which port has the lowest cost? This is pretty simple for the two bottom segments. The root bridge is directly connected to them; therefore, the ports on the root bridge are the designated ports for each of those segments.

   The two top segments are also pretty obvious. The tricky segment is the segment connecting MDF Cat1 and MDF Cat2. Again, the costs are equal. STP looks to the BID and settles on MDF Cat2 as the designated port for the segment due to its lower MAC address.

4. **Changing of the port states.** All ports that are either designated ports or root ports transition to the forwarding state. The ports that are neither a root port nor a designated port are put back into a blocking state. We have two blocked ports: IDF Cat3 the left port is blocked, and MDF Cat1 the right port is blocked. These two blocked ports eliminate any possible loops on the network. Remember, STP will block one port per physical loop. In Figure 4-12, there are two physical loops; therefore, STP needed to block two ports in order to eliminate these loops. Notice the single active path.

   Some ways in which this design could be optimized include:

   - You could modify the BID of one of the MDF switches, forcing it to become the root bridge. This would probably not be a bad idea, given the fact that the MDFs are centrally located on the network.

   - You could create a Fast EtherChannel bundle between the two MDFs to increase the bandwidth, and provide load balancing and redundancy between the two MDFs.

- You could enable PortFast on all of the ports connected to end-user workstations and servers on the network.
- If the design were left as is, you could enable UplinkFast on IDF Cat3 and MDF Cat1 to speed up STP convergence in the event of a directly connected link failure.
- You could also enable BackboneFast on all of the switches to speed up STP convergence in the event of a indirectly connected link failure.

You may have come up with some other ideas, as there are many different ways to fine-tune this Spanning Tree implementation. My hope is that this lab at least got you thinking along those lines.

If you had any trouble with this exercise, try going through it while referring back to the text in the chapter.

If you have access to sufficient lab equipment, try to implement this exercise in the lab environment. This will help solidify your understanding of the material covered in this chapter.

5
InterVLAN Routing Concepts

CERTIFICATION OBJECTIVES

5.01   InterVLAN Environments
5.02   Internal Route Processors
5.03   Commands
✓   Two-Minute Drill
Q&A   Self Test

The purpose of switches versus hubs is to better manage bandwidth in a broadcast domain by building a table of Media Access Control (MAC) addresses within the switching environment. As we discussed before, all these functions take place at Layer 2, the Data Link layer of the Open System Interconnection (OSI) model. Since switches flood broadcasts throughout the broadcast domain, replacing hubs with switches does not improve a situation where the amount of broadcast traffic hinders network operations. On of the key methods of reducing broadcast traffic in a large network is to fragment large broadcast domains into smaller ones and to place routers at their boundaries to enable communications between them. This brings a new element into switched internetworking: intervlan routing

InterVLAN routers, unlike switches, operate at Layer 3 of the OSI model, the Network layer. The Network layer makes use of network addresses in order to reach the destination system. This chapter covers the basics of network layer routing, and more specifically, how it applies to a switched intervlan environment. We will look at how routers are used to fragment large broadcast domains, and how specialized router platforms can be used to maximize routing functions by leveraging the capabilities of powerful switching engines like the Cisco Catalyst 5000 and 6000 series switch.

CERTIFICATION OBJECTIVE 5.01

InterVLAN Environments

In Chapter 3, "Virtual Local Area Networks (VLANs)," we discussed how switches can alleviate bandwidth problems by microsegmenting broadcast domains and carrying information only to the required switch ports. Switches, however, are still subject to broadcast traffic. Each VLAN created on a Catalyst switch represents a different broadcast domain. When a broadcast is sent on a broadcast domain, every node within the domain receives a copy of the broadcast frame. In a switching environment, the Catalyst engine accomplishes this by flooding the broadcast to every port associated with that VLAN. Every broadcast frame transmitted within a broadcast domain still needs to be flooded to every port in the domain. This can lead to reduced throughputs when the level of broadcast becomes excessive. The traditional method of reducing broadcast traffic is to fragment the broadcast domain into separate networks and to place routers at the boundary of each network. This restricts the propagation of broadcasts to the network on which they originated. Figure 5-1 shows the result of a network fragmentation.

Network fragmentation succeeds in limiting the propagation of broadcasts throughout the entire network. What, however, is the resulting effect on network communications? That depends on the protocol operating in the environment. Broadcast-based protocols such as Microsoft's NetBEUI are no longer capable of operating within the newly fragmented environment. Other routable protocols, such as TCP/IP, Novell IPX, or AppleTalk can be adapted to work in the new environment. What exactly has changed? All of a sudden, only nodes within a common domain can reach each other through broadcasts. NetBEUI uses broadcasts to reach other nodes. Such a protocol cannot be used in a routed environment because it does not use a Layer 3 network address. *Routed* protocols (not to be confused with *routing* protocols) can operate beyond the boundaries of a broadcast domain. Since a destination system is no longer directly accessible through the use of a destination MAC address in the broadcast domain, a new, higher-level mechanism needs to be put in place to enable the information to flow logically to the appropriate network and reach its target. This is done at Layer 3 through the use of Network layer protocols.

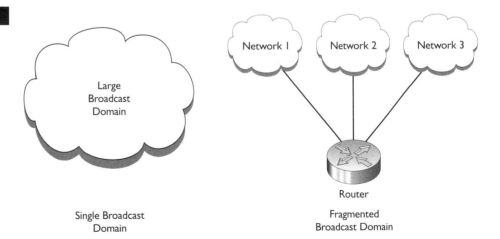

FIGURE 5-1

The result of network fragmentation

Remember that switching functions are performed at Layer 2 of the OSI protocol. Switches use MAC addresses to make decisions and encapsulate the information in a frame. Routing functions are performed at Layer 3 of the OSI protocol. Routers use routing tables to make decisions and encapsulate the information in a packet. We will also cover a special case in which packets at Layer 3 are switched directly by the Catalyst engine. This Layer 3 switching process is often referred to as routing.

Network layer information is used to route packets to their destination. The newly fragmented networks each have distinct network numbers that the routers can use to direct the flow of packets by using a routing table. Similar to a MAC address table, a routing table maps network numbers to an outbound router port or a next-hop destination router. An extensive explanation of routing and routing protocols is beyond the scope of this text. It is important, however, to understand the basic mechanism of routing (Layer 3) and its interaction with switching (Layer 2). We will concentrate our efforts on TCP/IP, since it is the most widely used network protocol today.

CERTIFICATION OBJECTIVE 5.02

Basic Routing Operations

When configuring a network endstation for TCP/IP operations, the three most important parameters are as follows:

- The IP address
- The subnet mask
- The default gateway

All other parameters, such as Domain Name Server (DNS) and Windows Internet Naming Service (WINS) server are complimentary services that run over TCP/IP. How does a node, being a computer, router, or any network-aware device, communicate with another node? In TCP/IP, the end-to-end communication occurs as discussed in the following section.

Network Communication Within a Common Network

Within a common network segment, node-to-node communication is accomplished without the use of a router. Unlike NetBEUI, where the entire communication is accomplished using broadcasts, unicast communication is accomplished by using the destination IP address. Keep in mind that the flow of communication must still traverse the lower layers of the OSI model before being transmitted across the wire. The following is the process used by the two nodes in Figure 5-2 that are communicating over a common segment:

Node A (Source)   IP: 172.21.1.1   subnet mask: 255.255.0.0

Node B (Destination)   IP: 172.21.1.5   subnet mask: 255.255.0.0

1. Node A examines the destination IP address of Node B and compares it to its own. Using the subnet mask, Node A determines that Node B is within its own network. The use of the default gateway will therefore not be necessary.

2. Node A sends an Address Resolution Protocol (ARP) broadcast, requesting that the node corresponding to IP address 10.1.1.2 send back its MAC address. Node B responds to Node A with its own MAC address. Node A now has an entry in its ARP table for Node B. An example of the output of an ARP table on a Microsoft Windows client is shown in Figure 5-3. Notice how the Layer 3 network address is mapped against a Layer 2 MAC address.

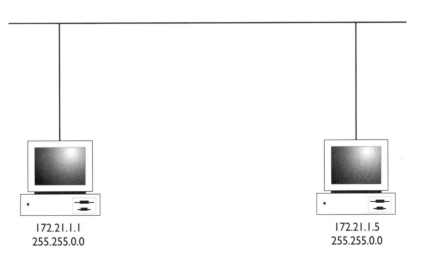

FIGURE 5-2

Two nodes on a common network

FIGURE 5-3

The ARP table of a Microsoft Windows client

```
C:\WINDOWS>arp -a
No ARP Entries Found

C:\WINDOWS>ping 172.21.1.5

Pinging 172.21.1.5 with 32 bytes of data:

Reply from 172.21.1.5: bytes=32 time=1ms TTL=128
Reply from 172.21.1.5: bytes=32 time<10ms TTL=128
Reply from 172.21.1.5: bytes=32 time<10ms TTL=128
Reply from 172.21.1.5: bytes=32 time<10ms TTL=128

Ping statistics for 172.21.1.5:
    Packets: Sent = 4, Received = 4, Lost = 0 (0% loss),
Approximate round trip times in milli-seconds:
    Minimum = 0ms, Maximum =  1ms, Average =  0ms

C:\WINDOWS>arp -a

Interface: 172.21.1.2 on Interface 0x3000004
  Internet Address      Physical Address      Type
  172.21.1.5            00-a0-c9-c9-13-c5     dynamic

C:\WINDOWS>
```

3. Node A encapsulates the data it needs to transmit to Node B into a Layer 3 IP packet and passes the packet to Layer 2. Notice how at Layer 3, units of transmissions are referred to as *packets*.

4. Layer 2 accepts the packet from Layer 3 and encapsulates the packet into a frame. It then places the frame on the wire for all the nodes to inspect.

5. All the nodes, including Node B, receive the frame and examine the destination MAC address. If the address matches its own MAC address, the node strips the frame encapsulation and passes the resulting packet up to Layer 3.

6. At Layer 3, the node looks at the destination IP address and compares it to its own. It recognizes its own IP address, strips the packet encapsulation, and passes the resulting data to the upper layers.

This simple process seems to make the use of a Layer 3 IP address unnecessary, since a match occurs at Layer 2 with the destination MAC address. This is only true, however, in a single-segment environment. We will now examine the same process in a multiple network environment using a default gateway.

Network Communication Between Multiple Networks

When going from one network to another, the communication needs to flow through one or more routers. The following parameters are used for the routers shown in Figure 5-4:

Node A (Source) IP: 172.21.1.1 subnet mask: 255.255.0.0
  Default Gateway: 172.21.1.6

Node B (Destination) IP: 10.32.128.1 subnet mask: 255.255.0.0
  Default Gateway: 10.32.128.6

1. Node A examines the destination IP address of Node B and compares it to its own. Using the subnet mask, Node A determines that Node B is not within its own network. The use of the default gateway will therefore be necessary.

2. Node A knows that in order to reach the destination node, it needs to send the information to its default gateway. Node A sends an ARP request for IP address 172.21.1.6, the IP address of the default gateway router.

3. The default gateway router recognizes its own MAC address in the ARP request and responds to Node A with its MAC address. Node A places the MAC address of the default gateway in its ARP table.

FIGURE 5-4

Two nodes on different segments

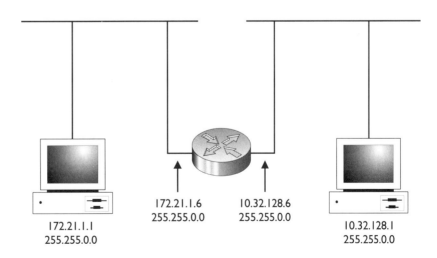

4. Node A encapsulates the information into a Layer 3 IP packet with a source IP address of 172.21.1.1 and a destination IP address of 10.32.128.1, and passes the packet to Layer 2.

5. Layer 2 encapsulates the packet into a frame with its own MAC as the source address, and the MAC address of the router as the destination MAC address. Note that at Layer 2, the destination MAC is the address of the default gateway, not the MAC address of the destination node. This is because the destination node could not respond to an ARP request since it is not on the same broadcast segment. Node A places the frame on the wire for every node on the segment to examine.

6. The router recognizes its destination MAC address, strips the frame encapsulation, and sends the resulting packet to the Network layer.

7. At the Network layer, the router examines the destination IP address. In this case, the destination IP address is not the IP address of the router, but the IP address of the destination node. The router performs a lookup in its routing table and finds that network 10.32.128.0 is directly connected to one of its Ethernet interfaces. This is where the routing decision is made.

8. The router passes the packet back to Layer 2 so it can transmit it on that Ethernet segment.

9. Layer 2 of the router encapsulates the packet once more and places its own MAC address as the source address, and the destination node's MAC address as the destination MAC address. It then places the frame on the new segment for every node to listen to.

10. Node B receives the frame and recognizes its destination MAC address. It strips the frame encapsulation and passes the remaining IP packet to Layer 3. Layer 3 compares the destination IP address and confirms that it is indeed the intended destination of the information. It strips the packet encapsulation and passes the remaining information to the upper layers for processing. Note how the source and destination IP addresses never change throughout the journey, while the source and destination MAC addresses change from hop to hop.

Figure 5-5 shows the flow of information between Node A and Node B in a fragmented network environment. Pay attention to the Source Address (SA) and the Destination Address (DA) for the MAC addresses and the network addresses. Notice

Basic Routing Operations **233**

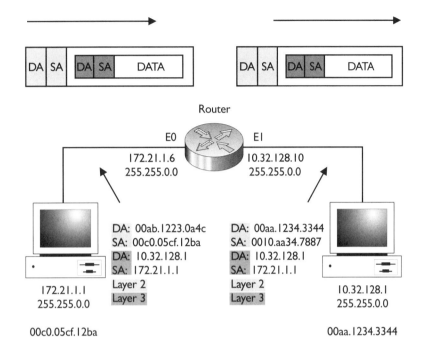

FIGURE 5-5

Information flow in a fragmented network

which ones change from hop to hop and which remain constant throughout the journey of a packet.

EXERCISE 5-1

Finding the Correct Address

In Figure 5-5, when Node A pings Node B, the pings come back as successful. You know that you have IP connectivity between the two nodes. Can you identify what should be contained in the ARP table of Node A?

Answer: Since Node B is on a different network, Node A will send the information to the default gateway. In order to do so, it needs the MAC address corresponding to the router's IP address on its subnet. This is the default gateway for that node. Since the node cannot send the packet directly to the destination address, it needs to hand the packet to the router. The node sends an ARP request on the segment, requesting the MAC address corresponding to IP address 172.21.1.6. Once it receives the ARP reply from the router with the proper MAC address, it puts the information in a frame with the router's MAC address as MAC DA. The resulting ARP table therefore shows the router's MAC address to IP address mapping, not the MAC address of Node B. Node A will never show MAC addresses belonging to nodes that are not on the same broadcast domain. This is because ARP requests are broadcasts, and these broadcasts cannot go beyond the boundary of the router.

Legacy Routing Environments

Fragmenting large broadcast domains into smaller networks to alleviate broadcast issues is nothing new. The traditional method of achieving this is to separate users on different hubs and to place a router between them. Whenever a broadcast domain is fragmented into smaller networks, each node on those new networks needs to be given a new network address corresponding to the network it is on. This used to be a huge and painful task on legacy TCP/IP networks, for each node had to be assigned a new, unique IP address. Nowadays, mechanisms such as Dynamic Host Configuration Protocol (DHCP) automate this process, making the fragmentation process much less difficult. Other routed protocols such as Novell's Internet Packet eXchange (IPX) protocol and Apple Computer's AppleTalk include automatic host network address configuration as an integral part of the protocol. Fragmenting broadcast domains using these protocols is much easier than with TCP/IP. What are the limitations of this process? The primary limitation is of a physical nature. All of a sudden, users need to be connected to the hubs belonging to their own network. This limits the geographic location of users and forces them to operate in a specific location in order to be in the appropriate network. The second limitation is the level of fragmentation allowed by the router. For each new network created, legacy routers need one physical interface connected to that network. The only way for network communication to occur from one network to another is through a router. This means that the level of fragmentation is limited by the router hardware itself. Once all the interfaces on a router have been used, another network cannot be added without either upgrading the router itself or going to a more higher-end router platform. The fragmented broadcast domain shown in Figure 5-1 is a very good example of a legacy router serving individual networks. The following code output shows the configuration of the legacy router shown in Figure 5-5. Since this chapter deals mostly with routing, all of the commands shown will be IOS-based commands unless otherwise specified.

```
Cisco-2514#conf t
Enter configuration commands, one per line.  End with CNTL/Z.
Cisco-2514(config)#interface ethernet 0
Cisco-2514(config-if)#ip address 172.21.1.6 255.255.0.0
Cisco-2514(config-if)#no shutdown
Cisco-2514(config-if)#
6w1d: %LINK-3-UPDOWN: Interface Ethernet0, changed state to up
6w1d: %LINEPROTO-5-UPDOWN: Line protocol on Interface Ethernet0,
 changed state to up
Cisco-2514(config-if)#interface ethernet 1
Cisco-2514(config-if)#ip address 10.32.128.10 255.255.0.0
Cisco-2514(config-if)#no shutdown
Cisco-2514(config-if)#
6w1d: %LINK-3-UPDOWN: Interface Ethernet1, changed state to up
Cisco-2514(config-if)#end
Cisco-2514#
6w1d: %SYS-5-CONFIG_I: Configured from console by console
Cisco-2514#
Cisco-2514#ping 172.21.1.6

Type escape sequence to abort.
Sending 5, 100-byte ICMP Echos to 172.21.1.6, timeout is 2 seconds:
!!!!!
Success rate is 100 percent (5/5), round-trip min/avg/max = 4/4/4 ms
Cisco-2514#show arp
Protocol  Address          Age (min)  Hardware Addr   Type   Interface
Internet  10.32.128.10        -       0060.4740.fc83  ARPA   Ethernet1
Internet  172.21.1.1          0       00e0.1e42.bbae  ARPA   Ethernet0
Internet  172.21.1.6          -       0060.4740.fc82  ARPA   Ethernet0
Cisco-2514#
Cisco-2514#show ip route
Codes: C - connected, S - static, I - IGRP, R - RIP, M - mobile, B - BGP
       D - EIGRP, EX - EIGRP external, O - OSPF, IA - OSPF inter area
       N1 - OSPF NSSA external type 1, N2 - OSPF NSSA external type 2
       E1 - OSPF external type 1, E2 - OSPF external type 2, E - EGP
       i - IS-IS, L1 - IS-IS level-1, L2 - IS-IS level-2, * - candidate default
       U - per-user static route, o - ODR

Gateway of last resort is not set

C    172.21.0.0/16 is directly connected, Ethernet0
C    10.32.0.0/16 is directly connected, Ethernet1
Cisco-2514#
```

Notice how the routing table shows that the router is aware of both networks 172.21.0.0 and 10.32.0.0. Each network has an outbound interface associated with it, enabling the router to make a routing decision based on the destination IP address of a packet.

Router-on-a-Stick

People normally use the terms *network* and *broadcast domain* interchangeably. This is not accurate. Generally, each IP network is deployed on a separate broadcast domain. The broadcast of a node on Network A will not reach the interface of any node on Network B because of the router placed between them. There is a special case, however, where multiple IP networks coexist on a common broadcast domain. In this case, broadcasts from one network will reach nodes on all the other networks since they essentially live on the same wire. All the nodes on the segment will examine the packet at Layer 2 and pass it up to Layer 3, since the destination MAC address was the broadcast address (ffff.ffff.ffff). Layer 3 processes the packet, determines that the packet came from a different IP network, and discards it. Even though the nodes on the various IP networks do not communicate directly with each other, they are still subject to broadcast-related problems emanating from the other networks.

In order for separate IP networks to talk to each other, a router is still required, even though the networks reside on the same segment. In this case, the router does not have individual interfaces in the various segments; instead, it has a single interface on the broadcast domain that responds to multiple IP addresses. The router therefore receives packets from Network A on its interface, makes a routing decision, and places the packet back onto the same segment for Network B. The term *router-on-a-stick* refers to a router that serves multiple networks out of a common interface. The name originates from the fact that on a network diagram, that router looks like a lollipop connected to a segment. Figure 5-6 shows two networks on a common broadcast domain, connected together using a router-on-a-stick.

A solid network design normally avoids this type of configuration, primarily because it makes each network subject to broadcast problems originating in the other networks sharing the broadcast domain. It is sometimes necessary to use such methods to accommodate temporary situations. For example, when a company

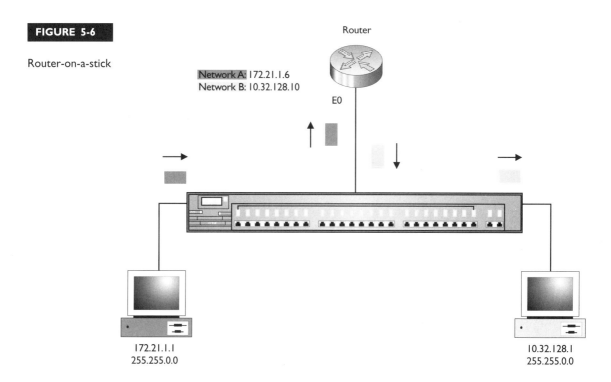

FIGURE 5-6

Router-on-a-stick

upgrades its Novell network, it may be required to change IPX encapsulations. IPX has four methods of encapsulating Ethernet packets: ETHERNET_II, ETHERNET_802.3, ETHERNET_802.2, and ETHERNET_SNAP. Different versions of the Novell Network Operating System use different kinds of encapsulation. Nodes using different encapsulations, however, cannot communicate directly with each other. Therefore, when upgrading a large Novell network, it is often necessary to upgrade systems incrementally. This means that different types of encapsulation can coexist on the same broadcast domain for the duration of the upgrade period. During that time, should connectivity be required between the old and new networks, a router-on-a-stick is often used to provide temporary connectivity between the two networks.

The configuration of a router-on-a-stick involves the use of a secondary network address on the same interface. The syntax is similar to declaring a primary network address, except for the *secondary* keyword added to the command line. The following code example shows the configuration of the router-on-a-stick in Figure 5-6. Notice how the routing table shows both networks as directly connected to interface Ethernet 0.

```
Cisco-2514#conf t
Enter configuration commands, one per line.  End with CNTL/Z.
Cisco-2514(config)#interface ethernet 0
Cisco-2514(config-if)#no shutdown
Cisco-2514(config-if)#ip address 172.21.1.6 255.255.0.0
Cisco-2514(config-if)#ip address 10.32.128.10 255.255.0.0 secondary
Cisco-2514(config-subif)#end
Cisco-2514#
Cisco-2514#show ip route
Codes: C - connected, S - static, I - IGRP, R - RIP, M - mobile, B - BGP
       D - EIGRP, EX - EIGRP external, O - OSPF, IA - OSPF inter area
       N1 - OSPF NSSA external type 1, N2 - OSPF NSSA external type 2
       E1 - OSPF external type 1, E2 - OSPF external type 2, E - EGP
       i - IS-IS, L1 - IS-IS level-1, L2 - IS-IS level-2, * - candidate default
       U - per-user static route, o - ODR

Gateway of last resort is not set

C    172.21.0.0/16 is directly connected, Ethernet0
     10.0.0.0/16 is subnetted, 1 subnets
C       10.32.0.0 is directly connected, Ethernet0
Cisco-2514#
```

on the job

A router-on-a-stick can solve temporary topology issues, but should not normally be used as a permanent routing solution. An exception to this would be a large flat network with hundreds of nodes, low broadcast traffic, and multiple different Class C addresses, based on availability, requiring routing for interconnection. By having all the nodes on a common broadcast domain, the router-on-a-stick approach negates the advantages of having multiple networks separated by a router. It is important to know the capabilities of routers, but is even more important to understand the importance of a proper network design.

VLAN Routing Environments

In an office building, if the network is fragmented among floors, the process is usually simple. Each hub on each floor belongs to a different network, and all the nodes on that floor are members of the same network. In today's network environments, however, workgroups rather than building floors drive network topologies. We saw in Chapter 3 how VLANs and trunking-capable switches can be used to provide that level of flexibility. Legacy routers can easily integrate to VLAN environments by having a physical interface in each VLAN. Figure 5-7 shows the integration of a legacy router in an InterVLAN environment.

This restores the flexibility of deploying VLAN ports throughout the network topology, with the legacy router providing connectivity between each VLAN. The disadvantage is that the legacy router consumes one switch port per VLAN. In an environment with a large number of VLANs, the number of physical router interfaces can become an issue. Furthermore, all InterVLAN communication must go through the physical links connecting the router to the VLANs. In a Token Ring

FIGURE 5-7

Legacy routing in a VLAN environment

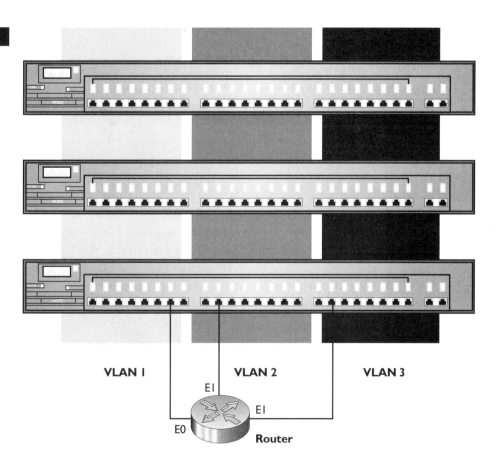

environment, for example, this would limit the entire intervlan traffic to 16 Mbps. In a network topology where a server farm resides on a separate VLAN with multiple client VLANs trying to access its resources, this can create a significant bottleneck, hindering network efficiency. The following is a sample configuration of an external router with physical interfaces connected to different segments on a switch, providing routing services between the VLANs.

```
Cisco-7206#conf t
Enter configuration commands, one per line.  End with CNTL/Z.
Cisco-7206(config)#interface ethernet 0/0
Cisco-7206(config-if)#no shutdown
Cisco-7206(config-if)#ip address 172.20.1.1 255.255.0.0
Cisco-7206(config-if)#exit
Cisco-7206(config)#interface ethernet 0/1
Cisco-7206(config-if)#no shutdown
Cisco-7206(config-if)#ip address 172.21.1.1 255.255.0.0
Cisco-7206(config-if)#exit
Cisco-7206(config)#interface ethernet 0/2
Cisco-7206(config-if)#no shutdown
Cisco-7206(config-if)#ip address 172.22.1.6 255.255.0.0
Cisco-7206(config-if)#
Cisco-7206(config-if)#end
Cisco-7206#
```

External Trunking Routers

One way to alleviate the port count on an external router is to use a router interface that supports trunking. Many high-end Cisco routers such as the Cisco 4500 series and 7200 series can be equipped with 10/100 Mbps Ethernet interfaces that natively support Cisco Inter Switch Link (ISL) and IEEE 802.1q trunking. When used in trunking mode, these interfaces *must* operate in 100 Mbps mode. This enables the router to have a single trunk connection to the switch, and allows it to perform routing functions between any VLAN present on that switch. This means that for a network comprised of 50 VLANs, we no longer need a router with 50 Ethernet interfaces using 50 switch ports on a switch—one Ethernet trunk can provide the same level of connectivity. Figure 5-8 shows a trunking router in action.

This configuration looks very similar to the router-on-a-stick approach, but offers isolation between VLANs. This means that, unlike the router-on-a-stick, broadcasts from one VLAN do not affect or reach the other VLANs in the management domain. The trunking router can create virtual software interfaces to handle every VLAN present in the switch. This solves the physical interface requirement problem

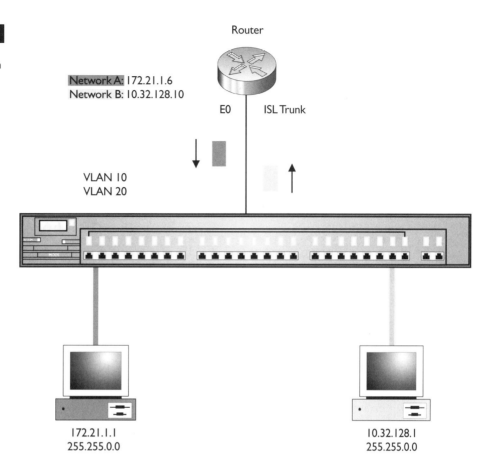

FIGURE 5-8

VLAN routing on an external trunking router

experienced by legacy routers when running multiple VLANs, but still presents the bandwidth problem of operating over a slow physical media. In fact, trunking routers create an even greater bottleneck, since *all* intervlan communications now go through a single connection. To improve throughput in these circumstances, Cisco Systems now provides optional 1000BaseSX Gigabit Ethernet modules that can operate at a speed of 1000 Mbps. Although this provides much-needed relief, it can still present a substantial bottleneck depending on the network computing needs.

The configuration of trunking routers requires the use of subinterfaces. Subinterfaces are virtual software interfaces that operate under the guidance of a major physical interface. The "ethernet 0" interface of a router, for example, can have multiple subinterfaces. These interfaces would be labeled "ethernet 0.1," "ethernet 0.2," and so on. The IOS considers these as individual interfaces, unlike the router-on-a-stick where the routing occurs on the same physical interface. In the case of a trunking router, each subinterface is programmed to access a specific VLAN in the management domain. The router must therefore be told which VLAN it needs to access, and which VLAN encapsulation to use. The following code shows the configuration of the trunking router shown in Figure 5-8. The encapsulation for each VLAN is ISL.

exam
ⓌatchThe only two types of encapsulation supported by routers are ISL for Ethernet and Token Ring networks, and Secure Data Exchange (SDE) for FDDI networks. IEEE 802.1q encapsulation is not supported by trunking routers.*

```
Cisco-7206#conf t
Enter configuration commands, one per line.  End with CNTL/Z.
Cisco-7206(config)#interface ethernet 0
Cisco-7206(config-if)#no shutdown
Cisco-7206(config-if)#interface ethernet 0.1
Cisco-7206(config-subif)#encapsulation isl 10
Cisco-7206(config-subif)#ip address 172.21.1.6 255.255.0.0
Cisco-7206(config-subif)#exit
Cisco-7206(config)#
Cisco-7206(config-if)#interface ethernet 0.2
Cisco-7206(config-subif)#encapsulation isl 20
Cisco-7206(config-subif)#ip address 10.32.128.10 255.255.0.0
Cisco-7206(config-subif)#end
Cisco-7206#
```

on the
ⒿobSubinterface numbers do not have to match the VLAN number. They are individual identifiers used to differentiate each subinterface. It is a good rule of thumb, however, to number them after the VLAN they support if possible. This simplifies troubleshooting and makes the configuration easier to understand.*

Internal Trunking Routers

The switching fabric speed of a high-end Cisco Catalyst switch ranges in the hundreds of Gigabits. Physical router interfaces do not come close to these speeds by multiple orders of magnitude. To take advantage of the speed of the switching fabric, Cisco developed routers that integrate directly in the chassis of the Catalyst switch. These routers interface directly with the backplane of the switch, accessing the VLANs at the speed of the switching fabric. These routers do not have any physical network interfaces connecting to the switch. Instead, virtual interfaces are created in the router's software to access any VLAN present on the host switch. The flexibility of creating practically any number of VLANs in a network environment is thereby extended to the router itself by enabling it to have virtual interfaces in each of these VLANs. The access speed of these virtual interfaces is no longer limited to the physical media used to connect them to the VLANs; instead, they approach the speed of the switching fabric on which the router connects to. These interfaces, although virtual, are configured and behave similarly to their physical counterparts. The next section concentrates on these internal route processors.

Now that you have a better understanding of routing in an intervlan environment, here are some possible scenario questions and their answers.

SCENARIO & SOLUTION

Are networks and broadcast domains the same?	No. Normally, a broadcast domain is associated with a single network, but there are situations when multiple networks reside on a common broadcast domain.
Will fragmenting a large broadcast domain into smaller VLANs and using an external trunking router to interconnect the newly formed fragments solve all broadcast related issues?	No, it may not. While the impact of broadcasts will be limited to a single VLAN, the ISL trunk used by the router might become congested by the broadcast it receives on that segment. This will impact the routing performance of the other VLANs supported by that ISL trunk.
How can a router help the transition from one IPX encapsulation to another, while maintaining network connectivity between the old and new networks?	A router-on-a-stick, which is a router with an interface configured with multiple network addresses, can adequately provide routing services between the two networks while nodes are being migrated to the new encapsulation.
How can an internal router provide routing services if it does not have physical interfaces to attach to each VLAN?	Internal routers use virtual interfaces to communicate directly with the switch. Since there is no hardware involved in the logical interfaces, a large number of virtual interfaces can be created to service every VLAN present on the switch.

CERTIFICATION OBJECTIVE 5.03

Internal Route Processors

Cisco provides optional internal routers for all of its high-end Catalyst switches. These "on-board" routers provide routing functions for all the VLANs in the management domain of the switch they are connected to. The backplane of the switch feeds the router directly at Gigabit speeds. The following is a list of Cisco Catalyst switches that can accommodate a directly attached router module:

- **Cisco Catalyst 5000 Series** Router Switch Module (RSM), or a Router Switch Feature Card (RSFC).
- **Cisco Catalyst 6000 Series** Multilayer Switch Module (MSM), or a Multilayer Switch Feature Card (MSFC).
- **Cisco Catalyst 8500 Campus Switch Router (CSR)** Switch Route Processor (SRP), or a MultiService Route Processor (MSRP).

In a management domain including multiple high-end switches, it is not necessary to have internal routers in every chassis. One router for the entire domain is normally all that is required to perform routing functions for the entire domain. It is common, however, to have a standby internal router on a separate chassis. This provides cross-platform router redundancy, ensuring the availability of the network as a whole. The technique by which routers can perform standby functions for each other is explained in Chapter 7, "Hot Standby Routing Protocol (HSRP)." Figure 5-9 shows the CiscoView output of a Catalyst 5509 switch with an RSM installed in slot 8.

Catalyst 5000 Series

The Catalyst 5000 series offers the possibility of integrating one or more Router Switch Modules (RSMs) into the chassis. This can be done in one of two ways. The method first uses an RSM, which is a module that slides into one of the slots in the Catalyst 5000 chassis. The RSM can only be inserted into specific slots of the chassis depending on the model. Table 5-1 lists the valid slots to install an RSM on a Catalyst 5000 series switch.

Once installed in the chassis, the RSM becomes an integral part of the Catalyst 5000 hardware. The RSM itself provides a physical console port to access the

Internal Route Processors **245**

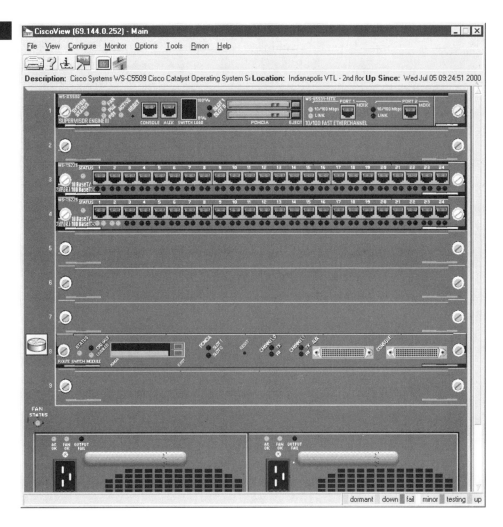

FIGURE 5-9

Catalyst 5509 with an RSM in slot 8

TABLE 5-1 Valid Slots for RSM Installation in a Catalyst 5000 Series Switch

Switch Model	Catalyst 5000/5005	Catalyst 5509	Catalyst 5500
Number of slots	5	9	13
Valid slots for RSM	2-5	2-9	2-12

router's command-line interface. The following is the output of the "show module" and "show port" commands on a Catalyst 5500 switch with an RSM in slot 12. Notice how the RSM appears as a switch trunk port to the Catalyst 5500 engine.

```
Cat-5500% show mod
Mod Module-Name         Ports Module-Type              Model     Serial-Num Status
--- -------------------  ----- ------------------------ --------- ---------- -------
1                         2    1000BaseSX Supervisor    WS-X5530  010059698  ok
2                         2    1000BaseSX Supervisor    WS-X5530  010433217  standby
3                         24   10/100BaseTX Ethernet    WS-X5225R 011794127  ok
12                        1    Route Switch             WS-X5302  010445943  ok

Mod MAC-Address(es)                                     Hw    Fw        Sw
--- -------------------------------------------------- ----- --------- ----------------
1   00-50-50-81-28-00 to 00-50-50-81-2b-ff 1.9          3.1.2    4.5(1)
2   00-50-50-81-28-00 to 00-50-50-81-2b-ff 1.9          3.1.2    4.5(1)
3   00-50-a2-f0-d5-c0 to 00-50-a2-f0-d5-d7 3.2          4.3(1)   4.5(1)
12  00-e0-1e-92-27-de to 00-e0-1e-92-27-df 7.0          20.14    11.3(7)WA4(10)

Mod Sub-Type Sub-Model  Sub-Serial  Sub-Hw
--- -------- ---------- ----------- ------
1   NFFC     WS-F5521   0010436652  1.0
1   uplink   WS-U5534   0013162768  1.0
2   NFFC     WS-F5521   0009995935  1.0
2   uplink   WS-U5534   0011459779  1.0
Cat-5500%
Cat-5500% show port 12
Port  Name              Status     Vlan       Level  Duplex Speed Type
----- ----------------- ---------- ---------- ------ ------ ----- ---------
12/1                    connected  trunk      normal half   400   Route Switch

Port   Trap      IfIndex
-----  --------- -------
12/1   enabled   223
Use 'session' command to see router counters.
Last-Time-Cleared
--------------------------
Tue May 30 2000, 11:41:33
Cat-5500%
```

The alternative to the RSM is the RSFC. Instead of occupying a slot in the Catalyst chassis, the RSFC is a daughter card mounted on the supervisory engine of the Catalyst 5000 switch. This allows the switch to host additional modules, and thus increase the port density of the chassis. One of the disadvantages of the RSFC is that network administrators lose the direct connectivity provided by a console port to access the Command Line Interface (CLI) of the router. The RSFC is accessed through the backplane of the switch by using the "session" command from the switch CLI. The RSFC normally occupies virtual slot 15 of the switch. To access the RSFC, the command "session 15" is issued from the switch CLI. The following output shows a successful connection to an RSFC from a Catalyst 5500 switch. This is the equivalent to an internal telnet connection. Notice the result of the command "show tcp" once logged in to the RSFC. The local and remote IP addresses show up as a 127.0.0.0 address, which is reserved by TCP/IP for loopback purposes. This means that the switch actually establishes a telnet connection to the RSFC using loopback addresses.

```
Cat-5500% session 15
Trying Router-15...
Connected to Router-15.
Escape character is '^]'.

User Access Verification

Password: XXX
RSFC-1> show tcp
tty2, virtual tty from host 127.0.0.2
Connection state is ESTAB, I/O status: 1, unread input bytes: 1
Local host: 127.0.0.13, Local port: 23
Foreign host: 127.0.0.2, Foreign port: 1036

Enqueued packets for retransmit: 0, input: 2  mis-ordered: 0 (0 bytes)

Event Timers (current time is 0x70A2C298):
Timer          Starts    Wakeups            Next
Retrans           28          0       0x70A2C639
TimeWait           0          0              0x0
AckHold           36         13              0x0
SendWnd            0          0              0x0
KeepAlive          0          0              0x0
GiveUp             0          0              0x0
PmtuAger           0          0              0x0
DeadWait           0          0              0x0

iss: 3011241323  snduna: 3011245122  sndnxt: 3011245714     sndwnd:  4096
irs: 1342567425  rcvnxt: 1342567492  rcvwnd:      4062   delrcvwnd:    66
```

```
SRTT: 319 ms, RTTO: 941 ms, RTV: 151 ms, KRTT: 0 ms
minRTT: 0 ms, maxRTT: 300 ms, ACK hold: 200 ms
Flags: passive open, higher precedence, retransmission timeout

Datagrams (max data segment is 1460 bytes):
Rcvd: 65 (out of order: 0), with data: 38, total data bytes: 67
Sent: 58 (retransmit: 0), with data: 41, total data bytes: 4780
RSFC-1>
```

As we have seen, the RSM and RSFC operate just like regular routers, but they offer much more flexibility and can operate at much faster speeds. There is another advantage to these onboard router devices. In addition to talking directly to the VLANs via the backplane of the switch, the RSM and RSFC can also talk directly to the switching engine itself about the traffic they carry. This requires the addition of a NetFlow Feature Card (NFFC) on a Supervisor III module of the Catalyst 5000 chassis when using an RSM. Using this additional hardware, the switch and the router exchange information about the flow of packets through the router and their resulting paths across the switching fabric of the switch. Once the RSM has routed a packet from one VLAN to another, the switch learns the inbound and outbound switch ports involved, and proceeds to switch the remainder of the conversation between the two endstations. This results in what is called "Layer 3 switching." This means that Layer 3 functions, which are normally the responsibility of a router, are now handled by the switch itself. This provides a tremendous increase in packet throughput, since switching functions are faster than routing functions by at least one order of magnitude. For the RSM and Catalyst 5000 series, MultiLayer Switching (MLS) is only available for the TCP/IP protocol in IOS versions 11 or earlier. As of version 12, IOS now offers MLS support for IPX as well. MLS is discussed in greater detail in Chapter 6 of this book. Other network protocols such as AppleTalk must go through the RSM and follow the normal routing path. MLS configuration and concepts are also covered in Chapter 6. Here are some of the key specifications for the RSM and RSFC:

- 32 Mbytes, 64 Mbytes, and 128 Mbytes configurations.
- 2 x 100MHz R4700 RISC1 processors.
- 2 x Synergy Advanced Gate array Engines (SAGE) Application-Specific Integrated Circuits (ASIC) used to interface with the Catalyst 5000 switching fabric. These ASICs are represented on the RSM as Channel 0 and Channel 1.
- One million packets-per-second processing capability.

Internal Route Processors **249**

- Provides routing for up to 256 VLANs.
- MLS support for TCP/IP.
- EIA/TIA-232 serial console port.
- Hot swappable to ensure uptime of the Catalyst 5000 chassis.

EXERCISE 5-2

Hardware Configuration of the RSFC

You need to provide a Catalyst 5500 platform for one of your clients. The client informs you that he will need 10 slots for Ethernet modules once you have delivered the switch. He informs you that he is not willing to purchase an additional Catalyst 5500. Furthermore, he wishes to have two integrated routing engines for redundancy. He doesn't care about supervisory engine redundancy, and would rather you saved costs by having a single supervisor engine if possible. What is the minimum hardware required to meet these needs, and explain your choice for the routing engine.

Answer: The Catalyst 5500 has 13 available slots. As we have seen, slot 13 can only be used by an ATM Switch Processor. In this example, the slot is therefore of no use to us. This leaves slots 1 through 12. Ten of these slots will be used by Ethernet modules. This leaves two free slots in the chassis. Slot 1 must be occupied by a supervisory engine. This supervisory engine *must* be equipped with an RSFC in order to meet the dual router requirement. The remaining slot can be occupied by a regular RSM, which would provide the second routing engine in the chassis. This configuration will work, but leaves the Catalyst 5500 vulnerable by having a single point of failure by having a single supervisor. A better design would have a second supervisory engine instead of the RSM module. That supervisory module would also be equipped with an RSFC, providing redundancy to both the router engine and the supervisory module. This becomes a cost trade-off that must be examined by the customer.

When configuring internal routing engines, network administrators create virtual router interfaces to connect to the various VLANs on the switch. These interfaces are named "vlan x," where "x" is the number of the VLAN to which the virtual interface will attach itself. If the RSM is installed on a switch that is configured to operate in VTP server or transparent mode, creating a virtual router interface for a

250   Chapter 5: InterVLAN Routing Concepts

VLAN that does not exist will actually create a default VLAN on the management domain of the switch. If the switch is in client mode, the RSM will create an interface, but not attach to any VLAN on the switch. The status of that interface will remain "Line is up, line protocol is down." Each virtual interface alternatively attaches itself to channels 0 and 1 upon creation. These channels are attached to the backplane of the switch through the two SAGE ASICs, and can be identified by the LEDs on the RSM module itself. The command "show controller c5ip" is used to show the internal state of these channels, including the channel allocation for each VLAN. The output of this command follows:

```
rsm>show controller c5ip
DMA Channel 0 (status ok)
  Received 455734671 packets, 50048657K bytes
    One minute rate, 8650 bits/s, 13 packets/s
    Ten minute rate, 12591 bits/s, 18 packets/s
  Dropped 4606796 packets
      689361 ignore, 0 line-down, 0 runt, 0 giant, 3917435 unicast-flood
      Last drop (0x81408A), vlan 138, length 64, rsm-discrim 0, result-bus 0x5
    Error counts, 0 crc, 0 index, 0 dmac-length, 0 dmac-synch, 0 dmac-timeout
  Transmitted 207017147 packets, 25806164K bytes
    One minute rate, 5131 bits/s, 6 packets/s
    Ten minute rate, 9153 bits/s, 9 packets/s

DMA Channel 1 (status ok)
  Received 262981085 packets, 28239032K bytes
    One minute rate, 5796 bits/s, 7 packets/s
    Ten minute rate, 6149 bits/s, 8 packets/s
  Dropped 7352369 packets
      7330444 ignore, 0 line-down, 0 runt, 0 giant, 21925 unicast-flood
      Last drop (0x9D412F), vlan 303, length 78, rsm-discrim 0, result-bus 0x5
    Error counts, 32594 crc, 0 index, 0 dmac-length, 0 dmac-synch, 0 dmac-timeout
  Transmitted 157488396 packets, 24387341K bytes
    One minute rate, 3343 bits/s, 4 packets/s
    Ten minute rate, 3936 bits/s, 5 packets/s

Vlan    Type        DMA Channel   Method
1       ethernet    1             auto
128     ethernet    0             auto
130     ethernet    1             auto
131     ethernet    0             auto
132     ethernet    1             auto
134     ethernet    0             auto
136     ethernet    1             auto
```

```
138       ethernet    0           auto
140       ethernet    1           auto
142       ethernet    0           auto

Inband IPC (status running)
  Pending messages, 0 queued, 0 awaiting acknowledgment

Vlan0 is up, line protocol is up
  Hardware is Cat5k Virtual Ethernet, address is 00e0.1e92.27de
 (bia 00e0.1e92.27de)
  Internet address is 127.0.0.13/8
  MTU 1500 bytes, BW 100000 Kbit, DLY 100 usec,
     reliability 255/255, txload 1/255, rxload 1/255
  Encapsulation ARPA, loopback not set, keepalive not supported
  ARP type: ARPA, ARP Timeout 04:00:00
  Last input 00:00:00, output 00:00:06, output hang never
  Last clearing of "show interface" counters 8w0d
  Queueing strategy: fifo
  Output queue 0/40, 0 drops; input queue 0/75, 0 drops
  5 minute input rate 0 bits/sec, 1 packets/sec
  5 minute output rate 1000 bits/sec, 1 packets/sec
     545 packets input, 32706 bytes, 0 no buffer
     Received 8 broadcasts, 0 runts, 0 giants, 0 throttles
     0 input errors, 0 CRC, 0 frame, 0 overrun, 0 ignored, 0 abort
     406 packets output, 38254 bytes, 0 underruns
     0 output errors, 0 interface resets
     0 output buffer failures, 0 output buffers swapped out
rsm>
```

> **on the Job**
>
> When planning your network design, pay attention to the channel allocation of your RSM. Try to maintain the balance between both channels. This will ensure that the channels are load balanced, providing the best possible throughput. In the preceding code example, had VLANs 128, 129, 130, 131, and 132 been created in order, the channel allocation for each VLAN to attach to the backplane of the switch would have been Channel 1 for VLANs 128, 130, and 132, and Channel 0 for VLANs 129, 131, and 133. If these last VLANs were later deleted to produce the VLAN configuration shown in the code, all the virtual interfaces of the RSM would be operating on Channel 0 only, causing an imbalance in the channel allocation. The RSM will not reallocate channels to better make use of the bandwidth once the virtual interface is created.

Aside from the nomenclature used to define the virtual interfaces, the configuration of the RSM is performed the same way as any other IOS-based router. Referring back to Figure 5-8, the RSM configuration required to perform routing functions for these two networks would be as follows:

```
rsm#conf t
Enter configuration commands, one per line.  End with CNTL/Z.
rsm(config)#interface vlan 10
rsm(config-if)#ip address 172.21.1.6 255.255.0.0
rsm(config-if)#interface vlan 20
rsm(config-if)#ip address 10.32.128.10 255.255.0.0
rsm(config-if)#end
.Jun 15 21:31:57: %SYS-5-CONFIG_I: Configured from console on vty0 (127.0.0.2)
rsm#
```

Catalyst 6000 Series

The Catalyst 6000 series offers the same "in-chassis" routing capabilities as the Catalyst 5000. Keep in mind that the modules for the Catalyst 5000, 6000, and 8500 series are not interchangeable, even though they perform similar functions. The routing engine for the 6000 series was conceived with multilayer switching in mind right from the start. The Multi-Layer Switch Module (MSM) and the Multi-Layer Switch Feature Card (MSFC) are the Layer 3 engines of the Catalyst 6000 switch. Like the RSM and RSFC, they can integrate into the chassis as either a switch module or a daughter card on the supervisory engine of the switch. In the case of an MSFC, should a second MSFC be required for redundancy, a second supervisory module is also required to accommodate the feature card, since the supervisory engine can only accommodate a single MSFC. Unlike the 5000 series, the MSM can occupy any slot within the Catalyst 6000 chassis.

As its name indicates, the MSM functionality includes MLS support for a broader range of network protocols. In addition to TCP/IP, the MLS supports Layer 3 switching functionality for IPX and IP multicast. Here are some of the key features of the MSM and MSFC:

- Multimegabit backplane interface providing 4 x 1 Gbps throughput
- 64MB DRAM system memory
- 4–6 million packets-per-second Layer 3 processing capability
- Provides routing for up to 64 VLANs
- MLS support for TCP/IP, IPX, and IP multicast

- EIA/TIA-232 serial console port
- Hot swappable to ensure uptime of the Catalyst 6000 chassis

The configuration of the MSM and MSFC is different from the Catalyst 5000 series. It requires getting a little more involved with the hardware itself and mimicking the configuration of an external trunking router. Unlike the RSM, the MSM does not have individual virtual VLAN interfaces that it can create at will. Instead, the MSM offers four GigabitEthernet interfaces that interface directly with the backplane of the Catalyst 6000 chassis. Conversely, each interface is associated with a switch port on the switch. Assuming that the MSM is in slot 6 of the Catalyst 6000 chassis, the basic configuration of the MSM and its host switch is as follows:

- Configure ports 6/1, 6/2, 6/3, and 6/4 to be in the appropriate VLANs. Each port represents one of the GigabitEthernet interfaces on the MSM.
- Configure each GigabitEthernet interface with the appropriate network address for the VLAN in which it was placed.

The configuration of the switch and the MSM to operate as the router shown in Figure 5-7 is as follows. First, the Catalyst 6000 switch:

```
Cat-6500> (enable)
Cat-6500> (enable) set vlan 1 6/1
VLAN  Mod/Ports
----  -----------------------
1     6/1

Cat-6500> (enable) set vlan 2 6/2
VLAN 2 modified
VLAN 1 modified
VLAN  Mod/Ports
----  -----------------------
2     6/2

Cat-6500> (enable) set vlan 3 6/3
VLAN 3 modified
VLAN 1 modified
VLAN  Mod/Ports
----  -----------------------
3     6/3

Cat-6500> (enable)
```

And now the configuration of the MSM:

```
MSM#
MSM#conf t
Enter configuration commands, one per line.  End with CNTL/Z.
MSM(config)#interface GigabitEthernet 1/0
MSM(config-if)#ip address 10.1.1.1 255.255.255.0
MSM(config-if)#exit
MSM(config)#interface GigabitEthernet 1/1
MSM(config-if)#ip address 10.2.1.1 255.255.255.0
MSM(config-if)#exit
MSM(config)#interface GigabitEthernet 1/3
MSM(config-if)#ip address 10.3.1.1 255.255.255.0
MSM(config-if)#end
MSM#
6w4d: %SYS-5-CONFIG_I: Configured from console by console
MSM#
```

This configuration poses a problem: with only four GigabitEthernet interfaces on the MSM, we seem to lose the flexibility of the VLAN interfaces of the RSM. Should there be five or more VLANs on the switch, four interfaces would not be enough to route all of them. One solution would be to use one GigabitEthernet interface and turn it into an ISL trunk. This way, the interface could support ISL subinterfaces for each VLAN. The problem here is that only one of the four GigabitEthernet interfaces would be in use, severely restricting the throughput of the MSM engine to the switch. Cisco provides a solution to this problem using a virtual interface and Fast EtherChannel technology. The interface, called "port-channel," is a virtual representation of all four GigabitEthernet interfaces placed in Fast EtherChannel mode. The port-channel therefore offers a total throughput of 4 Gbps to the Catalyst 6000 chassis. The port-channel is then configured as a trunk, and subinterfaces can be created at will, restoring the flexibility required to handle a large number of VLANs. The configuration of the switch and the MSM for port-channel operation is as follows. On the Catalyst switch, the switch ports associated with the four GigabitEthernet interfaces must be configured for Fast EtherChannel and trunking.

```
Cat-6500> (enable)
Cat-6500> (enable) set port channel 6/1-4 on
Port(s) 6/1-4 are assigned to admin group 70
Port(s) 6/1-4 channel mode set to on
Cat-6500> (enable)
Cat-6500> (enable) set trunk 6/1 on isl 1-1005
Adding vlans 1-1005 to allowed list.
```

```
Please use the 'clear trunk' command to remove vlans from allowed list.
Port(s) 6/1-4 allowed vlans modified to 1-1005.
Port(s) 6/1-4 trunk mode set to on.
Port(s) 6/1-4 trunk type set to isl.
Cat-6500> (enable)
```

Next, the MSM is configured for port-channel operation. The virtual interface must first be created, and then the individual GigabitEthernet interfaces are added to the port-channel bundle. At this point, the port-channel interface is ready to assume the routing functions. Subinterfaces are created and associated with the proper VLANs. In this example, the MSM will perform the routing functions of the router shown in Figure 5-8. Notice how the channel-group number defined on each GigabitEthernet interface matches the interface number of the port-channel interface. This is how the physical interfaces are associated with the virtual interface.

```
MSM#configure terminal
Enter configuration commands, one per line.  End with CNTL/Z.
MSM(config)# interface GigabitEthernet 1/0
MSM(config-if)# no ip address
MSM(config-if)# channel-group group 1 mode on
MSM(config-if)# exit
MSM(config)#
MSM(config)# interface GigabitEthernet 1/1
MSM(config-if)# no ip address
MSM(config-if)# channel-group group 1 mode on
MSM(config-if)# exit
MSM(config)#
MSM(config)# interface GigabitEthernet 1/2
MSM(config-if)# no ip address
MSM(config-if)# channel-group group 1 mode on
MSM(config-if)# exit
MSM(config)#
MSM(config)# interface GigabitEthernet 1/3
MSM(config-if)# no ip address
MSM(config-if)# channel-group group 1 mode on
MSM(config-if)# exit
MSM(config)#
MSM(config)#interface Port-channel 1
MSM(config-if)#
MSM(config-if)#interface Port-channel 1.1
MSM(config-subif)#encapsulation isl 10
MSM(config-subif)#ip address 172.21.1.6 255.255.0.0
MSM(config-subif)#exit
```

```
MSM(config)#
MSM(config)#interface Port-channel1.2
MSM(config-subif)#encapsulation isl 20
MSM(config-subif)#ip address 10.32.128.10 255.255.0.0
MSM(config-subif)#end
10w0d: %SYS-5-CONFIG_I: Configured from console by vty0 (127.0.0.2)
MSM#
```

> **exam Watch**
>
> *When configuring a port-channel interface, remember that the grouping of physical interfaces is done using Fast EtherChannel technology. This means that both ends of the physical interfaces must agree on the bundle. In this case, do not forget to configure Fast EtherChannel on the ports of the switch itself. Without these configurations, the router will bundle the interfaces on its end, but the switch will treat the interfaces as individual links. This will cause the Fast EtherChannel link to fail.*

Figure 5-10 shows CiscoView's representation of a Catalyst 6500 with redundant MSFCs. Notice how the router engine shows up as a part of the supervisory module. This is because feature cards are daughter boards on the supervisory engines themselves. They do not occupy physical slots inside the chassis.

Catalyst 8500 CSR Series

The Catalyst 8500 Campus Switch Router series combines ATM switching services with Layer 2 switching for Gigabit Ethernet into a single integrated chassis, providing high-performance switching and advanced Quality of Service (QoS) capabilities. When equipped with a Switch Route Processor (SRP), the switch operates as a Layer 3 switch only. When equipped with a Multiservice Route Processor (MSRP), the switch offers multiservice ATM switch capabilities in addition to the Layer 3 switching services of the SRP. Here are some of the key capabilities of the MSRP:

- 200MHz R5000 RISC-based processor
- 24 million packets-per-second Layer 3 processing capability
- MLS support for TCP/IP, IPX, IP multicast, and ATM LANE
- Embedded ATM switching capabilities
- Rich QoS features

FIGURE 5-10

MSFC daughter cards in a Catalyst 6500 switch

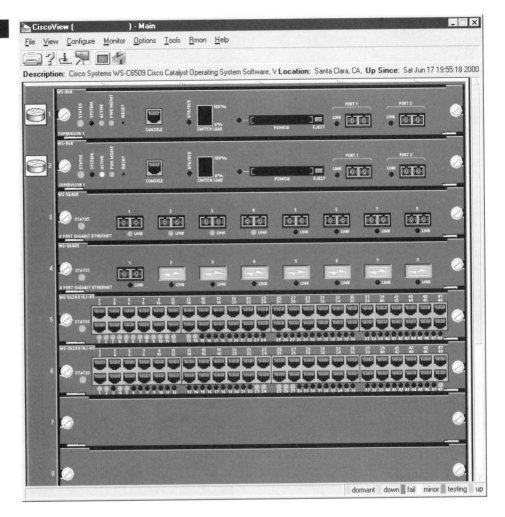

- EIA/TIA-232 serial console port
- Hot swappable to ensure uptime of the Catalyst 8500 chassis

The configuration of the ATM functionality of the 8500 series is beyond the scope of this book. The configuration of the SRP is identical to the configuration of the MSM in the Catalyst 6000 series.

Now that you have a better understanding of internal route processors, here are some possible scenario questions and their answers.

SCENARIO & SOLUTION

What are the main differences between an MSM and an MSFC?	The MSM is a module that occupies a slot in the Catalyst 6000 chassis. The MSFC is a daughter card that is housed on the supervisory engine of the switch itself. It occupies a virtual slot on the Catalyst 6000 software and can be accessed using the "session" command.
How many VLANs are supported by the RSM on the Catalyst 5000 series?	The RSM can support up to 256 simultaneous virtual interfaces, which is the VLAN limit of the Catalyst 5000 engine.
Are RSMs and MSMs hot swappable?	Yes. All modules in the Catalyst 5000 and 6000 series are hot swappable. Remember, however, that without a redundant router, pulling the router module out of the chassis will stop routing services between the VLANs. Traffic local to each VLAN will operate normally. Again, keep in mind that the routing modules of the 5000 and 6000 series are not interchangeable. They cannot be swapped around to fix an outage.

CERTIFICATION OBJECTIVE 5.04

Commands

This chapter covers many commands to configure intervlan routing functionality. This section describes in detail the use and syntax of each of these commands as they are applied in this chapter, along with additional commands covering other network protocols that were discussed earlier. It can be used as a reference tool when configuring VLAN routing in your network topology. The commands in this section are strictly IOS based.

enable

Perhaps the most powerful command in the IOS, this command places the router in "privileged exec" mode from the regular "exec" mode. Dubbed "enabled mode," privileged exec mode allows network administrators to modify the IOS configuration and view certain parameters not normally available to regular exec-level users. The prompt of the IOS device itself changes from ">" to "#", indicating that the exec level has changed to enabled mode. Normally, a password will be configured to restrict the access to this mode; however, it is not a mandatory requirement. When a new router is configured, access to privileged exec mode does not require an enable password. It is *not* recommended to operate your router without an enable password.

```
router>enable
Password:
router#
```

show running-config

Often truncated to "show run," this command displays the running configuration of an IOS router. This privileged exec-level command does not have any optional keywords. The following shows a brief output of this command on a Catalyst 5500 RSM:

```
lab-rsm#show running-config
Building configuration...

Current configuration:
!
version 11.3
service timestamps debug uptime
service timestamps log uptime
service password-encryption
!
hostname lab-rsm
!
enable password 7 XXXX
!
ip subnet-zero
ip tcp synwait-time 5
no ip domain-lookup
!
```

```
!
!interface Vlan1
 ip address 169.144.0.253 255.255.255.0
!
interface Vlan145
 ip address 169.145.254.254 255.255.0.0
!
interface Vlan801
 ip address 169.158.1.254 255.255.255.0
!
interface Vlan802
 ip address 169.158.2.254 255.255.255.0
!
interface Vlan803
 ip address 169.158.3.254 255.255.255.0
!
interface Vlan804
 ip address 169.158.4.254 255.255.255.0
!
interface Vlan805
 ip address 169.158.5.254 255.255.255.0
!
ip classless
ip route 0.0.0.0 0.0.0.0 169.144.0.254 200
!
line con 0
line aux 0
line vty 0 4
 password 7 XXX
 login
!
end
```

configure terminal

This privileged exec command is the first step in configuring any IOS device. Often truncated to "conf t," it places the router into configuration mode. Any command entered from that point impacts the configuration of the IOS device. The prompt of the IOS device changes from "#" to "(config)#," indicating that the router is in configuration mode. The following code listing shows a router being placed in configuration mode. Since this command is issued from privileged exec mode, which is the highest level of authority on the router, no additional passwords are required to enter configuration mode.

```
router#configure terminal
Enter configuration commands, one per line.  End with CNTL/Z.
router(config)#
```

ip routing

This command enables the ip routing process on the router. This command is enabled by default on all Cisco routers and will not show up in the configuration unless disabled by entering the command "no ip routing." It is important, however, to understand that this function is enabled on the router even though it is not apparent.

appletalk routing

This command enables the AppleTalk routing process on the router. Without this command, the router will not respond to any other AppleTalk command. Unlike the command "ip routing," which is enabled by default on the router, appletalk routing must manually be declared. It is important to know that not all versions of Cisco IOS support AppleTalk. When purchasing a version of IOS, pay attention to the feature set of the software.

ipx routing

Like the "appletalk routing" command, the command "ipx routing" must first be issued before any other IPX command will be accepted by the router. Not all versions of the IOS include IPX support. Be aware of this limitation when ordering IOS software.

interface

In configuring IOS functionality, the order of commands entered is important. This involves first selecting a resource to be configured, and then applying configuration commands to that resource. The "interface" command is used to select an interface resource to be configured. This does not make any changes to that interface; it simply selects the interface. Any further commands will be applied to that interface. The prompt of the router will change from "(config)#" to "(config-if)#" for a physical interface, or to "(config-subif)#" for a subinterface. The syntax of the command is "interface <interface type> <interface number>". The interface type depends on the hardware installed in the IOS device. The IOS device will report an error if a command is entered for hardware that is not present. Some of the most common interface commands include:

- interface ethernet 0
- interface token-ring 0
- interface GigabitEthernet 0
- interface serial 0
- interface atm0
- interface VLAN 1

There are many more interface types available, depending on the technology used. The preceding commands are the most common interface selection commands that you will find in this book. The following shows the successful selection of interface Ethernet 0 and the creation of subinterface Ethernet 0.1 on a Cisco router.

```
router(config)#
router(config)#interface ethernet 0
router(config-if)#
router(config-if)#interface ethernet 0.1
router(config-subif)#
```

encapsulation

The "encapsulation" command is used when configuring subinterfaces in a trunking environment. It is important to realize that not all hardware is capable of trunking. When selecting the proper hardware for any project, the selection of trunking-capable components is an important factor. The syntax of the command is "encapsulation <encapsulation type> <vlan ID>." The encapsulation type can be "isl" for Cisco Inter Switch Link encapsulation, "dot1q" for IEEE 802.1q encapsulation, "sde" for Secure Data Exchange in an 802.10 FDDI environment, or "tr-isl" for Token Ring ISL VLANs. The VLAN ID field refers to the VLAN number as it appears in the VLAN list of the switch itself. The following shows the configuration of a subinterface accessing VLAN 10 using ISL encapsulation.

```
Cisco-7206(config-if)#interface ethernet 0.1
Cisco-7206(config-subif)#encapsulation isl 10
```

ip address

This interface command applies an IP address to a selected interface. Be aware that the IOS device must already have an interface selected in order for this command to work. The syntax of this command is "ip address <ip address> <subnet mask> [secondary]." The *secondary* keyword at the end of the command enables network administrators to apply multiple IP addresses to the same interface. This is particularly useful in the router-on-a-stick configuration discussed earlier in this chapter. The following shows the successful configuration of an Ethernet interface with multiple IP addresses.

```
router(config)#
router(config)#interface ethernet 0
router(config-if)#ip address 10.1.1.1 255.255.255.0
router(config-if)#ip address 20.1.1.1 255.255.255.0 secondary
router(config-if)#ip address 30.1.1.1 255.255.255.0 secondary
router(config-if)#
```

ipx network

The interface command "ipx network" configures a selected interface with the IPX network number on which the interface will be operating. Unlike TCP/IP, where both network and node number are declared using the "ip address" command, IPX uses the interface's MAC address as the node address for IPX. The only configuration required is the IPX network. This means that a router having multiple interfaces in an IPX environment will have the same node number in each IPX network. The syntax for the command is as follows: "ipx network <1-FFFFFFFD> encapsulation <type> [secondary]." The network number is a 32-bit number expressed in hexadecimal format. The encapsulation types are listed in Table 5-2.

TABLE 5-2 Novell Encapsulations

Keyword	Encapsulation Type
Arpa	IPX Ethernet_II
Hdlc	High-level Data Link Control over serial links
novell-ether	IPX Ethernet_802.3
novell-fddi	IPX FDDI RAW
Sap	IEEE 802.2 on Ethernet, FDDI, Token Ring
Snap	IEEE 802.2 SNAP on Ethernet, Token Ring, and FDDI

The default encapsulation for IOS devices is "novell-ether." The optional *secondary* keyword is used to configure multiple IPX networks on the same interface. The following shows the configuration of an Ethernet interface to operate in IPX network 2a.

```
router(config)#interface ethernet 0
router(config-if)#ipx network 2a
router(config-if)#
```

exam Watch

It is important to remember the Cisco encapsulation types and their associated Novell counterparts. Also, remember that the default encapsulation type is "novell-ether."

appletalk

There are two main interface commands to configure AppleTalk on an interface: "appletalk cable-range" and "appletalk zone." First, the command "appletalk cable-range" configures a range of valid network numbers that can be used on that interface. The valid range is from 1 to 253. When an AppleTalk interface starts up, the router selects a network number within the declared cable range. Next, it picks a node address at random, and queries the network to see if that address is in use. If no other node on the network has already claimed that address, the router starts AppleTalk services. The syntax for this command is "appletalk cable-range <start>-<end>," where "start" is the lower boundary of the range, and "end" is the upper boundary of the cable range. The "appletalk zone" command is the second essential interface command for AppleTalk to operate properly. It associates a zone name with the cable range, enabling the AppleTalk Chooser application of Macintosh computers to see all the AppleTalk resources on the segment. The syntax for this command is "appletalk zone <zone name>," where "zone name" is a text field identifying the name of the zone. Cable ranges can have multiple zone names associated with them. If no zone name is declared, the cable range will not interact with other routers in the network. A proper cable range/zone name configuration is essential to the proper operation of an AppleTalk interface. The following shows the configuration of an Ethernet interface for AppleTalk operations.

```
router(config)#
router(config)#interface ethernet 0
router(config-if)#appletalk cable-range 10-19
router(config-if)#appletalk zone My_Zone
router(config-if)#
```

FROM THE CLASSROOM

Misconfiguring AppleTalk Zones

One common mistake when configuring AppleTalk is not paying enough attention when configuring AppleTalk zone names. AppleTalk zone names must match exactly in order for nodes on a common segment to operate properly. Besides being case sensitive, AppleTalk zone names are vulnerable to the space character. If an AppleTalk zone is entered with a trailing space character, the zone name will not match the other zone names entered on other routers on the segment. This means that the routers will not communicate properly. The command "show appletalk zone" will *not* show this trailing character. The only way to identify this mistake is to examine the router's configuration. The interface configuration will show a trailing ":20" following the zone name. This is the indication that the zone name was incorrectly configured. The following code output shows the configuration of an interface with an AppleTalk zone name incorrectly configured with a trailing space character.

```
router(config-if)#appletalk zone My_Zone
router(config-if)#description Zone has trailing <space> after My_Zone
router(config-if)#end
router# show running-config
...
interface Ethernet0
 appletalk cable-range 10-10 10.203
 appletalk zone My_Zone:20
!
```

In this case, all other routers properly configured with the AppleTalk zone name "My_Zone" would not be able to communicate with the misconfigured router. Be careful when configuring AppleTalk zone names.

—*Benoit Durand, CCIE #5754*

end

The "end" command places the IOS device from configuration mode back into privileged exec mode. There are no optional keywords for this command, and it can be entered from any point while in configuration mode.

```
router(config)#
router(config)#end
router#
05:53:38: %SYS-5-CONFIG_I: Configured from console by console
router
```

<ctrl>-z

The command "<ctrl-z>" serves the same function as the command "end"; it brings the router back from configuration mode to privileged exec. Notice in the following code how IOS suggests the use of <ctrl>-z when entering configuration mode.

```
router#conf t
```

Enter configuration commands, one per line. *End with CNTL/Z.*

```
router(config)#
router(config)#^Z
router#
```

show ip route

This command displays the entire IP routing table of a router. The command has multiple optional keywords that can be used to filter the output of the routing table. The following shows the available keywords for the command, along with a sample display of an IP routing table.

```
router#show ip route ?
  Hostname or A.B.C.D  Network to display information about or hostname
  bgp                  Border Gateway Protocol (BGP)
  connected            Connected
  egp                  Exterior Gateway Protocol (EGP)
  eigrp                Enhanced Interior Gateway Routing Protocol (EIGRP)
  igrp                 Interior Gateway Routing Protocol (IGRP)
  isis                 ISO IS-IS
  list                 IP Access list
  odr                  On Demand stub Routes
  ospf                 Open Shortest Path First (OSPF)
  profile              IP routing table profile
  rip                  Routing Information Protocol (RIP)
  static               Static routes
  summary              Summary of all routes
  supernets-only       Show supernet entries only
```

```
      traffic-engineering  Traffic engineered routes
      <cr>
router#show ip route
Codes: C - connected, S - static, I - IGRP, R - RIP, M - mobile, B - BGP
       D - EIGRP, EX - EIGRP external, O - OSPF, IA - OSPF inter area
       N1 - OSPF NSSA external type 1, N2 - OSPF NSSA external type 2
       E1 - OSPF external type 1, E2 - OSPF external type 2, E - EGP
       i - IS-IS, L1 - IS-IS level-1, L2 - IS-IS level-2, * - candidate default
       U - per-user static route, o - ODR

Gateway of last resort is not set

     20.0.0.0/24 is subnetted, 1 subnets
C       20.1.1.0 is directly connected, Ethernet0
     10.0.0.0/24 is subnetted, 1 subnets
C       10.1.1.0 is directly connected, Ethernet0
C    192.169.1.0/24 is directly connected, Ethernet1
     30.0.0.0/24 is subnetted, 1 subnets
C       30.1.1.0 is directly connected, Ethernet0
router#
```

EXERCISE 5-3

Showing Specific Route Entries

You wish to troubleshoot a routing problem on a router. You type the command "show ip route" and are inundated with tons and tons of routes. You try to sift through the routes looking for the networks that are directly attached to the router, but cannot locate all of them. How can you alleviate this problem and show only the networks that are directly attached to the router?

Answer: Use the command "show ip route connected." This will display only the route entries for networks that are directly connected to the router. These routing entries will show up with a route type of "C," which represents a connected route. When troubleshooting route entries, remember that a connected route will *not* show up in the routing table if its associated interface is down. If you are missing some connected routes in your routing table, ensure that the interfaces are not in shutdown state and are operating properly.

show ipx route

This command displays the entire IPX routing table of a router. The command has multiple optional keywords that can be used to filter the output of the routing table. The following shows the available keywords for the command, along with a sample display of an IPX routing table showing connected routes only. In most routing tables, the router will show routing entries received from neighboring routers through IPX RIP.

```
router#show ipx route ?
  <1-FFFFFFFE>  IPX network number
  default       Default route
  detailed      Comprehensive display
  <cr>

router#show ipx route
Codes: C - Connected primary network,    c - Connected secondary network
       S - Static, F - Floating static, L - Local (internal), W - IPXWAN
       R - RIP, E - EIGRP, N - NLSP, X - External, A - Aggregate
       s - seconds, u - uses, U - Per-user static

3 Total IPX routes. Up to 1 parallel paths and 16 hops allowed.

No default route known.

C          2A (NOVELL-ETHER),   Et0
C          3C (NOVELL-ETHER),   Et1
c          5F (ARPA),           Et1
router#
```

show appletalk route

This command displays the entire AppleTalk routing table of a router. The command has multiple optional keywords that can be used to filter the output of the routing table. The following shows the available keywords for the command, along with a sample display of an AppleTalk routing table.

```
router#show appletalk route ?
  <1-65279>   Network number
  Ethernet    IEEE 802.3
  Null        Null interface
  Serial      Serial
  <cr>
```

```
router#show appletalk route
Codes: R - RTMP derived, E - EIGRP derived, C - connected, A -
AURP
       S - static  P - proxy
2 routes in internet

The first zone listed for each entry is its default (primary)
zone.

C Net 10-19 directly connected, Ethernet0, zone Sales
C Net 20-29 directly connected, Ethernet1, zone Marketing
router#
```

exam watch

Notice how each cable-range has a zone name associated with it. A valid match of zone name to cable range must exit before the cable-range will appear in the routing table. If either is misconfigured, the router will drop the route. This is a basic point to remember when required to troubleshoot Appletalk.

ping

The exec command "ping" is used to verify network connectivity with other routers or nodes within the network. It can be used for multiple network protocols, including TCP/IP, IPX, and AppleTalk. By default, ping will use TCP/IP. The syntax for this command is "ping [protocol] <network address>." The "network address" format depends on the network protocol specified. By default, IOS will send five pings to the destination. Successful pings will show up as "!," while unsuccessful pings will show up as ".". The following shows successful pings for IP, IPX, and AppleTalk hosts.

```
router#ping 10.1.1.2

Type escape sequence to abort.
Sending 5, 100-byte ICMP Echos to 10.1.1.2, timeout is 2 seconds:
!!!!!
Success rate is 100 percent (5/5), round-trip min/avg/max = 4/4/4 ms
router#
router#ping ipx 2A.00e0.1e42.bbae

Type escape sequence to abort.
Sending 5, 100-byte IPXcisco Echoes to 2A.00e0.1e42.bbae, timeout is 2 seconds:
```

```
!!!!!
Success rate is 100 percent (5/5), round-trip min/avg/max = 4/24/104 ms
router#
router#ping appletalk 10.240

Type escape sequence to abort.
Sending 5, 100-byte AppleTalk Echos to 10.240, timeout is 2 seconds:
!!!!!
Success rate is 100 percent (5/5), round-trip min/avg/max = 8/10/12 ms
router#
```

The ping command has an extended mode only accessible from the privileged exec mode. By simply typing **ping** at the command prompt, multiple options are available to extend the functionality and flexibility of the ping command. The following shows an extended ping of an IP host. Notice all the available options.

```
router#ping
Protocol [ip]: ip
Target IP address: 10.1.1.2
Repeat count [5]: 1
Datagram size [100]: 100
Timeout in seconds [2]: 3
Extended commands [n]: yes
Source address or interface: ethernet 0
Type of service [0]: 0
Set DF bit in IP header? [no]: yes
Validate reply data? [no]: yes
Data pattern [0xABCD]:
Loose, Strict, Record, Timestamp, Verbose[none]: V
Sweep range of sizes [n]: yes
Sweep min size [36]: 100
Sweep max size [18024]: 1100
Sweep interval [1]: 200
Type escape sequence to abort.
Sending 6, [100..1100]-byte ICMP Echos to 10.1.1.2, timeout is 3 seconds:
Reply to request 0 (4 ms) (size 100)
Reply to request 1 (4 ms) (size 300)
Reply to request 2 (4 ms) (size 500)
Reply to request 3 (8 ms) (size 700)
Reply to request 4 (4 ms) (size 900)
Reply to request 5 (4 ms) (size 1100)
Success rate is 100 percent (6/6), round-trip min/avg/max = 4/4/8 ms
router#
```

traceroute

The "traceroute" command is used to verify end-to-end connectivity while gathering information about the routers along the way. This command can be used for multiple network protocols, but defaults to TCP/IP unless otherwise specified. The syntax for this command is "traceroute <protocol> <network address>." The following output shows the valid network protocols for the "traceroute" command, along with a sample traceroute output in an IP environment.

```
router#traceroute ?
  WORD       Trace route to destination address or hostname
  appletalk  AppleTalk Trace
  clns       ISO CLNS Trace
  ip         IP Trace
  ipx        IPX Trace
  oldvines   Vines Trace (Cisco)
  vines      Vines Trace (Banyan)
  <cr>

router# traceroute 204.50.58.11

Type escape sequence to abort.
Tracing the route to 204.50.58.11

  1 12.126.229.13 8 msec 8 msec 12 msec
  2 12.127.0.134 12 msec 12 msec 8 msec
  3 12.123.4.253 12 msec 12 msec 12 msec
  4 144.228.207.65 36 msec 36 msec 36 msec
  5 144.232.10.217 36 msec 32 msec 32 msec
  6 144.232.10.6 36 msec 36 msec 36 msec
  7 144.232.18.54 32 msec 32 msec 36 msec
  8 144.232.18.37 36 msec 32 msec 36 msec
  9 144.232.9.46 32 msec 32 msec 36 msec
 10 208.30.212.2 48 msec 48 msec 48 msec
 11 204.50.128.6 52 msec 48 msec 48 msec
 12 206.186.248.70 152 msec 132 msec 88 msec
 13 204.50.58.11 84 msec 176 msec 220 msec
router#
```

copy running-config startup-config

This command is the final step in configuring an IOS device. It saves the running configuration of the router to Non-Volatile Random Access Memory (NVRAM), which is where IOS devices store their configurations. Often shortened to "copy run start," this overwrites any previously saved configuration. The following shows the output of this command.

```
router#copy running-config startup-config
Destination filename [startup-config]?
Building configuration...
[OK]
router#
```

Now that you have a better understanding of intervlan routing commands, here are some possible scenario questions and their answers.

SCENARIO & SOLUTION	
You are looking for a specific IP route in the routing table, but the output of the command "show ip route" is long and unsorted. What do you do?	Use the optional keywords of the "show ip route" command, or specify the network address to be displayed.
You configured your RSM and Catalyst 5000 switch and verified the connectivity between various networks. Following a power outage, network connectivity between networks was lost. What is the likely cause?	The configuration of the RSM was not saved to NVRAM. Unlike set-based switches where a command is automatically saved as it is entered, IOS devices need to be instructed to save the configuration to NVRAM. This is accomplished with the command "copy running-config startup-config."
If the router prompt shows "router(config-if)#," what level of IOS configuration are you in?	The interface configuration mode. We know this from the "config-if" part of the prompt. Be aware of the various prompts possible and their associated configuration state.

CERTIFICATION SUMMARY

In today's networks, a common upgrade path is to simply replace every hub with a switch. Although this can provide a significant improvement in unicast traffic throughput, this does not resolve broadcast propagation issues. A solid network design will examine traffic patterns and the impact of broadcast traffic in the entire network. The method of restricting broadcasts to smaller domains is to break up broadcast domains and to interconnect them using routers. While broadcast domains operate at Layer 2 of the OSI model, the Data Link layer, routers interconnect broadcast domains at Layer 3, the Network layer.

Legacy routers employ physical interfaces to link broadcast domains. This method can severely restrict the flexibility of a network topology employing a large number of VLANs. Furthermore, today's high-end switching engines operate at speeds ranging in the hundreds of Gigabits per second. In order to harness the speed of these switches and provide the same flexibility of VLANs, Cisco developed routers that can interface directly with the backplane of its high-end switch chassis. These routers use virtual interfaces that connect to the virtual LANs present on the switch. Since they interface directly to the high-speed backplane, the possible bottleneck of physical media is avoided. This symbiotic relationship between the switch and the router module also enables them to provide multilayer switching services.

All routing modules are powered by the Cisco IOS. The configuration of these modules, although slightly different from their external counterparts, still follows the same configuration structures of IOS.

TWO-MINUTE DRILL

Here are some of the key points from each certification objective in Chapter 5.

InterVLAN Environments

- Switches do not solve broadcast problems in a large, single-segment network. The key is to fragment the broadcast domains into smaller entities and link them using routers.
- Switches operate at Layer 2 of the OSI model, the Data Link layer. Routers operate at Layer 3 of the OSI model, the Network layer.
- End nodes and routers keep a table of MAC address to Network address mappings called the ARP table.
- In a intervlan conversation, the source and destination MAC addresses change from hop to hop, while the source and destination network addresses remain constant throughout the entire path.
- Legacy routers normally have one physical interface in each network segment for which they route. A special case called router-on-a-stick enables a router to route for multiple networks located on the same physical segment.
- In a switched intervlan environment, a trunking-capable router can be used to route for all the VLANs through a single physical interface. Virtual subinterfaces are created on the router to represent each segment for which the router provides routing services.

Internal Route Processors

- Internal routers such as the MSM, RSM, and SRP interface directly with the chassis of the switch in which they reside. This provides them with high-speed channels to perform routing functions for the VLANs present on the switch.
- Most internal routers have a console port for network administrator to use when configuring the IOS. Internal routers that operate as a feature card on the supervisory engine of the switch can only be accessed through the "session" command from the command-line interface of the switch itself.

- On an RSM for a Catalyst 5000 series switch, virtual interfaces labeled "interface vlan x" are created, where "x" is the VLAN number. These interfaces attach directly to the backplane of the switch, offering routing services for these VLANs.
- On an MSM and SRP for the Catalyst 6000 and 8500 series, physical interfaces can be bundled using Fast EtherChannel technology and allocated to a single virtual interface labeled "port-channel x," where "x" represents the bundle number associated with the physical interfaces.
- Internal routers speak directly to the backplane of the switch they are housed in. This enables them to speak directly to the switching engine itself and perform multilayer switching functions, also called Layer 3 switching.

Commands

- The subinterface command "encapsulation isl x," where "x" is the VLAN number, is used by trunking routers to associate a VLAN to that subinterface.
- The interface command "ipx network x," where "x" is the network number, is used to configure an IPX interface. The router uses its own MAC address as its node number on that network.
- AppleTalk routing functions require two parameters to be configured: the cable range and the zone name. Without either of these parameters, AppleTalk will not operate successfully.
- The command "show ip route" is used to display the entire IP routing table of the router. Multiple keywords are available to filter the output of the entire table to display only the desired information.
- The commands "ping" and "traceroute" are used to verify Layer 3 connectivity. They can both be used for multiple network protocols.

SELF TEST

The following questions will help you measure your understanding of the material presented in this chapter. Read all the choices carefully, as there may be more than one correct answer. Choose all correct answers for each question.

InterVLAN Environments

1. You determine that the broadcast rate of your single-segment network is starting to cause problems for the users. Network response time is slow, even though you upgraded all the hubs to switches last year. UNIX systems use TCP/IP, Novell servers use IPX, and Windows machines use NetBEUI. You decide to fragment your network into smaller VLAN segments, and provide intervlan routing through the use of a trunking router. Following the fragmentation and configuration of new network addresses, the Windows users complain that the network is not functioning properly. UNIX and Novell users have no complaints. What is the likely cause of this problem, and what steps should you take to resolve it?

    A. The Windows server did not get its NetBEUI address changed correctly. This is why the Windows client cannot connect. Contact the network administrator and have him or her verify the NetBEUI address.

    B. Windows is not able to operate over multiple segments. You must place all the Windows users in the same segment in order for them to operate properly.

    C. The broadcast traffic generated by the UNIX and Novell nodes still impacts the Windows machines. In fact, since they now have to cross a router, the impact of the UNIX and Novell nodes is even worse than before. All Windows nodes must be placed on a separate VLAN used for Windows machines only.

    D. The Windows nodes use a protocol incompatible with routers and fragmented networks. The Windows machines should be migrated to NetBIOS over TCP/IP or IPX.

2. Your client wishes to migrate his Novell network to a new version of the Network Operating System. After some research, you find out that the two versions use a different IPX encapsulation. Your client informs you that you are not to change the physical infrastructure, and that the migration should be as seamless as possible. As such, he wants both networks to be able to interact with each other while nodes are being transitioned from one network to the other. What is the best method to accomplish this task?

    A. Configure a router-on-a-stick and perform IPX routing for both networks on the same physical interface.

B. Configure each network in a separate VLAN, and use a trunking-capable router to route between the two VLANs.

C. There is no way to accomplish this. Nodes of different IPX encapsulation cannot talk to each other.

D. Configure multilayer switching so that the Layer 2 encapsulation can be routed by the router operating at Layer 3.

3. Which of the following statement accurately describes the journey of a packet across multiple routers and segments?

   A. The MAC addresses and Network addresses remain the same throughout the journey.
   B. The MAC addresses remain the same, and the Network addresses change from hop to hop.
   C. The Mac addresses change from hop to hop, and the Network addresses remain the same.
   D. The MAC addresses and the Network addresses change from hop to hop.

4. Your client has a single Catalyst 5500 switch with every slot filled with 10/100 Ethernet modules. On these modules, a total of three ports are not in use. Your client informs you that he wishes to fragment his network into 10 VLANs that will need to be interconnected using a router. What is the best solution to meet his requirement on a restricted budget?

   A. Because the switch cannot handle an RSM due to the lack of an available slot, your client needs to reduce the number of VLANs to three, at which point a small external router can use the remaining Ethernet ports and perform routing services for all three VLANs.
   B. Configure an external router-on-a-stick and connect it to a single port on the switch. The router interface will have 10 network addresses, one for each VLAN, and provide routing between them.
   C. Reduce the number of nodes in order to free up one of the slots on the switch. Install an RSM and perform routing on the backplane of the switch. Connect a small workgroup switch to the Catalyst 5500 to handle the nodes that were disconnected from it.
   D. Configure an external router to use an ISL trunk to the switch. Use 10 subinterfaces on the router, one for each VLAN, to provide the routing between them.

5. An external trunking router is to be configured to route between VLANs 10 and 20. Select the configuration that will accomplish this task.

   A.
   ```
   interface vlan 10
     ip address 10.1.1.1 255.255.255.0
   interface vlan 20 ip address 20.1.1.1 255.255.255.0
   ```

B.
```
interface Ethernet 0
   ip address
interface Ethernet 0.10
   ip address 10.1.1.1 255.255.255.0
interface Ethernet 0.20
   ip address 20.1.1.1 255.255.255.0
```

C.
```
interface port-channel 1.1
   encapsulation isl 10
   ip address 10.1.1.1 255.255.255.0
interface port-channel 1.2
   encapsulation isl 20
   ip address 20.1.1.1 255.255.255.0
```

D.
```
interface Ethernet 0
   no ip address
interface Ethernet 0.1
   encapsulation isl 10
   ip address 10.1.1.1 255.255.255.0
interface Ethernet 0.2
   encapsulation isl 20
   ip address 20.1.1.1 255.255.255.0
```

6. Where do routers store the MAC addresses they dynamically learn in order to map them against network addresses?

   A. The Address Resolution Protocol table
   B. The Media Access Control table
   C. The Content Addressable Memory table
   D. The Routing table

7. What is the major limitation of external trunking routers over internal routers?

   A. External trunking routers cannot create VLAN interfaces like the internal routers. This limits the number of interfaces they can have, and would not be adequate in a management domain with a large number of VLANs.
   B. External trunking routers use physical segments to access the VLANs on a switch. The access speed provided by these physical links is much lower than the access speeds of internal routers accessing the VLANs through the backplane of the switch.
   C. External trunking routers cannot use Fast EtherChannel technology to create an interface bundle like internal routers. This reduces the possible throughput to the switch, creating a possible bottleneck.

D. Trunking routers do not have a console port; they need to be accessed using the "session" command on the Catalyst switch. This makes the router difficult to configure when access to the switch is not possible.

Internal Route Processors

8. You are to configure an MSM on a Catalyst 6000 switch in a management domain that has 40 VLANs. After loging on to the MSM, you realize that the platform does not support the "interface vlan x" type of command. Instead, the MSM has four GigabitEthernet internal adapters that interface directly with the backplane of the switch. Which of the configuration models is best suited to handle this requirement?

    A. Use ISL and create 10 subinterfaces on each of the four GigabitEthernet interfaces. This way, the load will be distributed between all four interfaces, and all 40 VLANs will be routed by the MSM.

    B. Use ISL and create 40 subinterfaces on each of the four GigabitEthernet interfaces. This way, each interface will have a presence in all 40 VLANs. Each interface can serve as a backup to the others, and the router will automatically load balance between all four GigabitEthernet interfaces.

    C. Bundle all four GigabitEthernet interfaces using EtherChannel technology, and use a virtual port-channel interface to represent the bundle. Configure the Port Channel interface to have 40 IP addresses using the "secondary" IP address command. This will provide high-speed access to all the VLANs, and enable the port-channel interface to route between all 40 VLANs.

    D. Bundle all four GigabitEthernet interfaces using EtherChannel technology, and use a virtual port-channel interface to represent the bundle. Use ISL trunking and create 40 subinterfaces on the port-channel. This will provide high-speed access to all the VLANs, and enable the port-channel subinterfaces to route between all 40 VLANs.

9. Your task is to configure a brand new Catalyst 5500 with an RSM on board. You create VLANs in the following order: 1, 3, 5, 7, 9, and then create 2, 4, 6, 8. All the VLANs have equal load distribution. You are then instructed to delete all the even-numbered VLANs on the switch. Will this create a problem in the channel allocation of the RSM?

    A. Yes it will. Because only the even-numbered VLANs remain, they will all be using the same channel on the backplane, leaving the second channel idle.

    B. No it will not. The RSM will reassign channel allocation in order to load balance the remaining VLANs.

280 Chapter 5: InterVLAN Routing Concepts

C. No it will not. Since the remaining VLANs 1, 3, 5, and 7 were originally created in order, they were assigned to alternating channels in the first place. The load remains well distributed between the RSM channels.

D. Yes it will. Since the VLANs are removed on the switch, the RSM does not know that its interfaces are no longer attached to anything. This will cause an internal routing loop.

10. Which ASIC is used by each channel of the RSM to controls its access to the backplane of the Catalyst 5000 series switch ?

   A. SAINT—Synergy Advanced Interface and Network Termination
   B. SAGE—Synergy Advanced Gate Array Engine
   C. SAMBA—Synergy Advanced Multipurpose Bus Arbiter
   D. EARL—Encoded Address Recognition Logic

11. Which of the following answers are possible combinations in a Catalyst 5500 chassis? (Choose all that apply.)

   A. One supervisory engine, one RSM in slot 12, one redundant RSM in slot 13
   B. One supervisory engine, one RSM in slot 5, one RSFC
   C. One supervisory engine, two RSFCs
   D. Two supervisory, two RSFCs, one RSM in slot 5, and one RSM in slot 9

12. The development team in the company you just started to work for have expressed the need for new VLANs to handle some new projects. On your first day of work, you were given the passwords to all the routers in the company. You unfortunately do not have the passwords of the Catalyst 5500 switch, but do have the password of the RSM. The switch is a critical networking piece that cannot be turned off. What are your options to meet this requirement?

   A. Log on to the RSM and create "interface vlan x," where "x" is the number of the VLAN you wish to create. Since you have enabled mode on the router, the switch will always create a new VLAN to accommodate the virtual interface.
   B. Recover the password of the Catalyst 5500 and create the VLANs from the CLI. Since you have physical access to the switch, there is no problem with recovering the lost password.
   C. Configure an external router to operate in ISL trunking mode, and create subinterfaces for each of the new VLANs. Since the link is a trunk between the router and the switch, VTP will propagate the new VLANs to the Catalyst 5500 as long as the router is in VTP server mode.

D. Log on to the RSM and create "interface vlan x," where "x" is the number of the VLAN you wish to create. If the switch is configured for VTP server or VTP transparent mode, the switch will create a new VLAN to accommodate the virtual interface.

13. How many virtual interfaces can the RSM handle in a intervlan routed environment?

   A. It depends on the memory configuration. The RSM can be configured with 32 Mbytes, 64 Mbytes, or 128 Mbytes. The number of virtual interfaces is proportional to the memory since they exist in software only.
   B. 256 virtual interfaces
   C. 128 virtual interfaces
   D. 64 virtual interfaces

14. You are charged with configuring a brand new Catalyst 6500 with an MSFC on board. After displaying the interfaces present on the MSFC, you notice that it has four internal GigabitEthernet interfaces. You decide to bundle all four interfaces and create a port-channel interface. Your configuration is as follows:

    ```
    interface GigabitEthernet 1/0
      channel-group group 10 mode on
    interface GigabitEthernet 1/1
      channel-group group 10 mode on
    interface GigabitEthernet 1/2
      channel-group group 10 mode on
    interface GigabitEthernet 1/3
      channel-group group 10 mode on
    !
    interface port-channel 1
      no ip address
    interface port-channel 1.1
      encapsulation isl 1
      ip address 10.1.1.1 255.255.255.0
      ipx network 2a
    ```

   After successfully creating the virtual interface, you notice that you do not have connectivity with any device on VLAN 1. What are possible causes of this?

   A. The Catalyst 6500 must have the ports associated with the MSFC configured for ISL trunking before the Port-Channel can successfully operate.
   B. The Port-Channel interface number does not match the Port-Group number declared on the GigabitEthernet interfaces. These parameters must match in order for the Port-Channel to operate successfully.

C. The Catalyst 6500 must have the ports associated with the MSFC configured for Fast EtherChannel technology before the Port-Channel can successfully operate.

D. All of the above

Commands

15. Privileged exec mode is accessed by issuing which command from the command-line of an IOS router?

    A. Enable
    B. Login
    C. Session
    D. Su

16. Which of the following prompts adequately represents a router in configuration mode that is ready to receive subinterface configuration commands?

    A. Router#
    B. Router(config)#
    C. Router(config-if)#
    D. Router(config-subif)#

17. Which keyword enables network administrators to configure multiple network addresses on the same interface?

    A. Encapsulation
    B. Secondary
    C. Cable-range
    D. Network

18. Novell administrators ask you to provide them with connectivity between two network segments. They do not know anything about routers, but they provide you with network numbers 10 and 20 for the two networks. You test your router by performing successful IPX pings of its interfaces and put it in operation. The Novell administrators inform you that they cannot see the remote network, let alone the router itself. You verify the network addresses and find that everything is in order. What is the likely cause of the problem?

    A. The interfaces are still in "shutdown" mode. The command "no shutdown" must be issued for each interface.

B. The command "ipx routing" was not entered. This command is off by default and will not let the router respond to IPX packets even though the interfaces are configured properly.

C. The default IPX encapsulation of the router is probably different from the encapsulation used by the Novell network. Consult the Novell administrators to identify which encapsulation to use.

D. IPX is not a routable protocol. It uses broadcasts as its means of communication and cannot go beyond the boundaries of a router.

19. Which of the following commands can be used to verify the connectivity between two routers?

   A. ping
   B. traceroute
   C. telnet
   D. session

20. The result of the command "copy running-config startup-config" saves the router's configuration to:

   A. DRAM memory
   B. Flash memory
   C. NVRAM memory
   D. ROM memory

21. Cisco uses IPX encapsulation nomenclature that is different from the one used by Novell. In the following list, which Cisco IPX encapsulation does not match to its equivalent Novell encapsulation?

   A. arpa   IPX Ethernet_II
   B. novell-ether IPX Ethernet 802.3
   C. sap   IEEE 802.3
   D. snap   IEEE 802.2 SNAP

LAB QUESTION

Your company recently purchased a new Catalyst 5500 switch equipped with an RSM to replace the hubs and small external routers that connect the company's entire internal network. Your mission, should you choose to accept it, will be to configure the RSM for routing operations. Assume that

VLANs 10 through 15 are present in the management domain of the switch. Your manager wants you to configure the RSM for IP, IPX, and AppleTalk services for all VLANs. The addressing plan is as follows:

VLAN	IP Address	IPX Network	AppleTalk Info
10	10.1.1.1/24	10	10-10 Zone_10
11	11.1.1.1/24	11	11-11 Zone_11
12	12.1.1.1/24	12	12-12 Zone_12
13	13.1.1.1/24	13	13-13 Zone_13
14	14.1.1.1/24	14	14-14 Zone_14
15	15.1.1.1/24	15	15-15 Zone_15

You must present a complete configuration for the RSM and show the routing tables for each network protocol.

SELF TEST ANSWERS

InterVLAN Environments

1. ☑ **D.** NetBEUI is a broadcast-based protocol that does not use Network layer addresses. It is incompatible with fragmented networks since it cannot reach beyond the router. Routable protocols such as TCP/IP and IPX can be used to transport NetBIOS, which would restore Windows connectivity across multiple segments and routers.
   ☒ **A** is incorrect because there are no network addresses to change in NetBEUI; the protocol operates strictly using broadcasts. **B** is incorrect because Windows is capable of operating over multiple segments when using the proper protocol. **C** is also incorrect because by segmenting the network, the level of broadcasts generated by the fraction of UNIX and Novell nodes on the segment would be lower than on the original large broadcast domain.

2. ☑ **A.** A router-on-a-stick is the perfect solution for Novell transitions of this sort. It will route for both networks without requiring any changes to the infrastructure.
   ☒ **B** is incorrect because assigning ports to VLANs and changing them as the nodes migrate would constitute a change in the network topology. **C** is also incorrect since there is a way to accomplish this. **D** is incorrect because multilayer switching would not solve IPX encapsulation problems.

3. ☑ **C.** The MAC address changes from hop to hop, but the source and destination Network addresses remain the same throughout the journey. This is so the destination station knows the point of origin of the packet so it knows to what destination address to reply. Remember that the sending station learned the MAC address of the next-hop router through the use of the Address Resolution Protocol (ARP). ARP enables TCP/IP hosts to create a MAC address to IP address table.
   ☒ **A**, **B**, and **D** are incorrect because they are not valid combinations.

4. ☑ **D.** An external ISL router will be much less expensive than adding an RSM to the switch. Furthermore, it will provide the flexibility to handle any number of VLANs as required.
   ☒ **A** is incorrect because through trunking, you can provide intervlan routing for all 10 VLANs; there is no need to reduce the number of VLANs in the management domain. **B** is incorrect because each VLAN represents a different segment. A router-on-a-stick is used to route between multiple networks operating on a single segment. **C** is also incorrect because adding an RSM and an additional switch is not the most affordable solution.

5. ☑ **D.** An external trunking router would be using a single physical connection, in this case an Ethernet interface, and configure multiple subinterfaces to handle each VLAN. The command "encapsulation isl x" is used to associate the subinterface with the VLAN ID on the ISL trunk.
    ☒ **A** is incorrect because it represents the configuration of an internal RSM on a Catalyst 5000 series switch. **B** is incorrect because the subinterface number does not attach it to a VLAN. The command "encapsulation" must be issued on the subinterface in order to link it to a specific VLAN. **C** is also incorrect because it represents the configuration of an MSM on board a Catalyst 6000 switch.

6. ☑ **A.** The Address Resolution Protocol (ARP) table. The table can be displayed on a router by entering the "show arp" command. Routing tables do not show MAC addresses, since they represent Layer 3 routing information by mapping networks to next-hop addresses or egress interfaces.
    ☒ **B** and **C** are incorrect because they pertain to the MAC address to switch port mappings of a switch. **D** is incorrect because it maps network addresses to outbound interfaces and next-hop network addresses.

7. ☑ **B.** The physical medium used by external trunking routers can often be a bottleneck, since all inter-VLAN traffic needs to go up to the router on one VLAN, be routed by the router, and sent back on another VLAN through the same physical connection. Some relief can be found by using Fast EtherChannel technology or GigabitEthernet links, but the speeds still pale in comparison to the backplane speed of a high-end switch.
    ☒ **A** is incorrect because using subinterfaces, the router can create an adequate number of interfaces to handle all the VLANs in a management domain. **C** is incorrect since Fast EtherChannel technology is available to external routers. **D** is incorrect because external routers all have a console port. Only certain models of internal routers do not have a console port.

Internal Route Processors

8. ☑ **D.** Bundling the interfaces and using ISL to handle all the VLANs provides VLAN flexibility and maximizes the throughput of the MSM.
    ☒ **A** is incorrect because it does not make the best use of the MSM's bandwidth. Imagine, for example, that the bulk of the network traffic is on VLANs 1 through 10. This means that the first GigabitEthernet interface would be congested, while the remaining three interface are almost idle. The router would not load balance across the four interfaces. **B** is incorrect because the MSM will not allow for two interfaces to be members of the same network. When entering IP addresses on the second GigabitEthernet subinterface, the router will report an address overlap. One router cannot serve as backup for itself. **C** is incorrect because it places all the IP

addresses in the same broadcast domain. The port-channel interface would have a presence in only one VLAN, so it could not perform routing functions for the remaining 39 VLANs.

9. ☑ **C.** The channel allocation was distributed properly at the creation of VLANs 1, 3, 5, and 7. Removing VLANs 2, 4, 6, and 8, which were created later, does not change the channel distribution on the RSM.
☒ **A** is incorrect because as we explained, the remaining VLANs will use alternating channels, distributing the bandwidth adequately. **B** is incorrect because the RSM does not reallocate channels once the VLANs have been created. **D** is incorrect because when a VLAN is removed from the switch without removing the interface on the RSM itself, the interface is placed in a "down" state—no routing loop is possible.

10. ☑ **B.** SAGE performs encapsulation of the frames before they cross the switching bus.
☒ **A, C,** and **D** are incorrect. They are ASICs that are used by the Catalyst 5000 engine itself to perform switching functions.

11. ☑ **B, D.** In **B**, the supervisory engine can house the daughter card for the RSFC, and the RSM can operate out of slot 5. In **D**, although the total number of routing engines on the switch is probably over the normal needed for redundancy, the switch has the capacity to handle all four routers.
☒ **A** is incorrect because slot 13 of the Catalyst 5500 is reserved for an ATM Switch Processor (ASP) module. The backplane of that slot cannot support an RSM or any other line module. **C** is incorrect because one supervisory module cannot house two RSFCs.

12. ☑ **D.** If the switch itself can create new VLANs on the management domain, an RSM in its chassis can cause the switch to create VLANs by creating VLAN interfaces on the router. This will not happen if the switch is in VTP client mode.
☒ **A** is incorrect because the switch does not depend on the exec level of the router in order to create VLANs on the management domain. Being in enabled mode on the router will not override a switch in VTP client mode. **B** is incorrect because recovering the password of the switch would mean rebooting the entire chassis. The question stated that the criticality of the switch required us not to turn the switch off. Finally, **C** is incorrect because routers do not operate as VTP servers or clients like switches do.

13. ☑ **B.** 256 interfaces also represent the maximum number of simultaneous VLANs that the Catalyst 5500 engine can support.
☒ **A** is incorrect because the amount of memory does not impact the number of interfaces. It normally pertains to the feature set of the IOS installed on the router. **C** is incorrect because

neither the router nor the switch is limited to 128 VLANs or interfaces. **D** is incorrect. It represents the limitation of an MSM, not an RSM.

14. ☑ **D.** These parameters are all required in order for a Port-Channel interface to operate properly.
    ☒ There are no incorrect choices.

Commands

15. ☑ **A.** The command "enable" is used to place the router in privileged exec mode. The router will then display a "#" in the prompt, indicating that it is in privileged exec mode.
    ☒ **B** is incorrect because the command "login" is not an exec-mode command. **C** is also incorrect because the command "session" is used on the CLI of a Catalyst switch to access one of its modules. **D** is incorrect because it represents the "super user" command on UNIX systems to bring the command line into "root" level access.

16. **D.** After receiving a command to place the router in subinterface configuration mode—for example "interface Ethernet 0.1"—the router will show a prompt with the words "config-subif."
    A is incorrect because it represents a router in privileged exec mode. **B** is also incorrect because it represents the global configuration mode. **C** is incorrect because it represents the interface configuration mode.

17. ☑ **B.** The *secondary* keyword is added at the end of network addressing commands such as "ip address" and "ipx network."
    ☒ **A** is incorrect because it attaches a VLAN to an interface; it does not have anything to do with network address configurations. **C** is incorrect because it pertains to AppleTalk configurations. **D** is incorrect because it represents a command used in routing protocol configuration. It does not cause multiple network addresses to be accepted on a single interface.

18. ☑ **C.** The default IPX encapsulation type is "novell-ether." If the encapsulation used by the Novell network is different, the router will not be able to communicate with the servers.
    ☒ **A** is incorrect because the interfaces were successfully pinged. An interface in shutdown mode would not respond to pings. **B** is also incorrect because a router that was not issued the command "ipx routing" would not allow for IPX interface configurations to be entered. Furthermore, pings would not be successful on the interfaces. **D** is incorrect because IPX is indeed a routable protocol, and does not rely solely on broadcasts to operate.

19. ☑ **A, B, C.** All three commands can be used to test the connectivity between two routers. Ping is the most basic command. Traceroute will trace the path between the two routers, and telnet will attempt to log on to the remote router, creating a TCP connection between the two.
    ☒ **D** is incorrect because it does not make use of a network connection. The "session" command is used on the CLI of a Catalyst switch to access an onboard router through the backplane.

20. ☑ **C.** The configuration of an IOS device is stored in Non-Volatile Random Access Memory (NVRAM).
    ☒ **A** is incorrect because DRAM memory is used by the router for operations and processes. It cannot store any information after the router has been powered off. **B** is incorrect because IOS devices use flash memory to store their copy of the IOS. **D** is also incorrect because ROM memory is not configurable. It is static memory that normally contains the bootstrap of the router and a stripped-down version of IOS used for disaster recovery.

21. ☑ **C.** sap encapsulation is the equivalent of IEEE 802.2 on Novell networks.
    ☒ **A, B,** and **D** all correctly match their Novell equivalents.

LAB ANSWER

The following are the configuration steps to achieve this configuration:

1. Place the RSM in privileged exec mode by issuing the command "enable" and entering the proper password if required.

2. Enter configuration mode by issuing the command "configure terminal."

3. Enable IPX services by issuing the command "ipx routing."

4. Enable AppleTalk services by issuing the command "appletalk routing."

5. Create and configure the virtual interfaces by issuing the command "interface vlan x," where "x" is the appropriate VLAN number. For example, VLAN 10 would be serviced by "interface vlan 10."

6. Enter the interface configurations for each virtual interface. The following example shows the proper configuration for the interface controlling VLAN 10. Repeat this configuration for each virtual interface with the appropriate network protocol information.

```
Interface vlan 10
ip address 10.1.1.1 255.255.255.0
ipx network 10
appletalk cable-range 10-10
appletalk zone Zone_10
```

7. Exit configuration mode by entering the command "end."

8. Save your configuration by entering the command "copy running-config startup-config."

9. Display each routing table by entering "show ip route" for TCP/IP, "show ipx route" for IPX networks, and "show appletalk route" for the AppleTalk networks.

6
MultiLayer Switching

CERTIFICATION OBJECTIVES

6.01   Data Flow

6.02   MLS-SE, MLS-RP, MLSP

6.03   Configuring the MLS-SE for IPX MLS

6.04   MLS Cache, Access-Lists, and Other MLS Restrictions

6.05   Commands

✓   Two-Minute Drill

Q&A   Self Test

In the previous chapters, we saw how switches use Media Access Control (MAC) addresses to switch information frames at Layer 2 of the OSI model, the Data Link layer. Switching was limited to a single broadcast domain. A router was required if information needed to go from one network to another. Routers make use of network addresses to route packets at Layer 3 of the OSI model, the Network layer. The big advantage of switching over routing is the speed at which operations are performed. Even with the best caching methods, the Layer 3 routing process is several orders of magnitude slower than the Layer 2 switching process.

In large computing environments, it is common to find a large number of VLANs within the internetwork. To go from one VLAN to another requires the interaction of a router. If one of the VLANs supports a data center or a server farm, most of the traffic flow from the other VLANs will traverse a router in order to reach the resources within that data center. This means that even though the individual VLANs can switch frames within their broadcast domain at very high speeds, when it comes to sending information to and from the data center, the communication speed is limited by the processing speed of the router. In this case, a network using switches to connect every workstation might not provide much benefit, since the router appears to create the bottleneck. Multilayer switching (MLS) can effectively remedy this situation. With the proper hardware and network topology, the switching engine itself can dynamically learn that flow of information through its ports, bypass the router altogether, and forward Layer 3 packets at switching speeds. This process is also known as Layer 3 *switching*, which is synonymous with routing. In this chapter, we discuss the mechanisms that MLS uses to perform these functions, the impact of MLS on other Layer 3 functions such as router access-lists, and how to configure MLS into a multi-VLAN environment.

CERTIFICATION OBJECTIVE 6.01

Data Flow

In Chapter 5, "InterVLAN Routing Concepts," we examined in detail the process an IP packet goes through in order to travel from one IP subnet to another. In a regular switched VLAN environment, an IP packet is placed in a Layer 2 frame and placed on a segment with the source MAC address of the sending workstation and the destination MAC address of the router. We saw how the router stripped the Layer 2 frame, examined the destination IP address in the Layer 3 packet information, made a routing decision, and put the packet back into a new Layer 2 frame, this time having the router's MAC address as source, and the next hop as destination MAC address. The network addresses in the IP packet never changed; only the source and destination MAC addresses in the Data Link frame were modified. Figure 6-1 shows the processing of MAC and IP addresses during the normal routing process as seen in Chapter 5.

Consider the situation shown in Figure 6-2. In this figure, a Catalyst 5505 switch connects two VLANs together through an RSM. The RSM is shown as external to the switch, but it really resides in one of the slots of the switch chassis itself.

In this situation, communication between the workstation and the server must go through the router. The switch itself takes an incoming frame from port 5/1, and switches it to the port belonging to the RSM in VLAN 1. Once the RSM finishes its routing functions, the frame destined for the server reappears at the port of the RSM in VLAN 2. The switch then does its normal duties of switching that frame to port

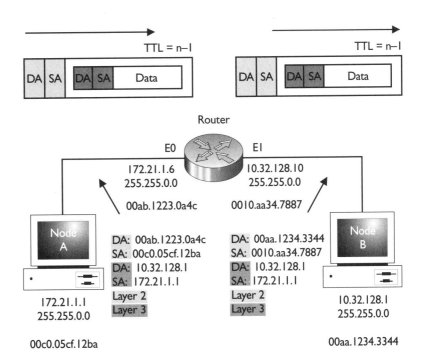

FIGURE 6-1

MAC and IP address changes in a normal routing environment

294 Chapter 6: MultiLayer Switching

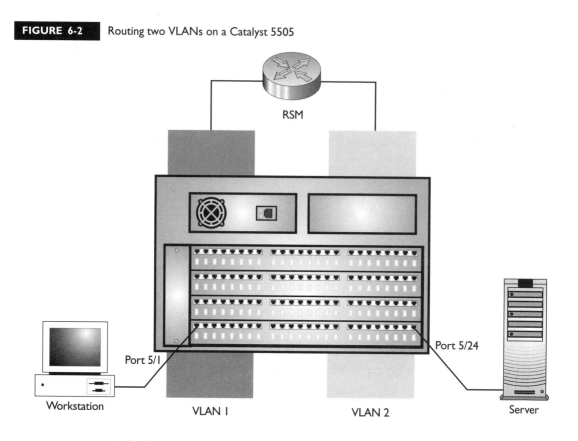

FIGURE 6-2 Routing two VLANs on a Catalyst 5505

5/24. This routing function is essential and cannot be avoided. But what if the switch could learn from experience? During a communication flow, multiple IP packets are sent from the source to the destination. MLS enables the switch to talk to the routing engine and learn about the flow of traffic. In this case, the first packet is through the router. Following this initial routing function, the switch and the router inform each other of the outcome. The switch then builds a shortcut or "flow" for this particular communication, and switches all subsequent packets internally from port 5/1 to port 5/24. This process is knows as "route once, switch many," since in a normal MLS environment, only the first packet needs to be routed by the router. Subsequent packets are all switched internally by the Catalyst switching engine.

This is not quite the same as normal switching. Remember that when the Catalyst switches a frame within a single broadcast domain, it looks up the destination MAC address of the frame and makes a switching decision as to which port to send the frame to. The switch itself does not make any modifications to the frame itself. In the case of MLS, when the frame switches the frame from one VLAN to another, it must enforce the change of MAC addresses that occur in a normal routing sequence. Therefore, when going from port 5/1 to port 5/24, the frame goes through a process called "MAC layer rewrite." This is one of the key responsibilities of MLS, and can only occur after the router has routed the initial packet and a shortcut has been established in the switch's MLS cache. Frames received on 5/1 would have the workstation's MAC address as source, and the router's MAC address as destination. Normally, they would be sent to the router for processing. When MLS is enabled and a flow has been established, the switch will rewrite the source and destination MAC addresses, and switch the frame directly onto port 5/24. The source MAC would reflect the router's MAC address, and the destination MAC would be the address of the server. As with the routing process, the Time To Live (TTL) field of the IP packet is decremented just as if the packet had crossed the boundary of a router. Finally, the switch recalculates the checksum value of the packet with the new values it has rewritten. To the workstation and server, the packet seems to have been routed normally, when in fact, the router has been bypassed entirely. Figure 6-3 shows the communication flow in an MLS environment.

> **exam**
> **ⓦatch**
>
> ***MLS flows are unidirectional entries in the MLS cache. They only represent a one-way communication between two endstations. In a bi-directional application such as Telnet, two flow entries are created in the MLS cache, one from source to destination and one from destination to source.***

The size of the MLS cache is 128k entries. Cisco recommends that the number of flow entries in the MLS cache be kept under 32k in order to ensure that all packets are properly switched. When the cache size goes above 32k entries, some packets may be sent to the router for regular processing.

As of Cisco IOS version 12.1, IPX MLS is also supported by MLS-capable routing platforms. The mechanisms through which an IPX packet is switched through MLS follows the same rules as an IP packet. The source and destination MAC addresses are rewritten by the switch; the IPX network addresses, node and socket numbers remain intact; and the Transport Control field is incremented by 1. In IPX, once the Transport Control field of an IPX packet exceeds the maximum value, the packet is discarded. The default value is 16. The IPX MLS does not have separate cache memory. It therefore competes with IP MLS for cache space. All other network protocols must be sent to the router for processing.

FIGURE 6-3 Traffic flow in an MLS environment

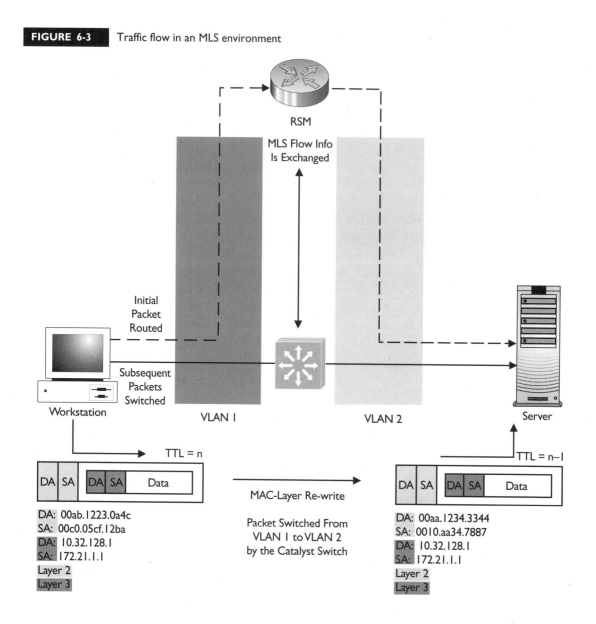

MLS Flow Mask

The MLS cache keeps a record of flows according to one of three different formats called *flow masks*. These flow masks define the type of information that is kept about each flow in the MLS cache. The type of flow mask selected also affects the number of flow entries entered in the MLS cache. The MLS cache is often used with a feature of the Catalyst switch called NetFlow Data Export (NDE) to collect flow statistics. Applications such as Cisco's Netflow Flow Collector and Netflow Data Analyzer use the data collected from NDE for network analysis or even billing purposes. The MLS environment can only use one flow mask type. If the flow mask type is changed, the MLS cache is flushed. The switches participating in MLS will adopt the most specific and most granular flow mask used within the MLS environment. A switch can be forced to use a minimum granularity flow mask using the command "set mls flow." This command does not dictate what flow mask the switch will actually use, but sets the minimum granularity flow mask to be used on that switch. If another switch or router in the MLS topology forces a higher granularity flow mask, all the other switches in the MLS topology will flush their MLS cache and start using this more granular flow mask as their own.

Access-lists used on the router are also directly related to the MLS flow mask used by the switches. When an outbound access-list is present on the router, the router receives a packet to be routed, examines it against its access-list, and discards it if the packet is not permitted by the access-list. Since the router does not return the packet to the switch, no flow entry is created in the MLS cache. The resulting flow mask used by the switches can therefore be dictated by the router's access-list. Extended access-lists, for example, use a granularity that includes information about source IP address, destination IP address, and port and protocols used. In order to support that type of access-list, the switch must use its highest level of flow mask granularity to match the precision of the router's access-list. The following sections list the flow masks supported by MLS and their respective granularity.

destination-ip

The destination-ip flow mask is the least specific flow mask. The MLS cache keeps an entry for each destination IP address. All flow to that destination will use this entry, no matter what source IP address it came from or what protocol or port it is using. The output of the cache table is as follows:

```
Switch> (enable) show mls entry
                Last Used           Last  Used
Destination IP  Source IP           Port  DstPrt SrcPrt Destination Mac   Vlan Port
--------------  --------------      ----  ------ ------ ----------------- ---- -----

MLS-RP 172.20.6.161:
172.20.6.2      172.20.26.9         UDP   6001   69     00-c0-aa-11-23-00 100  1/1
172.20.22.8     172.20.2.1          TCP   9023   Telnet 00-0d-e6-cc-00-08 101  1/2
172.20.28.11    172.20.8.4          UDP   6004   DNS    00-d3-00-a4-00-11 100  1/3
172.20.7.3      172.20.27.10        TCP   6010   FTP    00-c0-04-16-34-00 102  1/4
MLS-RP 10.32.16.1:
172.20.86.12    172.20.85.7         TCP   6007   SMTP   00-03-0d-00-00-12 86   3/1
172.20.85.7     172.20.86.12        TCP   6012   WWW    00-c0-ae-0f-00-07 85   3/2
Switch> (enable)
```

Notice in the output how the source IP address, port, and protocol used are labeled "last used." This is because MLS edits the flow entry each time the flow is used. Since there is only one entry per destination IP, the flow is edited every time an endstation communicates with the host having that destination IP address. This is the only flow mask mode supported by IPX MLS.

> **exam**
> **⑩atch**
>
> *The destination-ip flow mask is the default flow mask used by IP MLS. It is also the only flow mask supported by IPX MLS.*

source-destination ip

The source-destination ip flow mask is more specific. The MLS cache keeps an entry for each source and destination IP address pair. This means that if multiple workstations access the same server, a flow entry will be kept for each. The following output shows the MLS cache having a source-destination ip flow mask:

```
Switch> (enable) show mls entry
                                    Last  Used
Destination IP  Source IP           Port  DstPrt SrcPrt Destination Mac   Vlan Port
--------------  --------------      ----  ------ ------ ----------------- ---- -----

MLS-RP 172.20.6.161:
172.20.6.2      172.20.26.9         TCP   6001   WWW    00-c0-aa-11-23-00 100  1/1
172.20.6.2      172.20.26.10        TCP   8001   WWW    00-c0-aa-11-23-00 100  1/1
172.20.28.11    172.20.8.4          UDP   6004   DNS    00-d3-00-a4-00-11 100  1/3
172.20.7.3      172.20.27.10        TCP   6010   FTP    00-c0-04-16-34-00 102  1/4
Switch> (enable)
```

Notice how similar the output is to the destination-ip flow mask. The difference in this output is that there can be more than one entry with the same destination IP address. This is because the flow mask records individual entries for each source and destination IP address pair. The source IP address parameter in the MLS cache output therefore no longer shows "last used." The first two entries show a connection from endstations 172.20.26.9 and 172.26.10 to server 172.20.6.2. An MLS entry is kept for both endstations. In this case, the ports in use show a Web connection to the server (www). Should either endstation end its Web session and start a Telnet session to the same server, the MLS flow entry would be rewritten with the same source and destination IP addresses, but with the new ports used by the Telnet connection. Since more information is stored, this flow mask increases the MLS memory requirement. Aside from being more accurate, the source-destination ip flow mask can be a necessity for people using the NDE feature. By having characteristics on flows from specific source IP addresses, network administrators can compile usage statistics for specific users, and use that data to charge these users for network usage.

ip-flow

The final flow mask is ip-flow. It is the most memory-demanding flow mask in that it keeps a flow entry for every source and destination IP address, protocol, and port combination. There is no longer a "last used" field in the cache output. Should two workstations each open a Web and Telnet session to the same server, four unidirectional flows would be created in the MLS cache. The responses from the server to these sessions would create four more flows in the reverse direction. The following is the output of the MLS cache in ip-flow mode:

```
Switch> (enable) show mls entry

Destination IP    Source IP        Port DstPrt SrcPrt Destination Mac    Vlan Port
---------------   ---------------  ---- ------ ------ -----------------  ---- -----

MLS-RP 172.20.6.161:
172.20.6.2        172.20.26.9      TCP  6001   WWW    00-c0-aa-11-23-00  100  1/1
172.20.6.2        172.20.26.9      TCP  6023   Telnet 00-c0-aa-11-23-00  100  1/1
172.20.6.2        172.20.26.10     TCP  8001   WWW    00-c0-aa-11-23-00  100  1/1
172.20.6.2        172.20.26.10     TCP  8056   Telnet 00-c0-aa-11-23-00  100  1/1
172.20.28.11      172.20.8.4       UDP  6004   DNS    00-d3-00-a4-00-11  100  1/3
172.20.7.3        172.20.27.10     TCP  6010   FTP    00-c0-04-16-34-00  102  1/4
Switch> (enable)
```

The ip-flow flow cache may be needed in situations where NDE requires statistics about the applications running on the network. Through the data collected in ip-flow mode, network administrators can examine the amount of information that is being passed over Web, mail, or any other port-specific applications.

Be careful when using the ip-flow flow mask not to overflow your MLS cache usage. On a Catalyst 5500, for example, anything beyond 32k entries in the cache will increase the possibility that some packets are sent to the router for normal routing functions. If this happens, the performance of that communication is degraded, and the accuracy of your Netflow data export will be reduced.

EXERCISE 6-1

The Correct Flow Mask

You find that the number of MLS entries in your switch is rather high. In order to see what could be the issue, you examine the configurations of both the MLS-SE and MLS-RP. The relevant configurations are shown next. You decide to select destination-ip as flow mask specified on the MLS-SE. The configuration commands are shown after the configurations. Explain, if any, the resulting effect on the MLS cache.

The MLS-RP configurations:

```
mls rp ip
!
interface FastEthernet0/0
 ip address 10.1.1.1 255.255.255.0
 mls rp ip
 mls rp management-interface
!
interface FastEthernet0/0
 ip address 20.1.1.1 255.255.255.0
 ip access-group 101 out
 mls rp ip
!
access-list 101 permit tcp 10.0.0.0 0.255.255.255 host 20.1.1.10 eq telnet
access-list 101 deny ip any any
!
The MLS-SE Configurations:
#mls
set mls enable
set mls flow destination-source
set mls agingtime 256
```

```
set mls agingtime fast 0 0
set mls include 10.1.1.1
set mls nde disable
The command you enter:
Cat-5500> (enable) set mls flow destination
Configured IP flowmask is set to destination flow.
```

Solution: Changing the configured flow mask on the MLS-SE had no impact on the MLS cache. Remember the rule of highest granularity when selecting a flow cache within an MLS topology. In this scenario, we can clearly see that an outbound extended access-list is being used on the MLS-RP. This access-list will force the utilization of ip-flow as the flow cache used by MLS. Declaring destination-ip as the lowest granularity flow mask to be used by the switch will not change the actual flow mask used by the MLS process.

How Different Hardware Platforms Handle Flows of Data through MLS

The Catalyst 5000 and 6000 series switches are the LAN workhorses in Cisco's product line, and normally do the bulk of the multilayer switching in today's internetworking environments. From an operations standpoint, the 2948G, 4000, 5000, and 6000 series handle IP MLS in an identical way. They all have a 128k MLS cache to store IP MLS flows. However, the hardware used on each series is different. The Catalyst 5000 series, for example, has multiple configurations that can support MLS operations. When using a Supervisor III Engine, the module must be equipped with a NetFlow Feature Card (NFFC) II card in order to support MLS. When using a Supervisor IIIG Engine with a router switch feature card, MLS is supported natively without an NFFC. Make sure you are aware of the hardware requirements when ordering MLS-capable equipment. For the 6000 series, the Supervisor Engine must be equipped with a Policy Feature Card (PFC) in order to support MLS. Similar to the Catalyst 5000 series, the PFC controls the entries and operations of the MLS flow cache.

Now that you have a better understanding of MLS data flow, refer to the following Scenario & Solution.

SCENARIO & SOLUTION

What is a "MAC-layer rewrite?"	It is the process through which the switch rewrites the source and destination MAC addresses of a packet when switching it from one VLAN to another. This process is essential, since MAC addresses are locally significant to the broadcast domain they are on. When crossing a router boundary, a router rewrites these values before placing the packet back on the new segment. The switch must therefore perform the same modifications when switching a packet at Layer 3.
What is the default flow mask used by IP MLS?	The default flow mask used by IP MLS is destination-ip. It is also the only flow mask supported by IPX MLS.
Which flow mask is the most accurate?	The ip-flow mask is the most accurate flow mask, because it keeps a flow entry in the MLS cache for every combination of source MAC address, destination MAC address, and port/protocol combination.
Does the switch modify anything more than the source and destination MAC addresses when it performs a MAC-layer rewrite?	No. The switch also increments the TTL field of IP packets, decrements the Transmission Control field of IPX packets, and recomputes the checksum of the packet using the new values.

CERTIFICATION OBJECTIVE 6.02

MLS-SE, MLS-RP, MLSP

We have seen how MLS operates in concept. It is now time to tie these concepts in with specific MLS terminology and responsibilities.

MLS-SE

The Multilayer Switching-Switching Engine (MLS-SE) is the part of the Catalyst switch that performs all MLS functions. It exchanges information with the router about IP and IPX flows, and maintains the MLS cache. When a packet enters the switch, the MLS-SE compares it to its MLS cache. If the packet matches an entry in the MLS cache, the MLS-SE performs the MAC layer rewrite, and switches the packet onto the outbound port. If the packet does not match any entries in the cache, the MLS-SE sends the packet to the router as a "candidate packet." This candidate packet serves to establish the MLS cache flow for subsequent packets going to that destination. The switch expects the return of this packet once it has been routed by the router. Upon its return, this packet is identified as an "enabler packet."

Configuring the MLS-SE for IP MLS

The configuration of the MLS-SE for MLS IP is fairly simple. It involves enabling the MLS process on the switch itself and declaring which routers will be participating in MLS. By default, the MLS-SE uses destination-ip as its cache flow. The following code output show the successful configuration of a Catalyst 5500 switch to operate with an MLS-Route Processor (MLS-RP) that has the IP address 10.1.1.1. The default cache flow has been overridden with the source-destination ip cache flow:

```
Cat-550> (enable) set mls ?
  agingtime                Set agingtime for MLS cache entry
  disable                  Disable MLS in the switch
  enable                   Enable MLS in the switch
  nde                      Configure Netflow Data Export
  flow                     Set minimum flow mask
  include                  Include MLS-RP
  multicast                Set MLS feature for multicast
  statistics               Add protocols to protocol statistics list

Cat-5500> (enable)
Cat-5500> (enable) set mls enable
IP Multilayer switching is enabled.

Cat-5500> (enable) set mls include 10.1.1.1
IP Multilayer switching enabled for router 10.1.1.1.

Cat-5500> (enable) set mls flow ?
  destination              Set destination flow
  destination-source       Set destination-source flow
  full                     Set full flow
Cat-5500> (enable) set mls flow destination-source
Configured IP flowmask is set to destination-source flow.
Cat-5500> (enable) %MLS-5-FLOWMASKCHANGE:IP flowmask changed from DEST to DEST-SRC
```

```
Cat-5500> (enable) show mls include
IP:
Included IP MLS-RP
---------------------
10.1.1.1

Cat-5500> (enable)
Cat-5500> (enable) show mls
Total packets switched = 1102
Total Active MLS entries = 27
IP Multilayer switching enabled
IP Multilayer switching aging time = 256 seconds
IP Multilayer switching fast aging time = 0 seconds, packet threshold = 0
IP Current flow mask is Source-Destination flow
Configured flow mask is Source-Destination flow
Active IP MLS entries = 27
Netflow Data Export disabled
Netflow Data Export port/host is not configured.
Total packets exported = 0

IP MLS-RP IP      MLS-RP ID      XTAG MLS-RP MAC-Vlans
---------------   ------------   ---- -------------------------------
10.1.1.1          00906de3ac00    2   00-90-6d-e3-ac-00  1,10,20
Cat-5500> (enable)
```

These are the basic steps required to enable multilayer switching on the MLS-SE. Notice the message sent to the console when the flow mask was changed. The process of changing flow masks on the MLS-SE purged the MLS cache of all entries. The cache is then rebuilt using the new flow cache as candidate packets arrive at the switch. As we can see, the switch wasted no time in repopulating its MLS cache. The output of the command "show mls" already shows 27 active MLS entries. Remember that the command "set mls flow" only sets the minimal flow mask used by the switch. If an outbound extended access-list were configured on the router, this would have forced the switch to adopt the ip-flow mask in order to support the granularity of the extended access-list.

exam ⓦatch

When communicating with the router, the MLS-SE uses a unique parameter called XTag to identify each router. This parameter is displayed when showing the list of MLS-RP participating in the MLS process. The following code example shows the output of the command "show mls" on the MLS-SE. It shows the XTag associated with each MLS-RP.

```
Cat-5500> (enable) show mls
Total packets switched = 1674
Total Active MLS entries = 68
IP Multilayer switching enabled
IP Multilayer switching aging time = 256 seconds
IP Multilayer switching fast aging time = 0 seconds, packet threshold = 0
IP Current flow mask is Destination flow
Configured flow mask is Destination flow
Active IP MLS entries = 27
Netflow Data Export disabled
Netflow Data Export port/host is not configured.
Total packets exported = 0

IP MLS-RP IP      MLS-RP ID      XTAG MLS-RP MAC-Vlans
----------------  ------------   ---- --------------------------------
10.1.1.1          00906de3ac00    2   00-90-6d-e3-ac-00  1,10,20
10.1.1.3          00906de3a796    3   00-90-6d-e3-a7-96  1,10,20
Cat-5500> (enable)
```

CERTIFICATION OBJECTIVE 6.03

Configuring the MLS-SE for IPX MLS

As of version 12.1 of the Cisco IOS, IPX MLS has been added as a new feature of the MLS process. Routers running IOS 12.1 code and providing IPX routing services can now participate in IPX MLS to improve IPX routing performance. The configuration of the MLS-SE for IPX MLS is done the same way as for MLS IP. It involves enabling the MLS IPX process on the switch itself and declaring which routers will be participating in MLS IPX. IPX MLS only supports the destination-ip cache flow. The following code output shows the successful configuration of IPX MLS on a Catalyst 5500 switch.

```
Cat-5500> (enable) set mls enable ipx
IPX Multilayer switching is enabled.

Cat-5500> (enable) set mls include ipx 10.1.1.1
IPX Multilayer switching enabled for router 10.1.1.1.

Cat-5500> (enable)
```

Notice how IPX MLS uses TCP/IP to communicate between the MLS-SE and MLS-RP. This means that a viable IP network must be operating for IPX MLS to operate properly.

MLS-RP

The Multilayer Switching-Route Processor (MLS-RP) performs the routing function for packets that are not switched internally by the MLS-SE. The MLS-RP exchanges information with the MLS-SE about the packets it routes, changes in routing, and aging of flows. It remains in constant communication with the MLS-SE to ascertain the health of the MLS process. Not all routers can act as an MLS-RP. Cisco identifies the following platforms as MLS-capable routers:

- A Route Switch Module (RSM) or Route Switch Feature Card (RSFC) on a Catalyst 5000 series switch
- A Multilayer Switch Module (MSM) or Multilayer Switch Feature Card (MSFC) on a Catalyst 6000 series switch
- An externally connected Cisco 7500, 7200, 4700, 4500, or 3600 series router with MLS-capable software

Configuring the MLS-RP for IP MLS

Since the MLS-RP is a Cisco router running IOS, the commands to enable MLS on the MLS-RP are different from those on the MLS-SE. As with the MLS-SE, the first task is to enable the MLS process on the router. This is done with the global configuration command "mls ip rp". Next, the individual interfaces that participate in MLS must be configured. This task involves enabling the MLS process on that interface and declaring the VTP domain name of the MLS-SE that controls this VLAN. This domain name is case sensitive and must match exactly the VTP domain name that is configured on the switch in order for MLS to operate properly. Following this, one more task remains: the MLS-SE needs to be told which VLAN to use to communicate with the MLS-SE. MLS calls it the *management interface*. This will be the VLAN on which the MLS-SE's sc0 interface resides. In the following code, the router is configured to use interface VLAN 1 as the management interface. This assumes that the MLS-SE has a valid IP address and is configured to communicate using interface sc0 through VLAN 1. The router must have at least one management interface configured to operate on a VLAN that is participating in MLS. If a VLAN does not span across an entire internetwork, multiple management interfaces may be required on the MLS-RP in order to support MLS on all the switches in the VTP domain. For example, take a VTP domain having VLANs 1, 2, 3, and 4. Two switches connect to the MLS-RP, one carrying VLANs 1 and 2, and the other carrying VLANs 3 and 4. In order for MLS to operate with both MLS-SEs, the router must have two VLAN interfaces configured as an MLS

Configuring the MLS-SE for IPX MLS

management interface. In this case, declaring interfaces VLAN 1 and VLAN 3 as management interfaces would satisfy the MLS requirement of that topology.

```
RSM#configure terminal
Enter configuration commands, one per line.  End with CNTL/Z.
RSM(config)#mls rp ip
RSM(config)#
RSM(config)#interface VLAN 1
RSM(config-if)#ip address 10.1.1.2 255.255.255.0
RSM(config-if)#mls rp ip
RSM(config-if)#mls rp vtp-domain My_Domain
RSM(config-if)#mls rp management-interface
RSM(config-if)#exit
RSM(config)#
RSM(config)#interface VLAN 10
RSM(config-if)#ip address 10.10.1.2 255.255.255.0
RSM(config-if)#mls rp ip
RSM(config-if)#mls rp vtp-domain My_Domain
RSM(config-if)#exit
RSM(config)#
RSM(config)#interface VLAN 20
RSM(config-if)#ip address 10.20.1.2 255.255.255.0
RSM(config-if)#mls rp ip
RSM(config-if)#mls rp vtp-domain My_Domain
RSM(config-if)#exit
RSM(config)#end
2w3d: %SYS-5-CONFIG_I: Configured from console by vty0 (10.1.1.2)

RSM#show mls rp
ip multilayer switching is globally enabled
ipx multilayer switching is globally disabled
ipx mls inbound acl override is globally disabled
mls id is 0090.6de3.ac00
mls ip address 10.1.1.1
mls ip flow mask is source-destination
mls ipx flow mask is unknown
number of domains configured for mls 1

vlan domain name: My_Domain
   current ip flow mask: source-destination
   ip current/next global purge: false/false
   ip current/next purge count: 0/0
   current ipx flow mask: destination
   ipx current/next global purge: false/false
```

```
        ipx current/next purge count: 0/0
        current sequence number: 1643178053
        current/maximum retry count: 0/10
        current domain state: no-change
        domain uptime: 1w2d
        keepalive timer expires in 14 seconds
        retry timer not running
        change timer not running
        fcp subblock count = 14

        1 management interface(s) currently defined:
           vlan 1 on Vlan1

        3 mac-vlan(s) configured for multilayer switching

        3 mac-vlan(s) enabled for ip multilayer switching:

           mac 0090.6de3.ac00
              vlan id(s)
              1    10    20

        router currently aware of following 1 switch(es):
           switch id 0050.5081.2bff
RSM#
```

When using an external router, if the router is not connecting through an ISL or 802.1q trunk to the MLS-SE, that router does not understand or speak VTP with the MLS-SE. It therefore does not know how to identify its VLANs to the switch. In order to identify these VLANs, an additional interface command must be added on the MLS-RP to associate the VLAN with the corresponding VLAN ID on the MLS-SE. The following shows the configuration of the Fast Ethernet interface of a Cisco 7200 router. The interface is associated with VLAN 10 on the MLS-SE. Notice how the router does not make use of ISL or 802.1q in its configuration.

```
C-7200#configure terminal
Enter configuration commands, one per line.  End with CNTL/Z.
C-7200(config)#
C-7200(config)#mls rp ip
C-7200(config)#
C-7200(config)#interface FastEthernet 0/0
C-7200(config-if)#ip address 10.1.1.5 255.255.255.0
C-7200(config-if)#mls rp ip
C-7200(config-if)#mls rp vtp-domain My_Domain
```

```
C-7200(config-if)#mls rp vlan-id 10
C-7200(config-if)#exit
C-7200(config)#end
1w2d: %SYS-5-CONFIG_I: Configured from console by vty0 (10.1.1.2)
C-7200#
```

on the job

It is important to remember that not all versions of IOS support MLS. IOS in the 11.3WA, 12.0WA, and 12.1WA trains should be used in order to support MLS on the MLS-RP.

Configuring the MLS-RP for IPX MLS

The configuration of IPX MLS on the MLS-RP is almost identical to the configuration of MLS IP. It involves enabling the IPX MLS process in global configuration mode, specifying the VLAN interfaces that will participate in IPX MLS, and declaring the VTP domain name in these interfaces. The following code output shows the successful configuration of IPX MLS on an RSM.

```
RSM(config)#mls rp ipx
RSM(config)#
RSM(config)#interface VLAN 1
RSM(config-if)#ipx network 1A
RSM(config-if)#mls rp ipx
RSM(config-if)#mls rp vtp-domain My_Domain
RSM(config-if)#mls rp management-interface
RSM(config-if)#exit
RSM(config)#
RSM(config)#interface VLAN 10
RSM(config-if)#ipx network 10A
RSM(config-if)#mls rp ipx
RSM(config-if)#mls rp vtp-domain My_Domain
RSM(config-if)#exit
RSM(config)#
RSM(config)#interface VLAN 20
RSM(config-if)#ip network 20A
RSM(config-if)#mls rp ipx
RSM(config-if)#mls rp vtp-domain My_Domain
RSM(config-if)#exit
RSM(config)#end
2w3d: %SYS-5-CONFIG_I: Configured from console by vty0 (10.1.1.2)
RSM#
```

MLSP

The MultiLayer Switching Protocol (MLSP) is at the heart of the MLS process. It is the protocol used between the MLS-SE and the MLS-RP. The tasks of MLSP are as follows:

- Enable MLS between the MLS-SE and MLS-RP
- Installing, updating, and deleting flows in the MLS cache
- Managing and exporting flow information when NDE is enabled
- Help the MLS-SE learn the MAC address of the MLS-RP
- Check the flow mask of the MLS-RP
- Confirm that MLS is operational

MLSP sends hello packets between the MLS-SE and MLS-RP in order to ascertain that the MLS process is operational. The default interval for these hellos is 15 seconds. If three hellos are missed, the MLS-SE declares the MLS-RP as dead. When exchanging information with the MLS-RP, the MLS-SE identifies the router not by its IP address, but by an agreed parameter called XTag. In the MLS cache, the XTag is a unique numerical value that represents an MLS-RP with which the MLS-SE exchanges MLSP information. The following code output shows the XTags for two MLS-RPs connected to the MLS-SE.

```
Cat-5500> (enable) show mls
Total packets switched = 1674
Total Active MLS entries = 68
IP Multilayer switching enabled
IP Multilayer switching aging time = 256 seconds
IP Multilayer switching fast aging time = 0 seconds, packet threshold = 0
IP Current flow mask is Destination flow
Configured flow mask is Destination flow
Active IP MLS entries = 27
Netflow Data Export disabled
Netflow Data Export port/host is not configured.
Total packets exported = 0

IP MLS-RP IP    MLS-RP ID     XTAG MLS-RP MAC-Vlans
--------------- ------------- ---- -------------------------------
10.1.1.1        00906de3ac00    2  00-90-6d-e3-ac-00  1,10,20
10.1.1.3        00906de3a796    3  00-90-6d-e3-a7-96  1,10,20
Cat-5500> (enable)
```

There are three steps in the creation of a flow: candidate, enabler, and caching. When a packet arrives at the MLS-SE, the MLS-SE compares the packet with the MLS cache entries. If the packet doesn't match, it is sent to the MLS-RP as a *candidate* packet. This means that the packets subsequent to the candidate have the possibility of being Layer 3 switched. After passing the packet through the MLS flow mask and rewriting the Layer 2 information, the candidate packet is routed to the outbound interface. This outbound interface of the router connects to another port on the MLS-SE. This enabler packet, when returning to the MLS-SE on the outbound port of the router, becomes what is called an *enabler* packet. If the enabler packet originated on the MLS-SE as a candidate packet, an MLS cache entry is created for that packet, and subsequent packets will use the cache entry to be switched by the MLS-SE. This restriction limits the possible topologies supported by MLS. We will examine these topologies in the following section.

The same MLE-SE must see both the candidate packet and the enabler packet in order for the MLS cache entry to be created. Upon the arrival of an enabler packet at the interface of an MLS-SE, an MLS cache entry will not be created if that MLS-SE did not see the candidate packet for that flow beforehand.

MLS Topologies

The deployment of MLS in an existing internetwork or the design of a new internetwork using MLS should be done with care. Since MLS creates shortcuts across the internetwork topology, it is important to understand how MLS operates on the network. The rule of the candidate and enabler packets applies when designing the topology.

The most basic MLS topology was shown in Figure 6-2. In that figure, a single Catalyst switch works in tandem with an RSM to switch packets between VLANs. The switch, or MLS-SE, will always be able to match a candidate packet to any enabler packet that returns from the RSM, or MLS-RP. When the internetwork becomes more complicated, the candidate/enabler rule must be met. Figure 6-4 shows an expanded network based on the initial MLS topology.

In this topology, the candidate/enabler packet rule is respected. Router 2, the MLS-RP, can Layer-3 switch the packets it receives from R1 out to R3. Connectivity from station A to station B is routed normally at R1, Layer-3 switched

FIGURE 6-4 Valid MLS topology

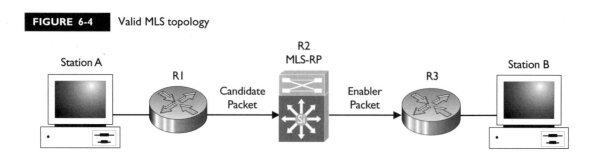

at R2, and routed normally at R3. On the other hand, the topology shown in Figure 6-5 does not respect the requirements for MLS to operate properly.

In this topology, external routers MLS-RP 1 and 2 are directly connected. MLS-SE 1 and 2 are also directly connected. Let's assume that the routing topology makes the packets flow from MLS-RP 1 to MLS-RP 2 on their common link instead of back through the switches. In this case, MLS-SE 1 receives a candidate packet from station A. It switches the packet to the interface of MLS-RP 1. MLS-RP 1 does not return an enabler packet to MLS-SE 1. Instead, it routes the packet to MLS-RP 2, which makes the routing decision to send the packet to MLS-SE 2. Since MLS-SE 1 never received the enabler packet for this communication, it cannot create a flow through MLS-SE 2 to bypass the two routers. The communication will be routed through MLS-RP 1 and 2 for the entire duration of the communication.

FIGURE 6-5 Invalid MLS topology

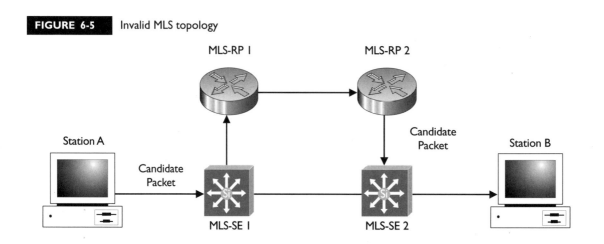

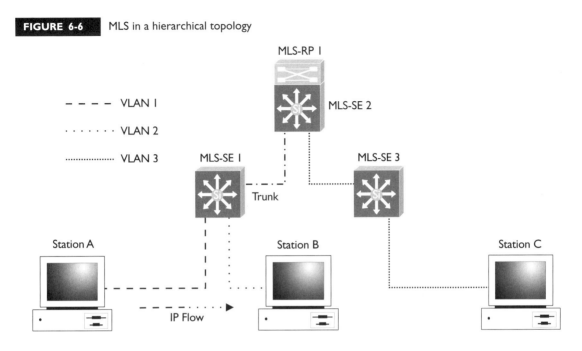

FIGURE 6-6   MLS in a hierarchical topology

One final topology shown in Figure 6-6 represents a successful MLS topology in a more complex, hierarchical topology.

In Figure 6-6, the initial packet from station A to station B flows through MLS-SE 1 and MLS-SE 2 to MLS-RP 1 for a routing decision. Both MLS-SE 1 and 2 treat this initial packet as a candidate packet. After being routed by MLS-RP 1, MLS-SE 2 receives the packet from the router in VLAN 2. It treats this packet as an enabler and creates an entry in the MLS cache for this flow. Any further packets for this flow would be Layer-3 switched by MLS-SE 2 internally. MLS-SE 2 then switches the packet back to MLS-SE 1, which also treats this returning packet as an enabler. MLS-SE 1 also creates an MLS entry in its cache for this flow. The following packets are therefore Layer-3 switched by MLS-SE 1. The MLS cache entry on MLS-SE 2 will eventually be removed when the aging-time is exceeded for that entry.

Now that you have a better understanding of MLS-SE, MLS-RP, and MLSP, refer to the following Scenario & Solution.

SCENARIO & SOLUTION

You have a Cisco 2500 series router with the latest version of IOS software running on it. Can you use this router be used in MLS?	No. Only Cisco 7500, 7200, 4700, 4500, or 3600 series routers are capable of participating in the MLS process.
Which two packet types must an MLS-SE process in order to create an entry in the MLS cache?	The MLS-SE must send a *candidate* packet to the MLS-RP and see an *enabler* packet come back from the router. Only then will the MLS-SE create a flow entry in the MLS cache.
Which parameter does the MLS-SE use to identify the MLS-capable routers with which it communicates?	The MLS-SE identifies the MLS-RPs it communicates with using a unique identifier called XTag.
Which hardware must be present on the MLS-SE in order to support MLS operation?	The Catalyst 5000 series switch must be equipped with a NetFlow Feature Card (NFFC) on its Supervisor III Engine. The Catalyst 6000 series switch must be equipped with a Policy Feature Card (PFC) in order to support MLS.
What is the hello interval of MLSP, and how long does an MLS-SE wait before declaring an MLS-RP dead?	The default interval for MLSP hellos is 15 seconds. If the MLS-SE misses three consecutive hellos from the MLS-RP, it declares that router as dead and removes it from the MLS process.

EXERCISE 6-2

MLS Topology Validation

You are hired by a high-tech computer firm to assess their plans to deploy MLS within their environment. Their network engineer has worked on a network topology that he thinks will support MLS. Their understanding of MLS is limited, so they require your expertise to determine if MLS will operate properly in their proposed topology. Figure 6-7 represents the network diagram that the network engineer has produced. Identify whether MLS will operate properly in this environment, and state the reasons that support your evaluation.

Solution: In this topology, MLS will *not* operate properly, because MLS-SE 1, which sends a candidate packet to MLS-RP 1, does not receive the enabler packet back from the router. That packet is sent to MLS-SE 3 on VLAN 3, which in turn switches the packet to the port belonging to station B. MLS-SE 1 never sees the

Configuring the MLS-SE for IPX MLS **315**

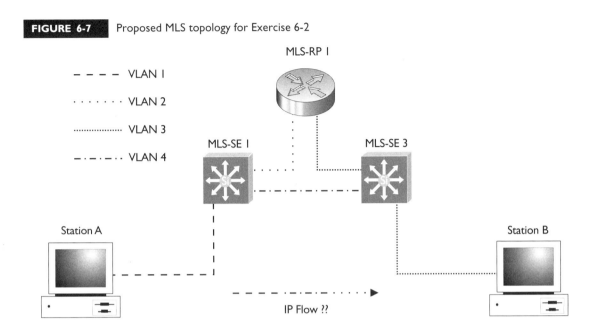

FIGURE 6-7 Proposed MLS topology for Exercise 6-2

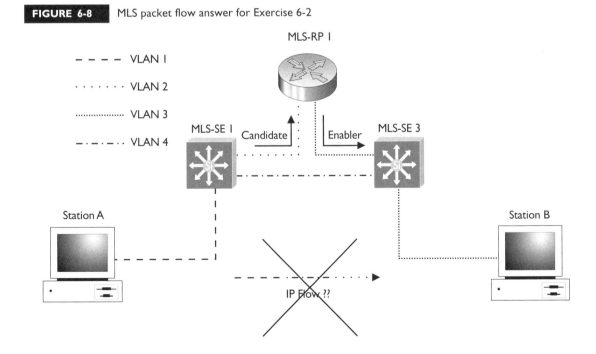

FIGURE 6-8 MLS packet flow answer for Exercise 6-2

enabler packet; therefore, no MLS cache entry can be created for that flow. Figure 6-8 shows the actual path of the candidate and enabler packets, and why no flow entry can be created from station A to station B.

CERTIFICATION OBJECTIVE 6.04

MLS Cache, Access-Lists, and Other MLS Restrictions

The primary function of MLS is to bypass the slower routing process by recognizing the flow of information and use the high-speed switching process of the Catalyst engine to forward packets to their destination. The router, however, performs many other services to ensure reliable network connectivity. Services such as Quality of Service (QoS), access-lists, or data encryption are all services performed by the router. These services cannot be duplicated by the MLS-SE. This section identifies the issues and restrictions of MLS when using other IP services on the router.

Disabling Combinations

The following is a list of combinations that either disable the IP service when MLS is enabled, or disable MLS when the IP service is enabled.

IP accounting   An MLS-enabled interface will disable any IP accounting functions configured on that interface.

Reflexive access-lists   When a reflexive access-list is configured on an interface, that interface can no longer participate in MLS.

Data encryption   Enabling data encryption on an interface disables MLS on that interface.

Input access-lists   An interface with an input access-list applied cannot participate in MLS. The solution is to translate the input access-list into an output access-list, and apply it to the outbound interface.

Output access-lists   MLS can operate with output access-lists configured on that interface. However, the following restrictions apply:

MLS Cache, Access-Lists, and Other MLS Restrictions

- Applying an output access-list on an MLS-enabled interface clears the MLS cache entries for that interface.
- Output access-lists that make the use of the log, precedence, tos (type of service) or establish options disable MLS on that interface.

Policy routing   Interfaces with policy route-maps applied to them disables MLS on that interface.

Network address translation (NAT)   MLS is disabled on any interface that participates in a NAT process.

TCP intercept   Although not a disabling feature, the use of TCP intercept with MLS may produce unstable or unpredictable results. IOS issues the following warning message to the console when both features are enabled on the same interface: Command accepted, interfaces with mls might cause inconsistent behavior.

Committed access rate (CAR)   Configuring CAR on an interface disables MLS on that interface.

IP security   All formats of the "ip security" command disable MLS on that interface.

TCP compression   The commands "ip tcp compression-connections" and "ip tcp header-compression" disable MLS on that interface.

Maximum Transfer Unit (MTU)   The MTU on interfaces participating in MLS must be 1500 bytes. Attempting to change the MTU on an MLS-enabled interface will generate an error. Conversely, attempting to configure MLS on an interface with an MTU other than 1500 will also generate an error.

- Covered above in output access lists.

exam
Watch

MLS only supports outbound access-lists. It does not support inbound, reflexive, or context-based access control (CBAC). Thankfully, most inbound access-lists can easily be converted into outbound access-lists. Inbound access-lists filter and discard packets before they reach the routing and MLS process of the router. The router therefore has no way to communicate information about denied packets to the switch so that the MLS cache table can be properly adjusted.

TABLE 6-1 Exercise 6-3 Chart

Feature	Disables MLS	Is disabled by MLS	No conflict with MLS
Data encryption			
Output access-list			
IP accounting			
NAT			
Ip route-cache			
Ip routing			
Ip security			

EXERCISE 6-3

A World Full of Features

Many features cannot be used in conjunction with MLS. Complete Table 6-1 with the appropriate answers pertaining to these combinations.

Solution: Table 6-2 shows the interaction of the listed features with the MLS process.

TABLE 6-2 Exercise 6-3 Solution

Feature	Disables MLS	Is disabled by MLS	No conflict with MLS
Data Encryption	X		
Output access-list			X
IP accounting		X	
NAT	X		
Ip route-cache			X
Ip routing			X
Ip security	X		

MLS Cache Issues

We mentioned earlier that the maximum number of flow entries in the MLS cache of the MLS-SE is 128k. Cisco, however, recommends that the number of flow entries be kept below 32k. Anything above 32k entries increases the possibility that packets having an entry in the MLS cache are sent to the MLS-RP to be routed. This means that having too many entries in your MLS cache reduces the efficiency of the Layer-3 switching process as the cache size increases.

Optimizing Cache

In order to keep the MLS cache size below 32k entries, the Catalyst operating system provides a few methods to reduce the number of flow entries in the cache. Each will affect the operation of MLS and should be adjusted with care. The command "show mls" displays general statistics of the MLS process on the MLS-SE, including the number of flow entries in the MLS cache. The following code listing is an example of the output of this command.

```
Cat-5500> show mls
Total packets switched = 1243529431
Total Active MLS entries = 932
IP Multilayer switching enabled
IP Multilayer switching aging time = 256 seconds
IP Multilayer switching fast aging time = 0 seconds, packet threshold = 0
IP Current flow mask is Destination flow
Configured flow mask is Destination flow
Active IP MLS entries = 932
Netflow Data Export disabled
Netflow Data Export port/host is not configured.
Total packets exported = 0

IP MLS-RP IP       MLS-RP ID      XTAG MLS-RP MAC-Vlans
----------------   ------------   ---- --------------------------------
192.168.10.254     00906de3ac00    2   00-90-6d-e3-ac-00  1,128,130-160
Cat-5500>
```

Flow Mask The easiest way to reduce the MLS cache size is to use the least granular flow mask. Of the three flow masks available in IP MLS, the destination-ip flow mask will use the least amount of memory. This is because destination-ip keeps a single flow entry per destination MAC address. Any number of workstations accessing a busy server on another subnet, for example, would use the same flow entry to reach it. In comparison, if source-destination ip were enabled, the MLS-SE would keep one flow entry per workstation trying to access that one server. It would use the same source-destination ip flow, whether the workstation tried to access that server via Telnet, ftp, or any other protocol. Finally, the ip-flow mask is the most memory intensive since it keeps a flow entry for each combination of source MAC, destination MAC, protocol, and ports used. Unless required for the purposes of NDE, it is recommended that MLS be configured with its default flow mask: destination-ip.

Remember that adjusting the flow mask on the switch only changes the minimum flow mask to be used by the switch. If you have an outbound access-list configured on one of the MLS-RPs, or have another switch that forces ip-flow as the lowest flow mask, adjusting the flow mask to destination-ip on your switch will not change the flow mask used in the MLS topology. Your switch will continue using ip-flow as its flow mask, and no economy of MLS cache entries will result from this command.

Aging-Time Another way to impact the size of the MLS cache is to adjust how long the flow entries remain in memory. The Catalyst switch offers two parameters for this purpose: the aging-time and the fast aging-time. By reducing the length of time that a flow can remain in the cache after it is no longer in use, we can eliminate unneeded flow entries and thus reduce the overall size of the MLS cache. Be careful when adjusting these parameters. Reducing the aging-time to a low value may cause the MLS-SE to drop entries while the communication between two endpoints is still ongoing. This would mean having packets switched and routed as the MLS-SE and MLS-RP keep renegotiating the candidate/enabler packet for that flow. On the other hand, if the MLS aging-time is set too high, the MLS flow entries will remain in the MLS cache much longer than required, unnecessarily increasing the number of entries in the MLS cache.

- **Adjusting the Aging-Time Value** Any flow entry that is not used within the specified aging-time is flushed from the MLS cache. This is the housekeeping process of MLS in order to keep only active flows in memory. The default value of the aging-time is 256 seconds. It can be adjusted anywhere between 8 to 2032 seconds, as a multiple of 8. This means that a configured aging-time of 17 seconds would be adjusted back to 16 seconds by the switch. The following code output shows the aging-time of MLS being adjusted to 128 seconds.

```
Cat-5500> (enable) set mls agingtime 128
Multilayer switching agingtime set to 128

Cat-5500> (enable)
```

- **Adjusting the Fast Aging-Time Value**   MLS works best with large streams between two endstations. For short communications such as DNS where a handful of packets are required, MLS does not provide much performance improvement. These short communications, however, still create entries in the MLS cache. The fast aging-time parameter of MLS lets network administrators control the size of the MLS cache by reducing the number of short flows in the cache. A threshold is set to indicate the minimum number of packets that need to be switched within the fast aging interval. For example, the aging-time of MLS can be set to its default 256 seconds. However, if we configure a fast aging-time of 32 seconds with a threshold of 15 packets, any flow that does not switch more than 15 packets within a 32-second interval is flushed from the MLS cache. Fast aging uses discrete values for interval and threshold. The fast aging-time interval can be set to 32, 64, 96, or 128 seconds, while the packet threshold can be set to 0, 1, 3, 7, 15, 31, or 63 packets. The following shows the configuration of fast aging on a Catalyst 5500. The fast aging parameters are set at a threshold of 7 packets in an interval of 32 seconds.

```
Cat-5500> (enable) set mls agingtime fast 32 7
Multilayer switching fast agingtime set to 32 seconds for
entry with no more than 7 packets switched

Cat-5500> (enable)
```

exam
Watch

The MLS cache can contain a maximum of 128k entries. Cisco recommends keeping the number of entries below 32k. In order to accomplish this, the flow cache, aging-time, and fast aging-time can be adjusted on the MLS-SE to reduce the number of entries in the MLS cache.

Now that you have a better understanding of the MLS cache, access-lists, and other MLS restrictions, refer to the following Scenario & Solution.

SCENARIO & SOLUTION

What is the maximum number of flow entries in the MLS cache?	The MLS cache can support up to 128k entries. Cisco, however, recommends maintaining the number of entries below 32k.
Will MLS stop functioning if you have 72k entries in your MLS cache?	No. The 32k limit ensures that all packets having an entry in the MLS cache will be properly Layer-3 switched. Anything beyond 32k entries increases the chance that packets having valid MLS flow entries in the cache get sent to the MLS-RP for normal routing instead of being switched. The packet is not lost and MLS does not stop functioning as a whole.
What measures can you take to ensure that the MLS cache size does not exceed 32k entries?	By selecting a less granular flow mask, less flow entries get create in the MLS cache. Also, the aging and fast aging-time of the MLS cache can be adjusted so that unused entries age out more rapidly.
Can access-lists be used in conjunction with MLS?	Only outbound access-lists are supported by MLS. Luckily, inbound access-lists can usually be translated into outbound access-lists.
If both NAT and MLS are configured on an interface, which of the two features will be disabled?	On an interface having both NAT and MLS configured, NAT will still function and MLS will be disabled for that interface.

CERTIFICATION OBJECTIVE 6.05

Commands

This section describes in detail the commands used to configure multilayer switching. It is divided into two categories: set-based commands that pertain to the configuration of the MLS-SE on a Catalyst switch, and IOS commands to configure the MLS-RP function of Cisco routers.

TABLE 6-3 The "set mls" Command

Set mls enable|disable	Enables or disables the MLS process.
Set mls agingtime <seconds>	Sets the aging-time of the cache entries. The value ranges from 8 to 2032 seconds in multiples of 8.
Set mls agingtime fast <seconds> <threshold>	Sets the fast aging-time and packet threshold of the cache entries. Time can be set to the following values: 32, 64, 96, or 128 seconds. Threshold can be set to 0, 1, 3, 7, 15, 31, 63, and 127 packets.
set mls flow destination|destination-source|full	Sets the flow mask to be used by the MLS process.
Set mls include <ip_address>	Defines the IP address of an MLS-RP that will be participating in the MLS process.
Set mls nde enable|disable	Enables or disables the NetFlow Data Export feature.

Set-Based Commands to Configure the MLS-SE

This section describes in detail the commands used in this chapter to configure and monitor multilayer switching on a Catalyst switch.

set mls

The set mls command enables and configures the MLS process on the MLS-SE. Its many functions are listed in Table 6-3.

clear mls

The clear MLS command is used to reset or clear certain characteristics of MLS. Table 6-4 lists the various forms of this command.

show mls

The command "show mls" displays different statistics about the MLS process on the MLS-SE. It also has several variants, which are listed in Table 6-5.

TABLE 6-4 The "clear mls" Command

Clear mls entry	Flushes out the entire MLS cache.
Clear mls rp <ip_address>|all	Removes an MLS-RP from the MLS process.
Clear mls statistics	Clears all MLS statistics on the switch.

TABLE 6-5 The "show mls" Command

Show mls	Displays general MLS configuration and status information.
Show mls entry rp|qos|rp <ip_address> |destination<ip_address> |source <ip_address> |flow|p*rotocol src_port dst_port*]	This command displays the MLS cache entries. It has multiple optional keywords that can be used to filter the output of the command: ip: Specifies to display IP MLS cache entries qos: Specifies QoS entries rp: Specifies the MLS-RP ip_addr: IP address or hostname of the MLS-RP destination: Specifies the destination IP address ip_addr_spec: Full IP address or a subnet address source: Specifies the source IP address flow: Specifies using flow information protocol: Protocol family (TCP, UDP, ICMP, etc.) src_port: Source protocol port dst_port: Destination protocol port ipx: Specifies to display IPX MLS cache entries ipx_addr_spec: Full IPX address or a network address
Show mls include	Displays information about the MLS-RPs that are participating in the MLS process
Show mls nde	Displays the status and configuration of the NDE process
Show mls rp ip|ipx <ip_address>	Displays information about a specific MLS-RP
Show mls statistics	Displays IP and IPX MLS statistics

FROM THE CLASSROOM

The "show mls entry" Command

The command "show mls entry" can show you detailed information of where the traffic flows within an internetwork. Using this information, it is possible to determine sensitive information such as the Web sites visited by specific users. Use this information judiciously. It is bad network etiquette to use this information to snoop on users unless it is a security or otherwise work-related necessity. You are encouraged to respect your user's privacy.

—*Benoit Durand, CCIE #5754*

EXERCISE 6-4

Filtering the Output of the MLS Cache Table

You notice that the MLS cache table of your switch exceeds 100k entries. This is much more than the usual 10k average entries that your switch normally contains. You understand that this can cause a problem with the operation of MLS in your network. You have noticed while walking around the building that many people are playing a new network game. Although playing games is discouraged, it is not against policy. Nonetheless, you suspect that this new game may have something to do with the increased number of entries in the MLS cache. After digging up the "Cool New Games" Web site, you find that the new game uses TCP port 6500 to communicate. The game uses a game server to perform the initial game setup, after which the players communicate from station to station without the use of the game server. The game server IP address is 10.1.1.1. Doing a "show mls entry" on the switch reveals too much information. All the entries for the entire network are displayed. Describe how you would best display the pertinent entries in the MLS cache to show only the flow entries associated with this new game. Also, explain how you would prevent employees from playing this game on your network, and its impact on the MLS cache.

Solution: The key is to display the flow entries having a destination port of 6500. In order to do so, the filter keyword "flow" of the command "show mls entry" is used to specify the flows for TCP source port 0 (any) and destination port 6500. The output of the command is shown here:

```
Cat-5500% show mls entry flow tcp 0 6000

Destination IP   Source IP      Prot DstPrt SrcPrt Destination Mac    Vlan Port
--------------   -------------  ---- ------ ------ -----------------  ---- ----
MLS-RP 10.1.1.1:
198.5.135.78     10.1.140.236   TCP  6500   36387  00-50-50-5c-70-00  15   4/23
207.25.71.29     10.1.134.13    TCP  6500   4016   00-50-50-5c-70-00  15   4/23
193.121.163.1    10.1.134.161   TCP  6500   4185   00-50-50-5c-70-00  15   4/23
139.72.190.50    10.1.134.161   TCP  6500   4205   00-50-50-5c-70-00  15   4/23
207.25.71.29     10.1.134.13    TCP  6500   4001   00-50-50-5c-70-00  15   4/23
207.25.71.29     10.1.134.13    TCP  6500   3986   00-50-50-5c-70-00  15   4/23
209.186.199.50   10.1.138.132   TCP  6500   4586   00-50-50-5c-70-00  15   4/23
207.25.71.29     10.1.140.236   TCP  6500   36488  00-50-50-5c-70-00  15   4/23
166.112.200.140  10.1.140.236   TCP  6500   36513  00-50-50-5c-70-00  15   4/23
207.25.71.29     10.1.140.236   TCP  6500   36420  00-50-50-5c-70-00  15   4/23
```

```
166.112.200.140  10.1.140.236   TCP  6500   36498  00-50-50-5c-70-00  15   4/23
198.3.103.147    10.1.138.147   TCP  6500   1095   00-50-50-5c-70-00  15   4/23
207.25.71.29     10.1.140.236   TCP  6500   36403  00-50-50-5c-70-00  15   4/23
207.25.71.29     10.1.140.236   TCP  6500   36386  00-50-50-5c-70-00  15   4/23
```

You find the total number of entries for that game to be excessive, and that it creates a negative impact on your network. The best way to restrict this traffic is through an outbound access-list on the router similar to the following:

```
Access-list 100 deny tcp any any eq 6500
Access-list 100 permit ip any any
```

The resulting impact of this outbound access-list on the MLS cache is to first flush the MLS cache for the interface on which it was applied. When the game tries to communicate, since there now are no MLS cache entries for that interface, the packet is sent to the MLS-RP as a candidate packet. The router examines its new access-list and determines that packets with a TCP destination port of 6500 must be denied; therefore, it drops the packet. No enabler packet is therefore returned to the MLS-SE, preventing the creation of MLS flow entries for that application. Note that installing an outbound access-list on the router also forces the flow mask in the entire MLS topology to adopt ip-flow, the highest granularity flow mask available to the MLS process.

IOS-Based Commands to Configure the MLS-RP

This section describes in detail the commands used in this chapter to configure and monitor multilayer switching on MLS-capable Cisco routers.

mls rp ip

In global configuration mode, this command enables the IP MLS process as a whole. This is a mandatory command in order for IP MLS to function properly. In interface configuration mode, this command identifies the interface as a participant in the MLS process.

exam
⚠atch

The command "mls rp ip" is both a global configuration command and an interface configuration command. Remember the usage of each form of this command.

mls rp ipx

In global configuration mode, this command enables the IPX MLS process as a whole. This is a mandatory command in order for IPX MLS to function properly. In interface configuration mode, this command identifies the interface as a participant in the MLS process.

mls rp vtp-domain <my_domain>

This interface configuration command identifies the Virtual Trunking Protocol (VTP) domain name *my_domain* as the domain to use when communicating with the MLS-SE.

mls rp management-interface

This interface command instructs the MLS process to use this particular interface to communicate with the MLS-SE. Unlike the MLS-SE where the IP address of the MLS-RP is specified, the router listens for MLSP on the interface configured with this command.

mls rp vlan-id <VLAN_ID>

This interface command is used only when the Cisco router participating in MLS is *not* an in-chassis router such as an RSM, or is *not* using ISL or 802.1q trunking to communicate with the MLS-SE. In such cases, trunking is not enabled between the MLS-SE and MLS-RP. This means that the router does not know the VLAN ID of the network it supports on that interface. The router must therefore be configured with the associated VLAN ID in order to supply this information to the MLS-SE when communicating over MLSP.

Now that you have a better understanding of the commands used to configure MLS on the MLS-SE and MLS-RP, here are some possible scenario questions and their answers:

SCENARIO & SOLUTION

Which two IOS commands are both global configuration commands and interface communication commands?	The commands "mls ip rp" and "mls ipx rp" are both interface and global configuration commands.
Which IOS interface configuration command is required when configuring an external MSL-RP that is not doing either ISL or 802.1q trunking with the MLS-SE? Why is this command required?	The interface configuration command "mls rp vlan-id <vlan_ID>" is required on external MLS routers that are not doing ISL or 802.1q trunking with the MLS-SE because the router has no way to identify to the switch which VLAN this interface supports. In order for the switch to marry the packets it receives with the VLANs it supports, the MLS process requires the router to specify this information. Routers doing trunking do not need this command, since the packets they send to the switch have either an ISL or 802.1q header that contains the VLAN ID of the packet.
Which set-based command is used on the MLS-SE to display the MLS cache flow entries?	The command "show mls entry" is used to display the contents of the MLS cache. Multiple keywords can be used to filter the output of this command and display only entries of interest.
In IPX MLS, can the MLS-SE declare an MLS-RP using the router's IPX address?	No. Even though only IPX MLS may be configured between the MLS-RP and MLS-SE, the IP address of the MLS-RP is used to declare it as a participant in the IPX MLS process. This means that an underlying IP network must be present in order to support IPX MLS.

CERTIFICATION SUMMARY

Multilayer switching can be a simple way to provide a substantial throughput improvement in an existing internetwork. With the proper care in designing a compatible network topology, MLS can alleviate the latency of the routing process by switching Layer 3 packets internally. The resulting process can increase the packet throughput performance by several orders of magnitude.

It is important to remember that there are several limitations and restrictions when using MLS. Many network services such as data encryption and quality of service are normally performed by a router. Since the essence of MLS is to bypass the routing process, such services are not compatible with MLS, since the switching engine cannot perform these duties on behalf of the router. There are also hardware and software restrictions to using MLS. Not all switching and routing platforms are capable of participating in MLS. It is important to remember these limitations when selecting network hardware or when implementing MLS in an existing topology.

MLS is relatively simple to configure. Some operating restrictions, such as the cache size limitation, are important to keep in mind. Cisco provides network administrators with the tools necessary to ensure that these operating limits are respected. A better understanding of the MLS process is the key to implementing MLS successfully.

TWO-MINUTE DRILL

Here are some of the key points from each certification objective in Chapter 6.

Data Flow

- ❑ The MLS process provides improved throughput by bypassing the routing process and switching Layer 3 packets on behalf of the router.
- ❑ When switching a Layer 3 packet, the switch performs a "MAC-layer rewrite" of the packet, which means it rewrites the source and destination MAC addresses of the packet. It also decrements the TTL counter of IP packets or increases the Transport Control field of IPX packets.
- ❑ The MLS cache uses one of three flow masks to determine how to enter information in the MLS cache: destination-ip, source-destination ip, or full flow. These flows affect the number of entries that are created in the MLS cache.
- ❑ MLS also supports the switching of IPX packets. Only the destination-ip flow is supported when switching IPX packets.

MLS-SE, MLS-RP, MLSE

- ❑ The MLS-SE is a switching engine that participates in the MLS process. It requires the proper hardware in order to support this feature.
- ❑ The MLS-RP a router that participates in the MLS process. The router platforms that support MLS are internal routers such as the RSM or MSM, or an externally connected Cisco 7500, 7200, 4700, 4500, or 3600 series router.
- ❑ When receiving a *candidate* packet, the MLS-SE sends the packet to the MLS-RP. The MLS-SE *must* receive the packet back from the MLS-RP in the form of an *enabler* packet in order to create a flow entry in the MLS cache. The rule of candidate/enabler must be respected when designing an MLS-compatible topology.

MLS Cache, Access-Lists, and Other MLS Restrictions

- ❑ MLS only supports outbound access-lists. Inbound, reflexive access-lists and context-based access control are not compatible. Inbound access-lists can easily be converted into outbound access-lists. Applying an outbound access-list to an interface participating in MLS flushes the MLS cache on the MLS-SE for entries belonging to that particular interface.

❑ The MLS cache can contain a maximum of 128k flow entries. Cisco, however, recommends keeping the size of the MLS cache below 32k entries to ensure that every packet that matches an entry in the MLS cache is properly switched.

❑ The MLS flow mask, the MLS fast aging-time, and the MLS aging-time are parameters that can be manipulated to minimize the MLS cache size.

❑ MLS is not compatible with many router functions such as data encryption, IP security, and IP accounting, and network address translation cannot operate in conjunction with MLS.

Commands

❑ On the MLS-SE, the command "set mls" is used to configure all MLS functions.

❑ On the MLS-RP, the command "mls ip rp" is both a global configuration command and an interface configuration command. In global configuration mode, this command enables the MLS process on the router. In interface configuration mode, the command identifies the interface as a participant in the MLS process on the MLS-RP.

❑ The command "show mls entry" is used on the MLS-SE to display the flow entries in the MLS cache. Many keywords are available to filter the output of this command to display only desired flow entries.

❑ The command "set mls agingtime" is used to configure both the aging-time and the fast aging-time of the MLS cache.

SELF TEST

The following questions will help you measure your understanding of the material presented in this chapter. Read all the choices carefully, as there may be more than one correct answer. Choose all correct answers for each question.

Data Flow

1. Which parameters are not changed by the MLS-SE when performing Layer 3 packet switching?
   A. The source and destination MAC addresses
   B. The source and destination IP addresses
   C. The Time To Live (TTL) field in IP or the Transport Control field in IPX
   D. The packet checksum

2. What is the primary function of MLS?
   A. To switch frames from one VLAN to another
   B. To switch frames from one router to another
   C. To switch packets from one VLAN to another
   D. To switch packets from one router to another

3. You find that your IP MLS cache is filling up with flow entries. The number of flow entries runs dangerously high. The present flow type is source-destination ip. Without changing the aging-time of the MLS cache, what measure can you take to alleviate the number of entries in the MLS cache?
   A. Periodically issue the command "clear mls entry" to refresh the MLS cache and ensure that only valid entries are inserted in the cache.
   B. Change the flow mask to ip-flow to have a less granular flow mask on the MLS-SE, thus having fewer entries in the MLS cache.
   C. Increase the amount of cache memory available to the MLS-SE.
   D. Change the flow mask to destination-ip to have a less granular flow mask on the MLS-SE, thus having fewer entries in the MLS cache.

4. What flow masks are supported by IPX MLS?
   A. destination
   B. source-destination

C. flow

   D. All of the above

5. Every month, your department incurs huge wide-area network bills for circuits to remote offices and dial-up lines. Your boss wishes to offload some of this cost to the various departments supported by the network. What solution are you likely to propose?

   A. Take periodical snapshots of the output of the "show mls entry" command. By using the source and destination addresses, you can compile statistics on network usage and bill the appropriate departments for network usage.

   B. Enable IP accounting on the router. In order to do so, you will need to disable MLS on these interfaces, since MLS and IP accounting are incompatible.

   C. Enable Network Data Export to collect data throughput information. By using tools such as NetFlow Data Analyzer, you will be able to provide flow statistics to your boss about network usage.

   D. Clear the counters on the router's interfaces and take monthly readings of the input and output packet counts.

MLS-SE, MLS-RP, MLSE

6. What type of packet is necessary for the MLS-SE to receive back from the MLS-RP in order to create an entry in the MLS cache?

   A. An enabler packer

   B. A candidate packet

   C. A broadcast packet

   D. An MLSP packet

7. You have a Catalyst 5500 switch with a Supervisor II Engine running Catalyst code version 5.4. The switch is also equipped with an RSM, which you upgraded with IOS version 12.1WA3 MLS-capable code. All your VLANs tie into this one Catalyst switch, and the RSM is the only router in the topology. You have ordered an NFFC-II daughter card for your Catalyst switch in order to support MLS on the MLS-SE. When the card arrives, you realize that you will not be able to deploy MLS after all. Why is that?

   A. Your topology does not support MLS. There is no way for candidate packets to come back from the router as enabler packets; therefore, no flow entries can be created within the MLS cache.

Chapter 6: MultiLayer Switching

    B. The NFFC-II card is not compatible with the Catalyst 5500. In fact, you should have ordered a Policy Feature Card (PFC) in order to support MLS on that platform.

    C. The Supervisor Engine is the wrong revision. The NFFC card is only supported on the Supervisor III Engine of the Catalyst 5500.

    D. The IOS image of the RSM does not support MLS functions.

8. You configured the basic parameters for MLS to operate on your network. You programmed an IP address on the sc0 interface of your Catalyst 6000 switch and can successfully ping the IP address of the VLAN 1 interface of your MSFC. You are sure that the switch points to the MSFC using the "set mls include" command. After enabling the MLS process on the Catalyst switch, you find that entries are not being created in the MLS cache. The configuration of the MLS-RP is shown next. What is the likely cause of MLS not working properly?

```
MSFC#configure terminal
Enter configuration commands, one per line.  End with CNTL/Z.
MSFC(config)#mls rp ip
MSFC(config)#
MSFC(config)#interface VLAN 1
MSFC(config-if)#ip address 10.1.1.2 255.255.255.0
MSFC(config-if)#mls rp ip
MSFC(config-if)#mls rp vtp-domain My_Domain
MSFC(config-if)#exit
MSFC(config)#
MSFC(config)#interface VLAN 10
MSFC(config-if)#ip address 10.10.1.2 255.255.255.0
MSFC(config-if)#mls rp ip
MSFC(config-if)#mls rp vtp-domain My_Domain
MSFC(config-if)#exit
MSFC(config)#
MSFC(config)#interface VLAN 20
MSFC(config-if)#ip address 10.20.1.2 255.255.255.0
MSFC(config-if)#mls rp ip
MSFC(config-if)#mls rp vtp-domain My_Domain
MSFC(config-if)#exit
MSFC(config)#end
2w3d: %SYS-5-CONFIG_I: Configured from console by vty0 (10.1.1.2)
```

    A. The versions of MLSP between the switch and the router are incompatible.

    B. The MSFC needs to have a global configuration command declaring the IP address of the MLS-SE; otherwise, it does not know who to communicate with.

C. The MSFC is not a compatible router to perform MLS functions. The version of IOS on the router permits the commands to be entered, but the hardware does not actually support MLS.

D. The management interface has not been declared on the MSFC. Therefore, the router does not know which interface to listen for the MLSP protocol.

9. What is the default hello interval for MLSP, and after how many missed hellos does the MLS-SE declare the MLS-RP as dead?

   A. 10 seconds, 3 missed hellos
   B. 15 seconds, 3 missed hellos
   C. 10 seconds, 5 missed hellos
   D. 15 seconds, 5 missed hellos
   E. 30 seconds, 3 missed hellos
   F. 30 seconds, 5 missed hellos

10. You are the network administrator of an IPX network. Your network consists of Catalyst 5500 switches, each equipped with RSMs and Supervisor III Engines with NFFC cards. Your boss has heard of IPX MLS and wants you to implement it within the existing internetwork. Which of the following must you do in order to deploy IPX MLS in your NetWare environment?

    A. Build an IP network overlaying your NetWare network.
    B. Gather the IPX addresses of the RSMs in order to create the MLS-RP tables on the Catalyst switches using the "set mls include" command.
    C. Select an appropriate IPX flow mask best suited for your environment.
    D. Upgrade the RSMs to MSFCs in order to support MLS in your network.

MLS Cache, Access-Lists, and Other MLS Restrictions

11. Which of the following type of access-list is compatible with the operation of MLS on that interface?

    A. Input access-list
    B. Output access-list
    C. Reflexive access-list
    D. Context-Based Access Control

12. What is the recommended maximum number of entries in the MLS cache?

    A. 256k entries

    B. 128k entries

    C. 72k entries

    D. 32k entries

    E. 16k entries

13. What is the immediate impact on MLS when applying an output access-list on an interface participating in MLS?

    A. MLSP packets are denied on that interface, and the router can no longer participate in MLS on that VLAN.

    B. The flow mask returns to the default destination-ip flow mask.

    C. The MLS cache on the MLS-SE is cleared of all entries belonging to that particular interface.

    D. The access-list on that interface is disabled because it is not compatible with the operation of MLS.

14. You successfully deploy MLS within your large internetwork. After enabling the MLS process on your routers and switches, you confirm that MLS entries are being created properly in the MLS cache of your switches. After a few days of operation, you notice that the traffic going through the interfaces of your routers has not decreased as much as you thought it would. After looking more carefully, you find that the routers are actually routing a large number of packets. Of the following possibilities, which is *not* a possible reason for this behavior?

    A. The routing protocol has converged on a new routing topology that causes the switches not to see a returning enabler packet after sending a candidate packet to the router.

    B. The MLS-SE has somehow missed three hellos from the router and has declared it dead. Packets are now being routed normally instead of being switched at Layer 3.

    C. The number of entries in the MLS cache far exceeds the recommended maximum of 32k. Many packets with matching MLS flow entries are actually being routed by the router instead of being switched at Layer 3.

    D. The NetFlow Data Export feature of MLS exceeded its maximum export amount of 128k entries. The MLS process is disabled by the MLS-SE until NDE can reset the MLS cache.

15. You issue the command "show mls" on your MLS-SE and find that the number of flow entries is dangerously close to the recommended 32k maximum. When displaying the MLS cache, you

find that most of the entries are flows directed at your DNS server farm. What is the most effective method of dealing with this massive number of DNS entries?

A. Select a less granular flow mask. This will reduce the number of entries created in the MLS cache. By going from ip-flow to source-destination, or from source-destination to destination-ip, the MLS-SE will store fewer entries in its cache.

B. Remove MLS from the interface connecting to the DNS server farm. DNS conversations are too small for MLS to provide any sort of throughput improvement.

C. Lower the MLS aging-time. By having a shorter aging-time, seldom-used MLS entries such as DNS will age out of the MLS cache more quickly.

D. Lower the MLS fast aging-time and configure an adequate packet threshold. By using a minimum packet threshold, MLS can clear out seldom-used entries such as DNS more quickly than larger flow entries.

Commands

16. What is the proper command on the MLS-SE to declare an IPX router as a member of the IPX MLS process?

    A. set mls rp 172.20.1.1
    B. set ipx mls include 172.20.1.1
    C. set mls include 1A.00c0.ac23.0c95
    D. set mls include 172.21.1.1

17. You are the junior network administrator in a company with a large internetwork. The network operates with IP MLS enabled, and all the flows seem to be created properly on all the switches. The senior network administrator wants you to implement security measures to restrict traffic on some of the routers. You gather the required information and deploy an outbound access-list on a few routers that also serve as MLS-RPs. The senior network administrator forgot to mention that NetFlow Data Export is enabled on every MLS-SE in the MLS topology. What was the impact of implementing these access-lists on the MLS process?

    A. Implementing the access-lists disabled MLS on those interfaces. Outbound access-lists are not compatible with MLS. Thankfully, they can easily be converted into inbound access-lists.

    B. Implementing the access-lists disabled the NDE feature on the MLS-SE for that interface. This means that there will no longer be any data collected in the MLS-SE for that interface.

C. Implementing the access-list flushed the MLS cache and forced the MLS-SE to recreate MLS flow entries from scratch. There will be a discrepancy in the exported NDE data, but both MLS and NDE will continue to operate properly.

D. Implementing the access-list has no impact on MLS or NDE, since it is an outbound access-list. The outbound access-list is the only access-list type supported by MLS.

18. You are connecting an external Cisco 7200 router to a Catalyst 5500 switch running MLS software. You wish to make the 7200 a member of MLS. The router has two interfaces, FastEthernet 0/0 and FastEthernet 0/1, connected to two ports on the same Catalyst 5500, the first port in VLAN 10 and the second port in VLAN 20, respectively. You enter the command "set mls include 10.1.1.1" on your Catalyst 5500 in order to include the 7200 as an MLS-RP in the MLS process. After letting the router and the switch run for a little while, you notice that MLS entries are not being created for the 7200 router. You verify the status of the router's interfaces and find that packets are being routed normally instead of being switched at Layer 3 by the MLS-SE. Using the 7200 router configuration shown next, what is the likely cause of MLS not operating properly for that MLS-RP?

```
7200-MLS#show running-config
Building configuration...

Current configuration:
!
version 12.0
service timestamps debug uptime
service timestamps log uptime
service password-encryption
!
hostname 7200-MLS
!
mls rp ip
!
interface FastEthernet0/0
 ip address 10.1.1.1 255.255.255.0
 no ip directed-broadcast
 mls rp ip
 mls rp management-interface
 duplex auto
 speed auto
!
interface FastEthernet0/0
 ip address 20.1.1.1 255.255.255.0
 no ip directed-broadcast
```

```
 ip access-group 100 out
 mls rp ip
 duplex auto
 speed auto
!
access-list 100 permit ip 10.0.0.0 0.255.255.255 any
access-list 100 ip deny any any
!
line con 0
 password My_Console
 login
line aux 0
line vty 0 4
 password My_Pass
 login
!
end

7200-MLS#
```

- A. The 7200 is configured properly. The version of IOS code probably does not support MLS functions. The router needs to be upgraded with the proper version of IOS.
- B. The VLAN ID is not specified by the router when talking to the MLS-SE. Therefore, the MLS-SE does not know how to handle these incoming VLANs. An additional command is required on both FastEthernet interfaces in order for the router to operate as an MLS-RP.
- C. The management interface for MLS is configured on the wrong interface. The router should actually expect to see MLSP messages on the FastEthernet 0/1 interface in order to participate in the MLS process.
- D. The topology does not support MLS operations. There is no way for the MLS-SE to receive enabler packets from the 7200 after is has sent the candidate packets to the router. Therefore, no MLS flow can be created in the MLS cache.

19. What is the outcome of the command "set mls disable"?
    - A. It entirely disables the MLS process on the MLS-SE.
    - B. It entirely disables the MLS process on the MLS-RP.
    - C. It disables the MLS process on that interface of the MLS-RP.
    - D. It disables the MLS process for that port on the MLS-SE.

20. Which of the following IOS commands are both global configuration commands and interface configuration commands?

   A. mls rp ip

   B. mls rp ipx

   C. mls ip rp

   D. mls ipx rp

LAB QUESTION

Last year, you successfully deployed MLS within your internetwork. All seemed well for many weeks as you monitored the performance of MLS and the number of cache entries. You took pleasure in spying on your users by displaying the MLS cache table and examining the Web sites they visit. After being reprimanded by your boss for intruding on the privacy of the people you support, your interest in the MLS cache faded. Now, months later, your company has grown by leaps and bounds. New VLANs were added to your internetwork, and hundreds of new users have attached to your network. The utilization LEDs of your Catalyst 5500 switch shows that your hardware is keeping up with the additional network load. You decide to look at the impact of these new users on the MLS process. The following is the result of the command "show mls" on the Catalyst 5500. All seems well in the network, but you feel that something may be happening. Identify, if any, the possible problems experienced by MLS, and document the steps you would take to alleviate these problems.

```
Cat-5500> (enable) show mls
Total packets switched = 253578956
Total Active MLS entries = 103673
IP Multilayer switching enabled
IP Multilayer switching aging time = 2032 seconds
IP Multilayer switching fast aging time = 128 seconds, packet threshold = 63
IP Current flow mask is Full flow
Configured flow mask is Full flow
Active IP MLS entries = 103673
Netflow Data Export disabled
Netflow Data Export port/host is not configured.
Total packets exported = 0

IP MLS-RP IP      MLS-RP ID      XTAG MLS-RP MAC-Vlans
----------------  ------------   ---- --------------------------------
10.1.1.1          00906de3ac00    2   00-90-6d-e3-ac-00  1,10,20
Cat-5500> (enable)
```

SELF TEST ANSWERS

1. ☑ **B.** The source and destination IP and IPX addresses are parameters that remain constant in a MAC-layer rewrite.
   ☒ **A, C, and D** are incorrect because they are all parameters that are changed by the switch in a MAC-layer rewrite.

2. ☑ **C.** The responsibilities of the MLS-SE are to bypass the routing process by switching Layer 3 packets from one VLAN to another.
   ☒ **A and B** are incorrect because frames are Layer 2 elements. MLS operates at Layers 3 and 4. **D** is incorrect because MLS is not restricted to switching packets between routers only. You could, for example, switch packets between a workstation and a server on a different VLAN.

3. ☑ **D.** The destination-ip cache flow is the least granular of the three flow masks available for IP MLS. It keeps only one entry for each destination IP address and reuses this entry for all the source IP, ports, and protocols.
   ☒ **A** is incorrect because clearing the MLS cache would not solve the problem. The MLS cache entries would eventually be recreated, and the problem would quickly reoccur. **B** is incorrect because the ip-flow mask is actually the most granular of the three IP flow masks. Selecting ip-flow would create even more MLS cache entries. **C** is incorrect because the maximum of MLS cache entries is fixed. Additional memory cannot be added to the Catalyst switch to alleviate high MLS cache utilization.

4. ☑ **A.** Unlike IP MLS, the destination flow mask is the only flow mask supported by IPX MLS.
   ☒ **B, C, and D** are incorrect because they refer to flow masks that are not supported by IPX MLS.

5. ☑ **C.** By using the NetFlow Data Export (NDE) feature of MLS, network administrators can compile statistics that can be used to analyze network usage by specific users or departments.
   ☒ **A** is incorrect because it does not provide a continuous description of all the MLS flows. The data derived from such a method would be difficult to tabulate and not very accurate in its measure. **B** is incorrect because the IP accounting feature of IOS does not provide the kind of granularity required for this purpose. Also, we do not want to disable the MLS process if it can be avoided. **D** is incorrect because it does not discriminate between the individual IP addresses. It would be impossible to distinguish traffic from the various departments using this method.

MLS-SE, MLS-RP, MLSE

6. ☑ **A.** The MLS-SE sends a candidate packet to the router and expects to see this packet return as an enabler packet. Without the return of this packet, an MLS flow entry cannot be created in the cache.

   ☒ **B** is incorrect because sending a candidate packet to the router does not create an entry in the MLS cache. **C** is incorrect because a broadcast packet does not cross the boundaries of a VLAN. As such, it does not get Layer-3 switched, nor does it create an entry in the MLS cache. **D** is incorrect because MLSP is the protocol used by the MLS-RP and MLS-SE to communicate with each other. It does not trigger the creation of flow entries in the MLS cache.

7. ☑ **C.** The NetFlow Feature card of the Catalyst 5500 engine is supported only on the Supervisor III Engine.

   ☒ **A** is incorrect because a single Catalyst 5500 with a single router being an RSM would provide a compatible MLS topology. **B** is incorrect because the NFFC-II card is indeed compatible with the Catalyst 5000 series. The PFC is used on a Catalyst 6000 series platform. **D** is incorrect because the 12.1WA train of IOS version supports MLS-RP functions.

8. ☑ **D.** A management interface needs to be declared on the MLS-RP in order for the router to know which interface to use when communicating with the MLS-SE.

   ☒ **A** is incorrect because MLSP does not have different versions to contend with. **B** is incorrect because the IP address of the MLS-SE does not have to be declared on the router. **C** is incorrect because the MSFC hardware is compatible with MLS functions. With the proper software, it can serve as an MLS-RP in the MLS process.

9. ☑ **B.** The default MLSP hello interval is 15 seconds. After three missed hellos from the MLS-RP, the MLS-SE declares the router as dead and removes it from the list of routers that are participating in the MLS process.

   ☒ **A, C, D, E,** and **F** are all incorrect because they do not represent the default settings of MLSP hellos.

10. ☑ **A.** In order to support IPX MLS, the routers and switches *must* be able to communicate via TCP/IP. The command "set mls include" on the MLS-SE only accepts an address in IP form to declare the participating routers.

    ☒ **B** is incorrect because the IPX address of the routers cannot be used to declare them as MLS-RPs. **C** is incorrect because only the destination flow mask is supported in IPX MLS. No decision as to flow mask selection is required. **D** is incorrect because the MSFC is a routing engine that operates in the chassis of a Catalyst 6000 series switch. It is not compatible with a Catalyst 5000 series chassis.

MLS Cache, Access-Lists, and Other MLS Restrictions

11. ☑ **B.** Output access-list are the only compatible types of access-lists. Input access-lists can normally be converted into output access-lists.
    ☒ **A**, **C**, and **D** are incorrect because they represent types of access-lists that are not compatible with the operation of MLS.

12. ☑ **D.** 32k entries is the maximum recommended number of flow entries recommended by Cisco. Anything over 32k increases the chance of packets having a valid MLS flow entry being sent to the router for normal routing.
    ☒ **A** is incorrect because it represents a value beyond the maximum number of entries that the MLS cache can actually hold. **B** is incorrect because although it represents the maximum number of entries that can be held in the MLS cache, it is not the maximum value recommended by Cisco for proper MLS operation. **C** is incorrect because it is above the maximum value recommended by Cisco. **E** is incorrect because it is below the maximum recommended by Cisco.

13. ☑ **C.** When applying an outbound access-list to an interface participating in MLS, the MLS-SE flushes the entire MLS cache.
    ☒ **A** and **B** are incorrect because they do not reflect the consequences of applying an outbound access-list to an interface participating in the MLS process. **D** is incorrect because outbound access-lists are compatible with the operation of MLS on that interface.

14. ☑ **D.** The NetFlow Data Export feature does not have the 128k entries limitation of the MLS cache. The NetFlow Data Collector can collect more than 128k worth of information.
    ☒ **A**, **B**, and **C** are incorrect because they are all possible reasons why an MLS-RP would be routing more packets than expected in an MLS topology.

15. ☑ **D.** Lowering the fast aging-time and providing a minimum packet threshold is the best method of dealing with entries that use a small number of packets such as DNS queries.
    ☒ **A**, **B**, and **C** are incorrect because although they represent valid methods of controlling the number of MLS cache entries, they are not the best-suited methods for dealing with flow entries such as DNS queries.

Commands

16. ☑ **D.** Even though we are setting up IPX MLS, the MLS-RP must be declared in the MLS-SE using the router's IP address, not the IPX address.

☒ **A, B,** and **C** are incorrect because they are not valid commands to configure an MLS-RP on the MLS-SE.

17. ☑ **C.** Applying an outbound access-list on an interface clears the MLS cache on the MLS-SE. The MLS process will start rebuilding the MLS cache as candidate packets are received and sent to the MLS-RP to be returned as enabler packets.
☒ **A** is incorrect because applying an outbound access-list to an interface does not disable the MLS process in that interface. **B** is incorrect because applying an outbound access-list does not disable NDE on the MLS-SE. **D** is incorrect because applying an outbound access-list does indeed affect MLS by clearing the MLS cache when the access-list is applied to the interface.

18. ☑ **B.** The command "mls rp vlan-id <VLAN_ID>" must be added to each FastEthernet interface to indicate which VLAN to attach to when talking with the MLS-SE. In this case, interface 0/0 would specify VLAN 10, and interface 0/1 would specify VLAN 20.
☒ **A** is incorrect because if the 7200 router did not have the proper version of IOS to support MLS, the MLS commands themselves would be rejected by the router and would not show up in the configuration. **C** is incorrect because the management interface on the router is properly configured on the interface that has the IP address specified by the MLS-SE using the "set mls include" command. **D** is incorrect because an MLS router connecting to an MLS-capable switch using only two connections to the same switch is a valid topology for MLS to operate. Every packet that the switch sends to the router for routing from VLAN 10 to VLAN 20 are returned by the router on the second port connecting it to the switch.

19. ☑ **A.** The command "set mls disable" disables the entire MLS process on the MLS-SE. It also clears the entire MLS cache and stops the NetFlow Data Export feature.
☒ **B** is incorrect. If the MLS-RP is connected to a single MLS-SE, then disabling MLS on that switch effectively disables MLS on the MLS-RP as well. However, if the MLS-RP participates in MLS with more than one MLS-SE, then disabling MLS on one of the MLS-SEs does not disable the MLS process on the MLS-RP. Remember that set-based commands are switch commands, not router IOS commands. **C** is incorrect because the MLS-RP can be connected to multiple MLS-SEs through a single interface. **D** is incorrect because the command does not disable individual ports in the MLS-SE. It disables the MLS process as a whole for that switch.

20. ☑ **A, B.** The commands "mls rp ip" and "mls rp ipx" are used at the global configuration level to enable the MLS processes on the router. At interface configuration level, these commands are used to identify the interface as participating in the MLS process.
☒ **C** and **D** are both incorrect because they have an invalid IOS syntax.

LAB ANSWER

The obvious concern in this scenario is the number of entries in the MLS cache. At 103673 entries, the MLS cache far exceeds the recommended maximum of 32k entries. It is very likely that the MLS-SE is sending many packets with a valid flow entry in the MLS cache up to the MLS-RP for normal routing, instead of switching the packet internally at Layer 3.

From the output of the "show mls" command, we see that we have a few options available to reduce the number of entries in the MLS cache. Here are the steps that are recommended to reduce the number of flow entries below the recommended maximum of 32k entries:

1. The flow mask is presently set at "Full flow," which means that the MLS-SE keeps a flow entry for each combination of source IP address, destination IP address, and port/protocol used. Since NetFlow Data Export is not enabled on that switch, we can safely move to a less granular MLS flow mask on the switch as follows:

   ```
   Cat-5500> (enable) set mls flow destination
   Configured IP flowmask is set to destination flow.
   Cat-5500> (enable) %MLS-5-FLOWMASKCHANGE:IP flowmask changed from FULL to DEST

   Cat-5500> (enable)
   ```

2. The second method we can use to reduce the number of entries is to lower the MLS aging-time. In this scenario, the MLS aging-time was obviously changed from its default value of 256 seconds to a whopping 2032 seconds. Let's put the aging-time back to its default value of 256 seconds. If we later find that these changes are not sufficient to reduce the number of entries below the recommended maximum, we can always reduce the aging-time from its default value.

   ```
   Cat-5500> (enable) set mls agingtime 256
   Multilayer switching agingtime set to 256
   Cat-5500> (enable)
   ```

3. Finally, the MLS fast aging-time has also been increased from its default value to a value of 128 seconds with a packet threshold of 63 packets. We can reduce these values to a more useful configuration by configuring the fast aging-time with an interval of 32 seconds with a packet threshold of 15 packets.

   ```
   Cat-5500> (enable) set mls agingtime fast 32 15
   Multilayer switching fast agingtime set to 32 seconds for
   entry with no more than 15 packets switched
   Cat-5500> (enable)
   ```

Fine-tuning MLS parameters is an iterative process. There is no magic solution to achieve a desired outcome. The preceding steps may not completely solve the cache size issue. An MLS-SE experiencing cache size problems should run for a certain time before you change the MLS settings again. This will give the switch time to rebuild the MLS cache and achieve a certain stability. If you find that the changes were not enough, you can play with the parameters some more until a desired effect is achieved.

7
Hot Standby Routing Protocol (HSRP)

CERTIFICATION OBJECTIVES

7.01	HSRP Groups, Virtual IP Address, HSRP Messaging Between Routers
7.02	Learn States
7.03	Commands
✓	Two-Minute Drill
Q&A	Self Test

Building fault tolerance into network solutions is extremely common for many businesses today for a few key reasons. First, the overall cost of adding redundancy into network designs is low, when compared with the potential loss of productivity caused from network outages that can impact the productivity of hundreds, even thousands of users. Second, the ability to recover from network failures dynamically lowers the operational costs associated with managing today's large, complex networks. Redundant networks offer end users the ability to continue using network services during failure of individual network components with very little impact to business operations until failed hardware can be replaced.

In the early years of networking, local area network (LAN) segments were large, bridged network segments containing workstations, servers, and printers. Now, with the growth of the Internet and client/server applications, it is rare that a Web server or file and print server is located on the same LAN segment as the end user. This implies that end users (workstations, servers, or printers, for example) must use a default gateway in order to communicate using Transmission Control Protocol/Internet Protocol (TCP/IP). The default gateway acts as the "traffic cop" and determines what remote subnets and networks an end device may reach.

Unfortunately, the default gateway has traditionally been a single point of failure for host-to-host communication—in the past, the failure of the entire router or interface(s) led to significant downtime for end users. Cisco offers a solution to this problem via Hot Standby Routing Protocol (HSRP). HSRP is a process you configure on Cisco routers to build dynamic redundancy for default gateway routers. It can help minimize, and possibly prevent any network downtime for your end users in the event of a default gateway failure.

There are several other traditional methods of providing some method of redundancy or dynamic failover for the default gateway functionality. The most popular methods before HSRP were 1) Proxy Arp, 2) RIP, and 3) IDRP. We will briefly discuss the limitations of each and why HSRP is a more scalable, flexible solution.

Proxy Arp allows you to configure your router to respond to packets arping directly for hosts not on the same subnet. Generally, devices using Proxy Arp do not support a default gateway, or sometimes, people purposefully configure Proxy Arp in environments where there are multiple exits. In the scenario where your end device does not support a default gateway, routers simply forward packets to the next hop, assuming they have a valid route or default route in their routing table. This can cause a lot of additional broadcast traffic on your subnet since the Proxy Arps are sent via Layer 2 broadcasts (the source device hopes some device with routing knowledge will see and route the request). In shared medium and switched medium topologies, this broadcast traffic could cripple your performance. At a minimum, every device must process every Layer 2 broadcast, effectively reducing performance and bandwidth available for other applications. Another significant risk of Proxy Arp is the inherent security risk. For example, as a malicious user, I do not need a valid IP address and default gateway to start looking for opportunities to inflict harm on corporate network resources. HSRP solves this issue by providing default gateway redundancy, as well as providing support for secure network designs (i.e., no Proxy Arp).

The second traditional method is the use of Routing Information Protocol (RIP). This solution essentially requires every device to participate in RIP routing updates, essentially "learning" the topology of the network as a router does. This presents several modern-day challenges. First, RIP is a legacy routing protocol, with no support for an efficient IP addressing scheme (i.e., no Variable Length Subnet Masking (VLSM)). Using this routing protocol requires you to run and redistribute between multiple routing protocols in your network if you have limited IP address space and need to efficiently address your LANs and WANs. A second major limitation of RIP is that routing processes are normally propagated by frequent broadcast traffic—again, this can limit the performance and effective bandwidth of your network. Another limitation of using RIP in your endstations is that it prevents you from easily migrating your router backbone to more efficient routing protocols like Open Shortest Path First (OSPF) and Enhanced Interior Gateway Routing Protocol (EIGRP). Finally, using RIP on your endstations can cause routing loops and backdoors, creating the potential for suboptimal routing. Since every device understands the routing topology, misconfiguration can lead to endstations routing packets instead of routers. Let your routers do this function, since they are built to route packets quickly and according to your network topology design.

As you can see, there are many different options for providing dynamic and redundant default gateway support. However, each method has severe scalability limitations, and HSRP is a better solution for almost all situations.

CERTIFICATION OBJECTIVE 7.01

HSRP Groups, Virtual IP Address, HSRP Messaging Between Routers

There are generally two methods of changing the default gateway assigned to your end devices. The first is using Dynamic Host Configuration Protocol (DHCP). DHCP supports the dynamic allocation of IP addresses for end-user workstations. DHCP allows the network administrator to instruct the workstation which IP address and default gateway IP address to use. When configuring your DHCP server, the default gateway refers to the router field that can be populated with an address for each scope. The scope is the subnet of IP addresses you are allocating. The address that you assign to the router field corresponds to the HSRP address and is synonymous with the default gateway. This allows network administrators to dynamically change the default gateway address; however, due to the lease time assigned to DHCP leases, this is not an effective way to quickly change this setting. The second method is manually assigning the IP address and default gateway—this method is frequently used with servers, printers, and other devices requiring static IP addresses. This method, however, prevents the network administrator from quickly changing the default gateway settings on each device to recover from default gateway failure. Obviously, these are not practical solutions for recovering from default gateway failures when the affected devices number in the hundreds or thousands. This is where HSRP can provide a cost-effective method of dynamically recovering from a default gateway failure.

HSRP is Cisco's method for providing default gateway redundancy in the absence of an approved Request for Comment (RFC) based standard. The three key requirements for implementing HSRP in your network are: 1) at least two Cisco routers connected to the same network segment, 2) those routers using IOS version 10.3 or higher, and 3) and Ethernet and/or Token Ring and/or Fiber Distributed Data Interface (FDDI) interface. First, let's cover what HSRP does and does not do.

HSRP should be used to provide default gateway redundancy for hosts using TCP/IP with a default gateway. This includes, but is not limited to, Voice over IP (VoIP) phones, servers (Web, application, database, file and print, etc), printers, and workstations. This redundancy can be transparent to the end devices, assuming they use a protocol that provides for guaranteed delivery of packets (like TCP/IP).

HSRP should not be used to directly control routing of traffic. HSRP is not intended for use in place of a routing protocol. If you wish to achieve load balancing, use a dynamic routing protocol like Open Shortest Path First (OSPF) or Enhanced Interior Gateway Routing Protocol (EIGRP).

Now that we have an introduction to HSRP, review some of the possible answers in the Scenario & Solution section below.

exam
⚙ atch

HSRP requires that you understand IP addressing and subnetting, since you will need to assign two (2) IP addresses to every HSRP group on your router interfaces. Make sure you understand how to subnet an IP address so that your default gateway/HSRP address is a valid IP address within the subnet you assign for each router's physical interface.

Basic Concepts

In this first section, we will discuss the inner workings of Address Resolution Protocol, and how hosts address packets destined for a remote end device. The TCP/IP protocol is extremely detailed, and a thorough understanding of the protocol is key to designing networks. A detailed review of TCP/IP is beyond the scope of this chapter, so let's discuss the basic concepts of how HSRP works from a technical point of view.

The Open Systems Interconnect (OSI) model allows two network devices to logically communicate at Layer 3 (IP). In order for communication between end devices to travel across different networks, however, the end devices must first

SCENARIO & SOLUTION

What interfaces can support the use of HSRP for providing default gateway redundancy?	HSRP supports Ethernet (and Fast Ethernet and Gigabit Ethernet), Token Ring, and FDDI. NOTE: Interfaces supporting InterSwitch Link (ISL) and ATM interfaces supporting LANE also support HSRP. See the Cisco documentation for specific details and caveats related to this functionality.
Can I use HSRP to control routing and ensure use of the optimal path?	HSRP is not intended for use as a routing protocol. If you desire fast and flexible dynamic routing, choose a routing protocol like OSPF or EIGRP.

communicate with their default gateway via their Layer 2 addresses. First, the end device determines that the remote IP address it is trying to reach is not on the same local segment. This signals to the end device that it should send the packets destined for the remote end device to the default gateway. Using Address Resolution Protocol (ARP), the end device associates the logical Layer 3 address of the default gateway with a Layer 2 address. The workstation then addresses the Layer 2 destination with the default gateway's Media Access Control (MAC) address. This mapping is stored in the memory of the workstation in an area we call the ARP cache. The ARP cache provides the workstation with the Layer 2 address that IP packets destined for remote networks must use. This process is completed every time a workstation requires to communicate with its default gateway. Due to the dynamic nature of ARP, we can provide default gateway redundancy using HSRP.

HSRP achieves default gateway redundancy by using a virtual IP address and virtual MAC address. When HSRP is working correctly, only one router is actually behaving as the default gateway at any one time. This router, called the Active router, actually listens and responds to ARP requests for this default gateway IP address from end devices, as well as routes packets from end devices on its locally attached segment. The other router, called the Standby router, "waits" for the possible failure or removal of the Active router, and dynamically takes over the default gateway function. No configuration changes are required on the end devices to begin using this new default gateway, since it is responding to requests for the default gateway with the virtual MAC address. (NOTE: There are situations where the default gateway MAC address will change, when using certain more advanced features discussed later.)

The routers participating in HSRP on a LAN segment communicate periodically using hello messages to verify the status of one another. These hello messages are sent via multicast packets. By default, HSRP routers send these hello packets every three seconds. After 10 seconds, by default, if HSRP routers do not receive hello packets from the other, they assume the other router is down and take control of the default gateway function. The HSRP MAC address used on Ethernet and FDDI by default is 00-00-0c-07-ac-01, which can be changed if necessary. The HSRP MAC address used on Token Ring by default is the functional address c0-00-00-01-00-00, which can be changed if necessary. We will discuss the more advanced configuration options and how to change these addresses later in this chapter.

Basic Configuration

It is extremely simple to configure HSRP in your network. The protocol requires three IP addresses to successfully configure default gateway redundancy:

- **Virtual IP address** This is the default gateway address configured on your end devices.
- **Real IP address for primary router** This is an IP address within the same subnet as the default gateway address.
- **Real IP address for secondary router** This is an IP address within the same subnet as the default gateway address.

Once you've reserved the IP addresses, the next step is to configure the protocol. Enter enable mode, and configure the interfaces connected to your LAN segment with a real IP address, and the necessary HSRP commands.

EXERCISE 7-1

Enabling HSRP

1. In a simple configuration, the following commands on your routers will enable HSRP. Configure your routers using the commands in the following code:

   ```
   Primary Router
   interface FastEthernet0
    ip address 172.30.51.2 255.255.255.0 (Real IP Address)
    no ip redirects (added by Cisco IOS by default)
    standby priority 200 (ensures this router is Active)
    standby ip 172.30.51.1 (Default Gateway/Virtual IP Address)
   Secondary Router
   interface FastEthernet0
    ip address 172.30.51.3 255.255.255.0 (Real IP Address)
    no ip redirects (added by Cisco IOS by default)
    standby ip 172.30.51.1 (Default Gateway/Virtual IP Address)
   ```

   The Primary Router will perform the duties of Active router and respond to all ARP requests for 172.30.51.1. End devices ARPing for the Layer 2 address associated with this IP address will receive ARP replies with the desired MAC address with a value of 00-00-0c-07-ac-01 from the Active router.

Note that in an example using Token Ring, this address would be c0-00-00-01-00-00, unless we are using the "standby use-bia" command that we will discuss later.

---

exam
⒲atch

Enabling HSRP only requires the "standby ip <ip address>" command. Ensure you know the correct default gateway address of your end users or the DHCP scope. If you use the wrong default gateway address with your standby command, you will not correctly provide the redundancy that HSRP offers to your end users.

CERTIFICATION OBJECTIVE 7.02

Learn States

In this section, we will review the different states that an HSRP router passes through before becoming the Active router. We will examine the four different states an HSRP router passes: 1) Init, 2) Listen, 3) Speak, and 4) Active/Standby.

EXERCISE 7-2

Using the Debug Feature on a Lab Router

A good method of really understanding HSRP is to use the debug feature on a lab router (**Note:** DO NOT use debug on your production routers unless instructed to do so by the Cisco TAC—this process can severely degrade performance on your router). Used properly in the lab, however, debug can provide a great deal of insight into the HSRP process. We provide an exercise later in the chapter for enabling debug on your router(s) so you can see the actual packet output related to HSRP. In this exercise, you will need to configure two routers with an Ethernet interface (or Token Ring) each. Configure Router A with IP address 172.16.20.1, a priority of 90, and a standby IP address of 172.16.20.5. Configure Router B with IP address

172.16.20.2 and a standby IP address of 172.16.20.5 (remember that default priority will be 100). Enable the process on both routers, and then type **debug stand** on Router A. You will see output similar to the code shown next. See the text following this example for an explanation of the steps we completed to simulate the different states an HSRP router follows. To turn off this debugging, issue the "no debug stand" command.

```
RouterA# debug stand
Hot standby protocol debugging is on
RouterA#
1  SB0:Ethernet0 Hello out 172.16.20.1 Standby pri 90 hel 3 hol 10 ip 172.16.20.5
2  SB0:Ethernet0 Hello in  172.16.20.2 Active  pri 100 hel 3 hol 10 ip 172.16.20.5
3  SB0:Ethernet0 Hello out 172.16.20.1 Standby pri 90 hel 3 hol 10 ip 172.16.20.5
4  SB0:Ethernet0 Hello in  172.16.20.2 Active  pri 100 hel 3 hol 10 ip 172.16.20.5
5  SB0:Ethernet0 Hello out 172.16.20.1 Standby pri 90 hel 3 hol 10 ip 172.16.20.5
6  SB0:Ethernet0 Resign in 172.16.20.2 Init    pri 100 hel 3 hol 10 ip 172.16.20.5
7  SB0: Ethernet0 state Standby -> Active
8  SB: Ethernet0 changing MAC address to 0000.0c07.ac00
9  SB0:Ethernet0 Hello out 172.16.20.1 Active pri 90 hel 3 hol 10 ip 172.16.20.5
10 SB0:Ethernet0 Hello out 172.16.20.1 Active pri 90 hel 3 hol 10 ip 172.16.20.5
11 SB0:Ethernet0 Hello out 172.16.20.1 Active pri 90 hel 3 hol 10 ip 172.16.20.5
12 SB0:Ethernet0 Coup in   172.16.20.2 Listen pri 100 hel 3 hol 10 ip 172.16.20.5
13 SB0: Ethernet0 state Active -> Speak
14 SB0:Ethernet0 Resign out 172.16.20.1 Speak  pri 90 hel 3 hol 10 ip 172.16.20.5
15 SB0:Ethernet0 Hello in   172.16.20.2 Active pri 100 hel 3 hol 10 ip 172.16.20.5
16 SB0:Ethernet0 Hello out  172.16.20.1 Speak  pri 90 hel 3 hol 10 ip 172.16.20.5
17 SB0:Ethernet0 Hello in   172.16.20.2 Active pri 100 hel 3 hol 10 ip 172.16.20.5
18 SB0:Ethernet0 Hello out  172.16.20.1 Speak  pri 90 hel 3 hol 10 ip 172.16.20.5
19 SB0: Ethernet0 state Speak -> Standby
20 SB0:Ethernet0 Hello in  172.16.20.2 Active  pri 100 hel 3 hol 10 ip 172.16.20.5
21 SB0:Ethernet0 Hello out 172.16.20.1 Standby pri 90 hel 3 hol 10 ip 172.16.20.5
22 SB0:Ethernet0 Hello in  172.16.20.2 Active  pri 100 hel 3 hol 10 ip 172.16.20.5
23 SB0:Ethernet0 Hello out 172.16.20.1 Standby pri 90 hel 3 hol 10 ip 172.16.20.5
```

In the preceding example, our HSRP debug shows the different states an HSRP router can enter. We have truncated many repetitive lines to shorten the output but still provide enough detail to let us walk you through the process.

The first six lines show normal HSRP behavior, where Router B is the active HSRP router, as evidenced by the inbound HSRP messages sourced from its IP address with a state of Active and the default priority of 100. The outbound messages sourced from Router A show its standby state due to its lower priority of 100. On line 7, we simulate a primary router resigning its active status, which forces the standby HSRP router, Router B, to change its MAC address (line 8) to the default HSRP MAC address for Ethernet (0000.0c07.ac00). Lines 9–11 show outbound messages from Router A as the active HSRP router. Then, in line 12, Router B (currently the active HSRP router) receives a message from Router A announcing its candidacy for Active status. Router B then enters Speak state (line 13), and sends a hello message resigning its Active status (line 14). Normal messages are exchanged in Lines 15–18, and Router A announces its permanent transition to Standby state (line 19). Lines 20–23 continue to show normal HSRP operation between our two routers. Next, we will provide examples of the different commands we can use to verify different modes of operation.

In the following code, the "show standby" command on a router displays the output of an HSRP router interface that is either physically down or administratively down. In this case, the local router's HSRP state shows as Init. This router is neither sending nor receiving hello packets, and the HSRP process is not running successfully on this interface. See the following code for an example of a router in Init state.

```
Router A# show standby
TokenRing0 - Group 0
  Local state is Init, priority 100
  Hellotime 3 holdtime 10
  Hot standby IP address is 172.30.41.1 configured
  Active router is unknown expired
  Standby router is unknown expired
Router A#
```

exam
⌚atch

The "show standby" command will also show an HSRP group in Init state if the router interface is shut down. Be sure to verify the up/up status of the physical/logical interfaces using the "show ip interface brief" command. Administrators will commonly assume that HSRP is not working on an interface when they see the INIT state—do not assume this. The interface may be shut down intentionally, causing the HSRP state to show as INIT. This will help you troubleshoot HSRP problems.

In the following code, the "show standby" command on a router displays the output of an HSRP router interface that is preparing to start the HSRP process. This router is still not sending hello packets, but is listening for hello packets to see if other HSRP routers are active on that LAN segment. Note the absence of a line stating when the next hello will be sent. See the following code for an example of a router in Listen state.

```
Router A# show standby
  TokenRing0 - Group 0
  Local state is Listen, priority 100
  Hellotime 3 holdtime 10
  Hot standby IP address is 172.30.41.1 configured
  Active router is unknown expires in 00:00:02
  Standby router is unknown expires in 00:00:02
Router A#
```

In the following code, the "show standby" command on a router displays the output of an HSRP router interface that is almost done with the HSRP startup process. This router is now sending hello packets (speaking), and still listening for hello packets to see if other HSRP routers are active on that LAN segment. Note the addition of the line stating when the next hello will be sent. The active and standby routers are still unknown.

```
Router A# show standby
TokenRing0 - Group 0
  Local state is Speak, priority 100
  Hellotime 3 holdtime 10
  Next hello sent in 00:00:02.868
Hot standby IP address is 172.30.41.1 configured
  Active router is unknown expires in 00:00:05
  Standby router is unknown expires in 00:00:05
Router A#
```

In the following code, the "show standby" command on a router displays the output of an HSRP router interface that is now the active HSRP router. This router is now sending hello packets (speaking), listening for hello packets, and responding to ARP requests for 172.30.41.1. Normally, you would see the real IP address of the standby router if another router had joined the HSRP process. (The standby router is unknown in our example since this is the only router running HSRP on that Token Ring segment.) The standby router would show similar output, except the Local State would be Standby, and the Active router and Standby router entries at the bottom of our example would be reversed. See the following code for an example of a router in Active state.

```
Router A# show standby
TokenRing0 - Group 0
  Local state is Active, priority 100
  Hellotime 3 holdtime 10
  Next hello sent in 00:00:02.868
  Hot standby IP address is 172.30.41.1 configured
  Active router is local
Standby router is 172.30.41.2 expires in 00:00:05
Router A#
```

Note that in the preceding code listing, the last two lines that show the Active router as local and the Standby router as 172.30.41.2. A common scenario after HSRP starts is to show the Standby router as unknown expired. This could occur in a couple of scenarios:

1. There is no other HSRP router configured for the same subnet. In this case, your router is the only HSRP router for that subnet. This will still act as the default gateway for the HSRP address, but in the event this router interface fails, your users will not have a Standby router to take over the HSRP active role.

2. The physical topology between your routers is not working correctly, and has cut off your two routers from being able to talk to one another. In this case, both routers will show as Active with the unknown expired Standby router. Obviously, this problem must be corrected since each router thinks it's attached to the same subnet (and thus has full connectivity to all devices in that subnet). A common example of this scenario involves the use of two physical LAN switches, connected by a trunk port (either a copper or fiber connection) that is sending and receiving packets on common VLANs between the two switches. In our case, assume the switches are only using VLAN 1, and the copper cable is disconnected. This problem will prevent communication between all devices on the same subnet but located on the physically separate switches. In addition, this will prevent remote devices from successfully communicating with end devices on this subnet.

CERTIFICATION OBJECTIVE 7.03

Commands

In this section, we will review, in detail, the configuration commands available with HSRP.

standby [group-number] ip [virtual ip-address [secondary]]

This command enables HSRP on your router(s) and is used in interface configuration mode. It is common to add the virtual IP address at the end of the command. If you do not specify an IP address, the router will learn the virtual IP address from another router(s) also configured with HSRP on that LAN segment. In order for this dynamic option to work, you must configure at least one router with the virtual IP address using the "standby ip" command.

The *secondary* keyword allows you to provide default gateway redundancy for secondary IP subnets configured on your router without using groups. In order to use this option, you must have a secondary IP address configured on the interface. You can use multiple HSRP secondary addresses in scenarios where you require support for multiple logical subnets on the same physical segment. See the following code for an example of a router using secondary HSRP addresses.

```
Primary Router
interface FastEthernet0
 ip address 172.30.51.2 255.255.255.0
 ip address 172.30.52.2 255.255.255.0 secondary
 no ip redirects
 standby priority 200
 standby preempt
 standby ip 172.30.51.1
 standby ip 172.30.52.1 secondary
```

on the Job *The use of multiple secondary addresses on router interfaces can lead to performance issues. By default, higher-end Cisco routers will only route packets destined for different logical subnets on the same physical interface using a route cache if the "ip route-cache same-interface" command is used (this is only supported on certain platforms). This command ensures the router will use the fast cache for packets coming in and going out of the same physical interface. This issue can have a dramatic adverse impact on CPU load of the router.*

By default, the group-number value is set at zero. When used on HSRP commands, the group number must be used on all commands associated with that same group. When providing default gateway redundancy for multiple subnets on an interface, using a different group-number for each subnet is recommended. This number can be any value between 1 and 255 for Ethernet/FDDI (256 groups total) and 1 and 3 for Token Ring (three groups total). This is not required, but helpful since using a group number changes the virtual MAC address. Remember, the default MAC address used with HSRP is 00-00-0c-07-ac-00; when using group numbers, the last number of the default MAC address is incremented by 1. For example, on a physical interface supporting two logical subnets, the HSRP MAC address will be different for each HSRP group. For example, on an Ethernet interface with Group 1 and Group 2, the virtual MAC addresses will be 00-00-0c-07-ac-01 for Group 1, and 00-00-0c-07-ac-02 for Group 2. See the following code for an example of a router configured with a secondary HSRP group.

```
Primary Router
interface FastEthernet0
 ip address 172.30.51.2 255.255.255.0
 ip address 172.30.52.2 255.255.255.0 secondary
 no ip redirects
 standby 1 priority 200
 standby 1 preempt
 standby 1 ip 172.30.51.1
 standby 2 priority 200
 standby 2 preempt
 standby 2 ip 172.30.52.1
```

Cisco IOS allows you to configure up to 256 groups on Ethernet or FDDI interfaces, and three groups on Token Ring. With the configuration just shown, the following code shows the router's ARP cache for the virtual IP and MAC addresses.

```
RouterA# show ip arp 172.30.51.1 (Primary)
Protocol  Address          Age (min)  Hardware Addr   Type  Interface
Internet  172.30.51.1          -      0000.0c07.ac00  ARPA  FastEthernet0
RouterA# show ip arp 172.30.52.1 (Secondary)
Protocol  Address          Age (min)  Hardware Addr   Type  Interface
Internet  172.30.52.1          -      0000.0c07.ac01  ARPA  FastEthernet0
```

standby [group-number] preempt [delay [delay in seconds]]

This command is optional and is used in interface configuration mode. When configured, preemption means that the HSRP router with the highest priority will become the active HSRP router, even if another lower-priority router is currently the active HSRP router. Without preemption, an HSRP router will only assume control if it does not receive confirmation via hello packets that another router is currently the active HSRP router. A higher-priority router will not take control from an Active lower-priority router without the preempt command.

The *delay* keyword, new in IOS version 12.0, allows you to prevent a router from taking control of HSRP from another router for some period of time (from 0 to 3600 seconds)—the default is 0 seconds. This means the router will take control immediately when it determines it should become the HSRP active router. The "delay" command would be helpful in scenarios where it takes your router some period of time to complete its routing table. Normally, there is the brief period of time when a router first starts up that it's building its routing table by receiving and processing routing information. If a router assumes control of HSRP (and responds to ARP requests) without routing information, it will not be able to effectively route packets.

The *group-number* keyword with the "preempt" command should be used in conjunction with the group-number used with the "standby ip" command. If you use HSRP groups on your "standby ip" commands, but do not use HSRP groups on your "preempt" commands, the features of the optional "preempt" command will not include this subnet.

standby [group-number] priority [number from 1 to 255]

This command is optional and is used in interface configuration mode. When configured, priority helps determine which router will assume control as the active HSRP router. The default value is 100, and values can range from 1 to 255. If no priority is configured and all routers have a default priority of 100, HSRP selects the router with the highest primary IP address. It's also important to note that preemption must be configured in order for a router with a higher priority to take control as active HSRP router from another lower-priority router while the lower-priority router is still active.

standby [group-number] timers hellotime holdtime

This command is optional and is used in interface configuration mode. This command changes the default timers HSRP uses to send hello packets (hellotime) and determine whether an active or standby HSRP router is down (holdtime). The default values are three seconds for hellotime, meaning HSRP routers send hello packets every three seconds. The default values are 10 seconds for holdtime, meaning HSRP routers will determine that partner routers are down if they do not receive a hello packet after 10 seconds. A router will take over as the HSRP active router from a partner router it has not heard from for 10 seconds, even if it is lower priority and is not configured to preempt.

The default values will normally work well for almost all environments. These timers should not be changed unless the defaults do not provide adequate default gateway failover time from the end device perspective. It is always easier to start with a simple HSRP configuration, and then make it more complex as required.

standby [group-number] authentication string

This command is optional and is used in interface configuration mode. This command includes an optional authentication string that can be up to eight characters. If no string is entered, the default string cisco is used. When configured, authentication is sent in HSRP hello packets in unencrypted format. This optional command must be configured on all routers on the same LAN segment to operate. If authentication is not configured on a router, or the string is incorrect, and other routers are using authentication, the router will not learn timer values or the standby address from other routers on that segment running HSRP.

standby [group-number] track type number [interface-priority]

This command is optional and is used in interface configuration mode. This command adds great flexibility to HSRP and allows it to adapt to network failures

FROM THE CLASSROOM

HSRP Group Authentication

It's important to note that authentication requires all routers in the same HSRP group to use authentication. IOS will warn you if routers on the same subnet are not all configured using the same authentication values. Assume our Active router has authentication configured using password *cisco* and the standby router does not have authentication configured. The following example shows the console messages you would see in this case.

```
From the STANDBY Router
%STANDBY-3-BADAUTH: Bad authentication from 172.30.75.2, remote state Standby
%STANDBY-3-BADAUTH: Bad authentication from 172.30.75.2, remote state Standby
%STANDBY-3-BADAUTH: Bad authentication from 172.30.75.2, remote state Standby
%STANDBY-3-BADAUTH: Bad authentication from 172.30.75.3, remote state Active
%STANDBY-3-BADAUTH: Bad authentication from 172.30.75.3, remote state Active
%STANDBY-3-BADAUTH: Bad authentication from 172.30.75.3, remote state Active
```

—*Herbert Borovansky, CCIE # 6037*

associated with other interfaces on the same router. When used correctly, tracking can help ensure your packets continue to be routed optimally.

For example, consider a scenario where you have an office with two HSRP-enabled routers with one Fast Ethernet interface each connected to the same LAN segment. In addition, the primary HSRP router has a T1 circuit providing WAN access out of the office, and the secondary HSRP router has a 56K circuit providing backup WAN access out of the office. Your network is configured to use EIGRP, meaning that normally, the T1 is the preferred path for WAN traffic to and from the office. Remember that HSRP turns off IP Redirection—this could create inoptimal routing in the event of the T1 circuit failing. Tracking allows you to ensure that your network routes packets optimally in certain scenarios.

Tracking could be configured in the scenario just described to ensure that if the T1 circuit fails, the secondary router assumes control of HSRP active router duties. This would ensure optimal routing since the router with the 56K circuit would become the active WAN path for traffic to and from the office once EIGRP activates this feasible successor. Tracking allows you to "watch" another interface(s) on the same router and increment or decrement the HSRP priority of that router based on the status of some other interface or multiple interfaces. In our example, we would tell the Active HSRP router to watch the Serial interface connected to the T1 circuit, and decrement the priority (to make the HSRP priority lower than the current standby router) if the interface goes down. Once the circuit is up, tracking can dynamically increment the HSRP priority. This is one scenario where preemption delay should be considered. In the event a circuit flaps, the primary HSRP router will increment and decrement the priority, causing the two routers to continue trading active router status. This could prevent the routers from successfully routing packets, since routing table information is constantly in flux from the flapping circuit.

The interface-priority value is optional and if no number is entered, a tracked interface will increment or decrement the HSRP priority by 10. You can track multiple interfaces on the same router, and if no interface-priority is entered, the priority will only be incremented or decremented by 10 even if multiple tracked interfaces are down. You can override this behavior by providing interface-priority values for each tracked interface. This allows you to customize the priority based on dynamic events in your network.

standby use-bia

This command is optional and is used in interface configuration mode. This command tells HSRP to use the interface's burned-in address as the virtual MAC address instead of the default virtual MAC address. This is highly recommended in a source-route bridged environment where your HSRP routers are located on physically different rings. HSRP can cause problems in this scenario without using the "standby use-bia" command since Token Ring uses the Routing Information Field (RIF) to direct packets when source-route bridging is enabled. This can cause problems if the virtual MAC is used, and the router Token Ring interfaces reside on physically different rings, since the RIF associated with the virtual MAC will direct the packets destined for the default gateway to the ring connected to the previous active HSRP router. By using the burned-in address, you ensure packets destined for the default gateway will use the real unique MAC address. This will prevent problems from occurring when using HSRP in this environment.

Cisco also notes there may be scenarios where end devices reject ARP replies with the source address set to a functional address from an HSRP router on Token Ring. In these situations, you may also want to consider using the burned-in address.

It's important to note the limited functionality of HSRP when using the burned-in address. As we discussed earlier, groups allow the use of multiple HSRP addresses. Since group numbers change the virtual MAC address, the use of the real MAC address for HSRP implies that groups cannot be used. Thus, groups cannot be used with the "standby use-bia" command, and you need to weigh the lost functionality in this scenario to determine which configuration to use.

on the job

Here's another way to implement HSRP in source-route bridged environments, and still provide the capability to use up to three groups. Place the router interfaces on the same physical Token Ring segment, ensuring that the RIF path to this virtual MAC address is identical, regardless of which HSRP router is active. In this case, the "standby use-bia" command is not needed since the use of the virtual MAC address should not cause the RIF issue described earlier. As with every solution, thorough testing should be completed to validate HSRP behavior in different scenarios.

Now that we have reviewed HSRP commands, here are some possible scenario questions and their answers:

show standby

In this section, we will review the commands used to verify and troubleshoot HSRP status.

SCENARIO & SOLUTION	
What is authentication?	Authentication is the process where HSRP routers exchange hello messages with an unencrypted password of up to eight characters. HSRP requires this password by all routers in the same HSRP routing process.
What is a limitation of using the "standby use-bia" command?	The use of the burned-in MAC address with HSRP prevents the use of groups, due to the inability to provide a unique MAC address for each HSRP group.

show standby [type number] [group] [brief]]

This command is optional and can be used in either enable mode or in read-only mode. The command provides the status of the local router's HSRP configuration (whether init, speaking, listening, active or standby), the priority, whether preemption is configured, the configured hello and hold timers, the Hot Standby IP address (virtual IP address used by end devices as default gateway), the standby or active router's IP address and when it expires (current status of hold timer), the state of tracked interface(s) and the interface-priority value to be incremented/decremented. The following code shows the output from an Active router, using default timers, preemption, and a priority of 200.

```
RouterA# show standby TokenRing 0
TokenRing0 - Group 0
  Local state is Active, priority 200, may preempt
  Hellotime 3 holdtime 10
  Next hello sent in 00:00:01.184
  Hot standby IP address is 172.30.75.1 configured
  Active router is local
  Standby router is 172.30.75.3 expires in 00:00:07
  Tracking interface states for 1 interface, 1 up:
     Up   FastEthernet0 Priority decrement: 150
```

In addition, you also have the option of using a shorter version of the "show standby" command with the *brief* keyword. This command will show you the interface(s) on the router using HSRP, the group number, if preemption is enabled, the Standby router's real IP address, and the virtual IP address (titled "Group addr"):

```
RouterA> show standby brief
                     P indicates configured to preempt.
                     |
Interface  Grp Prio P State    Active addr   Standby addr   Group addr
To0        0   200  P Active   local         172.30.75.3    172.30.75.1
RouterA>
```

Verifying HSRP in Switched Environments

Another way to verify HSRP status, if you are using Cisco Catalyst switches, is to check the Content Addressable Memory (CAM) or forwarding table. If you are using HSRP on an Ethernet segment, are not using groups, and want to verify the active router, try the following:

Look for the virtual MAC address in the switch's forwarding table. This virtual MAC address should point to the same port that the active HSRP router's physical interface is connected to. You will need to check the real MAC address of the router interface using the router command "show interface fastethernet0". In the following code, the real MAC address of our router is shown in bold.

```
RouterA> show interface fastethernet0
FastEthernet0 is up, line protocol is up
  Hardware is cyBus FastEthernet Interface,
address is 0050.71b7.c389 (bia 0050.71b7.c389)
  Description: Router A - VLAN A
  Internet address is 172.30.51.2/24
  MTU 1500 bytes, BW 100000 Kbit, DLY 100 usec, rely 255/255, load 1/255
  Encapsulation ARPA, loopback not set, keepalive set (10 sec)
  Full-duplex, 100Mb/s, 100BaseTX/FX
```

Another way of finding your router's real and virtual MAC addresses is to use the "show ip arp <ip address>" command. The following code shows the command issued twice to show the real and virtual IP addresses and their associated MAC addresses.

```
RouterA> show ip arp 172.30.51.2 (this is your real IP address)
Protocol  Address       Age (min)  Hardware Addr     Type   Interface
Internet  172.30.51.2      -       00-50-71-b7-c3-89 ARPA   FastEthernet0
RouterA> show ip arp 172.30.51.1 (this is your HSRP virtual IP address)
Protocol  Address       Age (min)  Hardware Addr     Type   Interface
Internet  172.30.51.1      -       00-00-0c-07-ac-00 ARPA   FastEthernet0
RouterA>
```

Once you know the router's real MAC address, look for this address in the switch's forwarding table using the "show cam <real MAC address>" switch command. This should show you which switch port the router interface is connected to. In the following code, the switch reports that the real MAC address is connected to switch port 2/1.

```
SwitchA> show cam 00-50-71-b7-c3-89
* = Static Entry. + = Permanent Entry. # = System Entry.
 R = Router Entry. X = Port Security Entry

        VLAN  Dest MAC/Route Des  Destination Ports or VCs / [Protocol Type]
        ----  ------------------  -----------------------------------------
        A     00-50-71-b7-c3-89   2/1 [ALL]
        Total Matching CAM Entries Displayed = 1
        SwitchA>
```

Next, we know the virtual MAC address should be associated with the same switch port as our router's real MAC address. Look for the virtual MAC address using the switch command "show cam 00-00-0c-07-ac-00". If the switch ports for your virtual and real MAC address are the same, congratulations! You have successfully identified your active HSRP router. The following code shows the "show cam <mac address>" command identifying the switch port associated with the HSRP virtual MAC address.

```
SwitchA> show cam 00-00-0c-07-ac-00
* = Static Entry. + = Permanent Entry. # = System Entry. R =
Router Entry. X = Port Security Entry

VLAN  Dest MAC/Route Des  Destination Ports or VCs / [Protocol Type]
----  -----------------   -------------------------------------------
A     00-00-0c-07-ac-00   2/1 [ALL]
Total Matching CAM Entries Displayed = 1
SwitchA>
```

Configuration Exercises

In this section, we will practice configuring HSRP with the basic features first, then continue to more advanced configurations. Each example builds on the previous example, so we recommend configuring your lab in the same order. It is important that your lab has two Cisco routers, preferably using IOS 11.3 or greater, and at least two active interfaces per router. If you only have one interface per router, that's OK, you will just need to skip the Tracking example.

EXERCISE 7-3

Configuring HSRP

Example 1 involves the use of the fewest commands required to enable HSRP.

1. Enter configuration mode on your first router (we'll call it Router A), and type the primary IP address and subnet mask on the FastEthernet0 interface.

2. Next, enable HSRP using the "standby ip" command with the default gateway/virtual IP address.

3. Repeat the same steps for Router B, changing only the real IP address of the router interface. HSRP is now running in your network! In this scenario,

Router A would assume control as the active router for HSRP—let's review why. As discussed earlier, HSRP uses priority to determine the active router, with the default priority of an HSRP set to 100. Since our example does not change the priority of either router, HSRP chooses the active router based on the highest real IP address. In our case, Router A has the highest real IP address. See the following code for a basic configuration example of HSRP.

```
Router A
interface FastEthernet0
 ip address 172.30.51.3 255.255.255.0 (Real IP Address)
 no ip redirects (added by Cisco IOS by default)
 standby ip 172.30.51.1 (Default Gateway/Virtual IP Address)
Router B
interface FastEthernet0
 ip address 172.30.51.2 255.255.255.0 (Real IP Address)
 no ip redirects (added by Cisco IOS by default)
 standby ip 172.30.51.1 (Default Gateway/Virtual IP Address)
```

Example 2 modifies the priority of Router B.

1. Enter configuration mode on Router B's FastEthernet0 interface, type **standby priority 200**, and exit configuration mode (see the following). In this scenario, Router A would retain control as the active router for HSRP until Router A is restarted or its FastEthernet0 interfaces goes down—let's review why. The default priority for an HSRP router is 100, which is the current priority of Router A. Our configuration change has incremented the priority of Router B to 200. Since HSRP uses priority as the first method of determining the active router, it would seem that Router B should have taken control as Active Router from Router A once we incremented its priority. This is only true if both routers are started at the same time and they complete the listening process. Changing a standby router's priority to a value higher than the Active router once HSRP has determined the Active router does not grant the Standby router the ability to take over Active router status. In our example, Router B will remain the Standby router until Router A's interface goes down, or is restarted. The next example will configure preemption, which will give Router B the ability to immediately seize Active router status from Router A.

```
Router A
interface FastEthernet0
ip address 172.30.51.3 255.255.255.0 (Real IP Address)
no ip redirects (added by Cisco IOS by default)
  standby ip 172.30.51.1 (Default Gateway/Virtual IP Address)
Router B
ip address 172.30.51.2 255.255.255.0 (Real IP Address)
no ip redirects (added by Cisco IOS by default)
standby priority 200 (this alone does not make Router B Active)
standby ip 172.30.51.1 (Default Gateway/Virtual IP Address)
```

Example 3 adds preemption to Router B.

1. Enter configuration mode on Router B's FastEthernet0 interface, type **standby preempt**, and exit configuration mode. In this scenario, Router B would take control as the Active router for HSRP, and Router A would become the Standby router—let's review why. In our example, Router A has a priority of 100, and Router B has a priority of 200. Our configuration change in the following code enables preemption on Router B, which tells it to take control of Active router status if it has the highest priority.

```
Router A
interface FastEthernet0
 ip address 172.30.51.3 255.255.255.0 (Real IP Address)
 no ip redirects (added by Cisco IOS by default)
 standby ip 172.30.51.1 (Default Gateway/Virtual IP Address)
Router B
ip address 172.30.51.2 255.255.255.0 (Real IP Address)
 no ip redirects (added by Cisco IOS by default)
 standby priority 200 (this alone does not make Router A Active)
standby preempt (this allows Router B to Become Active)
 standby ip 172.30.51.1 (Default Gateway/Virtual IP Address)
```

Let's review our current lab configuration—we now have HSRP running between Routers A and B. Router B is the active HSRP router since its priority is 200 and it is configured to preempt. Next, we will configure the more advanced options: Timers, Authentication, and Tracking.

Advanced HSRP Configuration Examples

Next, we will modify the default timers associated with HSRP, the hello timer and hold timer. Remember that, by default, HSRP routers send hello packets every three seconds. If HSRP routers don't see any partner's hello packets after 10 seconds, they will assume control of HSRP, regardless of priority and preemption settings. Let's presume you have an extremely time-sensitive application that requires no loss of packets and times out after six seconds. Your users have stated they can't tolerate having to restart their application sessions in the event of a network failure. The default HSRP timers will not meet your business requirements—you will need to alter and test the affect of changing the HSRP default hello and hold timers. Due to your requirements, we will configure your HSRP routers to assume control from the Active router after four seconds. Remember that by default, the hold timers are three times the hello timers. In our lab, we will need to send hello packets every second, and set the hold timer to four seconds.

Note: Changing the timers doesn't guarantee successful routing around network failures—you also need an extremely fast converging routing protocol like EIGRP or OSPF to ensure your Active routers always have routing table entries to successfully route packets.

```
Router A
interface FastEthernet0
  ip address 172.30.51.3 255.255.255.0 (Real IP Address)
  no ip redirects (added by Cisco IOS by default)
  standby timers 1 4 (required on all routers when modified)
  standby ip 172.30.51.1 (Default Gateway/Virtual IP Address)

Router B
  ip address 172.30.51.2 255.255.255.0 (Real IP Address)
  no ip redirects (added by Cisco IOS by default)
  standby priority 200 (this alone does not make Router A Active)
  standby preempt (this allows Router B to Become Active)
  standby timers 1 4 (required on all routers when modified)
  standby ip 172.30.51.1 (Default Gateway/Virtual IP Address)
```

Administrators should use caution when modifying the default timers associated with HSRP. The default timers are set to values that are usually sufficient for most applications. Changing default timers on HSRP to use different timers can cause erratic behavior, and you should keep the settings the same across each HSRP group. If you find the default timers are not sufficient, extra care should be taken by thoroughly testing the failover behavior of HSRP with the new HSRP hello and hold timers and your applications .

In the following code, we add authentication so hello messages include an unencrypted password. Note that once you add authentication to one HSRP router, you will need to add the same configuration string to the other HSRP router(s) watching that same virtual IP address.

```
Router A
interface FastEthernet0
  ip address 172.30.51.3 255.255.255.0 (Real IP Address)
  no ip redirects (added by Cisco IOS by default)
  standby authentication cisco (required on all routers when used)
  standby timers 5 15 (required on all routers when used)
  standby ip 172.30.51.1 (Default Gateway/Virtual IP Address)

Router B
  ip address 172.30.51.2 255.255.255.0 (Real IP Address)
  no ip redirects (added by Cisco IOS by default)
  standby priority 200 (this alone does not make Router A Active)
  standby preempt (this allows Router B to Become Active)
  standby authentication cisco (required on all routers when used)
  standby timers 5 15 (required on all routers when used)
  standby ip 172.30.51.1 (Default Gateway/Virtual IP Address)
```

Our final example adds tracking so our HSRP routers will watch another key interface and increment or decrement the routers' priority based on the physical status of that interface. In our example, both routers provide WAN connectivity—Router A is connected to a 56 K Frame Relay circuit, and Router B is connected to a T1 Frame Relay circuit. Since we are using EIGRP, the T1 connected to Router B is normally the preferred path. In the event our T1 fails, we want our network to dynamically reroute packets over the 56K circuit—EIGRP will handle this issue. EIGRP, however, will not ensure optimal routing since the traffic will first be sent to Router B, which will then have to send it to Router A (assuming EIGRP is not passive on that Fast Ethernet segment!). Thus, tracking let's us tell Router B to watch its Serial 0 interface, and decrement its priority by 150, thereby making its priority 50. In this case, Router A would now become the active HSRP router, with one additional modification. Remember that a lower-priority router will not take control of active HSRP status from an online higher priority router unless we add preemption. Thus, in the following code, we add the "standby preempt" command to Router A to ensure it takes control of HSRP active status when its priority becomes higher than Router B.

```
Router A
interface FastEthernet0
 ip address 172.30.51.3 255.255.255.0 (Real IP Address)
 no ip redirects (added by Cisco IOS by default)
 standby preempt (ensures Active status with higher priority)
 standby authentication cisco (required on all routers when used)
 standby timers 5 15 (required on all routers when used)
 standby ip 172.30.51.1 (Default Gateway/Virtual IP Address)
```

The configuration changes to Router B follow in the following code.

```
Router B
ip address 172.30.51.2 255.255.255.0 (Real IP Address)
 no ip redirects (added by Cisco IOS by default)
 standby priority 200 (this alone does not make Router A Active)
 standby preempt (this allows Router B to Become Active)
 standby authentication cisco (required on all routers when used)
 standby timers 5 15 (required on all routers when used)
 standby ip 172.30.51.1 (Default Gateway/Virtual IP Address)
 standby track Serial 0 150 (watch Serial 0 - decrement/increment
priority by 150 when Serial 0 is down/up)
```

Now that we have completed sample configurations, here are some possible scenario questions and their answers:

SCENARIO & SOLUTION

When should I use tracking?	Tracking is a desirable feature when you want to ensure the default gateway has the optimal path for routing remote packets. When your routing protocol is not running out your HSRP LAN interfaces, tracking ensures the active HSRP router moves to a router that has valid and optimal routing information.
What are the default and potential values for the priority of an HSRP router?	The default value of HSRP priority is 100. You can configure a value between 1 and 255 on an HSRP router.

Access List Configuration

Now we will provide an exercise to show the source and destination UDP ports. Again, we will use the debug option on our router to show the UDP packets sent from an HSRP router. On your Router B, you would see the following messages if you issue the "debug ip udp" command on your router. (NOTE: DO NOT use debug on your production routers unless instructed to do so by the Cisco TAC—this process can severely degrade performance on your router). From the command prompt, in enable mode, enter **debug udp ip** and you should see traffic similar to the following. To turn on this debugging, issue the "no debug ip udp" command.

When using HSRP with firewalls and access-lists, you must enable communication between the HSRP routers to ensure proper operation. HSRP communicates using UDP multicast packets on port 1985. The packets are sourced from the sending interface's real IP address and destined for the multicast address 224.0.0.2. An example of a Cisco extended access-list entry that permits HSRP traffic is shown in the following code. You would need to apply this entry to both extended access-lists in the scenario where both HSRP routers filter inbound or outbound traffic.

```
RouterB# debug ip udp
UDP: rcvd src=172.16.20.2(1985), dst=224.0.0.2(1985), length=28
UDP: rcvd src=172.16.20.2(1985), dst=224.0.0.2(1985), length=28
UDP: rcvd src=172.16.20.2(1985), dst=224.0.0.2(1985), length=28
```

```
UDP: rcvd src=172.16.20.2(1985), dst=224.0.0.2(1985), length=28
RouterB# no debug ip udp
UDP packet debugging is off
```

Here is the correct syntax of an extended access-list. This example covers an inbound access-list on the receiving router or outbound access-list on the sending router:

```
permit udp host <source ip> eq 1985 host 224.0.0.2 eq 1985
```

CERTIFICATION SUMMARY

The prevalent use of TCP/IP today in the Internet, extranets, and intranets creates a great dependence on the ability to send packets between remote hosts. Almost every end user communicates with remote IP hosts by sending traffic to his or her default gateway. This means the failure of your default gateway can severely impact the productivity of your business. Fortunately, Cisco addresses this need with Hot Standby Routing Protocol (HSRP).

HSRP requires at least two Cisco routers, running 10.3 IOS or greater. In addition, these routers must be connected to same logical network segment via similar interfaces. This protocol provides default gateway redundancy by creating a virtual IP and MAC address—these virtual addresses are shared between the two (or more) Cisco routers. The virtual IP address is the same IP address the endstations designate their default gateway. These routers also have at least one real IP address each, from the same subnet as the virtual IP address.

HSRP designates one router as the active router by election using either the highest IP address if priorities are the same, or the priority. These routers complete this election by sending and receiving UDP hello packets; by default, these packets are sent every three seconds. By default, if an HSRP router does not receive hello packets for a period of 10 seconds, it will assume the other router is down, and begin responding to ARP requests for the default gateway. In this case, the priority is no longer relevant since a lower-priority router will respond to ARP requests after failing to receive hellos from another HSRP router for 10 seconds.

HSRP also provides some advanced features, including group numbers, to support multiple logical networks on the same physical segment; authentication, to ensure the HSRP process is only controlled by legitimate routers; configurable timers to speed up or slow down how quickly HSRP routers will seize control after no hellos are received; and tracking, which allows you to control which path out of your network packets will take by monitoring the status of interfaces on the same router that you deem important. For source-route bridged environments, Cisco provides the option to use the interface's real MAC address. This prevents RIF confusion by ensuring a unique Layer 2 address.

In closing, HSRP provides a lot of flexibility to recover from default gateway failures. In the past, the failure of your router meant potentially significant downtime for your end users. Now, using HSRP, you can confidently predict that your network can recover from component failures.

TWO-MINUTE DRILL

Here are some of the key points from each certification objective in Chapter 7.

HSRP Groups, Virtual IP Address, HSRP Messaging Between Routers

- ❏ HSRP stands for Hot Standby Routing Protocol.
- ❏ The HSRP address that responds to default gateway requests is called the Virtual IP Address.
- ❏ Real IP Address is the IP address of the physical interface configured to respond to ARPs for default gateways
- ❏ ARP stands for Address Resolution Protocol. It is the process used by IP end devices to request the Layer 2 address of their default gateway.
- ❏ Groups is the HSRP method used to support multiple logical IP subnets via HSRP on the same physical router interface. HSRP supports 256 groups for Ethernet/FDDI and three groups for Token Ring.
- ❏ The MAC address sent by active HSRP routers to end devices that ARP for their default gateway's MAC address is called the Virtual MAC Address.
- ❏ Authentication is the HSRP method for authenticating HSRP messages using an unencrypted password.
- ❏ Tracking is the HSRP method of a router dynamically tracking its own, other non-HSRP interfaces. This router increments or decrements its HSRP priority based on that tracked interface's physical status (up or down).
- ❏ Burned-In Address is the HSRP method of using an HSRP router's real MAC address for ARP requests. This is helpful in source-route bridged environments where the HSRP routers are not physically connected to the same Token Ring segment, thereby creating a different RIF entry. This eliminates the ability to use groups on that interface.
- ❏ Multicast is the address HSRP hello packets use for communication.

Learn States
- Init
- Listen
- Speak
- Active
- Standby

Commands
- standby <group #> ip <ip address>
- standby <group #> authentication <password>
- standby <group #> priority <priority # from 1 to 255>
- standby <group #> preempt
- standby <group #> track
- standby <group #> timers
- standby use-bia
- show standby
- show standby brief
- show standby <interface>

SELF TEST

The following questions will help you measure your understanding of the material presented in this chapter. Read all of the choices carefully, as there may be more than one correct answer. Choose all correct answers for each question.

HSRP Groups, Virtual IP Address, HSRP Messaging Between Routers

1. How do you ensure that a router will seize control of Active router status?
   A. Configure it with the highest priority
   B. Configure it with preemption
   C. Configure it with preemption, and the highest priority
   D. Configure it with preemption, and the lowest priority

2. What default password is used with authentication by HSRP when no password is specified?
   A. real
   B. cisco
   C. virtual
   D. None, you must specify a password.

3. When using group numbers, how many are valid for Ethernet/FDDI, and how many are valid for Token Ring?
   A. 0 and 255 for Ethernet/FDDI, and 0 and 128 for Token Ring
   B. 1 and 255 for Ethernet/FDDI, and 0 and 3 for Token Ring
   C. 1 and 255 for Ethernet/FDDI, and 1 and 3 for Token Ring
   D. 0 and 128 for Ethernet/FDDI, and 0 and 255 for Token Ring

4. What HSRP phase is a router looking for other HSRP routers on the same segment?
   A. init
   B. listen
   C. speak
   D. standby

5. How many IP addresses, at a minimum, are required to configure HSRP between two Cisco routers?

   A. 1
   B. 2
   C. 3
   D. 5

6. What would the virtual MAC addresses be, respectively, for a router with groups 1 and 2 configured on a Fast Ethernet interface?

   A. 00-00-0c-07-ab-01 and 00-00-0c-07-ab-02
   B. 00-00-0c-07-ac-01 and 00-00-0c-07-ac-02
   C. 00-00-0c-07-ad-01 and 00-00-0c-07-ad-02
   D. 00-00-0c-07-ac-00 and 00-00-0c-07-ac-01

Learn States

7. What type of packets does HSRP use to send hellos?

   A. Multicast and unicast
   B. Broadcast
   C. Unicast
   D. Multicast

8. What F does HSRP use for hello packets?

   A. TCP, Port 1986
   B. UDP, Port 1985
   C. UDP, Port 1986
   D. TCP, Port 1985

9. What are the four states a router can report when configured with HSRP?

   A. Shutdown, Up, Waiting, Administratively Down
   B. Start, Listen, Speak, Active
   C. Start, Listen, Waiting, Active
   D. Init, Listen, Speak, Active/Standby

Commands

10. What other situation requires the "standby use-bia" command for Token Ring besides source-route bridged environments where your routers are located on different Token Ring segments?

    A. Token Ring end devices reject ARP replies with the destination address set to a functional address.

    B. Token Ring end devices reject ARP replies with the destination address set to a virtual MAC address.

    C. Token Ring end devices reject ARP requests with the destination address set to a functional address.

    D. None of the above.

11. What are default timers associated with HSRP?

    A. 20 seconds for hello timers, and 12 seconds for hold timers

    B. 3 seconds for hello timers, and 10 seconds for hold timers

    C. 10 seconds for hello timers, and 3 seconds for hold timers

    D. None of the above

12. What virtual MAC addresses are sent in ARP replies for Ethernet/FDDI and Token Ring by HSRP when groups are not used?

    A. 00-00-0c-07-ac-00 (Ethernet/FDDI) and c0-00-00-01-00-00 (Token Ring)

    B. 00-00-0c-07-ac-02 (Ethernet/FDDI) and c0-00-00-01-00-00 (Token Ring)

    C. ff-ff-ff-ff-ff-ff (Ethernet/FDDI) and ff-ff-ff-ff-ff-ff (Token Ring)

    D. None of the above

13. What is the default priority value of an HSRP router?

    A. 101

    B. 200

    C. 300

    D. 100

14. What HSRP command tells the router to verify HSRP messages using passwords?

    A. Timers

B. Encryption
C. Authentication
D. Adjacency

15. What happens to the priority of an HSRP router using tracking if multiple tracked interfaces are down and no interface-priority value is used with the "standby track" command?

    A. Increases by 100
    B. Decreases by 10
    C. Decreases by 100
    D. Increases by 10

16. What command forces HSRP routers to use their real MAC address instead of the virtual MAC address?

    A. standby use-bia
    B. standby use-mac
    C. standby preempt
    D. standby priority

17. What command is used to show the current status of HSRP without the detail?

    A. show standby
    B. show HSRP brief
    C. show standby brief
    D. none of the above

18. When and why is it recommended to use the "standby use-bia" command with HSRP?

    A. In Ethernet environments with many VLANs. This ensures the switch doesn't get confused and send a packet destined for the HSRP Virtual MAC Address from one VLAN to another VLAN.
    B. In Ethernet environments with multiple HSRP groups. This prevents the router from creating a unique MAC address for each group.
    C. In switched Token Ring environments. When the routers are connected to different rings, we need to ensure when failover occurs, that packets intended for the default gateway now use a different RIF.
    D. None of the above.

19. What are two router commands we can use to help identify HSRP interface real MAC addresses when trying to verify the switch port connection of the HSRP active router?

   A. show ip arp <virtual/real ip address> and show interface <interface>
   B. show ip route and show standby group
   C. show standby brief and show hsrp groups
   D. show interface <interface> and show ip eigrp neighbors

20. What HSRP command keyword provides support for multiple HSRP virtual IP addresses without using groups?

   A. secondary
   B. secondary group
   C. group
   D. standby secondary

21. What is the range of time, in seconds, you can configure HSRP to delay preemption using the *delay* keyword?

   A. 00-00-0c-07-ab-01 and 00-00-0c-07-ab-02
   B. 00-00-0c-07-ac-01 and 00-00-0c-07-ac-02
   C. 00-00-0c-07-ad-01 and 00-00-0c-07-ad-02
   D. 00-00-0c-07-ac-00 and 00-00-0c-07-ac-01

LAB QUESTION

Let's assume you have just experienced a lengthy outage to 225 users in the Tax and Accounting department due to their default gateway router interface failing. To make things worse, this problem appeared the week a major financial audit of the company was in progress. Your CIO insists that you now provide network redundancy to ensure this problem never happens again and wants a solution in place within two days. To make matters worse, DHCP was not implemented last year, so you don't even have the option of easily changing their default gateway using a short lease with DHCP.

You head down to your lab/storage room to find a second Cisco router. The primary router is a Cisco 7507 with a Fast Ethernet interface connected to the Tax and Accounting department switched Ethernet LAN, and a Fast Ethernet interface connected to your company's switched Ethernet metropolitan area network (MAN). All traffic from this department's LAN must cross the MAN in order to reach the Internet, other devices within your Intranet, or some extranet services.

Unfortunately, you don't have a spare 7507, but you do find a Cisco 3640 with two Ethernet interfaces.

Add this 3640 router to your network and ensure it acts as the backup to your 7507 for your Tax and Accounting users. During normal operation, the 7507 should always be the default gateway, but your design should ensure default gateway redundancy when either the LAN or MAN interfaces on your 7507 fail. What steps would you take to implement HSRP in your network?

SELF TEST ANSWERS

HSRP Groups, Virtual IP Address, HSRP Messaging Between Routers

1. ☑ **C.** Configure it with preemption, and the highest priority. Priority is used by HSRP to determine which router should have control of HSRP; however, it will not force a router to seize control (in the event priority changes). In scenarios where the priority of one router changes, due to tracking, for example, preemption must be configured on the normally lower-priority router to ensure it seizes control of the Active router status. The best way to control active router status is to configure preemption and at least one router's priority to be higher than the other.
   ☒ **A** is incorrect because a router with higher priority will not seize Active status from a lower-priority router unless preemption is configured. **B** is incorrect because a router will not seize control with only preemption—it must have preemption and a higher priority to seize active status from another HSRP router. **D** is incorrect because a router configured with preemption and a lower priority will not seize active status. The preemption is required, but priority must be higher as well in order for a router to seize Active status.

2. ☑ **B.** cisco. HSRP adds this password by default is no password is specified with the "standby authentication" command. The administrator has the option of specifying a password of up to eight characters, or leaving it blank, and thus defaulting to cisco.
   ☒ **A** and **C** are incorrect because the default value is cisco when no password is specified when using authentication with HSRP. **D** is untrue because specifying passwords with authentication is optional.

3. ☑ **C.** HSRP can support up to 256 groups on Ethernet/FDDI (0 is default, and you can add between 1 and 255); Token Ring can support up to three groups only.
   ☒ **A**, **B**, and **D** contain incorrect group numbers.

4. ☑ **B.** listen. This router is still not sending hello packets, but is listening for hello packets to see if other HSRP routers are active on that LAN segment.
   ☒ **A** is incorrect because an router HSRP in init phase is not sending or receiving hello packets, and the HSRP process is not active on that interface. **C** is incorrect because an HSRP router speaking has heard hellos from other routers. **D** is incorrect because an HSRP router in standby mode has found other routers and determined who is the active HSRP router. This router is available to take over HSRP active status after the HSRP hold timer has expired.

5. ☑ **C.** HSRP requires at least three IP addresses from the same subnet to successfully configure the protocol. One is called the virtual IP address, which equals the default gateway setting on your end devices. This IP address is shared between HSRP routers and can be either configured on all your routers running HSRP, or at least one, and learned by the others. This is configured using the "standby ip" command. The other two IP addresses are called real IP addresses, and they must match the subnet of your virtual IP address. These are configured using the normal "ip address" command on your router interface
☒ **A** is incorrect because one IP address will not correctly configure HSRP between two routers. **B** is incorrect because two IP addresses will not correctly configure HSRP between two routers. **D** is incorrect because five IP addresses are not required—at a minimum, three IP addresses are required to correctly configure at least one HSRP group.

6. ☑ **B.** 00-00-0c-07-ac-01 and 00-00-0c-07-ac-02. HSRP increments the virtual IP address by one for each successive group number. HSRP assigns the virtual MAC address 00-00-0c-07-ac-00 to group 0, which is the default, and used when no group number is specified.
☒ **A** is incorrect because HSRP uses virtual MAC addresses with "ac" where our example contains "ab". **C** is incorrect because HSRP uses virtual MAC addresses with "ac" where our example contains "ab". **D** is incorrect because we are using groups 1 and 2. HSRP adds one to the last pair of the virtual MAC address for each group number starting with 00-00-0c-07-ac-00 for group 0, 00-00-0c-07-ac-01 for group 1, 00-00-0c-07-ac-02 for group 2, etc. Our example shows the virtual MAC addresses HSRP would assign to group 0 and group 1.

Learn States

7. ☑ **D.** Multicast. HSRP sends hello packets to multicast address 224.0.0.2. This ensures that normal end devices will not see the packets unless they subscribe to that multicast group.
☒ **A** is only partially correct, because HSRP uses only multicast; unicast packets are not used. **B** and **C** are incorrect because HSRP uses only multicast.

8. ☑ **B.** UDP, Port 1985. HSRP uses User Datagram Protocol (UDP) Port 1985 for HSRP hello packets. You will need to permit access for this within your extended access-lists or application firewalls.
☒ **A** is incorrect because HSRP uses port 1985, not port 1986. **C** is incorrect because HSRP uses port 1985. **D** is incorrect because HSRP uses UDP, not TCP.

9. ☑ **D.** Init, Listen, Speak, Active/Standby.
☒ **A** is incorrect because Shutdown, Up, and Administratively Down are examples of router interface values and commands. Waiting is not a valid command or HSRP state. **B** is incorrect because Start is not a valid HSRP state. Listen, Speak, and Active are valid HSRP states. **C** is incorrect because Start and Waiting are not valid HSRP states. Listen and Speak are valid HSRP states.

Commands

10. ☑ **D.** None of the above. The correct answer is that in certain scenarios, Token Ring end devices reject ARP replies with the source address set to a functional address. By default, with Token Ring, HSRP uses the Token Ring functional address c0-00-00-01-00-00. In this case, you can force HSRP to use the burned-in address for ARP replies to ensure interoperability with all Token Ring devices in your network. Remember, the use of the burned-in address prevents you from using groups; thus, you should consider the loss of the group features when using "standby use-bia" on a case-by-case basis.
☒ **A** is incorrect because Token Ring end devices reject ARP replies with the source (not destination) address set to a functional address. **B** is incorrect because an end device would not process an ARP reply with a destination address set to a virtual MAC address—the end device would only process packets with a destination address set to its MAC address. **C** is incorrect because an ARP request is looking for the destination address associated with the destination IP address—the source address would be set to a functional address. An example of this would be the router sending an ARP request to identify the end device MAC address to deliver frames destined for that end device.

11. ☑ **B.** 3 seconds for hello timers, and 10 seconds for hold timers. By default, HSRP Hello packets are sent every 3 seconds; if, after 10 seconds, an HSRP router hasn't seen any hellos from its partner, it will become an Active router and respond to ARP requests for the default gateway address. The hold timers are set to more than three times the hello timers to ensure enough time for hello packets to reach partner HSRP routers.
☒ **A** is incorrect because 20 seconds for hello timers, and 12 seconds for hold timers are custom configured HSRP values. **C** is incorrect because 10 seconds for hello timers and 3 seconds for hold timers are incorrect—the hold timers are generally three times the hello timers. In answer C, these settings are reversed and HSRP would not work correctly. **D** is incorrect because the correct answer is listed in B.

12. ☑ **A.** Ethernet and FDDI use 00-00-0c-07-ac-00, and Token Ring uses the IEEE 802.5 functional address, c0-00-00-01-00-00.

☒ B, C, and D are incorrect. The virtual MAC used for Ethernet/FDDI in B is an example of when groups are used. The last examples in C are examples of broadcast Layer 2 addresses.

13. ☑ D. The default Priority of HSRP routers is 100—this can be changed using the "standby [group-number] priority [number]" command. The valid values are 1 to 255—if this command is not issued, the priority will be 100. Priority determines, in conjunction with preemption, which router will take Active state. In scenarios where you have not changed the priority on two routers, the router with the highest real IP address will win and assume control as active router.
    ☒ A, B, and C are incorrect because the default priority of an HSRP router is 100—A, B, and C are all examples of a router priority that was explicitly changed using the "standby [group-number] priority [number]" command.

14. ☑ C. Authentication. This is the process by which HSRP sends a password string of up to eight characters in unencrypted format. The "standby [group-number] authentication [string]" command configures authentication. The use of authentication on at least one router requires it be used on all your routers or none at all.
    ☒ A, B, and D are incorrect commands.

15. ☑ B. Decreases by 10. Tracking affects the priority of the local router only, and depends on the interface-priority value associated with the "standby track "command. The priority increases/decreases by a total of 10 for one or multiple tracked interfaces if no priority values are stated; the priority increases/decreases by the interface-priority value.
    ☒ A and C are incorrect because the change in default value of a router's priority when no interface-priority value is specified is 10. D is incorrect because the change in the default value of a router's priority when no interface-priority is specified is *decreased* by 10.

16. ☑ A. standby use-bia. This command forces HSRP to use the real MAC address of the router interface configure to run HSRP.
    ☒ B, C, and D are incorrect and do not affect the virtual MAC address used. The only other command that affects the virtual MAC is the use of HSRP groups.

17. ☑ C. show standby brief. This command shows an abbreviated version of the HSRP status on your router for all HSRP groups. In addition, you have the flexibility of adding an interface number after the "show standby" command instead of the brief keyword if you want to see HSRP status detail for just one of many interface.
    ☒ A is incorrect because the "show standby command" shows all of the detail associated with each HSRP group configured on your router. B is incorrect because "show HSRP brief" is not a valid command. D is incorrect because there is a correct choice.

18. ☑ **C.** In switched Token Ring environments. Remember that switched Token Ring environments use the RIF field to correctly forward packets to their end destination. In this example, pretend that we have not configured HSRP to use the burned-in address. If our two router's Token Ring router interfaces are located on different rings, the RIF value required to reach each router interface from the endstation will be different. Thus, when HSRP fails-over, the end device will continue sending packets to the virtual MAC address associated with the previous active router. Since the new active router is reachable via a different RIF, connectivity will be broken because end devices rely on their default gateway for remote connectivity.
☒ **A** is incorrect because a Layer 2 switch does not switch packets between VLANs based on MAC address; in fact, packets are never switched between VLANs by a Layer 2 switch. Layer 2 switches make forwarding decisions on a per-VLAN basis. A switch will forward a packet from an end device in VLAN 2 to another specific port in VLAN 2 (unicast), to all ports in VLAN 2 (broadcast), or some ports in VLAN 2 (multicast). **B** is incorrect because the use of "standby use-bia" prevents the use of HSRP groups. Remember that HSRP creates a unique virtual MAC address with each HSRP group, and the use of the burned-in MAC address prevents HSRP from creating more than one unique MAC address. **D** is incorrect because there is a correct choice.

19. ☑ **A.** "show ip arp <virtual/real ip address>" and "show interface <interface>". The "show ip arp" command is helpful in reporting what MAC address is associated with each IP address we query. The "show interface" command shows us the real MAC address associated with the router interface.
☒ **B** is incorrect because "show standby group" is not a real command. The "show ip route" command is not appropriate in this example because we are trying to find a MAC address associated with an IP address. **C** is incorrect because the "show standby brief" command does not report on the MAC address associated with the HSRP virtual or real IP addresses. The "show hsrp groups" command is not a real command. **D** is incorrect because "show ip eigrp neighbors" does not report on the MAC address associated with the HSRP virtual or real IP addresses.

20. ☑ **A.** secondary. HSRP allows you to support multiple virtual IP addresses on the same interface using either the *secondary* keyword, or groups.
☒ **B** is incorrect because *secondary group* is not a valid keyword. **C** is incorrect because *group* is not a valid keyword. **D** is incorrect because *standby secondary* is not a valid keyword.

21. ☑ **B.** 00-00-0c-07-ac-01 and 00-00-0c-07-ac-02. HSRP increments the virtual IP address by 1 for each successive group number. HSRP assigns the virtual MAC address 00-00-0c-07-ac-00 to group 0, which is the default, and used when no group number is specified.

☒ **A** is incorrect because HSRP uses virtual MAC addresses with "ac" where our example contains "ab". **C** is incorrect because HSRP uses virtual MAC addresses with "ac" where our example contains "ab". **D** is incorrect because we are using groups 1 and 2. HSRP adds 1 to the last pair of the virtual MAC address for each group number starting with 00-00-0c-07-ac-00 for group 0, 00-00-0c-07-ac-01 for group 1, 00-00-0c-07-ac-02 for group 2, etc. Our example shows the virtual MAC addresses HSRP would assign to group 0 and group 1.

LAB ANSWER

Remember certain portions of this solution are subjective and are not required to implement HSRP. Think of them as *On the Job* notes from the author's practical experience. Assume that your building engineering has installed the router in the rack, and provided the appropriate power connection. Also, assume the 3640 configuration is blank with no passwords and that your default network configuration includes your network's EIGRP configuration.

1. Check the IOS version on the 7507.
2. Log on to Cisco's Web site, CCO, and find the same version of code for the 3640.
3. Check that IOS version's release notes for any documented issues with HSRP in that version.
4. Install the IOS on your 3640.
5. Configure additional switch ports for each LAN and MAN connection for your new 3640 on the appropriate VLANs.
6. Connect the 3640's Ethernet interfaces to the switch ports (assume copper CAT 5 cables are used).
7. Connect via a console cable to your 3640.
8. Power on the 3640.
9. Enter enable mode.
10. Verify the IP subnets of your LAN and MAN and identify a unique IP address from each subnet for both routers' interfaces. You will need new addresses for both interfaces on the 3640 and a new address on the LAN segment for the 7507. Identify the default gateway IP address of your end users (the safest way is to check the existing 7507 Fast Ethernet interface).

11. Enter configuration mode on the 3640, configure the Ethernet interface connected to the LAN with the IP address you identified in Step 10, then enable the interface using the "no shutdown" command and exit configuration mode.

12. Ping the 7507 Fast Ethernet interface on the LAN segment from the 3640. Assume success.

13. Enter configuration mode on the 3640, configure the Ethernet interface connected to the MAN with the IP address you identified in Step 10, then enable the interface using the "no shutdown" command and exit configuration mode.

14. Ping the 7507 Fast Ethernet interface on the MAN segment from the 3640. Assume success.

15. Connect to the 7507 and enter configuration mode. Configure the Fast Ethernet interface connected to the LAN with the new IP address you identified in Step 10.

16. We should use the advanced feature tracking in HSRP in this solution, to ensure connectivity for our LAN users in the event our MAN connection goes down. See the following sample configuration for a possible solution using HSRP for our example. In addition, note that we have configured the 7507 to take control back from the 3640 once the MAN connection is active, because the 3640 only has Ethernet interfaces. These interfaces provide less total bandwidth to our end users, and we only want to use them as long as necessary until the 7507 is back in operation.

```
Cisco 7507 (Active HSRP Router)
interface FastEthernet0/0 (LAN Connection)
  ip address 172.29.1.3 255.255.255.0 (Real IP Address)
  standby priority 200 (ensures Active status by higher priority)
  standby preempt (ensures Active status with higher priority)
  standby ip 172.29.1.1 (Default Gateway/Virtual IP Address)
  standby track FastEthernet 0/1 150 (watch Fast Ethernet MAN connection -
decrement/increment priority by 150 when the interface is down/up)

interface FastEthernet0/1 (MAN Connection)
  ip address 172.29.2.3 255.255.255.224

Cisco 3640 (Standby HSRP Router)
interface Ethernet0/0
  ip address 172.29.1.2 255.255.255.0 (Real IP Address)
  standby ip 172.29.1.1 (Default Gateway/Virtual IP Address)

interface Ethernet0/1 (MAN Connection)
  ip address 172.29.2.2 255.255.255.224
```

17. Using the show HSRP show commands and your knowledge of HSRP, ensure that HSRP is functioning correctly within your network. Validate the design and implementation (during nonbusiness hours) to test several possible scenarios:

- Your 7507 LAN interface drops (3640 should become active).
- Your 7507 LAN interface returns to up/up (7507 should become active and 3640 becomes standby).
- Your 7507 MAN interface drops while LAN interface stays up (3640 should become active).
- Your 7507 MAN interface returns to up/up (7507 should become active and 3640 becomes standby).

8
Switching and Routing IP Multicasting

CERTIFICATION OBJECTIVES

8.01 Understanding the Differences Between Multicast, Broadcast, and Unicast Addresses

8.02 Translating Multicast to Ethernet Addresses

8.03 Understanding Multicast Protocols

8.04 Monitoring and Troubleshooting Commands

✓   Two-Minute Drill

Q&A Self Test

This chapter covers the fundamentals of IP Multicast. IP Multicast (IPMC) is a bandwidth-conserving technology that reduces traffic by delivering a single stream of traffic to a group of up to thousands of users. A student named Steve Deering created IP Multicast in 1989 as a research project at Stanford University. Since its inception, IPMC has gone through several changes. The first globally deployed IPMC network was called "MBONE," and was set up in 1992 by educational and research organizations as a way to broadcast audio and video from meetings of the Internet Engineering Task Force (IETF). Until recently, IPMC was an unpopular technology that very few networks implemented. As the demand for high-bandwidth streaming content has grown, the use of IPMC has grown in parallel. More and more networks are deploying IPMC each day. Several large Internet Service Providers (ISPs) and several large enterprise networks support IPMC today. As more networks connected to the MBONE, there was a realization that IP Multicast needed much more development to scale on a global level. Toward that end, many of the protocols discussed in this chapter were developed. The MBONE operates over the same physical network as the Internet, using the same routers and switches as other Internet traffic.

Increasing popularity of IPMC is partly due to the development of new protocols. As a result, IPMC is a more robust technology suited to run throughout an entire enterprise network. However, multicast is still maturing. Developments are being made every day, and various types of multicast protocols are being developed. Examples include router-to-client protocols, switching protocols, intra-domain routing protocols, inter-domain routing protocols, and reliability and security protocols. Because of these changes, the MBONE, and multicast in general, is a constantly changing and growing network.

Some of the applications that benefit from IPMC are streaming audio and video, distance learning programs, corporate communication software, video and audio conferencing systems, computer gaming software, and data warehousing applications. Let's look at a quick example of a multicast application. More and more computer games are being developed for multiplayer Internet-based game play. The problem that developers have when creating games like this is the limited amount of bandwidth people have available at their home. Because of this limitation, most games only allow four or eight simultaneous players in the same game. Let's assume that the bandwidth the update uses is 5 Kbps. If we have a four-player game and one player makes a single move, three copies of that 5 Kbps stream must be sent out. Now let's assume that this is a constantly updating game. In that same four-player game, each computer will be sending three 5 Kbps streams (a 15 Kbps stream) and receiving three 5 Kbps streams (a 15 Kbps stream). On a 28.8 Kbps modem (which can only send or receive data, not both), you will need 30 Kbps of bandwidth just to play. Let's expand our game to 1000 players. Each computer will now need 5 Mbps outgoing and 5 Mbps incoming to run correctly. Now, if we take that same game and run it over IPMC, you will only need one 5 Kbps outgoing and one 5 Kbps incoming stream for a total of 10 Kbps. Imagine playing a game of Quake with 1000 players! There are two different ways to overcome this problem. A game server can be used that acts as a central location for sending and receiving each update. This game server would require a very high-speed Internet connection and very high computing capacity to serve a few thousand players. The other solution would be to enable IP Multicast for each player. With this solution, no game server would be needed. Once each player (as well as the network that connected them together) runs multicast, everyone would subscribe to the same IPMC group. The group is an IP address that identifies what stream of multicast traffic to listen to. It also allows the network (routers and switches) to build proper routing paths for the data. When each player makes a move, his or her information is sent to the multicast group and distributed to everyone else. Since everyone subscribes to the same group, only one copy of each packet would be sent from each computer and replicated only where a network path split.

Now that you have a basic understanding of IP Multicast, refer to the following Scenario & Solution.

SCENARIO & SOLUTION

Isn't multicast the same as broadcast traffic?	No. Broadcast traffic is traffic that touches every device on a segment or network, regardless of whether they want to receive the traffic. Multicast traffic only reaches the network devices that want it.
If I want to send out a video broadcast over my network, wouldn't sending it to a broadcast address be easier than multicasting it out?	Yes, it would be easier, but not more efficient or more scaleable. With a broadcast video, every device on the network—routers, printers, servers, workstations—would have to process the entire video. Usually, when you want to send out a video, only the workstations need to see it.

Throughout this chapter, we will discuss how IPMC works in greater detail and the different protocols that comprise it. This chapter covers the most popular protocols in use today (at the time of writing this chapter). By the end of the chapter, you should be able to:

- Identify the difference between multicast, broadcast, and unicast traffic
- Convert a multicast IP address to a MAC address
- Explain what the different multicast protocols are and what they do
- Describe the different multicast modes
- Configure and troubleshoot IP Multicast

CERTIFICATION OBJECTIVE 8.01

Understanding the Differences Between Multicast, Broadcast, and Unicast Addresses

In order to understand the differences between multicast, broadcast, and unicast addresses, you must first understand each type of traffic. Before we discuss unicast, broadcast, and multicast, let's talk about the basic IP address. An IP address is a 32-bit number commonly represented in decimal form separated into octets (groups of 8 bits); for example, 172.16.10.102. Once you have the IP address, you can convert it to a binary number, and based on the binary number, you can identify to which class the address belongs. The following exercise covers in detail how to convert an IP address to binary. Once you understand that, you can build on that knowledge to quickly identify the network and broadcast address of a given IP address. It is also useful in determining the MAC address for multicast traffic. Both of these are illustrated in later examples.

EXERCISE 8-1

Converting an IP Address to Binary

1. Let's convert 172.16.10.102 to binary:

   First, take the 172. Find the largest power of 2 that it is larger than. The powers of 2 are listed in the following chart:

Powers of 2	1	2	4	8	16	32	64	128

   172 is larger than 128. Next, you subtract 128 from 172. 172 − 128 = 44. 44 is larger than 32. 44 − 32 = 12. 12 is larger than 8. 12 − 8 = 4. 4 is equal to 4.

   Now, based on the bit value for each subtracted number, set that place to 1. All other places will be set to 0. The following chart shows the bit values above their places in the binary number.

Bit Value	128	64	32	16	8	4	2	1
Binary Place	X	X	X	X	X	X	X	X

2. Next, we put a 1 in the 128, 32, 8, and 4 bits (all of the numbers that were subtracted from 172).

Bit Value	128	64	32	16	8	4	2	1
Binary Place	1	0	1	0	1	1	0	0

   That gives us the binary representation of 172.

3. Continue that for the next three octets.

16 = 16

Bit Value	128	64	32	16	8	4	2	1
Binary Place	0	0	0	1	0	0	0	0

10 is greater than 8. 10 – 8 = 2. 2 = 2.

Bit Value	128	64	32	16	8	4	2	1
Binary Place	0	0	0	0	1	0	1	0

102 is greater than 64. 102 – 64 = 38. 38 is greater than 32. 38 – 32 = 6. 6 is greater than 4. 6 – 4 = 2. 2 = 2.

Bit Value	128	64	32	16	8	4	2	1
Binary Place	0	1	1	0	0	1	1	0

Now, put all four of the binary octets together and you get the complete binary representation for 172.16.10.102: 10101100.00010000.00001010.01100110.

The first 4 bits in the IP address determine what class it is. If the first bit is 0, it is a Class A address. If the first 2 bits are 10, it is a Class B address (notice that in our example number the first 2 bits are 10, so 172.16.10.102 would be a Class B address). If the first 3 bits are 110, it is a Class C address. If the first four bits are 1110, it is a Class D address (multicast). Finally, if the first 4 bits are 1111, it is a Class E address.

Unicast traffic is communication between two devices on a network. All unicast traffic is addressed in the first three classes of addresses. Typical unicast traffic includes Web browsing, e-mail, file transfers, remote control, diagnostic tools (ping, traceroute, and Telnet), and many other applications. One device, typically a PC, will initiate a session such as a file transfer to another device. The traffic passing between the two devices is known as unicast, since it only goes from one device to another. A unicast IP address is in the range of 0.0.0.0 up to 223.255.255.255, with a few addresses and ranges excluded from use (including the beginning and end values of 0.0.0.0 and 223.255.255.255, and all network and broadcast addresses throughout the range). Unicast addresses are either Class A, Class B, or Class C addresses. A unicast IP address also contains a subnet mask in the packet header. The subnet mask is a number that identifies the size of the network. For more information on IP addressing and subnetting, you should refer to a book dedicated to IP addressing and subnetting. Along with the unicast address is the network address. The network address identifies the beginning of a network. That IP address is not a useable address for unicast traffic. An example of a network address is 172.16.1.0 with a subnet mask of 255.255.255.0.

Broadcast traffic is sent from one device destined for all other devices. There are several different types of broadcasts: directed broadcast, network broadcast, and all broadcast. The network broadcast is a message sent by a device destined for all other devices on that same broadcast medium—typically, an Ethernet segment. A directed broadcast is a broadcast that is destined for all devices in that same network. An all-broadcast message is a message destined for every device in the world. An example of a directed broadcast IP address would be 172.16.255.255, and an all-broadcast message would be 255.255.255.255.

Multicast IP addresses are Class D addresses. The valid range of multicast IP addresses is from 224.0.0.0 to 239.255.255.255. A multicast IP address will not have a subnet mask associated with it. An IP Multicast address is essentially the group or destination address for the multicast traffic. An IP Multicast address does not contain the IP address of the source of the multicast traffic.

The following exercise demonstrates how to determine the broadcast address for a given IP address with subnet mask.

EXERCISE 8-2

Calculating the Broadcast Address of a Given Network

You have been given an IP address of 192.168.142.101 with a subnet mask of 255.255.255.192. What is the network broadcast IP address for your computer?

The first step in calculating the broadcast address is to identify the network address and the subnet mask. The network address can be determined by converting the IP address and the subnet mask into binary.

192.168.142.101	11000000	10101000	10001110	01100101
255.255.255.192	11111111	11111111	11111111	11000000

1. Once you have calculated the binary values, you draw a vertical line between the 1s and 0s on both the IP address and subnet mask.

192.168.142.101	11000000	10101000	10001110	01	100101
255.255.255.192	11111111	11111111	11111111	11	000000

2. After the vertical line has been drawn, rewrite the first half of the IP address two times, once filling in the area after the line with all 0s (the network address) and the other time filling in the area after the line with all 1s (the broadcast address).

192.168.142.101	11000000	10101000	10001110	01	100101
255.255.255.192	11111111	11111111	11111111	11	000000
Network	11000000	10101000	10001110	01	000000
Broadcast	11000000	10101000	10001110	01	111111

3. Now, recalculate the IP addresses from the binary values.

Network =	192.168.142.64
Broadcast =	192.168.142.127

4. You now have both the network address and the broadcast address for the IP address 192.168.142.101 with the subnet mask of 255.255.255.192.

CERTIFICATION OBJECTIVE 8.02

Translating Multicast to Ethernet Addresses

Whenever two devices on an Ethernet network wish to talk to each other, they must first know each other's MAC address. The MAC address is usually associated with the physical adapter, or network interface card (NIC) for those devices. A MAC address is a 48-bit number usually represented in hexadecimal form; for example, 00-e0-b0-55-3a-2c. Each manufacturer gets a reserved portion of a MAC address and then gives each device its own unique number. IP addresses give humans an easy way to identify where a computer is (and DNS makes it even easier—now you only have to know the computer's name and domain name). As traffic flows throughout a network, it operates at Layer 2. IP addresses exist at Layer 3. Since the traffic runs at Layer 2, the computers have to translate all IP addresses to their equivalent Ethernet MAC addresses when on an Ethernet LAN. If multicast traffic is flowing over other Layer 2 topologies, there are other methods for translating the IP address to a Layer 2 identifier. The translation methodology for other Layer 2 topologies such as Frame Relay, Token Ring, ISDN, or Point-to-Point Serial lines are not covered in this book. When dealing with unicast traffic, both endpoints are known and both have a NIC, which in turn provides the MAC address.

Multicast, on the other hand, works differently. The endpoint (or receiver) in multicast traffic has an adapter and MAC address, but the multicast group as a whole does not physically belong to a single device. Since no single device owns the multicast group, there is no MAC associated with the group. Also, multicast does not use the Address Resolution Protocol (ARP), which prohibits devices from determining the associated MAC address with an IP Multicast address. This was an initial problem when developing IP multicast, and a solution had to be found. The solution was to reserve a fixed portion of a MAC address and use part of the multicast IP group address to determine the full MAC address. Steve Deering and Jon Postel purchased a reserved piece of a MAC address from the IEEE Organizational Unique Identifiers (OUI) organization for use with IP Multicast. The reserved OUI is 01-00-5E. That reserved piece only identifies half of the MAC address. The other half will be dynamically determined by all network devices based on the IP Multicast group address. Now, let's examine the details in converting an IP Multicast group address into its equivalent Ethernet MAC address.

Converting Multicast to Ethernet Addresses in Binary

Understanding how to convert an IP Multicast address to a multicast MAC address is important, because all Layer 2 devices talk at the MAC address level. When multicast traffic traverses a network, all switches that it passes only see the MAC address (no IP address). It is important to understand how the switches (and every other device) translate an IPMC group address into a multicast MAC address. As noted earlier, the first 24 bits of the multicast MAC address (represented in hexadecimal) are 01-00-5E. That covers 24 out of 48 bits. The next bit has been split between IPMC and future use for multicast, and is always set to 0. The last 23 bits of the MAC address map directly to the last 23 bits of the IP group address. That completes the 48 bits of the MAC address: 24 from the OUI, 1 set to 0, and the remaining 23 taken directly from the IPMC group address.

FROM THE CLASSROOM

Why Are There 32 Overlapping Addresses with IPMC?

Let's take a quick look at why there are 32 overlapping addresses. Remember earlier that when Steve was starting his work on IPMC, he realized that there needed to be a formal way to convert the Multicast IP group address into a MAC address. If there were 16 OUIs—one for each octet in the Class D address range (224, 225, …, 239)—then the translation would map perfectly between IP address and MAC address. Since Steve and Jon didn't have the budget for 16 OUIs (an OUI reservation costs $1000), they had to make do with what they had. Next, you ask, "how come there are 32 and not 16 overlapping addresses?" The answer to that question is that when Jon purchased the OUI 01-00-5E, he split it in half with Steve, allocating half of the MAC address bits for use with IPMC and keeping the other half for future research.

—*Andy McCullough, CCNA, CCDA*

Now let's look at the IPMC group address (the IP address for the multicast traffic). The last 23 bits have been used (translated directly to the MAC address) out of the 32-bit IP address, but the first 9 are ignored. Luckily, the first 4 bits in the IP address are always set to 1110 (designating a Class D address). That leaves us 5 bits in the IP address that can change, giving us 2^5, or 32 IP addresses mapping to the same MAC address.

Exercise 8-3 shows you how to convert an IP Multicast group address into its Ethernet MAC address.

EXERCISE 8-3

Converting an IPMC Address to Its MAC Address Equivalent

In this exercise, we will obtain the MAC address from the Class D Multicast IP address 228.10.128.240, and we will calculate the other 31 addresses that map to the same MAC address.

1. The first thing you need to do is to write the IP address out in binary.

```
228.10.128.240 = 11100100.00001010.10000000.11110000
```

2. Next, you drop the first 9 bits and convert the rest to hex.

```
xxxx xxxx . x000 1010 . 1000 0000 . 1111 0000
            0   A       8    0       F    0
```

3. Next, you prepend the OUI number.

```
01 – 00 – 5E + 0A – 80 – F0 = 01 – 00 – 5E – 0A – 80 – F0
```

That gives you the MAC address. Now we have to determine the overlapping IP addresses. Take the fifth through ninth bits of the IP address and cycle through all combinations. Refer to Figure 8-1.

4. That will give you the full list of 32 IP addresses that all map to the same Ethernet MAC address (Table 8-1).

FIGURE 8-1

Cycling chart of IP addresses

```
11100000.00001010.10000000.11110000 = 224.10.128.240
11100000.10001010.10000000.11110000 = 224.138.128.240
11100001.00001010.10000000.11110000 = 225.10.128.240
11100001.10001010.10000000.11110000 = 225.138.128.240
11100010.00001010.10000000.11110000 = 226.10.128.240
11100010.10001010.10000000.11110000 = 226.138.128.240
11100011.00001010.10000000.11110000 = 227.10.128.240
11100011.10001010.10000000.11110000 = 227.138.128.240
11100100.00001010.10000000.11110000 = 228.10.128.240
11100100.10001010.10000000.11110000 = 228.138.128.240
11100101.00001010.10000000.11110000 = 229.10.128.240
11100101.10001010.10000000.11110000 = 229.138.128.240
11100110.00001010.10000000.11110000 = 230.10.128.240
11100110.10001010.10000000.11110000 = 230.138.128.240
11100111.00001010.10000000.11110000 = 231.10.128.240
11100111.10001010.10000000.11110000 = 231.138.128.240
11101000.00001010.10000000.11110000 = 232.10.128.240
11101000.10001010.10000000.11110000 = 232.138.128.240
11101001.00001010.10000000.11110000 = 233.10.128.240
11101001.10001010.10000000.11110000 = 233.138.128.240
11101010.00001010.10000000.11110000 = 234.10.128.240
11101010.10001010.10000000.11110000 = 234.138.128.240
11101011.00001010.10000000.11110000 = 235.10.128.240
11101011.10001010.10000000.11110000 = 235.138.128.240
11101100.00001010.10000000.11110000 = 236.10.128.240
11101100.10001010.10000000.11110000 = 236.138.128.240
11101101.00001010.10000000.11110000 = 237.10.128.240
11101101.10001010.10000000.11110000 = 237.138.128.240
11101110.00001010.10000000.11110000 = 238.10.128.240
11101110.10001010.10000000.11110000 = 238.138.128.240
11101111.00001010.10000000.11110000 = 239.10.128.240
11101111.10001010.10000000.11110000 = 239.138.128.240
```

TABLE 8-1 Full List of IP Addresses for Exercise 8-3

224.10.128.240	225.10.128.240	226.10.128.240	227.10.128.240
228.10.128.240	229.10.128.240	230.10.128.240	231.10.128.240
232.10.128.240	233.10.128.240	234.10.128.240	235.10.128.240
236.10.128.240	237.10.128.240	238.10.128.240	239.10.128.240
224.138.128.240	225.138.128.240	226.138.128.240	227.138.128.240
228.138.128.240	229.138.128.240	230.138.128.240	231.138.128.240
232.138.128.240	233.138.128.240	234.138.128.240	235.138.128.240
236.138.128.240	237.138.128.240	238.138.128.240	239.138.128.240

CERTIFICATION OBJECTIVE 8.03

Understanding Multicast Protocols

IP Multicast consists of a suite of protocols that operate together, allowing multicast traffic to flow correctly. Some of the protocols are required, and others are optional. The multicast suite of protocols operates at all layers of the OSI model. Within the first three layers of the OSI model (Physical, Data Link, and Network), the protocols can be split into four categories:

- Client-to-router
- Switching
- Intra-domain routing
- Inter-domain routing

There is a multitude of protocols at Layers 4 through 7 that are outside the scope of this book.

Client-Router Protocols

There is one required protocol, the Internet Group Management Protocol (IGMP), that runs on both the router and client in order for IPMC to operate. IGMP allows for communication between the router and client, basically allowing a client to inform its router what IPMC group(s) it wishes to join. It also allows a router to query clients for group membership information. There are several different versions of IGMP. IGMP version 0 is the original version that was used at the Stanford University Lab when IPMC was developed. IGMPv0 is not in operation and was never deployed outside of Stanford. Since its inception, IGMP has been improved several times, and new versions have been developed. Currently, IGMP version 2 is the most widely used version of IGMP in operation today. IGMP version 3 is currently under development and will eventually replace version 2 as the most widely deployed version of IGMP. This section discusses IGMP versions 1, 2, and 3.

IGMP Version 1

IGMPv1 is defined in RFC 1112. The IGMPv1 packet is shown in Figure 8-2.

The IGMPv1 packet is 64 bits. The first four bits (0–3) are for the version. In IGMPv1, there is only one choice for version: version 1. Next, the type field is also 4 bits and can be either a membership report or a membership query. Membership reports and queries are explained in the next section. The unused field is set to 0. The checksum field is a number that is used for verification that the packet is complete (a 16-bit 1's complement of 1's complement of the sum of the IGMP message). It is used to verify whether the packet is valid. Finally, the group address is a 32-bit field and can be either a membership report, which is the IP address of the multicast group the client wishes to join, or set to 0 for a membership query (sent by the router).

IGMPv1 is composed of two main components, membership reports and membership queries. The next sections cover these in detail.

Membership Reports The client sends a membership report directly to the router. The report can be sent in response to a membership query or be sent manually. The membership report is a message that contains the IP Multicast group information that tells the router what multicast traffic it wishes to receive. It is sent with a Time To Live (TTL) value of 1, which prevents the packet from leaving its local subnet. If the packet were to leave the subnet, a different router (nonconnected router) could see the message and think that the message was intended for it, causing multicast traffic to be sent to subnets and/or networks that did not need it. One more function of the membership report is the report suppression mechanism. Report suppression is a function that allows only one client on a subnet to respond to a membership query. Report suppression is explained in further detail in the *Joining a Group* example with Figure 8-3.

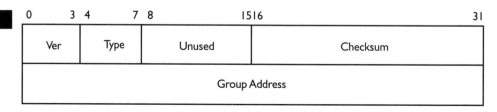

FIGURE 8-2 IGMPv1 packet format

Membership Queries Membership queries are sent by the router to establish what multicast groups have active listeners. The membership query is sent to the reserved IPMC address 224.0.0.1 (all hosts IP address). By default, the query is sent every 60 seconds. If no membership report is received within three queries, all IPMC traffic is cut off from the router interface that sends the query. An IGMP membership query is sent by the router to verify that there are still interested listeners on that interface. Without IGMP membership queries, the router would never know when to stop sending multicast traffic.

IGMPv1 Operation The following examples show how IGMPv1 operates. In these examples, there is a router and four hosts all running IGMP version 1. The examples show how a host joins a new multicast group, how a multicast group is maintained, and how a group is expired.

- **Joining a group** With IGMPv1, when a host wants to join a IPMC group, it simply sends an IGMP membership report for the group it wishes to join.

In Figure 8-3, Host1 sends an IGMP membership report to the IPMC address of the group that it wishes to join (226.10.10.1). The router sees the message and adds the Ethernet interface to receive multicast traffic destined for the multicast group 226.10.10.1. If Host1 through Host4 send any additional IGMP membership

FIGURE 8-3

IGMPv1 joining a group

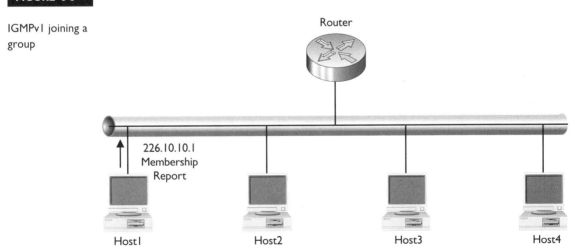

reports for the same IPMC group, the router simply resets its report timer for that group. If a membership report for a different IPMC group is sent, the router will add the Ethernet interface for the new group as well.

- **Maintaining a group** Once multicast traffic is flowing to an interface, the router will periodically (every 60 seconds) send a membership query to all hosts on that interface asking if anyone still wants the traffic. If a membership report is received, the router continues to send traffic. However, if after three queries no report is received, the router will turn off IPMC traffic to that interface. One of the features of IGMPv1 is report suppression. The way report suppression works is that when a membership query is received, all hosts that receive it start a countdown report timer. The value of the report timer is a randomly chosen value between 0 and 10 seconds. As soon as the first host reaches 0, it sends a membership report. If a host is counting down and sees a membership report for the same group, it simply disregards the query.

Figure 8-4 demonstrates report suppression. In this example, Host4 is the first to reach 0 and sends a membership report back to the router. All other hosts exercise report suppression and do nothing, and all multicast traffic continues.

- **Leaving a group** When a host is finished receiving the multicast traffic, it simply stops listening to that IPMC group address. There is no notification that it is finished. The only way a router knows if anyone is still interested in receiving the traffic is by its periodic membership queries. Once all hosts have silently left all multicast groups, the router will send three membership queries, each separated by 60 seconds. After the third query is sent with no

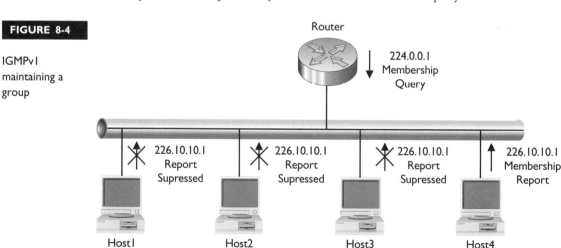

FIGURE 8-4

IGMPv1 maintaining a group

response back, the router will timeout that interface and stop sending multicast traffic to it. With IGMPv1, it can take between two and three minutes for multicast traffic to stop flowing once the last member has left (depending on how soon after a query the last host leaves). On Cisco routers, IGMPv2 has been available since IOS version 10.3. Prior to version 10.3, IGMPv1 was enabled by default. There are no commands required to configure IGMPv1. Additionally, most PCs (with a TCP/IP stack) support IGMPv2 today, and do not have to be configured to function.

IGMP Version 2

IGMPv2 is defined in RFC 2236, and is backward compatible with IGMPv1. Cisco IOS 10.3 and higher run IGMPv2, and IOS 11.1 and higher are set to version 2 by default. In versions 10.3 to 11.0, the router tries to automatically determine the correct version to run. The IGMPv2 packet is shown in Figure 8-5. By examining the packet format for both versions, you can see that no major changes were made, which is what allows version 2 to be backward compatible.

The IGMPv2 packet is also 64 bits long. The first two fields from version 1 have been combined to form the type field. The type field is now an 8-bit field and can be one of four types:

- Membership query, both general and group specific
- Version 1 membership report
- Version 2 membership report
- Leave group

The maximum response time field has replaced the unused field. By default in version 2, the maximum response time is a value in 1/10 of a second and is set to 100 (10 seconds). In IGMPv1, this field was permanently set to 10 seconds. The checksum field is still a 16-bit 1's complement of the sum of the IGMP message, and is used to verify whether the packet is valid. The Group address is still a 32-bit

FIGURE 8-5

IGMPv2 packet format

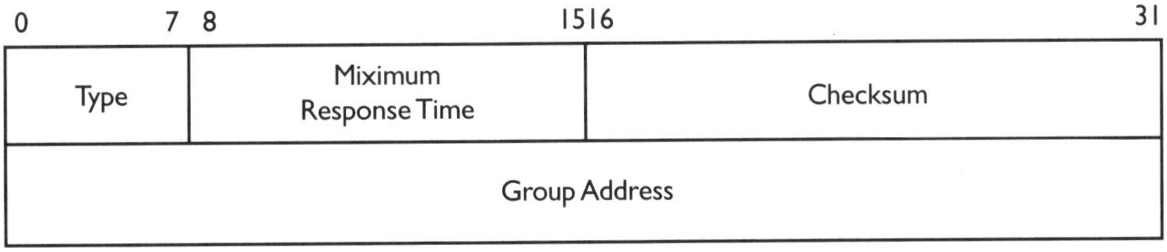

0	7	8	15	16	31
Type		Miximum Response Time		Checksum	
Group Address					

field, and can be 0 for a general membership query, or the IP address of the group in a group specific query, membership report, or leave group message.

In addition to the membership report and membership query, IGMPv2 has added a few functions, which are discussed in the following sections.

Querier Election   The querier election mechanism was added to IGMPv2 to provide a method of ensuring that one router will be elected as Designated Querier (DQ) for that segment. In an Ethernet network where there are two routers, both serving as the default gateway, the querier election process will occur, preventing both routers from sending membership queries. The querier election process is as follows:

1. As soon as the router begins IGMPv2, it sends a querier election message to the all-router reserved IP address of 224.0.0.2.
2. All other routers on that same broadcast network also send a querier election message.
3. All routers send the querier election message containing their IP address and the designation that they are the querier.
4. The router with the lowest IP address for that segment will keep the designation of querier, and all other routers will become backup queriers.

The querier will be responsible for sending and processing all IGMP membership reports and queries for that segment. If the querier shuts down, the backup querier will resume the role of DQ. During normal operation, the backup querier will still receive all IGMP membership reports from all clients on that segment, and will keep track of what groups are active.

Group Specific Query   In IGMPv2, a group specific query was added. The group specific query allows a router to specifically query an individual group to determine if there are any interested hosts that want to continue to receive that traffic. With IGMPv1, once there are multiple multicast groups active on an interface, all groups must remain active until all hosts for all groups have silently left. IGMPv2 now allows a router to timeout specific groups as soon as there are no listeners.

Leave Group Message   The leave group message is a function added to IGMPv2 that allows a host to notify its router that it wishes to leave a group. With this mechanism, routers now have the ability to timeout an interface much quicker than in version 1. As soon as a router receives a leave group message, it sends back a membership query for that same group. If there is no report sent back within three queries, the router can stop sending traffic for that group. With tuning of the query interval response timer, a router can now shut down a multicast group in as short as 0.3 seconds. A leave group message will be sent whenever a client closes down the multicast application, such as closing down Windows Media Player after listening to a multicast broadcast.

Query Interval Response Time   The query interval response timer allows a router to request a response to a membership query within a given time period. By default, this is set to 10 seconds. When a client first establishes communication with its router, it will determine what the query interval response time should be set to, and will use this value as its maximum value for the randomly generated number for report suppression.

IGMPv2 Operation   The following examples illustrate how IGMPv2 operates.

- **Joining a group**   Joining a group in IGMPv2 is exactly the same as in IGMPv1; when a host wants to join a IPMC group, it simply sends an IGMP membership report for the group it wishes to join.

In Figure 8-6, Host2 sends an IGMP membership report to the IPMC address of the group that it wishes to join (239.0.1.100). The router then sees the message and adds the Ethernet interface to receive multicast traffic destined for the multicast

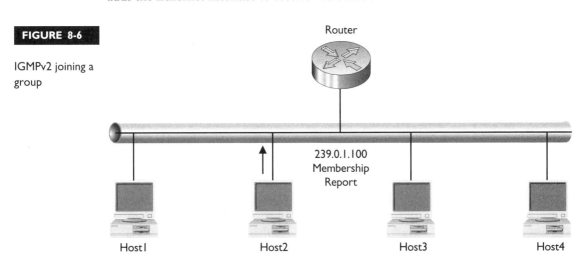

FIGURE 8-6

IGMPv2 joining a group

group 239.0.1.100. If Host1 through Host4 send any additional IGMP membership reports for the same IPMC group, the router simply resets its report timer for that group. If a membership report for a different IPMC group is sent, the router will add the Ethernet interface for the new group as well.

- **Maintaining a group** IGMPv2 is very similar to version 1 in the way multicast groups are maintained. The only difference between the two is that in version 2, the router will query each group that has members instead of querying every host. This allows the router to identify if there are any hosts for a particular group. The router will still periodically send a membership query to each group. The default query interval is 60 seconds. If no membership report is received in the query interval response time, the router will query two more times and then timeout that specific group.

on the job *Remember that with IGMPv2, the host can inform the router immediately of its departure to a specific group.*

IGMPv2 still uses the report suppression mechanism found in version 1; only now, the suppression timer can be changed from a default of 10 seconds to a value between 1/10 and 100 seconds.

- **Querier election** As soon as a router initializes any broadcast interface with IGMPv2, it sends out a querier election message to the all-router IP address of 224.0.0.2. This message is used to determine what router will become the designated querier. If no other messages are heard, the router will assume that role. Figure 8-6 illustrates the querier election process.

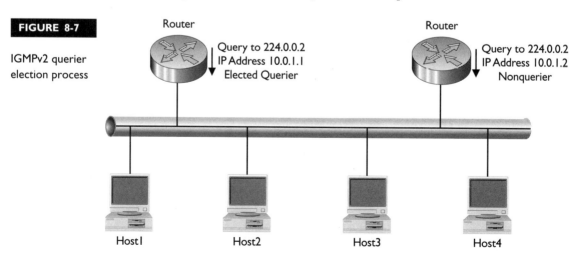

FIGURE 8-7

IGMPv2 querier election process

In Figure 8-7, Router1 has its Ethernet interface IP address set to 10.0.1.1, and Router2 has its Ethernet interface IP address set to 10.0.1.2. Both routers send out a querier election message to their Ethernet interface with their IP address. Router1 will do nothing since it does not see any IP addresses lower than its own. Router2 will become the nonquerier and silently listen to all future membership reports and queries. Both routers will periodically resend the querier election message to verify that the querier is still active.

- **Leaving a group** In IGMPv1, when a host finished receiving the multicast traffic, it simply stopped listening to that IPMC group address and silently left the group. IGMPv2 now allows the host to notify its router when it is finished. When a host is finished receiSving a specific multicast group, it sends a leave group message to the all-router IP address of 224.0.0.2 with the IP address of the group it no longer wants to receive. As soon as the querier router receives this message, it sends back a membership query to that same interface for that same group to determine if there are any other interested hosts. If a membership report is sent back, the router continues to forward on that group. If no membership report is received within three queries, the router will stop sending that multicast group out that interface.

on the job

It is important to understand what happens when IGMPv1 and IGMPv2 try to interoperate with each other. If there is an IGMPv1 host on a segment, the router will need to downgrade itself and only respond to version 1 features. If there is an IGMPv2 host and a IGMPv1 router, the router will not understand IGMPv2 membership reports. Also, all routers on a segment must be running the same version of IGMP. If there is a version 1 host and version 2 router, the router will automatically downgrade itself to version 1. Similarly, if there is a version 2 host and a version 1 router, the host will automatically downgrade itself to version 1. When there are two routers on the same segment, one running version 1, and the other running version 2, both running Cisco IOS 10.3 or higher, they will not automatically convert—that must be done manually. To change the IGMP version on a router, enter the interface configuration mode (for the Ethernet interface that needs to be changed) and type the command ip igmp version x, *where x is either 1 or 2.*

Configuring IGMP

IGMPv2 is on by default on all Cisco routers running IOS 10.3 and older. However, there are commands available to fine-tune IGMPv2. All IGMP commands are at the interface configuration level within Cisco IOS. Table 8-2 lists all configuration options for the command **ip igmp**.

ip igmp access-group <access-list> configures an IP access-list on the interface, which only allows multicast groups into that interface that pass the access-list.

ip igmp helper-address [address] configures an IGMP helper address, which causes all IGMP membership reports and leave group messages to be forwarded to the address configured.

ip igmp join-group [address] configures the router to join the multicast group specified.

ip igmp last-member-query-interval [time] configures how fast the query will be sent out an interface once a leave group message is received. The time is a value in milliseconds between 100 and 65535. By configuring this command, you can adjust the router to timeout a group quicker than the default 3 seconds.

ip igmp querier-timeout [time] configures the amount of time between a timeout of the elected querier on a segment where there are two or more routers. The time is a value in seconds between 60 and 300. The default value is 60 seconds.

ip igmp query-interval [time] configures the frequency at which IGMP membership queries are sent by the router. The time is a value in seconds between 1 and 65535. The default of this command is 60 seconds.

TABLE 8-2 ip igmp Command Options		
	access-group	IGMP group access group
	helper-address	IGMP helper address
	join-group	IGMP join multicast group
	last-member-query-interval	IGMP last member query interval
	quericr-timcout	IGMP previous querier timeout
	query-interval	IGMP host query interval
	query-max-response-time	IGMP max query response value
	static-group	IGMP static multicast group
	version	IGMP version

ip igmp query-max-response-time [time] configures the amount of time a host has to return a membership report in response to a membership query. The time is a value in seconds between 1 and 25, with the default being 10 seconds.

ip igmp static-group [address] configures a static connected member for the group specified on the interface.

ip igmp version [number] configures the version of IGMP running on that interface. The possible values are 1 or 2, with the default being version 2.

IGMP Version 3

At the time of writing this chapter, IGMPv3 was still under development and at the draft stage in the RFC process. IGMPv3 is expected to be backward compatible with both versions 1 and 2, and is expected to add support for source filtering multicast packets. What this will allow is that a host will now have the ability to request multicast traffic not only from a specific IPMC address, but also from a specific source. It will also allow a host to request multicast traffic from all but a specific source. This new feature will allow multicast to overcome one of its inherent problems of security. Today, it is possible for an untrusted source to begin sending out multicast traffic, and there are few mechanisms in place to prevent that traffic from flowing through the network and reaching the end user. IGMPv3 is expected to overcome that.

Now that you have an understanding of IGMP, here are some general scenario questions and their answers:

SCENARIO & SOLUTION

Do I have to run IGMP for multicast to operate correctly?	Yes. IGMP is used to inform routers what multicast groups are being requested. As soon as the router receives a new request, it can attempt to route the new multicast traffic to the client.
How do I find out what version of IGMP my desktops are using?	The best way to find out what version of IGMP your desktop is using is by visiting the Web site for the manufacturer of the operating system. Windows 98, NT 4.0 (SP4), and 2000 all run IGMPv2.

Multicast Switching Protocols

This section covers the two common protocols that operate on a Cisco switch at the time of writing this chapter. There are additional switching protocols under development that are outside the scope of this book.

Specific protocols were developed for switches in a multicast network to overcome the problem that by default, when a switch sees a multicast packet, it marks it as unknown and broadcasts it out all ports (except the port that the packet came in from). What this means it that if there is a 1M video stream being multicast to two hosts attached to a switch with 200 users on it, all 200 users will get the 1M video stream. Even if the users don't want the traffic, they will still have to process the traffic, which uses up resources and available bandwidth. Now imagine 20 different 1M video streams and 100 different 200K audio streams. Without a multicast switching protocol enabled on the switch, once all different streams have been subscribed (even if only one user subscribes to a different stream), every user attached to that switch would be getting 40M of traffic.

By turning on one of these switching protocols, the switch can now understand where the previously "unknown" multicast should go and forward it out the correct ports. The following sections discuss the two switching protocols in use today.

IGMP Snooping

Internet Group Membership Protocol Snooping (IGMP Snooping) is a protocol that operates on switches that allows them to dynamically learn about multicast traffic. IGMP Snooping, an industry standard, does what its name implies: it snoops all traffic listening for IGMP packets. Once it sees an IGMP packet, it dynamically learns what MAC address the traffic is destined for, and what MAC address the traffic comes from. Once the switch knows the MAC addresses, it can look up in its CAM table what port to send the traffic to.

exam
⚠atch

Be careful with IGMP Snooping. If the switch does not have Layer 3 capabilities, it will have to process ALL traffic entering it. This can severely overload the switch. To prevent this from happening, only Cisco switches with Layer 3 capabilities are capable of running IGMP Snooping.

When IGMP Snooping is turned on in the switch, it listens for all packets with a MAC address header of 01-00-5E and a Layer 3 header of IGMP. When a packet entering the switch meets both of those requirements, the switch will check to see if there is an entry in its CAM table for that MAC address (the translated MAC address from the multicast group address). If there is no entry for that MAC address, the switch will pass that packet over to the CPU for processing. The CPU will identify what MAC address sent the packet and what MAC address the packet is destined for. Once that is done, the switch will create a new entry in its CAM table for the MAC address of the multicast group and add the ports where the packet came in and was destined for. As additional IGMP membership reports come into the switch, it will dynamically continue adding to that CAM entry. If the switch intercepts a leave group message, it will dynamically remove that port from the CAM entry for that specific multicast group. Once the CAM table has been built for a specific multicast group, all other multicast traffic (other than IGMP messages) can bypass the CPU for processing and be switched by the switching engine. Figure 8-8 illustrates how IGMP Snooping operates.

FIGURE 8-8 IGMP Snooping operation—no multicast traffic

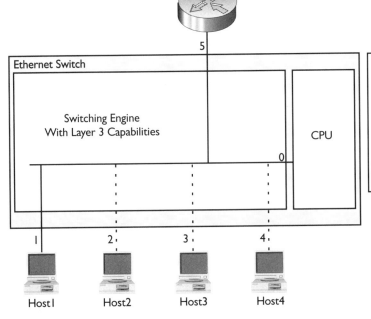

Figure 8-8 shows the architecture of a switch configured with IGMP Snooping before any IPMC traffic passes through the switch. Notice that there is an entry for the 0100.5EXX.XXXX MAC address and an associated Layer 3 header of IGMP already in the CAM table. This entry will allow the switch to intercept all traffic destined for the reserved multicast MAC address 01-00-5E-xx-xx-xx and examine the Layer 3 IP header to determine if it is an IGMP membership report, query, or leave group message. If the packet has the multicast MAC address, but is not an IGMP packet (!IGMP), the switch will pass that packet on to the proper ports.

In Figure 8-9, Host1 sends its IGMP membership report requesting to be added to the multicast group 239.0.1.2. Remember that all multicast groups are translated to their associated MAC address, which for 239.0.1.2 is 01-00-5E-00-01-02. Once

FIGURE 8-9 IGMP Snooping operation—first IGMP message

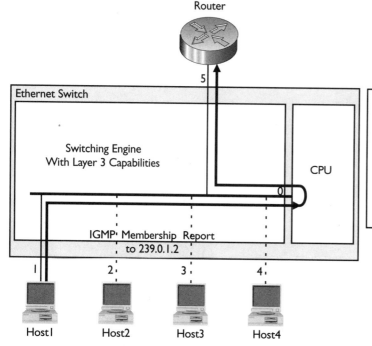

that first message is sent from Host1, the switch intercepts the packet (since the MAC address began with 01-00-5E and the IP packet header was set to IGMP) and creates a new entry in its CAM table for the specific MAC address. It then adds ports 1 and 5 to that CAM entry (the Source and Destination MAC address for that IGMP message). Now all additional non-IGMP packets destined for 239.0.1.2 will be sent only to ports 1 and 5.

As the second host joins (Figure 8-10), the switch will add that port to its CAM entry for the same multicast group and then forward that packet to ports 1 and 5. Once all of the hosts have joined the group, the switch will stop adding entries to its CAM table.

FIGURE 8-10 IGMP Snooping operation—second host joins

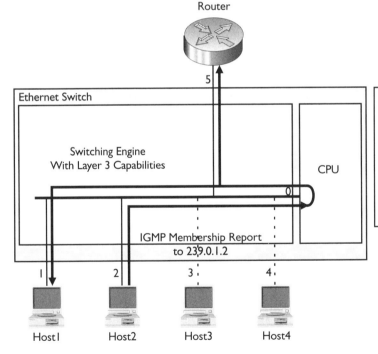

Once the multicast data begins to flow to 239.0.1.2 (Figure 8-11), the switch will forward that traffic on to only Host1 and Host2.

When a host sends a leave group message to the all-router IP address, the switch will process that message and forward it out to the correct ports. When the switch sees a leave group message, it will remove that port from its CAM table for that multicast MAC address.

In this example, if the switch were not Layer 3 capable, it would send every packet of the data stream to the CPU for processing. Imagine the impact on the switch if the data stream was a 2MB video stream!

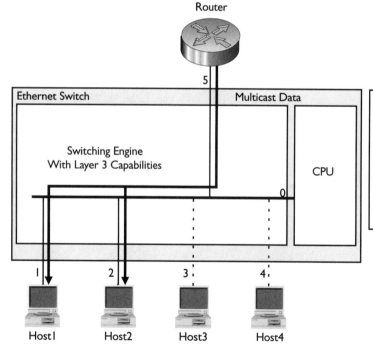

FIGURE 8-11 IGMP Snooping operation—multicast data flow

Configuring IGMP Snooping

IGMP Snooping is enabled by default on all Cisco switches that have Layer 3 capabilities. The command to turn on IGMP Snooping on a Catalyst switch is **set igmp enable**. There is nothing needed to configure IGMP Snooping on a router, and there are no fine-tuning or timer options for this command.

CGMP

Cisco Group Management Protocol (CGMP) is a Cisco proprietary protocol developed to overcome the Layer 3 requirements of IGMP Snooping. CGMP operates very differently from IGMP Snooping. CGMP runs on both the router and the switch, and requires that both the router and switch be Cisco and that they both support CGMP. CGMP runs only on Cisco routers and Cisco switches. It does not run on multicast sources or clients, and does not require any additional software on clients or servers.

> **exam Watch**
>
> *CGMP is not permitted on newer switch lines that are completely Layer 3 capable, such as the 6500 series switches. CGMP can be run on switches that can be Layer 2 only or Layer 2 and 3 (such as the 5500 and newer 4000 series). If the switch supports Layer 3 (5500 with a NetFlow Feature Card), it can run IGMP Snooping as well. Even though a Catalyst 5500 with Layer 3 support can run either CGMP or IGMP Snooping, it can't run both at the same time.*

The way CGMP operates is by the switch passing all multicast traffic to the router and allowing the router to determine what MAC addresses to add and remove from what multicast MAC entry. This is done over a well-known multicast MAC address that both the router and switch will listen for once CGMP is enabled. The MAC address 01-00-0C-DD-DD-DD has been reserved by Cisco and is specific to their hardware. Once a router sees an IGMP membership report or leave group message, it sends a CGMP packet to the switch at the MAC address 01-00-0C-DD-DD-DD with the following information:

- Type field (either Join or Leave)

Chapter 8: Switching and Routing IP Multicasting

- MAC address of the multicast client
- Multicast address of the group to be added or removed

Once the switch receives the CGMP packet from the router, it can dynamically maintain its CAM table for multicast traffic. The following series of figures explain the process visually.

In Figure 8-12, Host1 sends an IGMP membership report, and since the switch has no entry in its CAM table for that MAC address, it floods it out all ports.

Once the router receives the first IGMP membership report, it sends a CGMP join message back to the switch, telling it the MAC address of the client (USA) and

FIGURE 8-12 CGMP—first IGMP join

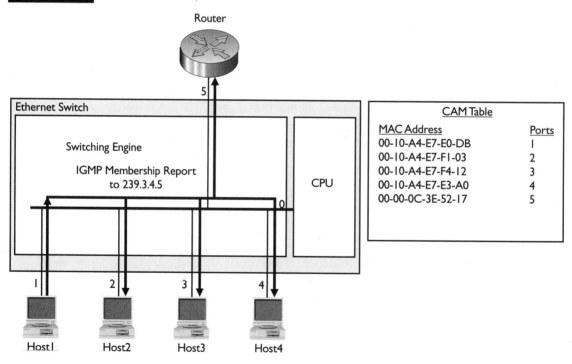

the MAC address of the multicast group (GDA). The switch now creates a new entry in its CAM table for the multicast group. The switch then looks up what port the MAC address for the client is in and adds that port along with the port for the router to the newly created CAM entry. In Figure 8-13, you can see that there is now a new entry in the CAM table for the multicast group 239.3.4.5. All traffic destined for that MAC address will now be sent to only those two ports.

When Host3 sends an IGMP membership report (Figure 8-14), the switch forwards it out to ports 1 and 5.

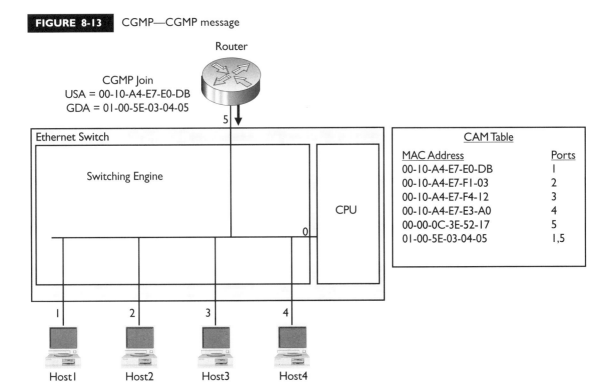

FIGURE 8-13 CGMP—CGMP message

424 Chapter 8: Switching and Routing IP Multicasting

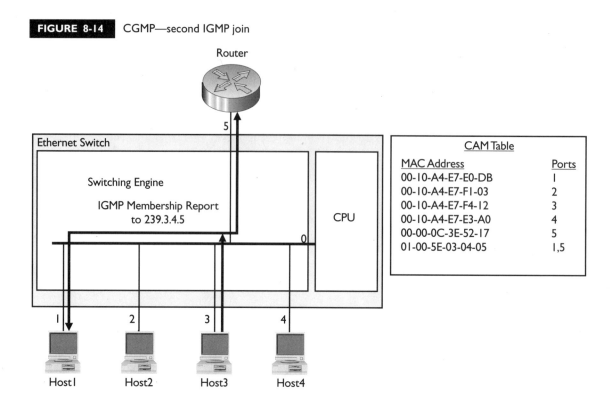

FIGURE 8-14   CGMP—second IGMP join

Once the router receives the IGMP membership report, it sends a CGMP join message back to the switch, this time with the MAC address of Host3.

exam 🐸 *atch*

Since the switch created the new entry in its CAM table based on information provided by an external source (the router), the CAM entry is entered as a static entry. With IGMP Snooping, the CAM entries are dynamically learned and entered as dynamic entries.

As soon as the switch receives the CGMP join message, it performs a lookup to find what port Host3 is on, and adds that port to the CAM table for the

01-00-5E-03-04-05 group (Figure 8-15). From now on, all traffic destined for the MAC address 01-00-5E-03-04-05 will be sent only to ports 1, 3, and 5.

Once the CAM table has been created, multicast traffic will be sent to the correct ports (Figure 8-16).

In Figure 8-17, Host1 sends an IGMP leave group message informing the router that it is finished receiving the multicast group.

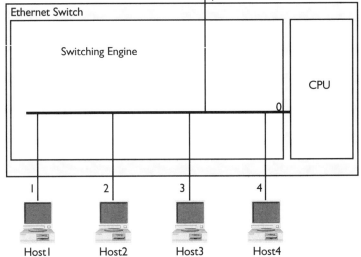

FIGURE 8-15   CGMP—CGMP message

426 Chapter 8: Switching and Routing IP Multicasting

FIGURE 8-16 CGMP—multicast data

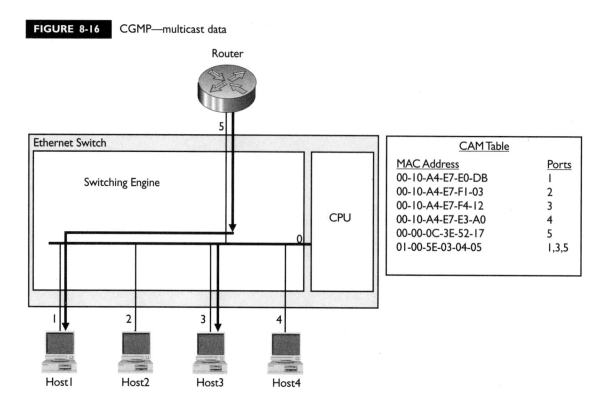

As soon as the router receives the IGMP leave group message, it sends a CGMP leave message back to the switch. The CGMP leave message tells the switch which MAC address to remove from what multicast MAC address (Figure 8-18).

Cisco's implementation of CGMP is a very good solution in the environment of smaller workgroup switches that don't have Layer 3 capabilities. It is important to remember that both the router and switch must be Cisco before CGMP will function properly.

Understanding Multicast Protocols **427**

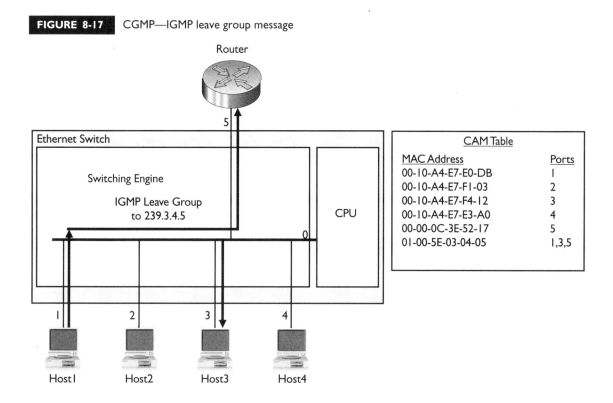

FIGURE 8-17 CGMP—IGMP leave group message

Configuring CGMP

The command to turn on CGMP on a Cisco Catalyst switch is **set cgmp enable**. From the interface configuration mode on the router directly connected to the switch, or a switch that runs IOS-based commands (e.g. 2900), the command to enable CGMP is **ip cgmp**. By default, all Cisco switches with Layer 2 capabilities only are configured for CGMP. Cisco routers are not configured for CGMP by default, and must be configured to support it. Like IGMP Snooping, there are no timer or optional parameters for this command.

FIGURE 8-18 CGMP—CGMP message

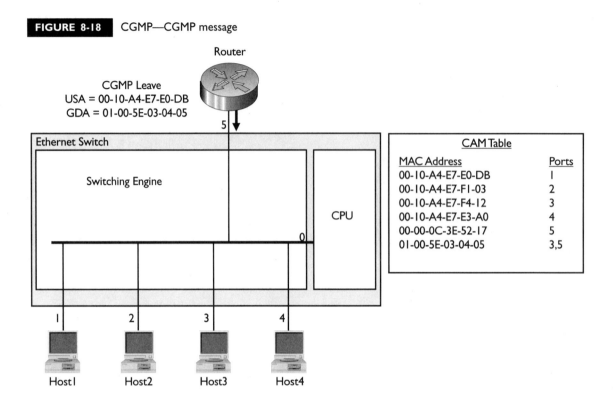

Multicast Routing Basics

Multicast routing works backward from unicast routing. In unicast routing, the packets are routed from the source to the destination. Each router along the way knows the destination and can determine the best route to take. In multicast routing, the source is not known and the destination is the origination point. This makes multicast routing much harder to accomplish. There are several different multicast routing protocols. They can be split into intra-domain and inter-domain protocols, whereas unicast routing protocols can be split into Interior Gateway Protocols (IGP) and Exterior Gateway Protocols (EGP). Unicast IGPs can be further split into Distance Vector (DV) and Link State (LS) routing protocols. Intra-domain multicast protocols can also be further split into Dense Mode (DM) and Sparse Mode (SM). Just as with Distance Vector and Link State, Dense Mode and Sparse Mode routing protocols have advantages and disadvantages over one another. The inter-domain multicast routing protocols, such as Border Gateway Multicast Protocol (BGMP), Multiprotocol Border Gateway Protocol (MBGP), and

Multicast Source Discovery Protocol (MSDP), are outside the scope of this book and will not be discussed. This section focuses on both Dense Mode and Sparse Mode intra-domain multicast routing protocols.

Since multicast routing operates backward from unicast routing, the router has to route from the receiver (destination) back to the source. In order for routers to accomplish this, there must be some kind of mechanism built into the routing protocol that will inform all other routers about all sources in the network at any given moment. There are two different approaches to informing all routers in the network about all active sources. The first approach is by flooding the information to all routers, which is the method Dense Mode routing protocols use. The second approach, which is used by Sparse Mode routing protocols, is by creating a centralized database, and every router queries the database for information about sources when needed. Both methods of informing routers about active multicast sources and groups will be explained in more detail in the Dense and Sparse Mode sections following.

Another job of a multicast routing protocol is to build and maintain distribution trees. A distribution tree is a set of routing information that tells the router what paths to use for specific multicast traffic. The distribution tree is built hop by hop, by determining the best next hop to the source for a specific multicast group. The distribution tree is maintained and verified through a process called Reverse Path Forwarding (RPF). RPF is an algorithm that is used to forward multicast datagrams. It is used to build the distribution tree in the following manner: a router will receive a multicast packet on an interface, and the router will then perform an RPF check to verify that the packet came in on the proper interface. If the packet came in on the proper interface, it is forwarded out all outbound interfaces for that multicast group. If the packet fails the RPF check, it is discarded. There are two different kinds of distribution trees: shortest path trees (also known as source trees) and shared trees. Sparse Mode routing protocols support both types of trees, whereas Dense Mode routing protocols only support source trees.

A source tree is denoted as (S,G), where the S is the unicast IP address of the source of the multicast traffic, and the G is the multicast IP address that the traffic is being sent to. A shared tree is denoted as (*,G), where the * denotes that there is no specific source, and the G is the multicast IP address that the traffic is being sent to. The reason that there is a * in a shared tree is that there can be multiple servers sending traffic to the same multicast group and they will all be part of the same tree. The * in this context refers to all sources. In certain networks, multiple sources can be configured to send the same multicast traffic, which increases the reliability of the traffic.

An example of this is a network that is broadcasting CNN. Two or three servers could be sending the same broadcast at the same time; some multicast clients will listen to the first server, and others will listen to the second server. The multicast routing protocol (e.g. OSPF, EIGRP, RIP) would determine what client listens to what source.

There will be one source tree built for each source in the network. Because each source gets its own tree, more memory will be used in the routers, but the routers will always have the best path back to each source (depending on both the multicast and unicast routing protocol), which will also in turn minimize network delay. Shared trees build one tree for each group instead of each source in the network. This will save memory in routers, but can lead to sub-optimal paths, which could introduce additional delay for the multicast traffic. Figures 8-19 and 8-20 illustrate the difference between shared trees and source trees.

FIGURE 8-19 Shared tree versus source tree—one source

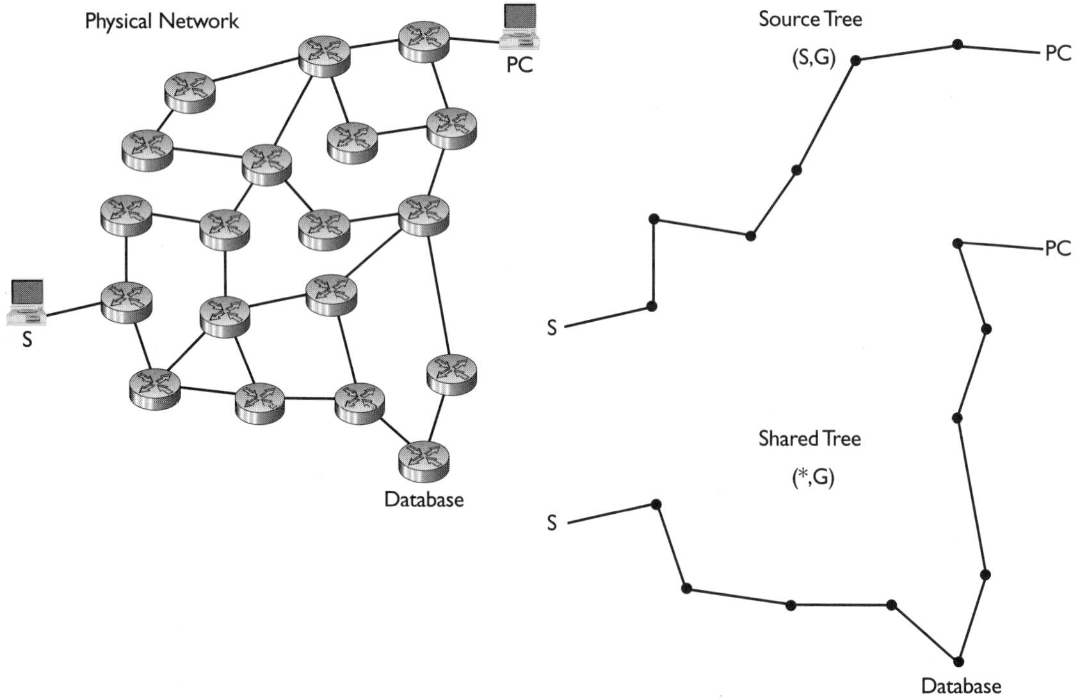

Figure 8-19 shows the difference between a shared tree and a source tree. Notice that how the shared tree is a much longer path. Remember that with a shared tree, all sources use the same tree. In an environment where there are several sources, this can significantly reduce the number of trees.

In Figure 8-20, there are two sources, each sending the same traffic to the same multicast group. In this example, you can see how using shared trees will reduce the number of trees. However, using shared trees doesn't always mean you will get a sub-optimal tree; you still may get the optimal path.

FIGURE 8-20 Shared tree versus source tree—two sources

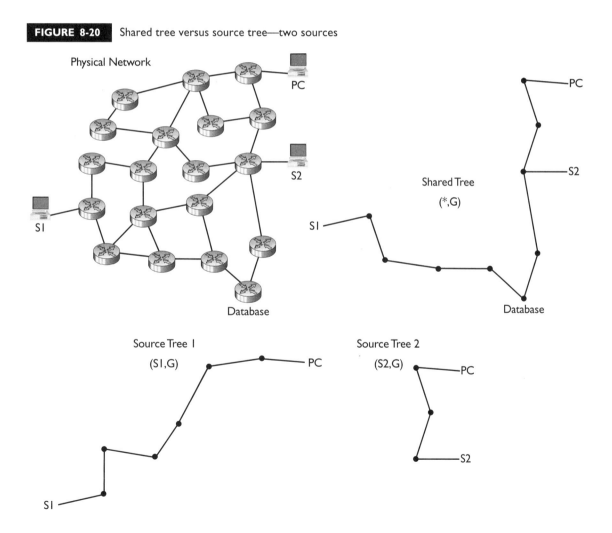

Another important part of multicast routing is the Outgoing Interface List (OIL). The OIL contains a list of interfaces that need to be copied on every incoming multicast packet. Each multicast group will have its own multicast routing entry (either a (*,G) or (S,G)). Included in the routing entry will be information on the incoming RPF interface and the outgoing interface list. Other information includes the multicast group address, timers, and flags. Additional information on the multicast routing table is covered in the section *Monitoring and Troubleshooting Commands* later in this chapter.

Dense Mode

Dense Mode multicast routing protocols work through a process of flooding all traffic and then specifically pruning back the interfaces and routers that do not wish to continue receiving it. As soon as a multicast source begins sending multicast traffic, its directly connected router will flood that traffic out all interfaces (including WAN links). After a period of time, the routers at the end of the network will begin pruning back the traffic if they do not wish to continue receiving it. Imagine what that could do if a server began multicasting out a 2MB video stream and you had a Dense Mode routing protocol configured for your network (including T1 WAN links). For a period of time, even if there were no interested listeners on the other side of the WAN link, the entire 2MB would fill the 1.5MB T1 line, stopping all other traffic from passing through. Dense Mode routing protocols run best in a pure LAN network, or a network with very high-speed WAN links. Because Dense Mode protocols have such a simple way of informing other routers of new groups and sources, they are usually very easy to configure and troubleshoot.

Sparse Mode

Sparse Mode multicast routing protocols, overcome the inherent flood and prune problem that Dense Mode protocols have. Instead of flooding multicast traffic out all interfaces, Sparse Mode protocols build a database containing a list of all multicast groups and all multicast sources. When a client wishes to begin receiving multicast traffic, its directly connected router contacts the database and finds the location of the source of the multicast traffic. Once a router knows the location of the source (IP address), a distribution tree can be built and the multicast traffic can flow down it. Sparse Mode protocols are best suited for networks that encompass WAN links where the multicast traffic may not be needed. Because of their more complex manner of maintaining information about multicast groups and sources, Sparse Mode protocols are typically more difficult to configure and troubleshoot.

Multicast Routing Protocols

The following sections cover three of the most popular Dense Mode multicast routing protocols: DVMRP, MOSPF, and PIM Dense Mode.

DVMRP

Distance Vector Multicast Routing Protocol (DVMRP) was the first multicast routing protocol developed to handle routing multicast traffic. DVMRP is defined in RFC 1075. DVMRP requires its own proprietary unicast routing protocol to function. Once DVMRP is configured on a network, a secondary unicast routing table will be built specifically for DVMRP. That secondary routing table will be built similarly to RIP. It is built solely on hop count, even if your IGP is OSPF. DVMRP has a hop limitation of 31 hops. Because it was the very first multicast routing protocol developed, it was adopted early in the development of MBONE. Recently, MBONE has begun replacing DVMRP with a newer, more robust sparse mode protocol: PIM Sparse Mode.

DVMRP runs on a flood and prune mechanism. It begins flooding out multicast traffic out all interfaces of every router in the entire network. If no interested clients request to keep receiving the traffic, the interfaces are pruned back one by one, until the smallest required number of interfaces and network paths are involved. Periodically, the router attached to the multicast source will reflood out all traffic to make sure that no additional interested clients are interested. Because of its limitation on hop count, slow convergence (RIP-like convergence), requirement of a hop-count based unicast routing protocol, and continual flooding of traffic, DVMRP is quickly becoming the least favorable multicast routing protocol.

Configuring DVMRP   Because DVMRP is losing its installed base and will soon be a dead protocol, similar to RIPv1, the commands to configure DVMRP are outside the scope of this book.

MOSPF

Multicast extension to OSPF (MOSPF) is defined in RFC 1584. Unlike DVMRP, MOSFP does not flood out multicast traffic out all interfaces. Instead, it uses LSAs (LSA type 6) and the link-state database in use by the unicast routing protocol to build its distribution trees. MOSPF only runs on an OSPF network. The OSPF network must encompass 100 percent of the network in order for MOSPF to work. This is the biggest problem encountered when trying to deploy MOSPF.

MOSPF uses the Dijkstra algorithm to calculate the shortest path tree. A potential problem, Dijkstra must be run for each multicast source for each group. In a network with 100 routers running 50 different multicast groups, each router will have to compute Dijkstra 50 times. Each time there is a change to the network, Dijkstra will need to be recalculated, again 50 times for each router. This can be a very significant load on the routers in a network.

Configuring MOSPF   Cisco currently does not support MOSPF. Hence, there are no commands to configure MOSPF.

PIM Dense Mode

Unlike DVMRP and MOSPF, Protocol Independent Multicasting Dense Mode (PIM Dense Mode) supports all underlying unicast routing protocols. PIM Dense Mode uses the routing table (not a routing protocol) to build its distribution trees. PIM Dense Mode, DVMRP, and MOSPF support only source trees. PIM Dense Mode is most effective in dense networks where a majority of the traffic will not traverse WAN links. Just like DVRMP, PIM Dense Mode operates on a flood and prune mechanism. As soon as a multicast source begins sending out multicast traffic, the routers begin flooding out the multicast traffic. Fifteen seconds after a leaf router (a router with no other connections to additional routers) receives the flooded multicast traffic, it can send a prune message upstream to the router that flooded the traffic. Every three minutes, all pruned interfaces get reflooded for an additional 15 seconds. Figure 8-21 illustrates the flood and prune operation of PIM Dense Mode.

Figure 8-21 shows how the flood mechanism works in a PIM Dense Mode network. As soon as Source1 begins sending multicast traffic to the group 224.1.1.1, RouterA floods it out all interfaces. Routers B, C, F, D, and E all get the multicast traffic and forward it out all interfaces. As the traffic flows, each router creates an (S,G) entry for the multicast source. The S will be populated with the IP address for Source1 (24.31.234.43), and the G will contain the multicast group that is being sent (232.125.226.56). The traffic will be continually flood out all interfaces in the entire network as long as the source continues to send and no router prunes back their interface.

FIGURE 8-21 PIM Dense Mode—flood

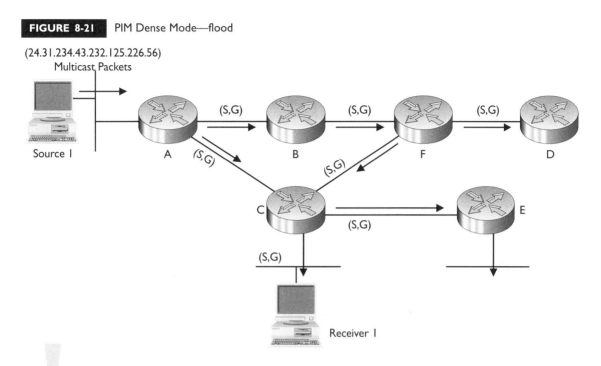

> **exam**
> **⊕atch**
>
> *Remember that PIM Dense Mode only supports source trees. When using PIM Dense Mode, you will not have any (*,G) trees.*

Figure 8-22 illustrates how each interface that doesn't have a client sends a prune message upstream. After the default 15 seconds of no traffic, RouterE, RouterC, and RouterD will send their prune messages upstream. As soon as RouterF receives both prunes from RouterC and RouterD, it cuts those interfaces off, and since it has no clients, sends a prune message up to RouterB. RouterB does the same and sends a prune message up to RouterA. One important thing to note here is that as soon as RouterC gets the prune from RouterE, it does not send that message upstream. Let's look at RouterB in more detail. After sending the prune message up to RouterA, it keeps the (S,G) entry in its multicast routing table with the prune flag set and begins a 3-minute timer. As soon as that timer reaches 0, it will remove the entry for (S,G). RouterA begins a 3-minute timer as well, and as soon as its timer reaches 0, it refloods out the traffic from Source1. RouterB will then reflood the traffic out to RouterF and so on. This 3-minute refresh will continue across the entire network until Source1 stops sending multicast traffic, even though there is only one receiver.

FIGURE 8-22   PIM Dense Mode—prune

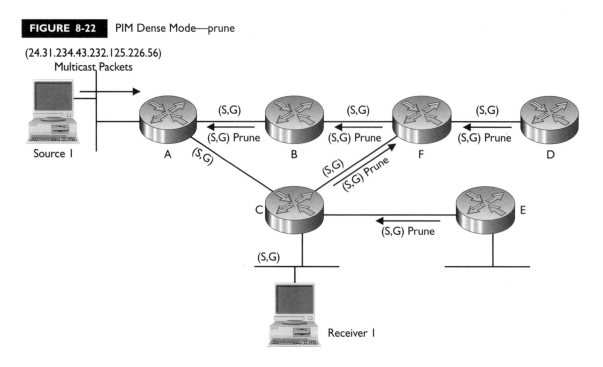

Configuring PIM Dense Mode   Because of its simple operation of flood and prune, PIM Dense Mode is a very easy multicast routing protocol to configure and troubleshoot. There are only two commands required on each router in the network to configure it: one global command **ip multicast-routing**, and one command on every interface **ip pim dense-mode** where multicast traffic is desired.

It is important to remember to configure PIM on all interfaces in the network. In certain circumstances, the unicast routing protocol could take a path that does not have multicast enabled, breaking multicast at that point in the network.

Now that you understand both CGMP and PIM Dense Mode, Exercise 8-4 tests you on how to configure them in a simple network.

EXERCISE 8-4

Configure PIM Dense Mode with CGMP

Configure Router1, Router2, and the switch from Figure 8-23 to support CGMP and PIM Dense Mode.

1. The first step is to configure Router1.

Router1(config)# ip multicast-routing
Router1(config)# interface Serial 0
Router1(config)# ip pim dense-mode

2. The second step is to configure Router2.

Router2(config)# ip multicast-routing
Router2(config)# interface Serial 0
Router2(config)# ip pim dense-mode
Router2(config)# interface Ethernet 0
Router2(config)# ip pim dense-mode
Router2(config)# ip cgmp

3. The last step is to configure the Switch.

Switch# set cgmp enable

FIGURE 8-23 Simple PIM Dense Mode and CGMP network

Sparse Mode

The following section covers the most popular Sparse Mode multicast routing protocol, PIM Sparse Mode.

PIM Sparse Mode   PIM Sparse Mode also supports all underlying unicast routing protocols. It uses the router's IP routing table to make RPF calculations and determine next-hop interfaces. Like other Sparse Mode routing protocols, PIM Sparse Mode supports both source trees and shared trees. Dense Mode protocols only support source trees, which means that a new tree must be built for each source in the network. The shared tree allows the routers to build one tree for each multicast group, conserving router memory. There is one potential problem with using the shared tree: the tree might not be on an optimal path. This could mean that additional network resources will be used, as well as increased latency in the multicast stream. PIM Sparse Mode uses the advantages of both source trees and shared trees. Shared trees rely on a central database as a way of informing other routers about active sources and groups. In PIM Sparse Mode, the database is called the Rendezvous Point (RP). The RP is a Cisco router (not a SQL database) that maintains a complete list of all multicast sources and groups in the network at all times. This is mostly just an added memory strain on the router. However, with memory size getting larger and price smaller (as opposed to the late 80's pricing), most current routers will not have a problem dedicating enough memory to act as the RP.

Since PIM Sparse Mode operates on an as-needed basis, no clients receive any multicast traffic until they specifically ask for it. Figure 8-24 details the process of requesting multicast traffic and the construction of the shared tree between the end router and the RP.

A client requests traffic by sending an IGMP membership report to its directly connected router, RouterE (Figure 8-24). The IGMP membership report will not have any information about the IP address of the source, only the IP address of the multicast group desired. As soon as RouterE receives the IGMP membership report, it looks for that entry in its multicast routing table. When it finds no entry, it creates an entry in its multicast routing table for that specific group (*,G).

Next, in Figure 8-25, RouterE will send a (*,G) join message upstream toward the RP. Each router in the path of this message will also perform a lookup for that multicast group. If no router on the path toward the RP has an entry for that group, the RP gets the join request and places that group in its database. If one of the routers in the path toward the RP already contains an entry for that group, the (*,G)

Understanding Multicast Protocols **439**

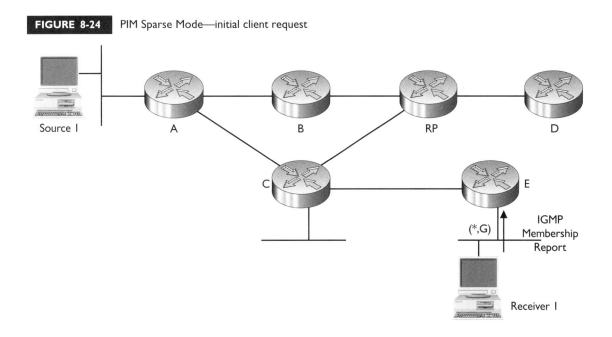

FIGURE 8-24 PIM Sparse Mode—initial client request

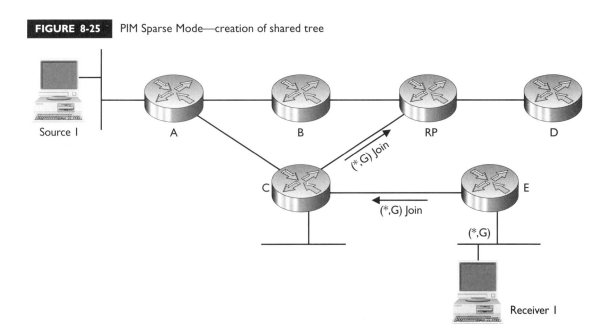

FIGURE 8-25 PIM Sparse Mode—creation of shared tree

join message is stopped and the router will add the interface where the join came from to its list of outgoing interfaces for that multicast group.

As soon as the (*,G) join message reaches the RP (Figure 8-26), it looks in its multicast routing table (which is the master database of all multicast traffic for the network) for the entry for that group. If an entry exists with an assigned source (S,G), the RP forwards the requested multicast traffic. If there is no existing entry for the specified multicast group, it creates a new (*,G) entry.

Pruning back the shared tree works similar to PIM Dense Mode. As soon as the last client leaves a particular group, its router will check to see if any other interfaces are interested. If there are no other interfaces in the outgoing interface list (OIL), the router will send a (*,G) prune message upstream. As soon as the upstream router receives the (*,G) prune message, it will do the same. This process will continue until either a router is encountered that has interested listeners, or the prune message reaches the RP.

Registering new traffic with the RP is done differently from Dense Mode protocols. Instead of flooding all multicast traffic out, the router directly attached to a new multicast source goes through a registration process. For the registration process, there are two possible scenarios:

- The source begins sending multicast traffic before any clients request it.

FIGURE 8-26 PIM Sparse Mode—creation of (*,G)

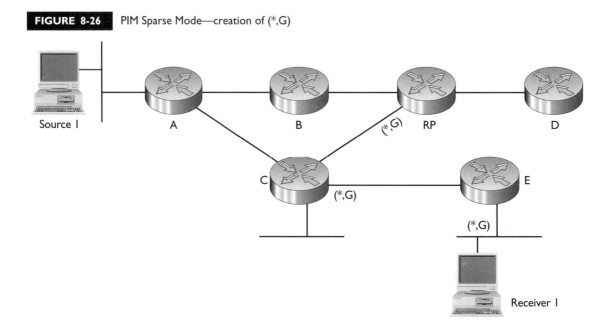

■ A client requests the multicast traffic before any source sends it.

Figure 8-25 shows the first scenario.

When Source1 begins sending traffic, its directly connected router (RouterA) will send a register message to the RP about what the multicast group is and what the IP address of the source is. The register message that RouterA sends to the RP contains the multicast source and group information, as well as the multicast payload, all encapsulated in a unicast packet (Figure 8-27).

From then on, the RP unicasts back a register stop message telling RouterA to stop unicasting the multicast traffic. The RP also creates a record in its database about that specific source and group. The RP keeps that entry until another router requests the multicast traffic or the default timeout timer of three minutes reaches zero, at which point the RP will remove the entry. Every three minutes, RouterA will reinitiate the register process with the RP (Figure 8-28).

In the second scenario, where the client joins the multicast group before the server begins sending traffic, the shared tree is built just as in Figures 8-24, 8-25,

FIGURE 8-27 PIM Sparse Mode—registering with the RP, source first

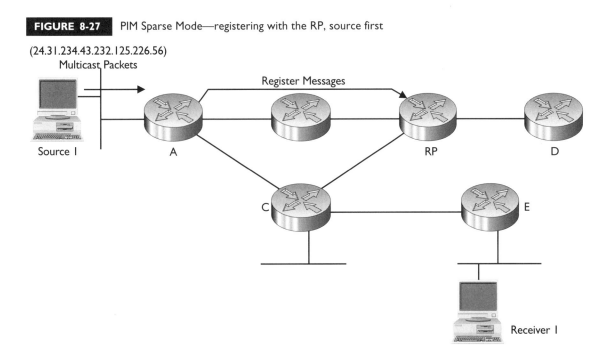

FIGURE 8-28   PIM Sparse Mode—registering with the RP, register stop

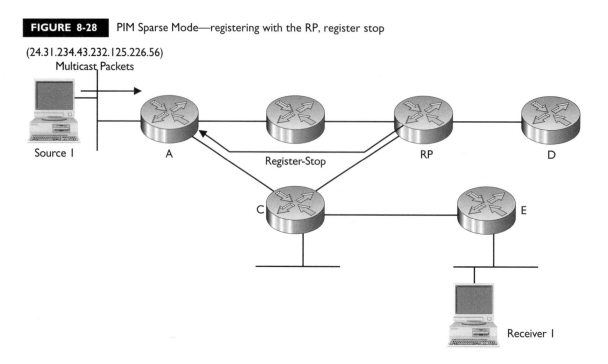

and 8-26. As soon as the first multicast packet is sent by the source, RouterA proceeds to register with the RP, just as in Figure 8-27.

Once the RP sees the multicast traffic that RouterC requested (Figure 8-29), it immediately decapsulates it and forwards it down the shared tree (RouterC forwards the traffic down its shared tree toward RouterE). At the same time, it sends a (S,G) join message up toward RouterB. RouterB then sends a (S,G) join up toward RouterA.

As soon as RouterA receives the (S,G) join from RouterB, it stops encapsulating the multicast packets and sends them as normal multicast down the newly created source tree to RouterB (Figure 8-30). Router B will then forward them down to the RP, and the RP will forward them down until the multicast packets reach Receiver1.

At this point, multicast traffic is flowing down the source tree from RouterA to the RP, and down the shared tree from the RP toward RouterE. As soon as RouterC sees the first packet with the source IP address identified, it has the option of switching over to the source tree. Since PIM Source Mode supports both types of distribution trees, a router can switch from the shared tree to the source tree as soon as it knows the unicast IP address of the source. By default, a Cisco router will try to

Understanding Multicast Protocols **443**

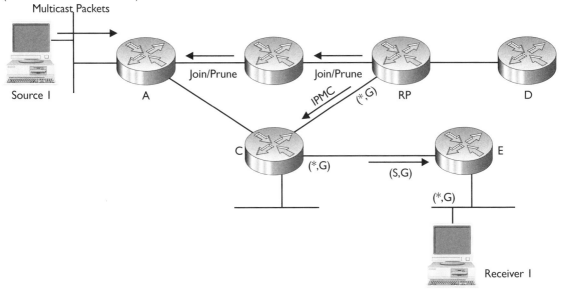

FIGURE 8-29 PIM Sparse Mode—forwarding multicast traffic

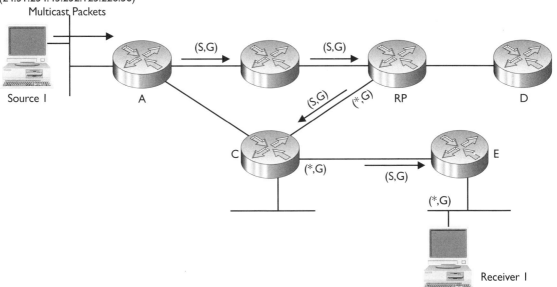

FIGURE 8-30 PIM Sparse Mode—traffic down shared tree

switch to the source tree as soon as the first packet arrives that identifies the source (by IP address). This value is configurable and can even be set to infinity, forcing a router to always stay on the shared tree.

In Figure 8-31, RouterC sends a (S,G) join message directly toward RouterA. As soon as RouterA receives the (S,G) message, it adds the interface connected to RouterC to the OIL for the specified multicast group. At this point, RouterC is getting the multicast traffic through both the source tree and the shared tree. Next, RouterC prunes back the shared tree by sending a (S,G) RP-bit prune message up to the RP. The RP will then stop sending multicast traffic down the shared tree, and if it has no other listeners, will prune the source tree back up to RouterA.

PIM Sparse-Dense Mode   In addition to PIM Dense Mode and PIM Sparse Mode, there is a third Cisco proprietary protocol: PIM Sparse-Dense Mode. PIM Sparse-Dense mode allows the router to operate in Dense Mode for all multicast groups where the RP has not yet been identified, and in Sparse Mode for all multicast groups where there is an RP. PIM Sparse-Dense Mode is the basis for Auto-RP.

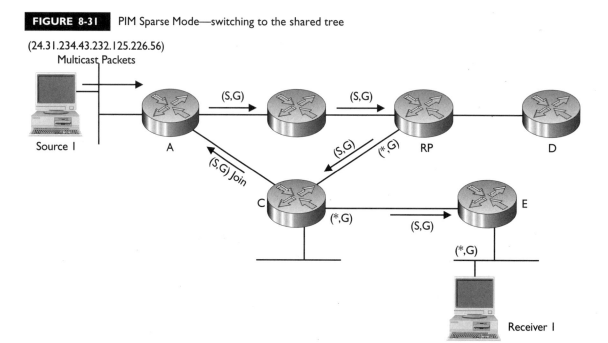

FIGURE 8-31   PIM Sparse Mode—switching to the shared tree

- **Configuring PIM Sparse-Dense Mode**   Just like PIM Dense Mode and PIM Sparse Mode, there are two commands required to configure PIM Sparse-Dense: one global command **ip multicast-routing**, and one interface command on every interface **ip pim sparse-dense-mode**. In addition to the two commands, the RP can be optionally configured either statically or by using Auto-RP. The next discussion covers Auto-RP and its configuration.

- **Auto-RP discussion**   Auto-RP is a Cisco proprietary protocol that can be used in conjunction with PIM Sparse-Dense Mode as a way to automatically configure the RP for a given network. Auto-RP allows a network to have multiple RPs available. Even though only one RP will be active for a particular multicast group, multiple RPs can be configured as a way of redundancy.

on the Job

There is another method of having multiple RPs for a given network: using MSDP in conjunction with the unicast routing protocol's ability to support duplicate IP addresses (EIGRP and OSPF). This method is referred to as Anycast-RP. Anycast-RP allows for multiple active RPs in a network, whereas Auto-RP only allows for a single active RP with multiple backup RPs. Anycast-RP and MSDP are considered advanced multicast topics and are outside the scope of this book. As with all other advanced multicast topics, additional information can be found at Cisco's multicast Web site: ftp://ftpeng.cisco.com/ipmulticast/index.html.

The way Auto-RP works is that instead of having every router in the network configured with the static IP address of an RP, the RP will be configured, and all other routers will simply learn the IP address for the RP. This only works in an all-Cisco network, and requires the use of PIM Sparse-Dense Mode. Auto-RP operates with two fundamental pieces, the mapping agent and the candidate RP. The candidate RP will multicast out RP-announcement messages to the reserved IPMC address 224.0.1.39 every 60 seconds. The RP-announcement message contains the IP address of the RP, the group range that the RP is willing to be the RP for (by default, it is the entire Class D range 224.0.0.0/4), and the holdtime (by default, the holdtime is 3 x the rp-announce-interval, or 3 x 60 seconds). The mapping agents listen for these RP-announcement messages and determine which router will be the active RP for the network. The candidate RP with the highest IP address will be chosen as the RP for the group range configured. Once the mapping agent has determined the RP, it sends a discovery message to the multicast group

224.0.1.40. The RP-discovery message contains the group-to-RP mapping cache. All routers in the network will use the cache as the configuration for the RP. By default, all Cisco routers will automatically join the group 224.0.1.40.

- **Configuring PIM Sparse Mode** PIM Sparse Mode is configured on a Cisco router by issuing the global command **ip multicast-routing** with the interface command (configured on all interfaces) **ip pim sparse-mode**. In addition to the two preceding commands, the RP must be configured.

- **Configuring Rendezvous Point** The rendezvous point is needed whenever you are using PIM Sparse Mode or PIM Sparse-Dense Mode. The RP is a router that contains a list of every multicast source and group in the network at any given moment. There are three different options for configuring the RP. The first is by statically configuring it with the global command **ip pim rp-address x.x.x.x** on every router in the network except the RP. The next option is to use PIM BootStrap Router (BSR). PIM BSR is also outside the scope of this chapter and will not be discussed. The third option is to use Auto-RP. In order for Auto-RP to operate correctly, you must also use PIM Sparse-Dense Mode. To configure Auto-RP, there are only two commands required, one for the mapping agent and one for the candidate RP (one router can be both the mapping agent and candidate RP). The command for the mapping agent is a global command **ip pim send-rp-discovery scope <ttl>**, where the ttl is the number of hops that the discovery message can go. The command for the candidate RP is **ip pim send-rp-announce <interface> scope <ttl> [group-list]**. The interface is the interface IP address that you want to advertise out to all routers as the RP address. The ttl is the number of hops that the announcement message can go. Make sure that the ttl for both the mapping agent and candidate RP is set high enough to reach every router in your network. The group-list optional parameter can be used to limit the RP to only specific multicast groups.

PIM can be a very complex protocol, just as complex as OSPF or BGP. The previous discussion on PIM is just a brief overview. For additional information on PIM, refer to Cisco's Web site on IPMC at ftp://ftpeng.cisco.com/ipmulticast/index.html.

Now that you have a better understanding of PIM Sparse Mode, refer to the following Scenario & Solution.

SCENARIO & SOLUTION

In my complex unicast network, there are some links that are redundant that I don't want my multicast traffic to flow down. How can I perform this and keep multicast traffic operational?	Currently, you can't do this. PIM version 3 will add support for static multicast route selection (there is no deadline yet as to when it will be available). PIM version 2 is available on certain versions of IOS. PIM version 2 adds the capability of BootStrap Router (BSR), which is outside the scope of this book.
I have a very large network and want to run PIM Sparse Mode. Can I configure two RPs to operate at the same time?	Yes. It requires running MSDP between the two RPs and having a unicast routing protocol running on your network that supports multiple paths to the same network such as EIGRP or OSPF. This is called Anycast RP. Information on Anycast and MSDP can be found on Cisco's multicast Web site.

CERTIFICATION OBJECTIVE 8.04

Monitoring and Troubleshooting Commands

The following section covers some of the commands used in monitoring and troubleshooting IP Multicast. Each command used has a sample output, along with a brief explanation of what the command does.

show ip route

Figure 8-32 shows the output of a unicast routing table. This command can be very useful in tracking down the RPF information when identifying multicast routing problems.

on the job

When troubleshooting any problems with multicast, it is very important that you have a complete understanding of the unicast routing path. If you expect a multicast path to follow a specific path, you might want to verify it by looking at how the unicast traffic flows.

FIGURE 8-32 show ip route

```
Router4#show ip route
Codes: C - connected, S - static, I - IGRP, R - RIP, M - mobile, B - BGP
       D - EIGRP, EX - EIGRP external, O - OSPF, IA - OSPF inter area
       N1 - OSPF NSSA external type 1, N2 - OSPF NSSA external type 2
       E1 - OSPF external type 1, E2 - OSPF external type 2, E - EGP
       i - IS-IS, L1 - IS-IS level-1, L2 - IS-IS level-2, * - candidate default
       U - per-user static route, o - ODR

Gateway of last resort is not set

     172.16.0.0/16 is variably subnetted, 6 subnets, 2 masks
C       172.16.44.0/24 is directly connected, Ethernet0
C       172.16.34.0/24 is directly connected, Serial0
O       172.16.23.0/24 [110/100] via 172.16.34.3, 2d09h, Serial0
O       172.16.12.0/24 [110/100] via 172.16.14.1, 2d09h, Serial1
C       172.16.14.0/24 is directly connected, Serial1
O       172.16.3.3/32 [110/51] via 172.16.34.3, 2d09h, Serial0
     24.0.0.0/26 is subnetted, 1 subnets
O IA    24.31.234.0 [110/60] via 172.16.14.1, 2d09h, Serial1
```

show ip igmp groups

A quick way to identify what multicast groups have been subscribed for a particular router is by using the command **show ip igmp groups**. This command, shown in Figure 8-33, quickly identifies what the multicast groups are, what interface has subscribed, how long the group has been active, when it expires, and what computer was the last to send a membership report.

FIGURE 8-33 show ip igmp groups

```
Router4#sh ip igmp groups
IGMP Connected Group Membership
Group Address      Interface         Uptime    Expires   Last Reporter
231.25.2.206       Ethernet0         00:01:47  00:02:50  172.16.44.3
232.125.226.56     Ethernet0         00:02:20  00:02:56  172.16.44.3
224.0.1.40         Ethernet0         2d11h     never     172.16.44.1
229.39.55.47       Ethernet0         00:03:25  00:02:52  172.16.44.3
224.243.35.236     Ethernet0         00:01:55  00:02:52  172.16.44.3
```

FIGURE 8-34 show ip igmp interface

```
Router4#show ip igmp interface Ethernet 0
Ethernet0 is up, line protocol is up
  Internet address is 172.16.44.1/24
  IGMP is enabled on interface
  Current IGMP version is 2
  CGMP is disabled on interface
  IGMP query interval is 60 seconds
  IGMP querier timeout is 120 seconds
  IGMP max query response time is 10 seconds
  Inbound IGMP access group is not set
  IGMP activity: 12 joins, 7 leaves
  Multicast routing is enabled on interface
  Multicast TTL threshold is 0
  Multicast designated router (DR) is 172.16.44.1 (this system)
  IGMP querying router is 172.16.44.1 (this system)
  Multicast groups joined: 224.0.1.40
```

show ip igmp interface

The command **show ip igmp interface** (Figure 8-34) is a useful command in identifying the version of IGMP and whether CGMP is enabled for a specific interface. It also gives you some information on various IGMP settings.

show ip pim interface

When using PIM, it is very important to verify that all interfaces are configured for it. The command **show ip pim interface** (Figure 8-35) is a way to identify what interfaces are running PIM, what mode of PIM, and whether there is a neighbor on that interface.

FIGURE 8-35 show ip pim interface

```
Router4#show ip pim interface

Address          Interface     Mode     Nbr    Query   DR
                                        Count  Intvl
172.16.44.1      Ethernet0     Sparse   0      30      172.16.44.1
172.16.34.4      Serial0       Sparse   1      30      0.0.0.0
172.16.14.4      Serial1       Sparse   1      30      0.0.0.0
```

FIGURE 8-36

show ip pim neighbor

```
Router4#show ip pim neighbor
PIM Neighbor Table
Neighbor Address    Interface           Uptime      Expires     Mode
172.16.34.3         Serial0             2d11h       00:01:13    Sparse
172.16.14.1         Serial1             2d11h       00:01:07    Sparse
```

show ip pim neighbor

A quick way to identify if the router is talking PIM with other routers is by issuing the command **show ip pim neighbor**. Figure 8-36 shows that this command will give you the IP address of the neighbors, what interface they are connected on, how long they have been connected, how long before they expire, and what mode of PIM they are talking.

show ip pim rp

The command **show ip pim rp** (Figure 8-37) gives information on the rendezvous point for the various multicast groups active on the router.

show ip rpf

The command **show ip rpf** [**source address**], shown in Figure 8-38, gives the information on the reverse path forwarding lookup for a particular multicast source. This command can be helpful in diagnosing problems with RPF failures.

FIGURE 8-37 show ip pim rp

```
Router4#show ip pim rp
Group: 234.254.143.183, RP: 172.16.3.3, uptime 2d11h, expires never
Group: 231.25.2.206, RP: 172.16.3.3, uptime 2d11h, expires never
Group: 232.125.226.56, RP: 172.16.3.3, uptime 2d11h, expires never
Group: 224.0.1.40, RP: 172.16.3.3, uptime 00:02:04, expires 00:00:55
Group: 229.39.55.47, RP: 172.16.3.3, uptime 2d11h, expires never
Group: 224.243.35.236, RP: 172.16.3.3, uptime 2d11h, expires never
Group: 224.0.1.24, RP: 172.16.3.3, uptime 2d11h, expires never
```

FIGURE 8-38

show ip rpf

```
Router4#show ip rpf 24.31.234.43
RPF information for ? (24.31.234.43)
  RPF interface: Serial1
  RPF neighbor: ? (172.16.14.1)
  RPF route/mask: 24.31.234.0/255.255.255.192
  RPF type: unicast
```

show ip mroute

Figures 8-39 and 8-40 show an output from the command **show ip mroute**. This is the most helpful command when monitoring and troubleshooting IPMC. There is a vast amount of information provided in the output. Because of this command's importance, the following is a more detailed explanation of two of the entries from Figure 8-39.

FIGURE 8-39

show ip mroute

```
Router4#show ip mroute
IP Multicast Routing Table
Flags: D - Dense, S - Sparse, C - Connected, L - Local, P - Pruned
       R - RP-bit set, F - Register flag, T - SPT-bit set, J - Join SPT
Timers: Uptime/Expires
Interface state: Interface, Next-Hop or VCD, State/Mode

(*, 234.254.143.183), 2d11h/00:02:59, RP 172.16.3.3, flags: SP
  Incoming interface: Serial0, RPF nbr 172.16.34.3
  Outgoing interface list: Null

(24.31.234.43/32, 234.254.143.183), 2d11h/00:02:24, flags: PT
  Incoming interface: Serial1, RPF nbr 172.16.14.1
  Outgoing interface list: Null

(*, 231.25.2.206), 2d11h/00:02:59, RP 172.16.3.3, flags: SJC
  Incoming interface: Serial0, RPF nbr 172.16.34.3
  Outgoing interface list:
    Ethernet0, Forward/Sparse, 00:09:13/00:02:28

(24.31.234.43/32, 231.25.2.206), 2d11h/00:02:59, flags: CT
  Incoming interface: Serial1, RPF nbr 172.16.14.1
  Outgoing interface list:
    Ethernet0, Forward/Sparse, 00:09:13/00:02:28
```

FIGURE 8-40 show ip mroute (continued)

```
(*, 224.0.1.40), 2d11h/00:00:00, RP 172.16.3.3, flags: SJCL
  Incoming interface: Serial0, RPF nbr 172.16.34.3
  Outgoing interface list:
    Serial1, Forward/Sparse, 2d09h/00:02:00
    Ethernet0, Forward/Sparse, 2d11h/00:02:26

(*, 229.39.55.47), 2d11h/00:02:59, RP 172.16.3.3, flags: SJC
  Incoming interface: Serial0, RPF nbr 172.16.34.3
  Outgoing interface list:
    Ethernet0, Forward/Sparse, 00:10:53/00:02:30

(24.31.234.43/32, 229.39.55.47), 2d11h/00:02:59, flags: CT
  Incoming interface: Serial1, RPF nbr 172.16.14.1
  Outgoing interface list:
    Ethernet0, Forward/Sparse, 00:10:54/00:02:29

(*, 224.243.35.236), 2d11h/00:02:59, RP 172.16.3.3, flags: SJC
  Incoming interface: Serial0, RPF nbr 172.16.34.3
  Outgoing interface list:
    Ethernet0, Forward/Sparse, 00:09:24/00:02:23

(*, 232.125.226.56), 2d11h/00:02:59, RP 172.16.3.3, flags: SJC
  Incoming interface: Serial0, RPF nbr 172.16.34.3
  Outgoing interface list:
    Ethernet0, Forward/Sparse, 00:09:47/00:02:31

(24.31.234.43/32, 232.125.226.56), 2d11h/00:02:59, flags: CT
  Incoming interface: Serial1, RPF nbr 172.16.14.1
  Outgoing interface list:
    Ethernet0, Forward/Sparse, 00:09:47/00:02:31

(24.31.234.43/32, 224.243.35.236), 2d11h/00:02:58, flags: CT
  Incoming interface: Serial1, RPF nbr 172.16.14.1
  Outgoing interface list:
    Ethernet0, Forward/Sparse, 00:09:24/00:02:23

(*, 224.0.1.24), 2d11h/00:02:46, RP 172.16.3.3, flags: S
  Incoming interface: Serial0, RPF nbr 172.16.34.3
  Outgoing interface list:
    Serial1, Forward/Sparse, 2d11h/00:02:46
```

Figure 8-41 is an excerpt from Figure 8-38. This section is the definition of the flags and values for the entries. The flags give detail to each multicast group entry as to its mode, and whether the entry is on a shared tree or source tree. The D, or Dense, flag denotes that the entry is running on Dense Mode. The S, or Sparse, flag denotes that the entry is running on Sparse Mode. The C, or Connected, flag identifies whether there is an interface with a connected IGMP listener. The L, or Local, flag identifies if the multicast group is sourced locally. The P, or Pruned, flag marks an entry that has no interested listeners and is in the final stages before being removed from the table. The R, or RP-bit set, flag identifies an entry that is in the process of switching from the shared tree to the source tree. The F, or Register, flag identifies if the group is in the process of being registered with the RP. The T, or SPT-bit set, flag is used on all entries that have switched to the source tree. Finally, the J, or Join SPT, flag identifies whether the entry has joined the shortest path tree. Next, we explain the routing entries for a specific multicast group.

Looking at the group routing entries in Figure 8-42, there are two different entries for the same multicast group 231.25.2.206. The first entry is a (*,G) entry denoting that it is the entry for the shared tree. It has identified the RP for the

FIGURE 8-41

show ip mroute—flags

```
IP Multicast Routing Table
Flags: D - Dense, S - Sparse, C - Connected, L - Local, P - Pruned
       R - RP-bit set, F - Register flag, T - SPT-bit set, J - Join SPT
Timers: Uptime/Expires
Interface state: Interface, Next-Hop or VCD, State/Mode
```

FIGURE 8-42

show ip mroute—detailed

```
(*, 231.25.2.206), 2d11h/00:02:59, RP 172.16.3.3, flags: SJC
   Incoming interface: Serial0, RPF nbr 172.16.34.3
   Outgoing interface list:
      Ethernet0, Forward/Sparse, 00:09:13/00:02:28

(24.31.234.43/32, 231.25.2.206), 2d11h/00:02:59, flags: CT
   Incoming interface: Serial1, RPF nbr 172.16.14.1
   Outgoing interface list:
      Ethernet0, Forward/Sparse, 00:09:13/00:02:28
```

group. The flags set are Source Mode, Join Source Tree, and Connected. It has identified the Serial0 interface as the incoming interface and the Ethernet0 interface as the outgoing interface. Also, the group has been active for 2 days and 11 hours and will expire in 2 minutes and 59 seconds. The second entry is the (S,G) entry for the same multicast group. Notice that instead of the *, it has identified the IP address of the source. The flags are set to Directly connected and SPT-bit or Source tree. This entry has also been active for 2 days and 11 hours and will expire in 2 minutes and 59 seconds. The incoming interface is different from the previous entry; however, the outgoing interface is the same. There is a lot of information contained in the **show ip mroute** command. The more experience you have with using it in a test environment, the better you can understand it.

show ip mroute summary

The command **show ip mroute summary**, shown in Figure 8-43, gives all of the detail as show ip mroute, except for incoming and outgoing interface information.

exam
Watch

Remember that the summary command will not provide the OIL information for each group.

show ip mroute active

The command **show ip mroute active** gives additional information on multicast groups than the **show ip mroute** command. In Figure 8-44, you can see that each group that is sending more than 4000bps of data is listed as active. The information provided is the group address, the name for the group (if configured), the source address with DNS name, and the rate of data over several time periods.

FIGURE 8-43

show ip mroute summary

```
Router4#show ip mroute summary
IP Multicast Routing Table
Flags: D - Dense, S - Sparse, C - Connected, L - Local, P - Pruned
       R - RP-bit set, F - Register flag, T - SPT-bit set, J - Join SPT
Timers: Uptime/Expires
Interface state: Interface, Next-Hop or VCD, State/Mode

(*, 234.254.143.183), 2d11h/00:02:58, RP 172.16.3.3, flags: SP
    (24.31.234.43/32, 234.254.143.183), 2d11h/00:02:49, flags: PT
(*, 231.25.2.206), 2d11h/00:02:58, RP 172.16.3.3, flags: SJC
    (24.31.234.43/32, 231.25.2.206), 2d11h/00:02:59, flags: CT
(*, 232.125.226.56), 2d11h/00:02:59, RP 172.16.3.3, flags: SJC
    (24.31.234.43/32, 232.125.226.56), 2d11h/00:02:59, flags: CT
(*, 224.0.1.40), 2d11h/00:00:00, RP 172.16.3.3, flags: SJCL
(*, 229.39.55.47), 2d11h/00:02:59, RP 172.16.3.3, flags: SJC
    (24.31.234.43/32, 229.39.55.47), 2d11h/00:02:59, flags: CT
(*, 224.243.35.236), 2d11h/00:02:59, RP 172.16.3.3, flags: SJC
    (24.31.234.43/32, 224.243.35.236), 2d11h/00:02:59, flags: CT
(*, 224.0.1.24), 2d11h/00:02:13, RP 172.16.3.3, flags: S
```

FIGURE 8-44 show ip mroute active

```
Router4#show ip mroute active
Active IP Multicast Sources - sending >= 4 kbps

Group: 231.25.2.206, (?)
   Source: 24.31.234.43 (?)
     Rate: 6 pps/53 kbps(1sec), 56 kbps(last 37 secs), 0 kbps(life avg)

Group: 232.125.226.56, (?)
   Source: 24.31.234.43 (?)
     Rate: 8 pps/71 kbps(1sec), 35 kbps(last 52 secs), 0 kbps(life avg)

Group: 229.39.55.47, (?)
   Source: 24.31.234.43 (?)
     Rate: 0 pps/0 kbps(1sec), 44 kbps(last 47 secs), 0 kbps(life avg)

Group: 224.243.35.236, (?)
   Source: 24.31.234.43 (?)
     Rate: 6 pps/37 kbps(1sec), 96 kbps(last 56 secs), 0 kbps(life avg)
```

debug ip igmp

Debug IP IGMP is a useful command to issue when identifying problems with host join failures. The output from this command, shown in Figure 8-45, can identify any problems with queries or membership reports. It also identifies what computer is sending the reports and for what group. Group leaves and group deletion are also shown.

debug ip pim

Debug ip pim when activated will cause all PIM packets to be displayed on the console. Figure 8-46 shows an output of the command. Some of the information that it provides is how the PIM trees are built, and how they are maintained.

debug ip mrouting

Debug ip mrouting, shown in Figure 8-47, gives information on routing updates, creation, and deletion. Some of the information it provides is (*,G) creation and updates, (S,G) creation and updates, and RPF information.

FIGURE 8-45   debug ip igmp

```
Router4#debug ip igmp
IGMP debugging is on
Router4#
2d12h: IGMP: Send v2 Query on Ethernet0 to 224.0.0.1
2d12h: IGMP: Set report delay time to 5.2 seconds for 224.0.1.40 on Ethernet0
2d12h: IGMP: Received v2 Report from 172.16.44.3 (Ethernet0) for 232.125.226.56
2d12h: IGMP: Received v2 Report from 172.16.44.3 (Ethernet0) for 224.243.35.236
2d12h: IGMP: Received v2 Report from 172.16.44.3 (Ethernet0) for 231.25.2.206
2d12h: IGMP: Received v2 Report from 172.16.44.3 (Ethernet0) for 229.39.55.47
2d12h: IGMP: Send v2 Report for 224.0.1.40 on Ethernet0
2d12h: IGMP: Received v2 Report from 172.16.44.1 (Ethernet0) for 224.0.1.40
2d12h: IGMP: Received v2 Report from 172.16.44.1 (Ethernet0) for 224.0.1.40
2d12h: IGMP: Received v2 Report from 172.16.44.3 (Ethernet0) for 234.254.143.183
2d12h: IGMP: Received Leave from 172.16.44.3 (Ethernet0) for 234.254.143.183
2d12h: IGMP: Send v2 Query on Ethernet0 to 234.254.143.183
2d12h: IGMP: Send v2 Query on Ethernet0 to 234.254.143.183
2d12h: IGMP: Deleting 234.254.143.183 on Ethernet0
```

FIGURE 8-46 debug ip pim

```
Router4#debug ip pim
PIM debugging is on
Router4#
2d12h: PIM: Building Join/Prune message for 224.0.1.24
2d12h: PIM: For RP, Join-list: 172.16.3.3/32, RP-bit, WC-bit
2d12h: PIM: Send periodic Join/Prune to RP via 172.16.34.3 (Serial0)
2d12h: PIM: Received Join/Prune on Serial1 from 172.16.14.1, to us
2d12h: PIM: Prune-list: (24.31.234.43/32, 229.39.55.47) RP-bit set
2d12h: PIM: Received Join/Prune on Serial1 from 172.16.14.1, to us
2d12h: PIM: Join-list: (*, 224.0.1.24) RP 172.16.3.3, RP-bit set, WC-bit set, S-bit set
2d12h: PIM: Add Serial1/172.16.14.1 to (*, 224.0.1.24), Forward state
2d12h: PIM: Send Router-Query on Ethernet0
2d12h: PIM: Received Join/Prune on Serial1 from 172.16.14.1, to us
2d12h: PIM: Prune-list: (24.31.234.43/32, 224.243.35.236) RP-bit set
2d12h: PIM: Send Router-Query on Serial1
2d12h: PIM: Send Router-Query on Serial0
2d12h: PIM: Received Router-Query on Serial1 from 172.16.14.1
2d12h: PIM: Received Join/Prune on Serial1 from 172.16.14.1, to us
2d12h: PIM: Join-list: (*, 224.0.1.40) RP 172.16.3.3, RP-bit set, WC-bit set, S-bit set
```

FIGURE 8-47 debug ip mrouting

```
Router4#debug ip mrouting
IP multicast routing debugging is on
2d12h: MRT: Create (*, 231.25.2.206), RPF Null, PC 0x335E67A
2d12h: MRT: Create (24.31.234.43/32, 231.25.2.206), RPF Serial1/172.16.14.1, PC0x335E778
2d12h: MRT: Create (*, 229.39.55.47), RPF Null, PC 0x335E67A
2d12h: MRT: Create (24.31.234.43/32, 229.39.55.47), RPF Serial1/172.16.14.1, PC0x335E778
2d12h: MRT: Create (*, 224.243.35.236), RPF Null, PC 0x335E67A
2d12h: MRT: Create (24.31.234.43/32, 224.243.35.236), RPF Serial1/172.16.14.1, PC 0x335E778
2d12h: MRT: Create (*, 232.125.226.56), RPF Null, PC 0x335E67A
2d12h: MRT: Create (24.31.234.43/32, 232.125.226.56), RPF Serial1/172.16.14.1, PC 0x335E778
2d12h: MRT: Create (*, 234.254.143.183)
2d12h: MRT: Create (24.31.234.43/32, 234.254.143.183), RPF Serial1/172.16.14.1,PC 0x3366A02
2d12h: MRT: RPF change 172.16.34.3/Serial0 for (24.31.234.43/32, 234.254.143.183) RP-bit
2d12h: MRT: Create (*, 224.0.1.40), RPF Null, PC 0x33564AE
2d12h: MRT: Update (*, 229.39.55.47), RPF Null, PC 0x33564AE
2d12h: MRT: Update (*, 232.125.226.56), RPF Null, PC 0x33564AE
2d12h: MRT: Update (*, 231.25.2.206), RPF Null, PC 0x33564AE
2d12h: MRT: Update (*, 224.243.35.236), RPF Null, PC 0x33564AE
2d12h: MRT: Update (*, 224.0.1.40), RPF Null, PC 0x33564AE
2d12h: MRT: Update (*, 224.0.1.40), RPF Null, PC 0x33564AE
2d12h: MRT: Create (*, 224.0.1.24), RPF Null, PC 0x3365F74
```

FIGURE 8-48 mtrace

```
Router4#mtrace 24.31.234.43 229.39.55.47
Type escape sequence to abort.
Mtrace from 24.31.234.43 to 172.16.14.4 via group 229.39.55.47
From source (?) to destination (?)
Querying full reverse path...
 0  172.16.14.4
-1  172.16.14.4 PIM   thresh^ 0   3 ms    [24.31.234.0/26]
-2  172.16.14.1 PIM   thresh^ 0   45579 ms [24.31.234.0/26]
-3  24.31.234.43
```

mtrace

mtrace is a very useful command when identifying the path a specific group flows. The syntax of the command is **mtrace** [**source**] [**group**]. Figure 8-48 shows an output of the command.

mstat

mstat is a useful command for gathering information about a specific multicast group coming from a specified source. The syntax of the command is **mstat** [**source**] [**group**]. Figure 8-49 shows an output from the command. The information it provides includes the path to the source, packet information, and gives a visual at each hop in the path.

FIGURE 8-49 mstat

```
Router4#mstat 24.31.234.43 229.39.55.47
Type escape sequence to abort.
Mtrace from 24.31.234.43 to 172.16.14.4 via group 229.39.55.47
From source (?) to destination (?)
Waiting to accumulate statistics......
Results after 10 seconds:

  Source         Response Dest    Packet Statistics For    Only For Traffic
24.31.234.43      172.16.14.4     All Multicast Traffic    From 24.31.234.43
     |          __/  rtt 11   ms  Lost/Sent = Pct  Rate    To 229.39.55.47
     v         /     hop 7    ms  --------------------     --------------------
24.31.234.1
172.16.14.1       ?
     |       ^      ttl   0
     v       |      hop 0    ms   0/350 = 0%      35 pps   0/50 = 0%   5 pps
172.16.14.4       ?
     |       \__    ttl   1
     v          \   hop 3    ms   0              0 pps     50          5 pps
172.16.14.4       172.16.14.4
   Receiver       Query Source
```

Exercise 8-6 will test your knowledge and understanding of the various monitoring and troubleshooting skills for IP Multicast.

EXERCISE 8-6

Monitoring and Troubleshooting IPMC

For this exercise, use the configuration from Exercise 8-4. Add to it a multicast source (Windows NT Server with Windows Media Services is an example) and a multicast receiver (Windows 95, 98, NT, 2000 with Windows Media Player). Refer to Figure 8-50 for a network diagram of the exercise setup.

1. Set up the Network as shown in Figure 8-50.
2. Configure Router1 and Router2 to run PIM Sparse Mode.
3. Configure Router2 as the RP.
4. Make sure that the computer can ping the server.
5. Begin sending out multicast traffic from the server and have the computer request multicast traffic.

FIGURE 8-50

IPMC network setup

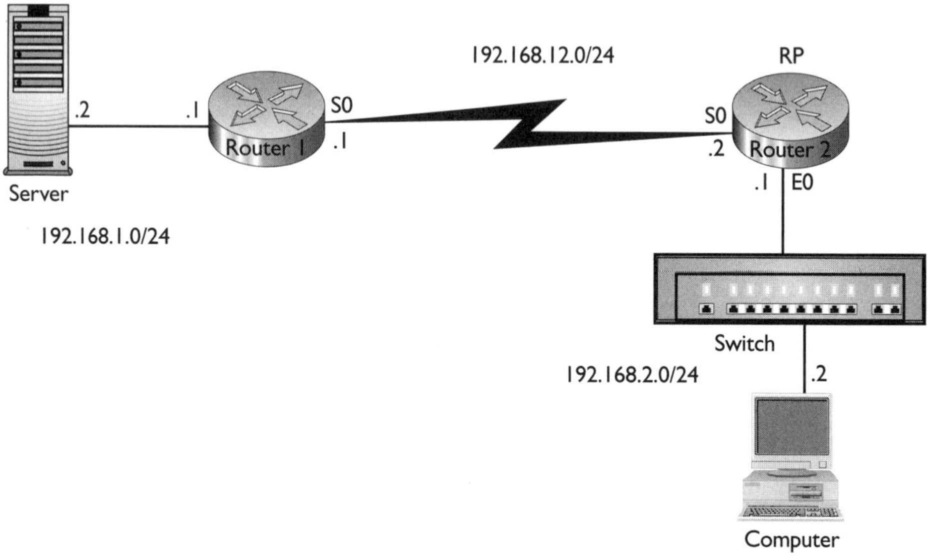

6. Once the multicast traffic is passing to the client, issue the commands necessary to perform the following:

- Identify all multicast sources that are sending more than 4000bps streams. This is done by issuing the command **show ip mroute active**.
- Identify the route that multicast traffic is taking from Router2 back to the Server. The command **mtrace [source] [group]** will give you the path back from Router2 to the source.
- Verify that all interfaces are running IGMPv2, and that Router2 is running CGMP. The command **show ip igmp interface** will identify what version of IGMP is running, as well as if CGMP is on or off.
- Identify all multicast groups on Router2. The command **show ip igmp groups** will list all of the multicast groups that have been subscribed to on Router2.
- Verify that both routers are running PIM Sparse Mode on all active interfaces. The command **show ip pim interface** will give a list of all interfaces that are running PIM and the mode they are in.

All of the monitoring and troubleshooting commands can be very useful tools in maintaining and fixing multicast networks. The best way to learn and better understand how they work is to try them out in a test environment. For more information on Microsoft's Windows Media Services, refer to Microsoft's Web site on Media Services at www.microsoft.com/windows/windowsmedia.

CERTIFICATION SUMMARY

IP Multicast is a protocol suite that allows for the distribution of streaming traffic (video, audio, live content, etc.) to a wide group of users. It operates by using the Class D address space, which is in the range of 224.0.0.0 to 239.255.255.255. All clients wanting to receive the multicast traffic will join a group. When the traffic is sent, all members of the group will receive it.

Various protocols within the suite can be classified as client to router, switch, routing, and others. The client-to-router protocols consist of several versions of Internet Group Management Protocol (IGMP), of which version 2 is the current standard, with version 3 under development. IGMP is a protocol that runs on both clients (MS, MAC, UNIX, etc.) and routers. IGMP is what a client uses to request multicast traffic. The switch protocols operate on both switches and routers. The Cisco Group Management Protocol (CGMP) runs on both Cisco routers and Cisco Layer 2 switches. IGMP Snooping runs only on switches with Layer 3 capabilities. Both CGMP and IGMP Snooping allow switches to dynamically learn about multicast groups and clients. By default, all switches treat multicast traffic as unknown and flood it out all ports; IGMP Snooping and CGMP prevent this. Routing protocols can be broken down to two different types: Dense and Sparse. Dense protocols operate by flooding multicast traffic out all ports and then prune back the interfaces that do not want it. Several of the most common dense protocols are Distance Vector Multicast Routing Protocol (DVMRP), Multicast extensions to OSPF (MOSPF), and Protocol Independent Multicasting (PIM) Dense Mode. All Dense Mode protocols are best suited for either small networks or networks with a very dense distribution of clients (a campus with no low-speed WAN links). Sparse protocols operate by creating a database that contains a list of all multicast sources and groups. When a new client requests a specific multicast group, the router will query the database to locate the source. Protocol Independent Multicasting (PIM) Sparse Mode is the most common Sparse protocol. It uses a Rendezvous Point (RP) as the centralized database. PIM Sparse Mode can switch to the more efficient source tree as soon as the source has been identified.

There are many options in configuring IPMC. There are enough variables to deploy a solution for almost situation. Within some of the protocols, such as IGMP and PIM, various timers can be adjusted to affect the performance of IPMC. In addition to the various timer adjustments that can be made, there are several different options to configure the RP within PIM Sparse Mode. All of these options allow multicast to be a more flexible protocol suite, which in turn will allow it to be more easily deployed on a global scale.

There is a wide range of show and debug commands and direct tools that can be used to monitor and troubleshoot the operation of an IP Multicast enabled network. With these commands and tools, even the most complex problems with IPMC can be identified and overcome.

This chapter introduced you to the protocol suite that makes up IP Multicast. There is a wide range of Data Link, Network, Transport, and Application protocols within the suite that are outside the scope of this book. These other protocols, along with the basic ones covered in this chapter, make IPMC a promising technology for the near future. With the growth of the Internet and the addition of multimedia across it, IPMC is gearing up to be the network that delivers high speed, high bandwidth, and live data all around the world. For additional study on IPMC, go to Cisco's Web site.

TWO-MINUTE DRILL

Here are some of the key points from each certification objective in Chapter 8.

Understanding the Differences between Multicast, Broadcast, and Unicast Addresses

- ❏ A multicast group address is in the range of 224.0.0.0 to 239.255.255.255.
- ❏ Multicast traffic is sent from a source or group of sources to a group of listeners.
- ❏ A broadcast address is the top IP address of a given network range, and is traffic that is directed to all machines in that network.

Translating Multicast to Ethernet Addresses

- ❏ Since no single computer belongs to a multicast group, a formal process for creating a MAC address for each group had to be made.
- ❏ To convert an IP Multicast address to its MAC address, prepend the reserved 01-00-5E protion to the octal representation of the last 23 bits of the IP address.
- ❏ There are 32 IP Multicast addresses that translate to the same MAC address.

Understanding Multicast Protocols

- ❏ IGMP is the protocol responsible for allowing clients to inform routers about what multicast groups they wish to receive.
- ❏ There are currently two versions of IGMP in use today.
- ❏ IGMP Snooping and CGMP are two protocols that allow switches to understand multicast traffic and dynamically add and remove ports to multicast MAC entries instead of flooding the traffic out all ports.
- ❏ Dense Mode routing protocols operate by flooding all multicast traffic out all interfaces and then pruning back interfaces that don't need it.
- ❏ Sparse Mode routing protocols operate by creating a centralized database (RP) containing the information of all multicast sources and groups.

- ❑ Dense Mode routing protocols are most effective in dense distribution of clients, such as a campus environment or a network with very little WAN connections.
- ❑ Sparse Mode routing protocols are most effective in sparsely populated networks including WAN links.

Monitoring and Troubleshooting Commands

- ❑ There are several show and debug commands to aid in monitoring and troubleshooting IP Multicast networks.
- ❑ It is important to understand both the unicast routing and multicast routing for a network.

SELF TEST

The following questions will help you gauge your understanding of the material presented in this chapter. Read all the choices carefully, as there may be more than one correct answer. Choose all correct answers for each question.

Understanding the Differences between Multicast, Broadcast, and Unicast Addresses

1. What class is the IP address 126.254.100.1?
   A. Class A
   B. Class B
   C. Class C
   D. Class D

2. What class is the IP address 233.100.100.1?
   A. Class A
   B. Class B
   C. Class C
   D. Class D

3. What type of IP address is 10.0.2.15 with a subnet mask of 255.255.255.240?
   A. Unicast
   B. Broadcast
   C. Multicast
   D. None of the above

4. You are trying to determine a valid IP address for a new multicast group. You have chosen to use the IP address of 329.100.0.1, and know there are other IP addresses that overlap. Which IP address overlaps with the multicast IP address 329.100.0.1?
   A. 224.100.0.1
   B. 230.0.100.1
   C. 239.228.0.1
   D. None of the above

Translating Multicast to Ethernet Addresses

5. After running multicast for several weeks with no problems, you get a call saying that multicast traffic is not operating properly. After conducting some initial research, you notice that all of the routers are configured correctly, and all of the switches are performing properly. You notice that the multicast groups that are running are 227.10.1.40, 231.138.1.40, and 227.10.1.41. What is the problem?

    A. You don't have enough information to determine the problem.
    B. You can't have two groups in the 227.10.1.x network.
    C. You can't have a multicast group running in the 231.x.x.x network.
    D. The 227.10.1.40 group and the 231.138.1.40 group share the same MAC address.

6. What is the multicast MAC address for the group address of 239.148.15.200?

    A. EF-94-0F-C8
    B. 01-00-5E-EF-94-0F
    C. 01-00-5E-14-0F-C8
    D. 01-00-5E-94-0F-C8

7. How many IP addresses share the same MAC address for the multicast IP address of 223.10.0.5 ?

    A. 31
    B. 32
    C. 16
    D. None of the above

Understanding Multicast Protocols

8. Which version of IGMP introduced report suppression ?

    A. Version 1
    B. Version 2
    C. Version 3
    D. None of the above

9. You are planning a multicast deployment across a Cisco network consisting of 3600 and 2600 routers and 2900 switches. What multicast switching protcol will you use and why?

    A. IGMP Snooping, because only IGMP Snooping supports switches with Layer 2 capabilities.
    B. CGMP, because only CGMP supports switches with Layer 2 capabilities.
    C. IGMP Snooping, because the 2900 switch has Layer 3 capabilities.
    D. Neither, because the 2600 doesn't support CGMP.

10. How many hops is DVMRP limited to?

    A. 15
    B. 16
    C. 31
    D. 32
    E. None of the above

11. You are planning to deploy IPMC on your corporate network consisting of several campuses, encompassing over 20 WAN links. The unicast routing protocol is OSPF. Several of the WAN links are low speed. Not every campus is expected to listen to every multicast group. What is the best multicast routing protcol to use?

    A. DVMRP
    B. MOSPF
    C. PIM Dense Mode
    D. PIM Sparse Mode

12. What is the difference between PIM Sparse Mode and PIM Dense Mode?

    A. PIM Sparse Mode uses any underlying unicast routing protocol, and PIM Dense Mode does not.
    B. PIM Dense Mode uses any underlying unicast routing protocol, and PIM Sparse Mode does not.
    C. PIM Dense Mode supports both types of distribution trees, and PIM Sparse Mode only supports source trees.
    D. PIM Sparse Mode supports both types of distribution trees, and PIM Dense Mode only supports source trees.
    E. There is no difference.

13. What is the command used to adjust how long before a router takes over as the querier?

    A. ip igmp query-max-response

    B. time

    B. ip igmp query-timeout

    C. ip igmp last-member-query-interval

    D. igmp query-interval

14. What is the command to statically join an interface to a specific multicast group?

    A. ip igmp join-group [group]

    B. ip igmp group-join [group]

    C. ip igmp join group [group]

    D. ip igmp group join [group]

15. You have been asked to ensure that the longest amount of time it takes to timeout a group is no more than 0.3 seconds. What command would you use to accomplish this?

    A. You can't have a client timeout faster than 1 second

    B. ip igmp query-max-response-time 100

    C. ip igmp last-member-query-interval 100

    D. ip igmp query-timeout 10

16. You are deploying IPMC across your network and are about to configure it between a Cisco router and Cisco Catylst 5500 switch. How do you find out if you need to run IGMP Snooping or CGMP on the switch?

    A. You don't have to; all switches are clearly marked with Layer 2 or Layer 3 capabilities.

    B. From the switch, type **set igmp enable** and **set cgmp enable** and see what works.

    C. From the router, type **show ip igmp interface**, which gives you the version of IGMP and whether CGMP is turned on.

    D. You can't find out; you must call Cisco to find out.

Monitoring and Troubleshooting Commands

17. What command would you use to identify what multicast groups are active on a router?

    A. show ip igmp groups

B. show ip mroute
C. show ip mroute active
D. All of the above

18. You are in the process of turning IPMC live on your network and are having problems. In certain areas, you have decided to not turn on PIM, because you have redundant links and don't want to clog up your secondary lines with multicast traffic in the event of a primary failure. Some segments are receiving the multicast traffic correctly, and others are not. You have isolated the problem down to one router where the traffic seems to stop. What would you check first, and what command would you use?

    A. Check the PIM neighbors by issuing the command **show ip pim neighbor**.
    B. Perform a reverse trace back to the source to verify the correct path through the network with **mtrace**.
    C. Check the multicast routing table with the command **show ip mroute**.
    D. Check the unicast routing table with the command **show ip route**.

19. What command would you use to identify what interface is forwarding multicast traffic for the group 239.0.1.20?

    A. **show ip igmp interface**
    B. **show ip mroute summary**
    C. **show ip mroute**
    D. Either A or C
    E. A, B, or C

20. The command **show ip mroute active** provides which of the following information? (Select all that apply.)

    A. A list of all multicast groups for the entire network.
    B. A list of all multicast groups through the router.
    C. The IP address of all sources.
    D. The DNS name of all sources.
    E. The data rate in packets per second (pps).
    F. The data rate in thousand bits per second (Kbps).

LAB QUESTION

For the following lab exercise, refer to Figure 8-50 for the setup and addressing. In this exercise, you will configure OSPF, PIM Sparse-Mode and multicast sources. You will need four routers, each with at least two serial lines. Two of the four must also have Ethernet ports. The multicast source can be any available multicast source, such as Microsoft Windows NT Server with Windows Media Services. For the client, any Microsoft computer with an Ethernet adapter and Windows Media Player will work. Once all of the equipment is physically set up and the correct version of software is loaded, you can begin the lab.

Working from Figure 8-51, perform the following steps:

1. Configure Routers 1, 2, 3, and 4 with the IP addresses and names given in the diagram.

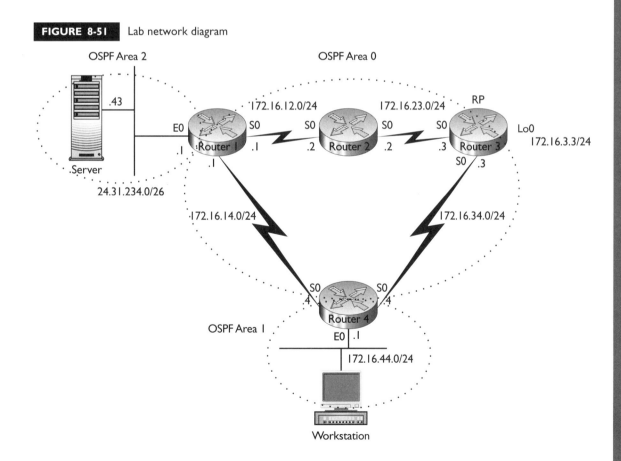

FIGURE 8-51 Lab network diagram

Configure OSPF for all four routers. Make the serial interfaces on all four routers area 0, the Ethernet on Router1 area 2, and the Ethernet on Router4 area 0.

2. Configure PIM Sparse Mode on all routers.
3. Configure Router4 to statically join the group 239.0.0.1.
4. Configure a loopback interface on Router 3, and make that interface the RP.
5. Verify that the workstation can ping the server.
6. Begin multicasting out traffic from the server.
7. Begin receiving multicast traffic on the workstation.

   Verify that the multicast traffic is flowing down the correct path. Use various show and debug commands during this process. The outputs from the *Monitoring and Troubleshooting Commands* section have been taken from this same lab setup and can be referenced if needed.

8. Verify that the group 239.0.0.1 has been joined and can be seen by Router1.

SELF TEST ANSWERS

Understanding the Differences between Multicast, Broadcast, and Unicast Addresses

1. ☑ **A.** All Class A addresses fall in the range of 0.0.0.0 up to 127.255.255.255.
   ☒ **B, C,** and **D** are incorrect because an IP address can't be in more than one class.

2. ☑ **D.** Multicast addresses are Class D addresses and fall in the range of 224.0.0.0 to 239.255.255.255.
   ☒ **A, B,** and **C** are all incorrect because the IP address is in the Class D range and can't be in more than one range.

3. ☑ **B.** For a 255.255.255.240 subnet mask, the broadcast address is every 16 IP addresses. Starting at 10.0.2.0 and counting up 16 address is 10.0.2.15, a broadcast address.
   ☒ **A** is incorrect because the IP address 10.0.2.15 255.255.255.240 is a broadcast address. **C** is incorrect because the IP address 10.0.2.15 is not in the Class D address range of 224.0.0.0 to 239.255.255.255.

4. ☑ **D.** The address 329.100.0.1 is invalid. The highest address for a multicast IP is 239.255.255.255. If you thought that this was a typo and the IP should have been 239.100.0.1, your answer would have been **A** and **C**. However, this was not a typo; it was a trick question to make sure you know the range of IP addresses.
   ☒ **A, B,** and **C** are all incorrect because the address 329.100.0.1 is not a valid IP address and therefore can have no overlaps.

Translating Multicast to Ethernet Addresses

5. ☑ **D.** Convert both groups to their MAC address and you will see that they are the same. When there are two multicast groups running at the same MAC address, switches will confuse them and can send both groups together, giving you garbage.
   ☒ **B** is incorrect because you can have multiple multicast groups in the same network. **C** is incorrect because the multicast group range is between 224 and 239. **A** is incorrect because there is enough information to determine the problem.

6. ☑ **C.** Refer to Exercise 8-3 for details on how to calculate the MAC address.
   ☒ **A** is incorrect because all IPMC MAC addresses begin with 01-00-5e. **B** is incorrect because the wrong octets were translated. **D** is incorrect because the 9th bit of the IP address was used in the calculation and should have been ignored, or set to 0.

7. ☑ **D.** 223.10.0.5 is not a multicast address.
   ☒ **A, B,** and **C** are incorrect because the valid range for multicast addresses is from 224.0.0.0 to 239.255.255.255.

Understanding Multicast Protocols

8. ☑ **A.** Version 1 of IGMP introduced report suppression. Report suppression is a mechanism that allows only one host per broadcast domain to respond to an IGMP query.
   ☒ **B** and **C** are incorrect because IGMP version 1 introduced report suppression. **D** is incorrect because there is a correct choice.

9. ☑ **B.** the 2900 switch only supports Layer 2. CGMP is the Cisco proprietary switching protocol that runs on Layer 2 switches. All Cisco access routers that support IPMC support CGMP.
   ☒ **A** is incorrect because IGMP Snooping is only supported on Layer 3 switches. **C** is incorrect because the 2900 does not support Layer 3. **D** is incorrect because the 2600 is a router, which does support CGMP.

10. ☑ **C.** DVMRP operates on hop count and has the limitation of 31 hops. This is the biggest reason why MBONE is phasing out DVMRP.
    ☒ **A, B,** and **D** are incorrect because the maximum number of hops that DVMRP supports is 31. **E** is incorrect because there is a correct choice.

11. ☑ **D.** PIM Sparse Mode is the best multicast routing protocol to use in a large WAN environment where the listeners are sparsely distributed.
    ☑ **A, B,** and **C** are incorrect because they are all Dense Mode protocols, which are best suited for dense distribution of multicast receivers with little or no WAN links.

12. ☑ **D.** PIM Sparse Mode can operate over both shared trees and source trees. It uses shared trees to first identify multicast groups and sources. As soon as the router knows where the source is, it switches to the more optimal source tree.
    ☒ **A** and **B** are both incorrect because both PIM Sparse Mode and PIM Dense Mode support any underlying unicast routing protocol. **C** is incorrect because PIM Dense Mode only supports source trees. It operates by flooding all multicast traffic everywhere in the network to identify new groups and sources. **E** is incorrect because there is a difference.

13. ☑ **B.** The command **ip igmp query-timeout** [seconds] specifies the timeout for the router to take over as the querier for the interface, after the previous querier has stopped querying. The default value is 2 * query-interval. If the router hears no queries for the "timeout" period, it becomes the querier.

☒ **A** is incorrect because the command **ip igmp query-max-response-time** would set the length of time that a client has to respond to a membership query (not a leave group query). **C** is incorrect because the command **ip igmp last-member-query-interval** would set the amount of time that a client has to respond to a membership query triggered by a leave-group message. **D** is incorrect because the command **ip igmp query-interval** configures the frequency that the router sends IGMP membership reports.

14. ☑ **A.** The proper syntax is **ip igmp join-group** [group].
    ☒ **B**, **C**, and **D** are invalid commands.

15. ☑ **C.** The command **ip igmp last-member-query-interval** [interval] is a timer that informs the clients how long they have to send leave messages, and is a value in milliseconds. The default value is 1000, which would take approximately 3 seconds to timeout a group. With a value of 100, it would take approximately 0.3 seconds to timeout a group.
    ☒ **A** is incorrect because you can have a client timeout as short as .3 seconds. **B** is incorrect because the command **ip igmp query-max-response-time 100** would set the length of time that a client has to respond to a membership query (not a leave group query). **D** is incorrect because the command **ip igmp query-timeout 10** configures the amount of time a nonquerier router takes over on a segment with more than one router.

16. ☑ **B.** If you have certain models of switches, you should already know. The 5500 with the NetFlow Feature Card (NFFC) has Layer 3 capabilities. Because of this, the code for the 5500 can run either, and the easiest way (with multicast commands) is to try both and see which one works.
    ☒ **A** is incorrect because the 5500 switch may or may not have Layer 3 capabilities (NFFC). The switch will not automatically run IGMP Snooping. **C** is incorrect, because the router will not know what type of switch it is connected to. **D** is incorrect, because you can determine it on your own and don't have to call Cisco.

Monitoring and Troubleshooting Commands

17. ☑ **D.** All of the above commands will show what multicast groups are running on a router.
    ☒ There are no incorrect choices.

18. ☑ **D.** The first thing to remember when troubleshooting IPMC is to verify that your unicast traffic is flowing the way you expect it to. If you have multiple paths to a network and haven't turned PIM on all links, the unicast table might be going over the link that doesn't have PIM on it. Even if the traffic flows down the alternate path, when the router on the other end

receives any multicast traffic, it will perform an RPF check against the unicast routing table and drop all packets.

☒ A, B, and C are incorrect because if you are not receiving any multicast traffic, you will not be able to see any PIM neighbors, multicast routes, or perform multicast traces back to the source.

19. **C.** The only command that will show all of the interfaces on the outgoing interface list (OIL) is **show ip mroute**.

☒ A, B, D, and E are incorrect. The other commands will show the multicast groups, but not the outgoing interfaces.

20. ☑ B, C, D, E, F. All of the answers except A are correct.

☒ A is incorrect, because every router doesn't necessarily know about all of the active multicast groups for the network, only if it happens to be subscribing to all of them.

LAB ANSWER

The following output is the verification that Router1 can see the group 239.0.0.1 (Figures 8-52, 8-53, 8-54, 8-55, and 8-56).

The following figures are outputs for the four router configurations.

FIGURE 8-52

Ping multicast group 239.0.0.1

```
Router1#ping 239.0.0.1

Type escape sequence to abort.
Sending 1, 100-byte ICMP Echos to 239.0.0.1, timeout is 2 seconds:

Reply to request 0 from 172.16.14.4, 12 ms
Reply to request 0 from 172.16.34.4, 48 ms
Reply to request 0 from 172.16.34.4, 36 ms
```

FIGURE 8-53

Router1 configuration

```
hostname Router1
!
ip multicast-routing
ip dvmrp route-limit 20000
!
interface Loopback1
 ip address 1.1.1.1 255.255.255.255
!
interface Ethernet0
 ip address 24.31.234.1 255.255.255.192
 ip pim sparse-mode
!
interface Serial0
 ip address 172.16.12.1 255.255.255.0
 ip pim sparse-mode
!
interface Serial1
 ip address 172.16.14.1 255.255.255.0
 ip pim sparse-mode
!
router ospf 7273
 network 24.31.234.0 0.0.0.255 area 2
 network 172.16.12.0 0.0.0.255 area 0
 network 172.16.14.0 0.0.0.255 area 0
!
ip pim rp-address 172.16.3.3
```

FIGURE 8-54

Router2 configuration

```
hostname Router2
!
ip multicast-routing
ip dvmrp route-limit 20000
!
interface Serial0
 ip address 172.16.12.2 255.255.255.0
 ip pim sparse-mode
!
interface Serial1
 ip address 172.16.23.2 255.255.255.0
 ip pim sparse-mode
!
router ospf 7273
 network 172.16.12.0 0.0.0.255 area 0
 network 172.16.23.0 0.0.0.255 area 0
!
ip pim rp-address 172.16.3.3
```

FIGURE 8-55

Router3 configuration

```
hostname Router3
!
ip multicast-routing
ip dvmrp route-limit 20000
!
interface Loopback0
 ip address 172.16.3.3 255.255.255.255
!
interface Serial0
 ip address 172.16.23.3 255.255.255.0
 ip pim sparse-mode
!
interface Serial1
 ip address 172.16.34.3 255.255.255.0
 ip pim sparse-mode
!
router ospf 7273
 network 172.16.3.3 0.0.0.0 area 0
 network 172.16.23.0 0.0.0.255 area 0
 network 172.16.34.0 0.0.0.255 area 0
```

FIGURE 8-56

Router4 configuration

```
hostname Router4
!
ip multicast-routing
ip dvmrp route-limit 20000
!
interface Ethernet0
 ip address 172.16.44.1 255.255.255.0
 ip pim sparse-mode
 ip igmp join-group 239.0.0.1
!
interface Serial0
 ip address 172.16.34.4 255.255.255.0
 ip pim sparse-mode
!
interface Serial1
 ip address 172.16.14.4 255.255.255.0
 ip pim sparse-mode
!
router ospf 7273
 network 172.16.14.0 0.0.0.255 area 0
 network 172.16.34.0 0.0.0.255 area 0
 network 172.16.44.0 0.0.0.255 area 1
!
ip pim rp-address 172.16.3.3
```

9
Switch Diagnostics and Remote Management

CERTIFICATION OBJECTIVES

9.01   SNMP Support

9.02   Remote Monitoring (RMON)

9.03   Switch Port Analyzer (SPAN)

✓   Two-Minute Drill

Q&A   Self Test

In a cost comparison, ongoing support almost always exceeds the original cost of both the equipment and the initial installation. This chapter deals with the management tools that Cisco includes with both its IOS command-based and set command-based switches. These tools allow both proactive and reactive monitoring of devices and events.

SNMP (Simple Network Management Protocol) is an industry-standard method of monitoring and modifying devices on a network. Based on the rights given, a user can be allowed to only monitor a device (read-only rights), or both monitor and make changes (read-write rights). This lets a network manager give the task of monitoring the network to the help desk, without worrying about them making detrimental changes. SNMP also allows proactive management by using *traps*. These traps are messages sent from the network device to a preconfigured workstation or server, often running network management software such as Cisco's CiscoWorks, IBM's NetView, or HP's OpenView. These messages are sent only when a certain preconfigured event occurs, such as an exceeded threshold error. RMON (Remote Monitoring) is a newer protocol that gives more in-depth data about a device, such as errors over time on a historical basis. Because of RMON's detail and overhead, Cisco has built RMON into hardware rather than using CPU cycles to compile the data. Together, SNMP and RMON can provide the network manager with the data necessary to proactively watch for problems and quickly pinpoint the source when a problem eventually happens.

SPAN (Switched Port ANalyzer) is a tool that allows an Ethernet switch to behave more like a standard hub/concentrator on the monitored port (not all ports without SPAN configured). In a hub/concentrator, all ports on the collision domain see all packets from that domain. An Ethernet switch (Cisco or otherwise) limits the collision domain to just two ports for unicast traffic—the source port and the destination port. While this is great for saving/increasing bandwidth, it prevents a protocol analyzer such as Network Associates' Sniffer from doing its job, which is to look at every packet on a network segment to find problems at Layers 2 through 7 of the OSI model. A protocol analyzer plugged in to a standard switch port would only see unicasts destined for that workstation, sent by that workstation, and broadcasts and multicasts sent from any workstation. Intrusion Detection packages also rely on watching all traffic on a segment to identify and stop hackers from doing damage. SPAN lets a switch duplicate packets from one or more ports to another port designated for management. A protocol analyzer attached to this port can then monitor traffic from the SPANed ports.

CERTIFICATION OBJECTIVE 9.01

SNMP Support

SNMP is unique in that it is easy to set up initially, and with some fine-tuning, you can have it report exactly what events you want, and ignore others that you feel aren't important. To allow interoperability between vendors, the concept of MIB (Management Information Base) came about. A MIB is a database of possible error conditions and statistics for a certain device. Multiple layers of security allow only certain individuals to make changes to devices, but allow others to obtain information from the device. User/password combinations called *community strings* are what separate the various levels of rights. The three community strings Cisco uses are Read-only, Read-Write, and Read-Write-all. The three most important parts of SNMP are *gets*, *sets*, and *traps*.

GET

Gets are used to obtain information from the network device. Typically, gets only need read-only rights. A user attempting to get information from a device needs to have the correct read-only community string for that device. Cisco and other manufacturers have chosen "public" as the default read-only community string. First, let's start with a set-based switch. For each function, the syntax is given for both switch types. If you have a switch accessible, please follow along on your own switch and use this chapter as an exercise. We're going to want to use the "set snmp" command. Do a "set snmp ?" now:

```
Engineering-2948> (enable) set snmp ?
Set snmp commands:
-----------------------------------------------------------------------
set snmp access             Set SNMP access group
set snmp community          Set SNMP community string
set snmp group              Set SNMP group
set snmp notify             Set SNMP notify
set snmp rmon               Set SNMP RMON
set snmp targetaddr         Set SNMP targetaddr
set snmp targetparams       Set SNMP targetparams
set snmp trap               Set SNMP trap information
```

```
set snmp user             Set SNMP user
set snmp view             Set SNMP view
```

From this point, we see that there is a command that starts with "set snmp community". Now do a "set snmp community ?" on the switch:

```
Engineering-2948> (enable) set snmp community ?
  read-only              Read-only access
  read-write             Read-write access
  read-write-all         Read-write-all access
```

Right now, we're only interested in the read-only community string. Do a "set snmp community read-only ?" now. You get:

```
Engineering-2948> (enable) set snmp community read-only ?
  <string>               Community_string
  <cr>
```

Pick a community string that you want to use. Let's use the string "public-ro". We now enter "set snmp community read-only public-ro ?" We get:

```
Engineering-2938> (enable) set snmp community read-only public-ro ?
  <string>               Community_string
  <cr>
```

Finally, we get to press ENTER. Press ENTER now:

```
Engineering-2948> (enable) set snmp community read-only public-ro
SNMP read-only community string set to 'public-ro'.
```

The switch comes back and tells you that it changed the read-only string to "public-ro". Now let's do a "sh snmp" to verify what we've changed:

```
Engineering-2948> (enable) sh snmp
RMON:                    Enabled
Traps Enabled:
Port,Module,Chassis,Bridge,Repeater,Vtp,Auth,ippermit,Vmps,
config,entity,stpx,syslog
Port Traps Enabled: 2/1-50

Community-Access         Community-String
----------------         ------------------
read-only                public-ro
```

```
read-write              private
read-write-all          secret

Trap-Rec-Address                              Trap-Rec-Community
----------------------------------------      --------------------
```

As you can see, now our read-only community string is "public-ro", as we intended. Now we'll try the same operation on an IOS command-based switch; in this case, a 3524XL. First, we need to get into global configuration mode, where most commands are entered that aren't specific to a particular port, interface, or line. From global configuration mode, the SNMP commands are under the "snmp-server" category. This can be abbreviated as "snmp". Do a "snmp ?" now:

```
3500-XL(config)#snmp ?
  chassis-id        String to uniquely identify this chassis
  community         Enable SNMP; set community string and access privs
  contact           Text for mib object sysContact
  enable            Enable SNMP Traps or Informs
  engineID          Configure a local or remote SNMPv3 engineID
  group             Define a User Security Model group
  host              Specify hosts to receive SNMP notifications
  location          Text for mib object sysLocation
  packetsize        Largest SNMP packet size
  queue-length      Message queue length for each TRAP host
  system-shutdown   Enable use of the SNMP reload command
  tftp-server-list  Limit TFTP servers used via SNMP
  trap-source       Assign an interface for the source address of all traps
  trap-timeout      Set timeout for TRAP message retransmissions
  user              Define a user who can access the SNMP engine
  view              Define an SNMPv2 MIB view
```

"Community" is what we're looking for. Now, enter "snmp community ?":

```
3500-XL(config)#snmp community ?
  WORD  SNMP community string
```

At this point, it's asking what community string we want to use. We'll use the same string we used on the set command-based switch—"public-ro". Enter "snmp community public-ro ?", and press ENTER:

```
3500-XL(config)#snmp community public-ro ?
  <1-99>       Std IP accesslist allowing access with this community string
  <1300-1999>  Expanded IP accesslist allowing access with this community
               string
```

```
ro            Read-only access with this community string
rw            Read-write access with this community string
view          Restrict this community to a named MIB view
<cr>
```

Now we're presented with the two levels of SNMP access, read-only and read-write. We want to associate read-only rights with our new "public-ro" community string, so we'll use the *ro* keyword. Now finish this command with a "?" to see if there are any other options to use: 3500-XL(config)#snmp community public-ro ro ?

```
<1-99>        Std IP accesslist allowing access with this community string
<1300-1999>   Expanded IP accesslist allowing access with this community
              string
<cr>
```

We're not interested in any access-lists, so press ENTER:

```
3500-XL(config)#snmp community public-ro ro
```

Note that the IOS command-based switches don't come back and tell you they changed anything. Essentially, what we just did was allow management workstations to view (but not change) the parameters and statistics of this switch, provided they are using the "public-ro" community string. Exit global config mode by typing **end**, **exit**, or pressing CTRL-Z. Now do a "show snmp group" or "sh snmp group" to see the results:

```
3500-XL#sh snmp group
groupname: public-ro                    security model:v1
readview :v1default                     writeview: <no writeview specified>
notifyview: <no notifyview specified>
row status: active

groupname: public-ro                    security model:v2c
readview :v1default                     writeview: <no writeview specified>
notifyview: <no notifyview specified>
row status: active
```

The groupname 'pubic-ro' is what we were looking for.

Note that the preceding examples use the community string "public-ro". If you use "public", keep in mind that this is a default, so using it in your own configurations may cause it to not show up when doing a "show run" (IOS based) or "show config" (set based) on your switch. For security purposes, it's a good idea to change all community strings to something other than the default.

> **exam**
> **ⓦatch**
>
> *Pay close attention to the task you are asked to perform, and what config mode is listed in the possible answers. For instance, if you're asked to set an IP address on an interface, you know the only way to do this is from interface configuration mode. Eliminate any answers that don't show (config-int) as part of the prompt, and you'll probably narrow it down to one or two possibilities.*

Most manufacturers use several standard SNMP parameters that define some physical information about a device: system name, location, and contact. Now we will attempt to enter these in the configuration of an IOS-based switch. Enter global configuration mode by typing "configure terminal" (or "conf t" for short) from privileged exec (enable) mode. Enter "snmp ?" and press ENTER:

```
3500-XL(config)#snmp ?
  chassis-id         String to uniquely identify this chassis
  community          Enable SNMP; set community string and access privs
  contact            Text for mib object sysContact
  enable             Enable SNMP Traps or Informs
  engineID           Configure a local or remote SNMPv3 engineID
  group              Define a User Security Model group
  host               Specify hosts to receive SNMP notifications
  location           Text for mib object sysLocation
  packetsize         Largest SNMP packet size
  queue-length       Message queue length for each TRAP host
  system-shutdown    Enable use of the SNMP reload command
  tftp-server-list   Limit TFTP servers used via SNMP
  trap-source        Assign an interface for the source address of all traps
  trap-timeout       Set timeout for TRAP message retransmissions
  user               Define a user who can access the SNMP engine
  view               Define an SNMPv2 MIB view
```

From this output, we see the three things we're looking for—chassis-id, contact, and location. These fields contain text that is useful for the network administrator to use, so any text is OK.

```
3500-XL(config)#snmp contact ?
  LINE   identification of the contact person for this managed node

3500-XL(config)#snmp contact John Doe, 555-1234 x567
```

This entered the contact information. Now let's do the chassis-id and location:

```
3500-XL(config)#snmp chassis-id ?
  LINE   Unique ID string

3500-XL(config)#snmp chassis-id Cisco 3524 XL switch
3500-XL(config)#snmp location ?
  LINE   The physical location of this node

3500-XL(config)#snmp location 1st floor wiring closet
```

Now a management workstation querying this device can learn this information from the switch, assuming that the workstation is using the correct read-only community string. Now we'll do the same with a set-based switch; in this case, a 2948G. Set-based switches hide the SNMP information under the "system" category. From enable mode, type "set system ?" and press ENTER. The output should look similar to this:

```
Engineering-2948> (enable) set system ?
  baud                  Set system console port baud rate
  contact               Set system contact
  countrycode           Set system country code
  location              Set system location
  modem                 Set system modem control (enable/disable)
  name                  Set system name
```

From this output, we find the three parameters we're looking for: contact, location, and name. Using this information, the correct commands to enter the required SNMP information on this switch are:

```
Engineering-2938> (enable) set system contact ?
  <string>              Contact string (256 characters max)
  <cr>
Engineering-2938> (enable) set system contact John Doe, 555-1234 x567
System contact set.
Engineering-2938> (enable) set system location ?
  <string>              Location string (256 characters max)
  <cr>
Engineering-2938> (enable) set system location 1st floor wiring closet
System location set.
Engineering-2938> (enable) set system name ?
  <name_string>         Name for the system
  <cr>
```

Keep in mind that with the set command-based switches, the snmp system name is actually the name of the switch. When you set the name, the switch's prompt will change to the new name.

```
Engineering-2938> (enable) set system name Cisco 2948 switch
System name set.
```

Now let's verify that what we entered is correct. Do a "sh system":

```
Cisco 2948 switch> (enable) sh system
PS1-Status  PS2-Status
----------  ----------
ok          none
Fan-Status  Temp-Alarm  Sys-Status  Uptime d,h:m:s  Logout
----------  ----------  ----------  --------------  --------
ok          off         ok          5,04:33:51      60 min
PS1-Type       PS2-Type
------------   ------------
other          none
Modem    Baud   Traffic  Peak  Peak-Time
-------  -----  -------  ----  ------------------------
disable  9600   0%       0%    Mon Jul 17 2000, 19:20:00
System Name             System Location          System Contact           CC
----------------------  -----------------------  -----------------------  ---
Cisco 2948 switch       1st floor wiring closet  John Doe, 555-1234 x567  US
```

Everything is just as we expected.

Set

SNMP sets are used to make changes to a network device, such as shutting down a port or interface. Since sets involve making changes, we don't want just anyone using sets on this device. Luckily, sets require read-write access, which involves a new community string. Read-write community strings (think of "community string" as a username and password combined into one) should only be given to those network managers who should be making changes to the device. This community string should always be different from the read-only community string for obvious security reasons. Cisco has chosen "Private" as the Read-write community string as a default. Since we now need set or read-write privileges, let's add the read-write community string to the two different switch types. The setting of the read-write community string is virtually the same as the read-only. Substitute "read-write" for "read-only" on the set command-based switches, and "rw" for "ro" for IOS command-based switches:

```
3500-XL(config)#snmp com private rw ?
  <1-99>       Std IP accesslist allowing access with this community string
  <1300-1999>  Expanded IP accesslist allowing access with this community
               string
  <cr>
3500-XL(config)#snmp com private rw
```

And for the set command-based switch:

```
Cisco 2948 switch> (enable) set snmp community read-write ?
  <string>              Community_string
  <cr>
Cisco 2948 switch> (enable) set snmp community read-write private
SNMP read-write community string set to 'private'.
```

Note that Cisco recently added a new community to its set command-based switches. Read-write-all allows all the gets and sets that read-write did, but also adds the capability of changing the community strings themselves.

Traps

Traps are the most useful of the SNMP messages. Where sets and gets are initiated by the network admin from a workstation, traps are initiated by the network device. This is an immediate message sent when a certain condition or threshold is met, such as an interface going down or a fan failure. These messages are sent only once, and no method of delivery confirmation is used. The unreliable protocol UDP is used because of its low overhead. SNMP messages are separate entities, as opposed to one message relying on the receipt of a previous or future message. That is why the successful transmission of traps does not need to be guaranteed. Using TCP would create unnecessary overhead for both the management workstation and the network device. Since only certain workstations are able to handle these trap messages, it wouldn't make sense to send the traps as a broadcast. Traps are sent only to preconfigured workstations, and the IP addresses of those particular workstations are entered individually into the configuration of the switch. These are called *trap targets* or *destinations*. These trap targets need to be running software designed to handle and act upon these messages. Packages such as Cisco's CiscoWorks, IBM's NetView, and HP's OpenView accept these messages and

FROM THE CLASSROOM

Building a Fault-Tolerant SNMP Management Strategy

While building your network to facilitate SNMP management, keep in mind what might happen if a particular device fails. By using some fault-tolerant features of the switches and routers, you can be sure that you receive all or most of the SNMP traps being sent.

- **HSRP** The Hot Standby Routing Protocol allows you to have two routers on a segment that share a virtual IP address, which is what the workstations and servers are configured for. They operate in an Active/Standby mode, so if the Active router dies, the Standby will take over. Using HSRP will therefore guarantee more IP accessibility to your switches, which is key for SNMP management.

- **Management Addresses and VLANs** On routers, it's a good idea to use loopback addresses for management, which makes the router reachable if an interface dies, but a redundant path exists. The same philosophy can be applied to switches. Interface VLAN 1 on IOS command-based switches and SC0 on set command-based switches are used for management. These by default exist on VLAN 1 of the switch. Make sure you have redundant VLAN 1 paths from the switch to other switches and routers. This will maximize uptime in the event of a single failure.

—Chuck Church, CCNP, MCNE, MCSE

categorize them. Based on the severity, the software can then act upon the message by notifying the network admin via e-mail, pager, etc. Let's add a trap target to a set-based switch now:

```
Engineering-2948> (enable) set snmp ?
  access                      Set SNMP access group
  community                   Set SNMP community string
  group                       Set SNMP group
  notify                      Set SNMP notify
  rmon                        Set SNMP RMON
  targetaddr                  Set SNMP targetaddr
```

```
targetparams            Set SNMP targetparams
trap                    Set SNMP trap information
user                    Set SNMP user
view                    Set SNMP view
```

Trap is the category we're looking for. Let's look at the trap subcommand:

```
Cisco 2948 switch> (enable) set snmp trap ?
  disable                   Disable SNMP trap
  enable                    Enable SNMP trap
  <host>                    IP address or hostname
Cisco 2948 switch> (enable) set snmp trap 192.168.1.2 ?
  <string>                  Receiver community string
Cisco 2948 switch> (enable) set snmp trap 192.168.1.2 private ?
  <cr>
Cisco 2948 switch> (enable) set snmp trap 192.168.1.2 private
SNMP trap receiver added.
```

You can set up to ten trap receivers.

exam ⓦatch

Sometimes Cisco tends to focus on small details on their exams and skip whole sections of other subjects. The maximum of 10 trap receivers may seem like a minute detail, but is a possible exam question. Also look for questions with multiple correct answers. Cisco also likes to trick testers into picking the first answer that looks right—this is a sure way to miss questions. Cisco states in their exam descriptions that you should pick the MOST correct answer, not just one that is correct. One answer may be more exact than the others, and that is what Cisco would want. Here's an example:
Which command will show the routes obtained from the OSPF routing protocol?

1. SH IP ROUTE
2. SH IP ROUTE ALL
3. SH IP ROUTE OSPF
4. SH ROUTE OSPF

If you've taken the BSCN course or exam, you probably know the answers. That's right, there are two possible solutions. Both 1 and 3 are correct, but number 3 will show only routes obtained from the OSPF process, while 1 will show you all routes, including the OSPF routes. However, since Cisco wants the more precise answer, number 3 would be the most correct.

It's also necessary to enable traps on the set-based switches. They are disabled by default:

```
Cisco 2948 switch> (enable) set snmp trap enable ?
  all                   All SNMP traps
  auth                  Authentication traps
  bridge                Bridge traps
  chassis               Chassis traps
  config                Configuration traps
  entity                Entity traps
  ippermit              IP permit traps
  module                Module traps
  repeater              Repeater traps
  stpx                  Spanning tree extension traps
  syslog                Syslog notification traps
  vmps                  Vlan Membership Policy Server traps
  vtp                   Vlan Trunk Protocol traps
  <cr>
```

Pressing ENTER will enable all traps. If you want only specific traps, you need to enter a category. The keyword is the category of traps that you want sent. The valid categories are All, Module, Chassis, Bridge, Repeater, Auth, Vtp, Ippermit, Vmps, Config, Entity, Stpx, and Syslog. The following is a brief description from Cisco of the various categories:

- **All**   Keyword that specifies all trap types. This includes all the below categories.
- **Module**   Keyword that specifies the moduleUp and moduleDown traps from the CISCO-STACK-MIB. This refers to the status of a particular module or card in the switch.
- **Chassis**   Keyword that specifies the ciscoSyslogMIB trap from the CISCO-SYSLOG-MIB. Chassis refers to the non-network devices in a switch; typically, the fans and power supplies
- **Bridge**   Keyword that specifies the newRoot and topologyChange traps from RFC 1493 (the BRIDGE-MIB). These bridge traps refer to changes caused by the Spanning Tree Protocol, which functions to eliminate Layer 2 loops while allowing redundancy.
- **Repeater**   Keyword that specifies the rptrHealth, rptrGroupChange, and rptrResetEvent traps from RFC 1516 (the SNMP-REPEATER-MIB). This

refers to the basic Ethernet repeater function of the switch. Collisions are tracked here.

- **Auth**   Keyword that specifies the authenticationFailure trap from RFC 1157. Auth traps are sent to alert the network manager of failed logons to the network device though telnet or other means.
- **Vtp**   Keyword that specifies the VTP from the CISCO-VTP-MIB. These traps are sent on changes to the VLAN domain due to the VTP protocol.
- **Ippermit**   Keyword that specifies the IP Permit Denied access from the CISCO-STACK-MIB. This refers to which addresses are allowed access to the management address for security purposes.
- **Vmps**   Keyword that specifies the vmVmpsChange trap from the CISCO-VLAN-MEMBERSHIP-MIB. Changes in VMPS will signal these traps.
- **Config**   Keyword that specifies the sysConfigChange trap from the CISCO-STACK-MIB. This is a trap to notify of changes to the configuration.
- **Entity**   Keyword that specifies the entityMIB trap from the ENTITY-MIB.
- **Stpx**   Keyword that specifies the STPX trap.
- **Syslog**   Keyword that specifies the system log. These traps refer to console messages that are sent to a syslog server, which is a collection point.

For our example, let's enable all traps:

```
Cisco 2948 switch> (enable) set snmp trap enable
All SNMP traps enabled.
```

Now let's check our work. Enter "sh snmp" on the switch:

```
Cisco 2948 switch> (enable) sh snmp
RMON:                     Enabled
Traps Enabled:
Port,Module,Chassis,Bridge,Repeater,Vtp,Auth,ippermit,Vmps,config,entity,stpx,
syslog
Port Traps Enabled: 2/1-50
Community-Access        Community-String
----------------        --------------------
read-only               public-ro
read-write              private
```

```
read-write-all       secret
Trap-Rec-Address                              Trap-Rec-Community
----------------------------------------      -------------------
192.168.1.2                                   private
```

As you can see, we now have all the traps enabled and are now sending traps to the IP host 192.168.1.2. Now we'll do the same on an IOS-based switch:

```
3524-XL(config)#snmp ?
  chassis-id        String to uniquely identify this chassis
  community         Enable SNMP; set community string and access privs
  contact           Text for mib object sysContact
  enable            Enable SNMP Traps or Informs
  engineID          Configure a local or remote SNMPv3 engineID
  group             Define a User Security Model group
  host              Specify hosts to receive SNMP notifications
  location          Text for mib object sysLocation
  packetsize        Largest SNMP packet size
  queue-length      Message queue length for each TRAP host
  system-shutdown   Enable use of the SNMP reload command
  tftp-server-list  Limit TFTP servers used via SNMP
  trap-source       Assign an interface for the source address of all traps
  trap-timeout      Set timeout for TRAP message retransmissions
  user              Define a user who can access the SNMP engine
  view              Define an SNMPv2 MIB view
```

"Host" is the category we want. Now enter "snmp host ?":

```
3524-XL(config)#snmp host ?
  Hostname or A.B.C.D  IP address of SNMP notification host
```

We want traps sent to the same host as before, so use 192.168.1.2:

```
3524-XL(config)#snmp host 192.168.1.2 ?
  WORD     SNMPv1/v2c community string or SNMPv3 user name
  informs  Send Inform messages to this host
  traps    Send Trap messages to this host
  version  SNMP version to use for notification messages
```

There are options for specifying SNMP version, and whether you want just traps or informs, but for now we'll just set the "public" community string:

```
3524-XL(config)#snmp host 192.168.1.2 public ?
  c2900      Allow SNMP C2900 Traps
  cluster    Allow Cluster Member Status traps
```

```
config              Allow SNMP config traps
entity              Allow SNMP entity traps
snmp                Allow SNMP-type notifications
tty                 Allow TCP connection traps
udp-port            The notification host's UDP port number
vlan-membership     Allow VLAN Membership traps
vtp                 Allow SNMP VTP traps
<cr>
```

We want all traps sent to this host, so just press ENTER:

```
3524-XL(config)#snmp host 192.168.1.2 public
```

Now we'll verify all of this with a "sh snmp":

```
3524-XL#sh snmp
Chassis: Cisco 3524 XL switch
Contact: John Doe, 555-1234 x567
Location: 1st floor wiring closet
0 SNMP packets input
    0 Bad SNMP version errors
    0 Unknown community name
    0 Illegal operation for community name supplied
    0 Encoding errors
    0 Number of requested variables
    0 Number of altered variables
    0 Get-request PDUs
    0 Get-next PDUs
    0 Set-request PDUs
0 SNMP packets output
    0 Too big errors (Maximum packet size 1500)
    0 No such name errors
    0 Bad values errors
    0 General errors
    0 Response PDUs
    0 Trap PDUs

SNMP logging: enabled
    Logging to 192.168.1.2.162, 0/10, 0 sent, 0 dropped.
```

Note that now we're sending traps to 192.168.1.2. The 162 at the end of the address refers to the UDP port that SNMP uses. Vendors such as Novell and Microsoft use UDP 161 for SNMP, so keep that in mind with your router's access-lists.

SNMP Support **493**

on the job

> *Make sure that your switch has a route table. Usually, a default (0.0.0.0) route is sufficient. Make sure this router exists on VLAN 1, which is the default VLAN for your management interfaces. This is easy to forget, since the switch, which operates at Layer 2, doesn't care about Layer 3 addresses. The switch will work fine without a route off the local subnet, but trap targets (as well as telnet and tftp) will not work from remote subnets.*

EXERCISE 9-1

Setting Up SNMP to Allow Access and Trap Acceptance

These steps will walk you through setting up SNMP on your switch to allow SNMP access and successful receipt of traps.

1. Install SNMP monitoring software on your workstation. This will allow your machine to send and receive SNMP messages and receive traps.

2. On both the workstation and the switch, configure identical community strings for both read-only and read-write.

3. On the switch, make sure a default gateway is configured, and that you can ping the workstation. IP connectivity is necessary for SNMP to work.

4. Enable SNMP and traps, and add your workstation as a trap destination.

MIBs

MIBs (Management Information Bases) are small databases that network hardware companies write to go along with the hardware they sell. If you want your management console to understand the trap that your Catalyst 5000 sends when a redundant power supply fails, you'll need to add the Cat 5000 MIBs to your management software. This process is known as *compiling* the MIBs. Once this is done, your software is set to understand all the messages that the switch is capable of sending. A MIB can be thought of as an upside-down tree, with an unnamed root node or object. Every node can be thought of as a group, with more groups or objects below it. Each node below the root has a decimal number associated with it. Below the root are three nodes: Consultative Committee for International Telegraph and Telephone (CCITT), International Organization for Standardization (ISO), and joint ISO/CCITT. Each of these root nodes is assigned a number: 1, 2, and 3, respectively. Most current MIB activity occurs in the portion of the ISO branch dedicated to the Internet community. Finding your way down the tree is how a MIB is defined. Cisco's private MIBs are under the MIB path 1.3.6.1.4.1.9. This was obtained by working down the MIB path—1 is for ISO. Under ISO is 3 for ORG, then DOD (6), Internet (1), Private (4), Enterprises (1), and finally Cisco (9). Under 1.3.6.1.4.1.9, there are many other nodes, over 500 objects. Cisco's private MIB supports DECnet, XNS, AppleTalk, VINES, and NetWare for routers. Port and interface states, power supply and fan states, and traffic thresholds are all objects for the switches. Cisco users can add private extensions to the MIB as required by adding a MIB ID to a Cisco hardware variable. This lets users customize the MIBs to their exact needs.

exam
Watch

Be sure to remember what the purpose of a trap is for the exam. Traps are sent from the network device to the management workstation to warn of a condition or problem.

Web Interface

While learning the SNMP CLI syntax is important for the switching exam, Cisco now has a much easier way of managing its IOS command-based switches. You may find it useful in your studies to make changes through the Web interface, and then look at the running configuration and see how it changed it. Once you have an IP address, default gateway, and enable password assigned to the switch, you can then manage the switch through a Web browser. Make sure that you're using a current browser, and that all the display options like JavaScript are enabled. If using MS Internet Explorer, make sure the IP address is in your trusted zone; otherwise, some objects will not display properly. Let's take a look at the Web interface. Point your browser to your switch's IP address. Figure 9-1 shows the opening screen of the 3524 XL switch we've been using.

The Visual Switch Manager link is the one we're interested in. Click on it. If prompted for a password, use the enable password with no username. Figure 9-2 shows the opening screen of the Visual Switch Manager.

Important things to note from this screen are the form boxes in the middle where you can change settings such as the SNMP parameters. On the top left, there is an APPLY button. You need to click this after making any changes so that they're

SNMP Support **495**

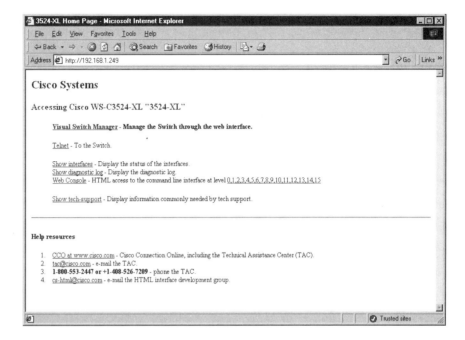

FIGURE 9-1

Web interface opening screen

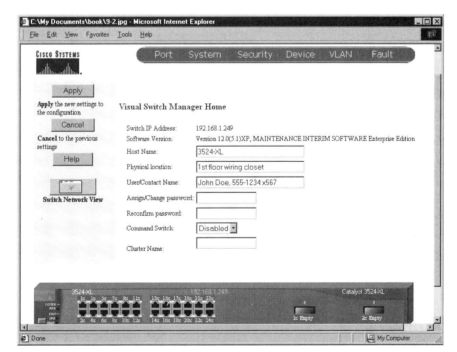

FIGURE 9-2

Visual Switch Manager opening screen

496 Chapter 9: Switch Diagnostics and Remote Management

permanent. The green bar at the top has menu items that you can click. For now, we're interested in looking at SNMP, so click System, and from the pull-down menu, select SNMP Configuration. Figure 9-3 shows the available parameters.

Please note that we omitted the top of the screen to show the trap configuration at the bottom of the page. Modify the settings here and click APPLY to instantly change the running configuration of the switch. Playing around with the settings here and seeing how the IOS configuration changes is a great learning tool for the switching test.

Now you know the basics behind SNMP, and how it pertains to Cisco IOS-based and set-based switches. The following Scenario & Solution questions reference possible SNMP issues and how to fix them.

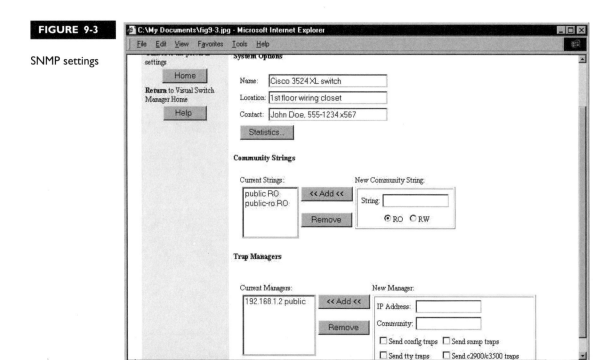

FIGURE 9-3

SNMP settings

SCENARIO & SOLUTION

My management console will not display the properties of a switch.	Can you ping the switch? Check the route table on both your workstation and the switch. From an MS Windows 95, 98, NT, or 2000 workstation, do a "route print" from a DOS window. You should have an entry with a destination and mask of all 0s. The gateway for this route should be a valid router on your network segment. On the switch, look at the configs for "ip default-gateway 192.168.1."254" on IOS command-based switches, and "set ip route 0.0.0.0/0.0.0.0 192.168.1.254" on set command-based switches. Is the read-only community string on the management software set to what the switch really is?
My management software doesn't seem to recognize the messages the switch is sending.	Have you compiled the Cisco MIBs into your network management software (NMS)? MIBs are like a dictionary for the management software to use to disseminate the traps. The process for compiling MIBs is unique for each network monitoring system (NMS), so check with your vendor's documentation.
I can ping the switch, but I don't receive any traps.	Are any routers filtering SNMP (UDP port 162) out between you and the switch? Have you configured the switch to send traps to your workstation?

CERTIFICATION OBJECTIVE 9.02

Remote Monitoring (RMON)

RMON and RMON2 are standards from the IETF (Internet Engineering Task Force). RMON is defined in RFCs 1757 and 1513. RMON2 adds an additional device and is defined in RFC 2021. The actual purpose of RMON is to add detailed port information such as error counts in real time. This type of data must be stored on the switch rather than sending a trap on every event. Because of this, SNMP by itself would not work because it doesn't maintain any previous data. RMON has hardware to compile data, and provide it to a management workstation. Because RMON is a very process-intensive type of monitoring, it is implemented in hardware, rather than relying on the switch's CPU. There are four main categories of RMON: History, Statistics, Alarm, and Event. History and Statistics are interface specific. They currently are supported on Ethernet, Fast Ethernet, Fast EtherChannel, Gigabit Ethernet, and Token Ring. Fast EtherChannel (FEC) is a Cisco-proprietary method of aggregating two or more links to another device. From Layer 2 and above, they appear as physical connection, but with two or more times the bandwidth. If one link fails, the rest continue to work, so FEC also adds some fault tolerance. Typically, FEC is used between switches, combined with VLAN trunks, but it can also be used to connect to a server if the NICs support FEC. Currently, NICs from Compaq and Intel support FEC. Currently, RMON monitoring requires an agent license from Cisco for their switches. Also, an NMS that supports RFCs 1513 and 1757 is required to comprehend the RMON data. Cisco's CiscoWorks is capable of reading such data. Since RMON and SNMP are so closely related, many of the commands for setting RMON are similar to SNMP commands. RMON is enabled by default on IOS command-based switches, but needs to be enabled on set command-based switches. Let's do that now on our 2948. Enter "set snmp ?", and hit ENTER:

```
Magnacom-2948> (enable) set snmp ?
  access                       Set SNMP access group
  community                    Set SNMP community string
  group                        Set SNMP group
  notify                       Set SNMP notify
  rmon                         Set SNMP RMON
  targetaddr                   Set SNMP targetaddr
  targetparams                 Set SNMP targetparams
  trap                         Set SNMP trap information
  user                         Set SNMP user
  view                         Set SNMP view
```

This time, the rmon category is what we want.

```
Magnacom-2948> (enable) set snmp rmon ?
  disable                      Disable RMON
  enable                       Enable RMON
Magnacom-2948> (enable) set snmp rmon enable
```

Doing so will enable the rmon process. Verify this with a "show snmp":

```
Magnacom-2948> (enable) sh snmp
RMON:                         Enabled
Traps Enabled:None
Port Traps Enabled: None

Community-Access        Community-String
----------------        ----------------
read-only               public
read-write              private
read-write-all          secret

Trap-Rec-Address                                       Trap-Rec-Community
----------------------------------------               ------------------
```

> **on the Job**
>
> *RMON can be a very hard system to set up. Cisco's Web site has some very good sample configurations that can help you get started with RMON. This would be an excellent place to start.*

This shows that RMON is now enabled. This embedded RMON agent is capable of looking only at the Data Link layer. Cisco does make a couple of products (SwitchProbe and Network Analysis Module) that integrate with RMON and enable the monitoring of higher layers. On the IOS command-based switches, you can define additional alarms and events. These are beyond the scope of this chapter, and well beyond the scope of the exam.

The following Scenario & Solution questions are a quick reference for getting RMON to work on your system:

SCENARIO & SOLUTION

RMON is configured on the switch, but the management workstation cannot access the information.	Are you using an RMON-compliant management product? Are you licensed to use RMON from Cisco? Do you have SNMP and IP configured properly on the switch?
RMON is configured at both the workstation and the switch, but I am receiving various error messages.	Make sure that you are using the same version of RMON at both locations. Currently, there is RMON 1 and 2. Version 3 is coming soon.

exam
⍥atch

Remember that RMON is a more in-depth version of SNMP, and has more specific requirements than pure SNMP. RMON also needs a license from Cisco. The exam covers switch setup, but does not cover any CiscoWorks, which is why we omitted that additional detail from this section. Most RMON data can be seen from the CLI using show commands such as "sh int", "sh port", "sh system", and "sh ver". This is an example of the information from "sh port" and "sh mac". As you can see, it details error counts and statistics.

Port	Align-Err	FCS-Err	Xmit-Err	Rcv-Err	UnderSize
2/1	-	0	2	0	0
2/3	-	0	1	0	0
2/4	-	0	1	0	0
2/5	-	0	2	0	0
2/6	-	0	1	0	0
2/7	-	1	0	2	0
2/11	-	1	2	2	0
2/13	-	0	1	0	0
2/17	-	0	1	0	0
2/18	-	0	1	0	0
2/19	-	0	1	0	0
2/21	-	0	1	0	0
2/22	-	0	1	0	0
2/24	-	0	1	0	0
2/27	-	1	2	2	0
2/32	-	0	2	0	0
2/34	-	0	2	0	0
2/36	-	0	1	0	0
2/38	-	1	1	2	0
2/44	-	0	1	0	0
2/46	-	0	1	0	0

Port	Single-Col	Multi-Coll	Late-Coll	Excess-Col	Carri-Sen	Runts	Giants
2/1	0	0	0	0	1	0	0
2/3	0	0	0	0	1	0	0
2/4	0	0	0	0	1	0	0
2/5	0	0	0	0	1	0	0
2/6	0	0	0	0	1	0	0
2/7	1	0	0	0	0	1	0
2/8	0	1	0	0	0	0	0
2/11	0	0	0	0	1	1	0
2/13	0	0	0	0	1	0	0
2/17	0	0	0	0	1	0	0
2/18	0	0	0	0	1	0	0

```
2/19            0           0           0           0        1         0         0
2/21            0           0           0           0        1         0         0
2/22            0           0           0           0        1         0         0
2/24            0           0           0           0        1         0         0
2/27            0           0           0           0        1         1         0
2/32            0           0           0           0        1         0         0
2/34            0           0           0           0        1         0         0
2/36           11           0           0           0        1         0         0
2/38            0           0           0           0        1         1         0
2/44            0           0           0           0        1         0         0
2/46            0           0           0           0        1         0         0

Last-Time-Cleared
-------------------------
Mon Jul 17 2000, 19:20:00


***************** show mac ******************


Port       Rcv-Unicast           Rcv-Multicast         Rcv-Broadcast
--------   --------------------  --------------------  --------------------
2/1                     32861                      0                     8
2/3                     97794                      0                  2496
2/4                      4393                    218                  1334
2/5                      6090                      1                     0
2/6                      8229                      1                  1117
2/7                     32474                    202                    17
2/8                     28981                      0                    15
2/11                     8985                     16                   124
2/13                        1                      0                     5
2/17                        0                      3                    34
2/21                        0                      3                    29
2/22                      273                      5                   253
2/24                        3                      3                    30
2/27                       39                      0                    85
2/32                       52                      0                    54
2/34                        0                     15                     0
2/36                    34579                   1011                   196
2/38                      734                      3                   182
2/44                     6881                      0                   476

Port       Xmit-Unicast          Xmit-Multicast        Xmit-Broadcast
--------   --------------------  --------------------  --------------------
2/1                     31960                   7483                  6300
2/3                     76734                   7460                  3759
```

```
2/4                       4381              7121            4973
2/5                       3769              6473             719
2/6                        902              1224            4472
2/7                      28981              6334              15
2/8                      30057              6135              17
2/11                     15442              1474            3413
2/13                        12              7484            6303
2/17                        10              5588            6247
2/18                        10              7486            6308
2/19                        10              7486            6308
2/21                        12              5586            6280
2/22                       288              5591            6054
2/24                        14              5584            6234
2/27                        43              7484            6223
2/32                        57              7486            6254
2/34                        10              7481            6308
2/36                     56067              6474            6112
2/38                      3961              7273            6171
2/44                      6961              7485            5832
2/46                        10              7484            6308

Port     Rcv-Octet          Xmit-Octet
-------  -----------------  -----------------
2/1              34647921            4407623
2/3              63960151           50791052
2/4                671243            1685323
2/5               5416176            1008019
2/6              10924504             884724
2/7              34694379            3278046
2/8               2808824           34900029
2/11               931080           14933861
2/13                  428            1391623
2/17                 2970            1254573
2/18                    0            1392062
2/19                    0            1392062
2/21                 2648            1257769
2/22                48491            1257464
2/24                 3056            1253608
2/27                25871            1374632
2/32                16803            1387933
2/34                  970            1391568
2/36             14439967           58189595
2/38               111067            6534993
2/44               744905            2015130
2/46                    0            1391934
```

```
MAC      Dely-Exced MTU-Exced  In-Discard Lrn-Discrd In-Lost    Out-Lost
-------- ---------- ---------- ---------- ---------- ---------- ----------
2/7               0          0          0          0          2          0
2/11              0          0          0          0          2          0
2/27              0          0          0          0          2          0
2/38              0          0          0          0          2          0

Last-Time-Cleared
-------------------------
Mon Jul 17 2000, 19:20:00
```

EXERCISE 9-2

Adding RMON Support to a Switch

This exercise will show you the few brief steps for configuring RMON. Most of the work to be done is actually on the management station, not the switch.

1. Install management software on your workstation to support RMON.
2. Set up your workstation to fully support SNMP, as in Exercise 9-1.
3. On the switch, enable RMON.

CERTIFICATION OBJECTIVE 9.03

Switch Port Analyzer (SPAN)

Switch Port Analyzer is Cisco's term for enabling a port to see traffic that normally it would not see. This would be useful for using a protocol analyzer or intrusion detection system on the switch. These products rely on seeing all traffic on a segment. For a little background, let's look at our 3524 switch. If you do a "sh mac", you'll see the MAC address table that the switch uses. On a set command-based switch, do a "sh cam dynamic 1" to see dynamic addresses on VLAN 1. The IOS command-based switch shows:

```
3524-XL#sh mac
Dynamic Address Count:                      2
Secure Address Count:                       0
Static Address (User-defined) Count:        0
System Self Address Count:                  49
Total MAC addresses:                        51
Maximum MAC addresses:                      8192
Non-static Address Table:
Destination Address    Address Type    VLAN    Destination Port
------------------     ------------    ----    ------------------
0010.4bd3.d0ab         Dynamic         1       FastEthernet0/24
0060.97f7.9742         Dynamic         1       FastEthernet0/21
```

This switch can keep track of a maximum of 8192 addresses, even those on other switches to which it has connections. The bottom portion is most important. It lists what port a frame would have to leave the switch to get to that MAC address. When the switch receives a frame from a port, it looks at the destination MAC address. If a match is found, it knows what port to send it out, and it sends it out only this port; thereby saving bandwidth on all other ports. If no entry is found, it sends it out all ports in that VLAN. Once it receives a response, it will create a new entry in the table for the new MAC address. But what if you have a network problem that requires a protocol analyzer and need to see all frames on a segment or a network? Cisco's SPAN works by designating a port as a monitor, and telling it what ports or VLAN that it can see. The switch will then duplicate any packets from the monitored ports onto the monitoring port. You can set the monitoring port to see frames being transmitted, received, or both on the monitored ports for set command-based switches. IOS command-based switches will only let you do both. You can set multiple monitoring ports, and each monitoring port can have one or more monitored ports. You can even allow a port to monitor an entire VLAN. Let's do it on an IOS command-based switch first. Remember that port monitoring is done on a per-interface basis, so you need to be in global configuration mode, and then enter an interface. Once in interface configuration mode, you want to change the port settings, so do a "port ?":

```
3524-XL(config-if)#port ?
  block           Forwarding of unknown uni/multi cast addresses
  group           Place this interface in a port group
  monitor         Monitor another interface
  network         Configure an interface to be a network port
  security        Configure an interface to be a secure port
  storm-control   Configure broadcast storm control parameters
```

"Monitor" is the command, so we'll follow command:

```
3524-XL(config-if)#port monitor ?
  FastEthernet     FastEthernet IEEE 802.3
  GigabitEthernet  GigabitEthernet IEEE 802.3z
  VLAN             Switch VLAN Virtual Interface
  <cr>
```

Let's have port Fast Ethernet 0/1 monitor all of VLAN 1. Use the *vlan* keyword, and "?" to see what's available:

```
3524-XL(config-if)#port monitor vlan ?
  <1-1000>  VLAN interface number
```

Use VLAN 1:

```
3524-XL(config-if)#port monitor vlan 1
```

Exit configuration mode, and do a "sh port mon" to see which ports are in a monitoring state:

```
3524-XL(config-if)#end
3524-XL#sh port mon
Monitor Port          Port Being Monitored
--------------------  --------------------
FastEthernet0/1       VLAN1
```

This shows that port Fa0/1 is monitoring all of VLAN 1. Let's say we want to monitor an additional port that is not in VLAN 1. As we did earlier, go into interface configuration mode for FastEthernet0/24. Now we'll pick an interface to monitor, rather than an entire VLAN:

```
3524-XL(config-if)#port monitor ?
  FastEthernet     FastEthernet IEEE 802.3
  GigabitEthernet  GigabitEthernet IEEE 802.3z
  VLAN             Switch VLAN Virtual Interface
  <cr>
```

We want to look at a Fast Ethernet port, so use that. I abbreviated it to "fa":

```
3524-XL(config-if)#port monitor fa ?
  <0-2>  FastEthernet interface number
3524-XL(config-if)#port monitor fastEthernet 0?
/
```

The "/" divides the group of ports: "0" from the actual port in the group "24":

```
3524-XL(config-if)#port monitor fastEthernet 0/?
  <1-24>  FastEthernet interface number
3524-XL(config-if)#port monitor fastEthernet 0/24?
:  <1-24>
```

The colon allows you to enter a range of ports such as "fa 0/10:12", which would include ports 10, 11, and 12 out of group 0. For this example, we want just 24:

```
3524-XL(config-if)#port monitor fastEthernet 0/24
3524-XL(config-if)#end
```

"End" to exit config mode. Now do a "sh port mon" again to see the change:

```
3524-XL#sh port mon
Monitor Port            Port Being Monitored
--------------------    --------------------
FastEthernet0/1         VLAN1
FastEthernet0/1         FastEthernet0/24
```

As we wanted, port Fa0/1 is now monitoring both VLAN 1 and port Fa0/24.

EXERCISE 9-3

Configuring SPAN for Port Analysis

This exercise will allow you to monitor a port or set of ports for protocol analysis.

1. Plug your network monitoring station into an unused port. Set this port to the fastest speed the workstation will support. Never monitor a port that is faster than your monitoring port.

2. On the switch, add the ports to be monitored to the monitoring ports SPAN list. Remember, the more ports you monitor, the more packets you'll see in the packet trace. If the problem you're trying to solve can be logically narrowed down to communication between two devices, only monitor those two.

3. Attach your workstation, and begin the protocol analysis.

Since we're on the IOS command-based switches, let's take a look at the Web interface, which can be used to set monitoring of other ports, but not entire VLANs. However, if you know all the ports that are in the VLAN, you can still set each port individually. Figure 9-4 shows the homepage of the Visual Switch Manager. Click Port at the top, and from the pull-down menu, select Switch Port Analyzer (SPAN).

After clicking on the SPAN menu item, you should see a screen similar to Figure 9-5 that shows a matrix of ports. Monitoring ports are along the left column, and monitored ports are along the top. For example, I've checked ports Fa0/3 and Fa0/4 to be monitored by Fa0/7. Click APPLY, and it's done.

on the job

Always use SPAN and protocol analyzers only as a last resort. First look at both the switch configurations and server/workstation configurations to make sure everything is OK. Then look at the port counters on the switch. You may find a large number of errors that may indicate a faulty NIC. Digging though a packet trace is time consuming, so eliminate the easy possibilities first.

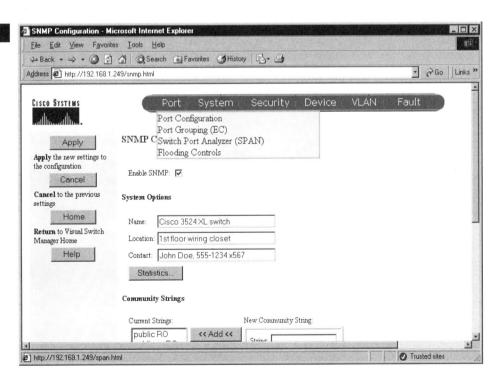

FIGURE 9-4

Visual Switch Manager with Port menu

FIGURE 9-5

SPAN Port screen

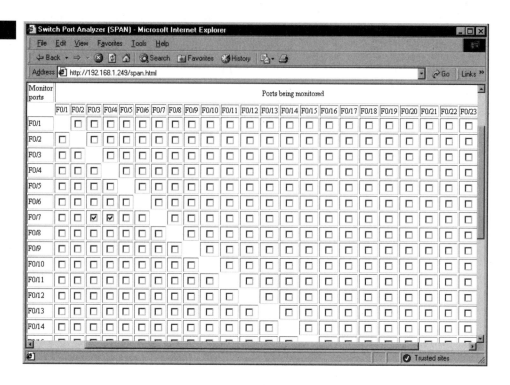

Now if we do a "sh port mon" from the CLI, we see:

```
3524-XL#sh port mon
Monitor Port                    Port Being Monitored
--------------------            --------------------
FastEthernet0/1                 VLAN1
FastEthernet0/1                 FastEthernet0/24
FastEthernet0/7                 FastEthernet0/3
FastEthernet0/7                 FastEthernet0/4
```

Port Fa0/7 is now monitoring Fa0/3 and Fa0/4 as intended. Now we'll do SPAN operations on a set command-based switch. First we'll do a "set span ?":

```
Magnacom-2948> (enable) set span ?
  disable                 Disable SPAN
  sc0                     Set SPAN on interface sc0
  <mod/port>              Source module and port numbers
  <vlan>                  Source VLAN numbers
```

We decided we need to analyze the traffic from the server on port 2/8, and the protocol analyzer is attached to port 2/9. Therefore, port 2/8 will be the source, and 2/9 will be the destination.

```
Magnacom-2948> (enable) set span 2/8 ?
  <mod/port>                 Destination module and port numbers
Magnacom-2948> (enable) set span 2/8 2/9 ?
  both                       Both receiving and transmitting traffic
  create                     Creating new SPAN session
  inpkts                     Enable/disable destination port incoming packets
  learning                   Enable/disable MAC address learning
  multicast                  Enable/disable multicast traffic
  rx                         Receiving traffic
  tx                         Transmitting traffic
  <cr>
```

We need to see port 2/8's received and transmitted traffic, so we use the keyword *both*. Another keyword you may use is *inpkts*. If you enable *inpkts*, you can use the destination port as a functional port for a workstation concurrently. Otherwise, the switch will not receive packets from the destination port. They do this so that when running an analyzer on a normal workstation, the traffic you would normally get is blocked, so that your own traffic isn't mixed with that of the monitoring ports. It's much easier to look at protocol traces if only two devices are involved. For this example, however, we'll enable "inpkts":

```
Magnacom-2948> (enable) set span 2/8 2/9 both inpk ?
  disable                    Disable destination port incoming packets
  enable                     Enable destination port incoming packets
Magnacom-2948> (enable) set span 2/8 2/9 both inpk en
Overwrote Port 2/9 to monitor transmit/receive traffic of Port 2/8
Incoming Packets enabled. Learning enabled.
```

Now we'll do a "sh span" to see if our changes took place:

```
Magnacom-2948> (enable) sh span

Destination       : Port 2/9
Admin Source      : Port 2/8
Oper Source       : Port 2/8
Direction         : transmit/receive
Incoming Packets: enabled
Learning          : enabled
```

As we hoped, traffic on port 2/8 (source) is now being duplicated on port 2/9 for both transmit and receive. Incoming packets (inpkts) are allowed, and learning is enabled, which means that the destination port will still learn MAC addresses from its connected devices. Now we'll have port 2/9 monitor VLAN 2:

```
Magnacom-2948> (enable) set span ?
  disable                 Disable SPAN
  sc0                     Set SPAN on interface sc0
  <mod/port>              Source module and port numbers
  <vlan>                  Source VLAN numbers
```

This time, we use just a single digit, which indicates a VLAN. Ports are always a module/port combination.

```
Magnacom-2948> (enable) set span 2 ?
  <mod/port>              Destination module and port numbers
```

Send the traffic to 2/9:

```
Magnacom-2948> (enable) set span 2 2/9 ?
  both                    Both receiving and transmitting traffic
  create                  Creating new SPAN session
  inpkts                  Enable/disable destination port incoming packets
  learning                Enable/disable MAC address learning
  multicast               Enable/disable multicast traffic
  rx                      Receiving traffic
  tx                      Transmitting traffic
  <cr>
```

Both received and transmitted packets will be duplicated:

```
Magnacom-2948> (enable) set span 2 2/9 both ?
  create                  Creating new SPAN session
  inpkts                  Enable/disable destination port incoming packets
  learning                Enable/disable MAC address learning
  multicast               Enable/disable multicast traffic
  <cr>
Magnacom-2948> (enable) set span 2 2/9 both inpkts
Created Port 2/9 to monitor transmit/receive traffic of VLAN 2
Incoming Packets enabled. Learning enabled.
```

Now we'll do a "sh span" to verify:

```
Magnacom-2948> (enable) sh span
Destination      : Port 2/9
Admin Source     : VLAN 2
Oper Source      : Port 2/7-8
Direction        : transmit/receive
Incoming Packets: enabled
Learning         : enabled
```

Port 2/9 is now monitoring VLAN 2. Where it says "Oper Source," these are the exact ports that it's monitoring. On this switch, ports 2/7–8 are the only ones in VLAN 2.

> **exam**
> **⊙atch**
>
> *Do not confuse SPAN with the Spanning Tree algorithm; they are not at all related. Also, remember the syntax. The set command-based switches use "sh span" to display port SPANing. If you use the same command on an IOS command-based switch, it's valid, but it will return information on Spanning Tree. Cisco may try to trick you on this for the exam. "show port monitor" is the correct command to use for IOS.*

The following Scenario & Solution questions will show you a few things to watch when configuring SPAN:

SCENARIO & SOLUTION	
I have configured one port to monitor another, but I don't see any traffic.	Make sure that your monitoring port is not part of an EtherChannel group or ATM. They are supported for SPAN monitoring; however, they can be monitored. Make sure that your NIC supports *promiscuous mode*, which allows it to see traffic not destined for it.
I cannot telnet from my monitoring workstation.	Make sure "inpkts" are enabled on the monitoring port; they are disabled by default. Inpkts allow the switch to accept packets from your monitoring port.
I am getting slow response from some network devices after configuring SPAN.	Check your SPAN monitoring ports. Make sure you never accidentally configure a router or server switch port as a monitoring port.

CERTIFICATION SUMMARY

As you have seen, Cisco has added many tools and features to its Catalyst line of switches to allow for easier management. Knowing when to use what is important for both the exam and in real life. SNMP and RMON, while closely related, serve different functions. SNMP typically is used for point-in-time monitoring, such as when an interface goes down, or a switch is overheating due to a fan or air-conditioning failure. RMON looks at statistical data at the port level, and can warn you of things such as an overused link between two switches. RMON also has more stringent requirements for the NMS. The switch's CPU handles SNMP, but RMON is implemented in application-specific integrated circuits (ASICs), which perform it quickly, and without burdening the CPU.

SPAN is not really related to RMON or SNMP, but is important in facilitating packet capture for protocol analysis or intrusion detection. It allows a network probe to see all traffic for a segment if need be, much like an Ethernet concentrator. SPAN is a major leap forward in Ethernet switch troubleshooting. If you deal with operating system support, chances are you'll need to set up SPANed ports sometime.

TWO-MINUTE DRILL

Here are some of the key points from each certification objective in Chapter 9.

SNMP Support
- SNMP supports both messages initiated by an NMS and by the network device.
- SNMP is implemented in the CPU, not in ASICs.
- SNMP uses unencrypted passwords called *community strings* for security.
- MIBs are databases that describe all the possible error conditions a particular network device can send. Some are universal; most are vendor specific.
- Traps are messages sent from the network device to the preconfigured trap destination, which needs to be running an NMS to understand the messages.

Remote Monitoring (RMON)
- RMON requires a license from Cisco to use.
- RMON is implemented in ASICs because of its overhead.
- RMON consists of history, alarms, events, and statistics.
- RMON can report much more per-interface information than SNMP.
- RMON requires an NMS complying with RFCs 1757 and 1513, which is very limiting.

Switch Port Analyzer (SPAN)
- SPAN duplicates traffic from a predetermined port or ports to another predetermined port.
- SPAN can monitor one port, multiple ports, or an entire VLAN.
- SPAN can monitor ISL and 802.1q trunks, in addition to standard 1 VLAN-only lines.
- Set command-based switches can specify traffic in one or both directions on the source port. IOS command-based switches can't specify, and must do both.
- If you allow "inpkts", a destination port can also be used by the monitoring station for normal functions and monitoring functions.

SELF TEST

The following questions will help you measure your understanding of the material presented in this chapter. Read all the choices carefully, as there might be more than one correct answer. Choose all correct answers for each question.

SNMP Support

1. What are the three levels of security for set command-based switches?
   A. Read-only
   B. Read-write
   C. Write-only
   D. Read-write-all
   E. Public

2. After an acquisition, your company's IP network was renumbered. What are two possible reasons why you don't get traps anymore from the devices?
   A. SNMP uses its own addresses and routing table, and needs to be redistributed into the new address scheme.
   B. The trap destinations configured on the switches need to be updated with the new addresses of the NMS machines.
   C. The new addresses fixed all your problems, so the devices don't need to send traps anymore.
   D. SNMP has the ability to self-reconfigure for the acquisition, so traps are automatically sent to the NMS machines of the acquiring company.
   D. The IP addresses and default gateways of the switches need to be updated to reflect the new address scheme.

3. Traps are sent from the NMS to the network device to monitor the various SNMP parameters. What is wrong with this statement?
   A. Traps are sent from the network device to the NMS to monitor SNMP parameters.
   B. Nothing is wrong, the statement is correct.
   C. Traps are sent to warn of possible issues, not for monitoring SNMP parameters.

4. You have just enabled the SNMP agent on your Windows NT workstation. You set your workstation as a trap target for a switch. What Windows utility do you use to view the traps?
   A. Trap Manager

B. Event Viewer

   C. Microsoft Management Console

   D. None of the above

5. Your NMS receives all the proper traps it should from your routers, but it only receives some of them from the Catalyst switches. You can ping all the switches from the NMS. What could be a possible cause?

   A. Your NMS is not a trap destination on the switches.

   B. Your NMS has not had the Catalyst MIBs compiled into it.

   C. SNMP packets from the switch cannot reach your NMS

   D. A router on the network is blocking some of the traps.

6. Your NMS was unplugged over the weekend. What will happen when you bring it back up?

   A. All the devices with queued traps will send them to your NMS.

   B. You'll start receiving current traps, but those from before the NMS was running are lost.

   C. Your NMS will poll all the devices for unsent trap messages.

   D. Your NMS is smart enough to tell the devices to use a backup NMS device while it is down.

7. SNMP relies on which two of the following protocols? Include all protocol layers.

   A. TCP

   B. IP

   C. UDP

   D. ICMP

Remote Monitoring (RMON)

8. You have just installed a Cisco SwitchProbe into your switch, but you cannot receive the RMON statistics from the switch. SNMP works fine, however. What are possible problems?

   A. The SwitchProbe is not an RMON device. It would never send any RMON statistics.

   B. Your NMS does not support RMON.

   C. You do not have IP connectivity between the NMS and the switch.

   D. SwitchProbe requires SPAN to be turned on before it can see all the traffic on the ports.

9. Which of the following does RMON *not* provide?

   A. History

B. Errors
C. Statistics
D. Events
E. Alarms

10. Why is RMON implemented in ASICs on the high-end Cisco switches?
    A. ASICs are a good money-making chip for Cisco, so they use them.
    B. ASICs are not used in switches, only in routers.
    C. ASICs offload the RMON processing from the main switch CPU.
    D. It is simpler to use ASICs than to require the switch to have a CPU.

11. Why don't many companies use RMON compared to SNMP?
    A. RMON is not yet an approved standard, so companies are waiting for its approval.
    B. RMON is Cisco proprietary, so only Cisco uses it.
    C. RMON requires a high-end NMS, typically UNIX-based that many smaller companies don't need or can't afford.
    D. SNMP does everything that RMON does, so it would be redundant.

12. An administrator is complaining that a RIP packet storm is occurring, and wonders why your Cisco switch running the embedded RMON agent didn't pick up the problem. What do you tell the administrator?
    A. "Sounds like a router problem, not mine."
    B. "RIP is a routing protocol, but the switch doesn't route, so it doesn't see the RIP updates."
    C. "The embedded RMON agent only looks at Layers 1 and 2. It looked like normal IP/IPX traffic to the switch."
    D. "RMON sent traps for the packet storm, but the CiscoWorks NMS doesn't accept RMON traps for routing protocols."

13. How does RMON work with SNMP on a switch?
    A. RMON replaces SNMP on the switch.
    B. RMON uses SNMP as a transport protocol.
    C. RMON is not used on switches, only on routers.

Switch Port Analyzer (SPAN)

14. You have a hub attached to a port you're monitoring via SPAN on your switch. What traffic from the hub will you see from the monitoring port?

    A. None

    B. Only those packets destined for the monitoring switch port

    C. All

15. You have configured one port from a Fast EtherChannel group as a monitored port. Why is this not a good idea?

    A. Monitoring EtherChannel ports is not supported.

    B. EtherChannel does load balancing between group members, so you need to monitor all ports in the group.

    C. EtherChannel is 3Com proprietary, and not compatible with Cisco's proprietary SPAN feature.

    D. To monitor EtherChannel, you would need to be monitoring from a Gigabit Ethernet port, which is not yet supported.

16. SPAN was designed to:

    A. Add RMON functionality to non-RMON compliant devices.

    B. Eliminate bridging loops by electing forwarding bridges.

    C. Let a switch port receive traffic that was destined for other ports for the purpose of monitoring.

    D. Allow hackers to use a protocol analyzer to get your credit card number.

17. SPAN lets one port see the other ports' traffic by:

    A. Putting all the ports in the same collision domain.

    B. Copying all packets from the monitored ports to the monitoring port.

    C. Putting all the ports in the same broadcast domain.

    D. Requesting the end devices to include the monitoring port device MAC address on all unicast packets.

    E. Bridging the traffic and using the CAM/MAC address tables.

18. If you enable SPAN, what happens to the monitoring and monitored ports?
    A. Packets seen on the monitored ports are copied to the monitoring port.
    B. They are put in the same collision domain. This lets the monitored port's traffic be seen on the monitoring port, and vice versa.
    C. The monitoring port's traffic is copied to the monitored port.

19. You have accidentally made a switches port that a router is connected to a monitoring port. This monitoring port is watching ports that are on four different VLANs. All of your routers use RIP. What will happen to the router that is now connected to the monitoring port?
    A. It will become horribly confused, as it sees RIP updates from four different segments that appear as local segments.
    B. It will see the problem, and sent an SNMP trap to your NMS, alerting you to your blunder.
    C. Your router will see these multiple VLANs, and convert its connection to an ISL trunk, improving performance.
    D. There would be no change; RIP is designed to handle such misconfiguration.

20. SPAN can handle which of the following protocols? (Choose all that apply.)
    A. IP
    B. IPX
    C. DECnet
    D. AppleTalk

LAB QUESTION

Figure 9-6 illustrates a portion of a typical large, switched environment. The core of this building's network uses a Catalyst 5000 switch. There are multiple VLANs on the switch, with each VLAN connecting to a workgroup switch dedicated to that VLAN. Two 4000 series routers using HSRP and ISL trunking handle the routing between the VLANs. There is a DHCP server on VLAN 1 that issues addresses to all the subnets/VLANs. IP helper is configured on the redundant routers to get the DHCP broadcasts to the DHCP server. Until recently, everything worked fine. Now the problem is that workstations on VLAN 3 are not getting issued IP addresses from the server. The

DHCP admin is on vacation, so you can't look at the server to see if the requests are getting to it. You decide you're going to use a protocol analyzer to try to diagnose the problem. Remember that the clients issue DHCP requests as broadcasts, the routers configured with IP helper see the broadcast, and forward it as a unicast to the preconfigured DHCP server. The DHCP server will then return the issued IP address as a unicast to the workstation. Where and how might you use the protocol analyzer to see how the DHCP process is failing in this problem? Will you need to use any of the features that were discussed in this chapter?

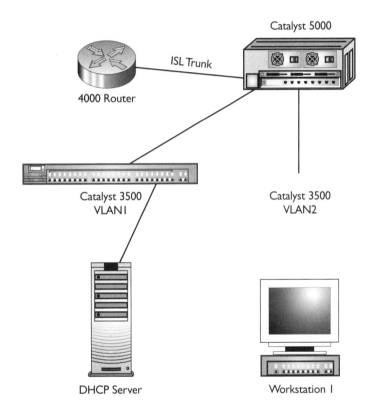

FIGURE 9-6

Example of a switched environment

SELF TEST ANSWERS

SNMP Support

1. ☑ **A, B, D.** All three are correct as defined by Cisco.
   ☒ **C** is incorrect; write-only does not exist. **E** is incorrect, as it is a default community string, but not a layer of security.

2. ☑ **B and E.** SNMP relies on IP, and the switches do not run routing protocols, so they need to be statically addressed and routed.
   ☒ **A** is incorrect because SNMP does not route or act as a routing protocol. It uses UDP on top of IP. **C** is incorrect because it's silly. No address change would fix all your network problems. **D** is incorrect for the same reason as **A**; it cannot reconfigure itself because it does not run a routing protocol.

3. ☑ **C.** Traps are sent from the network device to the NMS when a certain condition occurs.
   ☒ **A** is incorrect, as traps are not used for monitoring SNMP parameters of a device.

4. ☑ **D.** None of the above.
   ☒ **A, B,** and **C** are incapable of receiving traps. The SNMP agent of a workstation would allow it to send traps, but not receive them.

5. ☑ **B.** If your NMS has not had the unique Catalyst MIBs compiled into it, the NMS will not understand many of the traps the switches would send.
   ☒ **A** is incorrect because your NMS is receiving some of the traps currently, so it must be a destination. **C** is incorrect because it was stated that you could ping all the switches, which guarantees that IP is working. **D** is incorrect because a router would either block all SNMP or no SNMP on a per-device basis. All traps use the same port: UDP 162.

6. ☑ **B.** Your NMS will start receiving traps after it's loaded, but it cannot receive traps while it's down. Traps are only sent once by a device, and are never queued.
   ☒ **A** and **C** are incorrect because traps are never stored or queued on the network device. They are sent once immediately, and there is no verification process to see if they were ever received. **D** is incorrect because the NMS was unplugged. Since it had no warning that it was going to be unplugged (power or network, same result), it wouldn't have tried to initiate any fail-over anyway.

7. ☑ **B, C.** SNMP uses UDP port 161 (Layer 4) riding on top of IP (Layer 3) for communication.
   ☒ Neither **A** nor **D** are involved with SNMP.

Self Test Answers

Remote Monitoring (RMON)

8. ☑ **B.** If your NMS does not support RFCs 1757 and 1513, it will not be able to read RMON stats.
   ☒ **A** is incorrect, as the SwitchProbe is an RMON device. It lets the embedded RMON agent on high-end switches see higher than Layer 2. **C** is incorrect; since SNMP was working, IP connectivity must exist. **D** is incorrect because SPAN is only needed for external protocol analyzers. The SwitchProbe acts as an internal device, not a port-attached unit.

9. ☑ **B.** Errors are not one of the categories.
   ☒ **A, C, D,** and **E** are the four types of RMON data.

10. ☑ **C.** RMON uses a lot of CPU power, so moving its processing to an off-CPU chip makes everything faster.
    ☒ **A** is incorrect, as ASICs are actually expensive to design and make. **B** is incorrect, as most Cisco switches actually do have them. **D** is incorrect because all switches have a CPU, whether they use RMON ASICs or not.

11. ☑ **C.** Only high-end NMSs support RFCs 1757 and 1513, which define RMON.
    ☒ **A** is incorrect, since anything with an RFC number is an approved standard. **B** is incorrect for the same reason **A** is; anything that has been IETF approved cannot be proprietary. **D** is incorrect, as RMON does much more in-depth analysis of hardware than SNMP.

12. ☑ **C.** The embedded RMON agent only looks at Layers 1 and 2. Anything else requires extra hardware.
    ☒ **A** may be correct, but may get you fired. **B** is partially correct, but RIP uses broadcasts, so it actually does see all the RIP updates—it just doesn't know what they are. **D** is incorrect because the switch RMON agents would never send a trap for a routing protocol problem.

13. ☑ **B.** RMON uses SNMP protocols to move the data. It just provides more in-depth information than SNMP.
    ☒ **A** is incorrect, as RMON will not function with SNMP being set up on the switch. **C** is incorrect, as this chapter dealt with configuring RMON on a switch.

Switch Port Analyzer (SPAN)

14. ☑ **C.** Since it's a hub, it repeats its packets to all its ports. Therefore, any packet hitting the hub would be repeated to the switch port being monitored.
    ☒ **A** is incorrect, since the hub would send all its traffic to the switch. **B** would be correct if there was another switch connected to the switch port, but it was mentioned that it was a hub.

15. ☑ **B.** EtherChannel splits traffic across multiple physical links, so you need to monitor all members of the group to see all the traffic to and from this device.
    ☒ **A** is incorrect; only EtherChannel as a monitoring port is unsupported. **C** is incorrect, as EtherChannel is Cisco proprietary, not 3Com. **D** is partially correct, but **B** is more correct. A single Fast Ethernet port can monitor an EtherChannel group, but Gigabit may be better if the group has more traffic than the monitoring port will support.

16. ☑ **C.** SPAN lets a switch port see traffic that it normally would not see.
    ☒ **B** is incorrect, as it describes the Spanning Tree Protocol, not SPAN. **A** and **D** are partially correct, but they are not why SPAN was designed; they are more side effects. This is an example of Cisco's famous "most correct" answer.

17. ☑ **B.** The monitored ports have their packets copied to the monitoring port.
    ☒ **A** is incorrect because it's still a switch. None of the monitored ports will see any other monitored port's traffic. **C** is incorrect, as SPAN works on Layer 2, so all ports are always in the same broadcast domain. **D** is incorrect; SPAN functions transparently to the devices on monitored ports. **E** is incorrect, as switches already act as a high-speed, multiport bridge. A bridge wouldn't let you see traffic where you're neither the transmitter nor the receiver, much like a switch.

18. ☑ **A.** SPAN works by copying packets on monitored ports to the monitoring port.
    ☒ **B** is incorrect, as collision domains are not changed by SPAN. **C** is incorrect, as packets are never copied from the monitoring port to the monitored port. They are only copied from the monitored port(s) to the monitoring port.

19. ☑ **A.** Since RIP uses hop count, the router would see distant routers as one hop away, and make a mess of many routing tables.
    ☒ **B** and **C** are incorrect, as the router would have no way of knowing what is going on or how to fix it. **D** is incorrect; the remote RIP updates appearing local to the router will cause a great many problems. RIP wouldn't see this as a problem.

20. ☑ **A, B, C, D.** Switches and SPAN work at Layer 2, so any Ethernet frame, regardless of the Layer 3 information, would be handled by SPAN.
    ☒ There are no incorrect choices.

LAB ANSWER

In response to the last question: yes, you will use a feature from this chapter. Any time you see hear "protocol analyzer" mentioned in a switched environment, you should think SPAN. Focus on the workstation VLAN that doesn't work, although you may also want to look at the working VLAN to see exactly what packets are exchanged in a correctly working DHCP system. We might as well start from the beginning. Are the workstations on that segment really sending requests? Putting the analyzer on a port on the VLAN 3 switch and letting it see all the VLAN traffic ("port monitor vlan 3" from interface config mode of the VLAN 3 switch) should work. You expect to see DHCP requests in the trace. If you saw the requests there, check the VLAN 1 to see if the requests are making it as far as the server. If you did see them on VLAN 3, but didn't see them in unicast form on VLAN 1, it may indicate a problem with IP helper on the routers. Put the analyzer on VLAN 1, and let it see all traffic from VLAN 1. Did you see the unicast DHCP requests, now coming from the routers? If so, good. Now, since it appears that they're getting to the server, let's see if the server is responding with an address. Leaving the analyzer on VLAN 1, now look for DHCP response packets going back to the client, using the temporary destination of the router. If you see the response packets, and the Layer 2 and 3 addressing of the packets look good, move the analyzer back to VLAN 3. Are the DHCP response packets getting back to this VLAN and their destination workstations? If you've covered all these bases, you can probably blame the problem on the PCs. However, since it's unlikely that all the PCs are ignoring the response, the problem is most likely network related. Checking the routers for correct HSRP and IP helper would most likely uncover the problem.

10

Cisco Switching Product Line

CERTIFICATION OBJECTIVES

10.01	Cisco IOS-Based Switching Products
10.02	Cisco Set-Based Switching Products
✓	Two-Minute Drill
Q&A	Self Test

The focus of this chapter is on Cisco's Layer 2, Layer 3, and Multilayer Switching Catalyst product line. The importance of this chapter is twofold: first, to provide you with knowledge of the Cisco product line and what features are currently offered with each particular model, and second, to help you select the appropriate switch for a given application.

Cisco's focus throughout the BCMSN course is one of stable network design. Recognizing and implementing the software features, to provide network stability, have been covered thus far. Selecting the proper hardware to support the necessary features of this network is important. This chapter focuses on the Cisco switching hardware product line, singling out the different models and their supported features, both in hardware and in software. Selecting the appropriate switch to buy, given a set of network requirements, will be easy once you have identified the function of each switch model.

The Cisco Catalyst product line consists of switches that meet the requirements for small offices to large enterprises. The configuration of these switches, unlike the routers, is not standardized across the Catalyst product line. Cisco uses a variety of configuration options that differ from one switch to the next. Configuration options differ from menu configuration to Web browsers to command-line interfaces (CLIs).

Cisco categorizes the switches into layers per the hierarchical networking design model. Depending on business requirements, such as port speeds (10MB vs. 100MB), port densities, and features, there a few models of switches recommended at each layer. The following outlines Cisco's Catalyst switches and recommended layer in the hierarchical model; this will be covered in detail throughout the chapter.

- Access layer (Workgroup Connectivity) 1900/2900XL/3500XL/4000/5000
- Distribution layer (Workgroup Aggregation) 4840G/5000/6000
- Core layer (Network Backbone) Catalyst 5500/6000/8500

CERTIFICATION OBJECTIVE 10.01

Cisco IOS-Based Switching Products

Cisco classifies their switches in two categories: IOS-based switches and SET IOS-based switches. IOS-based switches offer a command-line interface (CLI) similar to that used in the router product line, but allows for configuration of Layer 2 settings through a configuration mode. The SET IOS-based switches use different commands, typically preceded by the word "SET" within the enable mode.

The IOS-based products consist of the 1900/2820, 2900XL, and 3500XL product line. These smaller switches were designed to be used at the Access layer, and offer easy configuration consistency for those already familiar with router configuration.

Catalyst 1900 and 2820

Beginning with Cisco's entry-level switches are the Catalyst 1900 and 2820. These switches were one of Cisco's first Layer 2 offerings, and are still a current product. These two switches have received a few facelifts over the years, since Cisco's entry into the switching market with acquisitions of companies like Grand Junction, from which these switches came. Originally only menu based, today the 1900 family of switches offers menu, Web, and IOS command-line configuration options depending on the version of software.

The Catalyst 1900 switch was designed as a fixed configuration Access layer switch providing 12 to 24 ports of 10BaseT desktop with two 100MB ports for scalability to servers or other switches. The Catalyst 2820 is a 24-port 1900 with two modular bays offering a more flexible higher-speed connectivity solution. Both switches use the same operating system, which is available in two versions: Standard and Enterprise.

on the job

The exam will only focus on general features and guidelines. In reality, though, there are many situations and configurations that may or may not be supported, depending upon the ports used, upgrades, memory, phase of the moon, positions of a canary in Japan, etc. (You get the idea.) To list every possible exception would fill a book twice as thick as this, and would be out of date in three months. To keep up to date on the newest features and models, you must become familiar with the Cisco Web site at www.cisco.com, and Cisco CD Documentation (which comes with every switch and is duplicated on their Web site). Make sure there are no special issues when planning upgrades or network designs, especially as it might apply to a new IOS feature. Many times, hardware upgrades are required for any IOS-related upgrades.

Hardware Features of the Catalyst 1900 and 2820

There are currently five models of Catalyst 1900, each available in both a Standard and Enterprise version. Each model has a 1 Gigabit backplane referred to as the Exchange Bus, 3MB shared memory buffer, support for 1024 entries in its CAM (content addressable memory) table, supports 12 or 24 10BaseT ports, an additional AUI Ethernet port on the back, and either 1 or 2 100BaseT or 100BaseFX multimode fiber ports. The 1900 series are fixed in configuration and offer no field-serviceable upgrades. The following list outlines the Catalyst 1900 series switch by model number.

- 1912   12 ports 10BaseT, 1 AUI, and 2 100BaseT ports
- 1912C   12 ports 10BaseT, 1 AUI, 1 100BaseT, and 1 100BaseFX
- 1924   24 ports 10BaseT, 1 AUI, and 2 100BaseT ports
- 1924C   24 ports 10BaseT, 1 AUI, 1 100BaseT, and 1 100BaseFX
- 1924F   24 ports 10BaseT, 1 AUI, 2 100BaseFX

The Catalyst 2820 originally came in two models, the Catalyst 2822 and Catalyst 2828, both available in Standard and Enterprise software versions. The only difference between the two was the number of entries supported in the CAM. The 2822 supported 2048 CAM entries, while the 2828 supported 8192—both have the same 1 Gigabit backplane as the 1900. Today only the 2828 is currently offered and the 2822 is not field upgradeable. Both models have 24 10BaseT ports with an additional AUI on the back, and 2 modular expansion ports. The expansion ports allow this switch to be integrated into a larger network by offering ATM and FDDI modules in addition to 100 Mbps Ethernet. The following is a list of modules offered:

- **155 Mb ATM UTP**   1 UTP RJ-45 connected ATM port
- **155 Mb ATM MM Fiber**   1 multimode fiber connected ATM port
- ***FDDI Fiber DAS**   FDDI fiber attached station provides dual ring connections for redundancy, also offering an optical bypass
- ***FDDI Fiber SAS**   Single FDDI fiber attached station
- ***FDDI UTP SAS**   Single CDDI UTP attached station
- **100BaseTX/1**   Single 100BaseT port
- **100Base FX/1**   Single 100BaseFX multimode fiber port

- **100BaseTX/8** Offering 8 shared ports, acting as a 100BaseT hub connected to a single switch port
- **100BaseFX/8** Offering 8 shared ports, acting as an 100BaseFX multimode fiber hub connected to a single switch port

Note: All FDDI modules for the 2820 will be discontinued on November 13, 2000.

All models of Catalyst 1900/2820 offer a number of LEDs to provide switch status from the chassis itself. There is a system LED that indicates the system status. An RPS LED lets you know the status of a redundant power supply. The redundant power supply is an option for an external power supply that can be used to provide power should the internal power supply fail. The same external power supply can also be used with the 2900XL, 3500XL, and Fasthub product line. LEDs above ports are also present and provide three varying meanings, depending on the mode status. Initially, the mode is set to stat (status), indicating whether an individual port is providing link. By pressing the MODE button once, the mode changes to UTL (utilization mode). In this mode, port LEDs light up sequentially and indicate the switch's current and highest utilization since booting. By pressing MODE a second time, the mode changes to FDUP (full-duplex mode). In this mode, each LAD that lights indicates which ports are currently set for full duplex. The 2820 additionally offers LEDs on each module indicating that module's status.

EXERCISE 10-1

Observing and Diagnosing Catalyst Issues Using the LED Indicators

1. Find a Catalyst 19*xx* switch (a 28*xx* will also do) that is in use in a production or lab environment.

2. Examine the front of the switch. Find the "System" LED on the left-hand side of the front of the switch. Examine the state of the System LED—a green LED indicates a working Catalyst switch. If the switch is yellow, this indicates that the switch is on, but there may have been a startup problem. If it's off, then so is the switch.

3. Next, examine the RPS LED. This is for the Redundant Power Supply. Note the color (or lack thereof) on the LED. A solid LED indicates the RPS is there and operational (although that doesn't mean it's running with the main

power supply). A green flashing LED will indicate that an RPS is present and both power supplies are running. (NOTE: On the 1900 series, Cisco doesn't recommend this—you'll want to check your RPS documentation and start the 1900 before starting the RPS.) An amber LED means the RPS is installed, but not operating. If there is no LED, then there is no RPS.

4. Look for the MODE button over on the left side and press it a couple of times (it's alright, you won't break anything). A series of LEDs will light up above the ports and above the button. Press MODE until you see "STAT" lit up above MODE. This indicates the status of each port on the switch. Examine the LEDs above the ports. A green light means the port is on, and if it's flashing, then traffic is flowing through the port. An amber light means there is a problem. Usually this is a physical problem like a bad network interface card (NIC), an unplugged cable, or a bad connection. Collisions can also cause the light to flash amber for a brief time. Notice that ports may have cables in them, but no lights are on above them. These machines aren't on, or there is no computer connected to them. (Unplugged cables don't light up LEDs, just bad ones and ones working at the Data Link layer.)

5. Press MODE again. This will light up the UTL LED. This is an indication of bandwidth usage. The LEDs don't follow a percentage, but rather a graphical scale of usage depending on whether the switch has 12–24 ports. Green indicates current bandwidth usage, and amber indicates usage within the default period (usually 24 hours). If you see spikes or increased usage, you should go into the CLI and run a usage report on bandwidth. This may aid in troubleshooting peaks and spikes in bandwidth. Notice what you currently have running and what the peak in the last 24 hours has been. Usually, if all LEDs are lit or are amber, it's a representation of 50+ percent utilization within the last 24 hours. (Time for a new switch with more bandwidth!)

6. Press MODE again. This should light up the FDUP LED. This displays which ports are running in full-duplex mode, and which are running in half-duplex mode. A green LED above the port indicates that the port is running in full-duplex mode, while no LED indicates half-duplex mode.

7. If the switch is a 2900XL series, you'll be able to press MODE one more time and see the "100" LED light up. This indicates which ports are running at 100 Mbps vs. 10 Mbps. If the LED above the port is on, it's running at 100 Mbps. If it's off, then the port is running at 10 Mbps.

If you see anything unusual or high, use the IOS, menu, or Web-based interface to go into the switch to get more details about the issue and what the problem may be. The LEDs are designed to be a quick guide to possible issues, but you'll still need the IOS and information accessible inside the switch to determine what the issues are, and whether they are a normal occurrence or a problem that needs to be resolved.

Software Features of the Catalyst 1900 and 2820

Software features on the 1900 and 2820 are dependent on Standard or Enterprise versions. The Standard version's features are as follows:

- **Menu-Driven Configuration**
- **CVSM**   Cisco Visual Switch Manager, Web-based graphical configuration option
- **CDP ver 2.0**   Cisco Discovery Protocol
- **Fragment-Free or Store-and-Forward Switching**   Selectable modified cut-through, or store and forward switching
- **CGMP**
- **SPAN**   Configuration of a switched port analyzer that allows for the mirroring of traffic to any other port for the purpose of protocol analysis
- **Telnet**
- **Network Port**   A selectable port for flood control, acts as a default gateway at Layer 2
- **SNMP**   Allows a switch to be configured and managed remotely using an SNMP management station
- **RMON**   Allows switches to gather SNMP statistics, history, alarms, and events
- **802.1d**   Spanning-Tree
- **Cluster Capable**   Can be linked to a 2900XL or 3500XL command switch and configured as one management entity

Cisco's Enterprise version of software on the 1900/2820 provides additional feature to the Standard edition, including the following:

- IOS Command-Line Interface
- **VLANs** Support for 64 active
- VTP
- **ISL** Support of ISL on the 100BaseT and 100BaseFX ports
- **Fast EtherChannel** Port aggregation of 100BaseT or 100BaseFX ports
- UplinkFast
- TACACS+

Catalyst 2900XL and 3500XL

The Catalyst 2900XL family of switches was the first in Cisco's new line of switches built on IOS configuration. The 2900XL, like the 1900/2820, is positioned as an Access layer switch, but is a step up from the 1900/2820 by providing flexible port speeds, 10/100Mb Ethernet, and Gigabit Ethernet support. With the addition of the 3500XL, Cisco extends the capabilities of the XL architecture beyond the 2900XL by adding a higher-capacity backplane and extending the capabilities beyond clustering by adding Gigabit stacking capabilities.

Cluster Architecture

Cisco introduced the concept of cluster architecture to ease the burden of management. Traditional management requires that each device be given its own IP address and configured individually. Within a cluster, one switch acts as the cluster manager and is assigned a single IP address that will be used to configure all of the other devices in the stack. Using the Cisco cluster Web management tool, a network administrator can configure or view any port in the cluster. Within a cluster is support for up to 16 switches, and 9 when using Gigastack design. Support for clustering is found only in the IOS-based architectures and requires CDP for communication. The cluster can consist of a mix of switches from the 1900, 2820, 2900XL, and 3500XL families, and can be connected using Ethernet, Fast Ethernet, Gigabit, or channeling.

Using the Gigabit architecture of the 2924MXL and 3500XL along with a Gigastack GBIC, Cisco can produce a high-performance stackable cluster yielding up to 2-gigabit, full-duplex performance between switches. Design of a cluster can be done in a bus architecture or a hub-and-spoke design. In the bus architecture, one switch is linked to the next using a single GBIC between switches. These switches are daisy-chained together and can form a loop. This scenario provides for redundancy of switch failure, but does not take full advantage of the full bandwidth available had both GBICs been cabled to the same switch. A hub-and-spoke architecture can be built using the 3508XL as the hub. There are, however, distance limitations on this design—all switches must be with one meter of each other.

In each case, when clustering, a Master Command switch is required to perform as the manager of the cluster. With respect to Gigastack, the IOS on the Master Command switch must be running version 12.0(5) or higher. Using clustering, management can now be simplified to manage over 750 ports, across switches, and on one screen.

Hardware Features of the Catalyst 2900XL

Currently, there are five models of Catalyst 2900XL. The models are analogous with the 1900/2820 product line, in that there are fixed configuration models and modular models. The modular versions are denoted by the letter "M" in the model number. Each switch offers 10BaseT/100BaseTX ports built on a 3.2 Gb switching fabric. The switch implements a 4MB shared buffer architecture. The following outlines the 2900XL product line:

- **2912XL**   12 10BaseT/100BaseTX ports
- **2912MF XL**   12 100BaseFx ports, 2 modular slots
- **2924 XL**   24 10BaseT/100BaseTX ports
- **2924C**   22 10BaseT/100BaseTX ports, 2 100BaseFX ports
- **2912M XL**   24 ports 10BaseT/100BaseTX, 2 modular slots

Modules that are currently available for the 2912MF and 2924M are:

- 4-port 10/100BaseTX switched
- 2-port 100BaseFX switched

- 4-port 100BaseFX switched
- 1-port 1000BASE-X module (2924XL only)
  - 1000BASE-SX GBIC enables short-wave laser multimode fiber
  - 1000BASE-LX/LH GBIC single-mode fiber
- 1-port 1000BaseT module
- ATM OC-3
  - Single-port UTP
  - Multimode fiber
  - Single-mode fiber
- Medium distance: 10 Km
- Long Distance: 40 Km

Hardware Features of the Catalyst 3500XL

There are currently four models of the Catalyst 3500 XL switch. Each provides an upgraded backplane of 10 GB, 4 MB shared memory buffer, and built-in support for Gigabit. These switches are fixed in configuration. The following is a list of Catalyst 3500XL models.

- **3508XL**   8 GBIC-based Gigabit Ethernet ports
- **3512XL**   12 10BaseT/100BaseTX, 2 GBIC-based Gigabit Ethernet ports
- **3524XL**   24 10BaseT/100BaseTX, 2 GBIC-based Gigabit Ethernet ports
- **3548XL**   48 10BaseT/100BaseTX, 2 GBIC- based Gigabit Ethernet ports

The 3508XL is ideal as an closet aggregation switch to create a 2900XL and 3500XL switch cluster using the Gigastack GBICS.

Like their IOS-based counterparts, 1900/2820, the Catalyst 2900XL/3500XLs share a common look and feel, including the LEDs. In addition to the port LEDs representing status, utilization, and full duplex, the 2900XL/3500XLs add an additional option for speed. The mode indicator moving to the fourth position, speed, will light the LED above the port if it is in 100 Mbps mode; otherwise, it is set for 10 Mbps.

Software Features of the Catalyst 2900XL and 3500XL

The Cisco software on the Catalyst 2900XL originally came in two versions: Standard and Enterprise like the Catalyst 1900. The Standard version provided all basic functions and supported 64 VLANs, but without the capability of trunking or VTP. The Enterprise edition added support for these and more. Some of today's standard features on the Catalyst 2900XL and Catalyst 3500XL are as follows:

- CVSM   Cisco Visual Switch Manager
- IOS CLI
- VLAN Support   64 active on the 2900XL, 250 active on the 3500XL
- VTP
- ISL and 802.1q trunking
- 802.1p priority queuing
- SPAN port designation
- CGMP
- Fast and Gigabit EtherChannel
- CMS   Cisco Cluster Management Suite
- Telnet
- SNMP
- CDP
- RMON   Statistics, history, alarms, and events
- 802.1d per VLAN Spanning-Tree
- UplinkFast
- TACACS+

FROM THE CLASSROOM

Purchasing the Right Switch

One of the most commonly asked questions during class is, "What model of switch do you recommend?" My standard response at this point is, "It depends. Each company has different requirements, and each situation needs to evaluated individually."

Before purchasing new equipment, you must know your own network. You need to understand what equipment you currently have, and how it is used. There are a number of questions you should be able to answer. What is your application traffic, types of data, network layer protocols, throughput utilization, and traffic patterns? What port density is required for each wiring closet? What type of cable is used from the wiring closet to the desktop? What type is used between wiring closets? Once you have answered these questions, then you can need to consider the future.

Decide what you expect the life span of the new equipment to be. On average, this should be between 3–5 years, as most accounting departments depreciate the equipment in this timeframe. How will your applications change in the next few years? Will you be running voice or video? As you begin to answer, try not to underestimate your needs, as you do not want to have to upgrade too soon. Once these questions are answered, you will be in a better position to choose the right equipment.

Now for considerations in the equipment itself: consider the size of the switch and its maximum port density, port speeds, throughput capability, redundancy, and suite of features. During product selection, try to select the equipment to meet both current and future requirements. Try not to overbuy—if you purchase an overpowered switch, you will be throwing your money away. Keep in mind that technology is constantly advancing, and what costs $1000 today may cost $500 in a year. Also consider that as technology advances, new switches will emerge in the market. Since this technology is built on the design of software implanted in hardware, upgrade capability is not always simple and can prove quite costly, so try not to cut too many corners. As this decision is not always the easiest, consult Cisco's Web site for the latest in product offerings—there is nothing worse than getting a new product and realizing it has just been discontinued.

—*Barry Gursky CCSI, CCNP*

SCENARIO & SOLUTION

Twelve users need to connect to each other and to an FDDI SAS connection in another location using fiber-optic cable.	Use a 2820 series switch with an FDDI-SAS module.
A client is building a switch cluster and wants to use GBIC ports and built-in redundancy with speeds of up to 1 Gbps.	Use the 3500XL series with GBICs linked together in a bus pattern.
Someone is setting up a test lab and needs three VLANs with six ports each for testing. No WAN connectivity is required.	Use the 1924 series and separate the ports into the required VLANs.
Someone else is setting up a workgroup, but because of high bandwidth requirements, the workgroup will require 23 100BaseTX ports for all their connections. There are no modules available for expansion, so all features must be built into the switch.	Use the 2924 series (the XL or the M XL series). Remember that the 2924 F series only has 22 100BaseTX ports.

CERTIFICATION OBJECTIVE 10.02

Cisco Set-Based Switching Products

The Cisco product line we'll discuss next will be referred to as the SET IOS-based switching line. The reason for the distinction here is the fact that there is a completely different command syntax for the next selection of switches. The SET IOS is based on three major commands: SET, SHOW, and CLEAR. Unlike the IOS switches, they do not require a special configuration mode to issue commands, but are SET directly from the privileged mode. The switches that make up this product line are the 4000, 5000, and 6000 series. Both the 4000 and 6000 are direct descendents from the older 5000 series, which comes from Cisco's acquisition of Crescendo in the mid-1990s.

The 5000 series was the family of switches that brought Cisco to the forefront of the switching industry, but today's technology needs are slowly dating this family of switches. The 5000 sales today are mostly for the purpose of high-density Access layer switches. However, in companies that have largely deployed the 5000, one could still leverage on the multilayer switching capabilities and include them in the

Distribution and Core layers. The 4000 series, originally designed for the wiring closet and offering only Layer 2 services, now has an addition to the family with Layer 3 IP and IPX switching. The 6000 family has the brightest future; Cisco is leveraging heavily on this box and has brought it into the limelight of the product line. The 6000 offers support for LAN, WAN, and voice technologies, with Layer 2, 3, and multilayer switching features. It serves best in the Distribution and Core layers, although large enterprises are deploying the 6000 throughout the company.

SET IOS Software Features

Across the SET IOS platforms exists a standard suite of features found each model. It seems appropriate to list this at the beginning of this section, rather than repeat standards throughout. All of the 4000, 5000, and 6000 series switches support the following:

- 16,000 CAM entries
- VLAN support for 250 active VLANs numbered in the range of 1–1000
- VTP
- CGMP
- CDP Cisco Discover Protocol
- PaGP Fast EtherChannel and Gigabit EtherChannel Port Aggregation Protocol
- SET command CLI
- Telnet
- SNMP management compatible with CiscoWorks for Switches Internetworks (CWSI)
- RMON, including statistics, history, alarms and events
- SPAN port mirroring
- 802.1d Spanning-Tree per VLAN
- UplinkFast
- PortFast

- BackboneFast
- ISL and 802.1q trunking
- TACACS+
- Environmental monitoring

This listing contains highlights of most of the major features, but by no means includes all of the features that can be found within the robust command set.

Catalyst 4000 Series

The Catalyst 4000 series was designed to leverage on the knowledge and ease of deployment of the Cisco's 5000 series SET IOS. The 4000 offers an upgraded backplane of 24 Gbps, and is an ideal switch for the Access layer wiring closet and server farm. The 4003 and 4006 models offer modularity, while fixed configurations are available in the 4912G and 4908G-L3.

Hardware Features of the Catalyst 4003 and 4006

The Catalyst 4003 and 4006 make up the modular variety of the 4000 family of switches. Designed with flexibility in mind, each offers a 24 Gbps backplane, options for redundant power supplies, hot-swappable fan trays, 10/100/1000 Mbps Ethernet, and optional support for Layer 3 switching. The two differences that set these switches apart are the number of slots within the chassis, which determines the overall port density, and the Supervisor Engine, which varies by model. The 4003 uses the Supervisor I engine as the brains behind the Layer 2 switching engine, while the 4006 uses the new Supervisor II. The only two differences between the models are the 10 Mbps port for out-of-band management on the Supervisor I vs. the 10/100 Mbps out-of-band management port on Supervisor II, and the addition of Dual Gigabit Ethernet ports on the Supervisor II.

Once the Supervisor is placed in slot 1 of either chassis, the remaining two or five ports are available for any of the following modular offerings:

- 24-port 10/100 Mbps (MT-RJ)
- 48-port 10/100 Mbps (RJ-45 or Telco)

- Layer 3 Engine with 32-port 10/100 Ethernet + 2-Gigabit Ethernet (GBIC) supporting routing IP, IPX, and IP multicast with hardware-based packet forwarding
- 32-port 10/100 Mbps Ethernet with 2-port Gigabit
- 32-port 10/100 Mbps Ethernet with Daughter Card Uplink Support
   - Uplink Daughter Card module with 4-port 100 Mbps fiber (MT-RJ)
- 6-port Gigabit Ethernet module (GBIC)
- 18-port Gigabit Ethernet module (GBIC)
- Recently added 12-port copper-based Gigabit 1000 Mbps (RJ-45), plus 2-port 1000BASE-X (GBIC slots).
- Recently announced line modules to support Cisco's AVVID architecture (IP telephony)

Hardware Features of the Catalyst 4908G-L3 and 4912G

The two fixed-configuration models in the 4000 series are the 4908G-L3 and the 4912G. While both switches feature the same software options as the 4003/4006, each was designed with a very specific goal in mind. The 4912G was designed as a gigabit aggregation switch. With only 12 ports of Gigabit Ethernet (GBIC), this switch is ideal for consolidating the wiring closet due to it nonblocking architecture. The 4908G-L3 was designed as a mid-size campus backbone aggregation switch with Layer 3 services in mind. Designed with only 8 ports of Gigabit Ethernet (GBIC), the 4908G-L3 provides routing functionality for IP, IPX, and IP multicast with hardware-based packet forwarding.

You will have to remember models and features and continue to keep up to date on the newer switches that are coming out (including new switches that may come out after the publication of this book). In the past, Cisco listed specific objectives on the switching exam for switch models. This resulted in the test quickly becoming obsolete and looking less like a switching exam and more like a sales brochure. Cisco now uses general guidelines for their test objectives, and therefore can update the exam at any time to reflect new technology without changing the guidelines. Keep an eye on features, and try to commit each series and switch model to memory.

Catalyst 5000 Family

The Catalyst 5000 family is divided into three separate product lines: the 2900, 5000, and 5500. In Cisco's current switching line, the 5000 family sales for the most part have been pushed aside to make room for the newer generation of SET IOS switches: the 4000/6000 families. Still the most widely deployed switch family to date, the 5x00 line still lives on in the current Cisco product line. With such a distributed installed base, Cisco continues to enhance the current product line, with new modules and updates that support Fast EtherChannel (up to 4 100 Mbps aggregated), Gigabit Ethernet, Token Ring, and Layer 2, Layer 3, and multilayer switching.

The positioning of this switch series is viewed across the enterprise as fitting the profile for deployment in the Access, Distribution, and Core layers. The 2900, non-XL, switch provides fixed configuration, and although most of the product line has been discontinued, support for a newer generation of 2900 has arisen. The 5000 models offer a modular chassis and support a variety of line modules, although they are limited to a 1.2 Gbps backplane. The 5500 series also provides a modular design, with support for the same line modules in the 5000 and additional options for gigabit. The 5500 series offers three separate 1.2 Gbps backplanes, and optionally provides additional redundancy for the Supervisor switching engine.

on the job

Although you will need to know the features of the Catalyst 5000 for the exam, you may not want to consider the Catalyst 5000 when designing a new network. Although Cisco has been updating the features of the 5000 series to support gigabit speeds and new forms of multilayer switching for companies that have spent a lot of money on a Catalyst 5000 infrastructure, there are now better solutions that can take advantage of the newest switching features. High cost, limited scalability, and newer switches are all better reasons to look at your network and determine if one of Cisco's 4000/6000/8500 series would better meet the needs of your enterprise. These days, Cisco recommends the Catalyst 5000 switch as a wiring closet solution, and other switches like the 6000/8500 as backbone and core switches.

Hardware Features of the Catalyst 2948G

All that remains today of the Catalyst 2900 family is the 2948G. Although classified under the heading of Catalyst 5000, the 2948G resembles more closely the architecture of the 4000 than its predecessor the 2926. With a 24 Gbps backplane, the 2948G features a fixed configuration of 48 ports 10/100 and 2-port Gigabit Ethernet (GBIC). This model of switch provides Layer 2 services and shares in the SET IOS configuration, with all of the standard software features. This switch is positioned for the wiring closet.

Hardware Features of the Catalyst 5000

The 500x switches offer modular design, available in both a 2-slot (5002) and 5-slot (5000) configuration. The 5002 and 5000 differ in only one feature other than the number of modules supported: the power supply. The 5002 has dual fixed power supplies, while the 5000 offers modular power supplies. Both switches provide a 1.2 Gbps backplane and require a Supervisor module in slot 1 to provides all switching functions.

Hardware Features of the Catalyst 5500

The 550x switches also offer a modular design just like their counterparts the 500x, and are available in three options: the 5505, a 5-slot chassis; the 5509, a 9-slot chassis; and the 5500, a 13-slot chassis. All three switches feature the same options as the 500x, but additionally supply three separate 1.2 Gbps backplanes and an option for a redundant Supervisor Engine in the second slot.

The 5500 switch stands out in its class, as the chassis itself has capabilities for Layer 2 LAN switching and can simultaneously house either an ATM LS1010 or Layer 3 8510 switch in the lower portion of the chassis. Just as slot 1 of each Catalyst is reserved for a Supervisor Engine, slot 13 is reserved for the LS1010 ASP, ATM Switch Processor, or a 8510 SRP (Switch Route Processor). If slot 13 is populated, slots 9–12 can be configured with either Catalyst 5000 LAN modules, which communicate back to the Supervisor along a 1.2 Gbps backplane located on the left side of the chassis, or LS1010 or 8510 modules, which communicate over an independent 5 Gbps backplane, on the right side, back to the ASP or SRP, respectively. The the Catalyst 5500 chassis was designed to consolidate the wiring closet.

Catalyst 5000/5500 Series Modules

The Catalyst 5000 family of switches offers a wide variety of modules to be shared throughout the various models. There are several models of Supervisor modules, the brains behind the switch. Beyond the necessity of the Supervisor are the switching ports that are available in 10/100/1000 Mbps Ethernet, Token Ring, FDDI, and ATM. Also available are Layer 3 switching options of the RSM (Route Switch Module) and RSFC (Route Switch Feature Card).

The Supervisor   The Layer 2 switching modules for the 5000 family consist of three models of Supervisors: Supervisor I, Supervisor II, and Supervisor III. The Supervisor I, now discontinued, was designed only to support the 5000, as it only supplied communications along one backplane. The Supervisor II, available for all 5000/5500 models, connects to all three backplanes, if present, and links them together providing for only 1.2 Gbps of throughput. The Supervisor III also connects to all three backplanes, if present, but maintains separation using ASIC technology, so that a total of 3.6 Gbps aggregate throughput is available. The Supervisor II and III models offer the capability of redundancy, and options for multilayer switching. Both Supervisors offer a number of variations:

- Supervisor II—Features 2-port 100BaseTX and MII, or 2-port 100BaseFX (multimode or single-mode)
- Supervisor IIG—Features integrated NFFC II and modular port configuration
- Modules currently available for the Supervisor IIG:
    - 2-port 1000BaseSX
    - 2-port 1000BaseLX/LH
    - 4-port 10/100BaseTX
    - 4-port 100BaseFX
- Supervisor Engine III with the NetFlow Feature Card (NFFC) or NFFCII features PCMCIA flash and modular uplinks
- Modules currently available for the Supervisor III:
    - 2-port 10/100BaseTX

- 2-port 100BaseFX
- 2-port 1000BaseSX
- 2-port 100BaseFX SMF
- 2-port 1000BaseLX/LH
- 4-port 10/100BaseTX
- 4-port 100BaseFX

■ Supervisor IIIG—Features integrated NFFC II and 2-port Gigabit Ethernet (GBIC)

The Supervisor IIG and IIIG engines support the optional RSFC (Route Switch Feature Card) daughter card, providing integrated Layer 2 and 3 operation on the Supervisor module.

With the addition of the NFFC and NFFC II feature card, the Supervisor takes the Catalyst 5xxx switch beyond Layer 2 and into multilayer switching. The NFFC boosts performance of Layer 3 and 4 switching to gigabit levels. Using the route-once switch-many model, the NFFC caches information from both the Layer 2 CAM and router processor switching tables while maintaining the integrity of traffic filters from traditional access lists. With this technology, the Catalyst 5xxx family is a viable solution for the Distribution layer in the hierarchical model.

SCENARIO & SOLUTION

You have a 1.2 Gbps backplane on the switch (a la 5005).	Use a Supervisor II, as it is more economical and will provide enough functionality.
You want the fastest Supervisor Engine for the 5500 switch.	The Supervisor III is the fastest, but you'll need NFFC cards and a Router/RSM to get MLS.
You want an economical solution for the 5500.	The Supervisor III F is the most economical, but least flexible Supervisor module.
You want a Supervisor Engine with built-in NFFC.	Either the Supervisor II G or III G has built-in NFFC onto the engine.

Line Modules As stated previously, there is a variety of line modules available in the current product offering:

- **48-port Group Switch module** Uses telco adapters and supports four 12-port collision domains on one module
- **24-port 100BaseTX Group Switch module** Supports three 8-port collision domains
- **12-port 10BaseFL** SC MMF
- **24-port 10BaseFL** MT-RJ MMF
- **48-port Ethernet switch module** Uses telco adapters, but each port is individually switched 10BaseT
- **12-port 100BaseFX** 6 ports MMF, 6 ports SMF
- **12-port 100BaseFX** MMF, Fast EtherChannel, ISL/802.1q
- **12-port 10/100BaseTX with Fast EtherChannel support**
- **24-port 10/100BaseTX and 100BaseFX switched Ethernet module** Varies by part number, depending on feature requirements such as Fast EtherChannel, ISL, 802.1q, and WRED
- **3-port Gigabit Ethernet module** GBIC (550x only)
- **9-port Gigabit Ethernet module** GBIC (550x only)
- **16-port Token Ring UTP and MMF**
- **Dual Attached FDDI** MMF and SMF
- **Dual Attached CDDI**
- **ATM OC-3 Lane/MPOA module** Dual Phy SMF, MMF and UTP
- **ATM OC-12 Lane/MPOA module** Dual Phy SMF and MMF
- **ATM DS-3** Dual Phy
- **ATM Fabric Integration module** Designed to bridge the frame and cell backplanes when using the LS1010 (5500 only)
- **5500/8500 Fabric Integration module** Designed to allow for Layer 3 switching directly from the catalyst backplane (5500 only)

- **Network Analysis module** Allows protocol analysis captures directly for any port of the overall backplane

RSM/RSFC The RSM Route Switch module is designed for high-performance VLAN routing built directly into the architecture of the 5000 family, making it ideal for the enterprise backbone. The RSM is built on the hardware of the 7500 RSP (Route Switch Processor). With the optional VIP2 (Versatile Interface Processor) module, the RSM can add additional ports of Serial, HSSI, ISDN, and ATM.

The RSFC (Route Switch Feature Card) is also designed for high-performance VLAN routing. The module attaches to either the Supervisor IIG or IIIG and does not require the use of a slot, thereby allowing the switch to reach higher densities. The RSFC is built on the hardware of the 7200 RSP.

The RSM and RSFC both run Cisco IOS software, including support for all major desktop protocols including IP, IPX, AppleTalk, Vines, DECnet, XNS, NetBIOS, and SNA when running the enterprise feature set. Features of the IOS include support for Cisco's MLSP, HSRP, and CGMP, to name a few.

Catalyst 6000 Family

Cisco's 6000 family is designed to address the Distribution and Core layers. The 6000 family (made up of four models: 6006, 6009, 6506, 6509) offers high performance, high throughput, Layer 2, 3, 4 and multilayer switching. These new models take their heritage from the 5500 and extend them to new levels. By offering Supervisor redundancy, Fast EtherChannel (up to 8 ports aggregated), Gigabit EtherChannel (up to 8 ports aggregated), and a 15 Mpps switching engine, the 6000 family certainly has earned its right as the flagship switch of the Cisco product line. Newer features take the 6000 series into the next generation. With options such as QOS supporting modules, voice modules, routing-capable WAN cards, server load-balancing support, and network monitoring (including intrusion detection), Cisco is truly integrating varying product features in one voice and data converged chassis.

With all of the new features available, Cisco has also developed a new version of the operating system. The traditional configuration of the 6000 has been distributed, much like the 5000, with the Layer 2 configurations using SET IOS, and the router functions being performed separately on IOS. With the newly released optional IOS, Cisco converges the configuration of Layer 2 and Layer 3 features into IOS. This new version has mixed reviews; so far, network mangers familiar with SET IOS say it takes more work to get the Layer 2 configurations completed.

Hardware Features of the Catalyst 6000

The Catalyst 6000 models come in two options: a 6-slot model (6006) and a 9-slot model (6009). Like the other members of the SET IOS switch families, the 6000 family utilizes the Supervisor Engine as the brain to the switch. Originally offering only a Supervisor I, an enhanced version the Supervisor IA is available to accommodate the Multilayer Switch Feature Card (MSFC) and the Policy Feature Card (PFC). The switch offers a 32Gbps backplane. Modular port options are shared with the 6500 models, and include LAN, WAN, and voice.

Hardware Features of the Catalyst 6500

The Catalyst 6500 model, like its 6000 counterpart, comes in two options: the 6506 and 6509, with 6 and 9 slots, respectively. The 6500 is breaking new ground with the latest release of the Supervisor II module. Originally supporting only the Supervisor I and IA, the 6500 offered a 32Gbps backplane. However, with the newly released Supervisor II and the Switch Fabric Module (SFM), the 6500 now uses an otherwise dormant second backplane and can scale to 265 Gbps. This new combination requires a new variety of Fabric Enabled switch modules. This power-packed combination, along with the MSFC and PFC, adds a new level in distributed architecture using Distributed Cisco Express Forwarding (dCEF) on new Gigabit Ethernet modules, if enabled with an optional Distributed Forwarding Daughter Card (DFC).

Catalyst 6000/6500 Series Modules

The Catalyst 6000 series family of switches offers an even wider variety of options over the previous Catalyst models covered. There are three models of Supervisor, several options of 10/100/1000 Mbps Ethernet, ATM, and Voice modules. Also available are Layer 3 switching options of the MSM (Multilayer Switch Module), MSFC (Multilayer Switch Feature Card), and PFC (Policy Feature Card).

The Supervisor   Three models of Supervisor include the now discontinued Supervisor I, Supervisor IA, and Supervisor II. Each model supports all of the bridging functions of the Catalyst switch, and each has two built-in Gigabit Ethernet ports. The Supervisor I and IA share many of the same features, such as

32 Gbps backplane support, 15 Mpps switching engine, and Supervisor redundancy. The feature that sets these two modules apart is the optional support for the MSFC/MSFC2 and PFC on the Supervisor IA. The newly released Supervisor II module designed exclusively for the 6500 supports all of the features of the Supervisor IA, while additionally extending the backplane with the Switch Fabric module to 256Gbps. Additionally, adding the Distributed Feature Card (DFC) on the Supervisor II, distributed Cisco Express Forwarding (dCEF) can distribute the contents of the multilayer cache down to fabric-enabled line switch modules. This allows traffic entering these special line modules to be switched locally, bypassing the need for the Supervisor II, central processing engine, to see it.

Line Modules The list of available line modules for 6000/6500 are as follows:

- 24-port 10BaseFL MMF
- 24- port 100 FX MMF
- 48-port 10/100BaseTX
- 48-port 10/100 TeloModule
- 48-port 10/100BaseTX, Voice Enhanced QoS
- 8-port Gigabit Ethernet GBICs
- 16-port Gigabit Ethernet GBICs
- 16 port Gigabit Ethernet MT-RJ
- 16-port Single Switch Fabric enabled Gigabit Ethernet with optional DFC—capable of local switching with DFC with performance rates of 15 Mpps
- 16-port Dual Switch Fabric enabled Gigabit Ethernet with DFC—capable of local switching rates of 24 Mpps
- Switch Fabric module—required to enable 256Gbps backplane and dCEF on the line modules
- 1-port ATM Lane/MPOA OC-12 MMF and SMF
- FXS Analog Interface module—24 FXS ports promote integration of legacy analog telephone services with Cisco's AVVID (Architecture for Voice, Video, and Integrated Data) technology
- 48-port Inline Power 10/100BaseTX Ethernet modules—support integrated IP telephone discovery

- 8-port voice T1 and services module—designed for trunking of voice across the campus and integration with the PBX
- Network Analysis module—Gathers multilayer service information about voice and data for analysis; integrated support of RMON/RMON2 statistics

MSM/MSFC/PFC   The MSM (Multilayer Switch Module), like the RSM, was designed to provide integrated VLAN routing across the backplane. The module would reside in a slot of the chassis and treat the physical connection as though there were four separate gigabit interfaces. The MSM has now been discontinued in favor of the MSFC.

The MSFC (Multilayer Switch Feature Card) and newly released MSFC2 provide Layer 3 routing capability integrated on the Supervisor. When combined with the Flexible WAN module, the 6000 can become a powerful wide-area router. The FlexWAN module like the VIPII module, for the RSM, accepts the 7200/7500 port adapters. The following is a list of supported adapters:

- T1/E1 port module
- T3/E3 port module
- OC-3 port module
- HSSI

With the integration of the Policy Feature Card (PFC), the Supervisor enables application-aware switching capabilities. This allows for the classification of traffic and permits server load balancing in conjunction with Cisco's Local Director, providing end-to-end QoS.

With the presence of the PFC and MSFC/MSFC2, the Supervisor becomes enabled for multilayer switching. The MSFC performance of the multilayer switching reaches 15 Mpps, while the new MSFC2 reaches 24 Mpps. The MSFC2 enables the dCEF capability when combined with the Distributed Forwarding Card (DFC) and Multilayer Switch Fabric module. With this feature enabled, the Layer 3 switching cache in the 6000 series Supervisor can reach switching performance approaching 100 Mpps.

The MSFC and MSFC2 offer the full suite of support from enterprise IOS, and provide support for IP, IPX, and IP Multicast with Layer 3 switching performance. Other protocols such as AppleTalk, DECnet, VINES, XNS, OSI, and CLNS obtain rates of 200,000pps utilizing the MSFC, and 680,000pps using an MSFC2.

Catalyst 8500CSR

The 8500CSR (Campus Switch Router) family is in a different class from the rest of the switches covered. As a switch router, commonly referred to as a Layer 3 switch, the 8500 provides a distributed packet forwarding engine. The 8500 product line supports 10/100/1000-Mbps Layer 3 switching, and can also serve as an ATM Layer 2 switch—this is the Multiservice Switch Router (MSR), which is not covered in this course. The 8510 shares the IOS of the Cisco router product line, making for ease of transition when moving from the traditional routing model. Available in two models—the 8510 providing a 5-slot chassis and the 8540 providing a 13-slot chassis—this switch meets today's needs for large enterprise environments, as Layer 3 campus backbone switches.

Hardware Features of the Catalyst 8510CSR

The 8510CSR is a modular 5-slot chassis with a 10Gbps backplane. Like other modular switches, the 8510CSR requires a switching module; in this case, Layer 3. The Switch Route Processor (SRP) provides this function, but unlike the Layer 2 Supervisor, the SRP resides in slot 3, central to line modules. This switching engine built on ASIC technology limits the support of the IOS feature set to IP, IPX, and IP Multicast only, at rates of 6 Mpps using Cisco's dCEF design. The modules of the 8510CSR can also be supported in slots 9–12 in the 5500 chassis once slot 13 has been populated with the SRP—this eliminates the need for a separate chassis.

Catalyst 8510CSR Modules   The Catalyst 8510CSR module series is limited in its offering to just three Ethernet family modules. Each module stores local cache tables to create the distributed Layer 3 switching environment. These modules offer support for Fast EtherChannel, up to 8 ports.

- 8-port 10/100 Mbps Fast Ethernet—UTP
- 8-port 100 Mbps Fast Ethernet—Multimode fiber
- 1-port Gigabit Ethernet—GBIC

Hardware Features of the Catalyst 8540CSR

The 8540CSR is also modular in design, but with a much larger 13-slot chassis this model runs on a 40Gbps backplane. Similar to the 6500's scalable design, the 8540 requires switch and route processing on two different modules. Two Fabric Switching modules provide the infrastructure for switching frames across the backplane, while the

SRP provides the Layer 3 processing engine. These modules are required; the SRP resides in slot 4, and the Fabric Switching modules reside in slots 5 and 6. There is also the optional support for redundancy of both the SRP and Fabric Switching modules within the chassis. Running IOS, this model supports the same features as the 8510. With distributed hardware forwarding using dCEF, the 8540 can scale to performance levels of 24 Mpps.

Catalyst 8540CSR Modules The 8540 is also limited in its module offering to just three modules, but with higher port densities. Note that the modules are not interchangeable between the 8510 and 8540. The modules of the 8540 support dCEF and vary in cache size. Each supports the capability of Fast EtherChannel and Gigabit EtherChannel.

- 16-port 10/100 Mbps Ethernet
- 16-port 100BaseFX Multimode
- 2-port Gigabit Ethernet—GBIC

SCENARIO & SOLUTION

A customer wants to install a new switch in a wiring closet at one of his remote sites. It will need about 50–100 100BaseTX ports, and the customer also wants to be able to have ATM operability.	The Catalyst 5500 switch can offer high port density and ATM switching backplane for wiring-closet solutions.
The fiber-optic backbone is acting up, and management wants to replace it with a high-speed Ethernet solution. What do you suggest?	The Catalyst 6000 series with Gigabit Ethernet and multilayer switching can serve as a replacement for backbone routers.
The e-commerce group wants to build a gigabit server farm using GBIC technology for 11 separate servers. What do you recommend?	The Catalyst 4912G series has 12 GBIC-enabled ports for server farm aggregation.
The networking group also wants a GBIC solution for their wiring closet, but they want to start getting the pieces in place for a Layer 3 switching network. Given this piece of information, what is the switch you would recommend?	The 4908G-L3 for multilayer switching will give them the option for Layer 3 switching right out of the box.
The Cisco 7500 router that the company uses for the entire network is being replaced. If you were to put in a switching/routing solution that could hook into an Ethernet backbone, what would you want to use?	The Catalyst 8500 CSR series can handle all the features and functions of a core router, and the CSR series is optimized for Ethernet backbones.

EXERCISE 10-2

Evaluating Products for Use in a LAN Environment

In this exercise, you will be evaluating the correct products to use based on a developing set of conditions. There may be more than one right answer per question, but try to plan a number of solutions you could use to deal with the requirements.

1. The call has just come down from management of the impending merger of your consulting company with another company. You will be migrating the company from a Token Ring to an Ethernet network. At this time, you are focused on the primary site that has about 150 workstations and 10–15 servers, all of which have to be connected in one LAN. What products can you use to meet these requirements?

2. The word just went out that the migration is taking place, and managers are demanding performance at least as good as the 16-Mbps quality of Token Ring. Therefore, you are not going to be using 10BaseT wiring. What products can be used to meet the requirements?

3. Some people in your company read in a trade magazine about VLANs, and want to set up a VLAN for each department (about nine of them). In addition, they'll want to set up routing between them, just in case it's a requirement (actually, they're trying to use up their budget—which sometimes happens in the real world). What will you use as a solution? If you are using 2900/3500XL switches, what would you want to use as opposed to a Catalyst 5000/6000 solution?

4. It has been determined that the new company has a network based on OSPF routing. As it stands, you're not going to be able to use OSPF on your old network router, so you decide to look at switching routers for a solution. Which Catalyst products discussed are switching routers?

5. Last but not least, some salespeople suggested that if they are going to sell a multilayer switching solution, they'll want someone to implement it so they can say so in the advertising. Therefore, the company's new network is going to be a guinea pig for the new technology. If you want to implement multilayer switching, what products are you going to use?

CERTIFICATION SUMMARY

In this chapter, you have been provided with a great deal of hardware information with respect to Cisco's comprehensive offering of Catalyst switches. Offering two completely different operating systems, Cisco supports a large number of features, including PVST (Per VLAN Spanning-Tree), ISL and 801.q trunking, Fast and Gigabit EtherChannel, and Layer 2, Layer 3, and multilayer switching. For the purposes of BCMSN, you are not required to memorize each module available, but you are expected to understand software and hardware features of each switch, including port densities. An understanding of where each switch is positioned within the campus network hierarchical model is imperative. The necessity to distinguish between Layer 2, Layer 3, and multilayer services and the equipment required to support these features is also required.

Keep in mind that depending on port density, you may choose the 1900/2820, 2900/3500XL, 4000, or 5000, or may even consider the 6000 at the Access layer. The 4908G-L3, 5000/5500, and 6000/6500 with support for multilayer switching fit best at the Distribution layer, while the 5500, 6000/6500, and 8500 are best utilized in the Core.

TWO-MINUTE DRILL

The following are some of the key points from each certification objective in Chapter 10.

Cisco IOS-Based Switching Products

- ❏ The Catalyst 1900/2820 series provides workgroup connectivity for desktop stations and wiring closets.
- ❏ The Catalyst 2900XL series is designed to service high-bandwidth users and switch clusters.
- ❏ The Catalyst 3500XL brings gigabit connectivity to the workgroup/wiring closet of LANs and server farms.

Cisco Set-Based Switching Products

- ❏ The Catalyst 4000 series provides concentrated bandwidth for workgroups or servers using gigabit technology based on Catalyst 5000 technology and Layer 3 switching.
- ❏ The Catalyst 5000 series is the old workhorse of the Catalyst series, and is ideal for large wiring closets or as the backbone for small/medium networks.
- ❏ The Catalyst 2900 series provides Catalyst 5000 functionality in a smaller, fixed configuration.
- ❏ The Catalyst 6000 series is Cisco's new gigabit-centered solution for campus and network backbones.
- ❏ The Catalyst 8500 is the large-scale "switching router" designed to be at the core of a campus LAN environment.
- ❏ The brain of a Catalyst 4000/5000/6000 switch is the Supervisor Engine module that resides in slot 1 of the switch.
- ❏ The Route Switch Module (RSM) provided an early routing solution for the Catalyst 5000 series.
- ❏ Cisco designed the Route Switch Feature Card (RSFC) to work with the Supervisor Engine to provide RSM functionality without requiring a module.

- ❏ To achieve multilayer switching, you need two devices: a device that provides routing and IOS functionality, and a device for caching/switching Layer 3 addresses.
- ❏ Newer Catalyst 5000 Supervisor Engines can support a Router Switch Feature Card (RSFC) and the NetFlow Feature Card (NFCC) to perform multilayer switching.
- ❏ Catalyst 6000 switches can use the Multilayer Switch Feature Card (MSFC and MSFC2) and Policy Feature Card (PFC) combination.
- ❏ The Catalyst 8500 series is primarily a router that uses Cisco Express Forwarding and dedicated ASICs to perform switching functions at Layer 3 of the OSI model.

SELF TEST

The following questions will help you measure your understanding of the material presented in this chapter. Read all of the choices carefully, as there may be more than one correct answer. Choose all correct answers for each question.

Cisco IOS-Based Switching Products

1. What is the name of the Web-based management interface for Catalyst switches that resides in the switch?

   A. RMON
   B. CVSM
   C. CWSI
   D. SPAN

2. You have a group of 1900 switches that you want to cluster and break up into six VLANs. Which steps you should take if you wish to accomplish these two goals?

   A. Upgrade the IOS to Enterprise Edition software
   B. Plug all the switches into the same power supply
   C. Create a Master switch to run the cluster
   D. All of the above

3. Management has about 15 Web servers they want clustered on their own segment. They will be using full-duplex 100BaseTX connections and will connect to the backbone using fiber-optic connections from the switch. What would be the best solution?

   A. Use a Catalyst 1924C and manually convert all ports to 100BaseTX
   B. Use a Catalyst 2820 and slap in a module for fiber optic
   C. Grab a Catalyst 2948G-:L3
   D. Use a Catalyst 2924XL

4. The development team is complaining that network response time is slow. They are blaming the 2924XL switch that all computers in the department use, saying it doesn't have the bandwidth capabilities. What can you do to check bandwidth usage and confirm that the switch is the problem?

   A. Unplug the switch and reset it

B. Press MODE until you get to % LED
   C. Press MODE until you get to STAT LED
   D. Press MODE until you get to UTIL LED

Cisco Set-Based Switching Products

5. What would be the most likely candidates as a command you would use on a Catalyst 5000? (Choose two.)

   A. Set port duplex
   B. Spanning-Tree Participate
   C. More System:startup-config
   D. Show config

6. Management has gotten the latest sales brochure and demands that you implement Catalyst 5000 multilayer switching on all switches. You just made a major purchase to the router infrastructure, investing in two Cisco 7500s. Given this bit of information, what would be the most cost-effective solution?

   A. Purchase Route Switch modules for your Catalyst 5000
   B. Purchase NFFCs for the Catalyst, and use the router-on-a-stick method
   C. Put in Multilayer Switch modules
   D. Do nothing. The Catalyst 5000 already does multilayer switching

7. Which of the following switches has the same look and feel as a Catalyst 5000? (Choose all that apply.)

   A. Catalyst 2900XL series
   B. Catalyst 2900G series
   C. Catalyst 3500XL series
   D. Catalyst 4000 series
   E. Catalyst 6000 series

8. Which module is the Supervisor module on a Catalyst 4006?

   A. Supervisor Engine I
   B. Supervisor Engine II
   C. Supervisor Engine III

D. Supervisor Engine III F

9. Which Supervisor Engine has the onboard NFFC integrated into the card?

   A. Supervisor Engine I
   B. Supervisor Engine II
   C. Supervisor Engine II G
   D. Supervisor Engine III

10. There is a malfunction in the RSFC on the Catalyst 5500 you use to run your company. You do have spare parts lying around. Which solution would you recommend to temporarily replace the functions of the 5500?

    A. Take out a port slot and put in an MSM
    B. Swap out the Supervisor III G with a Supervisor III F
    C. Take out a port slot and put in an RSM
    D. Swap the RSFC with one from a compatible Catalyst 8500

11. What does RSM stand for?

    A. Redundant Switch Module
    B. Route Switch Module
    C. Redundant Service Module
    D. Redundant Switch Module

12. When would you want to use an RSM to enable MLS on a Catalyst 6000?

    A. When you need to fill all available slots with modules
    B. When you have a Supervisor III G with NFFC
    C. When you have a Supervisor III with RSFC
    D. You wouldn't use an RSM with a Catalyst 6000 switch

13. Management has gotten the latest sales brochure and demands that you implement Catalyst 5000 multilayer switching on all switches. You just made a major purchase to the router infrastructure, investing in two Cisco 2500s. Given this bit of information, what would be the most cost-effective solution?

    A. Purchase Route Switch modules for your Catalyst 5000
    B. Purchase NFFCs for the Catalyst, and use the router-on-a-stick method

C. Put in Multilayer Switch modules

   D. Get the Supervisor III G and put a RSFC on it

14. What would you do to enable MLS on a Catalyst 6000? (Choose two.)

    A. Put in a Supervisor Engine III G with an RSFC on it

    B. Put in a Supervisor Engine I-A with an MSFC and a PFC on it

    C. Put in a Supervisor Engine II G with NFFC embedded

    D. Put in a MSM

15. What does NFFC stand for?

    A. NetFire Feature Card

    B. NetFlow Feature Card

    C. Network Function Feature Card

    D. NetFast Feature Card

16. What is the difference between an RSFC and MSFC?

    A. The RSFC is a card, and the MSFC is embedded.

    B. The RSFC works in a Catalyst 5000, and the MSFC works in a Catalyst 6000.

    C. The RSFC is an MLS-SE, and the MSFC is a MLS-RP.

    D. The RSFC works in a Catalyst 4000, and the MSFC works in a Catalyst 5000.

LAB QUESTION

In your company, you have an old set of hubs running 200 computers on an isolated segment. You are getting excessive collisions and bandwidth issues due to intensive network applications. You need a cheap and easy solution that will reduce network collisions. You also would like some features that aren't available to networked hubs, such as management from remote sites and Web-based interfaces, as well as some redundancy for the flow of traffic. Design a solution that will give you an easy, manageable replacement for stacked hubs.

SELF TEST ANSWERS

Cisco IOS-Based Switching Products

1. ☑ **B.** The Cisco Visual Switch Manager (CVSM) is the Web-based interface that resides in the switch memory.
   ☒ **A,** RMON, is incorrect because it is a monitoring standard (remote monitoring). **C,** CWSI, is incorrect because it is a switch manager, but it comes with Ciscoworks and doesn't reside in flash memory. **D,** SPAN, is incorrect because it is a port feature on a Catalyst switch.

2. ☑ **A, C.** To run more than four VLANs, you will need Enterprise Edition software. You also need a certain software version to work with Cluster Manager. You will also need a Master switch (like a 3500 or 2900XL) to run the cluster as the manager.
   ☒ **B** is incorrect, although they do need to be within so many feet of each other to work right. **D** is incorrect for the same reason.

3. ☑ **D.** A Catalyst 2924XL meets all requirements easily.
   ☒ **A** and **B** are incorrect because they don't support 100BaseTX from their ports. **C** is incorrect because it doesn't support 100BaseFX connections.

4. ☑ **D.** The UTIL mode is the one that displays how much bandwidth is being used on the switch. The lights over the ports light up on a scale from 1–100 percent to give you a basic visual idea of what percentage of the bandwidth is being used.
   ☒ **A** is incorrect because unplugging the switch and resetting it will not check bandwidth usage and confirm it is a switch. **B** doesn't exist, and **C** will only show you port statistics, not bandwidth usage.

Cisco Set-Based Switching Products

5. ☑ **A, D.** The Catalyst 5000 series uses the Set-based IOS configuration commands: "set" and "show."
   ☒ **B** is a menu choice on a Catalyst 1900, and **C** is what you use for a configuration on a Cisco 12.0 router.

6. ☑ **B.** By purchasing NFFCs to handle the switching and rewriting of packets, the router-on-a-stick method will handle IOS functions for MLS.
   ☒ **A** is incorrect because it doesn't implement MLS, and only duplicates features you can do with the Cisco 7500. **C** is incorrect because it works for the Catalyst 6000, but not the 5000. **D** is incorrect because the Catalyst 5000 does not have inherent multilayer switching built in.

7. ☑ B, D, and E all use the Set-based CLI.
   ☒ A and C are incorrect because they use an IOS-based CLI.

8. ☑ B. The Supervisor Engine II works in the 4006.
   ☒ A is usually for the 4003, while C and D are for the Catalyst 5000 series.

9. ☑ C. The NFFC comes embedded on the G series Supervisor Engine.
   ☒ A, B, and D are incorrect because none of them have an embedded NFFC, although the Supervisor III can get an NFFC as an expansion card.

10. ☑ C. The RSM will do the same functions as the RSFC.
    ☒ A is incorrect because the MSM doesn't work with the Catalyst 5000. B and D are incorrect because there is no RSFC on the Supervisor III F or in the Catalyst 8500.

11. ☑ B. RSM stands for Route Switch Module.
    ☒ A, C, and D are incorrect because they are not legitimate modules.

12. ☑ D is the correct answer for the Catalyst 6000.
    ☒ B would serve as a correct answer for a Catalyst 5000. A and C don't work on a 6000, and wouldn't enable MLS anyway.

13. ☑ D. This will perform MLS switching on the Catalyst 5000.
    ☒ A is incorrect because it is only part of a multilayer solution. B is incorrect because you can't perform MLS using the router-on-a-stick method with a Cisco 2500. C is incorrect because the MSM will work on a Catalyst 6000, but not on a Catalyst 5000.

14. ☑ B, D. You can meet the MLS switching requirements with either an MSM or the MSFC/PFC combo.
    ☒ Neither A nor C are designed for the Catalyst 6000; they work in the Catalyst 5000.

15. ☑ B. NFFC stands for NetFlow Feature Card.
    ☒ A, C, and D incorrect because they are fictitious.

16. ☑ B. The RSFC is the feature card for the Catalyst 5000, while the MSFC is the card for the Catalyst 6000. They are not interchangeable between models.
    ☒ A is incorrect because the MSFC is also a card. C is incorrect because the RSFC isn't an MLS-SE. D is incorrect because the MSFC doesn't work in a Catalyst 5000, and the RSFC isn't used in a Catalyst 4000.

LAB ANSWER

Probably the best solution for this sort of a situation would be a switch cluster with the 3500XL series. You can run nine 3524XLs in a Gigastack (24*9=216), and they can be looped in a bus so that if a link goes down between one switch, it will take the other path. This will give you gigabit speeds with enough ports without having to justify the purchase of a larger switch. Furthermore, the cluster can be managed using Cisco Visual Switch Manager and from a Web interface. This will allow complete management of all switches from one point.

A
About the CD

This CD-ROM contains the CertTrainer software. CertTrainer comes complete with ExamSim, Skill Assessment tests, and the e-book (electronic version of the book), and DriveTime. CertTrainer is easy to install on any Windows 98/NT/2000 computer and must be installed to access these features. You may, however, browse the e-book directly from the CD without installation.

Installing CertTrainer

If your computer CD-ROM drive is configured to autorun, the CD-ROM will automatically start up upon inserting the disk. From the opening screen you may either browse the e-book or install CertTrainer by pressing the *Install Now* button. This will begin the installation process and create a program group named "CertTrainer." To run CertTrainer use START | PROGRAMS | CERTTRAINER.

System Requirements

CertTrainer requires Windows 98 or higher and Internet Explorer 4.0 or above and 600 MB of hard disk space for full installation.

CertTrainer

CertTrainer provides a complete review of each exam objective, organized by chapter. You should read each objective summary and make certain that you understand it before proceeding to the SkillAssessor. If you still need more practice on the concepts of any objective, use the "In Depth" button to link to the corresponding section from the Study Guide.

Once you have completed the review(s) and feel comfortable with the material, launch the SkillAssessor quiz to test your grasp of each objective. Once you complete the quiz, you will be presented with your score for that chapter.

ExamSim

As its name implies, ExamSim provides you with a simulation of the actual exam. The number of questions, the type of questions, and the time allowed are intended to be an accurate representation of the exam environment. You will see the following screen when you are ready to begin ExamSim:

When you launch ExamSim, a digital clock display will appear in the upper left-hand corner of your screen. The clock will continue to count down to zero unless you choose to end the exam before the time expires.

There are three types of questions on the exam:

- **Multiple Choice** These questions have a single correct answer that you indicate by selecting the appropriate check box.
- **Multiple-Multiple Choice** These questions require more than one correct answer. Indicate each correct answer by selecting the appropriate check boxes.
- **Simulations** These questions simulate actual Windows 2000 menus and dialog boxes. After reading the question, you are required to select the appropriate settings to most accurately meet the objectives for that question.

Saving Scores as Cookies

Your ExamSim score is stored as a browser cookie. If you've configured your browser to accept cookies, your score will be stored in a file named *History*. If your browser is not configured to accept cookies, you cannot permanently save your scores. If you delete this History cookie, the scores will be deleted permanently.

E-Book

The entire contents of the Study Guide are provided in HTML form, as shown in the following screen. Although the files are optimized for Internet Explorer, they can also be viewed with other browsers including Netscape.

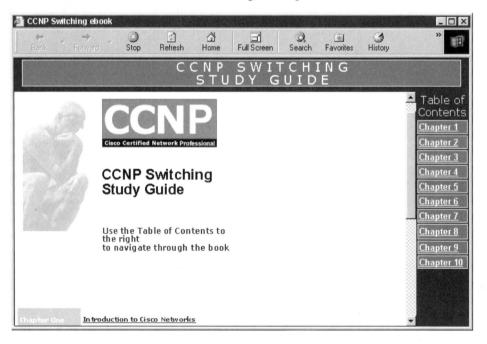

DriveTime

DriveTime audio tracks will automatically play when you insert the CD ROM into a standard CD player, such as the one in your car or home stereo. There is one track for each chapter. These tracks provide you with certification summaries for each chapter and are the perfect way to study while commuting.

Help

A help file is provided through a help button on the main ExamSim Gold screen in the lower right hand corner.

Upgrading

A button is provided on the main ExamSim screen for upgrades. This button will take you to www.syngress.com where you can download any available upgrades.

Glossary

10Base2   Ethernet specification using 50-ohm thin coaxial cable and a signaling rate of 10-Mbps baseband.

10Base5   Ethernet specification using standard (thick) 50-ohm baseband coaxial cable and a signaling rate of 10-Mbps baseband.

10BaseFL   Ethernet specification using fiber-optic cabling and a signaling rate of 10-Mbps baseband, and FOIRL.

10BaseT   Ethernet specification using two pairs of twisted-pair cabling (Category 3, 4, or 5): one pair for transmitting data and the other for receiving data, and a signaling rate of 10-Mbps baseband.

10Broad36   Ethernet specification using broadband coaxial cable and a signaling rate of 10 Mbps.

100BaseFX   Fast Ethernet specification using two strands of multimode fiber-optic cable per link and a signaling rate of 100-Mbps baseband. A 100BaseFX link cannot exceed 400 meters in length.

100BaseT   Fast Ethernet specification using UTP wiring and a signaling rate of 100-Mbps baseband. 100BaseT sends link pulses out on the wire when there is no data traffic present.

100BaseT4   Fast Ethernet specification using four pairs of Category 3, 4, or 5 UTP wiring and a signaling rate of 100-Mbps baseband. The maximum length of a 100BaseT4 segment is 100 meters.

100BaseTX   Fast Ethernet specification using two pairs of UTP or STP wiring and 100-Mbps baseband signaling. One pair of wires is used to receive data; the other is used to transmit. A 100BaseTX segment cannot exceed 100 meters in length.

100BaseX   100-Mbps baseband Fast Ethernet specification based on the IEEE 802.3 standard. 100BaseX refers to the whole 100Base family of standards for Fast Ethernet.

80/20 rule   General network standard that 80 percent of traffic on a given network is local (destined for targets in the same workgroup); and not more than 20 percent of traffic requires internetworking.

AAL (ATM adaptation layer)   Service-dependent sublayer of the Data Link layer. The function of the AAL is to accept data from different applications and present it to the ATM layer in 48-byte ATM segments.

AARP (AppleTalk Address Resolution Protocol)   The protocol that maps a data-link address to an AppleTalk network address.

ABR (area border router)   Router located on the border of an OSPF area, which connects that area to the backbone network. An ABR would be a member of both the OSPF backbone and the attached area. It maintains routing tables describing both the backbone topology and the topology of the other area.

access list   A sequential list of statements in a router configuration that identify network traffic for various purposes, including traffic and route filtering.

accounting   Cisco command option that, when applied to an interface, makes the router keep track of the number of bytes and packets sent between each pair of network addresses.

acknowledgment   Notification sent from one network device to another to acknowledge that a message or group of messages has been received. Sometimes abbreviated ACK. Opposite of **NACK**.

active hub   A multiport device that repeats and amplifies LAN signals at the Physical layer.

active monitor   A network device on a Token Ring that is responsible for managing ring operations. The active monitor ensures that tokens are not lost, or that frames do not circulate indefinitely on the ring.

address A numbering convention used to identify a unique entity or location on a network.

address mapping Technique that allows different protocols to operate together by associating addresses from one format with those of another.

address mask A string of bits, which, when combined with an address, describes which portion of an address refers to the network or subnet and which part refers to the host. *See also* **subnet mask**.

address resolution A technique for resolving differences between computer addressing schemes. Address resolution most often specifies a method for mapping network layer addresses to Data Link layer addresses. *See also* **address mapping**.

Address Resolution Protocol *See* ARP.

administrative distance A rating of the preferability of a routing information source. Administrative distance is expressed as a value between 0 and 255. The higher the value, the lower the preference.

advertising A process in which a router sends routing or service updates at frequent intervals so that other routers on the network can maintain lists of usable routes or services.

algorithm A specific process for arriving at a solution to a problem.

AMI (alternate mark inversion) The line-code type that is used on T1 and E1 circuits. In this code, zeros are represented by 01 during each bit cell, and ones are represented by 11 or 00, alternately, during each bit cell.

ANSI (American National Standards Institute) An organization of representatives of corporate, government, and other entities that coordinates standards-related activities, approves U.S. national standards, and develops positions for the United States in international standards organizations.

APaRT *(automated packet recognition/translation)* Technology that enables a server to be attached to CDDI or FDDI without necessitating the reconfiguration of applications or network protocols. APaRT recognizes specific data link layer encapsulation packet types; when these packet types are transferred to another medium, they are translated into the native format of the destination device.

AppleTalk A suite of communications protocols developed by Apple Computer for allowing communication among their devices over a network.

Application layer Layer 7 of the OSI reference model. This layer provides services to end-user application processes such as electronic mail, file transfer, and terminal emulation.

ARP (Address Resolution Protocol) Internet protocol used to map an IP address to a MAC address.

ASBR (autonomous system boundary router) An ASBR is an ABR connecting an OSPF autonomous system to a non-OSPF network. ASBRs run two protocols: OSPF and another routing protocol. ASBRs must be located in a nonstub OSPF area.

asynchronous transmission Describes digital signals that are transmitted without precise clocking or synchronization.

ATM (Asynchronous Transfer Mode) An international standard for cell relay suitable for carrying multiple service types (such as voice, video, or data) in fixed-length (53-byte) cells. Fixed-length cells allow cell processing to occur in hardware, thereby reducing latency.

ATM adaptation layer *See* AAL.

ATM Forum International organization founded in 1991 by Cisco Systems, NET/ADAPTIVE, Northern Telecom, and Sprint to develop and promote standards-based implementation agreements for ATM technology.

AUI (attachment unit interface)   An interface between an MAU and a NIC (network interface card) described in the IEEE 802.3 specification. AUI often refers to the physical port to which an AUI cable attaches.

auto-discovery   A mechanism used by many network management products, including CiscoWorks, to build a map of a network.

autonomous system   A group of networks under a common administration that share in a common routing strategy. Sometimes abbreviated AS.

B channel (Bearer channel)   An ISDN term meaning a full-duplex, 64-Kbps channel used to send user data.

B8ZS (binary 8-zero substitution)   The line-code type that is used on T1 and E1 circuits. With B8ZS, a special code is substituted whenever eight consecutive zeros are sent over the link. This code is then interpreted at the remote end of the connection.

backoff   The retransmission delay used by contention-based MAC protocols such as Ethernet, after a network node determines that the physical medium is already in use.

bandwidth   The difference between the highest and lowest frequencies available for network signals. The term may also describe the throughput capacity of a network link or segment.

baseband   A network technology in which a single carrier frequency is used. Ethernet is a common example of a baseband network technology.

baud   Unit of signaling speed equal to the number of separate signal elements transmitted in one second. Baud is synonymous with bits per second (bps), as long as each signal element represents exactly one bit.

bearer channel   *See* B channel.

BECN (backward explicit congestion notification)   A Frame Relay network facility that allows switches in the network to advise DTE devices of congestion. The BECN bit is set in frames traveling in the opposite direction of frames encountering a congested path.

best-effort delivery   Describes a network system that does not use a system of acknowledgment to guarantee reliable delivery of information.

BGP (Border Gateway Protocol)   An interdomain path-vector routing protocol. BGP exchanges reachability information with other BGP systems. It is defined by RFC 1163.

binary   A numbering system in which there are only two digits, ones and zeros.

bit stuffing   A 0 insertion and deletion process defined by HDLC. This technique ensures that actual data never appears as flag characters.

BNC connector   Standard connector used to connect coaxial cable to an MAU or line card.

BOOTP (Bootstrap Protocol)   Part of the TCP/IP suite of protocols, used by a network node to determine the IP address of its network interfaces, in order to boot from a network server.

BPDU (Bridge Protocol Data Unit)   A Layer 2 protocol used for communication among bridges.

bps   Bits per second.

BRI (Basic Rate Interface)   ISDN interface consisting of two B channels and one D channel for circuit-switched communication. ISDN BRI can carry voice, video, and data.

bridge   Device that connects and forwards packets between two network segments that use the same data-link communications protocol. Bridges operate at the Data Link layer of the OSI reference model. A bridge will filter, forward, or flood an incoming frame based on the MAC address of the frame.

broadband   A data transmission system that multiplexes multiple independent signals onto one cable. Also, in telecommunications, any channel with a bandwidth greater than 4 KHz. In LAN terminology, a coaxial cable using analog signaling.

broadcast   Data packet addressed to all nodes on a network. Broadcasts are identified by a broadcast address that matches all addresses on the network.

broadcast address   Special address reserved for sending a message to all stations. At the Data Link layer, a broadcast address is a MAC destination address of all 1s.

broadcast domain   The group of all devices that will receive the same broadcast frame originating from any device within the group. Because routers do not forward broadcast frames, broadcast domains are typically bounded by routers.

buffer   A memory storage area used for handling data in transit. Buffers are used in internetworking to compensate for differences in processing speed between network devices or signaling rates of segments. Bursts of packets can be stored in buffers until they can be handled by slower devices.

bus   Common physical path composed of wires or other media, across which signals are sent from one part of a computer to another.

bus topology   A topology used in LANs. Transmissions from network stations propagate the length of the medium and are then received by all other stations.

byte   A series of consecutive binary digits that are operated upon as a unit, usually eight bits.

cable   Transmission medium of copper wire or optical fiber wrapped in a protective cover.

cable range   A range of network numbers on an extended AppleTalk network. The cable range value can be a single network number or a contiguous sequence of several network numbers. Nodes assign addresses within the cable range values provided.

CAM   Content-addressable memory.

carrier   Electromagnetic wave or alternating current of a single frequency, suitable for modulation by another, data-bearing signal.

Carrier Detect   *See* CD.

carrier sense multiple access with collision detection   *See* CSMA/CD.

Category 5 cabling   One of five grades of UTP cabling described in the EIA/TIA-586 standard. Category 5 cabling can transmit data at speeds up to 100 Mbps.

CCITT (Consultative Committee for International Telegraphy and Telephony)   International organization responsible for the development of communications standards. Now called the ITU-T.
See also ITU-T.

CCO (Cisco Connection Online)   Self-help resource for Cisco customers. Available 24 hours a day, seven days a week at http://www.cisco.com. The CCO family includes CCO Documentation, CCO Open Forum, CCO CD-ROM, and the TAC (Technical Assistance Center).

CD (Carrier Detect)   Signal that indicates whether an interface is active.

CDDI (Copper Distributed Data Interface)   The implementation of FDDI protocols over STP and UTP cabling. CDDI transmits over distances of approximately 100 meters, providing data rates of 100 Mbps. CDDI uses a dual-ring architecture to provide redundancy.

CDP (Cisco Discovery Protocol) Used to discover neighboring Cisco devices, and used by network management software. The CiscoWorks network management software takes advantage of CDP.

cell The basic data unit for ATM switching and multiplexing. A cell consists of a five-byte header and 48 bytes of payload. Cells contain fields in their headers that identify the data stream to which they belong.

CHAP (Challenge Handshake Authentication Protocol) Security feature used with PPP encapsulation, which prevents unauthorized access by identifying the remote end. The router or access server determines whether that user is allowed access.

checksum Method for checking the integrity of transmitted data. A checksum is an integer value computed from a sequence of octets taken through a series of arithmetic operations. The value is recomputed at the receiving end and compared for verification.

CIDR (classless interdomain routing) Technique supported by BGP4 and based on route aggregation. CIDR allows routers to group routes together in order to cut down on the quantity of routing information carried by the core routers. With CIDR, several IP networks appear to networks outside the group as a single, larger entity. With CIDR, IP addresses and their subnet masks are written as four octets, separated by periods, followed by a forward slash and a two-digit number that represents the subnet mask.

CIR (committed information rate) The rate at which a Frame Relay network agrees to transfer information under normal conditions, averaged over a minimum increment of time. CIR, measured in bits per second, is one of the key negotiated tariff metrics.

circuit switching A system in which a dedicated physical path must exist between sender and receiver for the entire duration of a call. Used heavily in telephone networks.

CiscoWorks   Network management package that provides a graphical view of a network, collects statistical information about a network, and offers various network management components.

client   Node or software program, or front-end device, that requests services from a server.

CLNS (Connectionless Network Service)   An OSI network layer service, for which no circuit need be established before data can be transmitted. Routing of messages to their destinations is independent of other messages.

CMU SNMP   A free command-line SNMP management package that comes in source code form. Originally developed at the Carnegie Mellon University, and available at http://www.net.cmu.edu/projects/snmp/.

collision   In Ethernet, the result of two nodes transmitting simultaneously. The frames from each device cause an increase in voltage when they meet on the physical media, and are damaged.

collision domain   A group of nodes such that any two or more of the nodes transmitting simultaneously will result in a collision.

congestion   Traffic in excess of network capacity.

connectionless   Term used to describe data transfer without the prior existence of a circuit.

console   A DTE device, usually consisting of a keyboard and display unit, through which users interact with a host.

contention   Access method in which network devices compete for permission to access the physical medium. Compare with **circuit switching** and **token passing**.

cost   A value, typically based on media bandwidth or other measures, that is assigned by a network administrator and used by routing protocols to compare various paths through an internetwork environment. Cost values are used to determine the most favorable path to a particular destination—the lower the cost, the better the path.

count to infinity   A condition in which routers continuously increment the hop count to particular networks. Often occurs in routing algorithms that are slow to converge. Usually, some arbitrary hop count ceiling is imposed to limit the extent of this problem.

CPE (customer premises equipment)   Terminating equipment, such as terminals, telephones, and modems, installed at customer sites and connected to the telephone company network.

CRC (cyclic redundancy check)   An error-checking technique in which the receiving device performs a calculation on the frame contents and compares the calculated number to a value stored in the frame by the sending node.

CSMA/CD (carrier sense multiple access collision detect)
Media-access mechanism used by Ethernet and IEEE 802.3. Devices use CSMA/CD to check the channel for a carrier before transmitting data. If no carrier is sensed, the device transmits. If two devices transmit at the same time, the collision is detected by all colliding devices. Collisions delay retransmissions from those devices for a randomly chosen length of time.

CSU (channel service unit)   Digital interface device that connects end-user equipment to the local digital telephone loop. Often referred to together with DSU, as CSU/DSU.

D channel   Data channel. Full-duplex, 16-kbps (BRI) or 64-kbps (PRI) ISDN channel.

DAS (dual attachment station)   Device that is attached to both the primary and the secondary FDDI rings. Provides redundancy for the FDDI ring. Also called a Class A station. *See also* **SAS**.

datagram   Logical unit of information sent as a network layer unit over a transmission medium without prior establishment of a circuit.

Data Link layer   Layer 2 of the OSI reference model. This layer provides reliable transit of data across a physical link. The Data Link layer is concerned with physical addressing, network topology, access to the network medium, error detection, sequential delivery of frames, and flow control. The Data Link layer is divided into two sublayers: the MAC sublayer and the LLC sublayer.

DCE (data circuit-terminating equipment)   The devices and connections of a communications network that represent the network end of the user-to-network interface. The DCE provides a physical connection to the network and provides a clocking signal used to synchronize transmission between DCE and DTE devices. Modems and interface cards are examples of DCE devices.

DDR (dial-on-demand routing)   Technique whereby a router can automatically initiate and close a circuit-switched session as transmitting stations demand. The router spoofs keepalives so that end-stations treat the session as active. DDR permits routing over ISDN or telephone lines using an external ISDN terminal adapter or modem.

de facto standard   A standard that exists because of its widespread use.

de jure standard   Standard that exists because of its development or approval by an official standards body.

DECNet   Group of communications products (including a protocol suite) developed and supported by Digital Equipment Corporation. DECNet/OSI (also called DECNet Phase V) is the most recent iteration and supports both OSI protocols and proprietary Digital protocols. Phase IV Prime supports inherent MAC addresses that allow DECNet nodes to coexist with systems running other protocols that have MAC address restrictions. *See also* **DNA**.

dedicated line   Communications line that is indefinitely reserved for transmissions, rather than switched as transmission is required. *See also* **leased line**.

default gateway Another term for default router. The router that a host will use to reach another network when it has no specific information about how to reach that network.

default route A routing table entry that is used to direct packets when there is no explicit route present in the routing table.

delay The time between the initiation of a transaction by a sender and the first response received by the sender. Also, the time required to move a packet from source to destination over a network path.

demarc The demarcation point between telephone carrier equipment and CPE.

demultiplexing The separating of multiple streams of data that have been multiplexed into a common physical signal for transmission, back into multiple output streams. Opposite of **multiplexing**.

destination address Address of a network device to receive data.

DHCP (Dynamic Host Configuration Protocol) Provides a mechanism for allocating IP addresses dynamically so that addresses can be reassigned instead of belonging to only one host.

Dijkstra algorithm Dijkstra's algorithm is a graph algorithm used to find the shortest path from one node on a graph to all others. Used in networking to determine the shortest path between routers.

discovery mode Method by which an AppleTalk router acquires information about an attached network from an operational router and then uses this information to configure its own addressing information.

distance vector routing algorithm Class of routing algorithms that use the number of hops in a route to find a shortest path to a destination network. Distance vector routing algorithms call for each router to send its entire routing table in each update to each of its neighbors. Also called Bellman-Ford routing algorithm.

DLCI (data-link connection identifier) A value that specifies a virtual circuit in a Frame Relay network.

DNA (Digital Network Architecture) Network architecture that was developed by Digital Equipment Corporation. DECNet is the collective term for the products that comprise DNA (including communications protocols).

DNIC (Data Network Identification Code) Part of an X.121 address. DNICs are divided into two parts: the first specifying the country in which the addressed PSN is located and the second specifying the PSN itself. *See also* **X.121**.

DNS (Domain Name System) System used in the Internet for translating names of network nodes into addresses.

DSP (domain specific part) Part of an ATM address. A DSP is comprised of an area identifier, a station identifier, and a selector byte.

DTE (data terminal equipment) Device at the user end of a user-network interface that serves as a data source, destination, or both. DTE connects to a data network through a DCE device (for example, a modem) and typically uses clocking signals generated by the DCE. DTE includes such devices as computers, routers and multiplexers.

DUAL (Diffusing Update Algorithm) Convergence algorithm used in EIGRP. DUAL provides constant loop-free operation throughout a route computation by allowing routers involved in a topology change to synchronize at the same time, without involving routers that are unaffected by the change.

DVMRP (Distance Vector Multicast Routing Protocol) DVMRP is an internetwork gateway protocol that implements a typical dense mode IP multicast scheme. Using IGMP, DVMRP exchanges routing datagrams with its neighbors.

dynamic routing Routing that adjusts automatically to changes in network topology or traffic patterns.

E1 Wide-area digital transmission scheme used in Europe that carries data at a rate of 2.048 Mbps.

EIA/TIA-232 Common Physical layer interface standard, developed by EIA and TIA, that supports unbalanced circuits at signal speeds of up to 64 Kbps. Formerly known as RS-232.

EIGRP (Enhanced IGRP) A multiservice routing protocol supporting IPX, AppleTalk, and IP. BGP is used for interconnecting networks and defining strict routing policies.

encapsulation The process of attaching a particular protocol header to a unit of data prior to transmission on the network. For example, a frame of Ethernet data is given a specific Ethernet header before network transit.

endpoint Device at which a virtual circuit or virtual path begins or ends.

enterprise network A privately maintained network connecting most major points in a company or other organization. Usually spans a large geographic area and supports multiple protocols and services.

entity Generally, an individual, manageable network device. Sometimes called an alias.

error control Technique for detecting and correcting errors in data transmissions.

Ethernet Baseband LAN specification invented by Xerox Corporation and developed jointly by Xerox, Intel, and Digital Equipment Corporation. Ethernet networks use the CSMA/CD method of media access control and run over a variety of cable types at 10 Mbps. Ethernet is similar to the IEEE 802.3 series of standards.

EtherTalk Apple Computer's data-link product that allows an AppleTalk network to be connected by Ethernet cable.

EtherWave   A product from Netopia (formerly Farallon) used to connect AppleTalk devices with LocalTalk connectors to Ethernet networks. They are an alternative to LocalTalk-to-EtherTalk routers.

explorer packet   Generated by an end-station trying to find its way through a SRB network. Gathers a hop-by-hop description of a path through the network by being marked (updated) by each bridge that it traverses, thereby creating a complete topological map.

Fast Ethernet   Any of a number of 100-Mbps Ethernet specifications. Fast Ethernet offers a speed increase ten times that of the 10BaseT Ethernet specification, while preserving such qualities as frame format, MAC mechanisms, and MTU. Such similarities allow the use of existing 10BaseT applications and network management tools on Fast Ethernet networks. Based on an extension to the IEEE 802.3 specification. Compare with **Ethernet**. *See also* **100BaseFX; 100BaseT; 100BaseT4; 100BaseTX; 100BaseX; IEEE 802.3**.

FDDI (Fiber Distributed Data Interface)   LAN standard, defined by ANSI X3T9.5, specifying a 100-Mbps token-passing network using fiber-optic cable, with transmission distances of up to 2 km. FDDI uses a dual-ring architecture to provide redundancy. Compare with **CDDI**.

FECN (forward explicit congestion notification)   A facility in a Frame Relay network to inform DTE receiving the frame that congestion was experienced in the path from source to destination. DTE receiving frames with the FECN bit set can request that higher-level protocols take flow-control action as appropriate.

file transfer   Category of popular network applications that features movement of files from one network device to another.

filter   Generally, a process or device that screens network traffic for certain characteristics, such as source address, destination address, or protocol, and determines whether to forward or discard that traffic or routes based on the established criteria.

firewall Router or other computer designated as a buffer between public networks and a private network. A firewall router uses access lists and other methods to ensure the security of the private network.

Flash memory Nonvolatile storage that can be electrically erased and reprogrammed as necessary.

flash update Routing update sent asynchronously when a change in the network topology occurs.

flat addressing A system of addressing that does not incorporate a hierarchy to determine location.

flooding Traffic-passing technique used by switches and bridges in which traffic received on an interface is sent out all of the interfaces of that device except the interface on which the information was originally received.

flow control Technique for ensuring that a transmitting device, such as a modem, does not overwhelm a receiving device with data. When the buffers on the receiving device are full, a message is sent to the sending device to suspend transmission until it has processed the data in the buffers.

forwarding The process of sending a frame or packet toward its destination.

fragment Piece of a larger packet that has been broken down to smaller units.

fragmentation Process of breaking a packet into smaller units when transmitting over a network medium that is unable to support a transmission unit the original size of the packet.

frame Logical grouping of information sent as a Data Link layer unit over a transmission medium. Sometimes refers to the header and trailer, used for synchronization and error control, which surround the user data contained in the unit. The terms cell, datagram, message, packet, and segment are also used to describe logical information groupings at various layers of the OSI reference model and in various technology circles.

Frame Relay   Industry-standard, switched Data Link layer protocol that handles multiple virtual circuits over a single physical interface. Frame Relay is more efficient than X.25, for which it is generally considered a replacement.

Frame Relay Cloud   A generic term used to refer to a collective Frame Relay network. For Frame Relay carrier customers, it generally refers to the carrier's entire Frame Relay network. It's referred to as a "cloud" because the network layout is not visible to the customer.

frequency   Number of cycles, measured in hertz, of an alternating current signal per unit of time.

FTP (File Transfer Protocol)   An application protocol, part of the TCP/IP protocol stack, used for transferring files between hosts on a network.

full duplex   Capability for simultaneous data transmission and receipt of data between two devices.

full mesh   A network topology in which each network node has either a physical circuit or a virtual circuit connecting it to every other network node.

gateway   In the IP community, an older term referring to a routing device. Today, the term router is used to describe devices that perform this function, and gateway refers to a special-purpose device that performs an Application layer conversion of information from one protocol stack to another.

GB   Gigabyte. Approximately 1,000,000,000 bytes.

Gb   Gigabit. Approximately 1,000,000,000 bits.

GBps   Gigabytes per second.

Gbps   Gigabits per second.

giants   Ethernet frames over the maximum frame size.

GNS (Get Nearest Server)   Request packet sent by a client on an IPX network to locate the nearest active server of a particular type. An IPX network client issues a GNS request to solicit either a direct response from a connected server or a response from a router that tells it where on the internetwork the service can be located. GNS is part of the IPX SAP.

half-duplex   Capability for data transmission in only one direction at a time between a sending station and a receiving station.

handshake   Sequence of messages exchanged between two or more network devices to ensure transmission synchronization.

hardware address   *See* MAC address.

HDLC (High-level Data Link Control)   Bit-oriented synchronous Data Link layer protocol developed by ISO and derived from SDLC. HDLC specifies a data encapsulation method for synchronous serial links and includes frame characters and checksums in its headers.

header   Control information placed before data when encapsulating that data for network transmission.

Hello packet   Multicast packet that is used by routers for neighbor discovery and recovery. Hello packets also indicate that a client is still operating on the network.

Hello protocol   Protocol used by OSPF and other routing protocols for establishing and maintaining neighbor relationships.

hierarchical addressing   A scheme of addressing that uses a logical hierarchy to determine location. For example, IP addresses consist of network numbers, subnet numbers, and host numbers, which IP routing algorithms use to route the packet to the appropriate location.

holddown   State of a routing table entry in which routers will neither advertise the route nor accept advertisements about the route for a specific length of time (known as the holddown period).

hop   Term describing the passage of a data packet between two network nodes (for example, between two routers). *See also* **hop count**.

hop count   Routing metric used to measure the distance between a source and a destination. RIP uses hop count as its metric.

host   A computer system on a network. Similar to the term node except that host usually implies a computer system, whereas node can refer to any networked system, including routers.

host number   Part of an IP address that designates which node is being addressed. Also called a host address.

hub   A term used to describe a device that serves as the center of a star topology network; or, an Ethernet multiport repeater, sometimes referred to as a concentrator.

ICMP (Internet Control Message Protocol)   A network layer Internet protocol that provides reports of errors and other information about IP packet processing. ICMP is documented in RFC 792.

IEEE (Institute of Electrical and Electronics Engineers)   A professional organization among whose activities are the development of communications and networking standards. IEEE LAN standards are the most common LAN standards today.

IEEE 802.3   IEEE LAN protocol for the implementation of the Physical layer and the MAC sublayer of the Data Link layer. IEEE 802.3 uses CSMA/CD access at various speeds over various physical media.

IEEE 802.5   IEEE LAN protocol for the implementation of the Physical layer and MAC sublayer of the Data Link layer. Similar to Token Ring, IEEE 802.5 uses token-passing access over STP cabling.

IGP (Interior Gateway Protocol)   A generic term for an Internet routing protocol used to exchange routing information within an autonomous system. Examples of common Internet IGPs include IGRP, OSPF, and RIP.

InARP (Inverse Address Resolution Protocol)   A basic Frame Relay protocol that allows routers on the Frame network to learn the protocol addresses of other routers.

interface   A connection between two systems or devices; or in routing terminology, a network connection.

Internet   Term used to refer to the global internetwork that evolved from the ARPANET, that now connects tens of thousands of networks worldwide.

Internet protocol   Any protocol that is part of the TCP/IP protocol stack. *See* TCP/IP.

internetwork   Collection of networks interconnected by routers and other devices that functions (generally) as a single network.

internetworking   General term used to refer to the industry that has arisen around the problem of connecting networks together. The term may be used to refer to products, procedures, and technologies.

Inverse ARP (Inverse Address Resolution Protocol)   Method of building dynamic address mappings in a Frame Relay network. Allows a device to discover the network address of a device associated with a virtual circuit.

IP (Internet Protocol)   Network layer protocol in the TCP/IP stack offering a connectionless datagram service. IP provides features for addressing, type-of-service specification, fragmentation and reassembly, and security. Documented in RFC 791.

IP address A 32-bit address assigned to hosts using the TCP/IP suite of protocols. An IP address is written as four octets separated by dots (dotted decimal format). Each address consists of a network number, an optional subnetwork number, and a host number. The network and subnetwork numbers together are used for routing, while the host number is used to address an individual host within the network or subnetwork. A subnet mask is often used with the address to extract network and subnetwork information from the IP address.

IPX (Internetwork Packet Exchange) NetWare network layer (Layer 3) protocol used for transferring data from servers to workstations. IPX is similar to IP in that it is a connectionless datagram service.

IPXCP (IPX Control Protocol) The protocol that establishes and configures IPX over PPP.

IPXWAN A protocol that negotiates end-to-end options for new links on startup. When a link comes up, the first IPX packets sent across are IPXWAN packets negotiating the options for the link. When the IPXWAN options have been successfully determined, normal IPX transmission begins, and no more IPXWAN packets are sent. Defined by RFC 1362.

ISDN (Integrated Services Digital Network) Communication protocol, offered by telephone companies, that permits telephone networks to carry data, voice, and other source traffic.

ISL (Inter-Switch Link) Cisco's protocol for trunking VLANs over Fast Ethernet.

ITU-T (International Telecommunication Union Telecommunication Standardization Sector) International body dedicated to the development of worldwide standards for telecommunications technologies. ITU-T is the successor to CCITT.

jabbers   Long, continuous frames exceeding 1518 bytes that prevent all stations on the Ethernet network from transmitting data. Jabbering violates CSMA/CD implementation by prohibiting stations from transmitting data.

jam pattern   Initiated by Ethernet transmitting station when a collision is detected during transmission.

KB   Kilobyte. Approximately 1,000 bytes.

Kb   Kilobit. Approximately 1,000 bits.

KBps   Kilobytes per second.

Kbps   Kilobits per second.

keepalive interval   Period of time between keepalive messages sent by a network device.

keepalive message   Message sent by one network device to inform another network device that it is still active.

LAN (local area network)   High-speed, low-error data network covering a relatively small geographic area. LANs connect workstations, peripherals, terminals, and other devices in a single building or other geographically limited area. LAN standards specify cabling and signaling at the physical and Data Link layers of the OSI model. Ethernet, FDDI, and Token Ring are the most widely used LAN technologies.

LANE (LAN Emulation)   Technology that allows an ATM network to function as a LAN backbone. In this situation LANE provides multicast and broadcast support, address mapping (MAC-to-ATM), and virtual circuit management.

LAPB (Link Access Procedure, Balanced)   The Data Link layer protocol in the X.25 protocol stack. LAPB is a bit-oriented protocol derived from HDLC.

LAPD (Link Access Procedure on the D channel)   ISDN Data Link layer protocol for the D channel. LAPD was derived from the LAPB protocol and is designed to satisfy the signaling requirements of ISDN basic access. Defined by ITU-T Recommendations Q.920 and Q.921.

LAPF   Data link standard for Frame Relay.

late collision   Collision that is detected only after a station places a complete frame of the network.

latency   The amount of time elapsed between the time a device requests access to a network and the time it is allowed to transmit; or, amount of time between the point at which a device receives a frame and the time that frame is forwarded out the destination port.

LCP (Link Control Protocol)   A protocol used with PPP, which establishes, configures, and tests data-link connections.

leased line   Transmission line reserved by a communications carrier for the private use of a customer. A leased line is a type of dedicated line.

LEC (LAN Emulation Client)   Performs data forwarding, address resolution, and other control functions for a single end system within a single ELAN. Each LEC has a unique ATM address, and is associated with one or more MAC addresses reachable through that ATM address.

LECS (LAN Emulation Configuration Server)   Assigns LANE clients to ELANs by directing them to the LES that corresponds to the ELAN. There can be logically one LECS per administrative domain, which serves all ELANs within that domain.

LES (LAN Emulation Server)   Implements the control function for an ELAN. There can be only one logical LES per ELAN. It has a unique ATM address.

link Network communications channel consisting of a circuit or transmission path and all related equipment between a sender and a receiver. Most often used to refer to a WAN connection. Sometimes called a line or a transmission link.

link-state routing algorithm Routing algorithm in which each router broadcasts or multicasts information regarding the cost of reaching each of its neighbors to all nodes in the internetwork. Link state algorithms require that routers maintain a consistent view of the network and are therefore not prone to routing loops.

LLC (Logical Link Control) Higher of two Data Link layer sublayers defined by the IEEE. The LLC sublayer handles error control, flow control, framing, and MAC-sublayer addressing. The most common LLC protocol is IEEE 802.2, which includes both connectionless and connection-oriented types.

LMI (Local Management Interface) A set of enhancements to the basic Frame Relay specification. LMI includes support for keepalives, a multicast mechanism; global addressing, and a status mechanism.

load balancing In routing, the ability of a router to distribute traffic over all its network ports that are the same distance from the destination address. Load balancing increases the utilization of network segments, thus increasing total effective network bandwidth.

local loop A line from the premises of a telephone subscriber to the telephone company central office.

LocalTalk Apple Computer's proprietary baseband protocol that operates at the Data Link and Physical layers of the OSI reference model. LocalTalk uses CSMA/CA and supports transmissions at speeds of 230.4 Kbps.

loop A situation in which packets never reach their destination, but are forwarded in a cycle repeatedly through a group of network nodes.

MAC (Media Access Control)   Lower of the two sublayers of the Data Link layer defined by the IEEE. The MAC sublayer handles access to shared media.

MAC address   Standardized Data Link layer address that is required for every port or device that connects to a LAN. Other devices in the network use these addresses to locate specific ports in the network and to create and update routing tables and data structures. MAC addresses are 48 bits long and are controlled by the IEEE. Also known as a hardware address, a MAC-layer address, or a physical address.

MAN (metropolitan-area network)   A network that spans a metropolitan area. Generally, a MAN spans a larger geographic area than a LAN, but a smaller geographic area than a WAN.

Mb   Megabit. Approximately 1,000,000 bits.

Mbps   Megabits per second.

media   The various physical environments through which transmission signals pass. Common network media include cable (twisted-pair, coaxial, and fiber optic) and the atmosphere (through which microwave, laser, and infrared transmission occurs). Sometimes referred to as physical media.

Media Access Control   *See* MAC.

mesh   Network topology in which devices are organized in a segmented manner with redundant interconnections strategically placed between network nodes.

message   Application layer logical grouping of information, often composed of a number of lower-layer logical groupings such as packets.

MIB (Management Information Base)   Database for network management information; it is used and maintained by a network management protocol such as SNMP.

MSAU (multistation access unit) A wiring concentrator to which all end stations in a Token Ring network connect. Sometimes abbreviated MAU.

multiaccess network A network that allows multiple devices to connect and communicate by sharing the same medium, such as a LAN.

multicast A single packet copied by the network and sent to a specific subset of network addresses. These addresses are specified in the Destination Address field.

multicast address A single address that refers to multiple network devices. Sometimes called a group address.

multiplexing A technique that allows multiple logical signals to be transmitted simultaneously across a single physical channel.

mux A multiplexing device. A mux combines multiple input signals for transmission over a single line. The signals are demultiplexed, or separated, before they are used at the receiving end.

NACK (negative acknowledgment) A response sent from a receiving device to a sending device indicating that the information received contained errors.

name resolution The process of associating a symbolic name with a network location or address.

NAT (Network Address Translation) A technique for reducing the need for globally unique IP addresses. NAT allows an organization with addresses that may conflict with others in the IP address space, to connect to the Internet by translating those addresses into unique ones within the globally routable address space.

NBMA (nonbroadcast multiaccess) Term describing a multiaccess network that either does not support broadcasting (such as X.25) or in which broadcasting is not feasible.

NBP (Name Binding Protocol)   AppleTalk transport level protocol that translates a character string name into the DDP address of the corresponding socket client.

NCP (Network Control Protocol)   Protocols that establish and configure various network layer protocols. Used for AppleTalk over PPP.

NDS (NetWare Directory Services)   A feature added in NetWare 4.0 as a replacement for individual binderies. NDS allows NetWare and related resources to be grouped in a tree hierarchy to better provide central administration.

NetBIOS (Network Basic Input/Output System)   An application programming interface used by applications on an IBM LAN to request services from lower-level network processes such as session establishment and termination, and information transfer.

netmask   A number, usually used as a bit-mask, to separate an address into its network portion and host portion.

NetWare   A network operating system developed by Novell, Inc. Provides remote file access, print services, and numerous other distributed network services.

network   Collection of computers, printers, routers, switches, and other devices that are able to communicate with each other over some transmission medium.

network interface   Border between a carrier network and a privately owned installation.

Network layer   Layer 3 of the OSI reference model. This layer provides connectivity and path selection between two end systems. The Network layer is the layer at which routing takes place.

NLSP (NetWare Link Services Protocol)   Link-state routing protocol for IPX based on IS-IS.

node Endpoint of a network connection or a junction common to two or more lines in a network. Nodes can be processors, controllers, or workstations. Nodes, which vary in their functional capabilities, can be interconnected by links, and serve as control points in the network.

NVRAM (nonvolatile RAM) RAM that retains its contents when a device is powered off.

ODI Novell's Open Data-link Interface.

OSI reference model (Open System Interconnection reference model) A network architectural framework developed by ISO and ITU-T. The model describes seven layers, each of which specifies a particular network. The lowest layer, called the Physical layer, is closest to the media technology. The highest layer, the Application layer, is closest to the user. The OSI reference model is widely used as a way of understanding network functionality.

OSPF (Open Shortest Path First) A link-state, hierarchical IGP routing algorithm, which includes features such as least-cost routing, multipath routing, and load balancing. OSPF was based on an early version of the IS-IS protocol.

out-of-band signaling Transmission using frequencies or channels outside the frequencies or channels used for transfer of normal data. Out-of-band signaling is often used for error reporting when normal channels are unusable for communicating with network devices.

packet Logical grouping of information that includes a header containing control information and (usually) user data. Packets are most often used to refer to network layer units of data. The terms datagram, frame, message, and segment are also used to describe logical information groupings at various layers of the OSI reference model, and in various technology circles. *See also* **PDU**.

packet analyzer A software package (also sometimes including specialized hardware) used to monitor network traffic. Most packet analyzer packages will also do packet decoding, making the packets easier for humans to read.

packet burst   Allows multiple packets to be transmitted between Novell clients and servers in response to a single read or write request. It also allows file transfer to greatly improve throughput by reducing the number of acknowledgments.

packet starvation effect   On Ethernet, when packets experience latencies up to 100 times the average, or completely starve out due to 16 collisions. Occurs as a result of the CSMA/CD implementation.

PAP (Password Authentication Protocol)   Authentication protocol that allows PPP peers to authenticate one another. The remote router attempting to connect to the local router is required to send an authentication request. Unlike CHAP, PAP passes the password and host name or username in the clear (unencrypted). PAP does not itself prevent unauthorized access, but merely identifies the remote end. The router or access server then determines if that user is allowed access. PAP is supported only on PPP lines.

partial mesh   Term describing a network in which devices are organized in a mesh topology, with some network nodes organized in a full mesh, but with others that are only connected to one or two other nodes in the network. A partial mesh does not provide the level of redundancy of a full mesh topology, but is less expensive to implement. Partial mesh topologies are generally used in the peripheral networks that connect to a fully meshed backbone. *See also* **full mesh; mesh**.

PDU (protocol data unit)   The OSI term for a packet.

Physical layer   Layer 1 of the OSI reference model; it corresponds with the Physical control layer in the SNA model. The Physical layer defines the specifications for activating, maintaining, and deactivating the physical link between end systems.

ping (packet internet groper)   ICMP echo message and its reply. Often used in IP networks to test the reachability of a network device.

poison reverse updates   Routing updates that explicitly indicate that a network or subnet is unreachable, rather than implying that a network is unreachable by not including it in updates. Poison reverse updates are sent to defeat large routing loops.

port   1. Interface on an internetworking device (such as a router). 2. In IP terminology, an upper-layer process that receives information from lower layers. Ports are numbered, and each numbered port is associated with a specific process. For example, SMTP is associated with port 25. A port number is also known as a well-known address. 3. To rewrite software or microcode so that it will run on a different hardware platform or in a different software environment than that for which it was originally designed.

PPP (Point-to-Point Protocol)   A successor to SLIP that provides router-to-router and host-to-network connections over synchronous and asynchronous circuits. Whereas SLIP was designed to work with IP, PPP was designed to work with several network layer protocols, such as IP, IPX, and ARA. PPP also has built-in security mechanisms, such as CHAP and PAP. PPP relies on two protocols: LCP and NCP. *See also* **CHAP**; **LCP**; **NCP**; **PAP**; **SLIP**.

Presentation layer   Layer 6 of the OSI reference model. This layer ensures that information sent by the Application layer of one system will be readable by the Application layer of another. The Presentation layer is also concerned with the data structures used by programs and therefore negotiates data transfer syntax for the Application layer.

PRI (Primary Rate Interface)   ISDN interface to primary rate access. Primary rate access consists of a single 64-Kbps D channel plus 23 (T1) or 30 (E1) B channels for voice or data. Compare to **BRI**.

protocol   Formal description of a set of rules and conventions that govern how devices on a network exchange information.

protocol stack   Set of related communications protocols that operate together and, as a group, address communication at some or all of the seven layers of the OSI reference model. Not every protocol stack covers each layer of the model, and often a single protocol in the stack will address a number of layers at once. TCP/IP is a typical protocol stack.

proxy ARP (proxy Address Resolution Protocol)   Variation of the ARP protocol in which an intermediate device (for example, a router) sends an ARP response on behalf of an end node to the requesting host. Proxy ARP can lessen bandwidth use on slow-speed WAN links. *See also* **ARP**.

PVC (permanent virtual circuit)   Permanently established virtual circuits save bandwidth in situations where certain virtual circuits must exist all the time, such as during circuit establishment and tear down.

Q.921   ITU (International Telecommunication Union) standard document for ISDN Layer 2 (Data Link layer).

Q.931   ITU (International Telecommunication Union) standard document for ISDN Layer 3.

query   Message used to inquire about the value of some variable or set of variables.

queue   A backlog of packets stored in buffers and waiting to be forwarded over a router interface.

RAM (random-access memory)   Volatile memory that can be read and written by a computer.

reassembly   The putting back together of an IP datagram at the destination after it has been fragmented either at the source or at an intermediate node. *See also* **fragmentation**.

reload   The event of a Cisco router rebooting, or the command that causes the router to reboot.

reverse path forwarding If a packet server receives a packet through different interfaces from the same source, the server drops all packets after the first.

reverse Telnet Using a router to connect to a serial device, frequently a modem, in order to connect out. For example, telnetting to a special port on an access router in order to access a modem to dial out. Called "reverse" because it's the opposite of the router's usual function, to accept calls into the modem.

RFC (Request For Comments) Document series used as the primary means for communicating information about the Internet. Some RFCs are designated by the IAB as Internet standards.

ring Connection of two or more stations in a logically circular topology. Information is passed sequentially between active stations. Token Ring, FDDI, and CDDI are based on this topology.

ring topology Network topology that consists of a series of repeaters connected to one another by unidirectional transmission links to form a single closed loop. Each station on the network connects to the network at a repeater.

RIP (Routing Information Protocol) A routing protocol for TCP/IP networks. The most common routing protocol in the Internet. RIP uses hop count as a routing metric.

RMON (Remote monitor) A set of SNMP standards used to collect statistical network information. RMON is divided into groups, with each additional group providing more statistical information.

ROM (read-only memory) Nonvolatile memory that can be read, but not written, by the computer.

routed protocol Protocol that carries user data so it can be routed by a router. A router must be able to interpret the logical internetwork as specified by that routed protocol. Examples of routed protocols include AppleTalk, DECNet, and IP.

router   Network layer device that uses one or more metrics to determine the optimal path along which network traffic should be forwarded. Routers forward packets from one network to another based on network layer information.

routing   Process of finding a path to a destination host.

routing metric   Method by which a routing algorithm determines preferability of one route over another. This information is stored in routing tables. Metrics include bandwidth, communication cost, delay, hop count, load, MTU, path cost, and reliability. Sometimes referred to simply as a metric.

routing protocol   Protocol that accomplishes routing through the implementation of a specific routing algorithm. Examples of routing protocols include IGRP, OSPF, and RIP.

routing table   Table stored in a router or some other internetworking device that keeps track of routes to particular network destinations and, in some cases, metrics associated with those routes.

routing update   Message sent from a router to indicate network reachability and associated cost information. Routing updates are typically sent at regular intervals and after a change in network topology. Compare with **flash update**.

RSRB (remote source-route bridging)   Equivalent to an SRB over WAN links.

RTMP (Routing Table Maintenance Protocol)   The protocol used by AppleTalk devices to communicate routing information. Structurally similar to RIP.

runts   Ethernet frames that are smaller than 64 bytes.

SAP (service access point)   1. Field defined by the IEEE 802.2 specification that is part of an address specification. Thus, the destination plus the DSAP define the recipient of a packet. The same applies to the SSAP. 2. Service Advertising

Protocol. IPX protocol that provides a means of informing network routers and servers of the location of available network resources and services.

SAS (single attachment station)   Device attached to the primary ring of an FDDI ring. Also known as a Class B station. *See also* **DAS**.

segment   1. Section of a network that is bounded by bridges, routers, or switches. 2. In a LAN using a bus topology, a segment is a continuous electrical circuit that is often connected to other such segments with repeaters. 3. Term used in the TCP specification to describe a single Transport layer unit of information.

serial transmission   Method of data transmission in which the bits of a data character are transmitted sequentially over a single channel.

session   1. Related set of communications transactions between two or more network devices. 2. In SNA, a logical connection that enables two NAUs to communicate.

Session layer   Layer 5 of the OSI reference model. This layer establishes, manages, and terminates sessions between applications and manages data exchange between Presentation layer entities. Corresponds to the data flow control layer of the SNA model. *See also* **Application layer; Data Link layer; Network layer; Physical layer; Presentation layer; Transport layer.**

sliding window flow control   Method of flow control in which a receiver gives a transmitter permission to transmit data until a window is full. When the window is full, the transmitter must stop transmitting until the receiver acknowledges some of the data, or advertises a larger window. TCP, other transport protocols, and several Data Link layer protocols use this method of flow control.

SLIP (Serial Line Internet Protocol)   Uses a variation of TCP/IP to make point-to-point serial connections. Succeeded by PPP.

SNAP (Subnetwork Access Protocol)   Internet protocol that operates between a network entity in the subnetwork and a network entity in the end system.

SNAP specifies a standard method of encapsulating IP datagrams and ARP messages on IEEE networks.

SNMP (Simple Network Management Protocol)   Network management protocol used almost exclusively in TCP/IP networks. SNMP provides a means to monitor and control network devices, and to manage configurations, statistics collection, performance, and security.

SNMP Manager   Software used to manage network devices via SNMP. Often includes graphical representation of the network and individual devices, and the ability to set and respond to SNMP traps.

SNMP Trap   A threshold of some sort which, when reached, causes the SNMP managed device to notify the SNMP Manager. This allows for immediate notification, instead of having to wait for the SNMP Manager to poll again.

socket   Software structure operating as a communications endpoint within a network device.

SONET (Synchronous Optical Network)   High-speed synchronous network specification developed by Bellcore and designed to run on optical fiber.

source address   Address of a network device that is sending data.

spanning tree   Loop-free subset of a network topology. *See also* **Spanning Tree Protocol**.

Spanning Tree Protocol   Developed to eliminate loops in the network. The Spanning Tree Protocol ensures a loop-free path by placing one of the bridge ports in "blocking mode," preventing the forwarding of packets.

SPF (shortest path first algorithm)   Routing algorithm that sorts routes by length of path to determine a shortest-path spanning tree. Commonly used in link-state routing algorithms. Sometimes called Dijkstra's algorithm.

SPIDs (Service Profile Identifiers) These function as addresses for B channels on ISDN BRI circuits. When call information is passed over the D channel, the SPIDs are used to identify which channel is being referred to. SPIDs are usually some variant of the phone number for the channel.

split-horizon updates Routing technique in which information about routes is prevented from being advertised out the router interface through which that information was received. Split-horizon updates are used to prevent routing loops.

SPX (Sequenced Packet Exchange) Reliable, connection-oriented protocol at the Transport layer that supplements the datagram service provided by IPX.

SR/TLB (source-route translational bridging) Method of bridging that allows source-route stations to communicate with transparent bridge stations, using an intermediate bridge that translates between the two bridge protocols.

SRB (source-route bridging) Method of bridging in Token Ring networks. In an SRB network, before data is sent to a destination, the entire route to that destination is predetermined in real time.

SRT (source-route transparent bridging) IBM's merging of SRB and transparent bridging into one bridging scheme, which requires no translation between bridging protocols.

standard Set of rules or procedures that are either widely used or officially specified.

star topology LAN topology in which endpoints on a network are connected to a common central switch by point-to-point links. A ring topology that is organized as a star implements a unidirectional closed-loop star, instead of point-to-point links. Compare with **bus topology**, **ring topology**, and **tree topology**.

static route Route that is explicitly configured and entered into the routing table. Static routes take precedence over routes chosen by dynamic routing protocols.

subinterface   A virtual interface defined as a logical subdivision of a physical interface.

subnet address   Portion of an IP address that is specified as the subnetwork by the subnet mask. *See also* **IP address**; **subnet mask**; **subnetwork**.

subnet mask   32-bit address mask used in IP to indicate the bits of an IP address that are being used for the subnet address. Sometimes referred to simply as mask. *See also* **address mask**; **IP address**.

subnetwork   1. In IP networks, a network sharing a particular subnet address. 2. Subnetworks are networks arbitrarily segmented by a network administrator in order to provide a multilevel, hierarchical routing structure while shielding the subnetwork from the addressing complexity of attached networks. Sometimes called a subnet.

SVC (switched virtual circuit)   Virtual circuit that can be established dynamically on demand, and which is torn down after a transmission is complete. SVCs are used when data transmission is sporadic.

switch   1. Network device that filters, forwards, and floods frames based on the destination address of each frame. The switch operates at the Data Link layer of the OSI model. 2. General term applied to an electronic or mechanical device that allows a connection to be established as necessary and terminated when there is no longer a session to support.

T1   Digital WAN carrier facility. T1 transmits DS-1-formatted data at 1.544 Mbps through the telephone-switching network, using AMI or B8ZS coding. Compare with **E1**. *See also* **AMI**; **B8ZS**.

TCP (Transmission Control Protocol)   Connection-oriented Transport layer protocol that provides reliable full-duplex data transmission. TCP is part of the TCP/IP protocol stack.

TCP/IP (Transmission Control Protocol/Internet Protocol)   Common name for the suite of protocols developed by the U.S. DoD in the 1970s to support the construction of worldwide internetworks. TCP and IP are the two best-known protocols in the suite.

TDR (time-domain reflectometer) A TDR test is used to measure the length of a cable, or the distance to a break. This is accomplished by sending a signal down a wire, and measuring how long it takes for an echo of the signal to bounce back.

TEI (Terminal Endpoint Identifier) Field in the LAPD address that identifies a device on an ISDN interface.

TFTP (Trivial File Transfer Protocol) Simplified version of FTP that allows files to be transferred from one computer to another over a network.

three-way handshake The three required packets to set up a TCP connection. It consists of a SYN packet, acknowledged by a SYN+ACK packet, which is finally acknowledged by an ACK packet. During this handshake, sequence numbers are exchanged.

throughput Rate of information arriving at, and possibly passing through, a particular point in a network system.

timeout Event that occurs when one network device expects to hear from another network device within a specified period of time, but does not. A timeout usually results in a retransmission of information or the termination of the session between the two devices.

token Frame that contains only control information. Possession of the token allows a network device to transmit data onto the network. *See also* **token passing**.

token passing Method by which network devices access the physical medium based on possession of a small frame called a token. Compare this method to **circuit switching** and **contention**.

Token Ring Token-passing LAN developed and supported by IBM. Token Ring runs at 4 or 16 Mbps over a ring topology. Similar to IEEE 802.5. *See also* **IEEE 802.5; ring topology; token passing.**

TokenTalk Apple Computer's data-link product that allows an AppleTalk network to be connected by Token Ring cables.

transparent bridging Bridging scheme used in Ethernet and IEEE 802.3 networks. Allows bridges to pass frames along one hop at a time, based on tables that associate end nodes with bridge ports. Bridges are transparent to network end nodes.

Transport layer Layer 4 of the OSI reference model. This layer is responsible for reliable network communication between end nodes. The Transport layer provides mechanisms for the establishment, maintenance, and termination of virtual circuits, transport fault detection and recovery, and information flow control.

tree topology A LAN topology that resembles a bus topology. Tree networks can contain branches with multiple nodes. In a tree topology, transmissions from a station propagate the length of the physical medium, and are received by all other stations.

twisted-pair Relatively low-speed transmission medium consisting of two insulated wires arranged in a regular spiral pattern. The wires can be shielded or unshielded. Twisted-pair is common in telephony applications and is increasingly common in data networks.

UDP (User Datagram Protocol) Connectionless Transport layer protocol in the TCP/IP protocol stack. UDP is a simple protocol that exchanges datagrams without acknowledgments or guaranteed delivery, requiring that error processing and retransmission be handled by other protocols. UDP is defined in RFC 768.

unicast Regular IP packet sent from a single host to a single host.

UTP (unshielded twisted-pair) Four-pair wire medium used in a variety of networks. UTP does not require the fixed spacing between connections that is necessary with coaxial-type connections.

VCC (virtual channel connection) Logical circuit for carrying data between two endpoints in an ATM network.

virtual circuit Logical circuit created to ensure reliable communication between two network devices. A virtual circuit is defined by a VPI/VCI pair, and can be either permanent or switched. Virtual circuits are used in Frame Relay and X.25. In ATM, a virtual circuit is called a virtual channel. Sometimes abbreviated VC.

VLAN (virtual LAN) Group of devices on one or more LANs that are configured (using management software) so that they can communicate as if they were attached to the same wire, when in fact they are located on a number of different LAN segments. Because VLANs are based on logical instead of physical connections, they are extremely flexible.

VLSM (Variable-length Subnet Masking) Ability to specify a different length subnet mask for the same network number at different locations in the network. VLSM can help optimize available address space.

VTY (Virtual Terminal) VTYs work like physical terminal ports on routers so they can be managed across a network, usually via Telnet.

WAN (wide area network) Data communications network that serves users across a broad geographic area and often uses transmission devices provided by common carriers. Frame Relay, SMDS, and X.25 are examples of WANs. Compare with **LAN** and **MAN**.

wildcard mask 32-bit quantity used in conjunction with an IP address to determine which bits in an IP address should be matched and ignored when comparing that address with another IP address. A wildcard mask is specified when defining access list statements.

X.121 ITU-T standard describing an addressing scheme used in X.25 networks. X.121 addresses are sometimes called IDNs (International Data Numbers).

X.21 ITU-T standard for serial communications over synchronous digital lines. The X.21 protocol is used primarily in Europe and Japan.

X.25 ITU-T standard that defines how connections between DTE and DCE are maintained for remote terminal access and computer communications in public data networks. X.25 specifies LAPB, a Data Link layer protocol, and PLP, a network layer protocol. Frame Relay has to some degree superseded X.25.

ZIP broadcast storm Occurs when a route advertisement without a corresponding zone triggers the network with a flood of Zone Information Protocol requests.

zone In AppleTalk, a logical group of network devices.

Zone Information Protocol (ZIP) A protocol used in AppleTalk to communicate information about AppleTalk zone names and cable ranges.

Zone Information Table (ZIT) A table of zone name to cable range mappings in AppleTalk. These tables are maintained in each AppleTalk router.

INDEX

A

Access control lists (ACLs), 18
    HSRP configuration of, 374-375
    and MLS flow mask, 297
    MLS support for, 317
Access layer, 22-23
Active router, 352
Active sources, informing routers about, 429
Aging time, MLS cache, 320-321
Alarm category (RMON), 498
All category (traps), 489
All-broadcast message, 399
American Standards Institute (ANSI), 47
ANSI X3T11 FiberChannel, 47
AppleTalk, 234
    cable-range command, 264
    configuring on an interface, 264
    misconfigured zones, 265
    routing command, 261
    routing table, 268-269
    zone command, 264
    zone names, 265
Application layer (OSI model), 7-8
Application-specific integrated chips (ASICs), 3
APPLY button, 494
ARP (Address Resolution Protocol), 5, 351-354, 401
ARP broadcast, 229
ARP cache, 5, 352
ARP table, 5, 230
ATM (Asynchronous Transfer Mode) network, 13, 120-122
ATM devices, NSAP addresses on, 127
Atm lecs-address-default command, 127
Auth category (traps), 490
Auto-RP, 445

B

BackboneFast, 197-200
    commands, 198-199
    diagram, 197
    enabling, 199-200
Bad authentication messages (HSRP), 363
Bandwidth, need for, 39
Bandwidth use of Fast EtherChannel, 189
BID (bridge identifier) field, 176-177, 182
Bidirectional traffic between devices, 44

Binary
    converting IP addresses to, 397
    converting multicast to Ethernet addresses, 402
Blocked state port, 174
Blocking state (bridge ports), 179
Blocks, types of, 23-25
Blocks and their components, 25
Both keyword, 509
BPDUs (Bridge Protocol Data Units), 170, 174-176
    configuration BPDU packet decode, 181
    configuration frame, 175
    inferior, 198
    types of, 175
Bridge category (traps), 489
Bridge Identifier (BID) field, 176-177, 182
Bridge priorities, 176, 182
Bridge priority defaults, 176
Bridges, 9-10
    type of, 9-10
    use of the term, 170
Bridging loops, 170-172
Broadcast address, calculating for a network, 399-400
Broadcast domains, 14, 226
    defined, 236
    fragmented, 234
    reduction of, 15
    VLANs and, 95
Broadcast floods, 139
Broadcast storms, 15, 172
Broadcast Unknown Server (BUS), 124
Broadcasts, 226, 395
    issues of, 3-6
    types of, 399
Bundling multiple fast Ethernet ports, 188-190
Bus architecture, cluster design, 533

C

Cable-range zone name, 269
Cabling, 48-57
Cabling switch block devices, 57
CAM table, 18, 98
Campus network, 14-16
Candidate packet (MLSP), 311
Candidate packet (MLS-SE), 303
Catalyst 1900 series switches, 527
    back view of, 48

613

by model number, 528
console connections to, 51
console port connection, 48
Ethernet ports on, 56
expansion modules, 528-529
hardware features, 528-529
LED indicators, 529-531
software features, 531-532
Catalyst 2820 switches, 527
console connections to, 51
hardware features, 528-529
LED indicators, 529-531
software features, 531-532
Catalyst 2900 series switching commands, 70-71
Catalyst 2900XL switches, 532-535
console connections to, 51
hardware features, 533
software features, 535
Catalyst 2912MF switch modules, 533-534
Catalyst 2924M switch modules, 533-534
Catalyst 2948G switches, hardware features, 542
Catalyst 3500XL switches, 532-535
hardware features, 534-535
software features, 535
Catalyst 4000 series switches, 539-540
4003 and 4006 hardware features, 539
4003 and 4006 modules, 539-540
4908G-L3 hardware features, 540
4912G hardware features, 540
software features, 538-539
Catalyst 5000 series switches, 11, 49, 541-546
console connections to, 53
Ethernet module for, 56
hardware features, 542
line modules, 545-546
with RSMs, 244-252
series modules, 543-546
software features, 538-539
Catalyst 5500 switch
hardware features, 542
line modules, 545-546
RSFC connection to, 247
series modules, 543-546
Catalyst 5509 switch
with RSM in slot 8, 245
unpacking and installing, 99-100
Catalyst 6000 series switches, 252, 546-549
hardware features, 547
line modules for, 548-549
and MSM configuration, 253-254
series modules, 547-549
software features, 538-539
Supervisors, 547-548

Catalyst 6500 series
line modules for, 548-549
series modules, 547-549
Supervisors, 547-548
Catalyst 6500 switches
hardware features, 547
MSFC daughter cards in, 257
Catalyst 8500CSR (Campus Switch Router) series, 256-257, 550-551
Catalyst 8510CSR modules, 550
Catalyst 8540CSR modules, 551
Catalyst switches, 526-562
attachable router module, 244
categories of, 526
IOS or set-based interface, 58
selecting, 536
software platforms, 99
Category-five (CAT 5) cable, 41
CD-ROM (with this Guide), 563-567
CertTrainer software, installing, 564
CGMP (Cisco Group Management Protocol), 421-428
configuring, 427-428
configuring PIM Dense Mode with, 437
first IGMP join, 422
IGMP leave group message, 427
messages, 423, 425, 428
multicast data, 426
packet information, 421
second IGMP join, 424
Channel allocation of RSM, 251
Chassis category (traps), 489
Cisco cluster Web management tool, 532
Cisco IOS-based switching products, 526-535
Cisco set-based switching products, 537-552
Cisco switches. See Catalyst switches
Cisco Web site, using to keep up to date, 527
CiscoView, static VLAN membership using, 105
CiscoWorks, 486
Clear mls command, 323
Clear trunk command, 112, 145
Clear vlan command, 144
Clear vmps command, 145
Clear vtp command, 144
Client mode (VTP), 138
Client-router protocols, 405-415
Cluster architecture of Catalyst 2900XL and 3500XL, 532-533
Cluster Web management tool (Cisco), 532
Collisions, packet, 4
Combinations, disabling, 316
Command Line Interface (CLI), router, 247
Command session, 247
Common (Mono) Spanning Tree, 182
Communication between networks, 231-234

Communication within a network, 229-230
Community strings
    explained, 479
    public, 491
    read-only, 479
    read-write, 485
Component failure, 166
Components, 166
Config category (traps), 490
Configuration BPDU packet decode, 181
Configuration BPDUs, fields in, 175-176
Configuration Direct SVC, 124
Configure terminal (conf t) command, 260-261, 483
Connections, 48-57
Connectivity, verifying, 269-270
Console connections
    to 5000 series switches, 53
    to 1900/2800 switches, 51
    to PC/UNIX workstations, 51
    to 2900XL switches, 51
Console port (DTE) pinouts (RJ-45), 50
Content Addressable Memory (CAM), 17, 366
Content Addressable Memory (CAM) table, 18, 98
Control Direct SVC, 125
Control Distribute SVC, 125
Convergence (Spanning Tree), 179
Copy running-config startup-config command, 271-272
Core block, 24
Core Catalyst switch, unpacking and installing, 99-100
Core layer, 23
Core switch mod/port assignments, 82
CRC (cyclical redundancy check), 11, 109
Crossover cable pinout and wiring diagram, 55
CSMA/CD, 43
<Ctr-z> command, 266
Cut-through switching method, 11
Cyclic Redundancy Check (CRC), 11, 109

D

Data Direct SVC, 125
Data flow (MLS), 292-302
Data link layer (OSI model), 6-7
DB-9 connector, 49
DCEF (Distributed Cisco Express Forwarding), 547-548
Debug, using, 354-358
Debug ip igmp command, 455
Debug ip mrouting command, 455-456
Debug ip pim command, 455-456
Debug ip udp command, 374
DEC implementation of STP, 173
Default gateway routers, 348-350

Delay command, 361
Dense Mode (DM) routing, 428-429, 432. See also PIM Dense Mode
Descriptions, switch, 60-62
Design layer, 22-23
Designated port election (Spanning Tree), 178
Designated port (spanning tree), 174, 178
Designated Querier (DQ), 410
Destination Address (DA), 232
Destination-ip flow mask, 297-298, 319
Devices, defined, 60
Devices used in early networking, 2-3
DFC (Distributed Forwarding Card), 547-549
DHCP, 234, 350
DHCP leases, 350
Dijkstra algorithm, 434
Directed broadcasts, 399
Disabled port on a bridge, 179
Distance Vector (DV), 428
Distribution layer, 23
Distribution switch mod/port assignments, 82-83
Distribution trees, types of, 429. See also Shared trees; Source trees
Domain name entry, 135
DriveTime audio tracks, 566-567
DTP messages, 132
DTP trunking states, 130-131
Dumb terminals, 2
Duplex command parameters, 64
Duplex settings, 44-46
DVMRP (Distance Vector Multicast Routing Protocol), 433
Dynamic failover, for default gateway routers, 348
Dynamic Host Configuration Protocol (DHCP), 234, 350
Dynamic ISL (DISL) protocol, 130
Dynamic membership (port allocation), 105
Dynamic redundancy, for default gateway routers, 348
Dynamic vs. static VLANs, 103-108
Dynamic Trunking Protocol (DTP), 130-132

E

EARL (Early Address Recognition Logic) chip, 190
802.1d standard, 173
802.1q VLAN trunking, 114-116, 240
802.10 frame header, 117
802.10 VLANs, 116-120
802.3 Ethernet, 47
ELAN LEC joining sequence, 124
Emerging switching technologies, 1-35
Emulated LAN (ELAN), 122, 124
Enable password, 68-69
Enabled mode, router in, 259
Enabler packet (MLSP), 311

Enabler packet (MLS-SE), 303
Encapsulation command, 262
End command, 265-266
End System Identifier (ESI), 122
Enhanced Interior Gateway Routing Protocol (EIGRP), 349
Enterprise edition of Catalyst 2900XL/3500XL software, 535
Enterprise version of Catalyst 1900/2820 software, 532
Entity category (traps), 490
Ethernet, 3-4
    mixed with Fast Ethernet, 42
    usage and distance for, 41
Ethernet addresses, translating multicast to, 401-404
Ethernet Bundle Controller (EBC), 190
Ethernet connection to 10BaseT/100BaseT switch, 54-55
Ethernet to FDDI VLAN mapping, 118
Ethernet module for 5000 series switch, 56
Ethernet packets, IPX encapsulation of, 237
Ethernet ports on a 1900 series switch, 56
Event category (RMON), 498
ExamSim, 564-566
    help file, 567
    upgrades, 567
Exterior Gateway Protocol (EGP), 428
External trunking routers, 240-242

F

Fabric Switching modules, Catalyst 8540CSR, 550-551
Fallback VLAN, 107
Fast aging time, 320-321
Fast EtherChannel (FEC), 188-193, 254, 256, 498, 546, 550-551
    commands, 191-192
    enabling, 193
    features of, 189
    implementation, 189-190
    port groupings, 190
    specifications, 190
Fast Ethernet
    implementations, 41-43
    mixed with Ethernet, 42
Fast Ethernet interface of Cisco 7200 router, 308
Fast Ethernet ports, 188-193
Fault tolerance, building into networks, 348
Fault-tolerant SNMP management strategy, 487
FDDI VLAN linking, 116-120
FDDI-net VLAN, 98
FiberChannel, 47
Flood and prune mechanism, 432-436
Flow masks, 297-301, 319-320
Forward Delay timer (STP), 180
Forwarding state ports, 180, 194
Forwarding table, 366

Fragmentation, network, 227
Fragmented broadcast domain, 234
Fragmented network, information flow in, 233
Frame, explained, 228
Frame tagging, 18
FTP (File Transfer Protocol), 20
FTP queue, 20
Full duplex, 39-40, 44-46, 63-65
Full duplex devices, 65

G

Games, multiplayer Internet-based, 394
Gateway routers, 348-350
Get Nearest Server (GNS) broadcasts, 5
Gets (SNMP), 479-485
Gigabit aggregation switch, 540
Gigabit architecture, 533
Gigabit deployment, 47
Gigabit distance, 47
Gigabit EtherChannel, 546, 551
Gigabit Ethernet (GBIC), 46-47, 254, 540
Gigabit Switch Router (GSR12000), 23-24
Gigastack design of cluster architecture, 532
GNS request, 5
Group addresses, IPMC, 403
Group authentication, HSRP, 363
Group specific query, IGMP, 410
Grouping multiple fast Ethernet ports, 188-190
Group-number value, HSRP commands, 360-361

H

Half duplex, 44-46
Hardware configuration of RSFC, 249
Hardware features of Catalyst switches
    1900 and 2820, 528-529
    2900XL, 533
    2948G, 542
    3500XL, 534-535
    4003 and 4006, 539
    4908G-L3 and 4912G, 540
    5000, 542
    5500, 542
    6000, 547
    6500, 547
    8510CSR, 550
    8540CSR, 550-551
Hardware platforms, and MLS data flow, 301
Hello messages, 352, 356, 372
Hello packets, 310, 352, 356, 371

Hello Time (STP), 180
Hello timer (HSRP), 371
High-speed switching, push for, 3
History category (RMON), 498
Hold timer (HSRP), 371
Hostname and prompt example, 69
Hostnames, assigning on IOS-based switches, 68-69
HSRP (Hot Standby Routing Protocol), 347-392, 487
    access list configuration, 374-375
    adding preemption to a router, 370
    basic configuration, 353
    changing default timers, 371-372
    changing router priority, 369
    configuration commands, 359-375
    configuration exercises, 368-371
    enabling, 353-354, 368-371
    group authentication, 363
    group-number value, 360
    requirements for implementing, 350-351
    router states, 354
    tracking, 363-364, 372-373
    tracking preemption delay, 364
    UDP multicast packets, 374
    using burned-in addresses, 364-365
    using debug, 354-358
    using with firewalls and access-lists, 374
    verifying in switched environments, 366-368
HTML form of this Study Guide, 566
Hub-and-spoke architecture, cluster design, 533
Hubs, 8-9, 38-40
Hubs vs. switches (10BaseT), 38-40
HyperTerminal settings, 52-53

I

In-chassis routing, 252
IETF (Internet Engineering Task Force), 394, 497
IGMP (Internet Group Management Protocol), 405-415
    configuring, 413-414
    versions of, 405-413
IGMP Snooping, 416-420
    configuring, 421
    first IGMP message, 418
    multicast data flow, 420
    no multicast traffic, 417
    second host joins, 419
IGMP version 1, 406-409
    interoperating with IGMPv2, 413
    joining a group, 407-408
    leaving a group, 408-409
    maintaining a group, 408
    membership queries, 407
    membership reports, 406
    operation, 407-409
    packet format, 406
IGMP version 2, 409-413
    group specific query, 410
    interoperating with IGMPv1, 413
    joining a group, 411
    leave group message, 410-411
    leaving a group, 413
    maintaining a group, 412
    operation, 411-413
    packet format, 409
    querier election, 410, 412-413
    query interval response time, 411
    type field, 409
IGMP version 3, 415
Inferior BPDU, 198
Information flow in a fragmented network, 233
Init state, router in, 356
Inpkts keyword, 509
Integrity Check Value (ICV) field, 117
Inter Switch Link (ISL), 240
Inter-domain multicast routing protocols, 428
Interface commands, 261-262
Interim Local Management Interface (ILMI) PVC, 122
Interior Gateway Protocols (IGP), 428
Internal route processors, 244-257
Internal routing engines, configuring, 249
Internal trunking routers, 242-243
International Telecommunications Union (ITU), 122
Internet Control Message Protocol (ICMP), 65
Internet Protocol (IP) networks, 5
Internet Protocol (TCP/IP) properties dialog box, 86
Internet-based multiplayer games, 394
Internetworking equipment, 6-8
Inter-Switch Link (ISL), 18, 109-113, 183
InterVLAN environments, 226-228
InterVLAN routing
    concepts, 225-290
    configuration commands, 258-272
Intra-domain multicast routing protocols, 428
Intrusion detection, 503
IOS-based switching platforms, 98
IOS-based switching products (Cisco), 526-535
Ip address command, 263
IP addresses, 401
    basic, 396
    changes to in a normal routing environment, 293
    configuring, 58-60
    converting to binary, 397
    cycling chart of, 404
    for IOS-based devices, 59
    for primary router, 353

for secondary router, 353
for switch and management VLAN, 59-60
in trusted zones, 494
virtual, 352-353
IP broadcasts, 5
Ip cgmp command, 427
Ip igmp command, 414
IP MLS, configuring MLS-RP for, 306-309
Ip multicast-routing command, 436, 445
IP packet, Time To Live (TTL) field, 295, 406
Ip pim dense-mode command, 436
Ip pim send-rp-announce scope command, 446
Ip pim send-rp-discovery scope command, 446
Ip pim sparse-dense-mode command, 445
Ip route-cache same-interface command, 360
Ip routing command, 261
IP service and MLS disabling combinations, 316-317
IP Multicast addresses
    vs. broadcast traffic, 395
    vs. broadcast and unicast addresses, 396-399
    Class D addresses, 399
    translating to Ethernet addresses, 401-404
Ip-flow flow mask, 299-300, 320
IPMC addresses, converting to MAC addresses, 403-404
IPMC (IP Multicast), 393-476
    a bandwidth-conserving technology, 394
    commands, 447-459
    group addresses, 403
    monitoring and troubleshooting, 447-459
    network setup, 458
    switching and routing, 393-476
    32 overlapping addresses, 402
Ippermit category (traps), 490
IPX broadcasts, 5
IPX encapsulation of Ethernet packets, 237
IPX (Internet Packet eXchange) protocol, 5, 234
IPX MLS
    on a Catalyst 5500 switch, 305
    configuring MLS-RP for, 309
    configuring MLS-SE for, 305-316
Ipx network command, 263-264
IPX packet Transport Control field, 295
Ipx routing command, 261
IPX routing table, displaying, 268
ISL frame, 109
ISL frame header, 109
ISL-capable network interface card (NIC), 109
ITU specifications for signaling protocols, 122

J

Join messages (VTP), 140
Joined VLAN (pruning state), 140

L

LAN Emulation Address Resolution Protocol, 123
LAN Emulation Client (LEC), 123
LAN Emulation Configuration Server (LECS), 123
LAN Emulation Server (LES), 123
LAN environment, evaluating products for, 552
LAN (local area network) segments, 348
Lane command, 128
Lane database command, 127
LANE database configuration mode, 127
LANE (LAN Emulation), 120-130
    concepts, 122-124
    configuration, 125-130
    operation, 124-125
    starting, 128
LANE Network-Node Interface (LNNI) protocol, 124
LANs (local area networks), 2, 13, 348, 552
Layer 2 switching, 17-18
    bridges, 9-10
    switching functions, 228, 230
Layer 2 VLANs (switched VLANs), 13
Layer 3 routers, 10
Layer 3 switching, 18-19, 228, 248, 292
Layer 3 VLANs (routed VLANs), 13-15
Layer 4 switching, 19-20
Layers (OSI model), 6-8, 17-22
Learning state (bridge ports), 180
LE-ARP request, 123-125
Leave group message, 410
LEC sequence for joining an ELAN, 124
LECS NSAP address configuration, 127
LECS selector bytes, 126-128
LECs (LAN Emulation Clients), 123
LED indicators, on Catalyst 1900/2820, 529-531
Legacy equipment block, 24
Legacy routing environments, 234-236
Legacy routing in a VLAN environment, 239
LES service configuration, 124
LES/BUS pair, 124
Levels of authority, 69
Line modules
    for Catalyst 5000/5500, 545-546
    for Catalyst 6000/6500, 548-549
Link redundancy, 109
Link speed, 62
Link State (LS) routing protocols, 428
Listen state, router in, 357
Listening state (bridge ports), 179-180
Load balancing across a server farm, 20
Load balancing (Fast EtherChannel), 189
Load sharing, 109
Login passwords, types of, 68

Loops, bridging, 170-172
Lowest bridge priority wins, 182

M

MAC address, 4, 9, 228, 230, 352, 401-402
    changes to in a normal routing environment, 293
    converting IPMC addresses to, 403-404
    real, 367
    Source and Destination, 232
    virtual, 352, 367
MAC layer rewrite, 295
MAC (Media Access Control), 3
Management addresses, and VLANs, 487
Management domain
    creating, 135
    creating VLANs in, 100-103
Management interface, MLS, 306-307
Management tools (Cisco), 477-523
Master Command switch, 533
Max Age timer, 180, 196, 198
Maximum transfer unit (MTU), 100
MBONE, 394
Media type, choosing, 38, 44
Membership queries (IGMP), 407
Membership reports (IGMP), 406
Memorization lists, for exam preparation, 8
Metropolitan Area Networks (MANs), 117
MIBs (Management Information Bases), 479, 493-494
MLS cache, 297
    aging time, 320-321
    issues, 319-321
    number of flow entries, 319
    optimizing, 319-321
    size of, 295
MLS cache entry for a packet, 311
MLS cache output
    in destination-ip flow mode, 297-298
    in ip-flow flow mode, 299
    with source-destination ip flow mask, 298
MLS cache size, 295
MLS cache table, filtering output of, 325-326
MLS flow masks, 297-301, 319-320
MLS and IP service disabling combinations, 316-317
MLS (multilayer switching), 21, 248, 291-346
    access-list support, 317
    commands to configure, 322-327
    data flow, 292-302
    features that cannot be used with, 318
    in a hierarchical topology, 313
    management interface, 306-307
    packet flow, 315
    primary function of, 316
    route-once switch-many process, 294, 544
    topologies, 311-316
    topology validation, 314-315
Mls rp ip command, 306, 326
Mls rp ipx command, 327
Mls rp management-interface command, 327
Mls rp vlan-id command, 327
Mls rp vtp-domain command, 327
MLS topologies, 311-316
MLS topology validation, 314-315
MLS-capable routers, 295, 306
MLSP (MultiLayer Switching Protocol), 310-311. *See also* MLS
MLS-RP (MLS-Route Processor), 303-304
    configuring for IP MLS, 306-309
    configuring for IPX MLS, 309
    IOS-based commands, 326-327
MLS-SE (MultiLayer Switching-Switching Engine), 302-305
    configuring for IP MLS, 303-304
    configuring for IPX MLS, 305-316
    set-based commands, 323-326
    XTag parameter, 304
Module category (traps), 489
Monitoring ports with SPAN, 504-511
Mono (Common) Spanning Tree, 182
MOSPF (multicast extension to OSPF), 433
MSFC (Multilayer Switch Feature Card), 252, 257, 547, 549
MSM (Multilayer Switch Module), 252, 547, 549
    configuration for Catalyst 6000 switch, 254
    configuration for port-channel operation, 254-255
    features of, 252-253
MSR (Multiservice Switch Router), 550
MSRP (Multiservice Route Processor), 256-257
Mstat command, 457
Mtrace command, 457
MTU, standard for Ethernet segments, 100
Multicast applications, 394
Multicast Forward SVC, 125
Multicast frames, 174-176
Multicast IP addresses
    vs. broadcast traffic, 395
    vs. broadcast and unicast addresses, 396-399
    Class D addresses, 399
    translating to Ethernet addresses, 401-404
Multicast packets, 352
Multicast protocols, 405-447
    being developed, 394
    categories of, 405
    client-router, 405-415
Multicast routing basics, 428-433
Multicast routing protocols, 433-446
Multicast switching protocols, 416-428
Multilayer switching. *See* MLS

Multiplayer Internet-based games, 394
Multiple choice questions (on the exam), 565
Multiple path redundancy, 166
Multiple paths, providing, 170-188
Multiport NIC cards, 189

N

NeoTrace, 67
NetFlow Data Export (NDE), 297
NetFlow Feature Card (NFFC), 248, 301
NetView, 486
Network, defined, 236
Network address Source and Destination, 232
Network address translation (NAT), 17, 20
Network Analysis Module, 499
Network broadcasts, 399
Network communication between networks, 231-234
Network communication within a network, 229-230
Network connectivity, verifying, 269-270
Network design, stable, 526
Network fragmentation, result of, 227
Network interface card (NIC), 4, 109, 189
Network layer (OSI model), 7
    broadcasts, 4-5
    protocols, 4-5, 227
Network link redundancy, 166
Network operating systems (NOSs), 5
Network redundancy, 167-169, 348
Network topologies
    driven by workgroups, 239
    example, 66, 72
Networking devices, early, 2-3
Networking equipment, 6-8
NIC (network interface card), 4, 109, 189
No ip address command, 60
No switchport mode trunk command, 112
Nodes
    on a common network, 229
    on different segments, 231
Node-to-node communication, 229
Non-Volatile Random Access Memory (NVRAM), 271
Novell encapsulations, 263
Novell-ether encapsulation, 264
NSAP (Network Service Access Point) addresses, 121
    on ATM devices, 127
    configuration, 127
    resolution, 123, 125
    selector bytes, 126-127

O

On-board routers, 244
100BaseT, specifications for, 43
100BaseT switch, Ethernet connection to, 54-55
100BaseTX ports, 56
100-Mbps hubs or switches, 41-42
    between all layers, 43
    upgrading to, 42
Open Shortest Path First (OSPF), 349
Open Systems Interconnection (OSI) model, 6-8, 12, 17-22, 351
OpenView, 486
Organizational Unique Identifiers (OUI), 401
OSI layer matching, 12
OSI model layers, switching at, 17-22
Outgoing Interface List (OIL), 432, 440

P

Packet collisions, 4
Packet flow, MLS, 315
Packets
    explained, 228, 230
    switching between VLANs, 13
PAgP states, 191
Passwords (switch), 68-70
    IOS-based, 69
    set-based, 70
Path cost (Spanning Tree), 177-178
Per VLAN Spanning Tree (PVST), 182-183
Permanent Virtual Circuits (PVCs), 121-122
Personal computers (PCs), 2
PFC (Policy Feature Card), 301, 547, 549
Physical layer, 6
PIM BootStrap Router (BSR), 446
PIM (Protocol Independent Multicasting) Dense Mode, 434-437
    configuring, 436-437
    configuring with CGMP, 437
    flood, 434-435
    prune, 435-436
PIM Sparse Mode, 433, 438-444
    configuring, 446
    creation of prune message, 440
    creation of shared tree, 439
    forwarding multicast traffic, 443
    initial client request, 439
    registering with RP register stop, 442
    registering RP source first, 441
    switching to the shared tree, 444
    traffic down shared tree, 443
PIM Sparse-Dense Mode, 444-446
Ping utility, 64-66, 269-270

Platforms of Catalyst switches, 99
Point-to-multipoint topology, 121
Point-to-point topology, 121
Policy Feature Card (PFC), 301, 547, 549
Port ? command, 504
Port Aggregation Protocol (PAgP), 191
Port allocation, static vs. dynamic, 103-108
Port analysis, configuring SPAN for, 506
Port descriptions, 61
Port designations (STP), 186
Port monitoring (SPAN), 504-511
Port screen (SPAN), 508
Port speed, changing, 62
Port state bypassing, 194
Port states (STP), 179-180, 194
Port-channel interface, 254-256
PortFast, 194-195, 199-200
Ports assigned to a VLAN, 94-95
Presentation layer (OSI model), 7
Private Network-Node Interface (PNNI) protocol, 121
Privilege levels, 69
Privileged exec mode, router in, 259
Prompts, changing on set-based switches, 68
Protocol traces, viewing, 509
Proxy Arp, 348-349
Pruning, 138-141, 435-436
Pruning states (VLAN), 140
Public community string, 491

Q

Q (signaling protocol for ATM), 122
Q.SAAL, 122
Quality of service (QoS), 20, 256, 316
Querier election (IGMP), 410, 412-413
Query interval response time (IGMP), 411
Questions, types of on the exam, 565
Queuing strategies, 20

R

Read-only community strings, 479
Read-write community strings, 485
Real MAC address, 367
Redundancy
    for default gateway routers, 348, 350
    multiple path, 166
    need for, 167
    providing, 168
    using Fast EtherChannel, 189
Redundant link ports, blocking, 174

Redundant links, 166-170
Redundant network design, 167-169
Redundant networks, 348
Rendezvous Point (RP), 438, 446
Repeater category (traps), 489-490
Reverse Path Forwarding (RPF), 429
RJ-45 connector, 48-49
RMON (remote monitoring), 478, 497-503
    adding to a switch, 503
    categories of, 498
    process-intensive monitoring, 498
    viewing data using show commands, 500
RMON2 standard, 497
Rollover cable, 48-51
Root bridge election, 176-177, 182
Root bridge selection
    manual, 177
    set spantree and, 201-202
Root path cost (Spanning Tree), 177-178
Root port election (Spanning Tree), 177-178
Root port (spanning tree), 174
Route entries, showing specific, 267
Route processors, internal, 244-257
Route switch module (RSM), 13, 18, 244-252, 546
    channel allocation of, 251
    specifications for, 248-249
Route table, 493
Routed (layer 3) VLANs, 13-15
Routed protocols, explained, 227
Route-once switch-many model, 294, 544
Router module attachable Catalyst switches, 244
Routers, 10, 229
    on-board, 244
    router-on-a-stick, 236-238
Routing environments
    InterVLAN, 226-228
    legacy, 234-236
    VLAN, 238-243
Routing Information Field (RIF), 9, 364
Routing Information Indicator (RII), 9
Routing Information Protocol (RIP), 349
Routing operations, TCP/IP, 228-243
Routing protocols, explained, 227
Routing table, 228
RSFC (Route Switch Feature Card), 246, 546
    connection from Catalyst 5500 switch, 247
    hardware configuration of, 249
    specifications for, 248-249
RSM installation slots, Catalyst 5000 switch, 245
RSM (route switch module), 13, 18, 244-252, 248-249, 546

S

SAP table, 5
Secondary HSRP addresses, router using, 359
Secondary HSRP group, router configured with, 360
Secondary (keyword), 237, 263-264
Secondary network address, 237
Secure Data Exchange (SDE), 242
Security Association Identifier (SAID) value, 102, 117
Security problems of multicast traffic, 415
Series Q, 122
Server block (or farm), 20, 24
Server farm load balancing, 20
Server mode (VTP), 100, 138
Service Advertisement Protocol (SAP), 5
Session command, 125, 247
Session layer (OSI model), 7
Set cgmp enable command, 427
SET IOS major commands, 537
SET IOS switches, software features, 538
Set mls command, 323
Set mls flow command, 297, 304
Set port capabilities command, 192
Set port channel command, 192
Set port command, 144
Set port enable command, 64
Set snmp ? command, 498
Set snmp command, 479
Set snmp community command, 480
Set span ? command, 508
Set spantree command, 201-202, 205-206
    and cost, 202
    and root bridge selection, 201-202
    and STP timers, 202-203
Set system ? command, 484
Set trunk command, 111, 120, 142-143
Set vlan command, 118-119, 142-143
    output, 104
    parameters, 101
Set vlan mapping command, 116
Set vmps command, 107, 143-144
Set vtp command, 135, 142
Set vtp mode command, 137
Set-based switching platforms, 58, 98
Set-based switching products (Cisco), 537-552
Sets (SNMP), 485-486
SFM (Switch Fabric Module), 547
Shared buffer architecture, 533
Shared trees (multicast routing), 429-431, 438-439, 443-444
Shortest path trees, 429-431, 434, 438
Show appletalk route command, 268-269
Show appletalk zone command, 265
Show atm vc command, 122
Show cam command, 367-368
Show config command, 483
Show controller c5ip command, 250
Show interface command, 60
Show ip arp command, 367
Show ip command, 59
Show ip igmp groups command, 448-449
Show ip igmp interface command, 449
Show ip interface brief command, 356
Show ip mroute active command, 453-454
Show ip mroute command, 451-453
Show ip mroute summary command, 453-454
Show ip pim interface command, 449-450
Show ip pim neighbor command, 450
Show ip pim rp command, 450
Show ip route command, 266-267, 447-448
Show ip route connected command, 267
Show ip rpf command, 450-451
Show ipx route command, 268
Show lane command, 128
Show lane default-atm-addresses command, 126
Show lane server command, 129
Show mac command, 500, 503
Show mls command, 304, 319, 324-325
Show mls entry command, 324
Show module command, 246
Show port command, 63-64, 204, 246, 500
Show port mon command, 505, 508
Show running-config (show run) command, 259-260, 482
Show snmp command, 480, 482, 490, 492, 499
Show span command, 509-510
Show spantree command, 203-204, 206
Show spantree uplinkfast command, 205
Show standby brief command, 366
Show standby command, 356-357, 365-366
Show system command, 485
Show tcp command, 247
Show vlan command, 103, 119, 145, 148
Show vlan mapping command, 116
Show vmps command, 146, 149
Show vtp command, 145, 148
Show vtp domain command, 135
Show vtp status command, 136
Signaling protocols, ITU specifications for, 122
Simulation questions (on the exam), 565
Single point of failure, 166-168, 348
SMTP (Simple Mail Transport Protocol), 20
Sniffer (Network Associates), 478
Snmp ? command, 481, 483
Snmp community public-ro command, 481
Snmp community ? command, 481
Snmp host ? command, 491

SNMP (Simple Network Management Protocol), 478
    fault-tolerant management strategy, 487
    gets, 479-485
    MIBs, 493-494
    sets, 485-486
    setting up access and traps, 493
    settings screen, 496
    support for, 479-497
    traps, 478, 486-493
    UDP port used by, 492
    Web interface, 494-496
Software features of Catalyst switches
    4000/5000/6000 series, 538-539
    1900 and 2820, 531-532
    2900XL/3500XL, 535
SOHO (Small Office Home Office) environment, 8
Source Address (SA), 232
Source route bridging, 9
Source route translational bridging, 10
Source route transparent bridging, 10
Source trees, 429-431, 434, 438
Source-destination ip flow mask, 298-299, 319
SPAN (Switch Port Analyzer), 478, 503-511
    configuring for port analysis, 506
    designating a port as a monitor, 504
    Port screen, 508
Spanning Tree
    building, 173, 183-184
    enabling, 186-188
Spanning Tree algorithm, 108-109, 172-174, 511
Spanning Tree Protocol (STP), 172-188
    in action, 183-186
    cost values related to bandwidth, 178
    how it works, 173-179
    loop-breaking mechanism, 178
    port states, 179-180
    reducing convergence time, 195
    timers, 180, 202-203
    versions of, 173
Spanning Tree reconvergence, 174
Sparse Mode (SM) routing, 428-429, 432. *See also* PIM Sparse Mode
SRP (Switch Route Processor), 256, 542, 550
Stable network design, 526
Standard edition of Catalyst 1900/2820 software, 532
Standard version of Catalyst 2900XL/3500XL software, 535
Standby authentication string command, 362
Standby ip command, 354, 359
Standby preempt command, 361
Standby priority command, 361-362
Standby router, 352, 358
Standby timers hellotime holdtime command, 362
Standby track type number command, 362
Standby use-bia command, 364
Static VLAN membership using CiscoView, 105
Static VLANs, 103-108
Statistics category (RMON), 498
Store-and-forward switching method, 11
Stpx category (traps), 490
Straight-through cable pinout, 54
Straight-through cable wiring diagram, 54
Subinterface numbers, 242
Subinterfaces, 241-242
Subset advertisements (VTP), 134
Summary advertisements (VTP), 134
Supervisor Engines, 49, 301
    Catalyst 5000 series, 543-544
    Catalyst 6000/6500 series, 547-548
    Supervisor III Engine, 301
    Supervisor IIIG Engine, 301
Switch blocks, 22-25, 37-92
Switch description, 60-62
Switch Route Processor (SRP), 256, 542, 550
Switched network design, 22-25
Switched Virtual Circuits (SVCs), 121
Switched VLANs (layer 2), 13
Switches, 3, 10-11, 170. *See also* Catalyst switches
Switches vs. hubs (10BaseT), 38-40
Switching commands, 58-71
Switching layer characteristics, 22
Switching methods, 11
Switching packets between VLANs, 13
Switching products (Cisco), 526-562. *See also* Catalyst switches
Switching technologies, emerging, 1-35
Switchport access vlan command output, 104
Switchport command, 146
Switchport interface command, 148
Switchport mode trunk command, 111
SwitchProbe, 499
Syslog category (traps), 490

T

TCP/IP end-to-end communication, 228-243
TCP/IP (Transmission Control Protocol/Internet Protocol), 348, 351
10BaseT cabling, 43
10BaseT switch
    Ethernet connection to, 54-55
    vs. 10BaseT hub, 38-40
10-Mbps hubs, 41
Time To Live (TTL) field of IP packet, 295, 406
Token Ring-net VLAN, 98

T1, 14
Topologies
    driven by workgroups, 239
    example, 66, 72
Topology Change Notification (TCN) BPDUs, 175
Topology issues, solving with router-on-a-stick, 236-238
Traceroute utility, 67, 271
Traffic flow in an MLS environment, 296
Traffic shaping, 20
Translational bridging, 10
Transmission, accurate, 111
Transparent bridging, 9
Transparent failover, 167
Transparent mode (VTP), 100, 138
Transport Control field of an IPX packet, 295
Transport layer (OSI model), 7
Trap receivers, 488
Trap subcommand, 488
Trap targets (or destinations), 486-487
Traps, 478, 486-493
    categories of, 489-490
    purpose of, 494
Troubleshooting tools for WANs, 67
Trunk bandwidth, conserving, 138
Trunking, 108-132
Trunking capabilities of Catalyst family, 114
Trunking protocol, 18
Trunking routers
    external, 240-242
    internal, 242-243
Trunks, 108-132
    controlling VLAN presence on, 113
    making, 100
25-pin female connector, 49
25-pin male connector, 49

U

UDP multicast packets (HSRP), 374
UDP port, 374, 492
UDP protocol, 486
Unicast IP addresses, 399
Unicast routing protocols, 428
Unicast traffic, 398-399
Unshielded twisted-pair (UTP), 41
Untrusted source, multicast traffic from, 415
UplinkFast, 195-197
    commands, 196-197
    enabling, 199-200
    requirements, 196

V

Variable Length Subnet Masking (VLSM), 349
VIP2 (Versatile Interface Processor), 546
Virtual Channel Identifier (VCI), 121
Virtual interface, 250
Virtual IP addresses, 352-353
Virtual MAC addresses, 352, 367
Virtual Path Identifier (VPI), 121
Virtual router interfaces, 249
Virtual software interfaces, 241-242
Visual Route, 67
Visual switch block diagram, 81
Visual Switch Manager
    link, 494
    opening screen, 495
    with Port menu, 507
Vlan command, 102, 146
Vlan configuration command, 147
Vlan configuration mode, 102, 136
Vlan database command, 146
Vlan database configuration mode, 141
VLAN ID field, 262
VLAN ID tag, 98, 110, 117
Vlan keyword, 505
VLAN list, 113
VLAN mapping, 116
VLAN numbers, 116-117
VLAN trunking, 97, 108-132
VLAN trunking protocols (VTPs), 132-141
    DTP, 130-132
    802.1q, 114-116
    802.10, 116-120
    ISL, 109-113
    LANE, 120-130
    VTP, 132-141
VLANs (Virtual Local Area Networks), 13, 93-164, 226, 238-243
    adding to trunk list, 100
    and broadcast domains, 95
    command details, 142-149
    controlling presence of on a trunk, 113
    created through software only, 96
    creating, 98-103
    creating on an IOS switch, 102, 146-149
    creating in a management domain, 100-103
    creating on a set-based switch, 101, 142-146
    distributing between links, 108
    dynamic, 105-108
    eliminating unused, 138-139
    examples of, 16-17
    on an external trunking router, 241

Index **625**

fallback, 107
flexibility of in network topology, 97
frame processing, 98
introduction to, 13-17
IOS-based commands, 146-149
layer 3 (routed), 13-15
layer 2 (switched), 13
with legacy routing, 239
and management addresses, 487
mapping, 116
overview of, 94-149
ports on a switch assigned to, 94-95
pruning states, 140
routing on a Catalyst 5505, 293-294
set-based commands, 142-146
static, 104-105
static vs. dynamic, 103-108
in source-route bridging environments, 98
switching packets between, 13
types of, 97-98
Vmps category (traps), 490
Vmps command, 148
VMPS database file example, 106
VMPS queries, 107
VMPS Query Protocol (VQP), 107
VMPS (Virtual Management Policy Server), 106
Voice over IP (VoIP) phones, 350
VTP advertisement categories, 134

Vtp command, 146-147
VTP domain name, 135, 306
Vtp category (traps), 490
VTP operating modes, 100, 137
VTP pruning, 138-141
VTP (Virtual Trunking Protocol), 327

WAN block, 24
WAN links, 120
WAN (wide area network) troubleshooting tools, 67
Web browser, 494
Web interface, 494-496
Web interface opening screen, 495
Web management tool, Cisco cluster, 532
Windows network properties, 86
Workgroups, network topologies driven by, 239

XTags, 304, 310

Zone name, matching to cable range, 269

LICENSE AGREEMENT

THIS PRODUCT (THE "PRODUCT") CONTAINS PROPRIETARY SOFTWARE, DATA AND INFORMATION (INCLUDING DOCUMENTATION) OWNED BY THE McGRAW-HILL COMPANIES, INC. ("McGRAW-HILL") AND ITS LICENSORS. YOUR RIGHT TO USE THE PRODUCT IS GOVERNED BY THE TERMS AND CONDITIONS OF THIS AGREEMENT.

LICENSE: Throughout this License Agreement, "you" shall mean either the individual or the entity whose agent opens this package. You are granted a non-exclusive and non-transferable license to use the Product subject to the following terms:

(i) If you have licensed a single user version of the Product, the Product may only be used on a single computer (i.e., a single CPU). If you licensed and paid the fee applicable to a local area network or wide area network version of the Product, you are subject to the terms of the following subparagraph (ii).

(ii) If you have licensed a local area network version, you may use the Product on unlimited workstations located in one single building selected by you that is served by such local area network. If you have licensed a wide area network version, you may use the Product on unlimited workstations located in multiple buildings on the same site selected by you that is served by such wide area network; provided, however, that any building will not be considered located in the same site if it is more than five (5) miles away from any building included in such site. In addition, you may only use a local area or wide area network version of the Product on one single server. If you wish to use the Product on more than one server, you must obtain written authorization from McGraw-Hill and pay additional fees.

(iii) You may make one copy of the Product for back-up purposes only and you must maintain an accurate record as to the location of the back-up at all times.

COPYRIGHT; RESTRICTIONS ON USE AND TRANSFER: All rights (including copyright) in and to the Product are owned by McGraw-Hill and its licensors. You are the owner of the enclosed disc on which the Product is recorded. You may not use, copy, decompile, disassemble, reverse engineer, modify, reproduce, create derivative works, transmit, distribute, sublicense, store in a database or retrieval system of any kind, rent or transfer the Product, or any portion thereof, in any form or by any means (including electronically or otherwise) except as expressly provided for in this License Agreement. You must reproduce the copyright notices, trademark notices, legends and logos of McGraw-Hill and its licensors that appear on the Product on the back-up copy of the Product which you are permitted to make hereunder. All rights in the Product not expressly granted herein are reserved by McGraw-Hill and its licensors.

TERM: This License Agreement is effective until terminated. It will terminate if you fail to comply with any term or condition of this License Agreement. Upon termination, you are obligated to return to McGraw-Hill the Product together with all copies thereof and to purge all copies of the Product included in any and all servers and computer facilities.

DISCLAIMER OF WARRANTY: THE PRODUCT AND THE BACK-UP COPY OF THE PRODUCT ARE LICENSED "AS IS." McGRAW-HILL, ITS LICENSORS AND THE AUTHORS MAKE NO WARRANTIES, EXPRESS OR IMPLIED, AS TO RESULTS TO BE OBTAINED BY ANY PERSON OR ENTITY FROM USE OF THE PRODUCT AND/OR ANY INFORMATION OR DATA INCLUDED THEREIN. McGRAW-HILL, ITS LICENSORS, AND THE AUTHORS MAKE NO GUARANTEE THAT YOU WILL PASS ANY CERTIFICATION EXAM BY USING THIS PRODUCT. McGRAW-HILL, ITS LICENSORS AND THE AUTHORS MAKE NO EXPRESS OR IMPLIED WARRANTIES OF MERCHANTABILITY OR FITNESS FOR A PARTICULAR PURPOSE OR USE WITH RESPECT TO THE PRODUCT. NEITHER McGRAW-HILL, ANY OF ITS LICENSORS, NOR THE AUTHORS WARRANT THAT THE FUNCTIONS CONTAINED IN THE PRODUCT WILL MEET YOUR REQUIREMENTS OR THAT THE OPERATION OF THE PRODUCT WILL BE UNINTERRUPTED OR ERROR FREE. YOU ASSUME THE ENTIRE RISK WITH RESPECT TO THE QUALITY AND PERFORMANCE OF THE PRODUCT.

LIMITED WARRANTY FOR DISC: To the original licensee only, McGraw-Hill warrants that the enclosed disc on which the Product is recorded is free from defects in materials and workmanship under normal use and service for a period of ninety (90) days from the date of purchase. In the event of a defect in the disc covered by the foregoing warranty, McGraw-Hill will replace the disc.

LIMITATION OF LIABILITY: NEITHER McGRAW-HILL, ITS LICENSORS NOR THE AUTHORS SHALL BE LIABLE FOR ANY INDIRECT, SPECIAL OR CONSEQUENTIAL DAMAGES, SUCH AS BUT NOT LIMITED TO, LOSS OF ANTICIPATED PROFITS OR BENEFITS, RESULTING FROM THE USE OR INABILITY TO USE THE PRODUCT EVEN IF ANY OF THEM HAS BEEN ADVISED OF THE POSSIBILITY OF SUCH DAMAGES. THIS LIMITATION OF LIABILITY SHALL APPLY TO ANY CLAIM OR CAUSE WHATSOEVER WHETHER SUCH CLAIM OR CAUSE ARISES IN CONTRACT, TORT, OR OTHERWISE. Some states do not allow the exclusion or limitation of indirect, special or consequential damages, so the above limitation may not apply to you.

U.S. GOVERNMENT RESTRICTED RIGHTS: Any software included in the Product is provided with restricted rights subject to subparagraphs (c), (1) and (2) of the Commercial Computer Software-Restricted Rights clause at 48 C.F.R. 52.227-19. The terms of this Agreement applicable to the use of the data in the Product are those under which the data are generally made available to the general public by McGraw-Hill. Except as provided herein, no reproduction, use, or disclosure rights are granted with respect to the data included in the Product and no right to modify or create derivative works from any such data is hereby granted.

GENERAL: This License Agreement constitutes the entire agreement between the parties relating to the Product. The terms of any Purchase Order shall have no effect on the terms of this License Agreement. Failure of McGraw-Hill to insist at any time on strict compliance with this License Agreement shall not constitute a waiver of any rights under this License Agreement. This License Agreement shall be construed and governed in accordance with the laws of the State of New York. If any provision of this License Agreement is held to be contrary to law, that provision will be enforced to the maximum extent permissible and the remaining provisions will remain in full force and effect.